THE PSYCHOLOGY OF LANGUAGE

AN INTRODUCTION TO PSYCHOLINGUISTICS AND GENERATIVE GRAMMAR

McGRAW-HILL SERIES IN PSYCHOLOGY

Consulting Editors
Norman Garmezy
Richard L. Solomon
Lyle V. Jones
Harold W. Stevenson

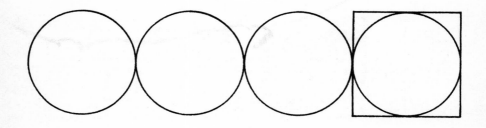

THE PSYCHOLOGY OF LANGUAGE

AN INTRODUCTION TO PSYCHOLINGUISTICS AND GENERATIVE GRAMMAR

J. A. FODOR
Massachusetts Institute of Technology

T. G. BEVER
Columbia University in the City of New York

M. F. GARRETT
Massachusetts Institute of Technology

McGRAW-HILL BOOK COMPANY

New York   St. Louis   San Francisco   Düsseldorf   Johannesburg
Kuala Lumpur   London   Mexico   Montreal   New Delhi
Panama   Paris   São Paulo   Singapore   Sydney   Tokyo   Toronto

Library of Congress Cataloging in Publication Data

Fodor, Jerry A
The psychology of language.

(McGraw-Hill series in psychology)
Bibliography: p.
1. Languages—Psychology.   2. Generative
grammar.   I. Bever, Thomas G., joint author.
II. Garrett, Merrill F., joint author.   III. Title.
[DNLM: 1. Psycholinguistics. BF455 F653p 1974]
P106.F6   401'.9   73-22088
ISBN 0-07-021412-3

THE PSYCHOLOGY OF LANGUAGE:
AN INTRODUCTION TO PSYCHOLINGUISTICS
AND GENERATIVE GRAMMAR

567890KPKP79

This book was set in Palatino by Textbook Services, Inc.
The editors were Robert P. Rainier and Susan Gamer;
the designer was Anne Canevari Green;
the production supervisor was Leroy A. Young.
The drawings were done by B. Handelman Associates Inc.
Kingsport Press, Inc., was printer and binder.

ACKNOWLEDGMENTS

Acknowledgment is made to the following for quoted material:

Excerpts from Brown, R. *Words and things*. New York: The Free Press, 1958, pp. 157–158. Copyright 1958 by Macmillan Publishing Co., Inc.

Excerpt from Brownowski, J., and Bellugi, U. *Science*, 1970, **168**, 669–673, pp. 462. Copyright 1970 by the American Association for the Advancement of Science. Reprinted by permission of author and publisher.

Excerpts from Gardner, R. A., and Gardener, B. T. Teaching sign language to a chimpanzee. *Science*, 1969, **165**, 664–672, pp. 441, 442. Copyright 1969 by the American Association for the Advancement of Science.

Excerpts pp. 153, 154 from the book A TREATISE OF HUMAN NATURE by David Hume. Intro. by A. D. Lindsay. Everyman's Library edition. Published by E. P. Dutton & Co., Inc., and used with their permission.

Excerpt from Kant, I. *Critique of pure reason*. N. K. Smith (Trans.). London: Macmillan, 1953, p. 12. Reprinted by permission of Macmillan, London and Basingstoke, and St. Martin's Press, Inc., New York.

Excerpt from Lackner, J. A developmental study of language behavior in retarded children. *Neuropsychologia*, 1968, **6**, 301–320, p. 453; reprinted with permission of microform international marketing corporation exclusive copyright licensee of Pergamon Press journal back files.

Excerpts pp. 142, 153 from the book AN ESSAY CONCERNING HUMAN UNDERSTANDING by John Locke. Ed. by Prof. J. W. Yolton. Everyman's Library Edition. Published by E. P. Dutton & Co., Inc., and used with their permission.

Excerpt from Luria, A. R., and Yudovich, F. IA. *Speech and the development of mental processes in the child*. London: Staples Press, 1959, p. 456. Copyright 1959 by Granada Publishing Limited. Reprinted by permission of authors and publisher.

Acknowledgment is made to the following for figures and tables:

Figure 2-2. Adapted from Osgood, C. E. On understanding and creating sentences. *American Psychologist*, 1963, **18**, 735–751. Copyright 1963 by the American Psychological Association. Reprinted by permission of the author and publisher.

Table 3-1. From Chomsky, N., and Halle, M. *The sound pattern of English*. New York: Harper and Row, 1968.

Figures 4-1 and 4-2. From Mowrer, O. H. *Learning theory and the symbolic processes*. New York: John Wiley, 1960.

Figure 5-1. From Marks, L., and Miller, G. The role of semantic and syntactic constraints in the memorization of English sentences. *Journal of Verbal Learning and Verbal Behavior*, 1964, **3**, 1–5.

Table 5-1. From Miller, G. A., and McKean, K. A chronometric study of some relations between sentences. *Quarterly Journal of Experimental Psychology*, 1964, **16**, 297–308.

Figure 5-2. Adapted from Miller, G. A. Some psychological studies of grammar. *American Psychologist*, 1962, **17**, 748–762. Copyright 1962 by the American Psychological Association. Reprinted by permission.

Figure 5-3. From Clifton, C., Kurcz, I., and Jenkins, J. Grammatical relations as determinants of sentence similarity. *Journal of Verbal Learning and Verbal Behavior*, 1965, **4**, 112–117.

Table 5-3. From Clifton, C., and Odom, P. Similarity relations among certain English sentence constructions. *Psychological Monographs*, 1966, **80** (5, Whole No. 613). Copyright 1966 by the American Psychological Association. Reprinted by permission.

Figure 5-4. Adapted from Clifton, C., and Odom, P. Similarity relations among certain English sentence constructions. *Psychological Monographs*, 1966, **80** (5, Whole No. 613).

Table 5-4. From Walker, E., Gough, P., and Wall, R. Grammatical relations and the search of sentences in immediate memory. *Proceedings of the Midwestern Psychological Association*, 1968.

Figure 5-5. From Clifton, C., and Odom, P. Similarity relations among certain English sentence constructions. *Psychological Monographs*, 1966, **80** (5, Whole No. 613). Copyright 1966 by the American Psychological Association. Reprinted by permission.

Figure 5-6. Adapted from Johnson, N. The psychological reality of phrase structure rules. *Journal of Verbal Learning and Verbal Behavior*, 1965, **4**, 469–475.

Figures 5-7, 5-8, and 5-9. From Levelt, W. J. M. A scaling approach to the study of syntactic relations. In G. B. Flores d'Arcais and W. J. M. Levelt (Eds.). *Advances in Psycholinguistics*. New York: American Elsevier, 1970.

Figure 5-10. From Walker, E. Grammatical relations in sentence memory. Doctoral dissertation, Indiana University, 1969.

Figures 5-12 and 5-13. From Wanner, E. On remembering, forgetting, and understanding sentences: A study of the deep structure hypothesis. Unpublished doctoral dissertation, Harvard University, 1968.

Figure 6-1. From Potter, R. K., Kopp, A. G., and Kopp, H. G. *Visible speech*. New York: Dover, 1966.

Figure 6-2. Adapted from Fairbanks, G., and Grubb, P. A psychological investigation of vowel formants. *Journal of Speech and Hearing Research*, 1961, **4**, 203–219.

Figure 6-3. From Miller, G. A. *Language and communication*. New York: McGraw-Hill, 1951.

Figure 6-4. From Liberman, A., Cooper, F. S., Shankweiler, D. P., and Studdert-Kennedy, M. Perception of the speech code. *Psychological Review*, 1967, **74**, 431–461. Copyright 1967 by the American Psychological Association. Reprinted by permission.

Figures 6-5 and 6-6. From Liberman, A., Harris, K., Eimas, P., Lisker, L., and Bastian, J. An effect of learning on speech perception: The discrimination of durations of silence with and without phonemic significance. *Language and Speech*, 1961, **4**, 175–195. Copyright 1961 by the American Psychological Association. Reprinted by permission.

Figure 6-9. From Halle, M., and Stevens, K. N. Speech recognition: A model and a program for research. In J. A. Fodor and J. J. Katz (Eds.). *The structure of language: Readings in the philosophy of language*. Englewood Cliffs, N.J.: Prentice Hall, 1964.

Figure 6-11. From Garrett, M., Bever, T. G., and Fodor, J. A. The active use of grammar in speech perception. *Perception and Psychophysics*, 1966, **1**, 30–32.

Figure 7-2. Adapted from Tannenbaum, P. H., and Williams, F. Generation of active and passive sentences as a function of subject and object focus. *Journal of Verbal Learning and Verbal Behavior*, 1968, **7**, 246–250.

Figure 7-7. Adapted from Forster, K. I. Sentence completion in left- and right-branching languages. *Journal of Verbal Learning and Verbal Behavior*, 1968, **7**, 296–299.

Figure 7-8. From Jarvella, R. Starting with psychological verbs. Paper presented at the Midwestern Psychological Association, Cleveland, 1972.

Figure 7-9. From Boomer, D. S. Hesitation and grammatical encoding. *Language and Speech*, 1965, **8**, 148–158.

Figure 8-1. Reprinted from *The genesis of language* by F. Smith and G. Miller (Eds.) by permission of the M.I.T. Press, Cambridge, Massachusetts. Copyright 1966 by the Massachusetts Institute of Technology.

Tables 8-1 and 8-2. From Brown, R., and Hanlon, C. Derivational complexity and order of acquisition in child speech. In J. R. Hayes (Ed.). *Cognition and the development of language*. New York: Wiley, 1970.

Figures 8-2 and 8-3. Reprinted from *Language development: Form and function in emerging grammars* by L. Bloom by permission of the M.I.T. Press, Cambridge, Massachusetts. Copyright 1970 by the Massachusetts Institute of Technology.

Figure 8-4. From Bever, T. G. The cognitive basis for linguistic structures. In J. R. Hayes (Ed.). *Cognition and the development of language*. New York: Wiley, 1970.

CONTENTS

	Preface	xi
1	Introduction	1
2	The Psycholinguistics of Taxonomic Grammar	23
3	Generative Grammars	79
4	Semantics	141
5	The Psychological Reality of Grammatical Structures	221
6	Sentence Perception	275
7	Sentence Production	373
8	First Language Learning	435
	Conclusion	505
	References	515
	Index	529

For Noam Chomsky and Morris Halle

This schematism of our understanding, in its application to appearances and their mere form, is an art concealed in the depths of the human soul, whose real modes of activity nature is hardly likely ever to allow us to discover, and to have open to our gaze....
Kant, 1781

But how does a person who has acquired systems of knowledge and belief then proceed to use them in his daily life? About this we are entirely in the dark....
N. Chomsky, 1972

PREFACE

The most exciting idea in contemporary psychology is that it may at last be possible to begin to construct an experimental mentalism: a psychology which does justice to the richness and complexity of the mental processes that cause behavior but is nevertheless empirically disciplined in the ways a science ought to be.

The goal of developing a science of the mental life of organisms is, of course, no novelty: it was implicit in the work of the Gestalt psychologists and of the Wurzburg school and in the methodology of Wundt and Tichner. Indeed, the notion that the mental processes which cause behavior (rather than behavior per se) are the subject matter of psychology is central to a tradition that reaches back at least to Descartes. Only in the context of twentieth century positivism did it seem plausible to deny that psychology is about how the mind works.

But if contemporary mentalism has a history, it is not a history of unmixed success. On the contrary, the strongest argument against mentalism in psychology is simply that by and large it has not worked. The assumption that overt behavior is normally contingent upon interactions among mental causes did not, in general, lead either to insightful theories of the presumed interactions or to an experimental elucidation of the presumed contingencies. Positivism provided a radical diagnosis of this failure which many psychologists were willing to accept: the mentalistic program was fundamentally misconceived; psychology should be a science of behavior, not of the mind.

It is possible to admit the failure while rejecting the diagnosis. In retrospect, much of what was wrong with traditional mentalism seems peripheral to its analysis of the goals of psychology. For example, because they believed that mental processes are necessarily conscious, many mentalists became committed to the view that psychology must rest upon special—introspective—modes of observation. Accordingly, much of the methodological controversy over traditional mentalism concerned the epistemological status of introspective reports—to the point where it began to seem that the claim that psychology is the science of mental phenomena and the claim that the data of psychology are introspections were not dissociable.

Whatever one makes of the epistemological issues about introspection, it seems clear as a matter of fact that there are only a few areas where the systematization of the subject's reports about his mental state yields interesting psychological theories. Psychophysics may be one. In most cases, however, the mental life of the subject appears to be as inscrutable to him as it is to the experimenter, so a science of mental processes must develop methods of experimentation more subtle than merely asking the subject what he's thinking. If overt behavior is usually the outcome of complexly interacting mental processes, as contemporary mentalists suppose, such methods may be hard to come by; the processes we are trying to study are only indirectly revealed in the processes we are able to observe. But this is a practical difficulty, not a principled one. There is, in short, nothing in the mentalist's construal of the goals of psychology which requires him to assume that experimental investigations are inappropriate to achieving those goals. We shall see, in the course of this book, that the development of theories of the mental processes underlying the use of language has fostered the development of appropriate experimental paradigms for the investigation of such processes.

It was not, however, solely the inadequacy of introspection as a research tool that bedeviled traditional mentalism. What proved far more damaging was the mentalist's inability to provide an account of his subject matter which permitted psychology to occupy a place among the empirical sciences. The following antimentalist argument often appeared inescapable: Insofar as the behavior of an organism is the joint product of its neurological states together with its stimulus inputs, a science which explains behavior may be couched either in the vocabulary of neurology or in the vocabulary of stimulus-response variables. In neither case, however, need psychological explanations refer to specifically mental constructs. But inasmuch as behavior is *not* the product of neurological states and stimulus inputs, it must be the consequence of factors which the physical sciences do not acknowledge. So the mentalist is posed with a dilemma: either one is a materialist, in which case one assumes that a complete account of the etiology of behavior need not mention mental processes, or one is a dualist, in which case one assumes that the causation of behavior is not explicable in the terms which physical sciences employ. Either mental constructs are unnecessary or they are occult. In neither case can a mentalistic psychology be an empirical science in methodological good standing.

A remarkable number of psychologists and philosophers have taken—and still take—this argument seriously. Yet what it urges is surely a paradox rather than a methodological insight. For if *anything* is clear in the area where psychologists work, it is that what people say and do is responsive to what they think, feel, want, and remember: Surely it is a truism that people often drink because they are thirsty, scratch because they have itches, and say what they say because they believe what they say. But what makes the truism true is precisely the contingency of forms of behavior upon mental states and processes. A serious psychology could hardly be grounded on a methodology which ignores such contingencies. Methodological principles are not, in short, self-validating. Why accept those which fly in the face of patent truths?

The other horn of the alleged dilemma is no more persuasive. Mental states and processes may finally prove to be neurological states and processes; but the possibility of explaining behavior by reference to beliefs, thirsts, and itches does not depend on knowing whether they will. Antimentalists have been inclined to argue that since psychological states *are* neurological states, the vocabulary of neurology must be the appropriate vocabulary for psychological theories. But this is not an argument; it's a pun on the word "are." One might as well say that since baseball players *are* taxpayers, it follows that the vocabulary of the 1040 form must be appropriate for the description of a squeeze play.

The truth of materialism—if it is true—does not dictate a theoretical vocabulary for psychology or, for that matter, for any of the other special sciences. Almost certainly, every hurricane is a physical event; but from the fact that hurricanes are not occult, it hardly follows that particle physics provides the appropriate vocabulary for doing meteorology. Analogously, it is no sane objection to chemistry that it worked with such notions as acid and base long before it was possible to give a physical account of the characteristic interactions of acids and bases.

It may, of course, be argued that a mentalistic psychology is at least constrained to prove compatible with neurological theory, on pain of exclusion from the scientific club. And so it certainly is. But compatibility is a *symmetrical* relation; psychological plausibility constrains model building in neurology quite as much as neurological plausibility conditions psychological theorizing. Materialism says that when psychologists and neurologists fall out, one of them must be wrong. But it doesn't say *which* one.

In fact, neurology and cognitive psychology have, thus far, had very little to do with one another. The theories in both fields are still too crude for either to provide serious conditions on the acceptability of the other. It is, for example, the sad truth that remarkably little has been learned about the psychology of language processes in normals from over a hundred years of aphasia study, and that nothing at all has been learned about possible neurological realizations of language from the psycholinguistic advances which this book will survey. To put it briefly: it is not only far from clear that neurology provides a useful theoretical vocabulary for psychology, it is even unclear that neurological theories will *ever* have much practical implication for the development of psychological models. The constraint that such models must be neurologically realizable may prove to be quite a *weak* constraint; think how many different programs may be realized on a computer without major alteration of its physical organization.

The analogy to machines is introduced here with malice aforethought. If contemporary mentalists are better situated than their forebears to provide an account of the place of psychology among the sciences, the invention of the general-purpose digital computer is in part responsible. For even though the computer is undoubtedly a physical system, characterizing its transformations of information is quite as important as characterizing its changes of physical state in any full description of the functioning of the machine. Since computers *are* physical systems, information-flow descriptions of computers are *true of* physical systems. But they are not descriptions in the vocabulary of physics, nor do they employ the same criteria of individuation that physical descriptions use. In particular, two machines of quite different physical composition may have the same computational capacities and the same information flow.

The analogy between mentalistic descriptions of organisms and information-flow descriptions of machines may, of course, eventually break down. At one time or another, psychologists have placed their faith in models based on mechanics, hydrodynamics, and telephone switchboards. In none of these cases has their faith been justified. But so long as the analogy holds, the burden of argument has shifted. Anyone who wants to urge that there are ontological problems inherent in mentalistic descriptions of organisms must show why there are not the *same* problems inherent in information-flow descriptions of machines.

The mere existence of computers provided one impetus for the development of contemporary mentalism. Computer mathematics provided another. An argument that has sometimes made stimulus-response psychology seem a viable alternative to mentalism is this: "The behavior of an organism is exhausted by the set of responses it makes throughout its lifetime. Insofar as what is interesting about an organism is its responsiveness to its environment, we can represent its psychology as a set of stimulus-response contingencies. Adding talk of mental states in no way enriches our ability to represent these contingencies; anything which can be said about them by a theory which acknowledges mental states can, at least in principle, be said by a theory which does not."

There is a trivial sense in which this argument is tenable. The behaviors actually produced by an organism, and the stimuli upon which its behaviors are contingent, can be represented by a list. It follows that insofar as the behavior of organisms provides the data to which a psychological theory must be responsive, these data can be captured by a theory whose vocabulary refers only to stimulus and response parameters. But even though this is true, it is thoroughly uninteresting. A scientific theory must predict not only what *did* occur but what *would have* occurred had the initial conditions been otherwise. (Mechanics tells us not only what did happen to objects that fall freely, but also what would have happened to any object had it been freely falling.) And though the actual responses of any organism can be represented by a list, the response *repertoire* of the organism usually cannot.

In short, it is not just the actual but also the potential behavior of an organism to which a theory of its psychology must be responsive. Once we have seen this, it can no longer be taken as self-evident that no theory can be more powerful than one defined over stimulus and response parameters solely. On the contrary, it is quite easy to show that there are describable behavioral repertoires which cannot be captured by such theories. In this sense, stimulus-response psychology is based on a relatively weak mathematical formalism.

It is a question of fact whether it is *too* weak. Much of what will be said in this book will argue that it is; that the regularities in language behavior can be captured only by theories which acknowledge elaborate and complicated mental processes on the part of speaker-hearers. Our present point is that stimulus-response systems occupy a relatively lowly position in the hierarchy of computers. There can be no a priori argument that such systems *must* be sufficiently powerful to represent the behavioral capacities of organisms.

There are thus several respects in which the new interest in mentalism is attributable to the development of computing machines, despite the fact that machine simulation per se has not proved so powerful a research tool as many cognitive psychologists had hoped it might. Very little of the theoretical work that will be reported in this book, for example, was done "on the machine." But analogies to machine operations are ubiquitous, the organization of programs is widely taken as a source of hypotheses about mental organization, and such formalism as is used is borrowed from logic and recursive function theory.

The other major impetus to the development of a mentalistic psychology comes from linguistics proper. Since the relation between linguistics and psychology will be the main theme of this book, suffice it to mention here just one of the reasons why the convergence of these disciplines has led in the direction of mentalism.

A truism mentalists like to stress is that what determines our behavior is not only the stimuli we are exposed to but also the way we interpret those stimuli. This was, of course, a fact that Gestalt made much of. Gestalt psychologists especially stressed perceptual ambiguities; cases in which precisely the same stimulus is seen sometimes in one way, sometimes in another, depending upon the "set" of the perceiver. Such phenomena are grist for the mentalist's mill, since they are pure examples of variation in the response without concomitant variation in the stimulus. Whatever happens when the duck-rabbit changes from duck to rabbit, or when the Necker cube "flips," cannot be explained in terms of *stimulus* variables, since it is precisely the stimulus which does *not* change with changes in the percept.

The figural ambiguities suggest a view of perception as the matching of *stimuli* to *descriptions*, with ambiguous stimuli being those which satisfy descriptions that are otherwise incompatible (a duck-rabbit looks like both a duck and a rabbit, but not in the same respects and not at the same time.) Gestalt theories of perception characteristically adopted this kind of view: perceptual integration was thought of as a matter of subsuming stimuli under "schema," these latter being construed as structural principles which the organism imposes upon its sensory field. A theory of the application of schema to stimuli would thus be a theory of mental processes insofar as they are revealed in the perceptual capacities of organisms.

If the Gestalt approach to perception never managed to produce more than a fragment of such a theory, this was at least in part because they lacked a detailed account of the kinds of descriptions available for the categorization of stimuli. It is in this respect that linguistics has made an essential contribution to the development of contemporary mentalism. Generative grammar has provided a theory of sentence structure which amounts to a detailed and sophisticated account of the categories in terms of which linguistic stimuli are perceptually integrated. Insofar as the account proves accurate, it becomes possible to pose the problem of characterizing the mental processes involved in effecting such integrations. When and if psycholinguistics is able to solve this problem, it will have provided a model for a mentalistic theory of perception.

Psycholinguistics may thus be taken as something of a test case for the possibility of an experimental mentalism. This book is in the nature of a progress report on recent attempts to develop a psycholinguistics that passes the test. Our primary aim has been to provide a critical summary of a decade of work on the mental processes involved in encoding and decoding the syntactic structure of sentences.

The volume of recent work in this field is impressive, and we have had to be selective in a number of respects. First, we have concentrated on work which either assumes or tests a transformational approach to syntax. Transformational models are by no means the last word on language structure, but they are the latest word and they give more promise of connecting with plausible psychological models than anything else in the field. This is, of course, a strong claim, but we shall see as we go along that there is considerable evidence in its favor.

Second, we have not come close to an exhaustive survey of the psycholinguistic literature. We do hope that we have reviewed those theories which have some chance of being true and those experimental paradigms which bear on the theories in interesting ways. We think that there is enough here to illustrate how psycholinguistics is done and why it is interesting to do it. There should be more than enough to refute the claim that mentalistic psychological theories are doomed to experimental sterility.

Finally, we have had to compromise in presenting the linguistics. Like psychology, linguistics is a developing discipline, and any brief survey of the current scene is sure to omit much that is important. Our aims in setting out the linguistic backgrounds to psycholinguistics have been threefold: first, to give the novice as much material as he needs to understand the presuppositions of the experimental literature; second, to give some indication of what argumentation in linguistics is like and what sorts of considerations have led to the highly abstract models of language structure that transformational grammarians accept; last, to indicate some of the current cruxes in the field and some of the directions in which inquiry is likely to proceed. We have done this in the context of examples drawn from English syntax, but the examples are only that. There is probably not a single syntactic rule discussed in this book to which no counterarguments are known.

These remarks apply equally to what we have had to say about semantics. We have thought it important to suggest some of the ways in which work in semantics within transformational grammar differs radically from what psychologists have traditionally thought about meaning. But we can discuss only a handful of the problems currently under investigation; even therein, we have limited ourselves to approaches which can be presented without assuming more formal logic than the casual reader is likely to know. In particular, we have omitted discussions of model theoretic approaches to semantics, since they presuppose some acquaintance with the mechanisms of modal logic.

We have had more than a little help from our friends. Much of what is true in this book we learned from students and colleagues. In particular, we wish to acknowledge our debt to Professors N. Block, Janet Dean Fodor, K. Forster, D. Hakes, M. Halle, S. J. Keyser, T. Langendoen, J. Limber, G. Miller, H. Polio, and H. L. Teuber, each of whom read, and commented helpfully upon, parts of the manuscript.

Cornelia Parkes did invaluable work on the references and bibliography, and Dianne Rice and Sarah Brill typed and retyped what we wrote and rewrote. To each of them we are endlessly grateful.

The enterprise was supported, to various extents and at various times, by the following grants: N.I.H. 5-TO1-HD-00011; N.I.M.H. 5-PO1-MH13390; N.I.M.H. HD05168-02; NGR 22-009-308; and by a grant from the Alfred P. Sloan Foundation.

The material in Part 1 of Chapter 4 is a somewhat revised version of a paper by Fodor, which first appeared in *The learning of language* (Reed, 1971) as "The ontogenesis of the problem of reference." Permission to reprint was granted by the National Council of Teachers of English, and is gratefully acknowledged.

J. A. Fodor
T. G. Bever
M. F. Garrett

THE PSYCHOLOGY OF LANGUAGE

AN INTRODUCTION TO PSYCHOLINGUISTICS AND GENERATIVE GRAMMAR

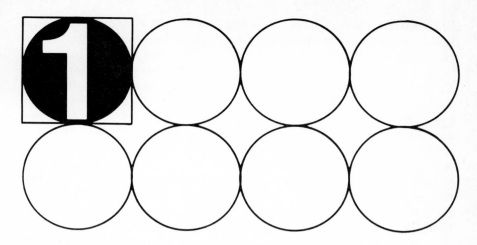

INTRODUCTION

This book is about the relation between theory and practice. In particular, it is about how organisms recruit the concepts at their disposal to organize their percepts and their behavior; how they apply what they know to what they do.

Such questions lie at the heart of problems about perception and action, and their solution must make up a major part of any successful account of memory. For example, it is a point of definition that perception involves determining whether a stimulus falls under a certain concept and that action involves integrating behavior in such a way as to satisfy the constraints some concept imposes. To perceive something as a car, a table, or a minuet involves determing that it has whatever properties the concepts "car," "table," or "minuet" require of their instances. Analogously, writing one's name, solving a maze, or getting married involves the production of behavioral integrations which satisfy the demands that the concepts "writing one's name," "solving a maze," or "getting married" place upon actions which instance them. In either case, the critical relation is the one between concepts and things that fall under them: perception involves *recognizing* cases of this relation and action involves *producing* them.

Similarly, it is an important fact about the functioning of memory that we are able to access classes of items to which a given concept applies. Our memories are so organized as to permit us to obey injunctions like: "list some people you know who were born in Minnesota" or "name twelve brands of automobiles not made in Detroit" or "tell me the phone numbers of two pretty girls." Patently, such questions can be phrased equally well as "list some people you know who satisfy the concept 'born in Minnesota'" or "name twelve brands of automobiles that instance the concept 'not made in Detroit'" or "provide the phone numbers of two individuals who fall under the concept 'pretty girl.'" This is, perhaps, more than a terminological exercise. We seem to be able to search our memories for instances of a given concept, just as we are able to scan the external environment for objects to which some concept applies. By viewing memory and perception as both fundamentally concerned with the relation between concepts and their instances, we stress important analogies between them. For example, the descriptions under which an item can be *recalled* must be intimately related to the ones under which it can be recognized, or we should not be able to remember what we have experienced. A theory of cognitive processes must explicate this relation.

In this way of looking at things, the explanation of perception, action, and memory involves two distinguishable kinds of theories. In the first place, there are theories which seek to analyze concepts; that is, to enumerate the constraints that concepts place upon their instances. Such theories typically attempt to answer questions like "What makes something a car?" or "What do minuets have in common?" by providing necessary and sufficient conditions for something being a car or a minuet.

In the second place, there are theories about how concepts are applied: theories of perceptual integration, which seek to describe the procedures an organism employs to determine which concept a given stimulus instances; theories of behavioral integration, which seek to explain how an organism produces responses which satisfy the constraints some concept places upon actions of a certain kind; and theories of recall, which seek to determine how the memory is searched for items which fall under a given concept. Such theories are characteristically concerned with answering questions like: "How do we recognize tables and triangles?" "How do we tie our shoes?" or "What features determine the associative set for a given word?"

In these various respects, much of the domain of what is traditionally called "cognitive psychology" turns out to be concerned with the problem of how organisms apply their concepts. The issues which emerge when one attempts to explore this domain are exceedingly complicated. To see what they are like, consider some ways in which appeals to concepts can enter into psychological explanations in even a relatively transparent case where the behavior of an organism is controlled by what it knows; consider the case of a man writing his name.

One way of analyzing what happens when a man writes his name would be the following: we give a detailed description of the instantaneous positions occupied by the man's fingers, hand, and arm during the course of writing. We thus seek to represent the man's behavior as a temporally ordered sequence of postures. Such a description could presumably be given equally well in terms of the behavior of the peripheral musculature controlling these postures. Indeed, whatever we take to be the effector mechanisms of the organism, it should always be possible, at least in principle, to provide a description of the actions of the organism as a temporally ordered series of states of such mechanisms. We might even consider identifying the action "writing one's name" with running through some specified series of effector states.

Many psychologists appear to think of the subject matter of their discipline in some such way. Tinbergen (1969, p.2), for example, characterizes the domain of the behavior sciences as "the total *movements* made by the intact animal," and Skinner (1938, p. 6) writes "By behavior . . . I mean simply the movement of an organism or of its parts in a frame of reference provided by the organism itself or by various external objects or fields of force. It is convenient to speak of this as the action of the organism upon the outside world. . . ."

In fact, however, we almost never speak in a way which identifies the *actions* of an organism with the sequence of *movements* it makes. (For example, we speak of a man as writing his name, not, normally, as moving a pen across the paper.) There is good reason for this. An account of the behavior of an organism misses a great deal if it is given solely in terms of states of the organism's effector system.

When we say of a man that he knows how to write his name, we do not mean that he is able to execute some specific sequence of gestures, nor that his muscles are capable of assuming some specific sequence of states. This is evident from the fact that a man who knows how to write his name at all knows how to do so under a variety of circumstances and in a variety of ways. There is, for example, no one who is able to write his name only in letters less than an inch high, or only with a pencil, or only on a blackboard. The commonsense explanation of this fact is that the man who writes his name is guided in his performance by some concept, plan, schema, idea, or mental content; and however he writes, large or small, in ink or in chalk, etc., there is some sense in which his behavior is guided by the *same* mental content on each of the occasions when what he writes is his name.

The commonsense view is thus that what determines which kind of action a given sequence of overt gestures realizes is often the mental state by which the sequence is controlled; the reason that markedly different sequences of gestures are often instances of the same behavior is simply that distinct gestures are often expressions of the same underlying mental state. One of the purposes for which commonsense explanations appeal to such (roughly equivalent) notions as concepts, plans, ideas, schemata, etc., is to provide criteria for the *individuation* of behaviors: we often answer the question "What is he doing?" by referring to the plan he has in mind. That is, we often suppose that behaviors are of the same kind when they are controlled by the same mental state.

There are at least two other roles that such appeals to mental contents may play in accounts of the integration of behavior. In the first place, we may appeal to the plan the organism is following when we are trying to make sense of its behavior. We do this whenever we account for a bit of behavior by referring to some organismic goal to which it is presumed to be a means. "Why is Smith writing an *S*?" "Because Smith is writing his name and his name begins with an *S*." Here we rationalize the behavior by referring to the plan that presumably controls it; we explain the behavior by showing how it fits into a pattern of action the organism is believed to be attempting to produce.

Finally, we may appeal to what the organism knows when we give a psychological account of the processes by which ongoing behavior is actually integrated. Let us return to the man who is writing his name. Suppose that his name is Frederick. We have just seen that is is plausible to argue that one has an idea of writing one's name that is distinct from the idea of running through any particular sequence of motor gestures. Lashley (1951) pointed out, in a classic article, that this sort of knowledge must control the details of ongoing behavior in a very intimate way. For example, when Frederick writes "Frederick," he must write *e* twice. Moreover, in writing his name, Frederick must distinguish the first time he writes *e* from the second time he does so, because the first time he writes *e*, he must follow it with a *d*, but the second time he writes *e*, he must follow it with an *r*.

The commonsense view is that the way he does it is to compare the temporally ordered motor output with a mental representation of the *in-*

tended output. Each of Frederick's overt gestures is thus internally represented not only as a discrete entity but also in terms of its relation to the plan which his ongoing behavior is in the process of realizing. In particular, the gestures involved in producing the two *e*'s in "Frederick" are distinguished not primarily by any intrinsic feature of their motor organization, but rather by their relation to the general plan that Frederick is executing when he writes his name.

Evidence for this sort of intimate relation between ongoing motor output and a persisting mental schema which guides its integration was pointed out by Lashley, who remarked upon the occurrence of preposition errors in typing (e.g., "elat" for "late"). Such errors strongly suggest that there must exist *some* level of representation at which linguistic units longer than single letters are present to the mind of the typist. Presumably this representation functions to provide a "simultaneous display" of the sequential information required to direct the typist's motor activity. Similarly, as Tolman and others have argued, an organism following a route through a city or a maze must be integrating its behavior by reference to some general analysis of its position vis-á-vis the geography of its environment. Unless one assumes some sort of internal "map" on which the organism locates itself, its ability to devise alternate routes to a given goal becomes inexplicable.

In short, in the analysis of behavior, we frequently find that while the *output* of the organism can be viewed as a temporally ordered sequence of gestures or of effector states, there is, nevertheless, reason to suppose that behavior is organized by reference to an internal representation of the action as a whole. It is common sense that one often knows what one is going to do before one does it, and that what one does now is often responsive to what one intends to do later on. Common sense appeals to current plans, strategies, intentions, etc., to account for this apparent determination of the present by the future; it is because one knows about painting oneself into a corner that one starts painting on the side of the room opposite the door; one paints here now because one intends to exit there later. There is no good reason why psychology should disagree with commonsense on any of these matters.

We have mentioned three ways in which appeals to the mental states of an organism may be involved in accounts of the way that the organism behaves. Such states may provide criteria for the *individuation* of behaviors, or they may serve to *rationalize* behavior, or they may function in the *integration* of behavior. It is implied by this view that any serious account of the behavior of an organism will have to say not only how (i.e., by virtue of what psychological mechanisms) the organism puts its knowledge to use, but also what it is that the organism knows; what concepts it has.

That the former of these problems is difficult is recognized by everyone who has thought about psychology at all. That the latter may be equally difficult follows from the consideration that there is no apparent limit to the complexity of the information that the organism may employ to organize its behavior. This is, once again, a claim that is obvious even at the level of common sense. What rationalizes my behavior in filling the tank of my car is the information I have about what the gas does. This information connects in subtle and elaborate ways with what I know about combustion, about the operation of cars, etc. Similarly, my knowledge of how to write my name connects with my knowledge of how to speak my name, with my knowledge of what my name is, and so on.

From the point of view of psychological theory, the most important feature of the way that concepts interconnect is that they characteristically form *productive* informational systems, in the sense that they determine the appropriate perceptual analysis, and the appropriate behavioral response, for types of stimuli on which the organism was not specifically trained. We have already remarked, for example, that the spatial concepts of an organism are normally interrelated in ways that permit it to calculate novel paths between points of known location. Similarly, it is obvious that mastery of the conceptual system that characterizes a complex game like chess involves the ability of the player to compute appropriate behaviors for any of a vast variety of chess positions that are novel to him. Presumably he does this by employing rules for relating new board configurations to configurations with which he is familiar and whose consequences he knows. Precisely analogous points can be made in the case of the concepts that mediate almoˈt any complex behavioral system; most notably, as we shall see, in the case of language.

The fact that the information in terms of which behavioral integrations are effected is characteristically productive has very important consequences for theories of action. It implies, in particular, that we cannot account for behavior if we assume that what the organism knows is exhausted by a fixed repertoire of static plans. (Cf. Miller, Galanter, and Pribram, 1960.) Rather, concepts must be organized bodies of information from which practical inferences about how to act in new situations can be drawn. In short, organisms are able to use the information at their disposal to construct new behavioral options by formulating new plans, and to reevaluate old responses when they encounter novel stimuli. An adequate theory of cognitive processes must so characterize their concepts as to account for the productivity and spontaneity of their behavior.

In the following pages we shall be trying to work out part of a theory of how certain facets of verbal behavior are controlled by the speaker's knowledge of the grammatical structure of his language. We shall see that this problem has two aspects: what is the speaker's concept of his language, i.e., what does the speaker know about his language by virtue of which he is able to speak it; and what are the psychological mechanisms which implement this knowledge, i.e., how does the speaker apply his concept of his language for the integration of verbal behavior. Before we turn to these questions, however, we wish to expand upon a point mentioned above: cognitive psychology is concerned not only with integration of behavior but also with perceptual integration, and there are important respects in which theories of behavior and of perception are symmetrical. In particular, the suggestion that the organization of action is effected by referring the behavioral output to an underlying mental model has an exact counterpart in the analysis of the organization of perception. Similarly, the productivity of the concepts with which organisms operate raises the same sorts of problems for theories of perception as for theories of action.

There is a well-known psychological demonstration experiment that works like this: A subject is presented with a stimulus array consisting of a screen with a small hole through which he can see an illuminated surface. He is then shown a series of color chips and asked to choose the one that most closely matches the color of the surface he sees. The experimental situation is arranged so that what the subject is actually viewing is a small part of the surface of a red apple illuminated by green light. Not surprisingly, under these conditions, subjects will choose a color chip which is greener than the true color of the surface of the apple.

Now, however, we introduce a subject to the same array *without* the interposed screen. That is, this second subject differs from the first in that he knows that he is seeing an apple, though, like the first subject, he does *not* know that he is seeing the apple under nonstandard illumination. The interesting point is that subjects in this second condition choose color chips closer to the true color of the apple (i.e., closer to the color it has when viewed in ordinary *white* light) than do subjects in the first condition.

We are dealing here with a fairly transparent instance of "perceptual constancy"; in this case, a constancy of the same type as one's ability to tolerate changes in the color of the illumination during the course of a day. Objects seen at twilight do not appear to be of a radically different color than when seen at noon. Yet the color of evening light is quite different from the color of broad daylight; hence the color of the light a given object is reflecting must change according to the time of day.

In these cases, then, the objective wavelength of the light falling on the subject's retina does *not* reliably predict the perceived colors that he reports. How is a theory of perception to account for this sort of fact?

Surely not by reference to any inherent limitations on our visual capacities; the magnitude of the color variations that are tolerated in the kinds of situations we have been discussing is far greater than the minimal color changes that the visual system can easily detect. The point appears to be, rather, that observers know the relevant facts about the "true" color of objects, and this knowledge is employed to compensate for the effects of nonstandard conditions of observation. To express the point in the terminology we used above, what determines the properties an object is perceived to have is not only its "objective" physical properties but also the concept that a subject applies in the process of perceptual organization. The perceived properties of an object are a complicated integration of the sensory input with our a priori expectations about objects of that kind. (For discussion, and further examples, cf. Bruner, 1957; Neisser, 1967; and Osgood, 1953.)

Cases of this sort are particularly striking, since they involve examples wherein the same percept is elicited by stimuli which are seen to be discriminably different when relevant features of their context are suppressed. However, insofar as it is an expression of the organism's ability to tolerate differences between stimuli to which it must respond uniformly, the phenomenon of perceptual constancy may be thought of as a special case of the much more general phenomenon of stimulus equivalence.

There are a vast variety of instances in which organisms treat stimuli which they are not disposed to *identify* as, nevertheless, in some respect equivalent. We are thinking of such workaday facts as that, on the one hand, one may have no difficulty in discriminating Fords from Ferraris, yet on the other, one may recognize both as instances of the concept "automobile." Analogously, no one has difficulty in discriminating between the following inscriptions: FREDERICK, Frederick, and *Frederick*. Yet, anyone who can read English automatically tolerates these differences and recognizes all three inscriptions as representations of the same word.

The problem to be faced here is the same one that arose in the discussion of the individuation of actions. We saw then that the variety of performances that can constitute writing one's name defies characterization in terms of an enumeration of sequences of motor gestures. This is because there is an indefinite number of such sequences, any of which may be an instance of writing one's name, depending upon the circumstances in which the performance happens to occur. For this reason, we found it plausible that in learning to write one's name, one learns not motor gestures but rather a schema of some fairly abstract kind. It is presumed to be the integration of this schema with information about local conditions (the size of the paper, the weight of the pencil, etc.) that determines which gestures one employs in writing one's name on a given occasion. Conversely, it is the fact that all instances of writing one's name are controlled by the same schema that makes all such behaviors behaviors of the same kind.

In strictly analogous fashion, we assume that the criterion for perceptual equivalence of stimuli is set by the schemata the organism employs for perceptual integration. As a first approximation, such schemata may be thought of as specifying the conditions a sensory array must meet if it is to qualify as being a percept of a certain kind.

This way of talking is useful in that it emphasizes the role that the concepts at the disposal of the organism play in shaping its perceptual world. It may, however, be misleading in at least the following way: it may encourage us to think of the conditions that schemata place on the perceptual integration of sensory arrays as being largely *sensory* conditions, i.e., to think of the criteria that must be satisfied if an object is to fall under a concept as statable largely in terms of the sensory properties of that object.

It is evident, however, that what determines whether a sensory array is an instance of a given concept may often be something quite abstract: consider the property by virtue of which the inscriptions FREDERICK, Frederick, and *Frederick* are all representations of the word "Frederick." Clearly, this property is not primarily a matter of any overt similarity of the inscriptions. Rather, in interpreting these inscriptions, we attend not only to such "sensory" properties as the absolute sizes or shapes of their elements but also to quite abstract geometric properties of the relations among the elements. It is presumably because readers are sensitive to abstract invariants of this sort that they can rapidly adjust to variations in type font or calligraphic style. A model which understands the mental processes underlying the identification of a percept as a search for invariant sensory features in a heterogeneous sensory array cannot, in general, account for that sort of capacity. (Some such error occurs in many treatments of perception by empiricists because of their habit of thinking of concepts as stored *images* and of perception as a a process of matching such images to inputs. Such views have often led empiricists to assume that it must be possible to characterize the conditions that concepts impose upon their instances in terms of imageable—i.e., sensory—properties of stimuli.)

These are considerations whose special relevance to the study of the psychological processes underlying language will presently be made clear. Suffice it for current purposes to emphasize that the scope of the problem of how an organism employs its concepts to effect its perceptual integrations does not begin to emerge so long as one thinks of the individuation and identification of percepts as determined largely by their sensory properties. So long as one supposes that stimuli are perceptually identical just in case their differences fall below discrimination thresholds and perceptually equivalent just in case they share criterial sensory attributes, it is possible to equate the problem of perception with the problem of how organisms learn to make discriminative responses to sensory invariants. This is, indeed, in large part the history of investigations of perception at the hands of American learning theorists. However, the existence of perceptual constancies demonstrates the impossibility of explaining perceptual identity in terms of relative indiscriminatibility, and the existence of abstract perceptual equivalences demonstrates that objects which are properly considered to be of the same kind need not therefore share criterial sensory properties. There may, for example, be nothing at all in common between the sensory arrays I produce when I write "Frederick" and when I say "Frederick." Yet everyone who can speak and read English recognizes these arrays as, in a relevant sense, perceptually equivalent. Some indication of the complexity of the conceptual system that mediates this equivalence can be gained by reflecting upon the fact that no theorist has yet produced a perspicuous account of the correspondence between the orthography and the phonology of English. Yet it is precisely this equivalence that is mastered in learning how to read; an accomplishment about which psychology knows primarily that it is extremely complicated.

When we discussed the integration of actions, we claimed not only that the concepts with which an organism operates are *abstract* but also that they are characteristically productive. The analogous consideration has important implications for perception. In particular, there seems to be no practical bound to the classifications into which we can sort our experiences, and a theory of perception must somehow account for this fact.

To appreciate the difficulty that theories of perception must face on this account, consider the number and range of categorizations of its experience that are available to the sophisticated human organism. A moderately well educated human can recognize spiral nebulae and cigarette butts, faces, misspellings, cabbages, kings, Oxford dons, scherzos, touchdowns, puns, certain kinds of social gaffes, teapots, friends of the family, his wife from a variety of angles and in a variety of lights, English accents, butlers, the taste of chicken, the cubist style in painting, etc. Corresponding to each of these ways of sorting he has an appropriate concept—i.e., a system of rules for determining when an individual satisfies the relevant description. How is this apparently boundless conceptual system organized? How is it recruited for perceptual organization?

We remarked above that virtually everything we have said about perception and action can also be said of memory. We are now in a position to see why this is so: the descriptions under which an item can be remembered are abstract and productive, just like the descriptions under which objects can be perceived and actions integrated. One can recall items under such descriptions as: "people I know under thirty," "states on the West Coast," "late symphonies of Beethoven," "persons with big noses," "neurotic dogs owned by friends of mine," "linguists who have been influenced by Noam Chomsky," and so on practically indefinitely. Conversely, a given item may be available under a variety of descriptions ranging from "my automobile" to "one of the things for which I am indebted to my bank." Certainly it is true that not every concept is equally available for accessing memory items (one might have some trouble listing Baroque composers whose last names begin with *t*, even if one can recognize, say, Telemann as satisfying that description), and not all the information available for a given item can be used with equal facility in "calling" that item from storage (it is usually easier to recall the telephone number that goes with a given name than the name that goes with a given telephone number.) Nevertheless, it seems clear that the set of descriptions under which the memory can be searched cannot be exhausted by a fixed set of cross-classifications any more than the structure of the perceptual system can be exhausted by a fixed set of perceptual categories. Analogously, just as perceptual categories cannot be specified solely by reference to the sensory characteristics of inputs, so there is no apparent bound on the abstractness of the descriptions that can be employed in recall. It is not noticeably easier to search the memory for objects which satisfy relatively concrete descriptions ("blue" or "round") than for things which satisfy relatively abstract, relational descriptions ("American" or "owned by me"). It is the abstractness and productivity of concepts which makes the problem of how organisms relate them to their instances interesting, and it seems that solving that problem is as essential to understanding how memory works as it is to understanding perception and action.

We have thought of the mature organism as possessing a productive system of concepts, rules, plans, strategies, etc., which is available for the recall of items from memory and for the organization and individuation of sensory inputs and motor outputs. In emphasizing the extent to which these concepts are abstractly related to their instances, we are implicitly diverging from views that have been widely held in theoretical psychology. In particular, we are assuming that the information at the organism's disposal is appropriately characterized *neither* as "perceptual information" nor as "motor information." Unlike the empiricists, we do not suppose that concepts resemble percepts (e.g., that they are images, or near kin to images). But also, unlike such psychologists as Piaget, Werner, Vygotsky, and Bruner, we do not suppose that concepts are fundamentally grounded in motor responses. The point here is that if we identify what the organism knows with instances of its perceptual integrations, we correspondingly make a mystery of its motor capacities; conversely, if we identify what the organism knows with instances of its motor skills, we necessarily make a mystery of perception. It argues against concepts being like images that they are routinely recruited for the integration of behavior. It argues against their being like gestures that they are routinely recruited for perceptual integration.

A theory which accounts for psychological phenomena in terms of the information an organism has at its disposal should, we believe, take cases of duality of perceptual and motor skills seriously. By and large, someone who can recognize triangles can draw them, and vice versa; by and large, someone who can speak a language can understand it, and vice versa. Granted that there is *some* level at which perceptual and motor systems are distinct (one speaks with one's mouth, not with one's ears), the tendency of perceptual and motor capacities to covary suggests that we ought not represent them as distinct vis-à-vis the concepts they employ. The model we shall be working with assumes that the mental representation of things like triangles and languages is not biased toward either perceptual or motor integration: it is a structure more like a definition than an image or a motor response. As such, concepts are equally available either for recognition or for the integration of behavior.

On this view, then, the central problem in cognitive psychology turns out to be what Kant called the problem of "schematism." If concepts are like rules or definitions, we must provide an account of how rules and definitions are employed to organize perception, motor integration, and memory. In the course of his discussion of perception, Kant remarks (1781; in Smith, 1953) that

It is schemata, not images of objects, which underlie our pure sensible concepts. No image could ever be adequate to the concept of a triangle in general. It would never attain that universality of the concept which renders it valid of all triangles, whether right-angled, obtuse-angled, or acute-angled; it would always be limited to a part only of this sphere. The schema of the triangle can exist nowhere but in thought. It is a rule of synthesis of the imagination, in respect to pure figures in space. Still less is an object of experience or its image ever adequate to the empirical concept; for this latter always stands in immediate relation to the schema of imagination, as a rule for the determination of our intuition, in accordance with some specific universal concept. The concept "dog" signifies a rule according to which my imagination can delineate the figure of a four-footed animal in a general manner, without limitation to any single determinate figure such as experience, or any possible image that I can represent *in concreto*, actually presents. This schematism of our understanding, in its application to appearances and their mere form, is an art concealed in the depths of the human soul, whose real modes of activity nature is hardly likely ever to allow us to discover, and to have open to our gaze [pp. 182–183].

Kant's argument is that concepts must be distinguished from images of the objects that fall under them. What we know about dogs or triangles cannot, in point of logic, be represented by an image of a prototypic triangle or dog; the "universality" of our concepts can be captured only by a theory which represents them as abstract. But, on the other hand, the work our concepts do primarily concerns the recognition and production of the concrete, individual objects to which they apply. It is by exploiting our *abstract* concept of triangle that we manage to recall, recognize, or produce an indefinite variety of *concrete* objects which *are* triangles. What, then, mediates the application of abstract concepts to their concrete instances? This is the problem whose answer Kant believed to be "concealed in the depths of the human soul."

It is a special case of this problem that concerns us in this book. We shall ask how a speaker-hearer applies his knowledge of the abstract structure of his language to understanding and producing utterances of sentences. But, insofar as it is correct to identify the problem of how concepts are applied as the central one in cognitive psychology, an examination of this special case should throw light on the entire range of cognitive phenomena.

In what respects is it plausible to view language processing as involving the application of concepts to their instances? In particular, what can be said for treating the production and perception of sentences as a special case of the use of concepts to effect perceptual and motor integration? We will approach these questions by first considering some very general features of communication exchanges which involve language.

No one has ever given a persuasive account of the necessary and sufficient conditions for understanding an utterance of a sentence. But it does seem clear that one of the necessary conditions be that the hearer determine *which* sentence the utterance he hears is an utterance of. The very least that the hearer must do if he is to grasp what has been said is to associate an acoustic event with a linguistic form. If, for the moment, we think of the hearer's knowledge of his language as represented by a list of the linguistic forms which constitute sentences of the language, then part of what the hearer must do in understanding an utterance is to associate it with one of the sentences on that list.

A first approximation to an analysis of speech exchanges thus suggests itself: the *speaker* in such an exchange chooses one of the sentences on his internal list and produces an acoustic event which, according to a certain scheme for *encoding* sentences into acoustic events, constitutes an utterance of that sentence. The hearer, receiving the utterance as input, looks through *his* internal list of sentences and finds the one with which it is associated by a scheme for *decoding* acoustic events into sentences. A necessary condition for mutual comprehension is that the sentence encoded by the speaker be the same sentence that is recovered by the hearer.

This model of speech exchanges clearly represents an enormous abstraction from the manifest behavior of speaker-hearers. For example, not every intelligible utterance is an utterance of a full sentence. Equivalently, not every output of the speech apparatus that is relevant to communication is properly decoded into sentential form.

Clearly, however, some such abstraction from the data will need to be made, since it is obvious that the data reflect the influence of variables which are only accidentally related to the ones a theory of the speech processes should represent. The manifest verbal behavior of the speaker-hearer includes, for example, hiccoughs, groans, sneezes, and other sounds which may have no relation to the speaker's communicative intentions. Similarly, the data reflect all sorts of misperformances and misperceptions when the intentions of the speaker-hearer are not accurately reflected by his actual behavior. That this is true is obvious from the very existence of cases in which we correct ourselves in the course of speech production or ask for correction in the course of speech perception.

Given that any model of the communication situation will be required to perform *some* abstraction upon the data, what justifies concentrating upon the production and comprehension of *sentences* rather than on some other linguistic unit? The ultimate answer to this question must be to show that the sentence is, as a matter of fact, the linguistic unit in whose structure the systematicity of language and language behavior is best revealed. Much of our discussion of grammar will be directed to reviewing evidence which bears upon this claim. Suffice it to remark here that the sentence is the smallest linguistic unit with which we can unambiguously make a statement, ask a question, give an order, etc. If, for example, one assumes that a fundamental semantic property of language is that it permits us to refer to an object to which we apply some predicate, then the sentence is the shortest linguistic form with which we can do this without relying upon nonlinguistic context. This is the sense in which utterances like "Run!" or "John" strike us as abbreviations of full sentences like "You run!" or "His name is John." Insofar as we are concerned with providing a theory of the speaker-hearer's mastery of such fundamental performances as making a statement, asking a question, or giving an order, it seems reasonable to concentrate upon the sentence as the linguistic vehicle of these performances.

Let us, then, continue to consider some of the implications of the analysis of the speech exchange suggested above. Crude though that analysis certainly is, it has the advantage of bringing two questions immediately to the fore. First, what is the nature of the internal representations of sentences which, we have supposed, are encoded into utterances by speakers and recovered by hearers? And second, what is the nature of the encoding and decoding systems employed to map from internal representations of sentences into utterances and back again?

Both questions will be discussed at length in the course of this book. The following remarks are thus preliminary.

Western Union employs a coding system in which certain complex but stereotyped messages are associated with numbers. What the sending telegrapher actually transmits is not, for example, "Am having a wonderful time, wish you were here, Sam," but rather something like "2 Sam." The receiving telegrapher, since he is privy to the encoding system which the sender employs, can recover the original message by substituting for "2" the stereotyped greeting with which it is associated by the code.

In the case of such codes, we might say that there is an *arbitrary* relation between the encoded form of the message and its unencoded form. The choice of "2" as the coded representation of "Am having a wonderful time, wish you were here" is, in an obvious sense, gratuitous; Western Union might equally have chosen "22" or "6" or, for that matter, "rabbit."

This sort of arbitrary code is possible only in a case in which there is a fixed set of messages to be transmitted, because the possibility of using the code depends on the sender and receiver's having arrived at a prior agreement about which message is to be represented by each symbol. In this kind of code, there is no general way of computing the encoded form of a message from a representation of its unencoded form, and no general way of recovering the message from its encoded representation.

Clearly, then, an arbitrary procedure for coding from internal representations of sentences to acoustic events, and vice versa, will not work in the case of full-blown language processes. For, as we remarked above, languages, like most other complex conceptual systems, are productive. They allow us continually to encode *new* messages—new sentences—and to recover the sentence encoded by novel utterances. Because languages are productive, the encoding-decoding procedures employed in language processing must be such as to permit speaker-hearers to compute the unencoded message from its encoded representation in some regular and nonarbitrary way.

In short, since most of the utterances a hearer experiences or a speaker produces are of sentences novel to both of them, it follows that the speaker and hearer cannot be employing a code which requires a prior agreement on what the encoded form of each sentence shall be. Rather, the encoding procedures must be such as to provide an appropriate acoustic form as output given an appropriate representation of any sentence in the language as input. Conversely, given as input an acoustic encoding of any sentence in the language, the decoding procedures must be adequate to recover the internal representation of that sentence.

Thus far we have been considering constraints on the speaker-hearer's encoding-decoding system which follow simply from the productivity of the messages that can be transmitted in natural language speech exchanges. Can analogous constraints be placed upon the speaker-hearer's *internal representation* of these messages, and, if so, what might these constraints be like?

Every language contains an indefinite number of distinct sentences, so the system of internal representations speaker-hearers use must distinguish between an indefinite number of objects. Moreover, as we have seen, the pairing of sentences and encodings must be nonarbitrary; there must be a general procedure for determining the encoding which corresponds to an internal representation, and vice versa. How is this to be accomplished? Roughly, the answer is that the representation assigned each sentence must specify whatever features of the sentence contribute to its individuation. To see how this works, it is only necessary to consider a system for representing sentences which *is*, in the relevant sense, nonarbitrary; such a system as, for example, the orthography of English.

"22" is an arbitrary representation of "having a wonderful time..." because the parts of the representation are in no systematic correspondence to the parts of the sentence. But the parts of the English orthographic sequence "having a wonderful time . . ." *do* correspond to parts of the sentence in the required way: for example, changing part of the representation results, in a systematic way, in changing the sentence it represents. Thus, "having a terrible time..." is an orthographic representation of a *different* sentence from the one represented by "having a wonderful time . . . ," and the difference falls, so to speak, in the right place: the *orthographic sequences* differ in that one has the subsequence "terrible" where the other has the subsequence "wonderful," and the corresponding *sentences* differ in that one has the word "terrible" where the other has the word "wonderful."

Roughly, English orthography is nonarbitrary in that parts of representations correspond to parts of sentences. It is only because this is true that English orthography can be employed to represent a productive set of linguistic objects. The same point can be made about whatever system of internal representations speaker-hearers use for the sentences of their language. Since the set of sentences is productive, each feature of a sentence which contributes to its individuation must correspond to some determinate part of the representation of that sentence.

If we knew what features of sentences contribute to their individuation, we would thus know a great deal about the system of internal representation that speaker-hearers use for their language. In fact, however, though it is easy to give examples of such features, it is extremely difficult to provide an exhaustive list of them. What is obvious is that the system of representation will at least have to mark such features of sentences as their lexical content and grammatical structures. For example, a system of representation rich enough to distinguish each sentence from every other will necessarily provide distinct representations for "a cat is on the mat" and "a dog is on the mat" and for "John loves Mary" and "Mary loves John." Since in such cases it is a difference in the grammatical organization of the sentences, or in their lexical content, which distinguishes among the members of the pairs, it follows that the speaker-hearer's system of representation for sentences of English must mark both such features. This is a kind of argument of great potential power: if the speaker-hearer's system of internal representation specifies the features of sentences upon which their individuation is contingent, and if there are two sentences which differ only in that one has the feature F and the other does not, then the presence or absence of F must be specified by the system of internal representation.

We have been considering some properties that internal representations must have if they are to distinguish among the sentences of a natural language. In particular, we suggested that they can do so only insofar as the internal representation of a sentence is a nonarbitrary representation of that sentence: one in which the parts of the representation correspond to the parts of the sentence in a systematic way. We may now add a further condition: the representations assigned to sentences must be abstract.

Suppose that the speaker-hearer internally represents sentences as strings of words; i.e., that his system of internal representation is essentially isomorphic to the one used by English orthography. That sort of representation satisfies the condition that it provides nonarbitrary representations for an indefinite set of sentences. It does *not*, however, satisfy the condition that each distinct sentence be distinctly represented. This is because it does not mark *all* the properties of sentences that can be relevant to their individuation. In particular, it fails to represent a variety of abstract properties.

Consider, for example, the string of words (1-1). It is clear that this

1-1 John likes old men and women.

string is a representation of not one but two sentences: one sentence corresponds to the interpretation "John likes old men and old women," and the other corresponds to the interpretation "John likes old men and all women." A system of representation rich enough to accommodate the fact that there is more than one English sentence with the orthographic shape of (1-1) must therefore have facilities for representing abstract structural features of sentences that the conventional orthography does not mark. For example, a representational system which specified each sentence as a *bracketed* orthographic string *would* be able to mark the ambiguity of (1-1). Given such a system, we could capture the fact that an utterance of (1-1) may be an instance of either the sentence (John) (likes ((old men) and (women))) or the sentence (John) (likes (old (men and women))).

The remark that the speaker-hearer's internal representation of sentences must include at least a specification of their bracketing is motivated by considerations other than the requirement that distinct sentences must have distinct representations, and some of these considerations are "behavioral" in even the grossest sense. Notice, for example, that the orthographic sequence (1-2) has two different *pronunciations,*

1-2 They are eating apples.

one corresponding to the bracketing (they) (are eating) (apples) and one corresponding to the bracketing (they) (are) (eating apples). (It also has two meanings, again with the difference in meaning corresponding precisely to the difference in grouping of the elements.) There are thus a variety of types of regularities which independently suggest that a representation of sentences as strings of words misses structural features which directly determine the way speaker-hearers perform with sentences. Indeed even the orthography is sporadically sensitive to the need for representing features of grouping. Note the difference between "they advertised for a light housekeeper" and "they advertised for a lighthouse keeper."

It now is clear that the requirement that the speaker-hearer's system of internal representation must distinguish among the sentences entails the requirement that that system be free of ambiguities. Ambiguities arise when a system of representation provides the same coding for more than one sentence; e.g., in the way that the conventional orthography provides the same coding for (John) (likes ((old men) and (women))) and for (John) (likes (old (men and women))). Any putative characterization of the speaker-hearer's system of representation which can be shown to permit such ambiguity is thereby shown to be too weak to capture the full resources at the disposal of the speaker-hearer, since it represents as univocal sequences to whose multiplicity of structures speaker-hearers are sensitive.

This argument can now be extended to show that the speaker-hearer must employ a system for representing sentences that are even more abstract than bracketed strings of words. For example, the bracketing system would not capture the fact that utterances of the kind produced by reading aloud the orthographic sequence of (1-3) can be instances of either of two distinct English sentences (one roughly synonymous with "they wouldn't quit drinking" and one roughly synonymous with "they wouldn't prevent drinking"). Both sentences share not only the orthographic representation of (1-3) but also the bracketed representation of (the police) ((wouldn't) (stop) (drinking)).

1-3 The police wouldn't stop drinking.

What we have here is an ambiguity generated not by the grouping of the parts of the sentences into constituents, but rather by the character of the grammatical relations between the parts. In one version, "police" is the subject of both "stop" and "drink." In the alternate version, "police" is the subject of "stop," while the subject of "drink" is "understood" or "implied" to be somebody other than the police.

We can now see one of the ways in which a theory of the speaker-hearer's internal representation of sentences connects with the theory of linguistic percepts. The process of speech recognition is essentially one of imposing a perceptual analysis upon the speech event, and a theory of the speaker-hearer's internal representation makes the character of this analysis explicit. Thus certain types of theories of the internal representation can be rejected simply on the grounds that they supply univocal descriptions for ambiguous utterances; i.e., for speech events which we know that the speaker-hearer can analyze in more than one way.

Our methodological principle that the internal representation of a sentence must mark the features relevant to its individuation is thus equivalent to the requirement that it mark the features relevant to its perceptual analysis. Consider another rather elementary example. Speakers easily distinguish the difference between words that rhyme and those that do not. This distinction is, in fact, partially marked in normal English orthography, where, in general, words that rhyme have partially identical spellings, the identically spelled parts being the rhyming parts. This generalization is, however, imperfect. Though it holds for such pairs as "tune" and "June," it does not hold for "right" and "bite," or "hate" and "bait."

Unlike the conventional orthography of English, an adequate theory of the speaker-hearer's internal representation must precisely capture the notion of rhyme by providing an "ideal orthography" in which the rhyming parts of rhyming words invariably receive identical representations. This follows from the more general requirement that the theory must represent the perceptual analysis which the speaker-hearer imposes upon utterances of words, since the perception of rhyme is presumably the perception of partial phonetic identities between the rhyming words.

In general, it seems clear that words are heard as complex sequences built up out of a relatively small number of elementary speech sounds (the *phones* of the language). For example, "boy" and "buy" are each heard as containing two speech sounds, the first of which they have in common, while "bad" and "dad" are heard as each consisting of three speech sounds, the last two of which they have in common. Each word in the *lexicon* of a language can thus be identified with some sequence of speech sounds drawn from the *phonological inventory* of the language. As has been widely noted, it is this decomposition of words into more elementary units which permits the language to represent a very large number of meaningful vocabulary items (half a million or so words, in the case of English) in terms of a relatively small number of meaningless elementary units (forty or so phonemes in the case of English).

Since each word is perceptually analyzed into a sequence of recurring elementary sounds, the phonological system used for internally representing utterances of a language may be thought of as cross-classifying the words into sets of partially identical items. (Thus "buy" and "boy" are classified as identical in their first item; "bad" and "dad" are classified as identical in their last two items, etc.) What a phonological theory claims to do, then, is to represent one facet of the coding system which speaker-hearers actually use in internally representing the utterances of their language, and to which they presumably appeal in making judgments about identity and difference of vocabulary items.

One can fully appreciate the significance of this claim only in light of the fact that there is, in general, no simple correspondence between the *perceptual* identities marked by the ideal orthography and any homogeneous *acoustic* feature of the utterance of words which have part of their phonetic representation in common. That is, the identification of rhyme (and of phonetic identity and difference in general) is, in the sense specified earlier in this chapter, a perceptual constancy; and the claim that is made for a theoretically adequate ideal orthography is that it precisely represents the perceptual objects this constancy engenders.

We have thus far mentioned a number of features of the perceptual analyses speaker-hearers impose upon the speech events which encode messages in their language. We have seen that a theory of the internal representations speakers encode and hearers recover must be rich enough to mark each such feature: each discrimination hearers make in interpreting utterances of their language corresponds to the *recovery* of some property of an internal representation, and each distinction speakers make in producing utterances of their language corresponds to the *encoding* of some property of an internal representation.

We can now propose some sort of answer to the questions with which this section was introduced: in what respects is it plausible to view language processing as the application of a concept to its instances?

A speech episode involves the encoding and decoding of an internal representation of a sentence. Such a representation marks certain linguistically relevant structural features of the sentence; that is, the sentence is represented by the speaker-hearer *as* an array of such features. It is in terms of these features that the message intended by the speaker and recovered by the hearer is presumed to be individuated. We have seen what some of these features are: bracketing, grammatical relations, phonological sequence, and so on.

Now, it is clear that a very complex coding system mediates between the internal representation and the speech event. Many of the structures that must be recovered in the perceptual analysis of a sentence are only very indirectly represented in the acoustic events which constitute utterances of the sentence. The problem of the perceptual analysis of speech is thus the problem of how the speaker recovers the appropriate internal representation of a given acoustic form (i.e., the representation intended by the utterer of the sentence), and the problem of the behavioral integration of speech is the problem of how the speaker, given that he has a certain internal representation of a sentence in mind, maps that representation onto the appropriate acoustic array (one which can be understood by a hearer who applys the decoding rules that are standard for the language). But this *is* merely a way of saying that speech production is a matter of constructing objects (utterances) which satisfy the constraints that certain concepts (internal representations of sentences) impose, and speech perception is a matter of determining which concepts such objects fall under.

Linguistic usage employs the term "structural description" for what we have been calling the speaker-hearer's internal representation of a sentence. That is, the structural description of a sentence is a representation which marks whichever of its features are relevant to the perceptual analysis of utterances of that sentence. Analogously, linguistic usage employs the term "grammar" for any system which is able to specify the set of structural descriptions characteristic of the sentences of a language. As a first approximation, then, the central question of psycholinguistics is: How does the speaker-hearer employ the knowledge of his language represented by a grammar to effect the encoding and decoding of speech?

The Psycholinguistics of Taxonomic Grammar

In this chapter, we survey some aspects of the history of psycholinguistics before 1960. We will be highly selective. The dramatic changes in linguistic theory identified with Noam Chomsky, Morris Halle, and their colleagues and students have brought about correspondingly radical alterations in the goals and methods of psycholinguistics, so that the relevance of much of the history of the discipline to current research has become equivocal. In the first place, many important insights captured by traditional continental theorizing about the psychology of language (see Blumenthal, 1970) can now be precisely explicated in terms of concepts developed within the context of generative grammars. Such concepts will be discussed in detail in later chapters. Second, until the early 1950s there was a curious lack of fruitful interaction between psychology and linguistics in the mainstream of American thinking: most psychologists treated problems about the assimilation and exploitation of linguistic structure as only ancillary to the general theory of learning, and the views of psychological mechanisms then current among many linguists can only be described as credulous (cf. Bloomfield, 1933).

Thus, in the American tradition, the earliest widely accepted psycholinguistic work which purported to provide an account of what speakers know about their language and of how that knowledge is implemented in verbal behavior is *c.* 1950. This account merits a detailed examination, not because it reached the goals it set out to achieve but rather because it provides a clear example of the ways that hypotheses about language structure can interact with hypotheses about the psychological mechanisms underlying behavior to produce relatively sophisticated psycholinguistic theories. In this chapter, we shall explore the theoretical synthesis that emerged in the 1950s as a result of the interaction of certain structuralist views of language with psychological theories deriving largely from the school of Clark Hull.

It is a fact of considerable interest that the initial development of psycholinguistics as a field of ongoing research in America occurred when psychologists with predominantly Hullean methodological prejudices first found out about structuralism in linguistics. That it should have been the inheritors of the Hullean tradition who produced the primary impetus to psycholinguistics within American learning theory is by no means an accident. There are specifiable features of the Hullean approach to psychology that led to a serious interest in the facts of language patterning on the part of a number of psychologists immersed in that tradition. To understand what they were, we must consider some characteristic differences between the treatment of serial patterning in behavior typical of Hulleans, on the one hand, and that of radical behaviorists like Watson and Skinner, on the other.

For the radical behaviorist, serial patterning in behavior is simply the consequence of response chaining: the organism's production of each response belonging to a behavior chain serves as a conditioned stimulus for its production of the next response in the chain. As Skinner (1938) says: "The response of one reflex may produce the eliciting or discriminative stimulus of another. . . . Most of the reflexes of the intact organism are parts of chains" (p. 52). Skinner is explicit in insisting that the behavior chain has no structure or organization beyond what is implied by the associative connections between the elementary behaviors which constitute it.

In every case what we have is a chain of reflexes, not a "chained reflex". The connections between parts are purely mechanical and may be broken at will. Any section of a chain may be elicited in isolation with the same properties which characterize it as part of the total chain. There is no reason to appeal to any unique property of the whole sample as an "act." I make these statements as explicitly as possible in view of prevailing opinions to the contrary [Skinner, 1938, pp. 54–55].

If serial order in behavior is viewed merely as the consequence of conditioned associations between elementary behavioral units, then serial structure in language must be the consequence of learned associations between elementary linguistic forms (presumably phonemes or words). A sentence is thus viewed as a behavior chain, each element of which provides a conditioned stimulus for the production of the succeeding element. Whatever grammatical structure the sentence has must thus be a function of the character of the associations between its elements. Skinner (1957), having defined an "autoclitic" as, in effect, a discriminated verbal response to one's own verbal behavior, argues that "An extension of the autoclitic formula permits us to deal with certain remaining verbal responses ... and [with] certain fragments of responses which occur in 'inflections' as well as with the order in which responses appear in larger samples of verbal behavior. Traditionally these comprise the subject matter of grammar and syntax" (p. 331).

There are, however, a number of compelling reasons for rejecting the view that serial order in language can be accounted for by reference to associative relations among elementary linguistic forms. For example, Lashley (1951) noticed that associative chain models cannot accommodate cases in which the structure of the initial segments of a speech event are sensitive to the character of *later* segments of that event.

Lashley's argument is, in effect, that cases in which the character of early portions of an utterance are determined by the intended character of later portions indicate that the utterance is integrated as a unit rather than as an associative chain. Such cases are legion in language. Agreement in syntax produces a variety of obvious examples of this kind; (2-1) is a sentence of English, but (2-2) is not (examples of

2-1   Are John and Mary coming?

2-2   *Is John and Mary coming?

ungrammatical forms will hereinafter be preceded by an asterisk). Here the number of the verb phrase is governed by the number of the noun phrase. But since the production of the verb phrase precedes the production of the noun phrase, the speaker's utterance of a plural verb cannot be a discriminated autoclitic response to his production of a plural noun.

Precisely analogous types of anticipation occur at other levels of language structure. For example, Halle (1959) writes: "In Russian, voicing is distinctive for all obstruents except /c/, /č/ and /x/, which do not possess voiced cognates. These three obstruents are voiceless unless followed by a voiced obstruent, in which case they are voiced. At the end of the word, however, this is true of all Russian obstruents: they are voiceless, unless the following word begins with a voiced obstruent, in which case they are voiced" (p. 22). Similar examples are equally easily found in English, where the form of the article is dictated by the phonological character of the noun that follows it: thus we have "*an* elephant" and "*a* dog" but not "*a* apple" or "*a* uncle." On the one hand, agreement clearly obtains between members of such pairs; and on the other, the direction of control is surely that the choice of the noun conditions the form of the article and not vice versa. Yet the actual order of production is "article, noun," so that the utterance of an article of a given phonological character cannot be a discriminated autoclitic to the production of its noun.

Such cases argue for a view of the integration of speech events according to which the output is planned in sequences longer than single elements. Somehow, we must account for the fact that sequences which occur relatively late in an utterance can control the character of sequences that occur relatively early, and this is precisely what a view of speech as a reflex chain does not permit us to do.

Similarly, if the speech event has no structure beyond what emerges from the putative associative bonds between elementary linguistic forms, how are we to account for even the gross facts about the organization of sentences into phrases? It is obvious that in a sentence like (2-3) there is some specially close relation between the words in "the

2-3 The boy and the girl left the house.

boy and the girl," on the one hand, and the words in "left the house," on the other. But this relation cannot be a consequence of the nature of the associative connection between any of the adjacent words, since the segmentation of a sentence into major phrases is independent of the particular lexical items occurring at the phase boundary. Notice, for example, that in (2-3) the major phrase boundary occurs between "girl" and "left," but in (2-4) it does not.

2-4 Where is the house the girl left?

There is a great deal of both linguistic and experimental literature which illustrates the kind of phrase integrity referred to here. We will review this literature at length in Chapters 5 and 6. Suffice it to say here that the relative degree of "connectedness" between adjacent lexical items in a sentence reflects features of the grouping of the sentence into phrases. Such features, however, cannot be captured by a view of syntax which assumes that the structure of the sentence consists solely of associations between adjacent lexical items. Rather, the sentence appears to have structure which is a "unique property of the whole sample as an act"; an acceptable account of serial order in verbal behavior will be required to explain the existence of this kind of structure and hence must employ concepts more powerful than that of the associative chain.

Many psychologists who have noticed these sorts of difficulties with associative chain theories of serially patterned behavior have attempted to remedy them by using the theoretical mechanisms of the Hullean analysis of learning. This is because Hull's methodological views allowed him to abandon the defining property of radical behaviorism: that theoretical constructs in psychology must be literally definable in terms of stimulus-response variables. Unlike radical behaviorists, Hulleans allow themselves to think of the production of observed behavioral integrations as being mediated by unobserved, internal variables whose precise character it is the goal of experimentation and theory construction in psychology to describe. In particular, the Hullean need not be committed, on methodological grounds, to the view that successive links in a behavior chain are conditioned responses associatively coupled to one another. Rather, when the data require him to do so, it is open to the Hullean to explain observed adjacencies between behavioral elements as the consequence of internal mediating processes.

The precise character of this methodological liberalization, and its consequences for analyses of language structure, will be discussed at length later in this chapter. Suffice it to remark here that the interest in formal linguistic structure evinced by many Hullean psychologists in the early 1950s may be understood as a consequence of their belief in the applicability of "mediation theoretic" learning models to the analysis of verbal behavior; in particular, to explaining the speaker-hearer's assimilation and exploitation of phonological and syntactic structure. We will see that the Hullean view of learning was particularly well adapted to account for certain features of the formation of stimulus and response hierarchies, and that it was precisely in terms of hierarchically arranged classes that the taxonomic (or "structuralist") linguistics of the 1950s sought to describe the organization of natural languages. The employment of mediation models in psychology thus appeared to permit an entente between the linguist's view of language structure and the psychologist's account of how languages are learned and used. But though this symmetry between their theories for a time occasioned considerable enthusiasm among both linguists and psychologists, it has turned out to be simply fortuitous in a number of respects.

STRUCTURALISM IN LINGUISTICS

We commence by outlining some major features of the view of language and of linguistic analysis that emerged within the American structuralist tradition between 1930 and 1950. We will try to locate some areas of consensus between such midcentury linguists as Bloomfield, Harris, Fries, and Twadell. It must be emphasized that we will be discussing only those areas of structuralism that had a serious impact upon theorizing among psycholinguists. Thus our characterization of the structuralist movement is highly selective and will do less than justice to the insights that structuralism achieved. Moreover, since it is intended to be a composite portrait, we do not claim that it precisely captures the views of any particular structural linguist. What we hope to do is to provide a succinct characterization of the underlying principles of structuralism which made it particularly appealing to mediational psychologists.

According to the structuralist account, the goal of linguistics is to produce *taxonomic grammatical descriptions* of natural languages. Such descriptions are required to exhibit certain features that were widely agreed upon by structural linguists. In particular, such descriptions are required to characterize the structure of the language under analysis at each of a fixed set of *levels of description*. These levels correspond, roughly, to the intuitive notions of *sounds, words,* and *phrases.*

A *level of description* is specified in the following way. First, one provides a *descriptive vocabulary*, the terms of which designate the entities whose behavior is described on the level under analysis. Characteristically the items in such a vocabulary were thought of as designating sets. For example, taxonomic grammars described the structure of each language at its *phonetic* level. The descriptive vocabulary at this level was taken to be a list of symbols, each of which designates a *phone*, where a phone, in turn, is thought of as a class of speech sounds. (To be precise, terms in the descriptive vocabulary were taken to designate linguistic *types*, where a type is extensionally identical with the indefinite class of utterances which constitute *tokens* of that type.)

Linguistically relevant distinctions between speech sounds are then represented by assigning the sounds to distinct phones. In English, for example, the descriptive vocabulary at the phonetic level includes the following items: $[\theta]$, $[d]$, and $[t]$. These terms designate classes of sounds, elements of which appear in utterances of such English words as "*th*in," "*t*ile," "*d*ial," and "s*t*yle."

It is important to understand the kinds of motivations that structural linguists considered relevant to deciding when a distinction should be represented at a given level of linguistic description and the kinds of theoretical consequences such decisions had. Let us consider, for example, what is involved in deciding when a given distinction between speech sounds is "linguistically relevant" (i.e., when such a distinction should be represented at the phonetic level of a grammatical description).

Clearly, utterances of speech sounds differ from one another in an indefinite variety of ways: every utterance of a speech sound is a unique physical event. But, equally clearly, not all such differences can or should be marked by the descriptive vocabulary of a phonetic theory; phones are not intended to designate unit classes, so a disciplined decision must be made about when two utterances of speech sounds are to be assigned to the same phone.

Structuralists often used the following principle for determining which kinds of differences between speech sounds were to be criterial for distinguishing between phones: every distinction between speech sounds which is relevant to distinguishing between *words* in any natural language must be represented as a distinction between *phones,* but a distinction between speech sounds which is *never* relevant to differentiating between words in any natural language must not be represented as a phonetic distinction. Intuitively speaking, the idea was that the phonetic system is to be rich enough to represent any distinction between speech sounds that can signal a distinction between meaningful items in any language, but not so rich as to mark distinctions between speech sounds that never serve to mark such a distinction.

There are, for example, no two words in English (no *minimal pair* of English words) which differ only in that one word has [tʰ] (an aspirated *t*) where the other word has [t] (an unaspirated *t*). Yet the contrast between [t] and [tʰ] *is* represented in the phonetic description of English. This is because there exist languages which do contain the relevant minimal pairs. In Hindi, for example, the distinction between aspirated and unaspirated speech sounds signals distinctions between words. Since the descriptive vocabulary of the phonetic level is intended to constitute a "rational orthography" for *any* natural language, it follows that even in languages which do not happen to use aspiration to signal lexical distinctions, aspirated utterances must be assigned to phones different from the ones to which unaspirated utterances are assigned.

We remarked that in Hindi [t] and [tʰ] determine minimal pairs and that such is not the case for English. How, then, is this difference between English and Hindi to be represented by a taxonomic grammar, given that such a grammar is committed to representing utterances of [t] and utterances of [tʰ] as phonetically distinct *both* in English *and* in Hindi? To put the problem slightly differently: the phonetic description of English distinguishes between the initial (aspirated) *t* in "tap" and the final (unaspirated) *t* in "pat." Yet, for the English speaker (though not, presumably, for the speaker of Hindi) these phones are mere functionally equivalent variants of the linguistic element *t.* Clearly, then, some formalism must be provided to distinguish the case where phones are alternate expressions of *the same* linguistic element in a language from cases where they express *different* linguistic elements in that language. Moreover, as our example suggests, we must expect to find that phones belonging to the same linguistic element in one language may turn out to belong to distinct linguistic elements in another language.

The formalism taxonomic linguists provided illustrates the character of their treatment of interrelations between levels of linguistic description. Suppose we assume that there exists a *phonological* level of description which is distinct from the *phonetic* level. The vocabulary items at the phonological level will be taken to designate *phonemes,* which are themselves taken to be classes of phones. We can now capture the notion that the aspirated and unaspirated English *t* are somehow expressions of the same linguistic element by saying that [t] and [tʰ] belong to (are *phonetic variants,* or *allophones,* of) the English phoneme /t/; the relevant difference between English and Hindi may now be succinctly expressed by saying that in Hindi, [t] and [tʰ] are allophones of distinct phonemes, while in English, they are allophones of the same phoneme.

What emerges from such examples is a hierarchy of sets. Lowest-level sets are phones, and their elements are utterances. Next higher-level sets are phonemes, and their members are phones. Functional *distinctness* between two linguistic entities is represented by assigning them to distinct sets at some level of description. Functional *equivalence* between two linguistic entities is represented by assigning them to the same set at some higher level. Thus, we represent the fact that aspirated and unaspirated *t* are functionally distinct (in some languages) by assigning them distinct representations at the phonetic level. We represent their functional equivalence in English by assigning them both to the same set at the next higher level (i.e., by assigning them to the same English phoneme).

This sort of interrelation between levels of description is characteristic of the organization of taxonomic grammars. A general constraint that such grammars were required to satisfy is that the entities postulated at the ith level of description must be sets (or sequences) of items at the $(i-1)$th level of description, down to the level of utterances. We shall refer to this constraint upon the organization of taxonomic grammars as the *taxonomic condition.* Its effect is to order the descriptive levels posited by a taxonomic grammar into a hierarchy of classes. We shall see later that the fact that structuralist analyses are required to satisfy the taxonomic condition is essential for reconciling taxonomic grammars with mediational accounts of the psychological processes involved in learning and using a language.

We can, in short, think of a taxonomic grammar as a finite set of descriptive levels: traditionally, the phonetic level, the phonemic level, the morphological level, and the syntactic level. Relations between the levels are controlled by the taxonomic condition, and each level acknowledges a fixed inventory of classes whose behavior is described at that level.

That the structure of natural languages can be described in terms of such sets of levels is, of course, an empirical claim—perhaps the most important substantive commitment undertaken by taxonomic grammars. We shall presently turn to a fairly detailed analysis of the structure languages were presumed to have at each of these levels and of the operations which were intended to establish their grammatical inventory. First, however, it is important to be aware of some purely methodological assumptions made by structural linguists.

If the major substantive constraint on structuralist grammars is expressed by the taxonomic condition, the overriding *methodological* constraint was what we shall call the *operationalist condition*: namely, that the proper analysis of the grammatical structure of a natural language should be the consequence of applying a well-defined discovery procedure to a sufficiently rich corpus of utterances drawn from that language. That is, the goal was to characterize a series of operational techniques (called "field procedures") for the analysis of utterances produced by native informants. The character of these techniques was supposed to ensure that their application to a representative corpus would automatically generate an analysis of structure at each level of description, and also to ensure that the interrelations between levels postulated by that analysis would automatically satisfy the taxonomic condition.

The requirement that field procedures should apply automatically was widely interpreted as further implying that the corpus must be taxonomized only in terms of its "objective" properties (like acoustic and distributional features) and not in terms of "subjective" properties that depend on appeals to informants. (It may be added, however, that this condition is slightly stronger than many structural linguists would have accepted, since it was often held that the linguist's data for the construction of a grammar must include not only a corpus of observed utterances but also enough judgments of similarity and difference of meaning of words in the language to define its minimal pairs.)

In short, then, the primary goal was that of imposing a taxonomy upon the utterances which constitute the corpus of observations of a language. The principles for classifying utterances were to be sufficiently clearly stated and sufficiently objective that their application would yield a unique solution for any representative corpus. Finally, the character of the taxonomy yielded by these principles should be such as to represent complex linguistic units (words, phrases, and sentences) as constructed from simpler units (phones and phonemes) by processes of which concatenation and set formation are the most important.

Given the view that the analysis of linguistic structure must be uniquely determined by automatic discovery procedures, we can best understand how structural linguists conceived of linguistic levels by considering the discovery procedures which defined them. In the following sections we shall examine the procedures in terms of which the phonological, morphological, and syntactic levels of taxonomic grammars were constructed. We shall also consider some features of linguistic organization which theories constructed in accordance with these procedures fail to capture.

Taxomonic phonetics and phonemics.   We remarked that in the taxonomic view, the relation between the phonetic level and the higher levels of linguistic description is regulated by the principle that phones are distinct if and only if there exists some language in which the contrast between them determines a minimal pair (equivalently, a and b are distinct phones if and only if there is a language in which a belongs to some phoneme to which b does not belong). Moreover, the techniques for assigning sounds to phones must satisfy the operationalist condition at least insofar as the field procedures for determining minimal pairs are capable of being rendered objective and automatic. Before taking up the problems encountered in defining the relations between the phonetic and phonemic levels, let us consider the implications of the operationalist condition for the relation between the phonetic level of description and the lowest (i.e., acoustic) level of analysis of speech signals.

It seems evident that in accepting the operationalist condition, taxonomic linguists assumed that the proper assignment of a speech signal to a phone must be settled by reference solely to the acoustic character of that signal. This point turns out to be important.

Clearly, even a highly detailed phonetic alphabet must abstract from the full richness of the acoustic signals produced by speakers. Two utterances of a phone by different speakers or by the same speaker at different times will differ in a variety of linguistically irrelevant acoustic properties (e.g., volume, absolute pitch, etc.). But the operationalist condition requires that we provide mechanical procedures for the assignment of phonetic descriptions to acoustic events. Such a mechanical procedure will thus be tantamount to a substantive theory—one which purports to distinguish between the linguistically relevant acoustic properties of utterances and the linguistically irrelevant ones. If, in short, we are to satisfy the operationalist requirement that the phonetic analysis of a corpus be purely mechanical, we must provide observational (presumably acoustic) criteria for the assignment of phonetic representations to speech samples.

The most natural assumption is that each phone can be associated with some distinctive constellation of acoustic features which, in turn, provide the necessary and sufficient conditions for assigning a speech signal to that phone. Whether a given speech signal exhibits one or another such constellation of features is, at least in principle, mechanically determinable. Hence given an acoustic definition of the phone, mechanical phonetic analysis is possible in principle. The form which the operationalist constraint takes at the phonetic level of grammatical description is thus the requirement that phones be acoustically defined.

Notice that while it may seem reasonable to assume that an acoustic specification of the conditions under which two sounds belong to the same phone ought to be forthcoming, this assumption is actually an extremely powerful one. In particular, it is tantamount to the assumption that the perceptual identity of phones is *not* an instance of perceptual constancy in the sense discussed in Chapter 1.

Powerful empirical assumptions thus turn out to be implicit in the acceptance of the operationalist condition, which requires "purely objective" criteria for the assignment of phonological analyses to utterances. In order to satisfy the requirement, one must therefore attempt to define phones in purely acoustic terms. But it must not be forgotten that the phone is primarily a perceptual entity; intuitively speaking, utterances should not be assigned to the same phone unless they *sound* the same to speakers of the language under analysis. Hence, in committing us to the acoustic definition of the phone, the operationalist principle also commits us to the assumption that when speech sounds are *perceptually* similar, it is because they are *acoustically* similar.

Thus, although the reasons for adopting the operationalist condition are purely methodological, once having accepted it we find ourselves committed to an extremely rigid account of the psychophysical relation for speech sounds. It would, in fact, be most surprising if any such account proved true. Readers acquainted with the psychological literature on visual, olfactory, and gustatory perception will recognize that there are hardly any cases in those modes for which the analogous psychophysical assumption would hold. In general, perceptual equivalences and differences among stimuli are *not* predictable in any simple way from their physical similarities and differences. If the psychophysics required by the principle that the phone must be acoustically definable were true, the perception of speech sounds would be a psychological anomaly.

We shall see in Chapter 6 that the problem of characterizing the psychophysical relation for speech sounds is an extremely difficult and interesting one. For the moment, let us assume, as structural linguists did, that mechanical procedures are in principle available for producing a correct phonetic transcription of any sufficiently large corpus of a natural language from a specification of the acoustic characteristics of the utterances in that corpus. On this assumption, the substantive procedures for grammar construction are allowed to presuppose a corpus represented in a rational orthography. The first problem seriously investigated by structural linguists was thus that of converting a *phonetic* transcription into a *phonemic* transcription by the application of well-defined taxonomic principles.

It will be remembered that a description of the structure of a language at the phonemic level is required to satisfy the following condition: every phoneme of the language must be identified with a unique set of phones of that language, and every occurrence of a phone must be unambiguously assignable to a phoneme. Moreover, the analysis must be such as to assign two phones to the same phoneme if and only if the contrast between those phones never determines a minimal pair in the language. (Thus, as we have seen, [t] and [tʰ] belong to the same English phoneme because there exists no pair of words in English that differ only in that one has [t] where the other has [tʰ]. To put it slightly differently, the members of every pair of English utterances that differ only by the presence or absence of aspirated /t/ count as repetitions of one another.)

It was a substantive issue among taxonomic phonologists whether there are purely mechanical procedures which assign phones to phonemes uniquely and also satisfy the condition that phones are assigned to distinct phonemes if and only if the contrast between them determines a minimal pair. What is at issue here is whether operations defined over a phonetic transcription would suffice to yield an acceptable phonemic analysis, or whether the linguist also required explicit appeals to informants' judgments about what words count as minimal pairs in their language. The question of the relation between the minimal-pair condition and the condition that phones be uniquely assigned to phonemes is complicated; we shall return to it presently.

To summarize the discussion thus far: a phonemic description of a given language is required to provide a unique assignment of its phones to its phonemes, and to do so in a way that assigns phones to distinct phonemes when and only when they contrast to form minimal pairs. The operationalist condition requires that procedures for yielding such descriptions be automatic, hence that they be definable over purely "objective" properties of the linguist's corpus. It must thus be asked what facts about the corpus can be exploited to construct a phonemic analysis satisfying these conditions.

The procedure classically employed by taxonomic phonologists was this: assign a pair of phones to the same phoneme just in case they are either in *free variation* or in *complementary distribution* in the corpus. The relations of free variation and complementary distribution will need to be discussed at length. We consider the latter notion first.

Complementary distribution as a criterion for assigning phones to phonemes. Two phones are said to be in complementary distribution in a language just in case there are phonetic environments in which the one occurs and from which the other is excluded. Intuitively, two phones are in complementary distribution if and only if they do not occupy the same positions in a word.

The basic idea is that whenever the relation of complementary distribution holds between phones belonging to a common phoneme, it does so because the phonetic value of that phoneme depends upon the phonetic environment in which it occurs. For example, in English the phonetic value of the phoneme /t/ is [tʰ] when it appears in the initial position in a word but [t] when it appears following word-initial /s/: thus, the *phonemic* sequence /top/ has the *phonetic* value [tʰop], while the phonemic sequence /stop/ has the phonetic value [stop]. The phonetic forms [t] and [tʰ] are thus in complementary distribution and may be considered positional variants of the phoneme /t/.

What is the relation between the notion of complementary distribution and the notion of a minimal pair? The question is important since, as we saw above, a pair of phones must be assigned to distinct phonemes in a language if and only if their contrast yields minimal pairs in that language.

Notice, first, that no pair of phones which are in fact in a complementary distribution can form a minimal pair. By definition, phones that form minimal pairs must contrast in the same linguistic enviroments; and, by definition, phones that are in complementary distribution cannot contrast since they are precluded from appearing in the same linguistic environment. Thus, for example, since [t] and [tʰ] are in complementary distribution in English, it follows that there exists no minimal pair [X t Y] and [X tʰ Y]. From these considerations it follows that any two phones in complementary distribution cannot determine minimal pairs and hence *must* be assigned to the same phoneme.

This conclusion, however, turns out to be unacceptable in two ways. In the first place, there arise cases in which the principle that phones in complementary distribution belong to a common phoneme does not provide for *any* well-defined assignment of phones to phonemes. And second, it often requires us to make an intuitively incorrect assignment of phones to phonemes.

An example of the second sort of failure arises from the fact that [ŋ] and [h] happen to be in complementary distribution in English, i.e., there exists no pair of English words in which they contrast. One has strong intuitions (which, moreover, are mirrored in the orthography of English) that this must somehow be an accident. That is, the fact that these two phones happen to be in complementary distribution should not be considered sufficient grounds for assigning them to the same phoneme. In particular, a linguist ought not consider them allophonic variants of a common form if his assignments are to reflect the intuitions of English speakers. (Cf. Gleason, 1955, for further discussion of this kind of case.)

The problem about the failure of the principle of contrastive distribution to effect unique assignments of phones to phonemes is still more serious. Consider the following pairs of English phones: [p, pʰ] and [t, tʰ]. The first member of each of these pairs is in complementary distribution with the second. But notice, moreover, that [p] is in complementary distribution with [tʰ] and that [t] is in complementary distribution with [pʰ]. This is a consequence of a general fact about English phonological structure; namely, that *all* aspirated unvoiced stops are in complementary distribution with all unaspirated unvoiced stops. By virtue of this consideration, however, we have two options for assigning such phones to phonemes. In particular, if complementary distribution is a sufficient condition for a pair of phones belonging to the same phoneme, *either* we can say that there are English phonemes /p/ and /t/, having, respectively, the allophonic variants [p, pʰ] and [t, tʰ] *or* we can say that there exist English phonemes */p/ and */t/ having, respectively, the allophonic variants [p, tʰ] and [t, pʰ].

To summarize, the principle of complementary distribution was selected to provide the operational definition of "phoneme" because it was assumed that only allophones of a common phoneme are ever in complementary distribution. It turns out, however, that this assumption is false. Not all phones in complementary distribution in a language do in fact belong to the same phoneme of that language so far as the intuitions of its speakers are concerned; and cases of complementary distribution between *classes* of phones provide instances where adherence to the principle of assignment by complementary distribution fails to give a unique mapping of the phonetic level onto the phonemic level.

The usual way of meeting these kinds of difficulties in taxonomic linguistics was to bolster the principle of complementary distribution with a principle of phonetic "similarity." Thus, *a* and *a'* are allophones of the same phoneme if (1) they are in complementary distribution and (2) they are phonetically similar in some sense that is presumably to be explicated by reference to their acoustic similarity. This principle now permits a resolution of the difficulties raised above. The phones [h] and [ŋ] are *not* allophones of the same phoneme because even though they are in complementary distribution, they are not "similar."

The phone [p] belongs to the phoneme which contains [pʰ]—and not to a phoneme which contains [tʰ]—because of the presumed acoustic similarity between [pʰ] and [p].

Resort to similarity between phones once again raises questions about the "purely objective" status of taxonomic description. As we suggested above, it is by no means obvious that the *perceptual* similarity between a pair of phones must inevitably be explicable in terms of a corresponding acoustic similarity between utterances of those phones. (It is by no means obvious, for example, that [p] and [pʰ] would even appear to be similar phones to a speaker of a language in which aspiration determines minimal pairs.) If similarity is used to define phonemes, then the "objectivity" of the mapping between the phonetic and the phonemic level is contingent on the assumption that necessary and sufficient conditions for perceptual similarity between phones can be acoustically characterized.

The kinds of difficulties that can arise when one attempts to supplement distributional procedures of phonemic analysis with appeals to hypothetical acoustic similarities between phones can be illustrated by the following examples. In certain cases, distinct phones do not correspond to distinct temporal segments of an utterance. Thus, for example, in some English dialects, [n] following a vowel and preceding a consonant (as in "cant") has *no* acoustic representation as a segment distinct from the vowel. In such dialects, "cant" is distinguished from "cat" not in the number of acoustic segments it contains but rather in the fact that in "cant" the /a/ is nasalized (spoken with the nasal cavity open).

The consequence of this sort of case is to pose a dilemma for the taxonomic principles. If we accept the view that the phonetic transcription must be acoustically determined, then the phonetic spelling of "cant" must be [cat]. But now the *phonemic* spelling of "cant" is surely /cant/; and since each phoneme is held to be extensionally identical with the set of its phonetic representatives, we appear to be committed to the view that [ã] is an allophone of /n/.

Analogously, in some English dialects, all medial consonants are represented by [D] (a flap produced by bringing the tip of the tongue against the roof of the mouth). Yet we have no trouble in distinguishing words like "ladder" and "latter," and, in fact, there *is* typically an acoustic distinction between utterances of these words: namely, that the first vowel of "ladder" is longer than the first vowel of "latter" owing to the operation of a general rule that lengthens English vowels before voiced consonants. Again, however, these facts pose a difficulty for the taxonomic principles. If we accept a phonetic transcription of "latter" and "ladder" as, respectively, [laDer] and [lāDer], then we are committed to a phonological analysis in which [a] is a phonetic representative of /t/. On the other hand, if we accept a phonetic transcription of "ladder" as [lader] and "latter" as [later], then we are abandoning a principle which is implicit in the assumption that the phone must be acoustically defined—namely, that the phonetic transcription must correspond, segment by segment, to the acoustic properties of the speech event. For, as we have seen, the *acoustic* fact that corresponds to the *phonetic* contrast between [t] and [d] concerns the length of the preceding segment. Clearly, the requirement that the phone be acoustically defined cannot be made compatible with the requirement that the phoneme be identified with the set of its phonetic representatives. One or the other or both of these principles will eventually have to be abandoned. In any event, appealing to acoustic similarities between phones to correct the inadequacies of the principle of complementary distribution looks unpromising.

The problem of "free variation." We have been discussing distributional procedures taxonomic phonologists employed for determining the appropriate assignment of phones to phonemes. In particular, we have considered the suggestion that phones should be assigned to the same phoneme whenever they are in complementary distribution and are acoustically similar.

This principle fails to determine the appropriate phonemic analysis in a kind of case we have not thus far discussed, namely, where distinct phones occur in the same linguistic environment (i.e., are not in complementary distribution) but nevertheless fail to determine minimal pairs. Cases of this sort in English include aspirated versus unaspirated consonants in word-final position, or contrasts like the one between the forms [ɛkənamiks] and [ikənamiks], both of which are possible phonetic renderings of "economics" in the dialect of many English speakers.

When distinct phones contrast in an environment without forming a minimal pair, they are said to be in *free variation*, and both intuition and taxonomic procedure dictates that they should be treated as allophonic variants of a common phoneme. Such cases, however, raise a serious problem with respect to the view that automatic principles of classification can establish a unique phonemic analysis of a corpus given only the phonetic analysis of that corpus as data. For, while the complementary distribution between phones can in principle be established by purely distributional analysis, it is far from obvious that any formal procedures will distinguish the case where contrasting phones determine minimal pairs from the case where they are in free variation. To put it slightly differently, contrast between phones in an environment is intended to be a sufficient condition for assigning the phones to distinct phonemes only where the contrasting phones determine minimal pairs, i.e., only where the substitution of one phone for another produces a difference in meaning. [ɛ] and [i] are thus allowed to be allophonic variants in the environment [_____ kənamiks] because the alternation between them does not involve a difference in meaning; [t] and [p], however, are *not* allowed to be allophones of a common phoneme because the substitution of one for the other always produces a change in meaning.

It appears, then, that the linguist's data for a phonemic transcription must include not only the corpus in correct phonetic analysis but also sufficiently many informants' judgments of identity and difference of meaning to decide which phonetic contrasts in the language determine minimal pairs. For obvious reasons this conclusion was resisted by some taxonomic linguists as seriously jeopardizing the objectivity of phonemic descriptions. If the characterization of the relation between the phonetic and the phonemic levels depends on which contrasts of phones determine differences of words, then the relation depends upon what is fundamentally a semantic distinction. For the notion of a *word*, as it is being used here, is, at least in part, a semantic notion. Thus, "board" and "bored" count as distinct words, despite the fact that they have the same phonetic and phonemic spellings. Correspondingly, [ɛkənamiks] and [ikənamiks] must count as phonetic renderings of the *same* word if the contrast between [i] and [ɛ] is to be attributed to free variation.

Judgments about minimal pairs must, then, involve judgments about similarity and difference of meaning, and a field procedure for determining the existence of minimal pairs must be a procedure for eliciting such judgments. The difficulty, however, is simply that no such procedure exists. Nor is it clear, even in principle, how such a procedure might be devised, given the notorious obscurity of such constructs as synonymy, homonymy, similarity and difference of meaning, etc. (For discussion, see Carnap, 1955; Katz, 1962.) In short, insofar as the taxonomic theory of the relation between the phonetic and phonemic levels rests upon a semantic construal of the notion "minimal pair," it rests on concepts and procedures of which no clear account has yet been given. But insofar as reliance upon semantic notions are to be prohibited in the assignment of phones to phonemes, it is correspondingly unclear how the critical relation of free variation between phones is to be defined.

Before we leave the discussion of the relation between phonetic and phonemic levels of taxonomic grammars, it may be well to make explicit an assumption we have been relying upon throughout: one *can* test putative principles for phonetic or phonemic analysis by determining whether they in fact yield correct characterization of the phonological and phonemic structure of a language. Presumably, many taxonomic linguists would not accept this assumption. It is possible, for example, to think of a taxonomic grammar as nothing more than a "conveniently abbreviated representation" of a corpus of observed utterances or, more generally, as an arbitrary formalism for which no psychological relevance is claimed. Some such view was, in fact, endemic among structural linguists, either because they believed that *no* scientific theory could claim to do more than provide a concise description of the scientist's observational data or because they thought that there was some peculiarity about linguistic descriptions which precluded making claims for the existence of the theoretical objects whose behavior they describe.

Such views of the goals of grammar construction seem to us to be of very little interest intrinsically or from the point of view of the argument of this book. Like the psycholinguists of the 1950s, we are interested in linguistic analyses primarily insofar as they may be claimed to represent the knowledge speaker-hearers have of the structure of their language. Clearly, the question of whether a given analysis *does* afford such a representation is an empirical one, to be treated like any other substantive issue in psychology. We will therefore assume throughout our discussion that it is possible, at least in principle, to distinguish between true theories of language and convenient descriptions of corpora, and that the crux of such a distinction is whether psychological reality can correctly be claimed for the constructs the linguistic analysis postulates.

Taxonomic morphology.   In our discussion of taxonomic phonology and phonemics, we suggested that a revealing way of investigating the kinds of phonological descriptions that structuralists accepted is to discuss the discovery procedures they used to generate the descriptions from data. An analogous approach may be taken for the levels of taxonomic morphology and syntax, since at these levels too, the operationalist constraint was considered to be the overriding methodological principle: that is, the proper analysis of structure at these levels was required to be the automatic consequence of applying mechanical discovery procedures to a corpus of observed utterances.

For purposes of morphological and syntactic analysis the corpus is, of course, thought of as represented by a phonemic transcription. That is, the input to the morphological and syntactic analysis procedures is thought of as provided by the output of the phonemic analysis procedures. It should be noted that the flow of information is thus conceived of as proceeding in one direction, from the phonology to the morphology and from the morphology to the syntax, just as we saw, in the preceding section, that the information flow between the phonetic and phonemic levels is unidirectional from the former to the latter. In general, excepting cases where analytic decisions were allowed to turn on semantic considerations, structuralists tended to accept the constraint that levels should be separate in the sense that information from higher levels of analysis must not be used to decide among alternative analyses at any lower level. This constraint, which is closely related to the structuralist's assumption that the population of any level of description is literally constructed out of classes of lower-level entities, is of some methodological importance. We will return to it later.

The first problem to be faced at the syntactic level is that of isolating those sequences of phonemes which constitute *morphemes* in the language under analysis. The notion of a morpheme may be thought of as an attempt to explicate the informal notion of a "minimal linguistic unit having a meaning." Intuitively the notion of a morpheme differs from the notion of a phoneme in that the latter is construed as the minimal linguistic unit whose alternations invariably determine *differences* of meaning. Thus, an appropriate analysis of English must represent /p/ and /k/ as *phonemes* because substituting one for the other characteristically produces a change of meaning (e.g., pairs of words like "cat" and "pat," and "pad" and "cad"). But /p/ and /k/ must *not* be represented as *morphemes* of English, since they are not themselves meaningful units. The problem of determining the morphological analysis of a language can thus be roughly characterized as that of providing taxonomic procedures which automatically isolate those sequences (including unit sequences and null sequences) of phonemes which "have a meaning."

The considerations that arise in attempts to isolate elements at the morpheme level are strikingly similar to those encountered in the isolation of phonemes, a point that taxonomic grammarians were sensitive to. Indeed, it is part of the appeal of the taxonomic approach that what are effectively the same analytic procedures are employed again and again at increasingly higher levels of analysis to isolate increasingly abstract taxonomic classes. In particular, the notions of complementary distribution, free variation, and minimal pair, which we saw play an essential role in the generation of taxonomic phonetic and phonological descriptions, are also the fundamental concepts involved in the isolation and classification of morphemes. As Gleason (1955) comments:

> The identification of morphemes is done almost wholly by variations and refinements of one basic technique. This is the comparison of pairs or sets of utterances which show partial contrast in both expression and content. Unless the contrast is partial (that is, unless there is some apparent identity somewhere in the utterances), and unless it exists in both expression and content, the comparison is fruitless. In many important respects this is the same general procedure as was used ... to identify English phonemes. For the identification of phonemes we wanted the smallest possible difference in expression with *any difference* in content whatever. For the identification of morphemes we seek the smallest differences of expression which exist with a *partial difference* of content. This difference of procedure rests in the fundamental difference between phoneme and morpheme. The phoneme is the smallest significant unit in the

expression which can be correlated with *any* difference in the content structure. The morpheme is the smallest significant unit in the expression which can be correlated with any *one particular* difference in the content structure [pp. 66–67].

The general view appears to be the following. A corpus in phonemic transcription will, of necessity, exhibit recurrences of certain phoneme sequences. That is, there will invariably be certain phoneme sequences which occur in more than one phonological environment. Single phonemes satisfy this trivially, and certain adventitious cases (like the /ur/ in /recur/ and the /ur/ in /fur/) yield recurrent nonmorphemic phoneme sequences. However, there are other cases which are of an intuitively different type; consider the /z/ in /dɔgz/, /flajz/, and /fajlz/ and, conversely, the /dɔg/ in /dɔg/ and /dɔgi/ but *not* in /bundɔgl/ and /dɔgmɑ/. The point is that some phoneme sequences recur because they represent lexical items in the language. The problem is to provide techniques which will segregate those recurrences from the ones that express only adventitious consequences of the organization of the language at the phonemic level. To put it slightly differently, the units at higher levels of structure in the language (phrases, sentences) are specified not directly in terms of phonemes but rather in terms of lexical items. Lexical items appear in the corpus as recurrent phoneme sequences. The operationalist constraint requires the taxonomic linguist to provide procedures which isolate those sequences.

As Gleason suggests, the essential insight is that the items in terms of which higher levels of linguistic structure are specified are precisely the items which are associated with stable meanings. This is the theoretical counterpart of the intuitive suggestion that phrases and sentences are fundamentally sequences of words, where words, in turn, are thought of as minimal semantic entities. If this view is correct, it should be possible to isolate those phoneme sequences which constitute morphemes by some procedure in which their presumed semantic stability is exploited.

The details of this procedure are not critical for our purposes; indeed, as we mentioned above, it is very much an open question whether reliable techniques could be formulated for eliciting semantic information from informants, given the unclarity of the fundamental semantic relations. At any event, the structuralists' intention was clearly to capitalize on the fact that a given morpheme has the same meaning in whatever linguistic environment it may occur. In particular, substituting some morpheme *m* for some other morpheme *m'* ought to produce the same semantic change in whatever linguistic environment the substitution is performed. Thus /kaet/ and /dɔg/ count as morphemes because, first, they contrast in a wide variety of phonemic environments (e.g., /the cat is on the rug/ versus /the dog is on the rug/) and, second, these contrasts are intuitively nonadventitious in the sense that they are associated with stable semantic differences. For example, it seems intuitively plausible to say that /the dog is on the rug/ differs in meaning from /the cat is on the rug/ in the same sort of way that /the dog likes liver/ differs in meaning from /the cat likes liver/. [For a carefully worked out attempt to formulate procedures for associating phonemic alternations with semantic alternations, see Ziff (1960); for critical discussion, see Katz (1962). For an attempt to construct purely distributional procedures for isolating morphemes, thereby avoiding appeals to the semantic intuitions of speakers, cf. Harris (1946).]

Suppose we assume that the notion of similarity of meaning is capable of being "operationalized" (e.g., in terms of field procedures for questioning informants) and that such procedures would permit a segmentation of the corpus into morphemes having the properties discussed above, i.e., that such procedures define a *morphemic level* of linguistic description. Even on that assumption, it is clear that there are regularities in the behavior of minimal semantic units which would not be captured at the morphemic level if the analytic procedures sketched thus far were considered to be exhaustive. For example, there are cases where morphemes have more than one sequence of phonemic representatives, and where the choice among such sequences is environmentally conditioned: the /s/ in /kæts/ is obviously synonymous with the /z/ in /dɔgz/ and with the /ız/ in /horsız/. It would therefore be desirable to be able to consider /s/, /z/, and /ız/ to be variants of a single "plural" morpheme. Yet that representation would be precluded by any definition of the morpheme which entailed that each morpheme has only one phonemic spelling. In particular, we want to be able to say that for each morpheme there exists a class of allomorphs (i.e., of distinct phonemic representations) which are related to it in essentially the same way that the allophones of a phoneme are related to that phoneme.

We saw above that there are two properties that phones are required to have if they are to be represented as allophones of the same phoneme: they must exhibit perceptual similarity; and they must be either in complementary distribution or in free variation across *phonetic* environments. Analogously, two *morphs* will be considered to be *allomorphs of a common morpheme* if and only if they are *semantically* similar and in complementary distribution or in free variation across *phonemic* environments. Thus /s, z/ and /ız/ are held to be allomorphs of a common morpheme because they are synonymous and in complementary distribution. (Roughly, /s/ pluralizes a noun which ends in an unvoiced phoneme, and /z/ pluralizes a noun which ends in a voiced phoneme, except that /ız/ pluralizes nouns which end in either /s/ or /z/.)

The intention in postulating allomorphs corresponding to morphemes is to distinguish those minimal semantic units which are, in- tuitively, merely variant phonemic spellings of the same lexical item from cases of synonymy between minimal semantic units which, intui- tively, constitute distinct lexical items. Thus the environmentally condi- tioned relation between the articles "a" and "an" should be distin- guished from the relation between distinct but synonymous lexical items like "perhaps" and "maybe." The intention is to make this dis- tinction by specifying that all and only those synonymous minimal sequences which are in complementary distribution or free variation shall count as allomorphs of a single morpheme.

In fact, however, it is very unclear that the distinction *can* be made in this way. If it is true, as many theorists have maintained, that synonymous expressions are usually intersubstitutable across linguistic environments, then the principles so far specified provide us with no technique for distinguishing free variation of allomorphs from substi- tutability of distinct but synonymous lexical items. Given that "perhaps he will come" and "maybe he will come" are phonemically distinct synonymous expressions in English, what principle is to prevent the representation of "perhaps" and "maybe" as freely varying allomorphic variants of some morpheme? Presumably, some further condition will have to be added to the ones so far employed to identify allomorphs. Perhaps it is that allomorphs of a morpheme not only must be either in complementary distribution or in free variation but also must be phonemically similar. Some such condition might be supposed to rule out "perhaps" and "maybe" as allomorphs of a common morpheme.

Notice that the problem raised here is fully analogous to one which occurred in the discussion of the relation between allophones and phonemes. We noted then that [pʰ] is in complementary distribution, in English, with both [p] and [t]. To avoid representing [pʰ] and [t] as allophones of a common phoneme, we were therefore required to demand *phonetic* similarity among allophones. Similarly, in the present case, to avoid representing intutively distinct but synonymous lexical items as allomorphs of a common morpheme, we must demand *phonemic* similarity among allomorphs. In neither case is this conse- quence a happy one; for just as the notion of phonetic similarity ap- pears to be susceptible of no simple explication, so is it possible to wonder *how much* phonemic similarity is going to be required for the establishment of allomorphs. What principle determines whether the semantic and phonological similarities between, say, the English prefixes "mal" and "mis" are sufficient to warrant assigning them to a common morpheme on grounds of complementary distribution (note: *malformed* and *misbegotten* but *misformed and *malbegotten)? This is similarly the case for classes of prefixes like "an," "non," "un," "in," all of which share a negative connotation.

It appears as though purely "objective" procedures for characterizing notions of adequate phonemic similarity between allomorphs are likely to be difficult to find if the taxonomy effected by such procedures is to be nonarbitrary. This is hardly surprising; a rational decision about whether synonymous items should be represented as lexically distinct should take account of such considerations as, for example, whether they are etymologically distinct. Clearly, considerations of this kind cannot be taken into account by a procedure which seeks to effect the individuation of morphemes solely in terms of formal properties of a corpus and the semantic judgments of speakers.

Taxonomic syntax.   We have commented upon the essential homogeneity of the procedures employed in isolating the linguistic classes that appear at the phonetic, phonemic, and morphemic levels of a taxonomic grammar: in each case, appeal is made to complementary distribution and free variation without change of meaning to provide the conditions under which linguistic elements belong to a common taxonomic class.

At the level of syntactic analysis, however, one finds a more or less tacit abandonment of these principles. Roughly, morphemes that belong to a common syntactic type *share* their privileges of occurrence (i.e., they are *not* in complementary distribution). What makes "boy" and "girl" both words of the same syntactic type is the similarity of their distributional pattern in English sentences. But while members of a common syntactic class do not exhibit complementary distribution, they do not exhibit free variation either, since their alternation in a linguistic environment characteristically determines changes of meaning. In short, new principles of class construction are required if the taxonomic approach is to be extended to the level of syntactic analysis.

There are clearly a vast number of cases in which distinct words occur in the same linguistic environments in any representative corpus of natural language utterances; thus, as we saw above, there is a very general overlap in the "privileges of occurrence" of such items as /dog/ and /cat/ and /boy/ and /girl/. This kind of fact suggests that it might be possible to represent the constraints on permissible *sequences* of morphemes in terms of equivalence classes of items having similar or identical privileges of occurrence. Thus if one thinks of /dog/, /cat/, /boy/, /girl/, etc., as members of a common *lexical class* (e.g., noun), it is possible to arrive at a compendious statement of such facts as the following: If the string "the dog is on the rug" is a permissible sequence of morphemes, so also will be the strings "the cat is on the rug," "the girl is on the rug," etc. One represents this fact by the "rule" that "the *noun* is on the rug" is a permissible sequence for any substitution instance of the class (noun).

The relevant procedure for characterizing taxonomic classes at the *syntactic* level of analysis is thus simply that of grouping into an equiva-lence class all morphemes which exhibit sufficiently similar privileges of occurrence in linguistic environments. What precisely is to count as sufficient similarity is a moot point in the taxonomic literature and will not concern us here. What *is* relevant is that given an inventory of the morpheme classes in a language, the taxonomic grammarian can provide an abstract representation of the *sentences* in his corpus by specifying the permissible *sequences* of morpheme classes. Thus one represents such facts as the "the cat is on the rug" and "a dog was under the table" are both sentences in the following way. (1) There is a lexical class (determiner=D) of which "the" and "a" are both members; there is a lexical class (animate noun=N_a) of which "cat" and "dog" are both members; there is a lexical class (verb=V) of which the morpheme "be" is a member; "is" and "are" are allomorphs of the morpheme "be"; there is a lexical class (preposition = P) of which "on" and "under" are members; there is a lexical class (inanimate noun = N_i) of which "rug" and "table" are members. (2) The sequence $D + N_a + V + P + D + N_i$ is a permissible sequence of morpheme classes in English.

We thus arrive at the notion of a level of syntactic description at which the language is represented by a set of sequences of morpheme classes. It is easy to see, however, that this kind of representation is it-self capable of being generalized, i.e., that there are facts of linguistic structure that such a representation fails to reveal. Thus, for example, just as there is patently an underlying similarity in the distributional privileges of such morphemes as "boy" and "girl," so there is an analo-gous similarity in the distribution privileges of such *phrases* as "the boy" and "the girl." If, then, similarity of distribution argues in favor of grouping "girl" and "boy" into a class like *N*, the same arguments would appear to support the recognition of a class noun phrase (*NP*) of which "the boy" and "the girl" are both members.

We can now characterize the richest notion of taxonomic linguistic description, which was widely influential in shaping the psycho-linguistics of the 1950s. The linguistically permissible sequences of a language are represented as sequences of phrases; phrases themselves are represented as sequences of morpheme classes; morpheme classes are classes of morphs; morphs are classes of phoneme sequences; and phonemes are classes of phones. Thus, for example, a typical taxonomic description of English might provide the representation for the English sentence "The cat is on the rug" shown in Figure 2-1. The claim for this description is not only that it provides the correct representation of the linguistic structure of "The cat is on the rug," but also that it appropri-ately represents the structural analogies that relate that sentence to others. Thus while the full description in Figure 2-1 suffices to distin-guish "The cat is on the rug" from any other English sentence, the repre-

Sentence :	The cat	is	on		the	rug.
Phrase structure :	((the cat)$_{NP}$	(is ((on (the rug)$_{NP}$	)$_{Prep. phrase}$	)$_{Pred. phrase}$	)$_S$	
Morpheme classes :	D N	V		Prep	D	N
Morphemes :	*the cat*	*be+present+singular*	*on*		*the*	*rug*
Phonemes :	/ði kæt	ɪz	ɔn		ði	rəg/
Phones :	[ðe kʰæt	ɪz	ɔn		ðə	rəg]

Figure 2-1   Taxonomic analysis of the sentence "The cat is on the rug."

sentation assigned at each level of description marks whatever similarities obtain between that sentence and other English sentences to which it
is grammatically related. While this view of sentence structure by no
means exhausts the conceptual resources of taxonomic linguistics, it does
provide a reasonable characterization of those aspects of taxonomic
theory that proved influential in psycholinguistics. More powerful versions of taxonomic syntax will be discussed in Chapter 3.

Summary remarks on taxonomic grammars.   In considering the taxonomic view of language structure as it has been presented here, one is
struck by the extent to which its character is determined by an acceptance of the operationalist principle. We can distinguish three major
themes in the taxonomic treatment of language, each of which can be
viewed as motivated by this principle.

1.   A taxonomic grammar of a language is a hierarchy of classes in
which the lowest-level elements are temporal segments of speech
events. That is, the grammar is in a strict sense *a taxonomy of speech
events.* In accepting this view, the taxonomic grammarian implicitly
adopts the typical operationalist notion that a scientific theory consists
fundamentally of an enumeration and taxonomy of the observables,
together with a statement of whatever generalizations about the behavior of the observables are inductively certifiable.

But this view of scientific theories must surely be rejected. Most
sciences do not have the form of a taxonomy; still less do they have the
form of a taxonomy of observables. Rather, sciences characteristically
are concerned with the way in which the behavior of observables is

contingent upon unobserved events and processes (e.g., micro-events such as particle interactions).

Because the taxonomic grammarian was committed to the methodological principle that linguistic theories must "emerge" from the data through the application of operational procedures, he was prohibited from viewing his data as the surface indication of underlying linguistic and psychological regularities and from viewing theory construction as the investigation of those regularities. He was thus committed to a view of linguistics as more similar to nineteenth-century botany than to twentieth-century physics.

2. Insofar as the principles for grammar construction are distributional, the flow of information through these principles goes in only one direction: no consideration of the character of the morphological system is allowed to influence decisions about the phonemic representation; no appeal to the character of phrase structure is made in deciding which sequences shall be included in the morphemic inventory; and so on.

It should be emphasized that to require decisions involved in theory construction at lower levels to be unresponsive to what the theorist knows about higher-level structure is to endorse an extremely questionable procedure. Normal methodological practice dictates that where a scientific theory is seeking to analyze structure at two levels of description, every attempt should be made to maximize the simplicity of the theory *as a whole* by taking account of the character of each of the levels in constructing the description of the other. That is, the description of each structural level is constrained to permit whatever simplifications of the whole theory are compatible with its empirical adequacy. As the philosopher Quine (1964) has put it:

> Total science is like a field of force whose boundary conditions are experience. A conflict with experience at the periphery occasions readjustments in the interior of the field. . . . But the total field is so underdetermined by its boundary conditions, experience, that there is much latitude of choice as to what statements to re-evaluate in the light of any single contrary experience. No particular experiences are linked with any particular statements in the interior of the field, except indirectly through considerations of equilibrium affecting the field as a whole. . . . Each man is given a scientific heritage plus a continuing barrage of sensory stimulation; and the considerations which guide him in warping his scientific heritage to fit his continuing sensory prompting are, where rational, pragmatic [pp. 42–46].

In short, in normal scientific practice, simplifications of the theory as a whole are achieved by constraining each level to account for the relevant data in a way that permits parsimonious characterizations of structure at other levels. Why, then, did structuralists accept the constraint that theory construction must preserve a unidirectional flow of information through the taxonomic principles rather than constrain the analysis at each level to contribute to the simplification of the theory as a whole?

Presumably because they were concerned with honoring the operation-alist principle that grammars should be generable from the data by well-defined discovery procedures. For, while it is obviously possible to define automatic principles for producing more or less ad hoc tax-onomies of linguistic entities, it is unlikely that such principles can be devised in a way that will automatically assign to each level that unique characterization which is compatible with the maximal simplicity of the grammar as a whole. This latter is an extremely strong requirement to place upon the discovery procedures for a grammar, and there is no reason whatever to believe it can be met by any principle of the kind proposed by taxonomic grammarians.

It might be added that insofar as these considerations argue against accepting the operationalist condition upon the construction of gram-mars, they argue equally against viewing the theory of grammars as primarily the theory of discovery procedures. It is a routine observation in the philosophy of science that the procedures by which one arrives at a scientific theory are irrelevant to either its truth or its level of confir-mation. In no serious science does the scientist take it as his goal to provide procedures for arriving at theories. Rather, the sole desidera-tum is that the theory, however arrived at, should be true. It is difficult to see why linguistics should be an exception to this rule.

3.   The classification of a linguistic element is determined by its dis-tribution. Clearly, some such principle for taxonomizing must be ac-cepted if the class membership of an item is to be determined by purely operational procedures.

Yet the appearance of objectivity purchased by accepting this con-straint is in a certain sense spurious, since the relevant sense of "dis-tributional similarity" cannot be specified in operational terms.

For example, in assigning morphemes to lexical classes, distribu-tional similarity between the morphemes is determined by reference to their cooccurrence in common linguistic environments. Yet it will hardly ever be the case that two members of a morpheme class will have *all* environments in common, so some theoretical insight must be exer-cised in determining which environments are to be "diagnostic" for a given class. If, for example, we choose to group together all and only morphemes which appear in the morphemic environment "-hood," we get a taxonomy which distinguishes between a lexical class containing "father" and "neighbor" on the one hand, and a lexical class which con-tains "uncle" on the other ("fatherhood" and "neighborhood" are words but "unclehood" is not). Given that this assignment is clearly unacceptable, we must avoid choosing the environment "-hood" as diagnostic for any morpheme class. But what operational principle dis-tinguishes between the acceptable and the unacceptable diagnostic environments? That is, given that one has selected appropriate diagnostic environments, it is clearly possible to taxonomize according to purely automatic procedures. But this fact is of no interest so long as the procedures for choosing acceptable diagnostic environments do not themselves satisfy the operationalist constraint.

It appears, then, that the operationalist constraint can at best be satisfied only in a post hoc fashion. Given that we have some intuitive or theoretical grounds for wishing to isolate a class of linguistic items, it is sometimes possible to find a distributional property common to just the members of that class, i.e., to provide some diagnostic formula for characterizing the class in a way that satisfies the operationalist constraint. But this will be equally true of classes which have *no* theoretical or intuitive interest; for example, the procedure which isolates all and only lexical items having a long vowel as their third phone is perfectly well defined and satisfies the operationalist constraints on classification as well as any procedures standardly employed in taxonomic linguistics. It happens, however, that this procedure isolates a class which has no theoretical interest: no important generalizations happen to be statable about the class of elements it defines. It is therefore of no interest to be able to claim that criteria for selecting members of this class are well defined.

To claim that a procedure for taxonomizing is operational is, therefore, to claim nothing of importance unless it is *also* demonstrable that the taxonomy which the procedure effects will group together elements whose behavior is in some theoretically relevant sense similar. The operationalist constraint ought therefore to demand that we accept only procedures which can be demonstrated to yield *theoretically relevant* taxonomies automatically. But there is no reason to believe that the principles of structural linguistics provide any basis for identifying such procedures or for distinguishing them from procedures which taxonomize automatically but uninterestingly.

In concluding our discussion of structuralist models of language, it must be added that though we have found many reasons for dissatisfaction with taxonomic grammars and with the methodological principles which motivated and justified them, there can be no doubt that many of the facts about linguistic structure that taxonomic grammarians set out to capture are real. Sentences in natural languages do satisfy a variety of types of constraints on their serial organization and do exhibit a characteristic decomposition of higher-level elements into lower-level elements. Any acceptable grammar will have to represent these sorts of features of the organization of sentences. In our discussion of generative grammars we shall consider ways of representing them which are immune to some, at least, of the criticisms we have raised against taxonomic models.

PSYCHOLINGUISTIC IMPLICATIONS OF TAXONOMIC GRAMMAR

A psychologist who accepts the view of language structure we discussed in the preceding section is faced with a twofold problem. First, he must explain how taxonomic structure is learned: in particular, he is responsible for describing the psychological mechanisms involved in the formation and concatenation of taxonomic classes, since those are the essential operations required to specify a level of a taxonomic grammar. Principles are thus needed which account for the child's ability to learn the grouping of elements into classes at each linguistic level and for his ability to learn the regularities underlying the serial distribution of these classes.

Second, the psychologist must provide a model for the way taxonomic information about language structure is employed by the adult to effect the organization of verbal behavior and the perceptual analysis of linguistic inputs. As Osgood and Sebeok (1969) remarked in an influential monograph, such a model is intended to exhibit the way the structure of "the message is related to decisions or choices made at each of these [taxonomic] levels of organization and what features in messages serve as boundary markers of these units" (p. 71). In short, the taxonomic linguist presented his psychological contemporaries with a picture of language structure as a hierarchy of levels interrelated by the taxonomic principle. The problem posed for psychology was to explain how verbal behavior could, in fact, come to exhibit such a structure.

Psycholinguistic treatments of serial order in language. The typical Hullean account of sequential order in verbal behavior was formulated in terms of the concept of *transition probability* developed in information theory. Let A and B be two elements or strings of elements, at a given level of linguistic description. Then, given a behavioral sequence S which contains A as a subsequence, let p be the probability that S contains B as the subsequence immediately following A. We will call p the *transition probability* from A to B. Thus suppose A is the element "noun phrase" and B is the element "verb"; then p_{AB} is the probability that a sentence which contains a sequence analyzable as (noun phrase$_i$) will contain a sequence analyzable as (noun phrase$_i$ verb). Similarly, suppose that A is the string of words "my brother" and B is the string of words "left the house," then p_{AB} is the probability that a sentence containing "my brother" contains "left the house" as the immediately succeeding phrase.

We can now relate the statistically defined notion of transition probability to a notion derived from the Hullean psychology of learning by simply assuming that the transition probability from A to B is a measure of the strength of the association of B to A. That is, it is assumed that the statistical fact that A has a determinate probability of being followed by B in a message in the language is to be explained by assuming that speakers of the language have the habit of producing (or expecting, or both) B to follow A, and that the value of p is to be explained by the assumption that p is an index of the strength of that habit.

A number of psychologists assumed that the learning of associations between linguistic items which cooccur in the speech environment of the child is a case of conditioning by stimulus-stimulus association. Such S-S integrations are characterized by the occurrence of learning which requires a high frequency of contiguity of the associated items in the experience of the learner, but which does not require specific reward (cf. Osgood, 1957, for discussion). Thus, for example, it is assumed that the transition probability from "my brother" to "left the house" measures the strength of the habit speakers have of producing "left the house" after having produced "my brother," and the explanation of the strength of this habit is just that in the child's speech environment, the latter sequence has been followed by the former with a certain probability. What saves this explanation from circularity is the presumed learning principle that when two stimuli cooccur with a certain frequency in the environment of an organism (in this case, in the speech environment of a child), the organism forms an association between them which has a strength proportional to that frequency.

It should be emphasized that the question of whether the learning of sequencing habits for verbal behavior is a case of "pure contiguity learning" (i.e., of S-S association) was a bone of contention among psychologists of this period. Many psychologists, particularly Skinnerians, thought it important to maintain that the formation of sequential associations between linguistic items was ineliminably dependent upon the occurrence of reinforcement, e.g., that the strength of an association between linguistic items A and B is determined by the frequency with which the response B to the discriminative stimulus A is reinforced during the linguistic training of the child. It is unnecessary for our purposes to enter into this dispute since, as we shall argue later, the entire attempt to construe sequential linguistic structure in terms of transitional probabilities, and the coordinate attempt to account for verbal patterning in terms of associative strength, was unsuccessful.

The important consideration for the present discussion is that whatever general associative principles may have been thought to be implicated in verbal association, there was quite widespread agreement that the sequential structure of language is representable in terms of some such notion as transition probability, and that the transition probabilities between items in a language are direct reflections of the associative habits of speakers of the language. We see here a very pervasive view of the way in which specifically linguistic theories of language structure may be supposed to cohere with psychological accounts of the integration of verbal behavior. As Osgood and Sebeok (1969) put it:

> The study of the sequential or transitional structure of behavior provides a meeting ground for linguistics, information theorists, and learning theorists. The linguist, applying his own methods of analysis, discovers hierarchies of more and more inclusive units; the information theorist, usually starting with lower level units such as letters or words, finds evidence for rather regular oscillations in transitional uncertainty in message sequences, the points of highest uncertainty often corresponding to unit boundaries as linguistically determined; and the learning theorist, working with notions like the habit-family hierarchy, finds it possible to make predictions about sequential psycholinguistic phenomena that can be tested with information theory techniques (p. 93).

The blending of psychology, linguistics, and information theory is characteristic of the Hullean style in psycholinguistics. Yet the treatment which appeals to laws of association to account for cooccurrences of items in the overt behavior of organisms is common to all schools of behaviorism, as is the assumption that frequency and habit strength are intimately related. To understand the *specifically* Hullean contributions to the development of psychological accounts of serial structure in verbal behavior, we must investigate the notion of a mediating response and the role it played in Hullean psychology.

It is well known that conditioning often exhibits local transitivity. For example, suppose a nonsense word B is conditioned in a paired associate learning task as the response to the nonsense word A. Next, the same subject is taught a pairing of B as stimulus with a different nonsense word C as response. That is, we teach the subject to respond to A by saying B and to respond to B by saying C. Given this training, subjects will often produce C as a response to A in transfer tests. Thus training on A-B and B-C can create an association between A and C, even though the subject is never specifically trained to produce an A-C pairing.

One might attempt to account for this kind of finding in the following way. We assume that whenever the subject responds to presentation of A by saying C he has, in fact, produced the "unobserved" or "implicit" mediating response B. That is, by virtue of the association that was produced in A-B training, presentations of A as a stimulus elicit covert occurrences of B as a mediating response. Correspondingly, the covert occurrence of B thus elicited mediates the production of an overt response C by virtue of the association established in B-C training.

There are, in fact, a large number of learning phenomena which, like this one, appear to require the assumption that the performance of the organism is integrated by the occurrence of unobserved, implicit, or "mediating" responses. Wherever associations occur between items in the behavior of an organism which have not been specifically paired in training, the mediation program envisages treating such associations as directly or indirectly derivative from associations between overt and implicit responses.

Thus, though sequential order in behavior is still to be explained by reference to associative chaining, the Hullean permits the following liberalization of radical behaviorist's methodology: some of the stimulus or response elements, or both, of associative chains may be thought of as de facto unobservable (e.g., as occurring in "abbreviated," or "reduced," form somewhere in the recesses of the organism's central nervous system). The postulation of such unobserved associative elements has the character of a theoretical inference: it is justified by reference to the simplicity and explanatory power of the theories in which it plays a role. The question naturally arises, then, to what extent this sort of liberalization leads to an increase in the theorist's ability to account for sequential organization in language.

To begin with, the Hullean liberalization goes some way toward permitting the learning theorist to make sense of the notion that language is simultaneously organized into units of a variety of levels of abstractness. This is a notion which, as we remarked at the beginning of this chapter, the radical behaviorist must find intractable. For, insofar as a psychologist is methodologically committed to full-blown operationalism, the only sort of associative relations his theories can countenance are those that hold between *overt* stimulus and response elements. But precisely what these elements should be taken to be in case of language is far from clear; one could imagine sequential associations being postulated to hold between sounds, articulatory gestures, words, phrases, etc. Which of these types of units is the radical behaviorist to choose as the "overt response" whose behavior his theory will account for?

Questions about the character of elementary responses in a verbal response chain often appear to be matters of indifference to radical behaviorists like Skinner. If, for example, we take literally Skinner's (1957) remark that a verbal operant is *any* response that occurs "as a function of certain variables" (p. 21), then, clearly, every linguistic entity from the phone to the discourse is an elementary linguistic unit, since every verbal effect surely has its sufficient cause. But it seems doubtful that even Skinner took this remark seriously, since he is quite happy both to consider grammatical inflections to be *fragments* of responses and to consider them to be discriminated autoclitics.

What, then, shall we say are the elementary behaviors out of which complex verbal responses are constructed? How shall we adjudicate between the claims of sounds, phones, phonemes, morphemes, words, phrases, sentences, and discourses to be the "real," "observable," "overt," etc., elements of which verbal behavior is composed? The point is precisely that language exhibits *simultaneous* organization on each of a number of levels, and this fact poses an intolerable dilemma for the radical behaviorist. He is methodologically committed to choosing one or another of these levels as the one which is said to be "overtly" observable. Yet, whichever he chooses, his theories will be unable to represent features of linguistic structure which hold among the linguistic entities at other levels. If, for example, he decides that words are to be behavioral units, then his theory will, in principle, be able to represent features of their serial order. But, by definition, behavioral *units* have no internal structure, so his theory will *not* be able to represent the phonological and phonemic regularities characteristic of the formation of words. Correspondingly, if he chooses to characterize the observable data in verbal behavior as the *sequences* of words, then his theory will be unable in principle to represent the fact that such sequences exhibit a characteristic organization into phrases, sentences, and discourses. Patently, the same sort of argument will hold for whatever level entities the radical behaviorist chooses as designata for terms in his observation language. Skinner appears to accept the consequences of this dilemma. He says that "although parts of . . . larger operants have the same form as parts of other operants or even of whole units, there may be no functional interaction" (1957, p. 21). This remark suggests, for example, that insofar as a sentence is under unitary functional control, it has no internal structure for its utterer. In particular, on this view, if the sentence "John went to the store" is under unitary functional control, it ipso facto does *not* contain any of the English words "John," "went," "to," "the," or "store." But this sort of paradox is surely intolerable. Clearly, some theoretical formalism must be found that will permit us to represent cases in which behavior exhibits simultaneous serial organization on a number of levels.

It was precisely this hierarchy of structure in language that taxonomic grammar sought to make explicit and that Hullean psycholinguistics sought to explain. Hulleans believed that they could account for the simultaneous organization of linguistic responses at a variety of levels in a way that the radical behaviorists' methodology precluded. In this account, the assumption that unobserved stimulus or response-like entities may mediate the integration of serially organized behavior plays a central role.

Since covert responses were assumed to obey whatever general associative laws govern overt behavior, it follows that covert responses can enter into association with one another. Hence implicit responses can themselves exhibit serial organization into chains. Suppose, then, that one were to identify the abstract entities which are specified in the higher levels of taxonomic grammars with mediating responses. In particular, while the psychological character of the lowest level of serial organization in language could be expressed by reference to associative relations between sounds or articulatory gestures, higher levels of serial organization could be characterized by postulating associations between concurrent implicit responses. The latter are thus conceived of as the psychological counterparts of such linguistic entities as phones, phonemes, words, and phrases, and serial ordering between such entities can be attributed to the action of the same associative principles that were presumed to control overt behavior.

If, for example, we think of "article" and "noun" as somehow the names of mediating responses, we can imagine an account of the organization of noun phrases in terms of associations between them. Thus, the taxonomic statement that, in English, the sequence "article noun" constitutes a phrase is to be explained by the psycholinguistic assumption that English speakers have formed a serial association which links the implicit response "article" with the implicit response "noun." Indeed the entire mechanism of transition probabilities can be invoked here in a manner strictly analogous to the one developed above. We can say, for example, that there exists a determinate transition probability from "article" to "noun" and that the size of that probability is an index of the strength of the habit English speakers have of providing the implicit response "noun" to the occurrence of an implicit response "article."

On this view, then, the fact that the production of a sentence is demonstrably the production of behavior which is serially ordered at a number of levels of description can be accounted for by the assumption that the speaker has developed associative connections between a corresponding number of types of implicit and explicit responses. The overt behavior of a speaker uttering a sentence in his language is thus the realization of a variety of habit structures, but since these structures are arranged in a hierarchy, the constraints they impose upon behavior have their effects simultaneously.

Osgood (1963) has provided a detailed outline of such a theory. He pointed out that "the notion of simultaneous, vertical hierarchies of units within units within units has been about as foreign to psychologists as the notion of probabilistic sequential hierarchies has been to linguistics" (pp. 741–742). Yet he suggested that it is precisely the former notion that psycholinguists require if they are appropriately to analyze processes of decision and control in verbal behavior. Psycholinguistic models are thus held to be inadequate insofar as they fail to describe serial linguistic structure at the more abstract levels of integration as well as at the level of directly observable behavioral output.

For Osgood, the identification of class markers (like noun, noun phrase, adjective, and so on) with implicit responses resolves the

Rewrite rules   Tree diagram

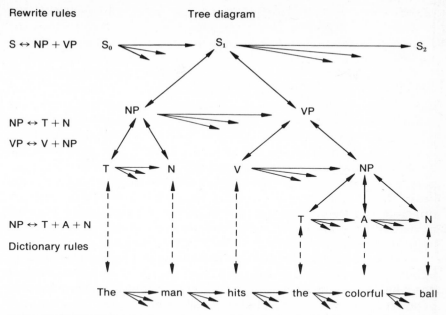

Figure 2-2 Sequential and simultaneous response hierarchies underlying the production/perception of the sentence "The man hits the colorful ball" (after Osgood, 1963).

dilemma. If transitional dependencies are assumed to organize verbal behavior simultaneously on a number of levels of description, we are in a position to reconsider the associationistic account of the organization of verbal behavior. Figure 2-2 suggests how sequential (probabilistic) and simultaneous (unitizing) hierarchies can be integrated. Divergent sequential hierarchies indicate that what follows within the noun phrase or within the verb phrase is in part optional and therefore probabilistically determined. An antecedent sentence (S_0) and a subsequent sentence (S_2) are shown to indicate that sentences as wholes are themselves probabilistically linked to units at their own level. Transitional decisions at supraordinate levels modify the probabilities of units at subordinate levels, but only partially; e.g., note that the noun class of *man* in the diagrammed sentence is jointly dependent upon its vertical relation to *NP* and its horizontal relation to *T* (Osgood, 1963, pp. 742–743).

What Osgood suggests is that serial organization can be explained in terms of transitional dependencies between items, not just at the level of "overt behavior," but also at the higher levels of implicit response. Briefly, at each level of description the occurrence of left-hand elements of a serial chain influences the probability of occurrence of right-hand elements in that chain. At the word level, then, the occurrence of "the" conditions the probability of occurrence of "man"; at higher levels, the occurrence of T conditions the probability of occurrence of N; the occurrence of NP conditions the probability of occurrence of VP; and the occurrence of S_0 conditions the probability of occurrences of S_1.

But though this model is appealing, if one accepts its associationistic premises, it is also untenable. To begin with, it has no resources for explaining the sort of right-to-left dependencies between linguistic elements that we illustrated by sentences like 2-1. What is still more important, to accept Osgood's proposal would entail abandoning a primary requirement upon any account of the organization of verbal behavior; namely, that the model should represent the fact that languages are productive: that the number of sentences in a language (and hence the number of sentences that the ideal speaker-hearer can, in principle, encode-decode) is unbounded. The incompatibility of such a model with the productivity of grammar is based on a rather subtle point which deserves to be explored at some length.

A grammar must be finite, but it must provide a representation of an infinite set of objects: the infinite set of sentences of the language it describes. For a grammar which represents sentences as hierarchically organized into words, morpheme classes, phrases, etc., this requirement can be satisfied in a way that the following examples should make clear.

Consider, first, a system of rules which describes the taxonomic structure of the sentence in Figure 2-2. These rules specify the grammatical category of sequences of linguistic elements. Thus, the rule $S \rightarrow NP + VP$ states that the sequence noun phrase + verb phrase belongs to the category *sentence*. Analogously, the rule $NP \rightarrow T + N$ states that the sequence article + noun belongs to the category *noun phrase*. The following sequence of rules of this sort can specify the taxonomic structure of "the man hits the colorful ball":

$$
\begin{aligned}
S &\rightarrow NP + VP \\
NP &\rightarrow T + N \quad \text{or} \quad T + A + N \\
VP &\rightarrow V + NP \\
T &\rightarrow \text{the} \\
N &\rightarrow \text{man or ball} \\
V &\rightarrow \text{hits} \\
A &\rightarrow \text{colorful}
\end{aligned}
$$

This system of rules is a *grammar* in the sense that it represents a variety of taxonomic structures, including the structure Figure 2-2 assigns to the "man hits the colorful ball." In particular, the rules can be employed to specify taxonomic analyses of sentences by constructing a set of trees in which the sequence of elements $B_1, B_2 \ldots, B_n$ is directly

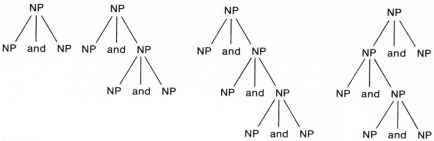

Figure 2-3

dominated by α in one or more of the trees if and only if the grammar contains a rule of the form $\alpha \rightarrow B_1, B_2, \ldots, B_n$.

The point to notice about the sort of formal system we have described so far is that its output is finite. The set of structures these rules assign to a given linguistic category can be represented by a finite disjunction, and the productive power of the grammar is exhausted when every disjunct is assigned to a category in every way permitted by the grammar. For example, in the grammar just given, the structures that are assigned to *NP* are only the two shown in Figure 2-2. The same is true of each of the other categories mentioned in these rules: the output of this grammar is a finite set of trees.

If, then, these sort of rules are to represent infinite sets (like the set of sentences in a language), their formal properties must be altered in some way. A sufficient liberalization is to permit at least one symbol designating a taxonomic category to appear *both* on the left-hand side of a rule *and* on the right-hand side of that same rule. That is, the grammar contains rules of the form $\alpha \rightarrow B_1 + \alpha + B_2$. For example, the grammar might contain a rule like the following:

2-5   *NP* → *NP* and *NP*

(This rule allows the specification of compound noun phrases like "the boy and the girl" and "the cat and the dog.") The interest of this kind of rule is that the set of structures it assigns to the category mentioned on its left cannot be specified by a finite list. This is immediately obvious from the fact that the rule can be applied over and over to its own output generating a new structure on each application. Thus it specifies infinitely many structures of the kind illustrated in Figure 2-3. One effect of this liberalization is that it allows a given element to dominate itself in trees specified by a grammar.

It should be noticed that the same effect can be obtained by slightly different formal means. Suppose that there is a pair of rules in the grammar which have the following features. Rule 1 has a symbol α on its left-hand side and a symbol β on its right-hand side; rule 2 has the symbol

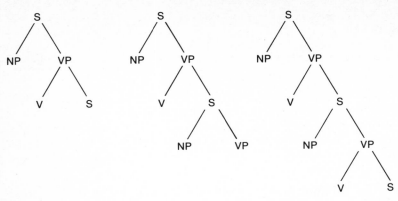

Figure 2-4

β on its left-hand side and the symbol α on its right-hand side. The grammar containing these two rules will now produce an infinite output. For example, consider a grammar which contains the following rules:

2-6 $S \rightarrow NP + VP$

2-7 $VP \rightarrow V + S$

(The latter of these rules might be implicated in the production of such sentences as "John knows the proposition is true," where "knows the proposition is true" is a verb phrase containing the verb "knows" and the sentence "the proposition is true.")

It is clear that a grammar containing rules (2-6) and (2-7), like a grammar containing rule (2-5), enumerates an infinite set of structures; for example, structures like those in Figure 2-4.

To summarize the argument thus far: a grammar which assigns a taxonomic analysis to sentences can be formalized by a finite set of rules, each of which determines the category of some sequence of linguistic elements. The grammar is said to be *recursive* when the rules permit a given element to directly or indirectly dominate itself in the trees which the grammar specifies. The grammar has an infinite output when there is no bound on the number of times a given element is allowed to dominate itself in a tree.

We can now see one reason why the kind of system Osgood suggested to reconcile grammatical and psycholinguistic models cannot be accepted. Osgood postulated "horizontal" probabilistic relations between linguistic elements at the *same* level of abstractness in a tree diagram. Thus, in the tree diagram for "the man hit the colorful ball," probabilistic relations are held to exist between *NP* and *VP*; between *T* and *N*; between "the" and "man"; and, in general, between the left and right members of each pair of elements at a given level in a tree. Clearly, however, for this proposal to be coherent, we must know what conditions need to be satisfied for two elements to be *at* the same level in a tree. That is, such a proposal is not well defined unless the notion "level of a tree" is well defined.

The difficulty is that there is no notion of a level of description for a grammar containing recursions of the kind we have discussed. We have seen that in such grammars an element may dominate itself indefinitely many times in a tree. Intuitively, this is equivalent to saying that when the grammar is recursive, each kind of element can occur at *any* structural level. This, in turn, is tantamount to saying that for a recursive grammar which assigns taxonomic structure, the notion of two elements being at *the same* level is simply undefined. As Chomsky (1957) has remarked:

> Phrase structure, taken as a linguistic level, has the ... character ... [that] ... we cannot set up a hierarchy among the various representations of [a sentence]; we cannot subdivide the system of phrase structure into a finite set of levels, ordered from higher to lower, with one representation for each sentence on each of these sublevels. For example, there is no way of ordering the elements *NP* and *VP* relative to one another. Noun phrases are contained within verb phrases, and verb phrases within noun phrases, in English. Phrase structure must be considered as a single level, with a set of representations for each sentence of the language [p. 32].

We thus find that there is a serious dilemma for views of the serial organization of language structure like the one Osgood proposed. Such views attempt to account for the fact that verbal behavior exhibits simultaneous organization at a variety of levels of description; the proposal is that behavior is integrated by the operation of transitional probabilities which hold between adjacent items at each such level. However, this assumption cannot be reconciled with the requirement that the language system must be productive. In particular, any such account could be undertaken only insofar as the knowledge of his language which the psycholinguistic theory ascribes to the speaker-hearer includes recursive rules. But the character of the structures recursive taxonomic rules specify precludes the definition of "adjacency between items at a level." And it is precisely that notion which theories like that offered by Osgood require to explain abstract aspects of linguistic organization.

The fact that transitional probabilities cannot be defined between adjacent elements in taxonomic trees is important, since solutions like the one Osgood proposed were widely accepted among psycholinguists in the Hullean tradition. Not only Osgood but also such theorists as Braine (1965), Jenkins and Palermo (1964), Berylyne (1965), Staats (1964), and others have assumed that the generalization of the notion of transitional probability from word strings to markers in tree structures could account for abstract constraints on the serial organization of sentences; and, insofar as such markers are identified with implicit responses, they could do so in a way that satisfies the methodological principles accepted by mediational learning theories. But we can generalize the notion of transition probability from strings of elements to trees only at the price of assuming the grammar to have a finite output. The incompatibility of such models with unbounded recursive rules in the specification of the speaker-hearer's linguistic information is thus a decisive difficulty for attempts to assimilate productive theories of grammatical structure to mediational views of behavior.

Mediational treatments of class formation.   A taxonomic grammar, as we have seen, characterizes linguistic structure by employing two main kinds of operations: those which assign linguistic elements to superordinate categories and those which concatenate such categories into sequences. A psycholinguistic theory constructed upon taxonomic assumptions must therefore contain not only principles which account for the learning of serial structure but also principles for the categorical assignment of linguistic elements.

To understand how Hullean psychologists proposed to deal with the assignment of linguistic elements to categories, we need the notion of *the associative set for the linguistic element* ϵ. The associative set for ϵ is defined to consist of all and only the responses that are associated to ϵ. We can use this concept to characterize the putative psychological counterpart of the equivalence classes in taxonomic grammar. Let $e_1, e_2, \ldots,$ e_n be elements at the ith level of taxonomic description. Let $E_1, E_2, \ldots, E_n$ be elements at the $(i + 1)$th level of taxonomic description. Then $e_1, e_2,$ $\ldots, e_n$ are members of the same linguistic class at the $(i + 1)$th level if and only if there exists an E_j such that E_j is in the associative set for e_1, and for $e_2, \ldots$ and for e_n.

Thus, for example, the taxonomic statement that "boy," "girl," "dog," "cat," etc., all belong to the category "noun" receives the following psychological translation at the hands of the mediation theorist: the implicit response "noun" is in the associative set for the stimuli "boy," "girl," "shoe," "dog," etc. Analogous treatment is afforded to taxonomic notion of category assignment at other levels of linguistic description. Thus when the taxonomic grammarian says that [p] and [p^h] are allophones of the phoneme /p/, the mediational psychologist "hears": the implicit responses /p/ is in the associative set of both [p] and [p^h].

The suggestion is that the notion of n-tuples of stimuli being instances of type T can be represented by assuming that each stimulus evokes an "implicit labeling response" T, and that it does so by virtue of the operation of associative principles. We shall argue that this account of what it is for something to be a thing of a certain kind is inadequate for the purposes of the psychology of language. It should be made clear, however, that in attempting to develop a theory of category membership which does not rely solely on appeal to the concepts of stimulus or response generalization, Hulleans were sensitive to a serious lacuna in other versions of behaviorism. In order to see why the Hullean treatment of class formation is an advance over other behaviorist treatments, consider briefly how one might appeal to the concept of generalization in an account of the conditions under which two things are of the same type.

In the pre-Hullean treatment of class formation, the notion of *generalization* is a fundamental conceptual building block, as it was in all empiricist theories of learning. It is invariably among the primary concepts that such theories appeal to in their attempts to explain stimulus and response equivalence, and in radical behaviorist theories it is the *only* concept used for this purpose. The principle of generalization may be stated in any of a number of ways. What all the standard formulations amount to is that training to a stimulus automatically transfers to any other stimulus which has sufficiently similar properties. It is held to be a fundamental fact about organisms that training is not specific to the trained stimulus. This is to say that the inherent structure of the organism determines equivalence relations among certain stimuli; namely, among any conditioned stimulus and all members of the class of generalized stimuli to which conditioning transfers.

The operation of the principle that *similarity* between CS (a conditioned stimulus) and GS (a stimulus to which conditioning generalizes) determines transfer of training, and hence determines how stimuli are grouped into categories, is among the cardinal tenets of cognitive psychology as developed by radical behaviorists. There are, however, well-known cases in which this principle appears to be inadequate. Among these are generalization to the octave of a conditioned tone, generalization across sensory modes, "semantic generalization," and so on. These cases are of considerable theoretical significance.

If the notion of generalization is to do any work in a psychological theory, it must provide an account of the kinds of stimulus properties that are capable of governing transfer of training. That is, if a theory is to employ the postulate that training transfers between similar stimuli, it must provide a way of distinguishing those kinds of similarity that are sufficient to mediate transfer from among the indefinitely many ways in which *any* two objects are similar. A natural way of meeting this requirement is the one that has usually been embraced by radical behaviorists: namely, to assume that training transfers between *physically* similar stimuli. If, however, this is to be the sole conceptual resource a theory employs for explaining stimulus equivalence, then for every case of transfer of training, the theory must show how the stimuli between which transfer occurs are relevantly physically similar, and, indeed, are *more* physically similar than items between which transfer does *not* take place.

In short, the principle of generalization is vacuous (i.e., is merely tautological) unless some way of determining the similarity between CS and GS is supplied that is independent of determining that training does, in fact, transfer from CS to GS. If similarity is to explain generalization, then the occurrence of generalization *cannot* be our metric of similarity. However, attempts to measure the degree of similarity between stimuli by reference to their physical properties fail to predict the observed pattern of generalization in the kinds of cases referred to above. Taken literally, the claim is untrue that physical similarity between stimuli is either necessary or sufficient for stimulus equivalence. (For an extensive discussion of the problems involved in providing a nonvacuous characterization of the laws governing transfer of training, see Osgood, 1953.)

In the case of psycholinguistics, appeal to generalization between physically similar stimuli is particularly unsatisfactory for explaining the formation of the kinds of equivalence classes postulated by taxonomic grammarians. The point at which this appeal seems initially most plausible is in accounts of the categorization of linguistic elements at the phonetic and phonemic levels of taxonomic description. For example, taxonomic grammar assures us that the first sound we produce when we utter "pin" belongs to the same phone as the first sound we produce when we utter "prick." The psychologist who accepts this analysis is beset with the problem of explaining the assignment of these sounds to the same phone in all its linguistic environments, and irrespective to broad variation in absolute pitch (children versus women; women versus men), amplitude (normal speech versus shouted speech), and so on.

The answer psycholinguistic theories have traditionally given to this problem is that all the utterances belonging to a phone form an equivalence class by virtue of their acoustic similarity. Conversely, on this view, speech sounds are assigned to *distinct* phones as the consequence of specifiable differences of values of their acoustic parameters. According to this kind of theory, what makes possible our mastery of the phonetic equivalences and differences among the speech sounds of our language is the reciprocal interaction of two psychological mechanisms: *generalization* (which may be thought of as assigning relatively similar sounds to a common phoneme), and *discrimination* (which may be thought of as excluding from a linguistic class any element that is not relevantly similar to the other members of that class). The important point to notice is that both generalization and discrimination are presumed to be responsive primarily to facts about the physical constitution of speech sounds: when generalization between speech sounds occurs, there must be some physical similarity to mediate the transfer of training. When discrimination occurs, there must be some physical feature common to the elements of one of the discriminated classes but not to the elements of the other.[1]

But the notion that the taxonomic classes in language are defined by the reciprocal action of generalization along physical parameters of stimuli and discrimination of physical differences between stimuli *clearly* fails for a number of types of higher-level classes that taxonomic grammarians wished to postulate. It would be absurd to suppose that what makes "John" and "The boy who left the room in a terrible hurry and returned several minutes later, looking embarrassed" both noun phrases is some physical feature common to them but not to any verb phrase. Precisely analogously, it seems hopeless to argue that what makes /s/, /iz/, and /z/ allomorphs of the plural morpheme is that they physically resemble one another more than any of them resemble any other arbitrarily selected phoneme sequences.

What is more surprising is a fact we alluded to in our discussion of the possibility of basing claims for the "objectivity" of phones on appeals to the acoustic similarity of the sounds belonging to them: that the presumed acoustic similarity is characteristically not found even among linguistic elements which the listener *hears* as similar. Not only the members of the class *noun phrase* but also the members of the class /p/ are heterogeneous in their acoustic properties. (See Chapter 6.)

Given the failure of appeals to generalization along parameters of physical similarity to account for the speaker-hearer's mastery of the

---

[1] There are a number of somewhat tendentious features of this discussion which might be mentioned, though they do not bear in any important way on the central question of the relevance of appeals to generalization in accounts of stimulus equivalence. For example, we have assumed, for purposes of discussion, that generalization and discrimination are to be treated as distinct psychological mechanisms. However, there is the possibility of considering the one to be merely the absence of the other. Similarly, we have not considered probabilistic models for generalization of verbal habits, though many psychologists would presumably balk at all-or-none assignments of sounds to phones or of phones to phonemes. But these considerations are all beside the point of the present argument since we wish to maintain that *however* the notion of generalization is to be construed, its applicability to explaining the formation of linguistic categories presupposes similarities between linguistic signals which, in fact, do not exist.

equivalence relations taxonomic grammars postulate, it can be seen that Hullean appeals to generalization *mediated by implicit responses* (hence to mediated stimulus and response equivalence) represented a conceptual advance. On the Hullean view, we can countenance the abstract equivalence of highly discriminable physical signals (like "the boy" and "a girl") because we can suppose such equivalences to be mediated by associations to a common implicit response. The psychologist thus adds to his repertoire for explaining stimulus equivalence the possibility that stimuli may become equivalent not only when they exhibit sufficient physical similarity but also when they have a common implicit response in their associative sets.

However, though this sort of suggestion adds power to the conceptual battery of general learning theory, it turns out to do less good in the analysis of language than might have been expected. Not even the sorts of class structure postulated by taxonomic grammarians can be plausibly accounted for by appeals to mediated stimulus-response equivalence. There are four considerations which argue conclusively to this effect.

Objections to the Hullean treatment of class formation

1. The Hullean treatment seems simply incompatible with the mediational treatment of *serial* organization. On the Hullean account, an item belongs to a class if the item is associated to the element which designates that class. But on the mediational view, the serial relation that holds between concatenated linguistic entities is explained by the assumption that the right member of any pair of such entities is an associate of the left member. For example, *NP VP* is a well-formed sequence of English phrase markers because *VP* is an associative response to *NP*, and similarly for any other serially ordered sequences postulated by a taxonomic grammar.

However, if the reason that *VP* follows *NP* in English sentences is that *VP* is an associate of *NP*, then it follows that *VP* is in the associative set for *NP* in the sense defined above. But we have seen that in the mediational view, being in the associative set for an element is sufficient for being subordinated to the element. Hence while the mediational explanation of the *serial* relationship between *NP* and *VP* entails that they must be elements at the same level of description, the mediational treatment of class formation entails that they must be elements at *different* levels of description (i.e., that *NP* must be subordinated to *VP*). Clearly these entailments are not compatible; hence the mediational account is inconsistent.

2. As Osgood has remarked, the associations that are postulated between an implicit response identified with a taxonomic class marker and the responses that are members of that taxonomic class must be bidirectional. This is because the mediational view identifies the *production* of a sentence with running through a tree from top to bottom and the *perception* of a sentence with running through the *same* tree from bottom to top. Commenting on Figure 2-2, Osgood (1963) remarks that

> Contrary to usual linguistic practice, in which the rewrite arrows and sequences within the tree are unidirectional (left-to-right and up-to-down), I have deliberately shown bidirectional arrows. The linguist's way of doing things reflects his too exclusive concern with the speaker, I think; that is, with generating or encoding sentences. The listener in the position of interpreting or decoding sentences begins with strings of words, combines them into large units and, finally, understands the sentence as a whole [p. 736].

The question of whether associations do, in fact, have the symmetrical character that Osgood requires is very much an open one (cf. Asch, 1968). What is more to the point, however, is that the assumption that linguistic associations are symmetrical is formally incompatible with the mediational treatment of the subordination-superordination relationship. In particular, if a sufficient condition for β being subordinated to α is that the latter be in the associative set of the former, then such associations can never be symmetrical. For, since each member of a pair of symmetrically associated elements is in the associative set of the other member, each member would be subordinated to the other, which is, of course, logically impossible. Yet Osgood is surely right in saying that his model fails to be a model of both sentence perception and production unless he assumes that the relations which impose vertical structure on trees *are* symmetrical.

We see here a classic example of the problems generated when one fails to distinguish between theories of language structure and theories of the computational mechanisms involved in the perception and production of speech. The domination relation exhibited by nodes in a tree is intended to represent features of the abstract phrasal organization of sentences. By taking this relation for a representation of the direction of information flow in both speech perception and production, one immediately falls into self-contradiction: subordination is an asymmetric relation, but information flow must go in both directions for the production and perception of speech. To claim that one phrase marker dominates another in the grammatical representation of a sentence is *not* to make any claim about the order in which the markers are computed in producing or understanding the sentence. In particular, Osgood's remark that the linguistic system is somehow biased toward the production of sentences is wrong. It is, in fact, a totally neutral representation of what is produced and perceived in speech exchanges.

3. Since the mediation theorist treats the case in which n-tuples of elements are members of a common class by assuming that the members of the n-tuple are each associated with a common implicit response, it follows that every such class is finite. It is self-evident that the speaker-hearer cannot learn more than a finite number of distinct associations in the course of his life. But clearly it is false that all linguistic classes are finite; not only the class "sentence" but also such classes as "noun phrase" and "verb phrase" are productive. That is, just as the speaker-hearer can encode-decode an infinite number of sentences, so he can also encode-decode an infinite number of noun phrases and verb phrases. This is because new noun phrases and verb phrases are constructible from sentences in very much the same way that new complex sentences are constructible from simple sentences. (See Chapter 3.)

4. If the mediators hypothesized to function in the establishment of taxonomic classes are associates in the usual sense, the question arises: What are the conditions under which two items come to be associated with the same mediator? Not surprisingly, the Hullean approach to this problem assumes that elements must become associated with a common mediator whenever they satisfy the distributional conditions taxonomic discovery procedures impose upon the commonality of class membership. Thus the arguments against the adequacy of taxonomic discovery procedures have close parallels in arguments against the adequacy of associationistic accounts of class formation.

Mediational psycholinguists have usually assumed that two linguistic elements become associated with the same implicit grammatical response under one of the following three kinds of conditions: they occur in approximately the same diagnostic environments and hence become associated with those environments; they occur in approximately the same ordinal positions in sentences and hence become associated with those positions; or they share some specifiable semantic features and hence become associated with stimuli which exhibit those features. Thus, on the first kind of account, a word is said to become associated with the mediating response characteristic of nouns if it commonly appears in one or more such "diagnostic" linguistic environments as "a _____," "an _____," "some _____," and "the _____." On the second account, an item is a noun if it commonly appears in, and hence is associated with, the second ordinal position in a sentence. (Thus a paradigmatic sentence of English is thought of as consisting of a first position which is filled with an article, followed by a second position which is filled with a noun, followed by a third position which is filled with a verb, etc.) In the third view, a word is a noun if it is associated with a referent which has some property as "thinghood," "objecthood," etc. That is, the defining property of "noun" is taken to be semantic rather than syntactic. Clearly, these views are not mutually exclusive.

It is fairly easy to see that none of these proposals can work. To begin with, neither ordinal position nor diagnostic environments can provide necessary and sufficient conditions for membership in linguistic classes. Thus, for example, one might attempt to define the diagnostic environment for the plural morpheme as "noun _____." One would thus identify the plural morpheme with the associative set for "noun." This suggestion fails since there exist linguistic items other than allomorphs of the plural morpheme that may appear immediately following a noun, e.g., any other affix (possessive *s* is a particularly compelling example, since it not only shares the environment that we had envisioned as diagnostic for allophones of the plural morpheme but it also has the same phonetic value as one of the realizations of that morpheme).

Similar problems arise at other levels. For example, it is impossible to define phonemes as associative responses to diagnostic environments since there exist phonemes which share identical privileges of occurrence. Any environment which specifies the phoneme /p/ will also specify the phoneme /t/, for one example.

For the same kinds of reasons, no analysis of higher-level syntactic markers as implicit responses to ordinal positions in sentences can conceivably deal with the existence of sentences which exhibit the same ordering of phrase types but which nevertheless differ in grammatical structure—for example, sentences like "John gave the book to Mary" and "John drove the car to New York." We want to say that these sentences do differ in structure: in particular, that "to Mary" is a quite different kind of phrase from "to New York." But we shall not be able to say this if we think of phrases as being of the same type when they share their ordinal positions in sentences, since these phrases can both occur in the position $NP\ V_{tr}\ NP$_____.

Indeed the entire attempt to specify the conditions under which items become associated with a common mediator in terms of shared ordinal positions is suspect. For example, the suggestion that "noun" is characteristic of the second position in an English sentence may hold for sentences like "the boy ran" (i.e., for sentences of the form TNV), but it clearly will not do for sentences like "birds fly" (i.e., sentences having the form NV) or for sentences like "the tall boy ran" (i.e., sentences having the form $TANV$). The ordinal position which a given type or linguistic element is capable of occupying would seem to be extremely variable, even in the case of "ordering" languages like English. (Cf. Braine, 1963; and Bever, Fodor, and Weksel, 1965a, 1965b.)

To summarize: if we think of a linguistic class marker as an associate to a class of linguistic items, we must provide some analysis of the conditions under which such associations arise. It is tempting to argue that linguistic items share an associate only in the case where they share linguistic environments. But no appeal to such environments, defined ordinally or otherwise, can assign linguistic items to distinct classes when they exhibit the same patterns of distribution. Yet there are very many cases in which the speaker-hearer does precisely that. In none of these cases can we interpret the notion of two elements belonging to the same taxonomic class by assuming that these elements are associated with a certain diagnostic environment.

Thus far we have argued that various distributional proposals for the conditions under which implicit grammatical responses are established cannot provide satisfactory accounts of the formation of grammatical classes. It might be supposed, however, that this argument is not forceful. Why not postulate *sets* of distinct implicit responses, each probabilistically associated with the same diagnostic environment? For example, why can we not think of "noun _____" as the diagnostic environment for *both* the implicit response "plural morpheme" *and* the implicit response "possessive morpheme," in the sense that each of these implicit responses has a finite but less than unitary probability of being elicited by the occurrence of a noun?

The difficulty with this suggestion is *not* that it invokes a notion of probability but rather that it begs the question the entire grammatical theory was constructed to answer, namely, "What individuates linguistic responses?" (For example, what makes the response [z] in "John's" a distinct response from the response [z] in "boys"?) The taxonomic answer to this question is that linguistic responses are distinct when, and only when, they belong to distinct higher-level classes. In the Hullean construal, this translates as: linguistic responses are distinct when and only when they are associated with distinct implicit responses. But this answer is patently question-begging unless we have some way of *individuating implicit responses*. The only suggestion in the field is that implicit responses are individuated by reference to the environments that are diagnostic for their occurrence, i.e., that what makes two linguistic mediating responses distinct is that they are responses to distinct diagnostic environments. However, if we now go on to permit *more* than one higher-level class to be associated with a given diagnostic environment (probabilistically or otherwise), the environment ceases to be "diagnostic," hence we are without conceptual resources for distinguishing between the classes such responses define, and the whole pattern of explanation collapses.

This sort of problem has led many psychologists (and linguists) to resort to semantic features of the referents of linguistic forms to provide criteria for distinguishing between them when they share all or most of their distribution.

Clearly, this strategy cannot work for levels of linguistic structures which involve non-meaning-bearing items like phones and phonemes. For example, we are not going to be able to distinguish between /p/ and the other stop consonants which share its distribution by reference to any homogeneous semantic properties of words containing /p/. Moreover, it seems dubious that this sort of proposal will work effectively at any other level of linguistic analysis.

For example, Braine (1965) remarks on the difficulty of accounting for the learning of equivalence classes solely in terms of diagnostic frames and ordinal positions:

> It is a fact that languages contain structures in which the same position can be occupied by two or more classes which are not differentially marked.... These "covert categories,"as they are called by Whorf (1956), may ultimately be based on semantic properties or relations. This notion would be consistent with the thinking behind my theory: class markers provide a device for making heterogeneous items similar (they all "go with" the marker); however, when items are already similar by virtue of a semantic property or relation of some sort, it would be readily understandable that the event marker might not be needed—the covert semantic marker would suffice to index the list [pp. 487–488]. (Cf. also Jenkins and Palermo, 1964.)

It does not clarify the situation much to suggest that the semantics will somehow provide a straightforward way of capturing taxonomic facts that elude the syntax, unless one gives some indication of what the character of this solution might be. Still less is it plausible to suppose that the semantic system, whatever its character, will itself be amenable to a treatment which can be assimilated to associationist principles. (We will discuss this question at length in Chapter 4.) But whether or not an associationistic treatment of semantics is plausible, it is impossible to assign linguistic forms to grammatical clauses by reference to their semantic behavior. This is because it is not the case that items which are semantically similar need exhibit the same syntactic behavior or even the same distribution. Hence, a syntactic classification based on semantic features often yields incorrect assignments of linguistic items to taxonomic classes. Gerunds and infinitives in English are cases in point. "Reading" and "to read" are presumably synonymous in such sentences as "He likes reading" and "He likes to read," but to assign them to the same syntactic category on the basis of that fact would be a mistake, since their syntactic behaviors differ in important ways. Thus there is an English sentence "John enjoys reading," but there is no English sentence "John enjoys to read." Similarly, generic reference in English can be achieved by employing any of at least three different syntactic forms (cf. "Latins are passionate lovers," "The Latin is a passionate lover," and "A Latin is a passionate lover").

Surely, however, this fact would not be a good reason for constructing a taxonomic class including as members "the," "a," and "plural."

In fact, no one has ever attempted to provide anything like a serious account of the kinds of semantic properties that the members of a taxonomic class are supposed to have in common. The point is not that we need to do more work in semantics (though that is true enough); it is rather that the kinds of formal relations in terms of which taxonomic grammarians and Hullean psycholinguists hoped to analyze language structure and verbal behavior are simply too weak to account for the facts. The appeal to unknown semantic properties of linguistic forms is symptomatic of the breakdown of the analysis.

SUMMARY AND CONCLUSION

We can now summarize the underlying considerations which appear to provide the basis for an entente between taxonomic grammar and Hullean psychology.

For the taxonomic grammarian, the structure of a language was determined by principles of sequential order and class formation. For the Hullean psychologist, order in behavior was construed either as the result of associations between elements of response chains or as the result of associations between overt behavioral elements and implicit mediators. In the former type of association the Hullean psychologist sought the basis of serial organization in language; in the latter he sought the principle responsible for the formation of linguistic classes.

There thus appeared to be a simple and persuasive model of the relation between linguistic structure and psychological laws: the operation of the associative principles which were assumed to produce the serial and hierarchical organization of behavior was taken to account for the serial and hierarchical structure which linguists find in languages.

We have seen, however, that the model that emerged from the interaction of mediational psychology and taxonomic grammar proved to be inadequate in a number of respects. In the first place, taxonomic grammar cannot account for a variety of facts about language structure. Hence in defining his task as that of describing psychological mechanisms which would account for the existence of taxonomic structure in language, the psychologist set for himself the wrong problem: he was attempting to explain facts about the organization of behavior which turned out to be, at best, only partially true. We shall see in the next chapter how much more complicated language structure is than what would be supposed from class and sequence models of grammar.

Even, however, if the taxonomic view of language were correct, the associative mechanisms which Hullean theory provided for the explanation of taxonomic structures are inherently inadequate to that task.

The attempt to treat the abstract symbols in terms of which linguistic descriptions are articulated as naming mediating responses foundered on the question: Under what condition do linguistic elements become associated with a given mediator? Similarly, the treatment of the more abstract types of linguistic organization (like phrase order) in terms of associations between implicit responses required a notion of linguistic level which we saw to be undefinable. Finally, the attempt to treat membership in a linguistic class as a case of association between members of that class and an implicit response involves a variety of formal and substantive difficulties which appear to us to be insuperable.

It remains to be remarked that these difficulties are symptomatic of a more profound disorder. What all mediational psycholinguists have had in common is the unquestioned assumption that the grammatical relations that hold among linguistic elements must ultimately be construed as special cases of associative relations. However, association is simply too impoverished a concept for these purposes. The notion that the rich and elaborate system of psychological processes that must surely underlie the performance of the speaker-hearer is somehow reducible to a single kind of psychological relation governed by a small set of psychological laws must certainly be rejected.

The mediating responses, which Hullean psychologists assumed structure behavior, must, by definition, themselves be governed by the same general associative principles that organize overt responses. (See Hull, 1943.) The mediation theorist hoped to describe the internal states of the organism in the same theoretical vocabulary used to describe its overt behavior, and to exploit the associative laws presumed to govern overt stimulus-response connections in explanations of the organization of mental life. There are two reasons for this commitment. First, the positive belief that associationism *is* the general fact about behavior of all sorts. Second, the consideration that unless *some* constraints are placed upon the character of the intervening variables postulated by mediation models, the model itself becomes vacuous: it reduces to the banal remark that something happens in the organism between the stimulus and the response. The Hullean, like all other empiricists, sought to avoid vacuous explanations in psychology by placing a priori restrictions on the kinds of theoretical entities that psychological theories could postulate.

In short, having abandoned the ontology or radical behaviorism, according to which the only psychologically relevant structures are those specifiable in the vocabulary of observable stimulus and response, the Hullean still sought some methodological constraint on the kinds of variables that could be postulated in psychological theory construction. The constraint he accepted is that internal variables should be like external variables in all respects except observability. In particular, mediating responses were assumed to obey the same principles of association that overt responses do. (Indeed they have often been construed as no more than reduced occurrences of overt behavior.) This sort of situation has occurred before in the history of science. Lucretius thought that physics must acknowledge the existence of unobservables (i.e., of micro-particles), but he took it to be self-evident that the laws governing their behavior were just the gross mechanical principles that can be observed to act at the macro-level. Hence, he was led to treat such phenomena as adhesion by postulating that micro-particles had hooks.

While vacuous explanation must, of course, be avoided, it is far from evident that the way to do so is by a priori constraints on the character of theoretical constructs. It has yet to be shown that psychologists need to require of the theories they accept more than that they be the simplest of those which account for the data. These are the principles on which the other sciences operate.

At any event, it appears that the difficulties that mediation theorists encountered are directly traceable to the two-front war they are forced to wage. On the one hand, they attempt to liberalize classical S-R theory by the introduction of unobserved S's and R's; but, on the other, they seek to retain the substance of associationism by constraining these unobserved entities to obey the associative laws. In the special case of language, this latter characteristic of mediation theories leads directly to trouble because of the implausibility of the claim that the relations between linguistic elements that order verbal behavior can be construed as associative. Association simply does not have the properties needed to explain the integrations speaker-hearers perform.

It is obvious that the choices involved in the production of a sentence are not independent of one another; parts of sentences constrain one another in relations like grammatical dependency, and the entire sentence exhibits a regular order of constituents and of formatives within constituents. Yet there are very striking differences between the phenomena of sentential order and the kinds of phenomena typical of serial learning in paradigmatic associationist experiments like the recall of word lists. Such differences suggest that quite aside from the details of Hullean theories of seriation in language, association is not the right *kind* of relation to explain sentence integration.

Consider just a few differences between typical associative relations and grammatical relations in sentences.

1. Associative relations in list learning are characteristically strongest between a given item and its immediate successor. That is, even where discontinuous items become associated during the rote learning of a list, such associations are invariably far weaker than asso-

ciations between contiguous items. (See, for example, McGoech, 1936.) Certainly if grammatical structure is essentially based upon association, then grammatical dependency between items other than adjacent ones should occur very rarely in sentences.

In fact, however, precisely the reverse is the case: the interpolation of material between syntactically interdependent parts of sentences is a fundamental principle of every language. Consider, for example, relativization in English, which routinely introduces material between a noun and its verb (e.g., in sentences like *"The boy* whom I met in Chicago *left the house"*). Or, consider the agreement in number between noun and verb in a sentence like *"John and Mary,* whom I knew very well when I was just a boy living on the lower East Side in New York, *have* both had *their* mortgages foreclosed." Presumably, speaker-hearers have very little difficulty with sentences like this one; yet it contains a grammatical dependency spanning nineteen lexical items—a prodigious feat of one-trial learning if the production or comprehension of a sentence really does depend upon the establishment of associative relations between the grammatically interdependent items which it contains.

2.   The character of grammatical dependencies is often intimately and intricately related to the linguistic structure of the material they subtend. For example, there is a dependency between the form of the verb and the form of the particle in "John *phoned* Mary *up"* (note that there is no sentence "John phoned Mary down"). But, though the particle that occurs depends upon which verb is chosen, the *position* the particle occupies is contingent upon the character of the *object* of the verb. (Thus "John phoned her up" is a sentence, but "John phoned up her" is not.) The rule is that the displacement of the particle around the direct object is mandatory when the direct object is a pronoun, but optional otherwise. It is very difficult to see how this pattern of relations could be reconstructed on an associationist account. One would have to say that in these cases where the direct object happens to be a pronoun, the associative relation between the particle and its verb is "suspended" in order to permit the association between the verb and its direct object to operate, and that the associative relation may be suspended "at the speaker's option" in the case where the direct object of the verb is any noun phrase other than a pronoun. The point, of course, is that the associative principles provide for no analog to the notion of an optional linguistic rule. Still less do they provide mechanisms for reconstructing the intricate interplay of optional and mandatory decisions involved in specifying the order relations among elements of a sentence. Associations differ in *strength*, while linguistic relations differ

in *quality*; the types of associations are not sufficiently heterogeneous to reconstruct the variety of types of relations that the operation of linguistic rules can mediate.

3. Associative strength is held to be a function of repetition (or reinforcement, or both). There is, however, no reason to believe that serial-order habits in normal language exchanges are either strengthened or weakened by repeated presentations of linguistic material; most sentences a speaker-hearer has to deal with are novel to him. In particular, since associative strength is a function of frequency, there can be no grounds for identifying the intimacy of the grammatical relation between elements of a sentence with the degree to which the elements are associated: elements of highly overlearned sequences need *not* exhibit grammatical interdependencies. For example, sentences like "How's life?" "What's new?" "Read any good books lately?" and so on.)

4. Many high-strength associations cannot, in fact, occur in grammatical sequences. The fact that associations like "black-white" and "long-short" are very strong does not serve to legitimate sentences like "The black white stick is long short." This is another instance of a recurrent difficulty with the associationist construal of linguistic relationships. Considered from the point of view of grammar, association may hold either between members of the same word class (hence "black-white") or between members of classes that occupy adjacent positions in sentences (hence, "boy-runs"). The associationist has no principled way of distinguishing the associations which are permitted to mediate the serial organization of sentences from those which are not.

It is difficult to resist the conclusion that most associationists have largely failed to realize the enormous problems that would have to be faced in providing a substantive associationistic account of structure in language. This is partly because of a failure to appreciate the intricacy of the organization exhibited by sentences; partly it is because of an unconscious adherence to a terminological convention whereby *any* structure is ipso facto *called* "associative" whether or not there is reason to believe that it has the logical properties characteristic of associations and whether or not there is reason to believe it satisfies associative laws.

In fact, verbalization, like other forms of intelligent behavior, resists treatment as a special case of a habit. Roughly speaking, the relation of association is locally transitive, probably irreflexive, and probably asymmetrical. In the case of any given organism, it holds between at most a finite number of pairs of behavioral elements, and its strength is highly responsive to the frequency with which the associated items cooccur in the organism's experience. Grammatical relations, on the other hand, are of a variety of different logical types; they characteristically hold between infinite sets of elements, and their mastery appears to be largely independent of the specific character of the experience of the speaker. In short, grammatical relations differ in practically every conceivable way from associative relations; it is difficult to imagine a less likely candidate than association for reconstructing the psychological processes of language use.

The interaction between taxonomic grammar and Hullean psychology failed to produce a viable account of either the structure of natural languages or the psychology of the speaker-hearer. Yet it was a very important episode in the development of American behavior theory. It marks the first attempt to use the principles of learning theory to deal seriously with a complex species-specific form of behavior. In so doing it served to mark a point beyond which appeals to those principles fail to be illuminating. And it was the occasion of the first sustained interaction between American psychologists and linguists. Though it failed to produce an acceptable psycholinguistic theory, it did commence the task of marking out the domain of such a theory. The attitude widely held before the Hullean incursion, that the linguist may make no psychological claims for his grammars and that the psychologist need have no particular concern with the facts of language structure, was explicitly abandoned. There was substituted a view of psycholinguistics as explicating the psychological operations underlying the assimilation and exploitation of the formal structures in language that grammars represent. This view continues to condition the research of investigators now working in the field.

GENERATIVE GRAMMARS

In the preceding chapter, we reviewed some aspects of the methods and goals of the "taxonomic" grammarians, who dominated linguistic science in America between 1930 and 1955. Taxonomic grammarians maintained the following two principles:

1. Grammar construction is to proceed by the manipulation of data according to well-defined techniques of classification. In some accounts, these data were to consist solely of observations of acoustic signals drawn from actual speech; in other accounts,

they were to consist of such observations together with informants' judgments of identity and difference of meaning.
2. The results of applying analytic techniques to a corpus of utterances is the partitioning of the corpus into classes. These classes are defined for several levels of description. A grammar consists of a hierarchy of descriptive levels, with the linguistic entities at each level consisting of classes of objects at the next lower level.

The previous chapter also reviewed several serious difficulties with these principles. In brief, the formal procedures for grammar construction required under principle 1 were not forthcoming, and it became increasingly evident that the kind of hierarchy of classes envisioned under principle 2 fails to fully express the grammatical structure of natural languages.

THE GOALS OF GRAMMATICAL DESCRIPTION

Among the more striking features of the taxonomic movement was a lack of consensus about the requirements that an adequate grammar of a natural language ought to satisfy. A variety of views were put forth on this issue. Sometimes it was suggested that since a grammar is merely a conveniently abbreviated form of the data included in the linguist's corpus, the best grammar is simply the one which provides the most economical abbreviation. Another popular proposal was that the appropriateness of a grammar is determined solely by the purpose to which the theorist intends to put it, so that there might be one English grammar that is "best" for machine translation, another that is best for information retrieval, a third that is best for theories of the hearer, a fourth that is best for theories of the speaker, etc.

Thus, taxonomic linguists held a variety of views about what conditions of adequacy a grammar ought to meet, and it seems that they did not consider consensus on this issue to be a matter of primary importance. This is perhaps because taxonomic grammarians often adhered to conventionalist views of the philosophy of science. Theoretical pluralism was in fashion. Scientific theories were conceived of as devices for generating predictions, or as abbreviated statements of observational data, or as "useful fictions"; in short, as anything except attempts to explain the observed phenomena by making true statements about the causal conditions upon which they are contingent. Martin Joos (1958), a prominent taxonomic linguist, remarked:

If the facts have been fully stated, it is perverse or childish to demand an explanation into the bargain. Explanation could serve only to facilitate filling out a fractional statement into a whole statement; or is explanation something magical? That is, if explanation is to have any useful difference in denotation from statement, it can only mean "statement of pattern," while statement is reserved for the meaning "statement of what is there and in what spot each item is": the same, but from a different viewpoint.

To ascribe any other efficacy to explanation is obfuscation; and to me that is the difference in connotation (between "explanation" and "statement"): that such obfuscation easily gets attached to explanation, but not to statement [p. v].

It is interesting to compare Joos's remarks with a recent discussion by Chomsky (1965). He remarks that it is not enough that a grammar should represent the corpus of observational data:

The grammar is justified to the extent that it correctly describes its object, namely the linguistic intuition—the tacit competence—of the native speaker. In this sense, the grammar is justified on *external* grounds, on grounds of correspondence to linguistic fact. On a much deeper and hence much more rarely attainable level (that of explanatory adequacy), a grammar is justified to the extent that it is a *principled* descriptively adequate system, in that the linguistic theory with which it is associated selects this grammar over others, given primary linguistic data with which all are compatible. In this sense, the grammar is justified on *internal* grounds, on grounds of its relation to a linguistic theory that constitutes an explanatory hypothesis about the form of language as such [p. 27].

Chomsky requires that a grammar be not only descriptively adequate, but that it exhibit "explanatory adequacy"; ultimately, it must be appropriately integrated with a theory of language learning, on the one hand, and of language universals, on the other.

In conflicts like that between Joos and Chomsky, we see a disagreement about scientific explanation in general, which issues in a disagreement about the status of grammatical theories in particular. While the paradigmatic taxonomic grammarian was conventionalistic about scientific explanation, the generative grammarian tends to be Realistic; he tends to hold that theoretical assertions in a science have a definite and, in principle, determinable, truth value, so that it is an objective, empirical question which of a number of competing theories ought to be accepted.

Thus, the discussion of the criteria a grammar must satisfy to correctly describe the structure of a language has been central in the literature on generative grammar. The following points have been widely agreed upon by generative linguists.

First, a grammar must enumerate the sentences of the language it describes. In particular, a grammar may be thought of as a program for a "machine" which is capable of enumerating all and only the well-formed sentences of a language. To demand that a grammar effect an exhaustive enumeration of the sentences of a language is to require that the grammar be *observationally adequate*.

Second, the grammar must be *descriptively adequate* in the sense that it is required to provide a correct *structural description* for each sentence. The notion of a structural description will be discussed at length in the course of this chapter. Roughly, a structural description must represent the grammatical relations exhibited by the sentence to which it is assigned, and must determine the decomposition of the sentence into its constituent parts.[1] A grammar which is both observationally and descriptively adequate must thus conform to the speaker-hearer's intuitions about which strings are sentences in his language and what structures those strings have (see Chomsky's remarks quoted above).

It is an empirical question whether a given grammar is adequate, observationally, descriptively, or both. For example, data about the intuitions of speakers are clearly relevant to deciding whether a grammar correctly enumerates the sentences of a language. All other things being equal, a grammar of English which claims that (3-1) is a sentence while (3-2) is not, is a better grammar than one which makes the opposite claim. Similarly, a grammar which marks "the boy" as a constituent of

3-1 The boy went to the store.

3-2 *store the to went boy the

(3-1) is closer to descriptive adequacy than a grammar which claims that "to the" is a constituent.

The second point is that the requirement that a grammar be observationally and descriptively adequate differs in kind from the requirement imposed by what we called the "operationalist principle" in our discussion of taxonomic grammar. While the taxonomic grammarian sought to constrain the *procedures* by which a grammar is constructed from data, the generative grammarian allows any techniques whatever for theory construction. He is indifferent to the *source* of his theoretical insights so long as it is possible to demonstrate that the data confirm the theory he eventually arrives at. Thus the taxonomic grammarian doubts that there is any sense to the attempt to construct the unique best grammar for a natural language, or even to the notion of empirical confirmation of a grammatical theory. But he is profoundly concerned with the character of the field procedures whereby grammars are produced. The generative grammarian, on the other hand, is indifferent to discovery procedures but very much concerned that his theory be confirmable in whatever sense any highly valued theory in science can be.

---

[1] A more precise way of making the distinction between descriptive and observational adequacy is to associate the latter with the requirement that the grammar enumerate the phonetic strings which constitute sentences, and the former with the requirement that the grammar assign correct phonological and syntactic descriptions to each string.

There are, however, limits to the clarity with which the distinction between observational adequacy and descriptive adequacy can be made. The criteria for observational adequacy must be relativized to the choice of a descriptive vocabulary for the representation of observations (e.g., to the choice of a phonetic system). But this choice is itself a theoretical issue; it must be defended by reference to the overall adequacy of the grammar—in particular, by reference to the level of descriptive and explanatory adequacy the grammar achieves.

THE LIMITATIONS OF TAXONOMIC SYNTAX

Although taxonomic grammarians may not have been primarily concerned with achieving observational and descriptive adequacy for the grammars they wrote, it is nevertheless reasonable to ask whether taxonomic grammars do in fact satisfy those conditions. Indeed, it is essential to raise this question insofar as one takes grammars to be theories of the speaker-hearer's knowledge about his language. A grammar which is not observationally and descriptively adequate could not be psychologically real.

Much of the discussion in Chapter 2 was an attempt to show that reasonable conditions of observational and descriptive adequacy are *not* satisfied by typical taxonomic accounts of phonetics, phonology, and morphology. We will now discuss the arguments which show that the type of syntactic theory developed in taxonomic grammar is too weak to achieve observational and descriptive adequacy for English (and presumably for any other natural language). We shall then discuss some varieties of transformational grammars for which observational and descriptive adequacy might conceivably be claimed.

We said that a taxonomic syntax is a set of descriptive levels so arranged that every item at a given level consists of one or more items at the next lower level. Thus, a sentence can consist of such sequences of phrase types as $NP + VP$; $NP + V + NP$; and so on. Analogously, a phrase type like NP can consist of such sequences of form classes as $T + N$; $T + A + N$; and so on.

A grammar of this kind can be represented as a system of rules for assigning parsing trees to sentences. The translation from conventional taxonomic notation into such a system of rules is, in fact, quite trivial. If the grammar says that $NP + VP$ is a possible realization of S, then add $S \rightarrow NP + VP$ to the system of rules. If the grammar says NP can be realized by $T + N$, then add $NP \rightarrow T + N$. In general, if the grammar says symbol A can be realized as the sequence of symbols $B, C, \ldots, D$, then add $A \rightarrow B, C, \ldots, D$ to the system of rules.

In short, most, if not all, of the syntaxes that have been suggested as taxonomic theories in the linguistic literature are realizations of a kind of formalism known as an immediate constituent (IC) grammar. We encountered such grammars in Chapter 2. An immediate constituent grammar consists of a finite set of rules each of which is a substitution instance of (3-3). In this schema, (1) the variables range over strings of one or more symbols, except that (2) X, Y, or both may be null; (3) A must

3-3 $XAY \rightarrow XBY$

be a single symbol; and (4) the intended interpretation of $\rightarrow$ is "is rewritten as" or "is expanded as." Thus, for example, the sequences in (3-4) are possible IC rules for an English grammar:

3-4 $S \rightarrow NP + VP$
     $NP \rightarrow T + N$
     $VP \rightarrow V + NP$

We shall not undertake to review the arguments that show that the formal notion of an IC grammar does, in fact, reconstruct much of the taxonomic account of syntactic structure (but see Chomsky, 1956, and Postal, 1964a). Our present concern is to investigate the question of whether any reasonably simple and plausible IC grammar could achieve descriptive or observational adequacy or both for natural languages.

We remarked in Chapter 2 that IC grammars, like taxonomic grammars in their conventional form, represent the structural descriptions of sentences as parsing trees. The easiest way to see this is to notice that any IC rule of the form $A \rightarrow B + C$ can be read as claiming that the sequence $B + C$ is a constituent of type A; this is tantamount to claiming that A *dominates* $B + C$ in some parsing tree. In general, given a set of IC rules, it is possible to provide a procedure for specifying their output in the form of trees. Thus, the sample IC grammar presented in (3-5) produces the sentences and structural descriptions in Figure 3-1, among others.

3-5   a. S $\rightarrow NP + VP.$

    b. NP $\rightarrow T + N$
              $T + Adj + N$

    c. VP $\rightarrow V$
              $V + Adj$
              $V + NP$

    d. T $\rightarrow$ The

    e. $Adj \rightarrow$ big, pretty, old, . . .

    f. N $\rightarrow$ boy, man, ball, . . .

    g. V $\rightarrow$ is, hit, likes, . . .

Questions about the observational and descriptive adequacy of IC grammars can thus be phrased as questions about the parsing trees they produce. To achieve observational adequacy, the system of IC rules must at least be capable of producing all the sequences of phones to which the parsing trees in a language can be assigned; and to achieve descriptive adequacy, it must at least assign the appropriate tree to each such sequence. Correspondingly, there are two sorts of difficulties with IC grammars that will be discussed here. The first concerns the unavoidable proliferation of rules and grammatical categories required to maintain the observational adequacy of such a grammar. We will see that this overelaborateness of IC grammars indicates not only a failure to conform to reasonable standards of simplicity but also, what is

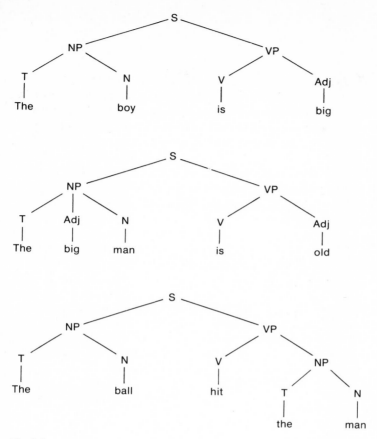

Fig. 3-1

considerably worse, a failure to represent significant generalizations about the structure of the language. The second difficulty relates to considerations of descriptive adequacy and involves cases in which the decision to employ IC rules commits us to inappropriate parsing trees. In such cases constituents are mislabeled, and sequences of items which *should* be represented as members of the same constituent are not so represented, etc.

OBSERVATIONAL AND DESCRIPTIVE ADEQUACY

Let us return to the rules given in (3-5). We can consider these rules as a candidate IC grammar of a fragment of English and use them to explore the kinds of problems we have just mentioned, altering them as the cases require. We shall see that as we attempt to supplement them in order to represent the variety of types of structures found in the language, and hence to maintain observational adequacy, the number of rules and categories that must be postulated goes up unnecessarily fast.

A striking example of this sort of difficulty arises from the attempt to treat grammatical dependencies between discontinuous items with a grammar containing only IC rules. It is easy to show that the treatment of such dependencies will commit us to adding a rule to the grammar for each type of grammatical structure that can appear between the dependent items.

Roughly speaking, item Y in a sentence is *dependent* upon item X if the occurrence of item X conditions the occurrence of item Y. Thus, in a sentence like (3-6), "up" is said to be dependent on "phoned," since all sentences as (3-7) are ungrammatical.

3-6   John phoned up Mary.

3-7   *John phoned over Mary.
*John phoned around Mary.
*John phoned towards Mary.

Grammatical dependencies have a natural treatment in IC grammars so long as the dependent items are adjacent. Thus, we can generate the verb phrase in (3-6) with a grammar that contains the rules in (3-8). However, consider a sentence like (3-9) in which the dependent items are *not* adjacent. For this sentence, we will need the rules in (3-10).[2]

3-8 $VP \rightarrow V_{part} + NP$
$V_{part} \rightarrow$ phone + up
$NP \rightarrow$ Mary

3-9   John phoned Mary up.

3-10 $VP \rightarrow V + NP + Part$
$V \rightarrow$ phone.
$Part \rightarrow$ up.

Since the rule in (3-10) expresses the fact that NP can appear between the dependent items "phone" and "up," a grammar which contains both (3-8) and (3-10) is observationally adequate vis à vis sentences (3-6) and (3-9). However, the price of observational adequacy

---

[2] Strictly speaking, what is dependent on "phoned" is $\begin{Bmatrix} up \\ \phi \end{Bmatrix}$, since "John phoned Mary" is well formed. Note further that (3-8) and (3-10) would actually work only if there were a *single* verb-particle pair in the language; since there are many, some device must be provided for ensuring that the expansion of *Part* is appropriate to the expansion of *V*. However this is accomplished, there will be two rules, one for the moved and one for the unmoved particle.

is that we now need two kinds of rules to express the behavior of "phone up"; one for the case in which the dependent items are contiguous, and one for the case in which they surround an *NP*. Clearly, this is a consequence we should avoid if we can.

An entirely analogous example arises in the case of the discontinuous connective "neither. . . nor." These elements can appear flanking a variety of types of constituents, as in (3-11). We can capture these distri-

3-11 Neither Sam nor Mary would leave.
Neither run nor walk to the nearest exit.
Work neither too rapidly nor too slowly.
Neither red nor pink cloth was available.

butional facts only if we permit ourselves a distinct rule for representing the behavior of "neither . . . nor" in each of these construction, for example, (3-12).

3-12 *Conj* → neither *NP* nor *NP*
Conj → neither *VP* nor *VP*
Conj → neither *Adv* nor *Adv*
Conj → neither *Adj* nor *Adj*

Once again, maintaining observational adequacy requires the proliferation of rules governing what appears prima facie to be a homogeneous construction type. In the present case, however, the use of an IC grammar to capture a grammatical relation between discontinuous elements also fails to represent an obvious generalization about the distribution of the form under analysis: namely, that the elements which can substitute for X and Y in schema (3-13) are required to be of the same syntactic type. Thus, (3-14) is well formed, but (3-15) is not [see (3-16)].

3-13 Neither *X* nor *Y*

3-14 Neither *NP* nor *NP*

3-15 *Neither *NP* nor *VP*

3-16 *Neither Sam nor work rapidly was available.

It should be emphasized that cases in which languages place constraints on discontinuous items are by no means exceptional; hence the failure of IC grammars to provide adequate mechanisms for the representation of such cases is a serious failure. Consider English "tag questions" like (3-17).

3-17 a. John should kiss Mary, *shouldn't he*?

b. John won't leave the Jaguar parked around the corner where the police are likely to give it a ticket, *will he*?

c. She is a nice girl, *isn't she*?

There are notable constraints on the form of the tags [italicized in

(3-17)] and the form of the sentences to which they are appended. First, when the main sentence is negative, the tag is affirmative, and vice versa.[3] Second, the auxiliary of the tag must match the auxiliary of the main sentence, so that "John will kiss Mary, shouldn't he?" is ungrammatical. What is especially interesting about tag questions, is the variety of types of structures that may appear between the dependent items; these include not only object *NP*'s but also any kind of conjunction, adverbials, etc., as in (3-18). To introduce tags in the grammar by using a separate rule for each structure that can intervene between the tag and

3-18 John did kiss Mary and then leave the party, didn't he?
John did kiss Mary in New York, didn't he?

its sentence not only would be unwieldy but would miss the generalization that the constraints that tags must satisfy are identical in all these cases.

The fact that there is no natural way to maintain observational adequacy for the treatment of discontinuous dependencies in IC grammars is closely connected to the fact that the structures they yield for sentences are not *descriptively* adequate in cases when the dependent but discontinuous items intuitively form a constituent. Thus, if (3-6) is produced by (3-8), "phone up" is marked as a constituent (i.e., the tree provided for that sentence has a node marked V_{part} which dominates only the sequence "phone up"). But "phone up" is *not* marked as a constituent in (3-9) if that sentence is generated by using (3-10); for the lowest node which dominates both "phone" and "up" also dominates "Mary" in the trees that (3-10) specifies. Analogously, "neither...nor" fails to be marked as a constituent in any of the trees generated by (3-12).

Thus far we have been arguing that achieving observational adequacy with an IC grammar requires an undesirable proliferation of rules in cases where a sentence exhibits grammatical dependencies among discontinuous parts. The same point can be made about the representation of order relations within an IC grammar. To say what constituent orderings are possible in the sentences of a language characteristically requires an unnaturally large number of rules. This is true even if we increase the power of the IC system by allowing rules that are sensitive to the context in which they are applied. Consider sentences (3-19), which exhibit a subset of the well-formed auxiliary expansions in English. If, for the moment, we ignore the behavior of tense, we can gener-

3-19 a. John is eating.

---

[3] Barring special emphasis, as in "John *did* kiss Mary, did he?"

b. John $\begin{Bmatrix} \text{should} \\ \text{may} \\ \text{can} \end{Bmatrix}$ eat.

c. John $\begin{Bmatrix} \text{should} \\ \text{may} \\ \text{can} \end{Bmatrix}$ be eating.

d. John has eaten.

e. John $\begin{Bmatrix} \text{should} \\ \text{may} \\ \text{can} \end{Bmatrix}$ have been eating.

ate these sentences with rules which acknowledge three auxiliary elements, together with *NP* and *VP*. The auxiliary elements will be *modal, have,* and *be.* Thus, to get *a* we use some such rule as (3-20):

3-20 *Aux → be V + ing* (when *Aux* precedes *V + ing*)

To generate *b* we use some such rule as (3-21):

3-21 *Aux → modal* (when *Aux* precedes $V_{infinitival}$)

To generate *c* we use some such rule as (3-22):

3-22 *Aux → modal* (when *Aux* precedes *be + V + ing*)

And so on.

We shall see, as our discussion develops, that there are a variety of serious difficulties with this approach to the auxiliary sustem; for example, it leads to trouble when we try to extend it to account for the behavior of tense and other affixal elements. Our present point, however, is that corresponding to (3-19) there is a distributionally parallel and syntactically related set of "yes-no" questions as in (3-23). If we are to capture *this* set of sentences in an IC grammar, we must pay the price of

3-23 a. Is John eating?

b. $\begin{Bmatrix} \text{Should} \\ \text{May} \\ \text{Can} \end{Bmatrix}$ John eat?

c. $\begin{Bmatrix} \text{Should} \\ \text{May} \\ \text{Can} \end{Bmatrix}$ John be eating?

d. Has John eaten?

e. $\begin{Bmatrix} \text{Should} \\ \text{May} \\ \text{Can} \end{Bmatrix}$ John have eaten?

f. $\begin{Bmatrix} \text{Should} \\ \text{May} \\ \text{Can} \end{Bmatrix}$ John have been eating?

adding an entirely new group of rules as (3-23) for *a*: *Aux* → *be* (when *Aux* precedes *NP* + *V* + *ing*); for *b*: *Aux* → *modal* (when *Aux* precedes *NP* + *V* ₙfinitival); for *c*: *Aux* → *modal* (when *Aux* precedes *NP* + *be* + *V* + *ing*); etc. Moreover, it seems clear that representing the question forms in this way misses an important point: each yes-no question is related to a corresponding declarative from which it can be constructed by permuting the subject *NP* of the declarative with an element of the *VP*.[4]

Thus far, we have seen that IC grammars require an undesirable proliferation of rules in cases where sentences exhibit discontinuous dependencies between their elements and in cases where interrelated sentences exhibit reorderings of constituents. The same sort of point may be made about cases in which sentential elements are deleted.

Consider the set of sentences (3-24):

3-24 a. John may have been eating an apple.

b. John may have been eating an apple or lasagna.

---

[4] We are making the usual assumption that IC grammars may not contain rules of permutation, and that the rules they do contain may not be employed in derivations which have the effect of permutation. The reasons for accepting these constraints are the following.

Suppose we had a rule which permitted the sequence *AB* to be written as the sequence *BA*. Such a rule rewrites more than one symbol at a time. But such rules fail to determine a unique tree structure for the strings they generate. If *BA* comes from *AB* by the application of the rule *AB* → *BA*, which of these trees is assigned?

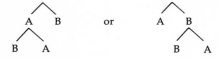

In short, we know that the rule *AB* → *BA* says *either* that *BA* is a constituent of type *A*, or that *BA* is a constituent of type *B*, but we do not know *which* it says. Hence, if we have such rules in an IC grammar, we must abandon the convention that the string of symbols produced by applying a rule is a constituent of the type designated by the element that the rule rewrites.

It is possible to permute elements with IC grammar without accepting permutation as a rewrite operation. For example, if we have a tree containing the sequence *AB*, we can derive a tree containing the sequence *BA* if the grammar acknowledges the rules *B* → *A* and *A* → *B*. However, employing such rules in grammars for natural languages will regularly lead to the generation of descriptively inadequate constituent structure analyses. For example, if we are to represent the permutation of *NP* and *modal* in questions like (3-23) in this fashion, we will have to have rules like *NP*→*modal* and *modal*→*NP*; these rules will apply to the sequence *NP* + *modal* in the constituent trees for such sentences as (3-19). However, the effect of applying these rules to those trees will be that "should" is labeled as an *NP* and "John" is analyzed as a modal in such sentences as "Should John be eating?"; and analogously for other examples.

    c.   **John may have been eating an apple or eating lasagna.**

    d.   **John may have been eating an apple or been eating lasagna.**

    e.   **John may have been eating an apple or have been eating lasagna.**

    f.   **John may have been eating an apple or may have been eating lasagna.**

    g.   **John may have been eating an apple or may have been eating a pear.**

    h.   **John may have been eating an apple or John may have been eating a pear.**

Notice that, excepting *a* and *b*, each sentence in (3-24) contains two occurrences of the auxiliary construction, one to the left of "or" and one to the right. Presumably an IC grammar could capture the leftmost of each of these occurrences by employing some such rules as in (3-20) to (3-22). However, it is clear that those rules cannot be the ones which generate the *right-hand* occurrences of the auxiliary construction in these sentences, for these constructions are not among the possible expansions that *Aux* can have in simple (i.e., nonconjoined) sentences. In particular, there is no sentence "John lasagna" corresponding to the right-hand part of *b*; there is no "John eating lasagna" corresponding to *c*; there is no "John been eating lasagna" corresponding to *d*; and there is no "John have been eating lasagna" corresponding to *e*. In short, if we want to capture the behavior of the auxiliary elements on the right of "or" in sentences like (3-24), we will have to add an entirely new set of *Aux* rules to the grammar. Moreover, it seems that such rules would have to be extremely cumbersome, since what auxiliary elements can appear to the right of "or" in a given sentence is clearly dependent on what appears on its left, and the rules would have to represent this context dependence. For example, there is no "*John ate an apple or have eaten a pear," though "John may have eaten an apple or have eaten a pear" is well formed.

    In fact, it is again obvious that the relevant generalization is missed by an IC grammar. Given a sentence that is symmetrical in the sense that *h* in (3-24) is, we may delete from the material after "or" the subject *NP* together with any number of elements in the verb phrase under the following conditions:

1.   We must start with the subject *NP*.
2.   We must delete only contiguous elements.
3.   We must delete only elements identical to elements on the left of "or."

Analogous generalizations hold for the conditions on deleting adverbial and prepositional elements in conjoined sentences, giving us "John may have been working or sleeping on Tuesday" from "John may have been working on Tuesday or John may have been sleeping on Tuesday" and "John may have been working or sleeping in Chicago" from "John may have been working in Chicago or John may have been sleeping in Chicago," etc.

It is worth remarking upon the similarity between these cases and the case of tag questions discussed above. In all these examples, what seems to be at issue is a requirement that conjoined sentences be symmetric in certain of their properties. This symmetry can be distorted by the optional or mandatory deletion of certain repeated elements, as in (3-24).

A particularly striking instance of this sort of pattern is found in the English comparative. Consider such sentences as (3-25). While the syntax of the comparative is in fact enormously complicated, the moral of

3-25   a.   John has more money than Harry.
      b.   John has more money than Harry has.
      c. *John has more money than Harry has money.
      d. *John has more money than Harry is tall.

these examples seems clear. Sentence *d* is ungrammatical because of a requirement on symmetry between the compared sentences: they must both have predicate adjectives or both have verbs; the mixed case is not allowed. Sentence *c*, though ungrammatical, is the model for understanding *a* and *b*. Clearly, the required analysis is to treat *c* as the symmetric paradigm from which *a* and *b* depart by optional deletion.

In short, there are a variety of structures in English all of which point to the same fundamental generalization: English permits symmetric conjoined sentences and deletion of repeated elements in such sentences under conditions that vary from construction to construction. This analysis appears to be required for examples like (3-24) and (3-25), and it is plausible for (3-17) on the assumption that sentences like (3-17*a*) are really deleted versions of some such structures as "John kissed Mary, didn't John kiss Mary?" Given the generality of this pattern of phenomena, it is worth emphasizing that it goes entirely unrepresented in an IC grammar.

DESCRIPTIVE ADEQUACY OF IC GRAMMARS

Thus far we have been arguing that IC grammars can maintain observational adequacy only at the price of proliferating rules and missing generalizations in cases where sentences exhibit dependencies, reorderings of constituents, or deletions. We now turn to a discussion of several cases in which we assume observational adequacy but where an IC grammar misdescribes the structure of the strings it generates: either sequences which are constituents fail to be so labeled or constituent structure is assigned at points where the sentence does not exhibit it.

We have already noted one case of the former sort. "Phone up" is (correctly) represented as a constituent in (3-6) but fails to be so labeled

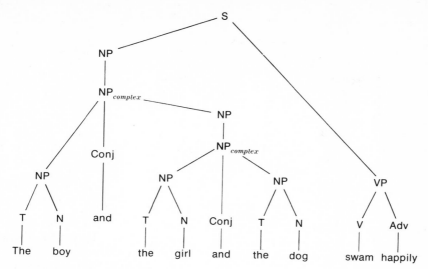

Fig. 3-2

in (3-9). An analogous situation arises in a variety of other cases. For example, *Aux* can be marked as a constituent in those declaratives where the auxiliary elements are adjacent, but it cannot be so marked in yes-no questions, where some of the elements of *Aux* have been permuted around a noun phrase. Similarly, a conjunction like *"neither...nor,"* whose elements are *never* adjacent in sentences, can never be represented as a constituent by an IC grammar. In fact, it is a general point that IC grammars will be able to represent only adjacent items as constituents; because the notion of a constituent can only be defined in such a system by reference to the immediately dominating node in a tree, no discontinuous constituents can be represented. Clearly, what is needed here is a redefinition of the notion "constituent" such that sequences of nonadjacent elements can qualify. When we discuss transformations, we will see how this idea can be made precise.

Conversely, the phrase structure trees generated by an IC grammar will often assign constituent structure which has no natural interpretation. Consider, for example, cases of true coordination like "the boy, and the girl and the dog swam happily." We can generate such sentences with IC rules like those in (3-26).

3-26   a.   *NP → NP_{complex}*
    b.   *NP_{complex} → NP and NP*

However, though such rules *will* produce the appropriate noun phrase sequences, they do so only at the price of assigning uninterpretable bracketing. Thus the tree in Figure 3-2 represents "the girl and the

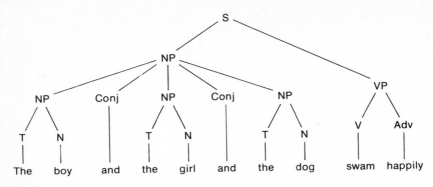

Fig. 3-3

dog" as a constituent of "the boy, and the girl and the dog swam happily" but fails to so represent "the boy and the girl." However, this seems completely arbitrary; the right tree would appear to be the one in Figure 3-3, where only coordinated constituent structure is assigned internal to the highest *NP*. However, the class of such trees cannot be enumerated with IC rules.

Exactly the same point applies for coordinated adjective sequences as in "the nice, old, bearded, German soldier fell ill." In the case of such sentences, the adjectives modify the noun, not one another. But for any IC rules we choose, it will be possible to find a coordinated adjective string to which the rules (incorrectly) assign internal bracketing. This sort of difficulty is intrinsic to IC rules. On the one hand, there is an upper bound to the number of symbols by which a given symbol can be rewritten; and on the other hand, every application of a rule in a derivation establishes a node in the corresponding tree. It follows that one cannot use IC rules to represent unbounded strings of coordinated items.

We now turn to a final, and very important, kind of case in which IC grammars fail to attain descriptive adequacy. Such grammars do not correctly represent the grammatical relations between constituents of sentences. In particular, they often fail to represent either the internal differences in grammatical structure between sentences which are superficially similar or the underlying similarity in grammatical structure between sentences which are superficially heterogeneous. For example, there are cases of ambiguities where two sentences can consist of the same sequence of constituents but nevertheless differ in the grammatical relations that hold between their constituents, and IC grammars cannot provide descriptively adequate representations of such cases.

Notice, in the first place, that there are sentential ambiguities which *are* naturally represented within the context of IC grammar.

What these cases have in common is that the ambiguity arises from the possibility of assigning more than one constituent structure tree to a given sentence. Thus, as we remarked in Chapter 1, the ambiguity of such sentences as (3-27) can be represented by reference to the alternative bracketings of "old men and women" shown in (3-28).

3-27 John likes old men and women.

**3-28 John likes (old men) and women.
John likes old (men and women).**

There are, however, ambiguities which turn not upon the existence of alternative constituent structure analyses but rather upon the existence of alternative interpretations of the grammatical relations which hold among constituents. Thus, a sentence like (3-29) is ambiguous depending upon whether we read it as "with a gun, Bill shot the man,"

3-29 Bill shot the man with a gun.

or "Bill shot the man who had a gun." But since there is no ambiguity in the bracketing of (3-29), there is no natural way of representing this ambiguity with constituent structure trees. IC grammars characteristically fail to represent the heterogeneity of grammatical structure that can be exhibited by sentences with similar or identical constituent analyses. We noted in Chapter 1 that this kind of fact strongly suggests that the speaker-hearer's internal representation of a sentence cannot consist just of a labeled bracketing.

The converse is also true: sentences whose constituents are identically grammatically related nevertheless frequently differ in their IC structure. We have already seen a number of such cases; IC grammars mark no particular structural relation between declaratives and their corresponding yes-no questions, though the grammatical relations among the sentence constituents are identical for the two. Similarly for such superficially heterogeneous pairs as active and passive, declaratives and imperatives, etc.: the sentences differ in constituent order but not in grammatical relations, and an IC grammar has no resources for expressing this fact. This is a point that we will return to in the discussion of transformational grammars. Suffice it to remark here that in all these cases observational adequacy of IC grammars is purchased at the price not only of proliferation of rules but also of descriptive inadequacy.

SUMMARY

In Chapter 2, we explored aspects of the taxonomic program in terms of the discovery procedures to which it was committed. We argued that the procedures which were intended to isolate classes of linguistc units at successively higher levels of analysis did not directly or uniquely yield such classes. In this chapter, we have argued that the kind of syntax envisioned as a result of applying the taxonomic procedures does not meet conditions of observational and descriptive adequacy in any natural way. In the first place, in order to use IC grammars to enumerate all the permissible sentences in the language, an enormous number of rules is required. That this is a consequence not of the inherent complexity of natural languages but rather of the inadequacies of IC grammars is suggested by the repeated failure of such grammars to capture relevant generalizations about linguistic structure. In the second place, IC grammars often fail to correctly describe the constituent structures of the sentences they generate or the grammatical relations among the constituents.

None of these arguments against taxonomic grammars is, however, decisive. Various ad hoc repairs could be offered to avoid the most glaring cases of misdescription, and the proliferation of rules characteristic of an IC attempt to represent grammatical structure could simply be accepted as a disagreeable but tolerable feature of any systematic descriptions of languages. What is needed is an alternative theory; one which avoids the difficulties so far mentioned and at the same time exhibits virtues that taxonomic systems do not. We turn now to a consideration of such alternatives.

TRANSFORMATIONAL GRAMMARS

A central theme in our discussion of IC grammars has been that they fail to represent certain types of syntactic relations among sentences. An important advance in modern grammatical theory was the attempt of Zellig Harris and his colleagues to develop a grammar which was broadly taxonomic in conception but which could appropriately represent such relations. Harris (1965) sought to develop a grammar which might be constructed by extensions of taxonomic procedures of classification but which would not be an IC grammar in the sense discussed above.

In a taxonomic grammar, elements are assigned to the same class at a certain level if they are in free variation. Part of Harris's proposal was to extend this principle to define *sentence classes* parallel to such traditional taxonomic classes as phones, phonemes, morphemes, and phrases. Roughly, two sentences belong to the same class if they can occur in the same discourse context without changing the meaning of the discourse. Thus, standard IC grammars can account for the fact that "John phoned up Mary" and "John looked up the number" are sentences of the same grammatical type since they are represented by the same sequence of phrase markers. Harris's grammar can also account for the fact that "John phoned up Mary" and "John phoned Mary up" belong to the same family of sentences since such pairs are presumed to be in free variation in discourses. That is, such sentences can substitute for one another in a discourse environment without altering the semantic interpretation of the entire discourse.

The other major condition under which elements are assigned to the same class in taxonomic grammar is complementary distribution: two elements belong to the same class if there are linguistic environments in which each can occur from which the other is excluded.

Harris proposed to extend this principle to sentences too, thereby providing for the construction of sentence classes whose members are syntactically related though nonsynonymous. For example, the extended application of the principle of complementary distribution, assigns "the prince changed into a frog" and "why did the prince change into a frog" to the same family of sentences because the former is precluded from such discourse positions as "and then the foolish princess asked..." in which the latter can occur, and the latter is precluded from such discourse positions as "and then the wise king stated..." in which the former can occur.

Harris's success in actually providing a detailed characterization of the discovery procedures for isolating classes of syntactically related sentences appears to have been rather limited. Indeed, the very fact that identity and difference of the *meanings* of discourses is taken as a primitive notion suggests that no formal (i.e., distributional) discovery procedures were seriously envisioned. Harris was, however, extremely interested in formally characterizing the membership of such classes for particular natural languages, and it is at this point that his program departs in an important way from the tradition of taxonomic grammar.

In a taxonomic syntax, the membership of an equivalence class like *NP*, *VP*, and so forth, is simply the set of strings which those symbols dominate in trees generated by an IC grammar. Hence, the membership of each such class is formally determined by a set of rewrite rules. Harris's innovation was to suggest that the membership of families of sentences must be specified by rules of a formally different type, i.e., by rules of "cooccurrence transformation" which operate to map phrase-structure trees onto other phrase-structure trees.

Consider a set of related sentences, (3-30), which presumably belong to the same sentence family (i.e., each sentence in the list is assumed to be either in free variation or in complementary distribution with every other such sentence in discourses produced by speakers).

3-30   a.   **Morris solved the problem.**   **Active**
       b.   **The problem was solved by Morris.**   **Passive**

c.	Morris didn't solve the problem.	Negative
d.	Did Morris solve the problem?	Question
e.	Was the problem solved by Morris?	Passive question
f.	The problem wasn't solved by Morris.	Negative passive
g.	Didn't Morris solve the problem?	Negative question
h.	Wasn't the problem solved by Morris?	Negative passive question

Among the cooccurrence transformations that represent the relations between sentences are (3-31). In particular, (3-31*b*) is a formula which

3-31 a. $NP_1 \; V + ed \; NP_2 \leftrightarrow NP_2 \; was \; V + ed \; by \; NP_1$
   b. $NP \; V + ed \; NP \leftrightarrow NP \; didn't \; V \; NP$
   c. $NP_1 \; V + ed \; NP_2 \leftrightarrow Did \; NP \; V \; NP$
   d. $NP_1 \; V + ed \; NP_2 \leftrightarrow was \; NP_2 \; V + ed \; by \; NP_1$
   e. $NP_1 \; V + ed \; NP_2 \leftrightarrow NP_2 \; wasn't \; V + ed \; by \; NP_1$
   f. $NP \; V + ed \; NP \leftrightarrow Didn't \; NP_1 \; V \; NP_2$
   g. $NP_1 \; V + ed \; NP_2 \leftrightarrow wasn't \; NP_2 \; V + ed \; by \; NP_1$

relates (3-30*a*) to (3-30*c*); (3-31*c*) is a formula which relates (3-30*a*) to (3-30*d*), etc.

Formulas like those in (3-31) serve, in obvious ways, to interrelate sentences which are presumed to satisfy the principles of free variation and complementary distribution, and hence belong to the same family. In particular, some of the transformations, like the one that relates actives and passives, preserve meaning and hold between sentences assumed to be in free variation. Other transformations, like the ones that relate actives to questions, do not preserve meaning and relate sentences which are presumed to be in complementary distribution.[5]

A syntax which includes cooccurrence transformations is able to meet several of the objections we raised against unelaborated IC grammars. For example, we mentioned that IC grammars afford no motivated way of representing relations that may obtain between sentences exhibiting different orders of constituents: "John phoned up Mary" and "John phoned Mary up" are represented as unrelated by IC grammars which, in fact, generate them by different systems of rules. But a grammar employing cooccurrence transformations could represent such a relation by some such transformational formula as: . . . $V + Prt + NP \ldots \leftrightarrow \ldots V + NP + Prt \ldots$ Similarly, the regular relation

---

[5] If, however, synonymy is a sufficient condition for free variation, then free variation cannot be a sufficient condition for membership in a sentence family, since it is obvious that synonymous sentences need not be syntactically related. In short, the notion that free variation, synonymy, and syntactic relatedness are somehow interdefinable for sentences is probably unworkable.

between actives and passives can be represented by a formula like (3-31a) and so on. In principle, a cooccurrence grammar can classify any type of sentence by reference to some other kind of sentence to which it bears a regular syntactic relation.

Implicit in the ability of cooccurrence transformations to represent syntactic relations between sentences exhibiting different constituent orders is their ability to represent differences between grammatical relations in sentences exhibiting the same constituent order. Thus, consider the well-known examples (3-32 and 3-33). There is no particular intuitive or formal motivation, given the considerations in terms of which IC grammars were constructed, for assigning different constituent analyses to these sentences. Prima facie, they are both of the form *NP + be + Pred* where *Pred* is *Adj + infinitival*. Yet it is clear that the fundamental grammatical relations between the constituents of these sentences are quite different. For example, in (3-32) "John" is understood to be the subject of "is eager" and of "please," while in (3-33) "John" is understood to be the object of "please."

3-32 John is eager to please.

3-33 John is easy to please.

In short, an IC grammar has no way of distinguishing between (3-32) and (3-33) other than by a gratuitous assignment of distinct labels to the two adjectives "easy" and "eager." A grammar which contains cooccurrence transformations can, however, represent these sentences as differing in structure. It does so by assigning them to different sets of transformationally interrelated sentences. In particular, it assigns (3-32) to a set which contains (3-34), and it assigns (3-33) to a set which contains (3-35). Notice that this *does* distinguish between the sentences, since there is no sentence "*It is eager for someone to please John," parallel in structure to (3-35), and there is no sentence "*John is easy to please someone" parallel in structure to (3-34). Thus, a grammar which contains both IC rules and cooccurrence transformations can employ the former to represent the fact that there is an aspect of analysis in which (3-32) and (3-33) have the same structure, and the latter to represent the fact that there is an aspect of analysis in which they differ in structure.

3-34 John is eager to please someone.

3-35 It is easy for someone to please John.

Since grammars employing cooccurrence transformations can distinguish between the structures of sentences which have identical constituent analyses, they can capture a variety of types of syntactic ambiguity which are beyond the representational power of an unelaborated IC grammar. We encountered an example of this type in (3-29) above. In fact, there is an indefinite number of such cases. When a pair of sentences are related in the way (3-32) and (3-33) are (i.e., they exhibit identical constituent order but differ in grammatical relations), there will often be a third sentence which is ambiguous between the structures they instantiate. Thus, related to (3-32) and (3-33) we have (3-36)

Or, consider (3-37) and (3-38). Here again, we have a pair of sentences which exhibit the same constituents in the same order, yet the grammati-

3-36   John is quick to please.

3-37 a. They asked the police to forbid drinking.

　　　 b. They asked the police to quit drinking.

3-38   They asked the police to stop drinking.

cal relations between constituents differ, as can be seen from the fact that "police" functions as the subject of "drinking" in (3-37b) but not in (3-37a). In this case too, the use of cooccurrence transformations will, in principle, permit us to distinguish between the structure of the sentences; namely by assigning (3-37a), but not (3-37b), to the class of sentences that contains, for example, "They asked the police to forbid someone's drinking." Notice there is no sentence "*They asked the police to quit someone's drinking." Notice too that we have the dividend that the ambiguity of (3-38) is explained by the fact that the transformations assign that sentence to both the sentence family containing (3-37a) and the family containing (3-37b).

Precisely analogous points can be made about such pairs as "The shouting at the children was impolite" and "The shouting by the children was impolite"; "Visiting relatives are unpleasant" and "Visiting relatives is unpleasant"; "John and Bill kissed both Mary and Sally" and "John and Bill kissed Mary and Sally respectively"; "I painted the boy a red picture" and "I painted the boy a red color." In each of these cases, the paired sentences share their constituent order but differ in their grammatical relations; and in each case we can find corresponding sentences that are ambiguous: "The shouting of the children was impolite"; "Visiting relatives can be unpleasant"; "John and Bill kissed Mary and Sally"; and "The magician made the prince a frog."

Thus, a grammar employing cooccurrence transformations can represent many of the structural distinctions native speakers intuitively make between superficially similar sentences in their language. Yet, in spite of this descriptive advantage over simple phrase-structure grammars, a cooccurrence transformation grammar has serious inadequacies of descriptive power.

For example, we remarked that sentences like "John is easy to please" and "John is eager to please" differ in structure precisely in that "John" is the subject of "please" in the latter but the object of "please" in the former. The use of cooccurrence transformations allows us to represent the fact that these sentences differ in structure, in that it allows us to group each of them with other sentences to which they are structurally similar. *But it fails to represent the facts about grammatical relations upon which the differences between the sentences turn.* In particular, the grammar has no way of saying that "John" is the subject of "please" in one sentence and the object of "please" in the other. Thus, cooccurrence transformations can group together sentences which exhibit identical grammatical relations. What they fail to do is represent what it is that the sentences grouped together have in common.

This is an important consideration for the following reason. If a syntactic theory fails to provide a characterization of the grammatical relations between the parts of a sentence, it thereby fails to characterize one of the syntactic properties of sentences that determine their meaning. If one does not know what constituent of a sentence is its subject, one can not know what the sentence means.

This failure to mark the grammatical relations between the constituents of a sentence counts so heavily against the descriptive adequacy of a grammar that it is worth tracing its source in grammars employing cooccurrence transformations. We remarked that the use of cooccurrence transformations will permit us to assign (3-33) to the same sentence family that contains (3-35). In so doing, it allows us to claim that the grammatical relations in these sentences are identical. So, it might be supposed, the grammar does, after all, provide a basis for analyzing "John" as the implicit object in (3-33); namely, by assigning that sentence to a family which also contains (3-35) in which "John" is the *explicit* object.

The trouble with this argument is that it is completely symmetrical; we might just as well have argued that "John" is the *implicit* subject of "easy" in (3-35) since it is the *explicit* subject of "easy" in (3-33) and, according to the grammar, both sentences belong to the same sentence family. What we need is some way of representing the fact that the grammatical relations that are explicit in (3-35) are the ones that are implicit in (3-33), and not the other way around. But since the cooccurrence transformations allow us to derive either sentence from the other, the grammar provides no formalism for marking this fact.

Harris has himself suggested a way out of this problem: that simple declarative sentences (roughly, sentences with only one predicate phrase) be used as the canonical or "kernel" instances of sentence types. On this proposal the *implicit* grammatical relations in any sentence are to be identified with those relations that are *explicit* in the kernel sentence assigned to its family. Thus, "John" is the subject of "please" in (3-32) since, by hypothesis, part of that sentence is transformationally related to "John pleases someone"; analogously, "John" is the object of "please" in (3-33) because that sentence is transformationally related to "someone pleases John."

Presumably, barring certain technical difficulties, this proposal will work: every sentence will be transformationally related to a simple declarative, and it will invariably be the simple declarative in which the grammatical relations characteristic of that sentence are explicit. Yet Harris's proposal leaves us with a serious unanswered question: *why* are the grammatical relations that appear explicitly in the declarative those which are implicit in related sentence types? Notice that insofar as the grammatical constraints provided by a cooccurrence grammar are concerned, the canonical sentence form could equally well have been taken to be the passive, or the negative question. Since all the cooccurrence transformations are symmetrical, either of a pair of related sentence forms can be derived (directly or indirectly) from the other. Yet the intuition is that it *is* the simple declarative in which grammatical relations are explicit. What is the explanation of this fact?

We want to pick out the declarative as the fundamental construction type, and we want this choice to be expressed by some feature of the grammar. What is causing the trouble is that any sentence in a class of transformationally interrelated sentences is derivable from any other by *some* formulable transformation. What we need is a way of breaking this symmetry.

A natural, and as we shall presently see, highly motivated, way of doing so is the following. Allow at least some of the transformations to be asymmetric, and impose the condition that there be a construction type such that (1) sentences belonging to it are never derived by transformation from sentences of any other constuction type, and (2) every sentence that does *not* belong to that construction type is derivable directly or indirectly from some sentence that *does*. It should be obvious that the natural choice for this underlying construction type is the simple active declarative. As we remarked above, every sentence will be transformationally related to a declarative in which its grammatical relations are made explicit, and this is not true of other construction types. For example, suppose we decided to try to take the passive as the underived construction type. It is clear that condition 2 would preclude our doing so, since we would be left without a transformational source for sentences like "the man slept an hour," "the book cost five dollars," etc. (There exists no "an hour was slept by the man" to serve as the derivational source of the first, and no "five dollars was cost by the book" to serve as the derivational source of the second.)

In short, if we assume that transformations can be asymmetric so that the notion of the transformational source of a sentence can be defined, we can explain why grammatical relations that are implicit in some sentences are explicit in others: the grammatical relations that are implicit in a sentence are simply those that are explicit in the source sentence from which it is derived. If we assume that the simple active declarative is the ultimate transformational source for all other construction types, we can explain why the declarative is the construction type in which grammatical relations are explicit: explicit grammatical relations are those which have not been affected by transformation, and the simple declarative is the only untransformed type.

Thus far we have been arguing that a descriptively adequate grammar should permit a uniform representation of grammatical relations and that the grammatical relations implicit in a sentence ought to be identified with those that are explicit in the simple declarative to which it is transformationally related. We have seen that we can simultaneously meet this condition and constrain the class of possible grammatical transformations if we (1) require that every sentence be derivable directly or indirectly from a simple declarative, and (2) require that at least some transformations be asymmetric. In short, by *adding* to the formal constraints the rules of the grammar are required to satisfy, we *increase* the descriptive adequacy of the grammar. This suggests that the added constraint should, in fact, be adopted.[6]

It is important to emphasize the gains in descriptive power that the sort of grammar we are now considering yields in comparison with traditional IC grammars. Recall the discussion of such examples as (3-17),(3-24), and (3-25) above. Our conclusion was that in these cases sentences form classes, each of which includes a relatively complex, fully parallel construction, together with a number of simpler, truncated versions. Moreover, all the simpler sentences appear to be formed by the mandatory or optional deletions of repeated elements in the fully parallel ones. We remarked that there is no way to state this generalization in an IC grammar. It can, however, be captured in a perfectly natural way by a grammar which allows the notion of transformational derivation: a transformational grammar can represent the sentences as

---

[6] The form of argument used here is one which is widely employed in every science: insofar as two theories are equally compatible with the data, accept the one which makes the stronger claims. In the present case, we are accepting a theory which claims that there are constraints on transformational derivations (they must start with a declarative, for example) over one which leaves the class of derivations unconstrained.

We should also note that Harris (1971) has himself pointed out that certain cooccurrence transformations do not operate symmetrically across a given corpus. Thus, a grammar something like the one we have been discussing is implicit in Harris's work. See Katz and Bever (forthcoming).

interrelated by sequences of transformation which derive the simpler ones from the parallel ones. These kinds of cases are in no way exceptional. As the chapter continues, we will see that there are a number of syntactic phenomena whose explanation depends upon the notion that sentences have transformational sources.

Thus far we have considered two kinds of arguments for the employment of transformational derivations in grammars: they permit a uniform explication of grammatical relations, and they permit a characterization of the patterns of derivation underlying a wide range of such syntactic phenomena as tag questions, comparatives, etc. It may be added that the use of transformational derivations also permits a uniform representation for such intuitively homogeneous sentence classes as questions, negatives, imperatives, declaratives, etc. That is, it seems intuitively clear that sentences like (3-30c, f, g, h) have some feature of their grammatical structure in common which the other sentences in (3-30) do not; they are all somehow negatives. On the other hand, (3-30d, e, g, h) seem to form a natural class in that they are all questions; etc. Thus, though all the sentences in (3-30) are transformationally interrelated, they are nevertheless cross-classified in intuitively important ways. It would be desirable if the grammar could be made to represent this cross-classification. It would be still more desirable if this representation could be made the consequence of accepting some constraint on the rules permissible in the grammar.

The first point to notice is that the rules given in (3-31) do not afford such a cross-classification in any natural way; for example, the rule which introduces negative in (3-31b) is completely different from the one which introduces negative in (3-31e). Clearly, the condition we would like to be able to impose is that there be at least one rule which appears in the derivation of all and only negatives; that there be at least one rule which appears in the derivation of all and only questions, etc. Thus, the derivation of a sentence like (3-30h) would contain both such rules, the derivation of a sentence like (3-30a) would contain neither, and so on. We will see presently that this sort of constraint on the descriptive adequacy of a grammar can be satisfied, though not in precisely the form in which we have stated it.

We started with the notion of a cooccurrence transformation as, in effect, any rule which relates sentences belonging to different construction types. We argued that a grammar which contains such transformations has important advantages compared with a standard IC grammar: primarily, it permits the representation of the syntactic relations between sentences which differ in their constituent structures, like the members of a sentence family (e.g., 3-30). We have also seen, however, that such a grammar has certain serious theoretical limitations. In particular, it fails to provide a natural representation for the grammatical relations in a sentence like subject and object, and it fails to reconstruct the intuition that such construction types as negative, question, imperative, etc., form homogeneous classes of sentences.

Both these failures can be traced to unwanted degrees of freedom in a cooccurrence transformation grammar. In effect, the rules actually proposed for such a grammar are an arbitrary selection from a larger set of rules which might equally well have been chosen. For example, for the eight sentence types related by the rules in (3-31), there are twenty-eight possible cooccurrence transformations. In general, if there are n transformationally interrelated sentences in a family, there are $n(n-1)/2$ possible cooccurrence transformations for that family, since every pair of sentences defines a possible transformational relation. But since any given cooccurrence grammar will *require* only $n - 1$ transformations to state the relation between n sentences, any grammar for n sentences will represent an arbitrary decision not to employ $n(n-1)/2-(n-1)$ transformations. Since these transformations are excluded arbitrarily, the fact that they are formulable represents an unwanted degree of freedom in the theory.

We suggested that the the way to exclude these unwanted degrees of freedom is to require the grammar to acknowledge only transformations which preserve grammatical relations by tracing every sentence to a transformational source in which its grammatical relations are explicit, and which introduce each construction type in only one way. Insofar as these conditions can be satisfied, we simultaneously eliminate unwanted degrees of freedom in the grammar and increase its descriptive adequacy.

The effect of these constraints is twofold: first, they introduce into a cooccurrence transformation grammar the notion of *the transformational source* from which a sentence is directly or indirectly derived. Second, they introduce at least a partial ordering on the application of rules. Consider, for example, the relation between passive and question. Roughly, question permutes the auxiliary of a sentence with its subject *NP*. It will thus apply correctly to passivized strings (i.e., strings of the form NP_2 *was* $V + ed$ *by* NP_1) to yield *was* $NP_2 V + ed$ *by* NP_1. If, on the other hand, we allow question to apply before passive, producing strings like *Aux* NP_1 V NP_2, we have a structure which cannot be passivized by the same rule which passivizes actives. There are thus three possibilities: either question and passive apply in order, or the grammar has no source for passive questions (and is observationally inadequate), or the grammar has two passive transformations, one for declaratives and one for questions (and is descriptively inadequate insofar as it fails to introduce all passives by the same rule). In short, a consequence of the requirement that the grammar supply homogeneous derivations for homogeneous constructions is that at least some of the rules in the grammar will have to apply in a fixed order.

THE DISTINCTION BETWEEN DEEP AND SUPERFICIAL STRUCTURE

We have argued that the attempt to satisfy requirements of observational and descriptive adequacy leads in the direction of establishing the simple declarative as the transformational source from which all the sentences belonging to a given family are derived. In fact precisely the same sorts of arguments, if systematically pursued, lead to the conclusion that simple declaratives must themselves have a transformational history. We will try to show that if one insists upon deriving construction types like passive, negative, question, etc., from declarative sentences, one must pay the price of complicating the grammar and failing to represent important generalizations about structure. On the other hand, the grammar can be simplified if one permits the ultimate transformational source of these constructions to be an abstract object in which grammatical relations are explicit and from which the declarative is itself derived.

Consider, again, the passive rule. If we apply the rule, as stated in (3-31a) above to a sentence like "the ball hit the dogs," it produces as output the ungrammatical sentence "*the dogs was hit by the ball." Similarly, if we apply the rule to the sentence "the man ate the turtles" it produces the ungrammatical sentence "*the turtles was eaten by the man." In general, the rule will produce an ungrammatical output whenever it is applied to a declarative with singular subject NP and plural object NP.

It is easy enough to see what is going wrong. Number agreement holds between the subject and verb of a sentence. When we passivize a declarative, we change the original object into the "derived" subject, and put the original subject into a derived adverbial phrase. As it turns out, it is the *derived* subject with which the main verb of a passive agrees in number. Unless the derivations of passives take account of this fact, the grammar will fail to achieve observational adequacy, for it will generate ungrammatical passives.

There are two ways of ensuring that passive number agreement is correctly represented by the grammar. The first depends upon the use of rule ordering: simply require that if the passive rule applies in a derivation, then it must apply before the rule that makes subject and verb agree in number. In the case of passives, the agreement rule will thus apply to make the verb agree with the *derived* subject; in the case of declaratives, where NP_1 and NP_2 are not interchanged, it will apply to make the verb agree with NP_1. In short, we can assure the correct number agreement by a simple convention on the ordering of two rules.

Notice, however, that to adopt this solution is to abandon the view that a passive literally derives from the corresponding active. On the contrary, the passive must be derived from a structure *for which number agreement has not been specified*—hence, from a structure which is not a sentence. On this account, at least some transformations do not apply to sentences.

There is an alternative solution which will preserve the principle that the declarative is literally the transformational source of the other construction types, namely, to have two passive rules, one applying to sentences which have singular objects and one applying to sentences which have plural objects; for example, (3-39*a* and *b*):

3-39   a. $NP_1 V + ed\ NP_{sg} \Rightarrow NP_{sg}\ was\ V + ed\ by\ NP_1$

      b. $NP_1\ V + ed\ NP_{pl} \Rightarrow NP_{pl}\ were\ V + ed\ by\ NP_1$

To accept this proposal is, however, to abandon the goal of introducing the passive by the same rule wherever it occurs. In addition, it is to suggest that the distinction between a passive with a plural subject and one with a singular subject is a distinction in construction type. Worse still, the grammar would be committed to the claim that this distinction exists *only* for passive; in contrast, actives with singular subjects would be constructed by the same rules that are employed to construct actives with plural subjects.

Thus, fragmenting the passive rule leads to counterintuitive claims about what the construction types in the language are. It also, obviously, leads to a proliferation of rules, which is undesirable in itself. Notice further that the number of rules we need to state the passive in a language will be a question not of the character of the passive, but rather of the kinds of agreement the language requires between verbs and their subject. Thus, in French, we will need *four* rules to characterize passive constructions because verbs agree with their subject both in number and in gender.

The strongest argument against fragmenting the passive rule is not, however, the resultant complexity of the grammar; rather it is the failure to represent important generalizations about the structure of the sentences under analysis. It is obvious that there is a simple regularity governing number agreement in *both* actives *and* passives: that verbs agree in number with their derived subjects. The problem is to reconcile this generalization with the generalization that the *subjects* of passives are the *objects* of their corresponding actives. This reconciliation *can* be brought about, but only by ordering the rule of number agreement after the passive rule; and, as we remarked, this solution involves applying the passive rule to structures containing verbs which are not yet specified for number, i.e., structures which are not sentences.

We have argued that the derivation of the passive starts with an abstract object which is unspecified for number and proceeds by the application of first the passive and then the number agreement transformation. We have also observed that number agreement in active and passive is an essentially homogeneous phenomenon, and therefore should be accomplished by the application of the same rule in both cases. This view has a very important consequence: it requires that the active itself have a transformational history—in particular, that the generation of the active involves at least the application of a number-agreement transformation. Notice that to endorse this view is to abandon the position, which we have provisionally accepted until now, that actives are unique in that they have no transformational history. In the present account, actives themselves derive from abstract, underlying structures by the application of one or more transformational rules.

That major simplifications result from the assumption that actives, too, have transformational histories can be seen from the following argument. We noted that the verb phrase of a sentence agrees in number with its subject noun phrase. Let us raise the question about where in the verb phrase the morpheme of number agreement occurs. Consider (3-40):

3-40	a.	They *eat* fish.	John *eats* fish
	b.	They *have* eaten fish.	John *has* eaten fish.
	c.	They *are* eating fish.	John *is* eating fish.
	d.	They *have* been eating fish.	John *has* been eating fish.
	e.	They *do* eat fish.	John *does* eat fish.
	f.	They may *have* eaten fish.	John may *have* eaten fish.

In each of these sentences, the verb phrase agrees with the noun phrase in number. But in each case, the number morpheme appears on a different element of the verb phrase. We could, of course, capture this fact by using a different rule to generate each of the sentences. There is, however, a more elegant solution—one which captures the simple generalization underlying these heterogeneous surface forms. Assume that the active, like other forms, derives transformationally from an abstract underlying structure. Assume, too, that the number morpheme is positioned as the leftmost element of the verb phrase in this structure. A single transformation now captures all the surface forms in (3-40) by simply attaching the number morpheme to the first element on its right.

We shall presently see that this same rule, which positions the number-agreement morpheme, can be generalized to position all affixal morphemes in the auxiliary (namely: tense, number, and the past participle morphemes associated with *be* and *have*; cf. Chomsky, 1957).

There are, in fact, a number of other facts which, like the ones just discussed, argue that sentences are transformationally derived from structures which are not themselves sentences. (Several of these facts will be described in detail when we consider the derivation of auxiliary constructions.) We have already encountered some cases for which the natural solution requires sentences to derive from nonsentential structures. For example, the presumptive source of (3-25a and b) is (3-25c); but (3-25c) is not itself an acceptable sentence. Similarly, the natural way to capture the relation between (3-6) and (3-9) is to derive the latter from the former by a rule which permutes the particle with the *NP*. But note that parity of treatment will require that (3-41) be derived from (3-42). This derivation has two important advantages: it avoids having two rules for introducing verbs with particles, and it permits us to explain why "phone up" is intuitively a constituent even in sentences like (3-41) where the verb and its particle are not adjacent. However, (3-42) is not an acceptable sentence, so if (3-41) derives from (3-42), (3-41) has a nonsentential source.

3-41   John phoned her up.

3-42 *John phoned up her.

It appears in light of the preceding arguments that actives are themselves derived linguistic forms and do not, in this respect, differ from other sentence types. If we have stressed this, it is not only because of its linguistic significance but also because of its importance for interpreting some of the experimental and theoretical issues raised by early work on the psycholinguistics of transformational grammars. We shall return to this point in Chapter 5.

SUMMARY

The preceding arguments take us beyond even the most sophisticated types of cooccurrence grammar; such cooccurrence grammars employ asymmetric transformations to connect each sentence with a corresponding active declarative. They thereby provide for a notion of the "transformational source" of a sentence in which its grammatical relations are made explicit.

For that conception, we have now substituted the notion of a grammar as consisting of a system of rules which map from abstract underlying structures onto the sentences of a language. It is this latter conception that we will be discussing in succeeding sections of this chapter.

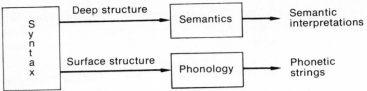

Fig. 3-4. Relation among components of a standard generative grammar.

"STANDARD" TRANSFORMATIONAL GRAMMARS

The idea that the syntactic component of a grammar maps a set of abstract objects onto the sentences of a language was introduced in Chomsky's monograph *Syntactic Structures* (1957). By 1965, a number of technical and substantive changes in this early form of the grammar had been widely accepted. The consequence of these developments was the elaboration of what is often referred to as the "standard" transformational theory of syntax. Though this theory has itself recently been undergoing substantial criticism and revision, it nevertheless provides a major point of reference for discussions in generative grammar and has been the primary source of linguistic assumptions for work in psycholinguistics. Indeed, recent alterations of the standard theory have tended primarily to effect its characterization of the relation between syntactic and semantic representations. They have not, so far, had any serious impact on the problem of characterizing the relation between syntactic models and theories of the speaker-hearer. We turn now to a discussion of standard transformational theory, the system of assumptions about syntax which will underlie much of the rest of this book. (For extended presentations of the standard theory, see Katz and Postal, 1964; Chomsky, 1965; Jacobs and Rosenbaum, 1968.)

In the standard theory, a grammar consists of three components: a syntax, a phonology, and a semantics. The syntax enumerates an infinite set of abstract, nonsentential tree structures (the so-called "deep syntactic structures") which are transformed into the trees that represent the surface constituent analyses of sentences. The phonology and semantic components accept these structures as inputs and associate them with phonological and semantic interpretations, respectively; specifically, deep syntactic structures are interpreted by the semantic component and surface syntactic structures are interpreted by the phonological component. We will take up the notion of a semantic representation in Chapter 4. A phonological interpretation may be thought of as representing a sentence as a phonetic string. Though we shall briefly discuss the functioning of the phonological system in mapping from a surface constituent structure tree onto a phonetic string, our primary interest will be in the organization of the syntactic component.

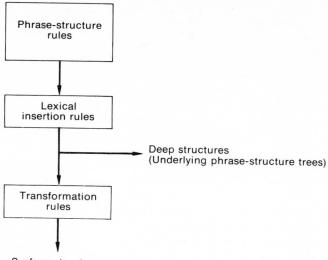

Fig. 3-5. The structure of the syntactic component.

Figure 3-4 shows the relations among components of a standard transformational grammar. Figure 3-5 shows the internal organization of the syntactic component. The syntax consists of a set of phrase structure rules (also called "the base" or "base structure component") which generate the population of deep structures characteristic of a language, and a set of ordered transformations which map these deep structures onto surface sentences together with their constituent structure trees. It should be noted that the phrase structure component is conceived of as a system of rewrite rules which expand syntactic symbols in the manner discussed previously for IC grammars. The basic notion of standard theory is thus that a syntax consists of an IC grammar which generates phrase-structure trees and a transformational grammar which acts in various ways to alter them.

Aside from these general claims about the organization of the syntax, four more specific hypotheses underlie much of the work on standard theories. :

3-43 a. Transformations do not change meaning (hence, the syntactic structures relevant to the semantic interpretation of a sentence are represented in its deep tree).

b. Grammatical relations are defined over deep structures.

c. Except for the insertion of lexical items into trees, transformations do not introduce structure: the effect of a transformation is to degrade the trees to which it applies.

    d. **Selection restrictions (that is, constraints upon cooccurrence of lexical items in sentences) are stated in the base and hence prior to the operation of any transformations other than lexical insertion.**

It should be emphasized that the principles in (3-43*a* to *d*) were conceived of not as ad hoc conventions but as empirical claims about the structure of the grammars of natural languages. In particular, the claim is that a grammar constructed in accordance with these principles will provide the intuitively correct analyses of sentences and that a grammar which violates them will provide correct analyses only at the cost of gratuitous complications.

    The easiest way to develop some understanding of how these general principles shaped the construction of standard transformational analyses is to run through some typical patterns of derivation. We will give a brief and very rough account of how five types of syntactic phenomena might be handled employing the mechanisms available to the standard theory: affix movement, passivization, relative clause construction, complementization, and lexical insertion. It must be emphasized that none of these treatments should be regarded as definitive. The arguments we will review have all had currency among standard theorists and are typical of the kinds of considerations that have motivated standard syntactic analyses. But few of the arguments are conclusive, and alternative derivations are possible in almost every case. Our goal here—as in preceding sections of this chapter—is not to provide a grammar of English, but rather to illustrate the considerations that have led generative grammarians to adopt successively deeper and more powerful accounts of the mechanisms of grammatical analysis. Contemporary linguistics is an unfinished science. Its methodology is, in many respects, more interesting than its firm results.

AFFIX MOVEMENT ACCORDING TO THE STANDARD THEORY
We pointed out above that if the passive transformation applies prior to number agreement, the notion of "passive construction" is captured directly within the grammar with a consequent reduction of the number of rules the grammar requires. This consequence of ordering transformations is revealed even more clearly in the treatment of the English auxiliary verb system.

    Consider the sentences in (3-44). The first observation is that the tense of each sentence occurs on the first element of the verb phrase. This regularity can be represented by permitting the IC component of

    3-44 a. **Morris solves the problem.**
           b. **Morris *is* solving the problem.**
           c. **Morris *must* be solving the problem.**

    d. Morris *solved* the problem.
    e. Morris *was* solving the problem.

the grammar to generate *tense* (present, future, past) to the left of the verb phrase in the deep structure and then using a *tense movement transformation* (3-45) to attach the tense to whatever word of the verb phrase occurs immediately to its right [e.g., to the main verb in (3-44*a,d*), to *be* in (3-44*b,e*), to *modal* in (3-44*c*)].[7]

    Now consider the sentences in (3-46). They demonstrate a regular

    3-45 (tense #X# ...) ⇒ #X + tense#

dependency between a form of the verb *be* and the progressive suffix (*ing*) which occurs on the end of the verbal element immediately follow-

    3-46 Morris *is* solv*ing* the problem.
    The problem *is* be*ing* solved by Morris.
    The problem will *be* be*ing* solved by Morris.
    The problem has *been* be*ing* solved by Morris.

ing *be*. This regularity can be represented if the phrase structure generates *be* + *prog* as a constituent in the base structure and rule (3-47) attaches the *prog* to the immediately succeeding verbal element (where the possible verbal elements are *be, have,* and main verbs).

    3-47 ing #V# ⇒ #V + prog#

    The final facts to consider are in (3-48). They reveal a dependency relation between a form of *have* and the past participle (*en* or *ed*) on the following verbal element. This can be accounted for by assuming that the

    3-48 a. Morris *has* solved the problem.
         b. Morris will *have* solved the problem.
         c. Morris could *have* been solving the problem.

base phrase structure generates *have* + *past participle* (*pp*) and that rule (3-49) attaches the *pp* to the immediately succeeding verbal element.

    3-49 pp V# ⇒ #V + pp#

    The similarity between the rules (3-45), (3-47), and (3-49) suggests that they should be collapsed together. Suppose that, in deep structure,

---

[7] We will adopt the following notational conventions: + indicates a boundary between syntactic elements of the same word; # indicates a boundary between words; ⇒ indicates a transformation (or a series of transformations); and { } indicates that the string enclosed stands for a deep-structure tree.

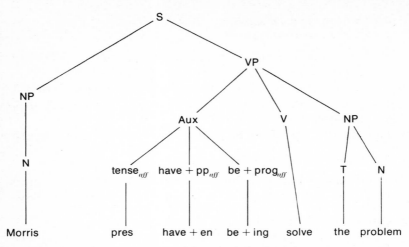

Fig. 3-6 Deep structure for "Morris has been solving the problem" prior to affix movement.

tense, prog, and *pp* are classified as *affix.* Rule (3-50) can now replace (3-45), (3-47), and (3-49). For example, (3-50) will apply to a structure like

3-50 *affix #X# ⇒ #X + affix#*

that shown in Figure 3-6 to produce sentence (3-51), in which *tense, pp,* and *prog* have each been permuted around a verbal element. We may note, finally, that rule (3-50) will now subsume the rule of number agreement on the assumption that number is an affixal element.

3-51 Morris has been solving the problem.

One consequence of this discussion is to provide further evidence that the passive transformation applies to an abstract structure rather than to an actual active sentence. We noted previously that unless number agreement applies *after* passive, unwarranted complications of the grammar ensue, and that since all actual sentences exhibit number agreement, it follows that passive does not apply to actual sentences. We can now see that the analogous argument holds for affixal elements other than number.

Suppose passive applies *after* (3-50) has positioned *tense, pp,* and *prog.* Notice that among the effects of passivization is the introduction of a discontinuous constituent *be + (en* or *ed).* [In (3-52) compare *a* with *b,* and *c*

3-52 a. John ate the cake.
 b. The cake *was* eat*en* by John.
 c. John will eat the cake.
 d. The cake will *be* eat*en* by John.

with *d.*] Now this *en* itself behaves just like an affix; that is, it behaves just like *prog* in (3-47) or *pp* in (3-48); it is attached to the verbal element immediately to the right of the "be" introduced by the passive. The rule of affix placement can therefore determine the surface position of the *en* that the passive introduces if we make the following two assumptions: first, the passive transformation introduces *be* + *pp* immediately to the left of the last verbal element in a *VP*; and, second, *en* is marked as an affix (*pp*) and hence falls under rule (3-50). Notice that if this pattern of derivation is accepted, passive must apply before affix movement. Hence it applies to a structure in which *tense*, *pp*, and *prog*, as well as number, all appear in the "wrong" positions; i.e., in positions they cannot occupy in actual surface sentences.

If on the other hand this pattern of derivation is *not* accepted, then we shall have to tolerate the usual proliferation of rules; we shall need a special passive rule for each possible development of the auxiliary.

Using this analysis of the auxiliary, we can provide still another argument to show that the structures transformations apply to are not actual sentences. Consider yes-no questions in English. Sentences (3-53) suggest a simple generalization about the derivation of yes-no ques-

3-53	a.	Will John come.	John will come.
	b.	Is John happy.	John is happy.
	c.	Has John eaten.	John has eaten.
	d.	Will John have eaten.	John will have eaten.
3-54		Did John eat.	John ate.

tions, namely, that they derive from the corresponding actives by permutation of the first *NP* with the first element of the auxiliary. This generalization can be preserved for case (3-54), if we assume that NP_1 has been permuted with *tense* and that *do* is a transformationally introduced element which attaches to *tense* when *tense* is the only element of the auxiliary. [It is worth noting that this analysis can be generalized to tag questions like (3-17).] However, this analysis assumes that *tense* appears as a separate element of the auxiliary in the structures to which question transformation and *do*-insertion apply. Since tense never occurs as a separate morphological element in actual sentences, this is tantamount to assuming that question transformation and *do*-insertion apply to abstract objects.

One further implication of these analyses should be noted. We are assuming that affixal elements are transformationally positioned in constructions like passives and questions. But then we shall have to make the *same* assumption about affix positioning in actives unless we are willing to tolerate a proliferation of affix-positioning rules. Hence, it follows from the analysis of affix movement and question formation (as from the analysis of number agreement) that actives themselves have a transformational history, i.e., that actives, like other sentences, derive from an abstract deep structure.

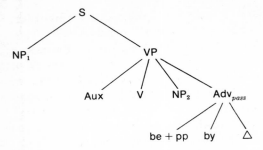

Fig. 3-7. Deep structure for a passive sentence.

PASSIVIZATION ACCORDING TO THE STANDARD THEORY

If the reader collects together the remarks we have made about passivization in the preceding two sections, it will be clear that the passive transformation can be formulated as shown in (3-55).[8] Notice, however, that the standard theory cannot employ this rule, since it violates principle (3-43c); in particular, it introduces an adverbial phrase ($by\ NP_1$)

3-55 $NP_1\ Aux\ V\ NP_2\ |\Rightarrow|\ NP_2\ Aux\ be + pp\ V\ by\ NP_1$

and the discontinuous constituent $be + pp$ in the surface structure of passives which are not present in the deep structure. In order, then, to avoid violating the injunction against "structure-building" transformations, we must assume that the deep tree which underlies passive sentences *does* contain an adverbial phrase; for example, as in Figure 3-7. The passive transformation will now be reformulated in the following way: the dummy marker in the adverbial phrase is replaced by NP_1, NP_2 is moved into the original NP_1 position, and the constituent $be + pp$ is placed immediately to the left of the main verb. Affix movement will then operate to attach pp to the right of the verb. On this view, the passive transformation will apply *mandatorily* to any deep structure containing the passive adverbial phrase rather than applying *optionally* to any tree of the form $NP\ Aux\ V\ NP$ as in the previous formulation.

It should be obvious from the above that it is possible to state the passive transformation in a way that makes it compatible with (3-43c). It is highly desirable, however, to have independent motivation for as-

---

[8] This rule applies to structures of the form $((NP_1)(Aux\ V\ NP_2)_{VP})_S$ to produce structures of the form $((NP_2)(Aux\ (be + pp)\ V\ (by\ NP_1)_{Adv})_{VP})_S$. It does so by (1) attaching $be + pp$ to the node VP at a position between the Aux and the main verb; (2) attaching the subtree $(by\ NP_1)_{Adv}$ to the VP; (3) deleting the original NP_1; (4) placing NP_2 in the position originally occupied by NP_1.

suming that the deep structures underlying sentences like passives (and, similarly, questions, negatives, imperatives, etc.) do in fact contain designated constituents which trigger the operation of the corresponding transformations. For, as we remarked above, principles like (3-43c) are supposed to be empirical hypotheses about the structure of language. If they are true, then constructing grammars which conform to them ought to lead to simplifications, and permit generalizations which would otherwise be missed.

There is evidence for this sort of independent motivation from arguments like the following. In discussing cooccurrence transformation grammars, we suggested that a reasonable constraint to place upon the descriptive adequacy of grammars is that they provide a basis for characterizing the notion of a construction type. A natural way to do so is to have each such type introduced by one and only one transformation. There are, however, good reasons for believing that this way of characterizing the notion of construction type will not work. Consider the three sentences in (3-56). It seems clear that the phrase "who is on the roof" has the force of a question in (3-56a and b) but not in (3-56c).

3-56   a.   Who is on the roof?
       b.   John asked who is on the roof.
       c.   John knows who is on the roof.

Yet the transformational history of "who is on the roof" is presumably identical for all three sentences. A natural solution to this problem is to differentiate between (3-56a and b) and (3-56c) at the level of deep structure by assuming that the former contains a "question" constituent which does not occur in the deep structure of the latter.

The same pattern explanation can be appealed to to represent the asymmetry between (3-57a and b). The operation of the imperative transformation is to delete a specified subject ("you") and a (future)

3-57   a.   Close the door and you will regret it.
       b.   Close the door and I will make you rich.

tense, so, for example, the source of (3-58) is presumed to be (3-59). But note that precisely the same transformational operations underly the

3-58   Close the door.

3-59   {You will close the door}

first clause of sentences like (3-57a) as well as (3-57b). Such clauses, like true imperatives, are always interpreted as having future reference, and the implied subject is always "you." Yet "close the door" is clearly not an imperative in (3-57a); on the contrary, the force of the sentence is precisely that you are *not* to close the door.

How, then are we to represent the fact that (3-57*a*) is a threat while (3-57*b*) contains an imperative, given that the first clause of each sentence is generated by precisely the same sequence of transformational operations? The suggestion, again, is that true imperatives have a characteristic imperative morpheme in their deep structures; the rule which derives all and only imperatives is the base structure rule which introduces this morpheme rather than the transformational operations of *you* deletion or *future-tense* deletion. It is an added virtue of this assumption that we can now give a straightforward account of the ungrammaticality of sentences like (3-60). If we assume that the base structure con-

3-60 *Probably close the door.
      ***Perhaps close the door.**

tains an imperative morpheme, it is possible to context-restrict the morpheme against the class of adverbs to which "probably" and "perhaps" belong without violating principle (3-43*d*) according to which all context restrictions are defined in the base.

RELATIVIZATION ACCORDING TO THE STANDARD THEORY

Thus far, throughout our entire discussion, we have been concentrating on "simple" sentences; roughly, sentences containing only one predicate phrase. We have said, first, that in the deep-structure trees underlying such sentences, morphemes occur in an order different from the ones they can exhibit in surface sentences; and, second, that the surface order of morphemes is a consequence of transformational operations. Finally, we have said that in the case of all simple sentences other than declaratives (e.g., passives, questions, imperatives, etc.) the deep structure contains a morpheme which is characteristic of the construction type, which triggers the operation of the appropriate transformations and which does not appear in the surface sentence. In the conventional jargon of linguistics, transformations which apply to the deep structures of simple sentences are called "singulary" transformations, and what we have been arguing is that the application of singulary transformations to the appropriately marked base trees is mandatory.

In the present section, we turn to the standard treatment of "complex" sentences (those sentences containing two or more predicate phrases). The basic idea is this: in the case of simple sentences, the underlying tree contains only one S node, and the operation of transformations is essentially that of rearranging the constituents within that node; in the case of complex sentences, the underlying structure contains two or more nodes labeled S and the operation of transformations

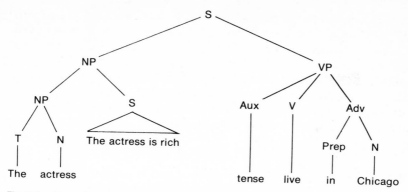

Fig. 3-8. Deep structure for a sentence containing a relative clause.

determines the surface relations of constituents within, *and between*, the subtrees they dominate.

Figure 3-8 gives a rough version of a standard-theory deep structure for sentence (3-61). It will be noticed that there are two nodes labeled S, one of which directly dominates "the actress lives in Chicago," and the

3-61 The actress who is rich lives in Chicago.

other of which directly dominates "the actress is rich." For convenience, we will often refer to the trees which underly complex sentences (i.e., to trees containing more than one node S) as *complex* trees, and to any subtree immediately dominated by S in a complex tree as a *sentoid*. (Katz and Postal, 1964, give a detailed presentation of the sentoid concept.)

Relativization of such complex trees proceeds in an apparently straightforward way. In particular, relativization acts on trees like those in Figure 3-8 by deleting the first *NP* in the subordinated sentence on the condition that it is identical with an *NP* in the next higher sentoid. (This transformational operation which deletes the subordinated *NP* of two identical *NP*'s is referred to as *equi-NP* deletion.)

However, there is more to an account of relativization than this deletion operation. In the first place, we must supply a source for the relative pronoun. Second, we must account for sentences like (3-62), in which the deleted *NP* occurs as the *second NP* in the subordinated sentoid. [We assume that (3-62) derives from a deep structure like (3-63).]

3-62 The boy whom the girl liked got sick.

3-63 {((The boy (the girl liked the boy)) got sick)}

Let us assume that in the deep structure of relatives, there occurs a *wh*-morpheme attached to one of the subordinated *NP*'s. A transformation (*wh*-attraction) operates mandatorily to place whichever *NP* contains the *wh*-morpheme at the front of the subordinated sentoid. In sentences like (3-61), where the *NP* containing *wh* is already the first *NP* of the subordinated sentoid, *wh*-attraction applies vacuously. In the case of sentences like (3-62), where the *NP* containing the *wh*-morpheme is the second *NP* of the subordinated sentoid, *wh*-attraction applies to produce an intermediate structure like (3-64). The relativization transformation is mandatory and is ordered after *wh*-attraction.

> **3-64** **((The boy ((*wh*-the boy) (the girl liked))) got sick)**

It should be noticed that the decision to distinguish *wh*-attraction from relativization per se is independently motivated by the fact that *wh*-attraction is precisely the same operation involved in forming *wh*-questions [like (3-65)]. In each of these sentences, a constituent containing a *wh*-morpheme has been carried to the front from its original

> **3-65** **a.** **Where does Sam eat snails?**
> **b.** **What does John want from Mary?**

position in the base. The presumptive deep structures for (3-65*a* and *b*) are (3-66*a* and *b*). We see here the source of the superficial similarity between relatives and questions illustrated by sentences like (3-56*b* and *c*).

> **3-66** **a.** **{(Sam eats snails (*wh*-somewhere))}**
> **b.** **{(John wants (*wh*-something) (from Mary))}**

Finally, consider the sentences (3-61) and (3-67). There are large

> **3-67** **The rich actress lived in Chicago.**

numbers of such sentence pairs where one member contains as a prenominal adjective what the other member contains as the predicate of a relative clause. This symmetry can be captured if we derive the adjectival form from the underlying form of the corresponding relative. The transformations involved are, in fact, easy to state. Given (3-68*a*), there is an optional transformation (*wh-is* deletion) which produces the intermediate structure (3-68). This structure is now in the domain of a mandatory transformation (*adj-preposing*) which places the predicate adjective from

> **3-68** **a.** **((the actress) (who is rich)) (lives in Chicago)**
> **b.** **((the actress) (rich)) (lives in Chicago)**

the reduced relative clause in front of the preceding *NP*, yielding sentences like (3-67).

Several points can be made about this pattern of derivation. First, *wh-is* deletion is independently motivated by the existence of such sentences as (3-69), which is clearly an optional variant of (3-70). In the former sentence, *wh-is* deletion has applied but *adj-preposing* has not.

3-69 The actress living in Chicago got arrested.

3-70 The actress who is living in Chicago got arrested.

This brings us to the second point, which is that while *adj-preposing* is mandatory for structures like (3-68b), it does not apply in the derivation of sentences like (3-69). Thus, there is neither a sentence (3-71), nor a sentence (3-72). To a first approximation *adj-preposing must* apply to simple

3-71 *the actress rich lived in Chicago

3-72 *the living in Chicago actress got arrested

adjective phrases and *may not* apply to complex adjective phrases (those containing a nonparticipial verb).

THE STANDARD THEORY OF COMPLEMENT CONSTRUCTIONS

Relative constructions derive from complex deep-structure trees in which a sentence appears as a modifier of a noun. Another kind of case in which sentences have complex trees in their underlying structure is *complementation*, where a subordinated sentence occurs in the scope of the verb in a higher sentoid [as in (3-73)].

3-73 John believed Bill was an idiot.
John expected Bill to leave.
John forced Bill to marry Sally.

There are a number of interesting ways in which complement constructions are cross-classified. For example, there is a class of verbs that take structures of the form *that S* as their objects [see (3-74)]. In such cases, the subordinated *S* can be realized as almost any well-formed declarative.

3-74 a. John admitted that Mary is beautiful.
     b. John doubts that Presidents ever lie.
     c. John doesn't know that Sally is deceiving him.

In this respect, *that-S* complements differ from two other kinds; *infinitival* complements (like "John requested Bill *to leave*") and *possessive-ing* complements (like "John disapproved of Bill's leav*ing*"). In these last two cases, the surface representation of the subordinated sentoid is a reduced version of a sentence.

What kinds of deep structures underlie these various types of complex sentences? One clue is their behavior under passivization. Since the passive transformation has the effect of moving the *object-NP* of a sentoid to the front of that sentoid, we can assume that any constituent of a complement construction that can be fronted by passivization must be an *object-NP* at the point in its derivation where pas-

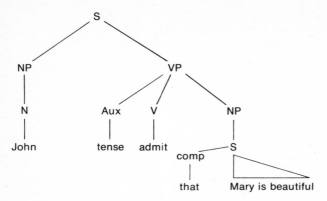

Fig. 3-9. Deep structure for a *"that-S"* complement.

sive applies. For example, *that-S* must be in the *object-NP* position somewhere in the derivation of *that-S* complements, since we have sentences like (3-75) corresponding to sentences like (3-74). Thus, the deep structure of sentences like (3-74*a*) must be as shown in Figure 3-9.

3-75 That Mary is beautiful was admitted by John.
That Presidents ever lie is doubted by John.
That Sally is deceiving him isn't known by John.

These cases are relatively straightforward. However, there are other cases whose behavior under passivization raises problems. Notice that corresponding to (3-76) we have not only the passive form of (3-77) but

3-76 Bill expected John to leave.

also the passive form of (3-78). In (3-77) the passive transformation has moved the whole subordinated sentoid "John leave." In (3-78), however,

3-77 For John to leave was expected by Bill.

3-78 John was expected to leave by Bill.

it has moved only the subject of the subordinated sentence ("John"); this suggests that, at some point in the derivation of (3-78) before the application of passive, "John" is the direct object of "expect." It is noteworthy that neither *that-S* complements nor *poss-ing* complements have passive forms like (3-78). Thus, there is no sentence (3-79*a*) corresponding to

3-79 a. *Mary was admitted that is beautiful by John
b. *Bill's was disapproved of leaving by John

3-80 John disapproved of Bill's leaving

(3-74*a*), and there is no sentence (3-79*b*) corresponding to (3-80). For such constructions, passive cannot apply to move the subject of the subordinated sentoid; hence, there is no reason to suppose that the subject of the

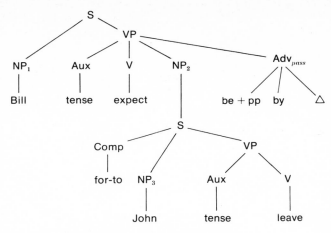

Fig. 3-10. Deep structure for a "for-to" complement.

subordinated sentoid ever appears as the direct object of a higher verb in the derivation of sentences containing *that-S* or *poss-ing* complements.

The discussion, thus far, suggests that passive must be able to apply in two different ways to the kinds of structures that underlie sentences like (3-76); at the point of the derivation where it applies to produce (3-77), the object of "expect" is "for John to leave," and at the point where it applies to produce (3-78), the object of "expect" is "John." How might this be arranged? There are a number of possible solutions in the standard transformational literature, all more or less similar to the following one.

Suppose that the deep structure of (3-77) has the general character of Figure 3-10. Since we are assuming that the subordinated sentence is dominated by *NP*, we have a straightforward account of the existence of (3-77); namely, passive applies in the usual way to permute NP_1 and NP_2, yielding the structure in Figure 3-11 as the tree for (3-77).

The alternative derivation, in which the *NP* moved is *not* a sentoid, as

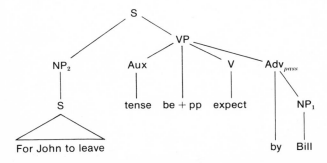

Fig. 3-11. Derived structure for (3-77) after the passive transformation.

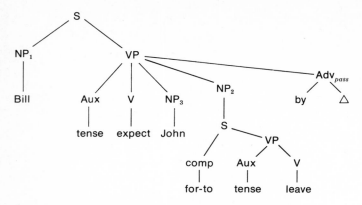

Fig. 3-12. Derived structure for (3-78) after subject raising.

in (3-78), is slightly more complicated. We have observed that the existence of such a "nonsentential" passive argues for a stage in the derivation at which the subject of the subordinated sentoid ("John") appears in the position of the direct object of the dominating verb. Suppose that we assume a transformation ("subject raising") which applies to the kind of structure in Figure 3-10 and has precisely the effect of attaching the first *NP* from the subordinated sentoid directly to the right of the verb in the dominating *VP* node. The application of this transformation to Figure 3-10 yields the intermediate tree Figure 3-12. Since NP_3 is now in object position for the main clause, passive applies to permute NP_3 and NP_1, yielding Figure 3-13 as the structure underlying (3-78).

To summarize: We have assumed that the existence of (3-78) requires "John" to be the direct object of "expect" at some point in the derivation of (3-76). But the existence of (3-77) indicates that "John" cannot be the direct object of "expect" in the base structure of (3-76).

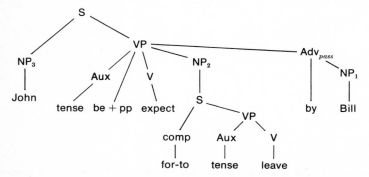

Fig. 3-13. Derived structure for (3-78) after subject raising and passive.

The present solution is to allow a transformation that raises "John" from its initial position in the subordinated sentoid to a derived position as object of the main clause verb. There is other evidence for this derived structure. Notice that reflexivization can apply to the subordinated *NP* in sentences like (3-76). That is, there exist forms like (3-81). But it is a general condition on reflexivization that it occurs only between identical *NP's belonging to the same sentoid*.[9] This suggests that the structure of

3-81   **John expected himself to leave.**

(3-81) must be (3-82) rather than (3-83) at the point at which reflexivization applies: that is, that in the derivation of (3-80), subject raising has applied before reflexivization.

3-82   **John (expects (John)$_{SP}$ (to leave)$_S$)$_{VP}$**

3-83   **John (expects (John to leave)$_S$)$_{VP}$**

In this same vein, it is instructive to compare verbs like "expect" with verbs like "persuade." Though we have sentences like (3-84) corresponding to sentences like (3-76), and although (3-84) has a nonsentential passive (3-85) corresponding to (3-78), (3-84) has no sentential passive corresponding to (3-77). In particular, (3-86) is ungrammatical.

3-84   **Bill persuaded John to leave.**

3-85   **John was persuaded to leave by Bill.**

3-86   ***For John to leave was persuaded by Bill.**

One can imagine two accounts of this asymmetry, both of which are compatible with the kind of treatment we have given (3-76). We could argue that the deep structure of (3-84) is precisely like the deep structure of (3-76) but that for verbs like "persuade," subject raising is *mandatory*. If, as we have been assuming, subject raising precedes passive, making subject raising mandatory for persuade-type verbs will assure that sentences like (3-84) have no corresponding sentential passive.

On the solution just proposed, "persuade" takes a sentential object *NP* in deep structure, just as "expect" does. There is an alternative solution, however, according to which "expect" and "persuade" differ in deep structure; in particular, "persuade," unlike "expect," has a *non-*

---

[9]Compare "John shaved himself" with "John asked the barber to shave himself." The former sentence means "John shaved John," but the latter means "John asked the barber to shave the barber"; it has no reading on which it means "John asked the barber to shave him." Such examples are taken to show that a noun in a subordinating sentence cannot reflexivize a noun in a subordinated sentence.

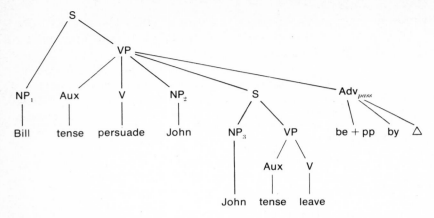

Fig. 3-14. Deep structure for (3-85).

sentential direct object in the base, as in Figure 3-14. In this configuration the complement sentoid is subordinated to the *VP* rather than to the direct object *NP*. Since, on this account {John leave} is not the object of "persuade" at any point in the derivation of (3-84), the passive transformation cannot be applied to yield (3-86). We will first sketch a derivation for (3-85) along the lines of this solution, and then give the argument which suggests that this derivation is correct.

Assume, then, that the deep structure of (3-85) is as shown in Figure 3-14. The transformations that apply in the derivation of (3-85) are *Equi-NP* (which, in this example, deletes NP_3 under identity with NP_2), and then the passive transformation, which permutes NP_1 and NP_2 in the usual way. Our discussion shows that the structure in Figure 3-14 is a plausible source for (3-85). Our present problem is to find grounds for choosing between that structure and one in which "persuade" takes a sentential object [as "expect" does in (3-76) and (3-77)]. The decision to choose Figure 3-14 as the source for (3-85) is based on an asymmetry between "expect" and "persuade" type verbs vis-à-vis the application of passive to the sentoids they dominate. Notice that we have the two passive forms (3-87*a* and *b*), which apparently correspond to the actives (3-88*a* and *b*). There is, however, the following difference. Sentences (3-87*a*) and (3-88*a*) are synonymous, but (3-87*b*) and (3-88*b*) are not. While the former sentence answers the question "Who did Bill persuade John to be examined by?", the latter answers the question "Who did Bill persuade the doctor to examine?" Thus, on the assumption that transformations do not change meaning, (3-87*b*) and (3-88*b*) cannot come from the same deep structure. On the other hand, it is plausible to hold that (3-87*a*) is a passive variant of (3-88*a*).

    3-87 a. Bill expected John to be examined by the doctor.
         b. Bill persuaded John to be examined by the doctor.

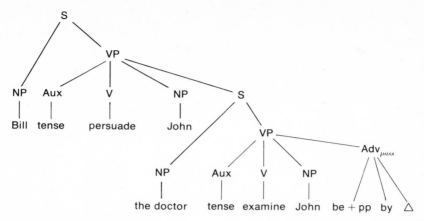

Fig. 3-15. Deep structure for (3-87b).

3-88 a. Bill expected the doctor to examine John.
b. Bill persuaded the doctor to examine John.

We can explain the asymmetry if we choose the solution according to which "expect" verbs and "persuade" verbs differ at the level of deep structure. For while (3-87a) is the result of passivizing the subordinated sentoid in (3-88a), (3-87b) is not transformationally related to (3-88b), but rather derives from the structure in Figure 3-15 with *equi-NP* applying to delete the subordinated occurrence of "John" after it has been fronted by passivization. Notice that there is no passive corresponding to (3-88b). That is, (3-89) is ungrammatical. This fact is predictable on the assumption which we have been making throughout: namely, that

3-89 *Bill persuaded the doctor John to be examined by him.

equi-NP deletion can apply only to the *first NP* in the subordinated sentence. On that assumption, (3-89) would have to come from the structure in Figure 3-16. However, the action of passivization on the subordinated sentoid in that structure will permute "the doctor" and "John," leaving us with the structure in Figure 3-17. Since *equi-NP* cannot apply here, the surface string in (3-89) cannot be derived.

In short, we have the following derivations: *Equi-NP* applies to {Bill persuaded the doctor (the doctor examine John)} and yields "Bill persuaded the doctor to examine John." {Bill persuaded the doctor (the doctor examine John (by *Adv* ₚₐₛₛ))} fails to meet the conditions upon *equi-NP* and yields no surface sentence. Analogously, {Bill persuaded John (the doctor examine John)} also fails to meet the conditions on *equi-NP* and blocks. {Bill persuaded John (the doctor examine John (by *Advₚₐₛₛ*))} does meet the conditions on *equi-NP* after passive has applied and yields "Bill persuaded John to be examined by the doctor."

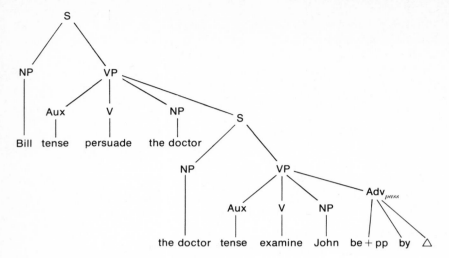

Fig. 3-16. Deep structure for *(3-89).

Notice that this analysis depends on assuming that "persuade" takes a direct object *NP* (rather than a complement sentence) in deep structure. In the opposed analysis which makes "persuade" like "expect," and makes subject raising mandatory in sentences with "persuade," we would have {Bill persuaded (the doctor examine John) (by Adv_{pass}))} as the source of *both* "Bill persuaded the doctor to examine John" (in case passive is *not* applied before subject raising) *and* "Bill persuaded John to be examined by the doctor" (in case passive *is* applied before subject

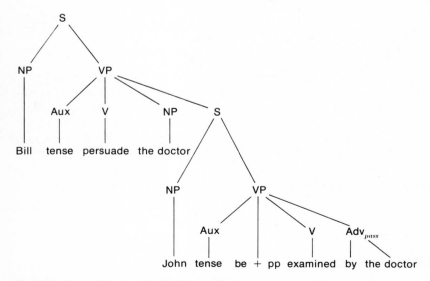

Fig. 3-17. Derived structure for *(3-89) after passive.

raising). But this would violate a fundamental principle of standard theory (3-43a), for it would commit us to the claim that the passive transformation changes meaning. Worse still, the meaning change would be restricted to complements on verbs like "persuade." The solution that "persuade" and "expect" differ in their deep structure clearly should be preferred, since it allows us to claim that passive does not change meaning in any complex sentences just as it does not in any simple sentences.

The upshot of this discussion is thus that, though (3-76) and (3-84) are indistinguishable at the level of surface structure, they differ in respect of the deep structure relation between "John" and the verbs. In (3-76), "John" is the deep subject of the subordinated verb; in (3-84) it is the deep object of the dominating verb.

THE TRANSFORMATIONAL CYCLE

We have argued that there are two types of infinitival complement constructions: the "persuade" type (i.e., a *VP-complement*), in which an *NP* is transformationally deleted from the subject position of a subordinated sentence on the condition that it is identical with the object *NP* in the subordinating sentence; and the "expect" type (i.e., an *NP-complement*), in which the subject *NP* of the subordinated sentence is transformationally "raised" to become the derived direct object of the subordinating verb.

It is significant that passivization *of the subordinated sentoid* must precede either of these operations. For example, passivization must apply to "the doctor examine John" before subject raising in the derivation of (3-87a). This is because (1) prior to passivization, "John" is not the first *NP* of the subordinated sentoid, and (2) after subject raising "John" is not even a constituent of the subordinated sentoid, so it could clearly not be affected by the application of passive to that sentoid. Precisely analogous considerations show that passivization must precede *equi-NP* deletion in (3-87b): *equi-NP* deletes the *first NP* in a subordinated sentoid, and "John" is the second *NP* of that sentoid until passivization has been applied. Compare Figure 3-15 with Figure 3-18, which illustrates the deep structure of (3-87b) after the application of passive but before the application of *equi-NP* deletion.

Notice, however, that we have already seen that passive can also apply *after* subject raising. Indeed, that was precisely the pattern of derivation that was required to produce the nonsentential passive (3-78). In fact, it is possible to find a sentence in which passive has applied *both* before *and* after subject raising, namely (3-90).

3-90 John was expected by Bill to be examined by the doctor.

In short, we appear to have a paradox: passive is required to *precede*

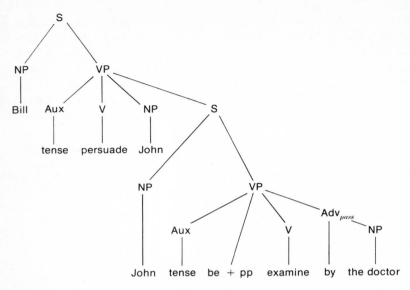

Fig. 3-18. Derived structure for (3-87*b*) after passive.

subject raising to account for one sort of sentence, to *follow* it to account for a second sort, and to both precede *and* follow it to account for a third.

However, the paradox is more apparent than real. For the application of passive that precedes subject raising is to the *subordinated* sentoid, while the application of passive that follows subject raising is to the *dominating* sentoid. The required ordering can be accommodated by arranging certain of the transformations (including subject raising, *equi-NP* deletion, and passive) in a cycle. In particular, on the standard analysis of a complex deep tree, all the cyclical transformations apply in fixed order to the lowest sentoid in the tree. They then reapply, in the same order, to the next highest sentoid in the tree, and so on, until the highest S node is reached.

If we assume that subject raising, *equi-NP* deletion, and passive are all cyclic transformations, we get the right set of outputs for the structures underlying sentences like (3-90). Thus, on cycle one, passive can apply to the embedded sentence in the deep structure of (3-90) to produce the intermediate structure (3-91). Subject raising now applies to the first sub-

3-91 (Bill (expected)) (John be examined by the doctor)

ordinated *NP*, producing (3-92), in which "John" is the direct object of

3-92 (Bill (expected) (John)) (be examined by the doctor)

"expect." On the *second* cycle, passive can now apply to the subordinating sentoid to permute "Bill" and "John," producing (3-90).

This solution turns out to be perfectly general. It is possible to distinguish between cyclical and noncyclical transformations in a way that provides the correct order of application of rules for all the known cases. For example, there are no known cases in which cyclic transformations must apply to a subordinating sentence in a complex tree before they apply to a subordinated sentence, and there are no known cases in which transformations must apply in one order in an early cycle but in a different order in a later cycle.

LEXICAL INSERTION ON THE STANDARD THEORY

In an IC grammar lexical items are incorporated into a constituent structure tree by a special class of nonbranching rules which rewrite class markers as single morphemes. Thus, trees like the one in Figure 3-1 might be generated by an IC grammar which includes a set of lexical rules like (3-5e to g).

On the standard transformational theory, two central claims are made about lexical insertion: first, that it is transformational and, second, that it occurs at the level of deep structure.

That lexical insertion must be transformational is shown by the following kinds of examples. Suppose we have a deep structure like {(John V (Bill was an impostor))}. Possible substitution for V are "believed" and "thought," but not "hit." What precludes "hit" is that the V for which we are to substitute dominates a subordinated sentoid. That is, the fact which precludes "hit" is a fact about the domination relations between nodes in the tree structure in which the V occurs. A rule which is sensitive to this kind of information is, however, a transformation rather than an IC rule since, by definition, IC rules are sensitive only to the left and right *linear* context of the symbol to be rewritten.

Two points should be noticed. First, lexical insertion transformations are counterexamples to the claim that no transformations introduce structure. Consider, for example, the transformation which introduces "phone up" under V in structures like {Joan V Mary}. The structure of "phone up" is presumably

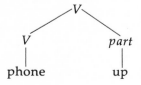

But this means that the lexical insertion transformation for "phone up" introduces a subtree into the trees it applies to, and in this sense is structure-building.

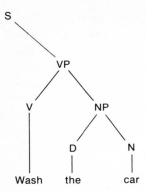

Fig. 3-19. Surface phrase structure for an imperative.

Second, if lexical insertion is to be accomplished by transformation, then the syntax will have to contain one transformation for each lexical item in the language. Presumably the transformation associated with each lexical item specifies the properties that must be exhibited by trees into which that item can be inserted. The operation of the transformation is simply to insert the item into trees which do exhibit those properties.

These sorts of considerations suggest the motivation for the claim that lexical insertion occurs only in deep structure. Suppose, for example, that we allowed lexical insertion to apply in surface structure, and consider a transformation like *you*-deletion which operates in the imperative. This transformation produces subjectless surface trees like Figure 3-19. But these trees do not satisfy the conditions on lexical insertion for verbs, since presumably these conditions refer to subject *NP*'s. To put it the other way around: if we allow lexical insertion after subject deletion, we will have no way of blocking such ungrammatical imperatives as "be divisible by five," which presumably violates a cooccurrence restriction between the predicate and the deleted subject.

It will be seen that the principle that lexical insertion occurs at deep structure and the principle that selection restrictions are stated at the level of deep structure are really two sides of the same coin. The preceding example shows that one of the functions of lexical insertion transformations is to ensure that lexical items are inserted only in structures where their selection restrictions are satisfied. The status of the claim that lexical insertion occurs only in deep structure, and hence that selection restrictions are stated at that level, is one of the central issues in the linguistic disputes that have centered on the standard theory. We will return to it at length in Chapter 4.

PHONOLOGY IN GENERATIVE GRAMMAR

The diagram in Figure 3-4 presents the general organization of a standard grammar. As we remarked above, the role of the phonological component is to map the surface syntactic structure onto sequences of phonetic segments. Unlike the syntactic component, the phonological component of generative grammar has occasioned little psycholinguistic research, so we present here only an outline of its main characteristics. The most important aspects of the phonological system are the following:

1. Phonemic and phonetic segments are defined in terms of distinctive features.
2. Features at the phonemic level provide an abstract classification of segments in the sense that they do not represent actual articulatory-acoustic parameters of the speech signal. Features at the phonetic level do represent such parameters.
3. The abstract phonemic sequences are mapped onto phonetic sequences by a set of ordered transformational rules which change features within segments.

1. During the period of taxonomic linguistics a number of researchers investigated the possibility of decomposing phones into a set of articulatory-acoustic *distinctive features.* Jakobson and others proposed that these features are binary—that is, a given phonetic segment is classified either as having (+) or not-having (−) each feature. Since every segment is a unique combination of such binary features and since there are usually no more than fifty phonemes in a language, a small number of features are adequate to describe the phonetic segments of each language. (See Table 3-1 for a presentation of the phonetic features describing some English phones.) This claim is interesting particularly in light of the variety of physical distinctions that the vocal tract *could* produce, and the variety of acoustic distinctions the ear can hear among non-speech stimuli. In Chapter 6 we return to a series of experiments on the perceptual "reality" of such features and their categorical nature. It is sufficient for our purposes here to note that they are the lowest level of phonological analysis treated within grammars. The phonetic feature matrices serve as instructions to the vocal tract and are thus interpreted by the presumably universal physiological mechanisms of speaking and hearing.

2. The basic representation of lexical sequences in the surface structures of sentences uses the same set of distinctive features as the phonetic description of segments. However, the distinctive features and

TABLE 3-1. DISTINCTIVE FEATURE COMPOSITION OF ENGLISH SEGMENTS

	ī	ū	ē	ō	ǣ	ā	ǣ	ɔ̄	i	u	e	o	ʌ	o	æ	ɔ	y	w	ɛ
vocalic	+	+	+	+	+	+	+	+	+	+	+	+	+	+	+	+	−	−	−
consonantal	−	−	−	−	−	−	−	−	−	−	−	−	−	−	−	−	−	−	−
high	+	+	−	−	−	−	−	−	+	+	−	−	−	−	−	−	+	+	−
back	−	+	−	+	−	+	−	+	−	+	−	+	+	+	−	+	−	+	−
low	−	−	−	−	+	+	+	+	−	−	−	−	−	−	+	+	−	−	−
anterior	−	−	−	−	−	−	−	−	−	−	−	−	−	−	−	−	−	−	−
coronal	−	−	−	−	−	−	−	−	−	−	−	−	−	−	−	−	−	−	−
round	−	+	−	+	−	−	−	+	−	+	−	+	−	+	−	+	−	+	−
tense	+	+	+	+	+	+	+	+	−	−	−	−	−	−	−	−	−	−	−
voice																			
continuant																			
nasal																			
strident																			

	r	l	p	b	f	v	m	t	d	θ	ð	s	n	z	c	c̆	ǰ	s̀	z̀	k	g	x	ŋ	h	kʷ	gʷ	xʷ
vocalic	+	+	−	−	−	−	−	−	−	−	−	−	−	−	−	−	−	−	−	−	−	−	−	−	−	−	−
consonantal	+	+	+	+	+	+	+	+	+	+	+	+	+	+	+	+	+	+	+	+	+	+	+	−	+	+	+
high	−	−	−	−	−	−	−	−	−	−	−	−	−	−	+	+	+	+	+	+	+	+	+	−	+	+	+
back	−	−	−	−	−	−	−	−	−	−	−	−	−	−	−	−	−	−	−	+	+	+	+	−	+	+	+
low	−	−	−	−	−	−	−	−	−	−	−	−	−	−	−	−	−	−	−	−	−	−	−	+	−	−	−
anterior	+	+	+	+	+	+	+	+	+	+	+	+	+	+	−	−	−	−	−	−	−	−	−	−	−	−	−
coronal	+	+	−	−	−	−	−	+	+	+	+	+	+	+	−	−	−	+	+	−	−	−	−	−	−	−	−
round																									+	+	+
tense																											
voice	+	+	−	+	−	+	+	−	+	−	+	−	+	+	−	−	+	−	+	−	+	−	+	−	−	+	−
continuant	+	+	−	−	+	+	−	−	−	+	+	+	−	+	−	−	−	+	+	−	−	+	−	+	−	−	+
nasal	−	−	−	−	−	−	+	−	−	−	−	−	+	−	−	−	−	−	−	−	−	−	+	−	−	−	−
strident	−	−	−	−	+	+	−	−	−	−	−	+	−	+	+	+	+	+	+	−	−	−	−	−	−	−	−

Source: After Chomsky and Halle, 1968, p. 176.

feature values that occur at the phonological level are not always paired with the articulatory or acoustic properties of the phonetic manifestations of the phonemes they describe. Rather, sequences of phonological rules intrude between the abstract level of phonological representation and the level of representation at which the distinctive features are realized as articulatory gestures and acoustic events.

For example, it would be difficult to find an articulatory or acoustic justification for treating /r/ and /l/ as both a consonant *and* a vowel. Nevertheless this formal analysis is justified in English by the following sorts of considerations. Like consonants, /r,l/ can precede, follow, and occur between all vowels and diphthongs (e.g., liar, rile, rail, lair, whaler, borrow, etc.). Another reflection of the fact that /r,l/ are consonants is the fact that they can stand alone with a vowel to form a syllable, while true vowels cannot. For example, /la, ra/ are syllables but /ea, ua/ are not. In these respects, it appears that /r,l/ should be considered consonants.

Yet like *vowels* (and unlike any other consonants), /r,l/ can follow two consonants ("stride," "splay") and precede three consonants ("bursts"). Furthermore, /r/ and /l/ can act syllabic nuclei as in the second syllable of "twaddle" and "bitter" in which there is no other clear vowel. In these respects, it appears that /r,l/ should be considered vowels.

One solution to this apparent contradiction would be to state the generalizations about basic sequences with /r,l/ classified as consonants (or as vowels), and then state exceptions for /r,l/; for example, if /r,l/ are classified as consonants:

Only two consonants can occur initially and only three finally unless one of them is /r,l/.

Only vowels can stand between consonants as the syllabic nucleus except /r,l/.

A different solution is to claim that /r,l/ are both vowels *and* consonants, and to state the basic morpheme structure generalizations in terms of "true" consonants and vowels; that is, in terms of those consonants that are marked as − *vocalic* and those vowels that are marked as − *consonantal* (see Table 3-1). On this solution /r,l/ are marked as + *vocalic* and + *consonantal*, which would be a contradiction at the *phonetic* level. It is, of course, physically impossible for a *phonetic* segment to be both a vowel and a consonant since the articulation of such a sound would require of the vocal tract both that it be open and that it be closed. However, this contradiction is irrelevant at the abstract phonological level since distinctive features at this level have no direct physical interpretation.

The consequence of this view is to allow for the simplification of phonological processes and an increase in their explanatory power. Such abstract classifications allow phonological processes to be formally represented and grouped together according to their distributional similarity despite their phonetic differences. Consider, for example, a formalization of the rules that account for the formation of plurals in English. Basically this process involves adding /s/ to a morpheme following an unvoiced consonant and adding /z/ following a voiced consonant or a vowel. A statement of this generalization in terms of distinctive features is given in (3-93). It should be noted that the rules in (3-93)

3-93 To form the plural noun from the singular noun
    1.   Add a phoneme S which is
        a. + *coronal* **(Made with the tip of the tongue)**
        b. + *continuant* **(A sound that can be sustained)**
        c. + *strident* **(Has a relatively large amount of noise)**
        d. − *vocalic* **(Is not a vowel)**
        e. + *consonantal* **(Is a consonant)**
    2. Assimilate the voicing of the plural morpheme to be the same as that of the immediately preceding segment.

suggest a sequential derivation of the final plural form that proceeds in stages, much like the syntactic derivation of sentences from their underlying syntactic structure. Thus, for example, after rule (3-93-1), the plural of "dog" would be "dogS," the plural of "dock" would be "dockS," and the plural of "saw," "sawS." This theoretical segment /S/ is *not* a representation of any *particular* sound since it is not specified as either voiced or unvoiced—rather it is a formal representative of a class of sounds which includes both /z/ and /s/. Rule (3-93-2) adjusts the voicing component of the sound to be the same as the preceding segment, yielding "dogz" and "docks" and "sawz." This representation captures the notion that plural formation in the kinds of cases we have been discussing involves only a single morpheme and affects only a single phonetic property of that morpheme, namely its voicing. Just as we have seen repeatedly in discussions of syntax, the theoretical assumption that there are abstract levels of representation not only simplifies the statements of the generative processes but also makes possible the representation of significant generalizations.

    3.   Like the syntactic rules, the phonological rules apply in a particular order. For example, rule (3-93-1) must precede (3-93-2) in order to produce the appropriate segments for voicing assimilation. A greater use of ordering can increase the scope of the generalizations that can be captured by the phonological rules. For example, the rules in (3-93) do not correctly derive the plural forms of nouns that end in affricates (a "harsh" sound); as they stand, they would make the plural of "bush" "*bushs" and the plural of "fudge" "*fudgz." One solution to this would be to add to rules (3-93) a stipulation that they do not apply to nouns that end in affricates, and a rule which inserts /əz/ following those sounds. But to do so would detract from the generality of (3-93). A solution which preserves the unity of pluralization makes use of the processes in (3-93), as in (3-94).

3-94 To form the plural noun from the singular noun
0. If a word ends in an affricate, add the vowel /ə/ ("uh")
1. Add _S_ to the word
2. Assimilate voicing of _S_ to the preceding segment

This ordering allows the plurals of nouns ending in harsh sounds to be derived by exactly the same rules as those which derive other plurals, as outlined in the derivations below.

bush	→	bushe	→	busheS	→	bushez
dock	→	dock	→	dockS	→	docks
dog	→	dog	→	dogS	→	dogz
saw	→	saw	→	sawS	→	sawz

It is clear that these rules must be applied in the stated order if they are to operate correctly.

The ordering among these rules clarifies the sense in which the input to the phonological component is abstract compared with the output: the input forms mark only those features which are unpredictable from the phonological context. For example, it is characteristic of English that consonants assimilate voicing to agree with a preceding consonant, so that at least that part of rule (3-94) can be stated as a general rule of English phonology. This has the consequence that the underlying phonological form of words with consonant clusters need not specify the value of the feature "voicing" for the second consonant: it is predictable from the first and can be filled in by rule.

The use of derivational rules applying to abstract phonological sequences allows quite generally for this sort of simplification of lexical representation. For example, in English, vowels are regularly lengthened before voiced consonants. If this is stated as a phonological rule, then each of the pairs of words in (3-95) can be represented with the same vowel. The technical simplification of using such a rule is that lexical indication of vowel length does not need to be included in such en-

3-95	let	led
	pat	pad
	sit	sid
	feet	feed

vironments. The parallel generalization is that vowel length in such environments is not a distinctive feature of English.

The fact that the underlying phonological structure is in this sense abstract is reflected in surprising analyses in which underlying theoretical forms are set up which can be quite "distant" from their surface appearance. For example, there is a regular process that softens /t/ to /ch/, as can be seen by comparing forms with final /t/ and those same forms with a suffix beginning in /y/. For example, the pairs in (3-96) reflect the fact that adding a suffix with initial /y/ to a word with final /t/ regularly softens it:

> **3-96** **gestate**............................**gestation**
> **digest**............................**digestion**

Once such a process is set up, words like "mention" can make use of the regularity to simplify their representation, even though they do not participate in the derivational processes exemplified in (3-96), i.e., even though there is no independent verb "ment." Thus, we set up *theoretical* forms like those in (3-97), in which phonetic /ch,sh/ is represented in the underlying forms as /t/. The regular *t*-softening rule that applies to

> **3-97** **station**............................**stetyon**
> **mention**............................**mentyon**

/t/ before /y/ automatically softens it to produce the correct phonetic output in the course of the phonological derivation. The force of such claims is, once again, to allow for the representation of phonological generalizations. For example, representing the underlying form of "station" as /stēt + yon/ reflects a claim that the root stem /stēt/ is the same one that underlies "state" and "static."

It is unclear as things now stand *how* abstract such underlying representations should be, since the phonological system might appear to give the theoretician power to state spurious regularities. It *is* clear, however, that the hypothesis of underlying phonological forms and rules that derive phonetic sequences from them resolves many empirical difficulties faced by the taxonomic grammarians. Consider, for example, the problem of assigning a phonetic segment to a particular phone when its presence in the phonetic sequence has differential effects only on an adjacent segment. We remarked in Chapter 2 that English has such a case for many speakers, who pronounce /d/ between two vowels as a "tongue flap" (/D/) and pronounce /t/ in the same position in the same way. However, the vowel preceding the tongue flap is lengthened if the tongue flap is a phonetic representation of /d/, as seen from the examples below:

> "latter" compares with "lādder"
> "writer" compares with "rīder"

This occurs as a function of the rule mentioned above which lengthens vowels before voiced consonants. The descriptive problem is handled straightforwardly if we assume two rules, one which lengthens vowels and a later one which merges intervocalic /d/ and /t/ to the same phonetic segment /D/, as shown in the following derivations:

/lædr/   →   /lǣ dr/   →   /læ Dr/

/lætr/   →   /læDr/

It is clear that this example would be difficult for a taxonomic grammar since it violates the principle that entities at successive levels of description should correspond segment by segment. In the intervocalic environment, there is no unique *phonetic* representation that differentiates the segment /t/ from /d/, only an effect on the preceding vowel. As in the case of syntax the assumption that surface forms are the products of derivations from underlying representations captures generalizations as well as resolving descriptive problems that have no natural solution in a taxonomic analysis.

SUMMARY: GRAMMATICAL UNIVERSALS

Thus far we have been discussing the standard theory's claims about the structure of grammars as they are set out in such principles as (3-43). But we might equally have represented the discussion as being about the standard theory's account of the universal syntactic properties of natural languages. The standard theory makes certain statements about the form of grammar that best describes a natural language. For example, it holds that we will never find a language for which the optimal grammar has a form other than that dictated by principles such as those in (3-43). To formulate the constraints that the standard theory places upon grammars of natural languages is thus tantamount to setting forth the claims the theory makes about what features of natural languages are linguistic universals.

Standard theory holds that every sentence in a natural language has both a deep structure and a surface structure; that the grammatical relations of each sentence are explicit in its deep structure, however much they may be obscured in its surface representation; that the deep structure of every sentence in every language is a tree configuration whose nodes are labeled by class markers, like *NP*, *S*, *VP*, and *Adj*, drawn from a finite universal list. The standard theory further claims that the deep structure of every sentence in language is generable by some finite set of phrase-structure rules; that transformations in general apply in a fixed order as determined by principles like (and including) the transformational cycle; that selection between constituents of sentences is definable at the level of deep structure; that lexical insertion applies to deep structures and is transformational; that no transformation has the effect of changing the meanings of the structures to which it applies; that the semantic interpretation of a sentence is defined over its deep structures and that the phonological interpretation of a sentence is defined over its surface structure.

Clearly, these claims amount to a substantive set of empirical hypotheses about the universal character of possible natural languages. We will see in the following chapters that many of them have extremely important consequences for the psycholinguistic theories of sentence perception, production, and the acquisition of language. This is, of course, not surprising. A standard grammar of a language purports to give an account of what the speaker-hearer of that language knows about its structure. Insofar as the account it gives is true, any theory of the mechanisms of speech production, of comprehension, or of language learning must show how the information represented by such a grammar is internalized and used.

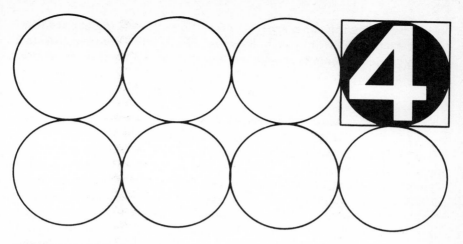

SEMANTICS

PART ONE.   SOME TRADITIONAL THEORIES OF LINGUISTIC SYMBOLS

Thus far our discussion of language structure has focused almost exclusively on syntax. Yet syntax has rarely been a matter of great concern to psychologists; in this respect, the Hullean developments discussed in Chapter 2 were departures from the main stream. What psychologists have largely cared about is semantics. In this chapter, we begin by reviewing some aspects of traditional theorizing about meaning in Anglo-American psychology and philosophy. We then turn to a survey of developments in' semantics within the context of generative grammar.

CENTRALITY OF THE NAMING PARADIGM

"The problem of language is the problem of meaning. The problem of meaning is the problem of reference. And the problem of reference is to explain how words name things." Until very recently, some such equivalence has recommended itself to many philosophers of language and to practically all psychologists. Its acceptance as self-evident has had much to do with the form that philosophical and psychological accounts of language have taken, at least since Locke. In the first part of this chapter, we will investigate several such accounts. But first we would do well to consider the assumptions that have made this version of the problem of reference a matter of such obsessive concern to students of language; to cast doubt upon such assumptions is to question the view that naming is the central relation to be explained by theories of meaning.

The view that calling someone by his name is the paradigm of reference is very nearly ubiquitous, both in traditional and in current accounts of the psychological processes underlying verbal behavior. Examples may be chosen almost at random. Thus Locke (1690), discussing the ontogenesis of language, traces the development of all general terms from prototypic proper nouns:

> There is nothing more evident than that the *ideas* of the persons children converse with ... are, like the persons themselves, only particular. ... The names they first gave to them are confined to ... individuals and the names of *nurse* and *mama* the child uses determine themselves to those persons. Afterwards, when time and a large acquaintance has made them observe that there are a great many other things in the world that, in some common agreements of shape and several other qualities, resemble their father and mother and those persons they have been used to, they frame an *idea*, which they find those many particulars do partake in and to that they give, with others, the name *man*, for example. And *thus they come to have a general name*, and a general *idea*. Wherein they make nothing new, but only leave out of the complex *idea* they had of *Peter* and *James*, *Mary* and *Jane*, that which is peculiar to each, and retain only what is common to all [vol. 2, p. 17].

Substantially identical approaches may be found throughout the contemporary literature, where the assumption that naming is the paradigmatic speech act is widely taken for granted. Carroll (1964) remarks: "There comes a stage ... when acquisition of vocabulary is amazingly rapid; this seems to occur when in his cognitive development the child has reached the point of perceiving that things, events, and properties have 'names'" (p. 32). Again, in one of the central theo-

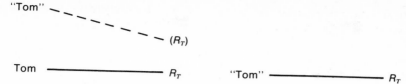

Fig. 4-1. Pattern of conditioning responsible for the understanding of the word "Tom" (after Mowrer, 1960).

retical passages of *Learning Theory and the Symbolic Process,* Mowrer (1960) argued that

> As Fig. [4-1] shows, the word "Tom" acquired its meaning, presumably, by being associated with, and occurring in the context of, Tom as a real person. Tom himself has elicited . . . a total reaction which we can label, R_T, of which r_T is a component. And as a result of the paired presentation or concurrence of "Tom"-the-word and Tom-the-person, the component or "detachable" reaction, r_T is shifted from the latter to the former. And similarly for the word "thief." As indicated in Fig. [4-2], this word is likewise presumed to have acquired its distinctive meaning by having been used in the presence of, or to have been, as we say "associated with," actual thieves [p. 144].

The reader will notice that Mowrer's figures are isomorphic; i.e., that the theory provides precisely similar treatments for predicates and for proper names.

It is not difficult to understand why so many theorists have located the nub of the reference relation in naming. In the first place, the one-to-one relation that holds between a name and its bearer suggests that it is sufficiently simple to be the aboriginal meaning relation from which all others differ in complexity but not in kind. One supposes that if the relation between a proper noun and its bearer is taken as primitive, the relations that hold between other sorts of words and what *they* stand for are easily defined in terms of it. Indeed, it is widely maintained that the

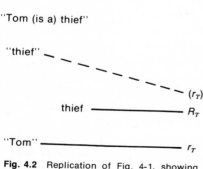

Fig. 4.2 Replication of Fig. 4-1, showing how the word "thief" acquires its distinctive meaning.

naming relation is everywhere the same, though it binds words to different sorts of entities in the case of each of the major syntactic word types. If a proper noun is a word which names an object, then a common noun is a word which can name sets of more objects than one. Analogously, verbs are to be thought of as naming actions, prepositions as naming relations, adjectives and adverbs as naming properties of objects and actions, respectively, and so on. This is presumably the semantic theory that everyone carries in his head and teaches to every child in grammar school.

A second reason for supposing that the naming relation between proper nouns and their bearers is semantic bedrock is perhaps that that model comports well with an associationistic view of psycholinguistic processes. This is a point we shall investigate in considerable detail later. But it is easy to see how it might be maintained that repeated cooccurrences of an object and utterances of its proper name set up in a child who is learning a language the habit of "expecting" the object when its name is uttered. Correspondingly, appropriate manipulation of patterns of reinforcement might be supposed to produce in the child an inclination to utter the name upon presentation of the object. If the existence of such habits and inclinations accounts for the fact that a proper name stands for what it names, and if naming is the fundamental semantic relation, then there is promise of a general characterization of the psychological processes underlying verbal meaning in terms of the same fundamental principles of association invoked to account for nonverbal learning.

Simplicity and compatibility with widely accepted psychological principles are certainly more than can be claimed for most theories about language. Nevertheless, there is reason to treat with considerable skepticism the view that naming is the central function that words perform. In the first place, there is a large class of words and phrases of which it is simply not reasonable to hold that they are kinds of names. Nor is this class of counterexamples homogeneous; the doctrine that all words are names admits of a number of different kinds of clear exceptions. Consider, for example, "for example," "hello," "and," "whether," "since," "of," "and so on," and so on. Though desperation might suggest that "hello" is the name of a situation in which persons are greeting one another, this is a case in which the counsels of desperation ought to be resisted. "What is the name of this situation?" is a bizarre question (compare "What is the name of this dog?") and "This situation is named 'hello' " is barely English (compare "This dog is named 'Posh' "). If it is still insisted that all words are kinds of names, then it must be replied that there must be as many kinds of names as there are kinds of words and that there is no reason for supposing that the relation between names like "Posh" and their bearers provides a model for the relation between names like "hello" and *their* bearers.[1]

It is no small matter that there exist many kinds of cases for which the name-bearer model of meaning is obviously not suitable. It means that, at the very best, a theory of meaning based upon this model will need to be held jointly with theories rich enough to account for the exceptions. This, in turn, means that the assertion that simplicity and psychological plausibility argues in favor of the naming model is not sound unless the theories that explain the exceptions are also simple and plausible. A theory that can handle "Mommy" but not "and" is clearly not good enough. And the (putative) fact that a theory that handles only the first is compatible with an associationistic psychology is no guarantee that a theory that handles both will be.

Another way to point out the implausibility of the view that a homogeneous relationship of naming is fundamental in semantics is to remark upon a striking difference between true names and all other sort of words: proper nouns are undefinable. Hence, in the sense of "meaning" in which having a meaning is having a definition, proper nouns have no meaning. (Notice that while it makes sense to ask "What does 'polarization' mean?" it makes no sense to ask "What does 'John Smith' mean?"—the only relevant question being "Who is John Smith?") But if it is true that names have no meaning, it seems odd to maintain that what bestows meaning upon other sorts of words is the fact that they bear to their referents the same sort of relation that "John Smith" bears to John Smith.

Third, it seems clear that the homogeneity of the naming relation can be maintained only at the expense of postulating metaphysical objects to stand in the sort of relation to common nouns, verbs, adjectives, prepositions, etc., that physical objects have to the proper nouns that name them. That is, the simplicity that is claimed for semantic theories based on naming is characteristically gained at the price of an extremely complicated (not to say extremely dubious) ontology. It is clear, for example, that adjectives cannot name the sorts of things that proper nouns do. For while the referent of a proper noun has a location, a date, an individual history, etc., not one of these things can be said about the referents of adjectives. If we nevertheless assume that adjectives *are* names we are ipso facto committed to the existence of a special kind of

---

[1] Cf. Carroll (1964), where it is asserted that "some signs, like *Hi* and *Thanks* bear referential relationship only to certain kinds of social situations" (p. 6). But if "Hi" refers to the situation in which people say "Hi," what does "the situation in which people say 'Hi'" refer to?

thing—a property or universal—that is tailor-made to be what adjectives are the names of. Similarly, "activity" becomes a technical word when it begins to be used as a cover term for the sort of thing a verb "names"; and one psychologist (Skinner, 1957, p. 121) has supposed that "pastness" must be "a subtle property of events" in order that there should be something named by the *ed* in "violated" and the *t* in "lost." One wonders, indeed, whether this project is not doomed to circularity. It is uninformative to say that all nouns name objects if it turns out that all such objects have in common is that they are named by nouns; nor is it easy to see what else of interest is common to, say, short naps and tall stories.

There is still further reason for taking a jaundiced view of the notion that the naming relation is fundamental, and that the primary task of semantics is to show how other kinds of meaning can be reduced to it. We have seen that one argument for taking naming seriously as the semantic primitive is that it appears to be a simple one-to-one relation, the extension of which is specified by such rules as "John Smith" names (the individual) John Smith; "snow" names (the stuff) snow; "white" names (the property) white; etc. If, however, the extension of the naming relation is specified in this way, it turns out that the rules determining the denotation of a word do not apply to every occurrence of the word. Moreover, it is by no means clear that the difficulty is not intrinsic; there is no obvious way to make the rules fully general. Consider, for example, the application of the rule " 'lions' names lions" to the sentence "John is hunting lions." The question is whether the rule holds for the occurrence of "lions" in this sentence. The answer appears to be that in one way of understanding the sentence, it does, but in another way of understanding it, it does not. If one understands "John is hunting lions" on the model of "John is hunting two lions, Leo and Lea," it is clear that the rule holds. For, "lions" evidently refers to lions in the latter case; in particular, it refers to Leo and Lea. However, consider the sentence "John is hunting lions but he won't find any." It is clear that the question "To which lions does the 'lions' of *this* sentence refer?" is a nonsense question. (Compare also "To which unicorns does 'unicorns' refer in 'There aren't any unicorns'?")

Hence there is a way of understanding "John is hunting lions" on which the obvious reference rule fails to apply, an interpretation on which the occurrence of "lions" in that sentence is nonreferential. What's more, this phenomenon is not by any means local. An indefinite number of examples may be constructed in which rules like " 'lions' refers to lions" fail in the scope of such verbs as "want," "desire," "think of," "believe," "hope for," and "intend to."

The problem of what to do about so-called "opaque contexts"—contexts in which reference rules fail to hold—is very much an open one in philosophy. We shall not review the solutions that have been proposed. What is relevant for our purposes is that the phenomenon of opacity reveals unexpected complexities in the notion of reference. Such complexities serve to undercut the argument that a semantic theory based on reference can make do with one fundamental word-object relation articulated by a reasonably simple and intuitive set of rules. The reverse turns out to be the case. It appears that we must either say that the naming relation does not obtain in opaque contexts, or that if it does, the reference rules for such contexts are so obscure as thus far to have defied unexceptionable formulation.

The arguments we have been examining suggest pretty strongly that one's view of language becomes seriously distorted when one holds that naming is *the* characteristic function of words. It would seem, rather, that naming is only one of a number of different functions that words can be used to perform; hence, the problem of characterizing the relation between names and their bearers is only one of a family of problems about meaning. Indeed, one way of summarizing the remarks we have made so far is to insist upon the necessity of distinguishing between problems about meaning and problems about reference. We have already seen that proper names have referents but do not have meanings. It may also be remarked that the distinction between meaning and reference is implicated in the problem of opaque contexts, for synonymous expressions can be interchanged in such contexts without altering truth value. But substitution of *non*synonymous expressions that share their referents may produce such alterations. Thus, if "John believes that the Metro runs through the biggest city in France" is true, it must also be true that John believes that the Metro runs through the largest city in France. But it need not be true that John believes that the Metro runs through Paris, since John may be under the misapprehension that the biggest city in France is Rheims.

Moreover, it is obvious that while synonymous expressions—i.e., expressions that are identical in *meaning*—must have the same referents (if they have any), the converse need not hold. "The largest city in France" has the same referent as "The city that the Metro runs through," though it is clear that these expressions are not synonymous. Paris would still be France's largest city even if the Metro were moved to Rheims.

While the distinction between meaning and reference is important, it is also subtle. Thus, we know that "round square" has no referent because we know that it follows from the meaning of "round" and "square" that anything that is square is not round. Similarly, we know that the referents of "bachelor" are all male because we know that "all bachelors are male" is analytically true (that is, true by virtue of the meanings of the constituent words), and we know that "the light box" may have two distinct kinds of referents because we know that "light" has two meanings. Although a theory that treats seriously of the *meaning* of words would presumably be concerned, in the first instance, with explaining why expressions like "round square" are linguistically incoherent, why expressions like "male bachelor" are redundant, and why expressions like "light box" are linguistically ambiguous, such a theory would have the indirect effect of explaining certain complexities in the relations between these words and their referents. Indeed, it seems a natural condition to place upon an adequate theory of meaning that it should account for phenomena of reference in these sorts of ways.

To say that the problem of reference is less general than it is sometimes supposed to be is not, therefore, to dismiss the problem. Still less is it to solve it. The problem of meaning is by no means identical with the problem of reference, but there is no use denying that the two problems are intricately related so that if we understood the mechanism of reference we would probably understand a good deal about meaning as well.

We do not propose to solve any of these puzzles. In fact, we shall suggest in the second part of this chapter that a critical element in this discussion of reference is one which has not yet been mentioned: the relation between rules of reference and rules which determine when a sentence is *true*. At present, however, our concerns are primarily historical. We wish to indicate what kind of problem the problem of reference was traditionally supposed to be and what kinds of solutions psychologists and philosophers have thought it amenable to. We shall try to show that there is a sense in which the nature of the problem has not itself been correctly grasped, so that the models that have been proposed for reference have been largely irrelevant to the exigencies of the problem that reference poses.

One way of seeing what the problem of reference was supposed to be is to raise the question of why reference was thought to be problematic. Why is it that, while so many deep problems about language have been ignored, there has been practically universal agreement that there is a puzzle about reference? What is it precisely that people thought needed to be explained?

CONVENTIONALISM AND THE PROBLEM OF REFERENCE

We make a start toward answering this question when we notice that theorists who hold that the problem of reference is the heart of the problem of language almost invariably also hold that it is characteristic of human languages that they are systems of conventions. We shall presently try to make the relation between these doctrines clear. For the moment, it is necessary to understand what is being claimed when the conventional aspect of language is stressed.

It is commonplace to remark upon a certain arbitrariness that attaches to facts about human languages. By this is meant not only that it is a matter of historical accident that a given language is spoken in one place and not another, but also that it is impossible to give any justification for persisting in particular linguistic usages other than the practical inconvenience of altering them. One (slightly misleading) way of putting this is to say that we could, in principle, alter any detail of our language simply by agreeing to do so, just as children do when they agree to converse in Pig Latin. This is meant to be analogous to saying, for example, that we could alter the conventions that determine what counts as correct evening dress simply by agreeing to do so, and to be *dis*analogous to saying that we could alter the way we walk simply by agreeing to limp. Precisely what is denied when the arbitrariness of facts about language is stressed is that something corresponds to a natural way of talking in the way that something does correspond to a natural way of walking.

This is a somewhat misleading way of making the point because it is evident that for an adult speaker set in his linguistic ways, adopting a new set of speech habits would involve considerably more difficulty than adopting a new set of conventions for formal attire. To emphasize the arbitrary character of linguistic rules is not, of course, to deny this. It is rather to assert that, in principle, we could equally easily have learned a way of talking quite different from the way of talking we did learn; presumably this is not true of alternative ways of walking.

That there must be something to the view when it is so stated is evident if only from the fact that human children born in different language communities all appear to be able to master their native tongues with approximately equal facility. What innate limits may be imposed upon this ability is not known, although we shall see in Chapter 8 that there is reason to believe that there may be such limitations. At any event, it is clear that the languages that actually exist are a somewhat accidental selection from a much larger set of possible human languages.

We could, to keep to quite simple examples, institute the following changes in English. We could henceforth adopt the practice of using the phonemic sequence represented by the conventional spelling of "boy" in just those cases in which the phonemic sequence represented by the conventional spelling of "girl" has hitherto been used, and vice versa. Or we could adopt the practice of pronouncing every other word in a sentence backward, or of replacing it by its translation in French, etc. Such considerations have led theorists to argue that since we could alter the facts about language by adopting the relevant *explicit* conventions, it is useful to think of such facts as obtaining by virtue of *tacit* conventions. In short, then, what lies behind the notion that facts about language are arbitrary is the view that, within whatever broad restrictions are placed upon the structure of languages by innate preferences for one or another kind of linguistic system, linguistic facts exist by virtue of a social rather than a logical or an empirical constraint.

"SYMBOLS" VERSUS "SIGNS"

The same point is sometimes made by saying of human languages that they are systems of *symbols* rather than systems of *signs*, and that this makes them essentially different from animal "languages." A symbol, in this view, is precisely an object whose meaning is conventional in the sense discussed above. A sign, on the other hand, is an object whose meaning is determined by some fixed relation it bears to a thing or situation. Thus, the warning rattle of the jackdaw[2] is a sign and not a symbol because the occasions on which it is uttered, its acoustic shape, and the behavior characteristic of its hearers are all fixed by causal laws.

One of the ways in which a sign may be related to what it signifies, then, is as effect to cause. The jackdaw's rattle presumably signifies the presence of its releaser (a black, dangling or fluttering object) in very much the same way, and in very much the same sense, that clouds signal rain and smoke signals fire. In such cases, the relation between the sign and its significate is, directly or indirectly, causal, although in the case of animal signs, the causal contingencies are presumably the local and specialized effect of the evolutionary process.

Cause and effect is not usually held to be the only relation capable of relating sign to significate. Another such "natural" (i.e., nonconventional, or nonsymbolic) relation which may provide a source of signs is resemblance. Thus it is widely maintained that while a word like "face" cannot conceivably be related to its referent by anything stronger than a convention, there is clearly some nonarbitrary element in the relation between that referent and the referent of Figure 4-3. Doubtless such figures are enormously stylized, so the ability to recognize what they are intended to portray must be to some extent the result of socialization (cf., for example, Gombrich, 1965). But though Figure 4-3 is a conventional representation in the sense that simplifications of a drastic sort are tolerated by anyone who recognizes it as a face, this conventionality is different in kind from the sort that would be operative if we decided to adopt Figure 4-4 as a symbol of faces.

---

[2]Cf. Lorenz, quoted by Brown (1958, p. 166).

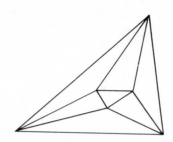

Fig. 4-3. Face schema

Fig. 4-4. Face symbol.

THE PROBLEM OF REFERENCE AND THE SIGN/SYMBOL DISTINCTION

It is notable that the problem of reference is always raised as a problem about symbols and never as a problem about signs. This is no accident. On the contrary, it provides a very clear insight into what the problem of reference has generally been taken to be.

We have seen that there is presumably a straightforward causal answer to the question of what relates the jackdaw's rattle to its referent. It is also possible to argue that there must be a relatively simple answer to the question of what relates Figure 4-3 to the objects it is capable of representing. But, now, what is to be said about the relation of the word "face" to its referent? To say that the relation is conventional is not to *explain* the relation but only to say that any acceptable explanation must account for its alterability-in-principle. Even to claim that the relation is *literally* the consequence of a tacit convention among speakers would leave open such questions as what the alleged conventions are, how they are learned, and what psychological mechanisms are involved when a speaker behaves in conformity with them. The notion that "conventional" reference relations literally rest upon conventions thus accounts for their alterability but for nothing else.[3]

To put the matter crudely, it is obvious what sticks signs to their significates: the glue is either causation or resemblance. That is why—bar-

---

[3] Probably, however, the social contract theory of language is no more intended to be taken literally than is the social contract theory of government. Indeed, so taken, the two theories suffer from analogous flaws.

ring worries about the nature of resemblance—no one has ever thought there was a problem about how signs refer. There *is* such a problem for symbols, however, since the conventional nature of the relation between a symbol and its referent apparently precludes attributing it either to a natural law or to resemblance, and it is unclear what other sorts of relations could account for reference. The problem thus has the form of a dilemma: the reference relations we can reasonably claim to understand depend upon causation or resemblance. Hence they cannot hold between arbitrarily selected objects. But the defining property of a symbol is that it *is* an arbitrarily selected object which, nevertheless, succeeds in referring.

Not only does the contrast between signs and symbols illuminate the connection between the problem of reference and the doctrine of conventionality, it also points to the form of traditional solutions of the problems of reference. Almost without exception, classical attempts to deal with reference have tried to break the dilemma by showing that the conventional relation between words and their referents can in fact be reduced to one or the other or both of the natural relations which hold between signs and their significates. That is, it has been almost universally assumed that the proper solution to the problem of reference must consist in showing how the relation between a word and its referent can, after all, be explained in terms of cause and effect, or resemblance, or both. The tantalizing analogy between signs and symbols has had so powerful a grasp on students of language that it has only been very recently recognized that the analogy may, in fact, be thoroughly misleading.

The terms of the problem admit of only three ways that one might try to reduce conventional relations to natural ones. One might say that the symbol-referent relation can be explained (1) by an appeal to causation and resemblance operating jointly, (2) by an appeal to resemblance operating alone, or (3) by an appeal to causation operating alone. Not surprisingly, all three positions have been occupied at one time or another. We shall review each in some detail.

(1) REFERENCE EXPLAINED BY APPEAL TO CAUSATION AND RESEMBLANCE

The view that the relation of a word to its referent can be accounted for by a simultaneous appeal to the notions of causation and resemblance is characteristic of the philosophy of language shared by the British empiricists and by the psychologists whom they directly influenced.

To understand what empiricists say about reference, it is necessary to bear in mind the following complication. For the empiricist, the referent of a word is characteristically a mental content. In particular, what a word refers to is either a *simple idea* (as: red, moist, bitter, or some other sensation, or "qualia"); or a *complex idea* (as: the idea of a particular material object or of a particular person) which is in turn presumed to be reducible in principle to some concatenation of simple ideas; or an *abstract idea* (as: the idea of color, triangularity, etc.) which is supposed to be the idea of a common property of the members of a set of simple or complex ideas.

Though it must be borne in mind in reading the empiricists that everything they say is, so to speak, at one degree of remove from the world—so that what "box" refers to is not boxes but the mental idea or representation of boxes—it should also be mentioned that this feature of the empiricists' idealism is not intrinsic to their view of language. It is rather a carryover from their doctrines about epistemology according to which our knowledge of objects is indirect via

> *our senses* [which] conversant about particular sensible objects, do *convey into the mind* several distinct *perceptions* of things, according to those various ways wherein those objects do affect them [pp. 77–78] ... since there appear not to be any *ideas* in the mind before the senses have conveyed any in, I conceive that *ideas* in the understanding are coeval with *sensation*; which is such an impression or motion made in some part of the body, as produces some perception in the understanding [Locke, in 1960 edition, vol. 1, p. 89].

Upon the distinction between simple, abstract, and complex ideas mentioned above, empiricists superimposed a further distinction between sensory impressions and perceptions on the one hand and memories, thoughts, reflections, etc., on the other.[4] It is extremely characteristic of the movement that this was held to be a distinction of degree rather than of kind. A recollection of an object agrees with a perception of the object in being a mental image. It differs only in the force, vivacity, liveliness, etc., with which the image presents itself. Thus Hume wrote (1739):

> All the perceptions of the human mind resolve themselves into two distinct kinds,

---

[4] Certain unavoidable confusions enter into any exposition of the empiricists as a result of their failure to agree upon a uniform terminology. We have followed Locke in using "idea" as a coverword for any mental content. It is thus possible to save "impression" as a synonym for "sensation" or "perception," where these latter words have something like their current psychological meaning. Hume (1739), on the other hand, uses "perception" where we have "idea," "idea" where we have "memory," "thought," or "reflection," and "impression" for "any sensation, passion, [or] emotion." The modern notion of a percept has no very important role in Hume, largely because the only sort of organization of sensory input Hume envisages is the summation of atomic "simple ideas" into molecular "complex ideas." Insofar as anything in Hume corresponds to perceptual integration, it is perhaps forming a complex impression.

which I shall call *impressions* and *ideas*. The difference betwixt these consists in the degrees of force and liveliness, with which they strike upon the mind, and make their way into our thought or consciousness. Those perceptions, which enter with most force and violence, we may name *impressions*; and, under this name, I comprehend all our sensations, passions, and emotions as they make their first appearance in the soul. By *ideas*, I mean the faint images of these in thinking and reasoning; such as, for instance, are all the perceptions excited by the present discourse, excepting only those which arise from the sight and touch, and excepting the immediate pleasure or uneasiness it may occasion [p. 11 in 1960 edition].

And again:

The first circumstance that strikes my eye, is the great resemblance betwixt our impressions and ideas in every other particular, excepting their degree of force and vivacity. The one seem to be, in a manner, the reflexion of the other; so that all the perceptions of the mind are double, and appear both as impressions and ideas [p. 12 in 1960 edition].

Hume proceeds to qualify this remark by noting that some *complex* ideas may exist as objects of imagination or reflection though they never existed as impressions. But though my complex idea of a unicorn has no sensory counterpart, it is to be supposed that each of the constituent simple ideas (white, having a horn, having four legs, etc.) from which that complex is constructed must have entered the mind as a sensation. The empiricist principle, correctly stated, is not that there is no idea that does not originate in sensation, but rather that there is no such *simple* idea.[5]

After the most accurate examination of which I am capable, I venture to affirm, that the rule here holds without any exception, and that every simple idea has a simple impression, which resembles it, and every simple impression a correspondent idea [p. 13 in 1960 edition].

Such passages form the groundwork for the empiricist theory of reference: the edifice is completed with the assumption of the usual associationistic principles of psychological causation, in particular the principle that "two objects are connected together in the imagination . . . when the one is immediately . . . contiguous to . . . the other [in experience]" (Hume, p. 20 in 1960 edition). Granted this principle, the empiricist may now argue as follows. First, the utterance of a word (i.e., the occurrence of an acoustic sensory image of a word) causes in the hearer memory images of whatever perceptions have previously been frequently associated with utterances of that word. Such would be the

---

[5] We are leaving out of consideration as irrelevant to our discussion the so-called ideas of reflection which were supposedly derived not from sensations but from the mind's introspective examination of its own processes.

image of a bed which presumably arises in the mind of anyone who has very often heard the word "bed" uttered simultaneously with perceiving a bed, or the image of a car which presumably arises in the mind of anyone who has often heard the word "car" uttered simultaneously with perceiving a car, and so on through the entire vocabulary. But second, the memory image elicited by a word resembles, and thus can represent, the sensory contents to which the word refers. Roughly, "bed" refers to beds because its utterances elicit memory images which resemble beds.

It will be remembered that, according to our analysis, the classical problem of reference arises from the conventional character of the relation between a word and its referent, and solutions of the problem have traditionally been attempts to reduce this conventional relation to "natural" relations of resemblance or causation, or both. We can now see how closely this analysis fits the empiricist approach. For while, in the empiricist's view, the relation between a word and its referent is conventional, the relation between a word and the memory image it evokes is presumably not. This latter relation is supposed to be mediated by the operation of psychological laws of association, and has thus as much claim to be rooted in a law of nature as the relation between smoke and fire. Moreover, just as the relation between a word and the memory image it elicits is a "natural" one, so too is the relation between a memory image and its corresponding sensory image. For this relation is explicitly one of resemblance: what makes a memory a memory and not a sensory impression is its relative lack of force and vivacity. But what makes it a memory of one sensory impression rather than another is precisely the resemblance it bears to that impression.

It is thus the empiricist's view that though reference is a conventional rather than a natural relation, it may nevertheless be explained solely by appeal to the natural relations of causation and resemblance. Though words do not themselves resemble their referents and are not directly causally connected to them, each word *is* causally connected with a memory image and that image *does* resemble the referent of the word.

Despite its reduction of reference to the natural relations of causation and resemblance, the empiricist's theory succeeds in accounting for the conventionality (i.e., for the alterability-in-principle) of the word-referent relation. Since the principle of association purports to hold for *arbitrarily* selected pairs of ideas (since, that is, it states that *any* two ideas that are sufficiently frequently conjoined will eventually tend to evoke one another), it follows that no restrictions are placed upon the acoustic shape of a word by any feature of its referent. Hence, given the appropriate training of speakers, any pronounceable sequence of sounds could be used in place of any other. But, as we saw above, this is precisely what is meant when it is claimed that the reference relation is arbitrary or conventional.

The empiricist theory of language thus manages to resolve the dilemma that we saw was at the heart of the traditional construal of the puzzle about reference. On the one hand, it accounts for the fact that words can stand for things without resorting to any relation not already required to account for the bond between natural signs and their significates. On the other hand, it achieves this without prejudice to the conventional character of the word-referent relation. In short, it shows how the meaning of a word might be accounted for by causation and resemblance without denying that it is an historical accident that a word means what it does.

Moreover, it is clear that we must credit the empiricists with having devised the first "two-stage," or "mediational," account of meaning. A memory image is properly described as a mediator between a word—to which it is related as effect to cause—and the referent of the word which, presumably, it resembles. In effect, the empiricist is arguing that it is not words but the memory images associated with words which, in the first instance, have referents. It is the employment of such images to mediate the word-referent relation that is the characteristic feature of the empiricist's approach to language. Given that the relation between a memory image and the sensory image it "refers" to is one of resemblance, there is presumably no more problem about how the former can stand for the latter than there is about how a portrait can represent its subject. Given that each word is causally associated with such a mediating image, the problem of reference is reduced to the problem of representation.

OBJECTIONS TO THE EMPIRICIST ACCOUNT

We have seen that it is essential to the empiricist view that words evoke images and that images resemble the referents of the words that evoke them. That the latter postulate has undesirable consequences was recognized rather early in the empiricist movement in connection with the problem of abstract or general ideas. It was Berkeley (1710) who first pointed out that if abstract ideas are supposed to represent common features of classes of objects, then images are uniquely unsuited to be the vehicle of such representations; for images are unalterably particular. Thus, it is clear how an image can represent, say, a particular triangle (i.e., by resembling the triangle more than it resembles any other). But it is unclear how an image can represent triangularity *in general*, since this would require it to resemble all triangles equally and simultaneously. To do this, the image would need to possess incompatible properties: e.g., it would have to be both scaline and obtuse, and this is clearly impossible.

Hume's solution to this difficulty was typical of the empiricists who followed Berkeley. In the case of an abstract idea, the vehicle of representation is indeed an image, but "the image in the mind is only that of a particular object, tho' the application of it in our reasoning be the same as if it were universal" (Hume, p. 28 in 1960 edition). Our image of triangularity is the image of a particular triangle, but we ignore its irrelevant details when we use it in reasoning about (or, presumably, in mediating references to) triangularity in general.

It seems unlikely that any of the empiricists recognized how enormous a concession was involved in this proposal. In the case of general terms it meant acknowledging that the mediator in reference must be not only an image but a set of rules for applying the image. In short, when an image mediates the reference of an abstract word, its relation to what it images cannot be accounted for solely on the basis of resemblance, for an image cannot resemble an abstract object. But if an appeal to rules for applying the image is essential to explaining how the image associated with "triangle" represents the abstract property of triangularity, then the program of reducing all cases of reference to natural relations has been tacitly abandoned.[6]

Moreover, to suggest that the vehicle of reference is *both* an image and rules for its application appears to be unnecessary, since if rules are allowed, the need for the image drops out. Consider, for example, the features of an image of a triangle that are relevant when the image is to be taken as a representation of triangularity in general. Among such features are having three sides and being a closed figure. Among the irrelevant features are the length of the sides and the size of the angles. In fact, the relevant features necessarily include just the defining features of triangles. In this sense, the rules which specify the features that an image must possess if it is to represent triangularity are equivalent to a general definition of "triangle." It is, however, unclear why a speaker who has associated such a definition with the word "triangle" would also need an image in order to use the word correctly to refer to triangles.

---

[6] On this point the psychologists were occasionally more faithful to the unadulterated image theory than were the philosophers. "Titchener is one of the few men who has ever claimed to see an image of Locke's abstract triangle . . . 'a flashy thing, come and gone from moment to moment: it hints 2 or 3 red angles with the red lines deepening into black, seen on a dark green ground. It is not there long enough for me to say whether the angles join to form the complete figure or even whether all 3 of the necessary angles are given'" [Titchener quoted by Brown (1958, p. 91)].

Since the word refers to all and only those things that satisfy the defini-tion, given the definition appeals to the image would be redundant. Thus, whatever heuristic role images may play in cognition (see, for ex-ample, Shepard and Chipman, 1970), it is clear that associating an image with a word is neither necessary nor sufficient for learning the referent of the word. We see in all this the beginnings of a redefinition of the problem of reference. Rather than attempt to reduce reference to a natural relation, what seems to be required is to explain referring as a species of rule-governed behavior. This is a point to which we shall presently re-turn.

Not only are images inadequate as the vehicles of reference in cases which involve abstract words, they are also notoriously unreliable. The content of the images associated with particular words seems to vary considerably from person to person; many subjects report no im-agery whatever in the course of normal conversations and some report none even when introspection is encouraged. Yet it will hardly do to say that this intersubjective variation indicates that speakers who belong to the same speech community and manage to communicate without difficulty nevertheless do not mean the same things by the words they use. It is a condition upon whatever state, object, psycholo-gical content, or mechanism we choose to identify with the meaning of a word that all speakers who communicate successfully by employing that word must have that state, object, content, or mechanism in com-mon. Hence interpersonal variation in the imagery associated with words is an argument for the semantic irrelevance of such imagery.

The incidental character of the imagery associated with words is brought out most strikingly by the fact that subjects occasionally report such images even in the case of words which cannot possibly be sup-posed to have referents. Thus, "Titchener's image of 'but' was of the back of the head of a speaker who often used this word while Titchener sat behind him on a platform" (Brown, 1958, p. 91). Such an association is doubly irrelevant: first, it is idiosyncratic and thus can have nothing to do with the linguistic meaning of "but"—a meaning that is presum-ably known by all speakers of English—and second, the knowledge speakers of English have of the meaning of "but" can not conceivably take the form of an image of its referent, since "but" does not have a ref-erent and does not mean anything that can be imaged.

In this respect image theory shares a common difficulty that all asso-ciationistic accounts of meaning are heir to: their intrinsic inability to provide a plausible answer to the question of how speakers arrive at a consensus about the meaning of words despite what must be very con-siderable differences in their linguistic experience. That such a con-sensus must be achieved is evident, since it is a precondition of com-munication. That it is unlikely to be accounted for by an associationistic model is evidenced by the prevalence of such idiosyncratic associations as those Titchener reports. Since, according to such theories, what a given speaker associates with a word is very much dependent upon what cooccurrences between utterances of that word and states of affairs happen to have been frequent in that speaker's experience, associationistic models automatically predict that the meanings of words ought to vary approximately as much as the personal histories of speakers do. Such theories are thus especially sensitive to features of personal history in determining their predictions about the meaning a speaker will associate with a word. But this feature of associationistic models makes them unfit for explaining the existence of communication within speech communities. A theory of language learning must account for our extraordinary achievement in speaking the same language despite considerable variation in the conditions under which we learn to talk.

What led to the abandonment of the empiricist approach to language was not, however, the sorts of arguments we have been discussing here. Rather, philosophers and psychologists arrived at a general methodological agreement to forego explanations that invoke mental contents like ideas and images in favor of explanations couched in terms of entities whose observation does not depend upon introspection. That the basis for the abandonment of the empiricist *solution* to the problem of reference was essentially methodological was important, since it meant that the integrity of the empiricists' *analysis* of the problem was never seriously challenged. In general, psychologists did not abandon the view that the problem of reference is that of providing *some* sort of reduction of conventional to natural relations. In fact, the empiricists' failure to provide a theory that accounts for reference in terms of causation and resemblance operating together was, somewhat paradoxically, interpreted as showing that reference must be accounted for as the result of one or the other operating alone. Thus, the history of the problem of reference in gestalt psychology has largely been an attempt to treat reference solely in terms of resemblance, and the history of the problem in learning theory has been largely an attempt to treat reference solely in terms of causation.

The attempt to account for reference in terms of causation alone is compatible with holding that the relation is essentially a conventional one. In particular, both the association of ideas and the conditioning of behavior provide for the possibility of establishing causal connections between events not previously so related. The essence of the principle of conventionality—that reference relations are alterable in principle—is thus preserved on a view of reference in which either mechanism plays the central role.

But adopting the view that reference is to be accounted for by an appeal to resemblance operating alone is tantamount to denying the conventionality of reference. If a word needs to resemble what it refers to, then it is not possible that any word whatever could refer to anything whatever. It is perhaps because holding that reference depends directly upon resemblance is not compatible with holding a version of the principle of conventionality that relatively few philosophers or psychologists have seriously defended this view.

(2) REFERENCE EXPLAINED BY APPEAL TO RESEMBLANCE ALONE

There are, nevertheless, some arguments for the resemblance theory, and these have often been stressed by psychologists in the gestalt tradition. The most striking of such arguments comes from the apparently universal occurrence of onomatopoeia. It appears that every language contains at least a few words the sound of which clearly imitates nonverbal sounds: "cuckoo," "splash," and so on, in English.

Direct onomatopoeia is, however, presumably too rarely a phenomenon to be of more than anecdotal interest from the point of view of a general theory of reference. While it need not be denied that onomatopoetic words provide a counterexample to the claim that reference is *universally* a purely conventional relation, they scarcely argue against the claim that reference is *characteristically* a conventional relation. Moreover, it must be stressed that onomatopoetic words do not violate the phonemic rules of the language in which they occur. If their relation to their referents is not fully conventional, it is at least conventionalized. Finally, what is striking about the sound systems of languages is that they are chosen from among an extremely limited subset of the vocalizations physiologically possible to a human being. This is precisely what one would *not* expect if imitation played any essential role in reference.

But though the sounds of words appear to be largely irrelevant to their semantic behavior, it is sometimes maintained that their more subtle "physiognomic" properties are not. Thus, Werner and Kaplan (1967) have claimed that

> At genetically early levels of representation, the vehicle is produced or taken as a mimetic facsimile of the referent: for example, there are the onomatopoetic vehicles that represent referents by phonemically imitating noises characteristic of the referents. A developmentally more advanced representation is indicated by a relation between vehicles and referents still formed by a bond of external "similarity" where, however, the similarity is carried by *different* modalities: thus, phonic properties may "synaesthetically" represent shapes, sizes, or colors of figures (for example, "zigzag"). Still more advanced genetically are representations by conventionalized patterns; here the external forms of vehicle and referent have lost most, if not all, of their surface similarity. Thus, there is a progressive distancing—a decrease in tangible "likeness"—between the external forms of vehicle and referent [pp. 47–48].

Werner and Kaplan also refer to Köhler's demonstration (1947) that subjects spontaneously recognize a relation between drawings of sharp objects and nonsense words like "takete." This is taken to point up the dynamic similarity of phenomena in different sensory modes in terms of which the resemblance between words and their referents is supposed to be explicated.

Two things need to be proved if this sort of view is to be taken seriously as an account of the nature of reference. First, that words and their referents do in fact characteristically share some underlying "dynamic similarity" despite the contrary surface appearances, and second that this similarity plays some part in establishing linguistic reference relations. The difficulty in demonstrating the first is, of course, that there is often no way of precluding the possibility that when words are treated as if they resemble objects, it is because the speaker has formed an associative bond between the word and the object, not because he has perceived an inherent dynamic similarity between them. If the resemblance theory is to be maintained, it must be shown that the perceived similarity between word and object is a *condition* rather than a *consequence* of the existence of a reference relation. To take one example, Werner and Kaplan claim that Kaden et al. (1955) have demonstrated that there is a characteristic error in judgments of the elevation of projected images of words like "climbing," and that this error is opposite in direction from that which infects similar judgments for words like "falling." They construe this as a demonstration of inherent dynamic similarity between a word and its referent. On their view, the result pertains to an effect of directional dynamics inherent in the perception of certain objects on the apparent location of words which designate those objects; the latter are seen relatively higher or lower depending on whether the dynamics of the former are upwards or downwards. Yet, it is unclear why the experiment must be interpreted this way, since we might equally hold that what has been demonstrated is just response transference from an object to the word which refers to it. Such transference would be predicted on the usual associationistic principle that responses characteristically elicited by a stimulus will, under appropriate circumstances, transfer to other stimuli with which it is paired.

The example quoted from Köhler cannot, however, plausibly be treated as a case of response generalization, since it concerns a response to a novel stimulus word. In this case, we do appear to be dealing with a spontaneous tendency to see cross-modal correspondences between acoustic and visual nonsense patterns. It might be argued that such tendencies represent the consequence of generalizations based upon repeated pairings of phonemically similar words with objects sharing certain nonlinguistic properties. That is, it might be maintained that "takete" suggests angularity to English speakers because tacks, tools, tips, and trowels are all often sharp. But, first, there is no empirical evidence that speakers will pair "maluma" and "takete" with the appropriate drawings only if their language contains many words that commence with *m* and refer to smooth objects and many words which commence with *t* and refer to sharp ones. Second, even if this could be shown, it would at best serve to replace the question of how cross-modal correspondences are to be accounted for with the question of why, if reference is an arbitrary relation, we should find so many cases where classes of words which partially correspond phonemically refer to partially similar objects.

However, the question raised by such examples is not only whether they show a spontaneous recognition of the "inherent similarity" of perceptual objects in different sensory modes, but also whether such correspondences are of more than marginal significance in determining meaning relations. Here it is worth noticing that there is no apparent tendency for full synonyms to exhibit phonemic features in common ("perhaps" and "maybe," "bachelor" and "unmarried man"), while, conversely, words that are literally phonemically identical ("box" as a verb and as a noun, "bank" when it refers to the institution and "bank" when it refers to the side of a river) need exhibit no similarity of referent. While such cases do not prove that the sort of similarity mentioned by Köhler and by Werner and Kaplan plays *no* role in the establishment of reference relations, they do show that the presence of such similarities is neither necessary nor sufficient to determine identity of reference.[7]

(3) SYMBOLS EXPLAINED BY APPEAL TO CAUSATION ALONE

Of the three possible treatments of reference in terms of the "natural" relations of causation and resemblance, the one most characteristic of contemporary psychological theory has been the attempt to account for reference just in terms of causation. In particular, reference is to be accounted for in terms of certain features of the conditioning of the behavior of speakers, when conditioning is thought of as establishing a causal relation between environmental stimuli and organic behaviors. On this view a word refers to an object if, first, speakers have been conditioned to respond to the presence of the object with utterances of the word and, second, speakers have been conditioned to respond to utterances of the word with behavior that would be appropriate to the object.

---

[7]For an extensive discussion of Werner and Kaplan's views, see Fodor (1964).

For the most part, there has been a clear consensus in American psychology that the stickleback which responds to an aggressive male by raising his spines, the rat which responds to an intense light by pressing a bar, and the human who tells the dentist to stop when the drilling begins to hurt, are all exhibiting essentially the same sort of behavior. In each case, either as the result of innate endowment or as the result of a history of conditioning, the organism is able to produce some quite specific response which may usually be relied upon to terminate aversive stimulation. Conversely, the stickleback which produces a fighting response when exposed to a schematic fish, the rat which learns to choose the door marked with a triangle, the human who learns to bring his umbrella when the morning is cloudy, and the human who learns to bring his umbrella when the weather forecaster says "rain today" are also exhibiting behaviors that differ in degree of complexity but not in kind. In each case, the organism has either learned or developed the capacity to respond differentially on the basis of "natural" relations between the stimulus and some other object. The stickleback responds to the schematic fish because, to its benighted eyes, the schematic fish resembles the male stickleback to which its fighting response is innately associated. The rat chooses the door with the triangle because the experimenter has so arranged the causal contingencies that going through that door has regularly been followed by food. The human brings his umbrella in the first instance because it has previously been his experience that clouds are regularly followed by rain, and rain by unpleasant sensations. He brings his umbrella in the second instance because it has previously been his experience that utterances of the acoustic shape "rain today" are also regularly followed by rain and discomfort. As Osgood (1963a) summarized this view, "I believe . . . that we neither wish nor require *any special theory of language*. Just because language behavior is intimately associated with abstract thinking and symbolizing does not necessarily imply that it is different in kind from ordinary behavior" (p. 21).

The question we must thus investigate is whether this kind of causal theory of reference is tenable. In particular, we must ask whether it can be convincingly maintained that the relation between a word and its referent is that of a conditioned response to its discriminative stimulus.

To begin with, while there can be no objection to considering the verbalizations of fluent speakers to be "linguistic responses," one must not suppose that, in this context, "response" means what it usually means: "A stimulus-occasioned act. An [act] correlated with stimuli, whether the correlation is untrained or the result of training."[8] On the

---

[8] This is the definition given in standard texts like Hilgard and Marquis (1940).

contrary, a striking feature of linguistic behavior is its freedom from the control of specifiable local stimuli or independently identifiable drive states. In typical situations, what is said may have no obvious relation whatever to stimulus conditions in the immediate locality of the speaker or to his recent history of deprivation or reward. Conversely, the situation in which such correlations *do* obtain (the man dying of thirst who predictably gasps "water!") are intuitively highly atypical.

Indeed, the evidence for the claim that linguistic responses are responses *in the strict sense* would appear to be nonexistent. There is no more reason to believe that the probability of an utterance of "book" is a function of the number of books in the immediate locale than there is to believe that the probability of an utterance of the word "person" or "thing" is a function of the number of persons or things in view. Lacking such evidence, what prompts one to these beliefs is, first, a confusion of the strict sense of "response" ("a stimulus-correlated act") with the loose sense in which the term applies to *any* bit of behavior, stimulus-correlated or otherwise, and second, a philosophy of science which erroneously supposes that unless all behavior is held to consist of responses in the strict sense, some fundamental canon of scientific method is violated. But the claim that behavior consists solely of responses cannot be established on methodological grounds alone. On the contrary, such a claim constitutes an extremely general (and quite implausible) empirical hypothesis about the extent to which behavior is under the control of specifiable local stimulation.

It is implausible because it would seem, prima facie, that the way an organism behaves is characteristically determined not just by the state of its local environment but also by its mental states—in particular, by its beliefs and its utilities. If this is true, then the output an organism will supply for a given input cannot, in general, be predicted unless we know what mental state the organism is in. In the case of complex organisms, where internal states play a preponderant role in the selection of behavior, there is no reason to expect that responses should prove to be correlated with stimuli in any way at all.

This point is absolutely fundamental, since it implies that what one has learned when one has learned the semantic structure of one's language *cannot* be a set of response contingencies. On the contrary, the response dispositions characteristic of two speakers of the same language may differ arbitrarily insofar as their beliefs or their utilities differ. If what we are disposed to utter when exposed to a particular stimulus is determined by an *interaction* of our knowledge of word meanings with our beliefs and our utilities, then knowing the meaning of a word cannot be identified with being disposed to utter that word in specified stimulus situations.

The second inadequacy of simple conditioning models of language is also a consequence of the identification of verbalizations with responses. In laboratory situations, an organism is said to have mastered a response when it can be shown that it produces any of an indefinite number of functionally equivalent acts under the appropriate stimulus conditions. That some reasonable notion of functional equivalence can be specified is essential, since we cannot, in general, require of two actions that they be identical either in observable properties or in their physiological basis in order to be manifestations of the same response. Thus, a rat has "got" the bar-press response if and only if it habitually presses the bar upon food deprivation. Whether it presses with its left or right front paw or with 3 or 6 grams of pressure is, or may be, irrelevant. Training is to some previously determined criterion of homogeneity of performance, which is another way of saying that what we are primarily concerned with are functional aspects of the organism's behavior. In short, a response is so characterized as to establish an equivalence relation among the actions which can belong to it. Any response for which such a relation has *not* been established is ipso facto inadequately described.

We have just suggested that it is not in general possible to find stimuli with which verbal responses are reliably correlated. It may now be remarked that it is not in general possible to determine when two utterances are functionally equivalent; i.e., when they are instances of the same verbal response. This point is easily overlooked, since it is natural to suppose that functional equivalence of verbal responses can be established on the basis of phonetic or phonemic identity. That is, however, untrue. Just as two physiologically distinct actions may both be instances of a bar-press response, so, it is perfectly obvious, two phonemically distinct utterances may be functionally equivalent for a given speaker or in a given language. Innumerable examples of suitable synonymous expressions (e.g. "brother" and "male sibling," "perhaps" and "maybe") can be produced by any speaker. Conversely, just as an action is not an instance of a bar-press response (however much it may resemble actions that are) unless it bears the correct functional relation to the bar, so may two phonemically identical utterances (as, for example, "bank" in "the bank is around the corner" and "The plane banked at fifty-five degrees"), when syntactic and semantic considerations are taken into account, prove to be instances of quite different verbal responses.

The problem of establishing identity conditions for verbal responses is compounded by a further consideration. There are, in general, indefinitely many ways of referring to a given thing (e.g., indefinitely many distinct English phrases which have a common referent). It seems obvious that not every such phrase can have been associatively coupled with the object referred to in the history of each speaker of the language. In short, just as associative theories fail to account for the productivity of the sentences in a natural language, so too they fail to account for the productivity of its referring expressions.[9]

Again, the identification of verbalizations with responses suffers from the difficulty that verbalizations do not normally admit of such indices of response strength as frequency, intensity, and resistance to extinction. It is obvious, but nevertheless pertinent, that "meaningfulness" in the technical associationist sense has nothing to do with meaningfulness *tout court*; that verbal responses which are equally part of the speaker's repertoire may differ vastly in their relative frequency of occurrence ("heliotrope" and "and" are examples in the case of the author's ideolects), that intensity and frequency do not covary (the morpheme in an utterance receiving emphatic stress is not particularly likely to be a conjunction, article, preposition, etc., yet these "grammatical" morphemes are easily the most frequently occurring ones); and that extinction of verbal responses is extremely rare except in such pathologies as aphasia. What is perhaps true is that one can vary the frequency or intensity of a verbal response by the usual techniques of selective reinforcement (cf. Krasner, 1958). This shows that verbal behavior can be conditioned, but it lends no support to the hypothesis that semantic relations are fundamentally associative.

There would thus appear to be very little or no basis for the view that the referent of a word is a discriminative stimulus prone to raise the probability of utterances of the word. There would seem to be still less basis for the view that understanding a word consists in being prone to produce a characteristic form of behavior when the word is uttered (e.g., that understanding a word is responding to it in ways that would be appropriate to its referent). It is literally the case that no one has ever provided a plausible candidate for the relevant "characteristic" behavior for any word in any language. And, everyone knows that in the vast majority of cases, the answer to the question "What do we do when people speak?" is "Listen."

---

[9] It might be supposed that we can identify response types by adopting the principle that two responses are of the same type just in case they are under the control of the same stimulus. But, as we remarked above, a given stimulus may elicit any response (or none), depending upon the beliefs and utilities of the responding organism. One of the more vicious circles that conditioning theories are prone to is that of identifying response types by reference to the presumed controlling stimulus, and then identifying the controlling stimulus by reference to the type of response it elicits.

REDEFINITION OF THE PROBLEM: REFERRING AS RULE-GOVERNED BEHAVIOR

We have now considered three sorts of attempts to show that the relation between a word and its referent can be accounted for either by an appeal to resemblance or by an appeal to causation or by both. We have seen that such attempts are motivated by a certain analysis of the problem of reference: the problem is to show that the relations that confer meaning upon signs also confer meaning upon symbols.

This analysis may, after all, prove to be correct. But the failure of three sorts of theories which accept it to provide an adequate account of reference surely argues against that possibility. We might, therefore, tentatively raise the question: What options would remain if we were to abandon the analysis; if, that is, we were to give up the view that a correct theory of meaning must demonstrate either that a relation of resemblance connects a word to its referent or that a relation of causation does?

Consider playing tag. Children who learn to play this game also learn when it is appropriate to designate someone as *it*. Learning this would appear to be a perfectly legitimate case of learning how to apply a noun to its referent: being *it* is, from a semantic point of view, comparable to being president: like "president," "it" is a title for which practically anyone of a certain age may qualify, though only one person may hold it at a time.

What is interesting about this rather frivolous example is that it is so clearly misdescribed by any of the kinds of theories of reference we have been discussing. For example, it is simply irrelevant to whether or not a child has learned to use the word "it" that he has or has not got images when he hears "it" uttered. It is, of course, relevant to deciding whether he has learned the word that he respond correctly to utterances of "it." But this surely does not mean that he must respond to utterances of "it" the way he responds to the player who is *it*, or that he must respond to the player who is *it* by uttering "it." On the contrary, the appropriate responses to the player who is *it* is not to say "it" but to run. Conversely, the occasions upon which it *is* appropriate to say "it" are, in large part, fixed by the rules of the game. Since alteration of these rules would alter the occasions on which "it" gets uttered, it is implausible to argue that any pattern of conditioning could be prerequisite to mastering the use of the word. Finally, it is not only irrelevant but absurd to ask whether, or in what way, the word "it" and the child who happens to *be it* resemble one another. To be the referent of "it" pro tem, all you need to be is in the game and slow on your feet. There is clearly no place here for an appeal to even the most refined sort of onomatopeia.

We can see that the theories of reference we have been discussing are irrelevant to explaining what the child learns when he learns how to use "it," because we know how to describe what he does in fact learn. What he learns is that a player is *it* just in case he is in the game and (1) he was chosen *it* at the beginning of the game and has touched no one in play since he was chosen, or (2) he was touched by someone who was *it* and has touched no one in play since. Granted that a child understands that a player is *it* only when one or another of these conditions is satisfied, no further question about the child's imagery or about his verbal or nonverbal responses need be raised. Learning that it is correct (i.e., *true*) to refer to a player as "it" only when one or another of these conditions is satisfied just *is* learning to determine the referent of "it" under the specialized conditions imposed by tag. To put the idea (only slightly) differently, what the child learns when he learns about "it" is a rule which determines necessary and sufficient conditions for the truth of sentences of the form "X is it"; i.e., X is *it*, for any X who is in the game, if and only if either 1 or 2 is a true description of X.

It is an open question to what extent this example offers a paradigm for learning the referent of words in less artificial cases. However, a number of interesting points arise upon the assumption that it is not atypical. In the first place, the question, "What is the nature of the bond that ties a word to its referent?" seems much less pressing once we maintain that reference as a feature of symbols is a different *kind* of property than reference as a feature of signs. If what makes an object the referent of a word is that it satisfies the conditions articulated by rules for using the word to make true statements, then there is no theoretical motivation for trying to find some reduction of reference to causation or resemblance. Involved in the notion that reference is essentially a relation determined by rules is the abandonment of the analogy between signs and symbols, an analogy which, as we have seen, has dominated much of the classical psycholinguistic literature.

Second, if learning the referent of a word involves learning rules that determine when the word is correctly or truly applied, there is reason to abandon the supposition that verbal behavior differs from paradigmatic conditioned behavior only in relative complexity. Conditioning models are notoriously unsuited for explaining the learning and application of rules. This is because the occasion for rule-governed behavior need not be identifiable in terms of any physical feature of the "stimulus" situation in which that behavior is appropriate. What makes a child *it* is his role in the game, and that is not a "stimulus property" of the child in the sense that his height or hair color are. Similarly, what makes a response conformable to a rule need not be identifiable in terms of the topology of the response. What distinguishes a pawn's move in chess from a rook's move is not some special feature of the gesture of the player's hand, it is the way the move is related to the rules of chess, to the board, and to the state of the game.

Third, implicating the notion of a linguistic rule in the explanation of reference is incompatible with the view that reference is a simple, primitive, and homogeneous relation. It is evident at once that three such different sorts of words as "John," "thief," and "today," though they may perhaps all be properly said to have referents, must be controlled by quite different sorts of reference rules.

Finally, on the view that reference is a rule-governed relation (or family of relations), it becomes relevant to ask how much information about the reference rules for a word can be elicited from an examination of, for example, the syntactic rules governing the word, and what interconnections may obtain between the reference rules and the rules that determine such other semantic features as synonymy, antonymy, copredicability, and so on. Seen in this light it is plausible to argue that reference may be determined by complicated interrelations between different sorts of linguistic rules and thus can best be studied only after those other rules are fairly clearly understood. Thus, it must be at least in part a consequence of the operation of syntactic rules that the Pope is referred to in "I want to meet the Pope" but not in "I want to be the Pope." A theory of reference adequate to deal with the asymmetry between such sentences will thus need to use information about their syntactic differences.

There is a moral to these reflections, fragmentary and unsatisfactory though they surely are. It is that the problem of reference is probably more like other problems about language than has traditionally been supposed. That is, it is likely that problems about reference, like problems about syntax and problems about phonology, are essentially problems about rule-governed behavior—problems which involve explaining how rules are learned and applied. But while this conclusion is agreeable in that it holds out the ultimate promise of an integrated treatment of the psychology of language, it must also be admitted that the part of cognitive psychology that is currently least well understood is precisely that part which concerns the assimilation and manipulation of rules. If, as we have been trying to suggest, there is very little in contemporary psychological theories of reference that was not proposed by Locke and refuted by Berkeley, that is perhaps because most psychologists have supposed that reference is the one part of linguistic competence that can be forced to fit familiar learning paradigms. But as the analogies and interdependencies between reference and other linguistic relations becomes clearer, one is increasingly impressed both with the coherence of language structure and with the inadequacy of current psychological models to cope with it.

PART TWO. SEMANTICS IN GENERATIVE GRAMMAR

THE GOALS OF SEMANTIC ANALYSIS: PRELIMINARY FORMULATION

The discussion in the first half of this chapter implicitly assumed that *words* (or, at any event, lexical formatives) are the linguistic entities with whose behavior semantic theories are primarily concerned. We have explored this assumption at such length because it has been common to practically all psychological accounts of linguistic meaning. Nor is the existence of this traditional consensus unintelligible. If words are the minimal meaningful linguistic elements, it is natural to assume that the behavior of words is what semantic theories seek, in the first instance, to explain.

But whatever may be the case with *meaning*, there are a variety of other semantic properties which are exhibited not by words but by *sentences*. As we noted in Chapter 1, it is by employing sentences that we unambiguously effect such acts as making assertions or asking questions, giving orders or issuing denials, promising, referring, implying, presupposing, and the rest. It is thus at the level of the sentence rather than the word that we first encounter the appropriate linguistic vehicle for saying things that are true or false, asking questions that are pertinent or otherwise, making promises that are or are not binding, and so on. Insofar as a semantic theory concerns itself with the analysis of performances like these, the natural domain of such a theory is the sentences of a language rather than its lexicon.

It is not simply a matter of taste whether one decides to treat sentences or words as the primary objects for semantic analysis. Rather, one's decision on this issue is likely to determine the general character of the semantic theory one espouses. If, for example, one takes the utterance of single words as the paradigm of language behavior, one must perforce look for the essence of word meaning in a relation between words and nonlinguistic objects. Thus, in Part 1 of this chapter, we reviewed a number of theories according to which the paradigmatic speech act is that of naming something and the paradigmatic semantic relation is one which is alleged to hold between a word and the thing it names; i.e., the relation by virtue of which a word symbolizes, stands for, or refers to something nonlinguistic.

If, on the other hand, we assume that the *sentence* is the primary vehicle of linguistic communication, and that speech acts like making assertions are the paradigms of verbal behavior, our conception of word meaning will be correspondingly altered. To give the meaning of a word, in this latter view, is not to specify the object it names. Rather, it is to give an account of the effect that the presence of the word has in determining what speech acts can be performed with sentences in which it occurs. In short, a representation of the semantic properties of a *sentence* determines the class of speech acts the sentence can be used to perform. A representation of the semantic properties of a *word* determines the effect the word has upon the semantic properties of sentences which contain it. The meanings of sentences are thus related to the meaning of words by the following principle: one determinant of the speech acts which can be performed by uttering a given sentence is the lexical content of that sentence.

For example, the assertion standardly made by uttering (4-1) is different from the assertion standardly made by uttering (4-2). We can see

4-1   The cat is on the mat.

4-2   The dog is on the mat.

this if only from the fact that the conditions under which the former assertion is true are different from, and logically independent of, the conditions under which the latter assertion is true. Now, this difference in truth conditions is surely attributable to differences of meaning between the words "cat" and "dog." In the present view, specifying the meanings of "cat" and "dog" involves formulating principles which account for the difference in truth conditions exhibited by the assertions standardly made with sentences like (4-1) and (4-2). More generally, what is wanted is a rule which at least determines how the truth conditions of sentences having the form ϕ (*dog*) differ from the truth conditions upon sentences of the form ϕ (cat).[10] As a first approximation, knowledge of such a rule might well be identified with knowledge of how "cat" and "dog" differ in meaning.[11] In this kind of theory, as Quine has elegantly remarked, representations of the meaning of words are "mere clauses in recursive definitions of the meaning of sentences."

We are thus making four assumptions: first, that speech acts such as making assertions are the paradigms of verbal behavior; second, that

---

[10] It will be convenient to speak of the "truth conditions upon a sentence" as a shorthand for the "truth conditions upon the assertion the sentence is standardly used to make." This way of talking masks some difficult problems, admittedly.

[11] For an extended treatment which seeks to handle the relation between word meaning and sentence meaning in this general way, see Ziff (1960). See also the review by Katz (1962).

the characteristic linguistic vehicle for the performance of a speech act is a sentence; third, that the theoretically important semantic properties of a sentence are those which determine what speech acts it is standardly used to perform; and fourth, that the semantic properties of a sentence are themselves determined, in part, by its lexical content.

These suggestions are evidently in need of sharpening, and we will return to them presently. But it should already be clear that they run counter to the entire tradition which sees the study of the semantics of natural languages as a branch of "semiotics" (i.e., of a science which concerns itself primarily with the relations between signs and what they signify). In particular, they run counter to the kinds of accounts of linguistic meaning discussed in Part 1 of this chapter. It has seemed evident to many psychologists that the paradigm of speech behavior is the utterance of a word that names some stimulus, and that the primary goal of a semantic theory must therefore be to enumerate the stimulus variables which control such verbalizations. The contrary view will be explored in what follows. It holds that language relates to the world primarily at the sentence level, that the paradigm of this sort of relation is achieved when a speaker performs a speech act correctly (e.g., uses a sentence to say something true about the world), and that to give the meaning of a word cannot be to characterize the stimuli that elicit it, since practically any stimulus could elicit practically any word, given an appropriately motivated speaker. Rather, to give the meaning of a word is to characterize the kinds of contributions its presence makes to determine the semantic properties of the sentences in which it occurs.

The following may be suggested, then, as a preliminary formulation of the goals a semantic theory of a natural language should be required to meet. In the first place, it should enumerate (and, presumably, define) the semantic properties that the sentences of the language can exhibit. In particular, it should enumerate the types of speech acts that sentences can be used to perform, together with the conditions necessary and sufficient for their successful performance. If, for example, promising is a kind of speech act that certain of the sentences in a language are standardly used to perform, then a semantic theory of the language should state the conditions under which the utterance of such a sentence counts as making a promise. [For examples of attempts to provide analyses of this kind, see Searle (1969).]

The second constraint a semantic theory might plausibly be required to meet is that it explain how the semantic properties of particular sentences are determined by their lexical contents. There are indefinitely many sentences of a given natural language; and, barring sentential synonyms, each sentence is associated with a different bundle of semantic properties; in particular, each sentence is the standard linguistic vehicle for a distinctive speech act.[12] Given the usual idealizations, a fluent speaker is able to determine which sentence is the appropriate linguistic vehicle for each such act. Hence, to explain how the content of a sentence determines the speech acts that it can be used to perform is part of explaining the speaker-hearer's ability to produce and understand novel sentences. Presumably, such an explanation refers that ability to the speaker-hearer's knowledge of the lexicon of his language and of the compositional mechanisms whereby the semantic properties of sentences are determined by the meanings of the lexical items they contain.

However, neither of these suggestions about the goals of semantic analysis will do as they stand. To begin with, any enumeration of the possible semantic properties of sentences must belong to "general linguistic theory" rather than to the semantic analyses of particular natural languages. Just as, at the level of syntactic description, some sentences in every natural language may be described as "grammatical," or "imperative," or "containing a nominalization," etc., so, too, at the level of semantic analysis, some sentences in every natural language can be described as standardly used to perform such speech acts as stating, ordering, asking, promising, and so on. In the former case, it is natural to argue that the problem of defining universal syntactic properties belongs to the syntactic component of general linguistic theory and not to the grammar of any particular natural language. This suggestion applies equally to the definition of whatever kinds of speech acts sentences are universally available to perform; since reference to these speech acts is required for the description of the semantic properties of sentences in any language whatever, the problem of enumerating and defining them belongs to general linguistic theory rather than to the semantic analysis of particular natural languages.

We might suggest that what *does* belong to the semantic analysis of a particular natural language is the task of showing how the semantic properties of each of the sentences of the language are determined by

---

[12] Strictly speaking, each sentence will be associated with a certain speech act by virtue of its distinctive syntactic form and lexical content, and with a variety of speech acts simply by virtue of its being a sentence. Thus, any sentence can be said ironically, any sentence can be quoted, etc. Similarly, there is a class of speech acts which is associated with sentences by virtue of quite general properties of their structure: any sentence that can be used to ask a question can be used to ask a rhetorical question, many sentences that can be used to express a wish can be used to express a demand, and so on. There are a variety of subtleties concerning the relation between sentences and their standard uses that we shall ignore in what follows, and these are among them.

the meanings of the words of which the sentence is composed. However, this formulation is defective too. As we have seen throughout this book, to understand a sentence it is necessary to know more than just the meaning of the words that it contains. One must also know what syntactic structural description the sentence bears. Since, for example, (4-3) differs in meaning from (4-4), it must be not merely the words in a

4-3   John loves Mary.

4-4   Mary loves John.

sentence but also its higher-level constituents and the grammatical relations which obtain among them that determine the semantic properties of the sentence.

We thus arrive at something like the following view: the goal of a semantic theory of a natural language is to explain how the semantic properties of its sentences are determined by their lexical content and syntactic structure. That is, a semantic theory of language L may be thought of as a device which, given a full syntactic structural description of any sentence in L and a specification of the lexical items it contains, automatically predicts the semantic properties of the sentence. The properties a semantic theory may assign to a sentence in the language it describes are themselves enumerated and defined by the semantic component of general linguistic theory. And, in every case, the semantic properties assigned a sentence will be those which determine the speech acts it is standardly used to perform.

A word needs to be said about the notion of the *standard* use of a sentence. Since indefinitely many of the sentences in a language are never uttered, to say that a sentence is *standardly* used to perform a certain speech act is not to say that it is *frequently* used to perform that speech act. Rather, a sentence is standardly associated with a certain speech act if the fact that it can be used to perform that speech act is determined solely by its syntactic form and lexical content. Thus, as semanticists, we are interested in such facts as that (4-1) can be used to assert of some contextually determined cat that is on the mat; and that (4-5) can be used

4-5   Is the cat on the mat?

to ask if some contextually determined cat is on the mat, etc. We are not, however, interested in such facts as that either sentence could be used, by prearrangement, as a code phrase meaning, say, "meet me by the fountain at four in the morning." The speech act of asserting the cat is on the mat is associated with (4-1) solely by virtue of the syntactic form and lexical content of that sentence. That is why any speaker who knows English can determine, by virtue of his linguistic knowledge alone, that (4-1) is the (an) appropriate linguistic vehicle for making that assertion. And that is why an adequate semantic theory of English must show how that sentence and that assertion are paired.

THE GOALS OF SEMANTIC ANALYSIS (continued)

We shall want to consider, in barest outline, how a theory might operate to associate sentences of a natural language with representations which formally determine the class of speech acts that they are standardly used to perform. Preliminary to doing so, let us ask what this requirement comes to in the special case of declarative sentences.

Many declarative sentences are standardly used to make assertions, and it is presumably a truism that using a sentence to make an assertion is using it to commit oneself to the claim that a certain state of affairs obtains. To say what that state of affairs is, is normally to give the content of the assertion. Thus, one way a semantic theory might seek to characterize the declarative sentences of a language is by assigning to each a representation which determines what a speaker would standardly be taken to commit himself to were he to use the sentence to make an assertion.

Consider a simple example. If a man makes the assertion standardly made by using the form of words in sentence (4-6), he is thereby committed to the assertion standardly made by using the form of words in (4-7) and to the assertion standardly made by using the form of words in (4-8). That is, he cannot consistently make the first assertion and

4-6   John went to the store and Mary went to the store.

4-7   John went to the store.

4-8   Mary went to the store.

deny either of the latter two. Similarly, he cannot consistently make the first statement and deny the statements standardly made by using such forms of words as in (4-9), (4-10), (4-11), etc.

4-9   John went somewhere.

4-10   Mary did something.

4-11   John did something that Mary did.

When two sentences are so related that whoever uses the first to make the statement that it is standardly used to make is thereby committed to the truth of the statement that the second is standardly used to make, we will say that the first sentence *entails* the second. We can now say that an important goal of a semantic theory is to assign to each sentence which is standardly used to make an assertion a representation that formally determines its entailments. Understanding such a sentence, on this view, either is or involves computing such a representation.[13] In particular, understanding such a sentence involves recovering whatever features of its grammatical structure and lexical content are relevant to determining what must be true if the statement standardly made by using the sentence is true.[14]

But, it might be argued, this is to require at once too little and too much. Too little because there are meaningful sentences (like interrogatives, imperatives, and certain types of declaratives) which are *not* standardly used to make assertions, and a semantic theory ought to say something about them; too much because the notion that what one is committed to by asserting a sentence is determined, at least in part, by the semantic properties of that sentence may itself be tendentious.

The former of these objections need not much concern us, first, because a semantic theory that works only for specified types of declaratives is clearly better than no semantic theory at all, and second,

---

[13] The present suggestion is that understanding a sentence involves computing a representation *which formally determines* the entailments of that sentence; not that it involves computing those entailments. This distinction is important, since every sentence that has any entailments has indefinitely many, and understanding a sentence must not be represented as requiring more than a finite amount of computation.

[14] This is not quite to say that a representation of a sentence which formally determines its entailments is ipso facto a representation of its meaning. For if that were so, then any pair of sentences that entail one another would be synonymous, and this appears not to be true. It is, for example, at best dubious that (*a*) and (*b*) are synonymous. On

  a Two is larger than one.
  b The only even prime is larger than one.

the contrary, one is inclined to say that the assertion standardly made by using (*a*) is distinct from the assertion standardly made by using (*b*) though, in point of logic, each of these statements is true if and only if the other is.

  Such cases suggest that we need a notion of sentential *synonymy* such that assertions of synonymous sentences are identical assertions and such that mutual entailment ("logical equivalence") of sentences is a necessary but not sufficient condition for their synonymy.

  As things stand, however, it is a moot point whether a distinction between synonymy and logical equivalence can be made clear. [Clear intuitions are hard to come by in this area. For example, is a passive sentence synonymous with its corresponding active or merely logically equivalent to it? Prima facie, (*c*) says something about John, while (*d*) says something about the ball. So, it might be argued, actives and

  c John hit the ball.
  d The ball was hit by John.

passives are converses, not synonyms.]

because it is quite likely that declaratives of the type standardly used for making assertions are the fundamental sentence types from the point of view of semantic analysis. A semantic theory might well seek to treat questions by reference to the class of declaratives that would serve as their possible answers, promises by reference to the class of declaratives the promiser obligates himself to make true, etc.

One must, however, take the second objection more seriously. It is that no clear sense can be made of the claim that among the various commitments one undertakes by asserting a sentence, there are some which derive solely from the linguistic structure of the sentence that one asserts.

Theorists who have made this objection have usually done so on the grounds that it is de facto impossible to distinguish such commitments from others which are undertaken by asserting a sentence but which cannot be attributed solely to the meaning of the sentence. It might, for example, plausibly be maintained that anyone who asserts (4-12) thereby commits himself to the claim that someone or something has moved his briefcase. Yet that commitment surely cannot be a consequence

4-12 My briefcase isn't where I left it.

(merely) of the semantic properties of the sentence asserted. It is, rather, a consequence of our shared belief that briefcases do not move themselves (or just disappear, etc.), and *that* belief derives, in turn, from

---

There is, however, at least a pious hope that there will prove to be a formally distinguishable subclass of the logically equivalent sentences which can plausibly be identified with the synonymous ones (for example, sentences which differ only in synonymous lexical items, sentences which differ only in "stylistic" transformations such as passive or extraposition, sentences which have identical base structures). After all, the rules which assign semantic representations to sentences must be "compositional" [see Katz and Fodor (1963)] in the sense that they must make such assignments on the basis of the lexical and syntactic structure of the sentences to which they apply. Since such rules must also be general in the sense that they apply to *every* sentence in the language, it is quite conceivable that of the indefinitely many logically equivalent representations of a sentence, there may be only one which reasonably simple and general rules can compositionally associate with the sentence. If that should prove to be true, then we would have theoretical justification for saying that sentences which receive the same such representation are synonymous and are standardly used to make the same assertions, while sentences whose representations are formally distinct but interconvertible by valid rules are merely logically equivalent. Of course, this begs very deep questions about what shall count as a semantic rule and what shall count as a rule of logic, but it is not self-evident that such questions are in principle unanswerable.

what we know about briefcases, not from what we know about English [see (4-13)].

4-13   My turtle isn't where I left it.

Is there, then, any reason to believe that those commitments we undertake solely by asserting a sentence with a certain linguistic form can be distinguished from those that are consequences of nonlinguistic beliefs we share with other members of our speech community? That is, is there any reason to believe that a clear line of division can be drawn between the semantic structure of a natural language and the cognitive structure of the speaker-hearers who use the language? This is not an innocent question, and it is not one we can resolve here. Suffice it to make one or two remarks which may justify begging a more extensive treatment.

To begin with, there appear to be cases in which it is simply indubitable that the validity of an inference is determined solely by the fact that the sentences in which it is couched have a certain lexical and syntactic structure. We are thinking not only of such traditional examples of analytic inferences as (4-14), where the entailment relation turns on the meanings of certain of the lexical items, but also of such utterly untendentious examples as (4-15), where the analyticity of the inference is guaranteed by the syntactic form of the sentences involved. In these latter cases especially, even the hardened philosophical skeptic is unlikely

**4-14   If John is a bachelor, then John is unmarried.
   If the Pope knows that it is raining, then it is raining.**

**4-15   If it is surprising that John left the house, then that John left the house is surprising.
   If the butler kissed the parlor maid, then the parlor maid was kissed by the butler.**

to deny that the validity of the inference is determined solely by the linguistic character of the sentences. Patently, then, there seem to be *some* commitments which derive from the semantic properties of the linguistic vehicle employed to make an assertion. Clear cases argue for the possibility of a clear distinction, so such cases provide prima facie reasons for believing that a semantic theory might be developed in such a way as to distinguish these commitments from all others.[15]

---

[15] To claim that there are some analytic sentences is, however, not to claim that *all* sentences are either analytic or synthetic. It is also not to claim that all necessary sentences are analytic or that all synthetic sentences are empirically defeasible. It is also not to claim that there are any *interesting* analytic sentences. Part, at least, of what is wrong with the traditional notion of analyticity is what philosophers have tried to make of it

It may be added that semantics is no worse off in this respect than syntax. It is true that there are many cases in which it is unclear whether the commitments a speaker undertakes by asserting a sentence ought to be attributed to the semantic properties of the sentence, but it is equally true that there are many cases where we lack strong intuitions about whether some feature of a sentence ought to be attributed to *syntactic* regularities. It is, for example, possible to doubt whether a sentence like (4-16) is ungrammatical or merely barbarous, and serious issues in syntax have occasionally failed of resolution because of the unclarity of informant's judgments about such cases. Yet it is unreasonable to argue that the exis-

4-16   He called a girl he had known in Chicago who had inherited a fortune in grain futures and purchased a 32-foot sloop and an E-type Jaguar up.

tence of these cases vitiates the notion of grammaticality or indicates the impossibility of developing syntactic theories. Rather, the primary motivation for such theories derives from the speaker's intuitions about clear cases like (4-17) versus (4-18) and the independently motivated theory is then permitted to adjudicate the cases where intuition is

4-17   John went to the store.

4-18   store the to went John

unclear. Nothing, of course, guarantees that this strategy will work. It is quite conceivable that the clear data do not determine a unique solution for the unclear cases. But the fact that there is no such guarantee has not been thought to make the employment of this strategy irrational in syntax, and it is not apparent why the same considerations should not hold for semantics. Nothing *ever* guarantees success in an empirical science, which is no good reason for giving up on science. [For a discussion of these and related issues, cf. Quine (1967) and Katz (1967).]

We assume, then, that some sense can ultimately be made of the notion that among the commitments undertaken in asserting a sentence, there are some which are determined solely by the lexical form and syntactic content of the sentence. We will require that a semantic theory provide a correct account of these commitments. That is, insofar as it concerns itself with those of the declarative sentences of a language which are standardly used to make assertions, a semantic theory must ascribe properties to each such sentence so as formally to determine the

---

in fields like philosophy of mind and ethics. It is *not* going to turn out to be analytic that people who scratch have itches, or that what most people approve of is good, or that reasons aren't causes, etc. Nor is it a reasonable constraint upon a good semantic theory that it should certify bad philosophy.

commitments a speaker undertakes when he uses the sentence to make whatever assertion it is standardly used to make.

SEMANTIC REPRESENTATIONS AND LOGICAL FORCE

Let us say any representation of a sentence which satisfies the condition just mentioned is a representation of its *logical force*. We can then say that a semantic theory of a natural language ought to explain how the logical force of a sentence is determined by its lexical and syntactic structure. The rest of this chapter will be devoted, in large part, to making this suggestion clearer. A few preliminary remarks are in order here.

We suggested that it is an aspect of the logical force of (4-6) that it entails (4-7) and (4-8). We might develop a fragment of a semantic theory which captures this aspect of the logical force of (4-6) in some such way as the following. First, we adopt rule 1, which assigns a semantic representation to sentences having the syntactic structure of (4-6). We then adopt rule 2, which determines (certain of) the entailments into which the semantic representation may enter.

1.   Any sentence of the syntactic form S_1 *and* S_2 has the semantic representation P *and* Q, where $P = S_1$ and $Q = S_2$.
2.   A formula of the form P *and* Q entails a formula of the form P and a formula of the form Q.

These two rules mediate the entailment from (4-6) to (4-7) and to (4-8). They have, to that extent, some right to be considered a part of a semantic theory of English. But, of course, they do not account for entailments like the ones from (4-6) to (4-9), (4-10), and (4-11). So, if rules 1 and 2 are part of the semantic theory of English, they are a very small part.

Still, there are some implications to draw. Notice, first, that we have used two kinds of rules to capture this fraction of the semantic behavior of (4-6). Rule 1 assigns a semantic representation to (4-6) on the basis of its syntactic form and its lexical content. Rule 2 tells us something about the entailments that can be drawn from a sentence which has that semantic representation. The preliminary suggestion, then, is that a semantic theory contain two kinds of rules: rules of *assignment*, which determine the semantic representation of a sentence, and rules of *inference*, which determine the entailments that can be drawn from a sentence by virtue of its semantic representation.

That some system of rules of inference forms an important part of a semantic theory appears to be self-evident. But we are also assuming that rules of assignment apply nontrivially to determine semantic representations of sentences; that is, that the semantic representation of a sentence is, at any event, distinct from its surface representation as an orthographic or phonetic string. That this must be true can be seen from the existence of ambiguous surface representations like (4-19). We have seen throughout this book that a given such sequence may represent

4-19   They are eating apples.

more than one syntactic structure. We now note that, in consequence, a given surface sequence may represent more than one *semantic* structure; in particular, (4-19), taken on one reading, entails (4-20); but taken on the other reading, it entails (4-21), and these entailments are, presum-

4-20   They are eating.

4-21   They are apples.

ably, mutually exclusive. Hence, we know this much about the system of representations of the logical force of English declaratives: it is not identical to the system of conventional orthographic or phonetic representations of English sentences. [The same point can be made by saying that (4-19) cannot be a representation of the logical force of a sentence since it does not provide a univocal domain for the application of rules of inference; since (4-19) is ambiguous, such rules cannot apply to it merely in virtue of its form.]

In fact, we are in a position to make a somewhat stronger point. It is clear not only that the surface representation of a sentence is *distinct* from a representation of its logical force but also that the mapping of surface representations of sentences of natural languages onto their semantic representations is, in general, extremely complicated. Sentences of natural languages do not usually wear their logical force on their sleeves. As Strawson (1952) has remarked,

> The existence of a framework of separate words (or other devices) suitable for quotation in a logician's rule [i.e., a rule of inference] is not...a *sine qua non* of our noticing a formal analogy [between the semantic representations of sentences which differ in lexical content or surface syntactic structure]. For sometimes the resemblances in the verbal patterns of valid inferences may be sufficiently striking for us to speak of their sharing a common form, even when there is no detachable framework of words for which we can lay down a logician's rule [p. 45].

That is, the logical force of a sentence often cannot be determined in any simple way by examining the surface features of the sentence; sentences of similar logical force may exhibit no corresponding similarity in surface organization, and vice versa.

Thus, a tradition has grown up, in the philosophical literature, of contrasting the "logical form" of a sentence, as given by its semantic representation, with its "grammatical form," as represented by its (surface) syntactic analysis. Some such contrast would certainly appear to be warranted. For example, Strawson (1952, pp. 45-46) points out that sentences of the form (4-22) all enter into valid inferences of the form of

4-22   *x* is congruent with *y*.
      x is an ancestor of *y*.
      x is faster than *y*.
      x entails *y*.
      etc.

(4-23), whereas none of the sentences in (4-24) enter validly into such

4-23   *x R y* and *y R z*, therefore *x R z*.

4-24   *x* loves *y*.
      x hates *y*.
      x abuses *y*.
      x employs *y*.
      etc.

inferences. Thus, if the semantic representation assigned to a sentence is to provide an explicit representation of its logical force, the semantic representations of the sentences in (4-22) will have to be uniformly different from the semantic representations of the sentences in (4-24).

In the present case, the difficulty is simply that the surface structures of sentences contain no explicit marker of the transitivity or intransitivity of their predicates.[17] Strawson remarks that "some logicians have felt that all those words which, substituted for *R* in [4-24], would yield valid inference patterns *ought* to have some common verbal feature which would make it possible to frame a principle of inference incorporating a quoted formula" (p. 46); that is, a principle whose applicability would be mechanical in the sense that it applies to sentences if and only if they exhibit the verbal feature in question. It is precisely this sort of defect of the surface representations of sentences that their semantic representations seek to remedy. In short, if the semantic representation of a sentence is one which captures its logical force, then the representation of sentences like (4-22) must contain some such feature as + *transitive* and that of sentences like (4-24) must be assigned the minus value of this feature. Given that the representations of these sentences do contain such features, and given that the rules of inference associated with the semantic theory include some such principle as (4-25),

4-25   *(x (R + trans) y)* and *(y (R + trans) z)* entails *(x (R + trans) z)*

---

[17] In syntax a verb is said to be transitive if it takes a nonsentential direct object. In logic a relation is said to be transitive if it satisfies (4-23). Thus some, but not all, syntactically transitive verbs express logically transitive relations.

the class of entailments into which sentences enter by virtue of the logical transitivity of their predicates will have been appropriately determined. An analogous story could presumably be told in the case of other fundamental logical properties of predicates.

Distinguishing between transitive and intransitive predicates thus requires the construction of semantic representations which differ from surface syntactic representations primarily in that the former make explicit a semantic feature that has no uniform representation in the latter. How is this to be accomplished? It seems clear that the question of whether a sentence contains a transitive predicate or an intransitive one is often (though, as we shall see, not always) determined by the lexical content of its main verb. Thus, two sentences of precisely the same syntactic structure may, nevertheless, differ in transitivity [see (4-26) versus (4-27)].

4-26 *x* loves *y.*

4-27 *x* precedes *y.*

In at least some cases, then, transitivity is a lexically carried feature and, in such cases, construction of semantic representations which distinguish transitive from intransitive sentences can proceed in a relatively straightforward way. Roughly, the problem can be solved if we assume that the semantic theory includes a *dictionary* in which "equals," "entails," etc., are represented as + *transitive*, and "loves," "touches," etc., are represented as − *transitive*, and that the rules for assigning semantic representations to sentences have access to this dictionary.

However, this solution is certainly inadequate. For example, it fails in the case of sentences containing comparative constructions. Thus, the lexical item "similar" must be marked as − *transitive* to account for the invalidity of such inferences as (4-28); yet a sentence of the form of

4-28 John is similar to Mary, Mary is similar to Peter, therefore John is similar to Peter.

4-29 *x* is more similar to *y* than *w* is to *z.*

(4-29) contains a transitive predicate.[18] (In general, every predicate occurring in a comparative construction will express a logically transitive relation.) From the semantic point of view, the syntactic operation of forming the comparative has the effect of taking an *n*-place predicate, which may be either transitive or intransitive into a 2*n*-place predicate

---

[18] That is, the following inference is valid: "*x* is more similar to *y* than *w* is to *z*; *w* is more similar to *z* than *a* is to *b*; therefore, *x* is more similar to *y* than *a* is to *b.*"

which is invariably transitive. Thus (4-30), which is (trivially) intransitive, becomes (4-31), which is transitive. Analogously, (4-32) becomes (4-29); (4-33) becomes (4-34); and so on.

4-30 x is tall.

4-31 x is taller than y.

4-32 x is similar to y.

4-33 x is close to y.

4-34 x is closer to y than w is to z.

Thus far, then, we have seen two kinds of cases: one in which the transitivity of a predicate is directly attributable to the transitivity of a lexical item, and another in which it is determined by a feature of grammatical form. In the first case, we say that (4-27) is transitive because it contains a lexically transitive main verb. In the second case, we say that (4-29) is transitive because it is a comparative. It seems clear, from such examples, that the interaction between lexical and syntactic aspects of sentences will have to be taken into account in computing their semantic representations.

Let us summarize the discussion thus far. We have thought of a semantic theory as containing a set of rules of assignment which map natural language sentences onto semantic representations. We have seen that assignment rules are, in general, sensitive to the syntactic form and the lexical content of the sentences upon which they operate, and that the mapping they effect of sentences onto semantic representations is quite complicated.

The system of semantic representations may itself be thought of as constituting a language. In particular, it must contain an infinite set of well-formed formulas. (Since there are infinitely many natural language sentences of distinct logical force, there must be infinitely many distinct semantic representations.) But the system of semantic representations differs from the system of orthographic or surface syntactic representations of English sentences in a critical way: namely, that rules of inference apply to semantic representations simply by virtue of their form. Thus, as a first approximation, a semantic theory consists of

1. A system of semantic representations
2. A set of rules of assignment which carry natural language sentences onto their semantic representations
3. A set of inference rules which apply mechanically to semantic representations

Such a theory is adequate only if, first, each of the sentences in a natural language which is standardly used to make an assertion receives a semantic representation under the assignment rules, and, second, the semantic representation interacts with the inference rules to determine the entailments of the sentence and thereby captures its logical force.[19]

We have thus loosely characterized a set of goals for semantic theories of natural languages, and it is reasonable to ask how close we are to being able to realize these goals. The answer is not encouraging. The mapping from natural language sentences onto their semantic representations is so complicated that no general procedure for effecting it now exists for any natural language. That is, there is no natural language for which we are currently able to formulate rules of assignment. Still more perplexing, we are currently unable to construct systems of semantic representations which appropriately represent the range of entailments associated with sentences in any natural language. In general, we find that given a system of semantic representations rich enough to represent the entailments of each natural language sentence, we do not know how to formulate rules of inference for the formulas of that system. Conversely, given a system of semantic representations poor enough so that we are able to formally characterize the rules of inference that govern its formulas, we discover that it does not provide distinct representations for each natural language sentence of distinct logical force.

For example, there is a philosophical tradition in which some version of first-order predicate logic is taken as the system of semantic representations for sentences. What one finds is that, even on the (highly dubious) assumption that each assertable natural language sentence has a unique best translation in some logical system, its translation apparently cannot, in general, be claimed to be a representation of its logical force.

This is true for two kinds of reasons: first, such systems typically provide no rules for determining inferences generated by the lexical content of sentences insofar as they turn on items other than certain quantified expressions and certain connectives. Second, there are grounds for believing that the syntax of natural languages is inherently richer than

---

[19] To put this requirement more exactly: a sentence which is standardly used to make any of n distinct assertions must receive precisely n distinct semantic representations under the assignment rules of the theory. R is a semantic representation of the sentence S if and only if

1. R corresponds to S under the assignment rules of the semantic theory.
2. The inference rules of that theory apply mechanically to R.
3. F is a formula derivable from R under the inference rules if and only if F is a formula which corresponds under the assignment rules to a sentence entailed by S.

THE PSYCHOLOGY OF LANGUAGE

the syntax of the standard formal languages, and that this extra syntactic complexity has semantic import.

To start with the first kinds of cases, it is notorious that the standard predicate logic fails to provide a reconstruction of inferences like the one from "x is red" to "x is colored"; or from "x is a son" to "someone is the parent of x"; or from "x is a bachelor" to "x has no wife"; or from "x sold y to z" to "z acquired y from x"; etc. Similarly, the standard predicate logic fails to provide a reconstruction of inferences which depend upon tense relations between sentences, or of inferences which involve modal terms (like "possibly" and "necessarily"), or of inferences involving clauses governed by "opaque" verbs (like "believe," "hope," "intend,").

These kinds of limitations are well known, and recent work in modal, epistemic, and tense logic may profitably be viewed as an attempt to remedy some of them by increasing the range of natural language sentences for which the logic provides semantic representations. There is, however, another kind of difference between natural and standard formal languages which has been less often discussed, though it seems an equally important source of difficulty for any attempt to use the formulas of logic to represent the semantic force of sentences.

The syntactic resources available to formal languages for the construction of complex sentences and for the representation of such relations as modification clearly include only a part of those available to natural languages. In particular, in the standard formal languages, complex sentences are composed from simpler ones by concatenation with sentential connectives of one or more places (typically, "not," "or," "and," and "if then"). Natural languages, however, have available a variety of other syntactic devices for the construction of complex sentential structures, of which sentential subordination is a particularly pertinent example. Thus, even at the level of syntactic deep structure, a sentence like (4-35) presumably has a different geometry from that of (4-36), and this syntactic fact is closely related to the semantic fact that

4-35 John ate the ice cream and Mary wept.

4-36 John ate the ice cream because Mary wept.

(4-36) is not a truth-function of "John ate the ice cream" and "Mary wept." [In particular, (4-36) may be false when these two sentences are true.] In short, insofar as we think of a semantic theory as expressing the logical import of whatever syntactic mechanisms a language has available for the construction of complex sentences, we must take note of the prima facie difficulties implicit in the fact that the languages for which formal rules of inference can now be formulated have fewer such mechanisms than do natural languages.

Again, seen from the point of view of the natural languages, the formal languages have a relatively impoverished set of mechanisms for expressing such key syntactic relations as modification. Roughly speaking, modification in formal languages is expressed by the relation between a predicate term and its variables or constants; by sentential conjunctions; and by sentential operators. [Thus, we have formulas like those in (4-37) corresponding to sentences like those in (4-38); formulas like those in (4-39) corresponding to sentences like those in (4-40); and formulas like those in (4-41) corresponding to sentences like those in (4-42).] Natural languages, however, have access to all these mechanisms and some others besides—notably modifiers over nonsentential

4-37   Purple (John)

4-38   John is purple.

4-39   ∃ x (x is an elephant) and (x is friendly)

4-40   There are friendly elephants.

4-41   Possibly (John eats bagels)

4-42   It is possible that John eats bagels.

constituents other than constants and variables. Thus, a sentence like (4-43) is clearly not a conjunction of (4-44); and there is one reading of (4-45) (the preferred one) on which it is not equivalent to (4-46). It is plausible to locate the difficulty in the fact that (4-43) and (4-45) contain

4-43   John is a good doctor.

4-44   John is good; John is a doctor.

4-45   John aimed his gun at the target.

4-46   John was at the target and John aimed his gun.

modifiers over nonsentential predicate phrases [e.g., that the deep structures are, roughly, (4-47) and (4-48)]. If this diagnosis is correct,

4-47   {John is a (good (doctor))}

4-48   {John ((aimed) at the target) his gun}

then the fact that we find trouble in translating such sentences into the standard predicate logic comports with the fact that they exhibit syntactic structures for which the logic offers no counterpart. [For further discussion, see Fodor (1970b).]

In short, as things now stand, we can say that formal logic offers a theory of some aspects of the logical force of some sentences of kinds that presumably are found in all natural languages. But, from the point of view of the long-range goals of semantic analysis as we have been characterizing them, it is a crude theory.

To summarize the discussion thus far: we want the semantic theory of a natural language to associate each (declarative) sentence with a semantic representation which formally determines the inferences it can enter into. By doing so, the semantic representation of a sentence determines the commitments undertaken by speakers who use the sentence to make whatever assertion it is standardly used to make.

If these are accepted as rational goals for theory construction in semantics, it follows that the semanticist is faced with three distinct but related problems. First, he must develop a notation rich enough to permit the representation of the logical force of the sentences in the language under investigation. Second, he must formulate the rules of inference which determine the behavior of formulas in that notation. And, third, he must develop assignment rules which associate the sentences with their semantic representations. We have suggested that formal logic provides a partial solution to the first two of these problems. It is an open, and interesting, question to what extent formal syntax can provide a solution to the third.

SEMANTIC REPRESENTATION AND DEEP STRUCTURE

We remarked in the preceding section that the semantic representation of a sentence is not, in general, determined by its surface syntactic analysis, and that this is true even if the surface representation is augmented by lexically carried semantic features. That this must be correct is evident from the existence of sentences like (4-49), whose ambiguity cannot be resolved at the level of surface structure.

4-49　The shooting of the hunters was heard.

A natural hypothesis to consider, then, is that the semantic representation of a sentence is determined in some simple way by its lexical content together with its *deep* syntactic analysis. There are, in fact, a number of considerations that appear to support this view. We saw in Chapter 3, for example, that many kinds of sentential ambiguities which cannot be resolved by surface representations do yield distinct deep structures for each term of the ambiguity. Thus, the ambiguity of (4-49) is resolved by deriving the surface form from two deep trees, in one of which there occurs the sentoid "the hunters shoot" and in the other of which there occurs "somebody shoots the hunters." It seems certain, from such cases, that the syntactic deep structure of a sentence often supplies semantically relevant information which is unmarked in its surface representation; hence that deep structure must be at least one of the determinants of the semantic representation of a sentence.

Or, consider sentences like (4-50). Given only the superficial disparity of the two verb phrases, one might be tempted to assume that

4-50　John won't eat spinach and Mary won't either.

this sentence has the semantic representation "F (John) and G (Mary)."

That is, one might be tempted to assume that "won't either" is a predicate on all fours with but distinct from "won't eat spinach." But, patently, this analysis won't do. Rather, it is obvious that the semantic representation we want for this sentence is either identical to, or very like, the one we want for (4-51). In both cases, we want the semantic

4-51 John won't eat spinach and Mary won't eat spinach.

representation to be something like "F (John) and F (Mary)"; "won't either" must be analyzed as a pro-form for "won't eat spinach" if the semantic representation of (4-50) is to determine its logical force.

Here, then, is another kind of case where the search for the semantic representation of a sentence yields an object reasonably like the one we encounter when we seek its base structure. For, just as (4-51) will do as an approximation to the semantic representation (4-50), so will it also do as an approximate representation of the transformational source of that sentence. This can be seen from the fact that for every sentence of the form in (4-52), there exists a corresponding sentence which differs

4-52 NP_1 won't VP_i and NP_2 won't VP_i either.

only in the deletion of the second occurrence of VP_i. Insofar as the syntax is presumed to be responsible for representing this sort of symmetry of structures, it is plausible to suppose that sentences of the reduced form are transformationally derived from the same deep structures that underlie their fully explicit counterparts.[20]

---

[20] An extremely interesting problem arises when one attempts to characterize the relations other than identity which can hold between VP's in sentences of the form of (4-52). On the one hand, not every choice of VP is allowed. For example, (a) is not well formed unless there is contrastive stress on "tomatoes." On the other hand, (b) and (c) appear to be grammatical by virtue of the particular character of the relations which hold between the properties denoted by their VP's. [Compare (d) and (e).] In short, if one accepts that the difference between (b) and (c) on the one hand, and (d) and (e) on the other, *is* a difference in grammaticality, then there appear to be some sentences whose well-formedness is a function of conceptual or factural relations between the properties denoted by their constituents. Insofar as this is the case, there must be some doubt whether the conditions for syntactic well-formedness can be specified in terms of purely formal relations between strings. For further discussion, see Lakoff (1970) and Chomsky (1972).

a *John won't eat spinach and Mary won't eat tomatoes either.

b John won't take a plane and Mary won't go by air either.

c John lives in New York and Bill doesn't live on the West Coast either.

d *John won't take a plane and Mary won't go by land either.

e *John lives in San Francisco and Bill doesn't live on the West Coast either.

Such examples might, indeed, convince one that the deepest syntactic representation of a sentence simply is identical with its semantic representation—that a sufficient condition for a pair of sentences to be synonymous is that they should have the same deep syntactic structure. This is a suggestion that has recently been quite seriously entertained by linguists associated with the "generative semantics" movement. We shall consider it here in some detail. [For some standard papers in generative semantics, the reader should consult the following: Lakoff (1965), Lakoff (1971), Postal (1970), Ross (1970), McCawley (1968), and Gruber (1965).]

In early discussions of the semantic component of generative grammars [Katz and Fodor (1963), Katz and Postal (1964), Chomsky (1965), for example], it was generally assumed that the semantic theory is a function over full (i.e., lexically interpreted) deep-structure trees, and that this function might perform quite complicated transformations upon its input in the process of pairing a sentence with its semantic representation. Indeed, it was part of the orthodoxy of what we called in Chapter 3 "standard" generative theories that there is a sort of symmetry in the organization of a grammar: the strictly generative (syntactic) component maps an initial string S onto surface structures by first producing and then transforming deep-structure trees. Two interpretive components (the phonology and the semantics) operate, respectively, to map surface structures onto sequences of phones (i.e., onto lowest-level representations of waveforms) and onto "semantic interpretations" (i.e., onto representations of meanings).

The proposal that deep structures should be identified with semantic representations simplifies this system by eliminating one of the interpretive components. In particular, if syntactic deep structure is itself taken to be representation of logical force, then the assignment rules, which pair sentences with their semantic representations, turn out simply to be the syntactic rules of a generative grammar.

But while this proposal appears to be an attractive one, it in fact turns out to be difficult to state clearly and still more difficult to evaluate empirically. Ideally, one would wish to argue as follows: there are a set of constraints that syntactic deep structures must satisfy (see Chapter 3) and a set of constraints that semantic representations must satisfy (principally, in the case of assertable sentences, that they determine the entailments of the sentences to which they are assigned). It is simply an empirical question whether it is possible to construct a level of representation which simultaneously satisfies both these constraints without abandoning simplicity or rigor. This sort of argument presupposes independently motivated syntactic and semantic structures. A precisely analogous argument would presuppose the existence of independently motivated syntactic and semantic rules. Thus, one would like to argue that there are a set of constraints that syntactic transformations must satisfy (that they associate deep syntactic trees with surface structures) and a set of constraints that assignment rules must satisfy (that they associate sentences with representations of their logical force), and it is simply an empirical question whether these constraints can be simultaneously satisfied by the same set of rules.

As it turns out, however, the problem is considerably less clear than these formulations might suggest; the issues of fact are, apparently, inextricably meshed with issues of methodology. The reasons for this unclarity include the following.

First, as we remarked above, there exists no known system of semantic representations rich enough to capture the logical force of sentences in natural languages. It is difficult to find a clear answer to the question whether the semantic representation of a sentence is identical with its base structure when one does not know what, in general, the semantic representations of sentences look like.

Second, just as philosophers are far from agreeing on the general characteristics of semantic representations, so are linguists far from agreeing on the properties of syntactic base structures. In particular, there is disagreement on which distributional properties of sentences these structures should represent. But unless we are able to specify these properties, it is hard to tell whether, or to what extent, a representation which determines distributional symmetries also determines entailments.

There are a number of heuristic tests that can be applied in deciding whether two linguistic forms should be assigned the same deep syntactic representation. For example, there is a strong inclination to say that forms that have the same selections should have the same base structures. Thus, one argues that actives and passives have common base structure because whatever noun phrase can be subject of the former can be object of the latter, and vice versa. If actives and passives share a base representation, this symmetry of selection need be stated only once, since it will be carried over by the transformations which convert the base representation into a surface active on one hand and a surface passive on the other. (See Chapter 3, where this sort of argument was used extensively.)

However, it seems clear that symmetry of selection is *no more* than a heuristic test for identity of base structure, since there are cases where distributional symmetry is clearly independent of syntactic relatedness between the structures involved. For example, the possible values of NP_1 and NP_2 are identical for the sentence forms in (4-53), but surely, no

4-53 NP_1 **bought** NP_3 **from** NP_2.
NP_2 **sold** NP_3 **to** NP_1.

one would argue that these forms are transformationally related or that they share a common base.

This conclusion is important because, for a wide variety of cases, it will turn out that items which are synonymous, or otherwise semantically related, have the same selections. Thus, if we were to take the existence of selectional symmetry as a sufficient condition for the asssignment of a common base, we would ipso facto be required to say that synonymous forms have the same deep structure, and would thus be a long way on the road to identifying deep structures with semantic representations by methodological fiat.

The difficulty is that, while some aspects of selection seem to mirror facts about syntactic relatedness, others do not. In (4-53) we appear to have selectional symmetry based on semantic (nonsyntactic) relatedness. There is also the converse case, where there appears to be selectional asymmetry based on distinctions of syntactic form between semantically closely related items. Thus, as Katz (1972) has pointed out, even items whose semantic relation is as close as "shoes" and "footwear" may differ quite markedly in their distributional properties. "Shoes" is a *count* noun, accepting number names as quantifiers ("one shoe, two shoes," etc.); whereas "footwear" is a *mass* noun, accepting only such nonnumerical quantifiers as "some."

In this respect it is worth citing a striking example of selectional symmetry without semantic relatedness noted by Jackendoff (reported in Chomsky, 1972). He notes that there is a large class of predicates which concatenate indiscriminately with singular *NP*'s, plural *NP*'s, generic *NP*'s, indefinite *NP*'s definite *NP*'s, and demonstratives to yield well-formed sentences. Thus, we have any choice (which preserves number agreement) from:

$$
\left\{
\begin{array}{l}
\text{the beaver} \\
\text{a beaver} \\
\text{beavers} \\
\text{some beavers} \\
\text{that beaver}
\end{array}
\right\}
\quad be \quad
\left\{
\begin{array}{l}
\text{a house builder} \\
\text{dangerous} \\
\text{a warm-blooded animal} \\
\quad \cdot \\
\quad \cdot \\
\quad \cdot \\
\quad \text{etc.}
\end{array}
\right\}
$$

The symmetry is not perfect, since generics do not take locatives in this sort of construction: *"the (generic) beaver is in my basement." Nevertheless, to a first approximation, if any of these types of *NP* yields a well-formed substitution instance in (T) *NP* be *A*, then so will the others. Yet this symmetry of selection cannot be a consequence of semantic similarities among the *NP*'s, since they differ in meaning about as much as any two *NP*'s with the same lexical content can. The moral appears to be that there is a level of syntactic representation which groups together linguistic forms that are widely different in their semantic behavior; a conclusion which should worry any theorist who thinks that all syntactic phenomena are semantic at heart, or even that syntactic structure exists primarily to define the domain of semantic rules.

In fact, these points can be generalized from the consideration of selectional symmetry to other aspects of syntactic behavior: there is a rather surprising number of cases in which we find failures of *syntactic* parallelism between forms which would appear to be very nearly identical in their semantic properties. Thus, "father's brother" and "paternal uncle" are semantically closely related if any two predicates are, yet they behave differently *vis-a-vis* syntactic phenomena like anaphora. In particular, (4-54) is ambiguous, with "him" referring either to Hamlet or to Hamlet's father. But (4-55) is univocal, and the pronoun can refer

4-54 Hamlet's father's brother killed him.

4-55 Hamlet's paternal uncle killed him.

only to Hamlet. Such cases suggest that some types, at least, of syntactic heterogeneity are quite compatible with a pair of forms receiving the same representation at the semantic level.

Analogously, a pair of sentences like (4-56) and (4-57) are, presumably, as close to synonymous as sentences can get, and one notes that

4-56 *John* took the *dog* for a walk.

4-57 *John* walked the *dog*.

the pairs of *NP*'s that can substitute for the italicized items are identical in the two sentences. Yet, despite the selectional and semantic symmetries between the sentences, they behave differently in respects that concern the details of their syntactic organization. In particular, because "a walk" occurs as an *NP* in (4-56), that sentence can be relativized in ways that (4-57) cannot. Contrast the ambiguity of (4-58), where the scope of the relative can be either "a walk" or "John took the dog for a walk," with the univocality of (4-59), where the scope of the relative must be the entire first clause.

4-58 John took the dog for a walk (,) which they both enjoyed.

4-59 John walked the dog, which they both enjoyed.

Of course, to suggest that there are many cases where semantic similarity may be independent of syntactic parallelism between linguistic forms is by no means to defeat the claim that semantically similar forms have identical *deep* syntactic structures. For it is quite possible that such syntactic heterogeneity as semantically related forms may exhibit can be attributed to relatively superficial aspects of their syntactic organization. If, in short, we opt for a common base structure in cases like (4-56) and (4-57), we account for their synonymy and for certain similarities between their syntactic behavior. We also, however, incur the obligation of providing some motivated reason for attributing their failures of syntactic parallelism to aspects of their structure that are *not* represented at the deepest level of syntactic analysis. It is probably fair to say that there exist no really decisive arguments for deciding whether this can be done in all of the relevant cases—and hence that no one is very clear on the status of the claim that semantic and syntactic representations might turn out to be identical at some level of analysis.

We remarked that selectional symmetry can at best be a heuristic test for identity of base structures, since (4-53) and similar cases show that one can have symmetry of selection without grammatical relatedness. It may now be added that, even in those cases where distributional symmetry between structures *can* plausibly be attributed to their grammatical relatedness, it is still probably a mistake to argue that symmetric structures must have a common base. Roughly, given a class of items C, whose members occur in two distinct linguistic environments, α— and β—, we have three different kinds of options for capturing the symmetry. We can say that despite the symmetry, α and β are syntactically unrelated [like the sentences in (4-53)]; or we can say that α C and β C derive by dis-

4-60 It was surprising that John left.
That John left was surprising.

tinct transformational routes from a common base (like actives and passives) or like (4-60); or we can say that α and β are transformationally unrelated, but that items in C are lexically marked for insertion into α— and β—. This last option is especially relevant to any evaluation of the relation between deep syntactic structures and semantic representations. Suppose, for example, that we decide to represent (4-58) and (4-59) as syntactically related in order to account for the selectional symmetries they exhibit. It would then be open to us to attempt to develop (and justify) transformations which convert the base for (4-58) into (4-59), or vice versa. But it is also open to us to generate {*NP took NP for an N*} and {*NP Ved NP*} as distinct base structures, and mark some lexical items (like "walk") as having features which permit them to substitute for N and V, thus tacitly locating the syntactic relation between (4-58) and (4-59) in a property of their lexical content.

As things stand in linguistics now, there is no definite consensus on the sufficient conditions for exploiting one or another of these options to represent a given distributional symmetry. In particular, as we remarked above, there is no definite consensus on the sufficient conditions for assigning identical base structures to superficially distinct forms. This is, clearly, a fault in the theory. We are offered more degrees of freedom than we are able to interpret, which is to say that the theory is, thus far, inadequately constrained by the data. [See Chomsky

(1970b) for a discussion of some of the considerations which might motivate decisions to assign distinct deep structures to distributionally symmetric forms.]

We have been considering difficulties in the way of an empirical assessment of the claim that semantic representations are identical with syntactic deep structures. Thus far we have remarked that there exists no acceptable characterization of the class of semantic representations for a natural language, and that this creates problems for the project of comparing the properties of semantic representations with those of base structures. We have also remarked that there exists no general consensus on the question of when symmetric linguistic forms should be assigned a common base, so that one cannot argue directly from the syntactic symmetries between synonymous linguistic forms to their deep identity. We now turn to a third consideration that must be kept in mind in attempting to evaluate the relation between syntactic deep structures and semantic representations.

A given formula represents the logical force of a sentence only relative to some postulated set of rules of inference for deriving the entailments of that formula. For example, we said that a candidate representation for a sentence like (4-6) might be P and Q, where the system contains a rule of inference which allows us to infer from P and Q to P, Q. But, of course, the pertinence of the representation depends on the availability of the rule. If we have no rule which specifies the entailments of formulas of the form P and Q, we gain nothing by assigning such formulas to sentences of natural languages.

If, then, we ask whether base structure represents logical force, we must have some system of inference rules in mind for drawing out the entailments of base structures. But this opens a further possibility for the treatment of semantically related but syntactically disparate natural language forms. In particular, we have the option of saying of forms like (4-58) and (4-59) that (1) they are syntactically unrelated at the level of base structure; (2) they are unrelated by assignment rules (i.e., they do not receive identical linguistic representations at any level of description); but (3) they are interconvertible by some rule of inference [i.e., the inference rule component of the semantic theory allows us to infer from the semantic representation of (4-58) to that of (4-59), and also vice versa]. Standard logical formalisms do not, of course, envision the employment of rules of inference exhibiting this degree of detail. But, as we have repeatedly remarked, the standard logical formalisms almost certainly do not provide formulas which represent the logical force of all the assertion-making sentences of any natural language. Presumably any semantic theory that does so will have to incorporate a system of inference rules that is far more articulate than those associated with such formalisms. [Cf. Fodor (1970b) and Fillmore (1971).]

THE PRIMITIVE VOCABULARY OF A SEMANTIC THEORY

Thus far we have been discussing the structure of the formulas which semantic theories may be supposed to assign as representations to sentences of natural languages. We have assumed that the characteristic property of such formulas is that they determine the entailments of the sentences they represent and that they do so by formally determining the rules of inference under which the sentences fall. It is a theoretical question of considerable importance (and, as we have seen, of some unclarity) whether formulas which satisfy that condition can be so constructed as to serve as deep syntactic structures.

A related, but distinct, question concerns the vocabulary in which semantic representations are to be couched. This is a question which turns out to have profound implications for psychological theorizing; we will return to it in Chapter 7 in the context of a discussion of some aspects of the relation between thought and language. For the present, we consider it in its specifically linguistic form.

When the structure of an "object" language is to be represented in some other, ("meta") language, two simplifying assumptions are often made—first, that the entire nonlogical vocabulary of the former is included in the primitive vocabulary of the latter; and second, that unquantified atomic formulas of the object language (i.e., formulas consisting solely of predicates or relations and referring expressions) are logically independent of (do not entail) one another. The effect of these assumptions is to restrict the class of valid inferences in the object language to those which are determined by the behavior of quantifiers and connectives—hence, to simplify the task of providing a formal account of such inferences in the metalanguage.

These assumptions cannot, however, be safely made when the object language is a natural language, since it is implausible to hold that the elementary predicates of natural languages are logically independent of one another. This consideration raises a variety of problems for the construction of a semantic theory which seeks to provide a formal account of the inferences into which the sentences of a natural language may enter. Since, for example, there are logical relations between such English language predicates as "above" and "below," "left" and "right," "red" and "colored," some device is going to be required which permits a semantic theory of English to represent the entailments such relations engender. Again, if the object language recognizes synonymies between lexical items (like "bachelor") and phrases (like "unmarried man"), it may be thought uneconomical for the metalanguage to contain both. Rather, it may be argued that the vocabulary of the metalanguage ought to contain at most that part of the vocabulary of the natural language which is not eliminable by definitions. What is thus primarily at issue in the discussion of the nonlogical vocabulary of a semantic theory is how to represent those entailments of natural language sentences, and those synonymies between natural language sentences, which depend upon relatively specific aspects of their lexical content.

This is, in fact, a kind of question we have already encountered in a slightly different guise. We remarked above that the distributional symmetries between sentences like (4-56) and (4-57) might be considered grounds for deriving one from the other [say (4-57) from (4-56)]. But if such derivations are allowed, then, so far as the present case is concerned, it is tantamount to saying that $walked_{V_{tr}}$ is not an item in the base structure of English sentences. If we now make the standard assumption that the assignment rules of a semantic theory interpret only base structure, it follows that $walked_{V_{tr}}$ need not appear as an item in the vocabulary of a semantic theory of English. Rather, $walked_{V_{tr}}$ is viewed as introduced into surface English sentences by a syntactic transformation, and the sentences containing it inherit their entailments from those determined by $walk_N$ which does, presumably, appear in the primitive vocabulary of the semantic theory.

We remarked, in discussing this sort of example, that there appear to be at least three possible treatments of such cases: roughly, (1) the solution just sketched, according to which the existence of entailment relations mediated by items in the nonlogical vocabulary of a natural language provides presumptive evidence for the syntactic derivation of the items from a common deep-structure source; (2) the assumption that such semantic relations are represented by a semantic lexicon; (3) the assumption that such relations are represented by local rules of inference enumerated in the metatheory. In this section, we shall consider each of these options in some detail.

TRANSFORMATIONALIST SOLUTIONS

Lakoff (1965) has suggested that sentences like (4-61) derive from deep structures like (4-62)—hence that there is at least one case in which a "simple" predicate of a natural language $melt_{V_{itr}}$ derives transformationally from a complex predicate with which it is synonymous [(*cause to melt*)$_{V_{itr}}$]. This transformationalist analysis of "causal" verbs is a paradigm for transformationalist treatments of logical relations involving simple predicates. [For another well-known example, see Postal (1970).]

Prima facie, there would appear to be a variety of types of facts which support this derivation. Notice, for example, that for many speakers one or more versions of (4-63) is ambiguous in just the way that the derivation of (4-61) from (4-62) would predict: namely, what is said to have

4-61 Floyd melted the glass.

4-62 {(Floyd caused (the glass melt))}

4-63 Floyd melted the glass $\left\{\begin{array}{l}\text{and that}\\ \text{and it}\\ \text{which}\end{array}\right\}$ surprised me.

surprised me can be either that Floyd melted the glass or that the glass melted. Now, if (4-62) is the deep structure of (4-61), these ambiguities are easily explained. On one reading of (4-63) the pro-forms have replaced the constituent "(Floyd caused (the glass melt)) ," and, on the other reading, they have replaced only the subordinated constituent, "(the glass melt)." The ambiguity of (4-63) thus appears to provide strong evidence that (4-61) is not the simple sentence it seems to be; in particular, it contains two sentoids in its deep structure. This, in turn, supports the view that a word has been derived from a phrase in the course of generating (4-61).

Further arguments might be alleged for the same conclusion. Thus, the italicized pronoun in (4-64), like the ones in (4-63), appears to refer to the glass melting rather than to Floyd melting the glass, and this

4-64 Floyd melted the glass though it surprised me that he was able to bring *it* about.

would follow naturally from the view that "(the glass melts)" is a constituent of the deep structure of (4-61). Finally, it may be noted that (4-61) has two associated *do so* forms, namely (4-65) and (4-66). Once again the natural treatment would appear to require that (4-62) be the deep structure of (4-61) since, on that account, we could say that (4-65) is

4-65 Floyd melted the glass, though it surprised me that he would do so.

4-66 Floyd melted the glass, though it surprised me that it would do so.

a case of *do so* replacing the higher *VP* and (4-66) is a case of *do so* replacing the subordinated *VP*.

If (4-61) is derived from (4-62), the derivation presumably involves two transformations: *predicate raising* of the embedded predicate, which permits us to map (4-62) onto the intermediate form (4-67), and *lexicalization*, which permits the transformational substitution of a word

4-67 (Floyd (caused (to melt (the glass))))

for a phrase [in the present case, $(\text{cause (to melt)}_{V_{itr}}) \Rightarrow (\text{melt}_{V_{tr}})$]. If this analysis is correct, it follows, first, that there are transformations which derive words from underlying phrases and, second, that at least one apparently simple sentence containing a surface transitive main verb derives from a complex deep structure containing an intransitive embedded verb. The derivation of (4-61) from (4-62) thus provides a precedent for such derivations as $\text{break}_{V_{tr}}$ from *cause to* $\text{break}_{V_{itr}}$; $\text{tear}_{V_{tr}}$ from *cause to* $\text{tear}_{V_{itr}}$; etc. But, moreover, it indirectly supports such surprising derivations as $kill_{V_{tr}}$ from *cause to die*. The suggestion is that from a semantic point of view, (4-68) is related to (4-69) and (4-70) in very much the same way that (4-71) is related to (4-61) and (4-72). The syntax

4-68 John caused Mary to die.

4-69 John killed Mary.

4-70 Mary died.

4-71 Floyd caused the glass to melt.

4-72 The glass melted.

mirrors these relations by deriving (4-69) from (4-68) in a way that strictly parallels the derivation of (4-61) from (4-62).

This argument is obviously appealing; no one could fail to be pleased if the theory of syntax were to support the theory of entailment in this surprising way. It is appealing, too, in that it appears to provide definite empirical data on the status of one of the fundamental principles of "standard" transformational theory; namely, the claim that lexical items are inserted into derivational trees only at the level of deep structure. If the present analysis is correct, then this claim can be regarded as disproved, since "lexicalization" transformations have precisely the function of introducing lexical items into trees which have already undergone transformation [e.g., lexicalization applies *after* predicate-raising in the derivation of (4-61) and (4-69)].

Nevertheless, there is good reason to doubt that the deep structure of (4-61) is (4-62) or that (4-69) is derived from (4-68). In what follows we will review two of the considerations which raise these doubts and then suggest an alternative account of the ambiguity of (4-64) and the well-formedness of (4-65) and (4-66). Taken all in all, the discussion will suggest that the analysis of causal verbs provides little support for transformationalist treatments of semantic relations and some arguments against them.[21]

We remarked that part of the interest of the derivation of (4-61) from (4-62) is that it appears to provide a precedent for the derivation of (4-69) from (4-68). This appearance, however, is probably illusory. The distributional characteristics of "kill/cause to die" are different from those of "melt/cause to melt" in ways that militate against handling these pairs symmetrically in the syntax.

To see why this is so, we must first consider the analysis of (4-69), which derives it from (4-68). It is noteworthy, to begin with, that corresponding to (4-68) we have both (4-73), in which *do so* replaces the higher *VP* "caused Mary to die" and (4-74), in which *do so* replaces the

---

[21] What follows is an abbreviated version of some arguments first given in Fodor (1970a). The interested reader should consult that article for further details.

4-73 John caused Mary to die and it surprised me that he did so.

4-74 John caused Mary to die and it surprised me that she did so.

embedded *VP* "Mary die." Now, if both "cause Mary to die" and "Mary die" are constituents of the deep structure of (4-69), we might expect that the *do so* transformation should operate on that structure to produce both (4-75), which is in fact well formed, and (4-76), which, however, is not. In short, it argues against the presence of a constituent

4-75 John killed Mary and it surprised me that he did so.

4-76 *John killed Mary and it surprised me that she did so.

"Mary die" in the deep structure of (4-69) that there is no well-formed sentence (4-76) in which that constituent has been replaced by *do so*.[22] To put it briefly, if the existence of (4-66) argues for a causal analyses of *melt$_{tr}$* the *non*existence of (4-76) argues against a causal analysis of *kill*. In fact, there are independent grounds for doubting that the transformationalist account is correct for either verb.

To begin with, notice that there are a variety of types of instrumental adverbial phrases which share *NP*'s with the verbs they modify, and that these phrases invariably share the *subject-NP*'s of those verbs. Thus, (4-77) means that John (rather than Mary) used the telephone, and there is no surface sentence corresponding to (4-78).

4-77 John contacted Mary by using the telephone.

4-78 *{(John contacted Mary by (Mary used the telephone))}

This generalization, that instrumental adverbs share *NP* with the *subjects* of the verbs they modify, holds, too, for instrumental adverbs on embedded verbs. For example, in (4-79), as in (4-77), it is John who

4-79 I believe that John contacted Mary by using the telephone.

does the phoning. Thus, it appears that a necessary condition upon the well-formedness of sentences containing *NP*-sharing instrumental adverbs is that it be the *subject-NP* of the modified verb that is shared. But it also appears that this is a *sufficient* condition for this kind of *NP* sharing. That is, given that an *NP* is the deep subject of a verb, it ipso facto can be shared by an instrumental adverb which modifies that verb (i.e., it can be the implicit subject of such an adverbial modifier). This is apparently true quite independent of the surface position that the *NP* comes to occupy. For example,

---

[22] This asymmetry between *melt$_{tr}$* and *kill* vis-à-vis *do so* transformation has been independently noticed by Bouton (1969).

1.   An *NP* which has been "raised" from deep subject of an embedded verb to surface object of a higher verb can nevertheless be the implicit subject of an instrumental adverbial on the embedded verb, as is the case for "Mary" in (4-80).

4-80   John expected Mary to treat her cold by taking aspirin.

2.   An *NP* can be shared by an instrumental adverb despite nominalization of the sentoid of which it is the subject, as in (4-81).

4-81   John's breaking windows by using a hammer surprised me.

3.   An *NP* can be shared with an instrumental adverbial on an embedded verb even after having been raised from deep subject of that verb to superficial subject of a higher verb, as in (4-82) [which presumably derives from (4-83) by a transformation which substitutes "John" for "it"].

4-82   John seems to break windows by using a hammer.

4-83   {It seems that John breaks windows by using a hammer.}

4.   A *subject-NP* can be shared with an instrumental adverbial after deletion of its verb by "gapping," as in (4-84).

4-84   John breaks windows by using a hammer and Bill by using a brick.

5.   Finally, an (implicit) *subject-NP* can be shared with an instrumental adverbial even after it has been deleted, as in (4-85) where it is not Mary but the unspecified "someone" who found Mary who is understood to have used the radar.

4-85   Mary was found by using radar.

All this strongly suggests the correctness of the claim that a structurally necessary and sufficient condition for an *NP* being shared with an instrumental adverbial is that the *NP* be the deep subject of the verb which the instrumental modifies. However, we will have to abandon this claim if we permit derivations like (4-69) from (4-68) or, *mutatis mutandis*, (4-61) from (4-62).

Notice that there is a deep structure, (4-86), which transforms into the surface sentence (4-87); (4-87) is ambiguous, just as the principle that

4-86   {John (caused (Bill die) (by (Bill swallows Bill's tongue)))}

4-87   John caused Bill to die by swallowing his tongue.

any deep subject can be shared by an instrumental adverbial requires. [That is, (4-87) has the source (4-88) as well as the source (4-86).] Now,

4-88   {John (caused (Bill die) (by (John swallows Bill's tongue)))}

if we suppose that predicate raising and lexicalization are transformations, we can derive not only (4-87) but also (4-89) from (4-86). But this will not do, since (4-89) has no reading on which it means what (4-86)

4-89   John killed Bill by swallowing his tongue.

predicts; (4-89) unlike (4-87) is univocal in that it is clearly John rather than Bill who does the swallowing.

In short, "Bill" cannot be shared with an instrumental adverbial in (4-89) despite the fact that "Bill" is the subject of a verb in (4-86) and, *ex hypothesi*, (4-86) is a deep-structure source of (4-89). Hence, if we want to save lexicalization and predicate raising as transformations, we will have to do so at the price of abandoning the generalization [which appears to be firmly supported by sentences (4-80) to (4-85)] that all deep subjects can be shared by instrumental adverbials. On the present evidence, then, it looks as though "Bill" is not the subject of any verb in the deep–structure of (4-89) but simply the object of "kill"—an undramatic but thoroughly intuitive conclusion.

It is worth pausing to reflect upon the moral of the preceding arguments. Lexicalization is a transformation which derives words from phrases. But phrases are syntactically complex in ways that words are apparently not. We might thus expect that phrases will exhibit distributional characteristics which differ from those even of words with which they are synonymous. That is, simply because they have internal syntactic structure, phrases can interact with syntactic rules in ways that appear to be incompatible with lexicalization. There are two instrumental adverb positions in (4-68) but only one in (4-69). This follows simply from the fact that (4-68) is a two-verb sentence while (4-69) is a one-verb sentence. But this difference between the structures produces an embarrassment of adverbs if we attempt to lexicalize (4-68) into (4-69). In particular, lexicalization predicts surface structures in which instrumental adverbs are inherited from both the main and the subordinate sentoids in (4-68), and such structures do not exist.

In short, even where a phrase and a word are synonymous, the former will characteristically exhibit degrees of syntactic freedom unavailable to the latter; independent of their meaning, two-verb sentences are different in their syntactic behavior from one-verb sentences. There is thus a dilemma. Either lexicalization carries these unwanted degrees of freedom over into surface structure, thereby predicting sentences which are in fact ungrammatical, or special, ad hoc constraints have to be instituted to ensure that lexicalization does not apply to phrases in which these degrees of freedom have been exploited.

The arguments just presented throw considerable doubt upon the transformational analysis of verbs like "melt" and "kill." But it remains to try to find some alternative explanation of the fact that (4-63) is ambiguous and that we have the two *do so* forms in sentences (4-74) and

(4-66). It was these facts that provided the strongest evidence for the transformational derivation of $melt_{tr}$ from *cause to melt$_{itr}$*.

It is tempting to argue that we are faced, not with a fact about "causal" verbs but rather with a fact about pro-forms like "do so" and "it." In particular, it seems that the widely held view that such forms enter into surface structure only as a result of deletion under identity (i.e., that they must invariably "refer back to" or "replace" material actually present in the base structure of a sentence) may be false. In certain cases, pro-forms may refer to material which is semantically and phonologically related to (but not identical with) material actually contained in the sentence in which the pro-form occurs. Thus, given a verb V which, like "melt" and "break" (but unlike "kill") has the same phonological shape in its transitive and intransitive forms, and where x V y entails y V_{itr}, it will generally be found that one or more of the pro-forms ("it," "do so," etc.) can "refer" to the intransitive form even when the pro-form occurs in transitive sentences like (4-63). It is this "loosening" of the conditions on the anaphoric functioning of pro-forms which explains why (4-63) is ambiguous and why both (4-65) and (4-66) are well formed.

It may be maintained that this explanation requires an ad hoc exception to the otherwise tidy rule that pro-forms can refer only to material actually present in the sentences in which they occur. This *is* a nice rule, but, unfortunately, it has to be abandoned on independent grounds. Sentences containing logically "symmetrical" verbs (i.e., where x V y entails y V x) behave very much like "melt," "break," etc., with respect to pro-forms. Thus, we have not only (4-90) but also (4-91). In the latter

4-90 John married Mary though we were surprised that he was willing to do it.

4-91 John married Mary though we were surprised that she was willing to do it.

case, "it" refers to "Mary marries John," which surely is *not* a constituent in the base structure of (4-91).

In short, given a structure A, which is not present in, but which bears appropriate phonological and semantic relations to items in the deep structure of sentence S, pro-forms in S may refer to A. It seems likely that this is true, but how one goes about saying that it is in the framework of generative syntax is very much an open problem.

LEXICALIST TREATMENTS OF LOGICAL RELATIONS

Some, though by no means all, of the difficulties that we have seen attach to transformational syntactic treatments of logical relations appear to point toward a *lexicalist* analysis of such relations. In the lexicalist account, one accepts the standard theory's assumption that there is a semantic component of the grammar which is independent of the syntactic component. One also assumes that the semantic component includes a richly structured dictionary, which functions primarily to assign semantic features to lexical items. For example, one might assume that properties like being a causal verb are simultaneously syntactic features (in that they govern selection) and semantic features (in that they govern entailments). By marking the verb *melt*$_{tr}$ as a causal verb in the *syntactic* lexicon, we determine that it occurs in the same linguistic environments as other verbs that are so marked (e.g., "break," "tear," "cause," etc.). By entering it as a causal verb in the *semantic* lexicon, we determine that sentences like (4-61) entail sentences like (4-92).

4-92   Floyd caused something to happen.

This sort of treatment has obvious disadvantages. In the first place, the claims it makes are weaker than those made by the transformationalist treatment in the sense that the lexicalist account does not predict distributional syntactic parallelism between words and the phrases with which they are synonymous. Obviously, we would prefer to accept the stronger of two theories wherever the data allow us to do so. Again, the lexicalist account suggests that the assignment of such syntactic features as + *causal* to a verb like "melt" is fully independent of the assignment of the homophonic semantic feature. And, while there are well-known examples where the syntactic and semantic behavior of a lexical item split apart ("ship" pronominalizes with "she" but presumably does not receive the semantic feature +*female*), it seems perfectly clear that the syntactic and semantic behavior of a word are intimately interrelated in the general case. By postulating independent syntactic and semantic lexicons, the lexicalist account seems to have made a move in the direction away from an account of this relationship.

On the other hand, the lexicalist treatment has the virtues of its defects. For example, precisely because it does not attempt to exhibit transformational relations between pairs like "kill" and "cause to die," it is able to handle word-to-phrase synonymies in a way that is homogeneous with its handling of word-to-word synonymies.

On the lexicalist view, the semantic theory consists essentially of a dictionary and a set of "projection rules" for applying the dictionary to lexically filled deep syntactic trees. [See Katz and Fodor (1963); Katz (1972).] In a given sentential environment E, a word w is synonymous with a phrase p or with another word w' if and only if we get the same result (i.e., the same semantic representation) whether we apply the dictionary to w in E, or to p in E, or to w' in E. Full synonymy between a pair of items is the case in which this condition is satisfied for any choice of E. Thus, in principle at least, the lexicalist theory can provide for a homogeneous treatment of such prima facie heterogeneous facts as in (4-93). One feels that this is as it should be. Whether a given language

4-93 a. "occulist" is synonymous with "eye doctor"

   b. "eye doctor" is synonymous with "doctor whose professional speciali-
       zation is the treatment and care of eyes"

   c. "bank" is synonymous with "financial institution" in "they robbed a
       ____," but not in "they sat by the river ____"

codes a given concept with a single word or with a phrase would appear
to be very much a matter of accident. If this is true, then semantic
theories ought to provide a treatment of word-to-phrase and phrase-to-
phrase synonymies that is essentially uniform with their treatment of
word-to-word synonymies.

We have assumed that the dictionary assigns semantic features to
words. That is, each word listed in the dictionary receives some constellation of semantic features as its entry. This constellation of features
must be sufficiently rich to determine, via the "projection rules," all the
effects the word can have upon the semantic properties of the sentences
in which the word occurs. In this sort of view, then, a primary problem
in general semantic theory is to decide what kinds of features a dictionary can assign to lexical items.

A traditional answer to this question is that, at least in the case of a
large number of types of words, the function of the dictionary is to
provide a definition which specifies the superordinate classes to which
the designata of the word belong. A cat, for example, is a thing; and
within the class of things, it is a living thing; and within the class of living things, it is an animal; and within the class of animals, it is a feline;
and within the class of felines, it is a domestic feline. The presumption,
therefore, is that semantic features designating each of these classes are
to be listed against the word "cat" in the semantic lexicon of English. In
effect, the semantic representation of sentences containing words like
"cat" replaces that word with a conjunction of semantic features which
may, in turn, be thought of as belonging to the primitive vocabulary of
the semantic theory.

There are three kinds of evidence that have been alleged in favor of
the view that some, at least, of the speaker-hearer's knowledge of the
semantic structure of his language can be faithfully represented by a
lexicon in which the semantic representation assigned to lexical items is
of this general kind.

In the first place, it seems at least plausible to represent the assertions
standardly made with such sentences as (4-94) as true by virtue of the

4-94 a. If something is a cat, then it is an animal.
      b. If something is a bachelor, then it is a male.

meanings of "cat" and "bachelor," respectively. If this is correct, and if
the semantic representation of a sentence is to determine those of its entailments which hold by virtue of the meanings of its constituent lex-

ical items, then the representation of sentences containing "cat" will have to include the fact that cats are animals, and the representation of sentences containing "bachelor" will have to include the fact that bachelors are males.

The second line of argument for this kind of semantic feature analysis appeals to the intuition that the meanings of sets of words like "mother," "sister," "aunt," "niece," "vixen," and "spinster," share some meaning component. It seems natural to represent this intuition by permitting the lexicon to assign to all these words some such feature as + *female*. Once again, the effect of this kind of decision is that the theory comes to represent words by providing semantic markers corresponding to the superordinate classes to which their designata belong.

Finally, there is a line of evidence that derives from specifically psychological research: results with at least two paradigms point to the existence of parts of the lexicon which are organized in terms of some sort of feature hierarchy.

The first of these paradigms is the standard "free" association technique. There are a variety of ways of analyzing free association data, but for present purposes the most interesting is perhaps the one used by Deese (1965). In essence, Deese's technique involves calculating the degree of association between two stimulus words by reference to the number of response words which they elicit in common. Since a frequent associate for certain kinds of concrete nouns is an abstract noun which designates a superordinate set, the use of this technique yields something like a class hierarchy for many nouns. Deese comments that

> Whenever a common category name exists in common use within the language, it will reveal its presence by a particular pattern of associative intersection that it has with a large and representative sample of instances of the category. That pattern can be described by two characteristics: (1) the category name will have the largest summed intersection with all the instances found in the matrix, and (2) the intersections of the category name with the instances will be more or less evenly distributed [p. 153].

This is the pattern Deese finds for the associative relation between the word "animal" and such words as "cat," and "dog."

A second technique which has recently provided evidence for a partial organization of the lexicon into a feature hierarchy was used by Miller and his colleagues. [See Miller (1969) and Anglin (1970).] This technique is extremely straightforward. Subjects are asked to sort a list of words by similarity of meaning. Scaling procedures are then employed to generate a representation of the resulting data as a space in which the distance between two items is inversely proportional to the number of subjects who sort them together. It is possible to demonstrate that for some groups of words, the resultant space exhibits the properties of a hierarchy.

Several points must be borne in mind when interpreting these results. First, it is quite clear (and both Miller and Deese stress this point) that the lexicon in toto does not form a hierarchy. This can be seen most easily from an observation by Chomsky (1965). Chomsky points out that there are sets of words, of which "male," "female," "married," "unmarried," are pertinent examples, which cannot be organized into a tree structure; that is, there is no way of representing the relations between the four classes as a taxonomy, inasmuch as both males and females can be either married or unmarried. In fact, the importance of Chomsky's insight has been rather widely missed in psychological discussions, since it often applies *even* to cases which, at first glance, seem susceptible to hierarchical analysis. For example, it is widely held that there is a lexical hierarchy which subdivides *animate* into *animal* and *vegetable* and then subdivides each of these into species. However, animal and vegetable are cross-classified by such categories as *edible-inedible*, *domestic-nondomestic*, etc. Hence, though it is true that such patterns of inference as "*x* is a dog" implies "*x* is an animal" implies "*x* is animate" can be captured on the assumption that the lexical entries for "dog," "animal," and "animate" are organized into a hierarchy, there is other information available to speakers which cross-classifies the elements of this hierarchy. The point to bear in mind is that any system which can be represented as a hierarchy can also be represented by a feature matrix where some features are redundant; but the converse is *not* true. Feature systems which permit cross-classification cannot, in general, be represented by a hierarchy. The arguments we have just considered suggest that the appearance of hierarchy in the lexicon is probably just an artifact of feature redundancies.

At best, then, the data provide an argument for the claim that parts of an analysis of the lexicon form a hierarchy. In fact, they may show a good deal less.

The results we have been discussing would be important if they demonstrated not merely that what speaker-hearers know *can* be (partially) represented by a hierarchy, but also that it *is* so represented in the mind of the speaker-hearer. In short, what needs to be shown is that, in the information storage system that speakers use, "dog," "cat," etc., are assigned to a subclass of the class animal. "Bachelor," "father," etc., are assigned to a subclass of the class male, and so on.

Do the data show this? It is difficult to argue that the card-sorting experiments do, since it is obvious that subjects are capable of sorting in ways in which do not directly reflect the organization of their internal system of data storage. For example, given a list of words, subjects can sort them into those which end in *w* and those which do not. This shows that subjects know which words end in *w*. It hardly shows that his representation of the lexicon is organized into two classes, one of which contains words ending in w and the other of which is its complement. In effect, to show that the subject can perform the sorting task is *only* to show that the truth or falsity of "x ends in w" is *derivable* from what the subject knows about each x. Namely, it shows that the subject knows how to spell. But it tells us nothing at all about the categories in terms of which the subject's information about x is organized. Of course, it *might* be supposed that merely instructing the subject to sort according to "meaning" somehow guarantees that the way he sorts will reflect the organization of his system of information storage. But it is difficult to see how one could justify this assumption.

The inference from the character of free-association data to the organization of the information storage system is also dubious. For example, if the associates to an item are intimately determined by the way in which it is stored, we should be able to predict the accessibility of information about stimulus from a knowledge of its associates. But it is immediately evident that we cannot always do so. For example, everyone who knows about tigers knows that they have noses. But the probability of "nose" as a free associate to "tiger" is, effectively, nil.

Perhaps the most direct evidence for the construct validity of associative measures for illuminating the organization of the internal lexicon is that of Collins and Quillian (1969). They hypothesized the same kind of hierarchically organized system that emerges from the work of Miller and Deese. They have attempted to show that the relations of superordination and subordination between pairs of items in the hierarchy *do* predict their relative accessibility. In particular, Collins and Quillian investigated subjects' reaction times in making true-false judgments about sentences in the subject-predicate form. The manipulated variable was the number of nodes in the hierarchy that would need to be traversed in order to relate the subject to the predicate. Thus, for example, Collins and Quillian predicted that judgments which depend on knowing that a canary is a bird would be faster than judgments which depend upon knowing that a canary is an animal, since "canary" is presumed to be directly dominated by "bird" in its hierarchy, while it is only indirectly dominated by "animal." Such predictions tended, in general, to be confirmed in their data.

But even though the Collins and Quillian results appear to provide strong support for hierarchial organization of the lexicon, their theory is in fact subject to serious difficulties. For example, Conrad (1972) investigated the extent to which the Collins and Quillian results can be attributed to response biases. Like Collins and Quillian, Conrad compared reaction time for true-false judgments for sentences in the subject-predicate form, where the manipulated variable was the distance in the hierarchy that separated the subject information from the predicate information. However, unlike Collins and Quillian, Conrad pretested the material in order to rank the predicates for the relative frequency with which they occur in elicited descriptions of the subject term. Conrad found the Collins and Quillian result—that relative distance between items in the hierarchy predicts relative differences in reaction time—only for comparisons where the frequency of the predicate decreases with increase in the distance between the subject and predicate. Conversely, when the predicates are equated for frequency in elicited descriptions, the Collins and Quillian results are *not* found. This suggests that distance through the presumed hierarchy is psychologically effective only where it happens to correspond to the response biases of subjects; i.e., that the Collins and Quillian results do not provide unequivocal support for the existence of the hierarchy.

To summarize: even though the claim that part of the lexicon is organized into a feature hierarchy is an extremely weak one, such psychological data as have been alleged in its favor are not persuasive. What these data do strongly suggest is what has never been in doubt: among the kinds of information that speakers have about the designata of lexical items is some which concerns superordinate classes to which the items belong. Somehow, what subjects know about dogs implies that dogs are animals; what they know about bachelors implies that bachelors are males, etc. What the data do *not* show is what the lexicalist would like to prove: that the form of representation for "dog" is a feature hierarchy in which it is dominated by *animal* and that the form of representation for "bachelor" is a feature hierarchy in which it is dominated by *male*. The psychological evidence for lexicalism must, therefore, be judged to be equivocal thus far.

Some objections to lexicalism.   We have been assuming that the lexicalist position has two fundamental claims to make about the structure of dictionary entries in the semantic lexicon: first, that such entries assign semantic features to lexical items; second, that the characteristic function of such features is to specify the system of superordinate classes to which the designata of the item belongs.

The first of these assumptions has received occasional criticism from theorists who do not like the componential, atomistic approach to meaning that it implies. [For a useful discussion, see Bolinger (1965).] But even among theorists who accept a componential approach to lexical analysis, it is now universally accepted that there are semantic phenomena which cannot be accounted for by the postulation of superordination relations among semantic features.

The kinds of facts most naturally treated by appeal to a semantic lexicon of the kind we have been discussing include the entailment of (4-92) by (4-61) and the analyticity of (4-94). In these cases, the phenomena to be explained turn on such facts as that breaking is a kind of causing, or that a cat is a kind of animal. The semantic consequences of these facts can plausibly be represented by assigning to the lexical item "break" the semantic feature + *causal* and to the lexical item "cat" the semantic feature + *animal*. The plausibility of this treatment is not impugned by the admission that the system of features probably does not form a hierarchy.

But as Bar-Hillel (1967a) and others have pointed out, it is clear that this approach will not do for the representation of a wide variety of types of semantic phenomena, especially for those concerned with relational terms. Consider, for example, such sentences as those in (4-95). It is immediately clear that the truth of these sentences does not arise from the meaning of the constituent lexical items in anything like the way the truth of "Tabby is a cat implies Tabby is an animal" arises from the meaning of "cat" and "animal." This is not, of course, to say that the lexicalist cannot list the semantic facts upon which (4-95) turns and call such lists dictionary entries. It is simply that the dictionary entries for "left," "right," "before," "after," etc., are going to have very little in common with those for "animal," "bachelor," etc., and the relations between semantic features that must be postulated for the first kind of

4-95   x is to the right of y implies y is to the left of x.
      x occurred before y implies y occurred after x.
      x purchased y from z implies z sold y to x.
      x married y implies y married x.

entry will be quite different from the relations that must be postulated for the second.

This seems to us a very damaging concession for the lexicalist to have to make. The substance of the lexicalist theory lies largely in his proposal of a normal form for dictionary entries; patently, if *anything* can in principle be a semantic feature, if any feature can in principle apply to any word, and if any logical relation can in principle hold among features, then the claim that the semantic behavior of words can be captured by a feature analysis is tantamount to the claim that it can be finitely described, which is a vacuous claim. The lexicalist must, therefore, provide some constraints on what can appear in a dictionary entry, and his theory will be persuasive only insofar as obeying those constraints permits us to construct entries that are simple and uniform. If, in short, the lexicalist must admit that he can provide no general account of the types of definitions that there may turn out to be, or of the ways in which definitions may turn out to determine entailments, it does not appear that much substance remains to the claim that lexicalism is true beyond the dogged determination to designate whatever part of the semantic theory represents the behavior of vocabulary items as a semantic lexicon. As Bar-Hillel (1967b) has properly remarked, "Some meaning rules can be conveniently put into a dictionary format. But there is a large number of other meaning rules for which this format is not adequate. So why not present them in a different format?" (pp. 413–414).

There are further, and rather subtle, difficulties that lexicalist treatments are prone to. Consider, for example, the (hypothetical) dictionary entry Katz presents for "bachelor" in *The Philosophy of Language* (1966, p. 155):

bachelor: (i) (Physical Object), (Living), (Human), (Male), (Adult), (Never Married); . . .

(ii) (Physical Object), (Living), (Human), (Young), (Knight), (Serving under the standard of another); . . .

(iii) (Physical Object), (Living), (Human), (Having the academic degree for the completion of the first four years of college); . . .

(iv) (Physical Object), (Living), (Animal), (Male), (Seal), (Without a mate at breeding time).

Each of the four senses of "bachelor" is here represented as a conjunction of semantic features; e.g., a bachelor in sense iii is a physical object, and living, and human . . . , etc. Certain of these features are, in turn, designated by single symbols in the vocabulary of the metalanguage (e.g., "human," "living") or by metalinguistic phrases which are themselves simply equivalent to conjunctions (e.g., a "physical object" is presumably something that is both an object and physical). So far this is unobjectionable, since conjunction is a well-behaved truth-functional relationship such that P *and* Q if and only if P is true and Q is true. However, Katz also uses, as semantic features, quite complex metalinguistic phrases such as "serving under the standard of another," and "having the academic degree for the completion of the first four years of college." There is no clear way to avoid doing this, since the metalanguage being used is, to all intents and purposes, English; and English has no way of expressing the required concept short of using syntactically complicated phrases.

Dictionaries, of course, characteristically employ the full syntactic and semantic resources of a language in describing the language. But dictionaries are not formal theories, nor do they seek to provide an explicit account of entailment. By contrast, a semantic theory is supposed to provide a formal analysis of the behavior of, for example, sentences containing subordinate constructions, sentences containing modifiers, and sentences containing modals. But if the analysis is given in a metalanguage which itself employs these kinds of syntactic devices, the problems of object language analysis that the theory is intended to explain simply recur when one attempts to characterize the rules of inference that govern the behavior of formulas in the metalanguage. For example, we are presumably allowed to infer from the metalinguistic formula ((Physical object) . . . (Without a mate at breeding time)) to the metalinguistic formula ((Physical Object) . . . (Without a mate)), and hence from the object language formula "x is a bachelor" (sense iv) to the object language formula "x is without a mate." But the theory lacks the conceptual resources to account for the validity of the latter inference precisely because it lacks the conceptual resources to account for the validity of the former one.

To put the point briefly, it is difficult to analyze English in terms of another language with equivalent syntactic and semantic resources (like French or, for that matter, English). But what a semantic theory seeks to do is still more difficult: namely, to analyze English in a language for whose formulas explicit rules of entailment can be stated. If formulas of the metalanguage are allowed to take as primitive precisely the sorts of syntactic structures that occur unanalyzed in the object language, this goal will not be realized.

"MEANING RULES"

We have been assuming that a grammar will contain both a syntax, which captures transformational relations between linguistic structures, and a lexicon, which represents the meanings of words. The preceding discussion shows, in effect, that these assumptions must somehow be restricted. As things now stand, they permit us to represent word-to-phrase synonymies *either* as transformational relations *or* as lexical relations, and we have no very convincing grounds for choosing between the two types of representation.

In fact, the situation is even worse than this suggests. For not only must a completed grammar arguably contain both a transformational syntax and a lexicon, it must also contain a system of inference rules which determine entailment relations among the semantic representations that the theory assigns to sentences. But, as we remarked above, this opens a further possibility for the treatment of semantically related natural language forms. Roughly, we can suppose such forms to be related *either* in the syntax *or* in the lexicon, *or* by relatively special-purpose "meaning rules." While most recent discussions of semantics have centered on one or another of the first two types of solution, it is becoming increasingly clear that the third type cannot be ignored [see Fodor (1970b) and Fillmore (1971)]. In particular, it seems likely that some types of valid natural language inferences cannot be represented in the lexicon or formalized in systems of logic which are restricted to standard rules of inference. Consider example (4-96). It is clear that *a* entails *b*, and

4-96 a. John met Bill in New York.
b. John met Bill.

that the entailment turns not upon lexical properties of the words in the sentence, but rather upon the structural relation between a verb phrase and its adverbial modifier. The standard inference rules of formal logic do not, however, provide us with principles which mediate inferences that turn upon such relations. The moral would appear to be that a formal system which represents inferences like (4-96) will have to have some richer notion of rule of inference than standard logical formalisms employ.[23] (Indeed, dictionary entries could themselves be viewed as merely special cases of such rules.) On this view, a semantic theory contains a list of rules of inference, the most general of which are the principles of logic and the most specific of which explicate the content of lexical items. Such rules would mediate all semantic relations between linguistic forms that are distinct at the level of syntactic deep structure.

We cannot dismiss this proposal out of hand, but it is worth noticing that it has certain features which make it a priori less attractive than either lexicalism or transformationalism. In particular, lexicalist and transformationalist approaches to semantics both provide for a sharp distinction between *synonymy* and *equivalence* among sentences. In transformationalist accounts, synonymous sentences are syntactically related while sentences which are (merely) equivalent are not. In lexicalist accounts, synonymous sentences, and only these, receive identical semantic representations under the projection rules; sentences which are logically equivalent receive distinct semantic representations that are interconvertible under standard rules of logical inference.

It is clear that these are uncashed checks: neither lexicalist nor transformationalist accounts of the structure of even small parts of natural language convincingly draw the required distinction between logical equivalence and synonymy. The present point is that both lexicalist and transformationalist approaches envision drawing that distinction and have available theoretical mechanisms for its representation.

If, however, we assume that all valid inference in a natural language is to be determined by an otherwise undifferentiated set of inference rules, so that there is no formal distinction drawn between, say, (4-95)

---

[23] It has been suggested that sentences like (4-96*a*) are actually conjunctions, of which sentences like (4-96*b*) are conjuncts. If this is true, then the inference from the former sentence to the latter could be carried through by a standard rule of inference— simplification of conjunction. But there are some good reasons for supposing that such is not true. For discussion of this and related problems, see Davidson (1967) and Fodor (1970b).

and (4-97), it is extremely difficult to see how the distiction between

4-97   not (not Q) implies (*P* v *q*)

logical equivalence and synonymy is to be preserved. To put the same point another way, if we abandon the notion of a semantic lexicon, we presumably also abandon the notion that definitions have a special role to play in the establishment of semantic relations. But once we have given up the notion of a definition, it is unclear why the inference rule which introduces a predicate such as "parent of" ought not to be, say, (4-98) rather than (4-99).

4-98   (*x* and *y* are parents of *z*) if and only if (*w*) ((*w* would be an aunt or uncle of *z*) ≡ (*w* were a sibling of *x* or *y*))

4-99   *x* and *y* are parents of *z* if and only if *z* is a child of *x* and *y*.

In short, insofar as a semantic theory is supposed to distinguish synonymies from equivalences, it is unlikely that the theory can consist of a set of inference rules. Whether this shows more than that the distinction between synonymy and equivalence ought to be abandoned is, however, an open question.

SURFACE STRUCTURE AND SEMANTIC INTERPRETATION

The discussion in the last three sections turns largely upon the claim, widely accepted in standard generative theory, that lexical insertion occurs (only) at the level of deep structure. Roughly, this claim is compatible with lexicalist and meaning-rule approaches to semantics, but not with "generative semantics" approaches. This is not, however, the only principle of standard theory that has recently come into question. It is a central tenet of standard theory that all semantically relevant syntactic concepts are defined over base structure. Current work is bringing this principle into doubt.

4-100   a.   John met Mary in New York.
b.   It was in New York that John met Mary.

Consider, for example, sentences (4-100*a* and *b*). Though these two sentences are presumably transforms of the same base, it seems clear that they differ in some semantically relevant respect variously characterized as their "topic," "theme," "focus," "presupposition," or simply "what they are about." This can be seen in a variety of ways—for example, from the fact that *a*, but not *b*, is a possible answer to "Whom did John meet in New York?" Notice that the fact that *a* and *b* are answers to different questions is intimately related to the fact that their standard uses have different presuppositions. A speaker who asserts *a* would normally be *presupposing* that John met someone in New York and *saying* that the someone in question was Mary. A speaker who asserts *b* would normally be presupposing that John met Mary somewhere and *saying* that the somewhere in question was New York.

It appears that questions of "aboutness" and presupposition are related in a quite regular way to details of the *surface* organization of sentences. In particular, any change in constituent order which produces a corresponding alteration in the intonation center of a sentence will characteristically produce an alteration of its focus and presupposition. For example, the dative transformation produces such changes in sentence pairs like (4-101*a* and *b*). (The normal intona-

4-101 a. **John gave Mary the *book*.**
    b. **John gave the book to *Mary*.**

tion center is indicated by italics.) It seems correct to say that these sentences differ in presupposition in precisely the respect that *a* presupposes John gave Mary something, while *b* presupposes that John gave the book to someone. Chomsky (1970a) suggests that any constituent containing the intonation center of a sentence can serve as the focus of the sentence, and that the corresponding presupposition can be specified by replacing the focus with a variable.[24]

But while it seems reasonably certain that some semantic properties of sentences are determined by their surface organization, it is not

---

[24] It is possible to maintain the principle that semantically relevant syntactic concepts are defined over base structures even in the face of the apparently intimate relation between surface structure, focus, and presupposition. For example, Lakoff (1970) has suggested that deep structures should consist of *pairs* of constituent trees and representations of presuppositions. A *derivational constraint* rejects any route through the transformations unless the resulting surface sentence has the presuppositions that the base structure specifies.

This approach permits presupposition to be specified in the base, but only at the risk of trivializing the claim that base structure is the natural vehicle for representing semantically relevant syntactic relations. Suppose, for example, that one wanted to require that the phonetic length of a sentence be represented in its base structure. The notion of a derivational constraint will allow one to do this. Thus, a deep structure would consist of a pair of a constituent tree and a number, and a derivational constraint would reject any route through the transformations unless the number of phones in the terminal string was equal to the number that is specified in the base. Clearly, by allowing ourselves computational mechanisms of this power, we can guarantee that *any* property of sentences we choose can be represented as a property of their base structures. This suggests that *not* allowing the unlimited exploitation of such mechanisms is a condition of making our claims about what is in the base substantive.

known which properties these are or what, if anything, they have in common. For example, it is obviously an important question whether features of entailment are determined by surface structure, and the answer to this question is by no means clear.

Partly this is because the relation between presupposition, focus, etc., and entailment is itself unclear. Thus, one wants to say that sentences (4-100a and b) differ in their presuppositions, but it is less obvious whether one wants to say that they differ in their entailments. Consider the case in which it was Sally whom John met in New York. Then a would be false, since a says that it was Mary whom John met. But if the condition for a sentence's being false is that what it *says* is false, then b can have no truth value whatever, since what is false is not what b *says* but what it *presupposes*.

Clearly, if one accepts this view, and if one wants to maintain the principle that sentences with the same deep structure are synonymous, something will have to be done by way of changing the intended notion of sentential synonymy. The present examples suggest that we will have to abandon the notion that synonymous sentences have the same truth value, and substitute for it some such notion as the following: *Two sentences are synonymous only under the following condition: If they both have a truth value, then they both have the same truth value*. In this account, the members of such pairs as (4-100) and (4-101) could be considered synonymous. In the troublesome case in which the presupposition of one member of the pair is false, the sentences will not *differ* in truth value; rather, one will have a truth value and the other will have none.

There is, however, a serious question of whether, even in this revised view of synonymy, sentences which share a base structure are synonymous whatever their surface structures may be. It is probably fair to say that no one knows the answer to this question. For example, Chomsky (1970a) and Jackendoff (1969) have argued that the scope of such elements as quantifiers is determined by surface structure. If this is true, then even this reduced sense of synonymy is not determined by base structure, since pairs of sentences which differ in quantifier scope will often have opposed truth values. The examples on which the claim that surface structure determines the scope of quantifiers rests seem, however, to be very equivocal.

Consider, for example, such pairs as (4-102a and b). In the first place,

4-102　a.　**Many men read few books.**
　　　　b.　**Few books are read by many men.**

though these sentences have the same base, they do seem to differ in meaning: a would naturally be taken to mean "many men are not book readers" and b to mean "(only) a few books are widely read." It is quite natural to represent this difference in meaning as a difference in the scope of the quantifiers "few" and "many." In particular, in *a* the scope relations might be represented as "(many men) (they read few books)" while in *b* the scope relations are "(few books) (many men read them)." The upshot is that cases such as (4-102) make it seem plausible to associate quantifier scope with surface quantifier order, the general principle being that the leftmost surface quantifier is the one with longest scope.

The situation is, however, less clear than these examples suggest. In the first place, the difference in meaning between (4-102*a* and *b*) seems to depend not only on a change in the scope of the quantifiers but also on the way that the quantifiers interact with the negative element "few." Notice that *both* members of the pair in (4-103) are ambiguous.

> 4-103 a. **You can fool all of the people some of the time.**
> b. **You can fool some of the people all of the time.**

There may be some tendency in cases like (4-103) to take the leftmost quantifier in surface structure to be the one with longest scope, but this tendency is clearly far less pronounced than in cases where the quantifiers interact with negatives; and this fact is not explained by an account which says that surface quantifier order determines scope.

More worrying still is the fact that there seem to be surface structures in which the principle "leftmost quantifier has longest scope" fails even when the quantifiers *are* interacting with negative elements. Consider the pair in (4-104). It might possibly be maintained that both these sentences are ambiguous. What seems entirely clear is that (4-104 *b*) does not

> 4-104 a. **John reads most people few poems.**
> b. **John reads few poems to most people.**

unambiguously mean "(few poems) (John reads them to most people)." If it did, then "John says few words to most people" could be questioned by "Which words?"

In short, the question of whether entailment is ever a phenomenon of surface structure remains open. Certainly this is a question with which psychologists interested in syntax recognition ought to be concerned. What we will have to say about recognition in Chapter 6 will assume that the primary problem in understanding a sentence is that of determining its base structure, and that the computation of its surface representations is a matter of secondary concern. It is an open question to what extent cases like (4-102) put that assumption in dispute.

SUMMARY AND CONCLUSION

The preceding should serve to make clear how far we are from the solution of even preliminary problems about the organization of semantic theories of natural languages; certain conclusions do, however, seem to be relatively firm.

1. The most fruitful approaches to semantics currently available are those which take the sentence (as opposed to the word) to be the fundamental unit under examination. In particular, the "problem of language and the world" is primarily the problem of providing an adequate account of the standard uses of sentences.

2. Sentences are used to perform speech acts. Of these, assertion seems to be paradigmatic for many kinds of declarative sentences. Part of a semantic theory ought thus to give an account of the speech acts and especially of assertion. In particular, we require a specification of the conditions under which an utterance of a sentence *counts* as an assertion, and of the conditions under which an assertion counts as being true.

Presumably all languages contain linguistic forms whose standard use is making assertions, and all language users distinguish between true assertions and false ones. Hence, the part of a semantic theory which is concerned with analyzing assertion belongs to "general linguistic theory." Analogous remarks hold for such other uses of sentences as asking questions, giving commands, making promises, etc.

3. Each sentence in a given language can be associated with a certain speech act, or class of speech acts, by virtue of the lexical content and syntactic form of the sentence. In this sense, there is for each sentence, a characteristic act, or class of acts, for the performance of which that sentence is the standard linguistic vehicle. Synonymous sentences will be standardly associated with the same class of speech acts.

4. Since both the set of speech acts and the set of sentences is infinite, sentences must be associated with speech acts by some recursive procedure.

5. A part of a semantic theory must thus be a function which assigns to each sentence a representation that formally determines the speech acts it can standardly be used to perform. It seems certain that this function must be defined over the syntactic form and lexical content of a sentence. But it is highly unclear, as things now stand, how the function operates, or precisely what kinds of formal representations of sentences it provides.

6. In case of a sentence standardly used to make assertions, the theory must assign representations which determine which assertion the sentence is standardly used to make. In particular, this representation, in combination with appropriate rules of inference, must formally determine the entailments of the sentence, since assertions are presumably to be analyzed as truth claims and two assertions make the same truth claims only if they have their entailments in common.

7. It follows from 5 and 6 that the representations a semantic theory assigns to sentences are sensitive to two sorts of constraints: "linguistic" constraints, in that they must be mechanically computable given the appropriate syntactic and lexical analysis of the sentence; and "logical" constraints, in that they must provide appropriate domains for rules of inference.

At this point, such clarity as is currently available seems to run out, and the issues become very murky. In particular:

a. We do not have an adequate account of the entailments of most kinds of sentences. Hence, with relatively few exceptions, we do not know what the output of a semantic theory ought to be for any given sentence as input. It is patently impossible to do serious research on a formal procedure for the assignment of semantic representations to sentences until we have a fairly good idea of what structures we want the procedures to assign; and, since what such structures are supposed to do is determine entailments, we will not know what structures we want to assign until we know more about what entailments various kinds of sentences have.

b. Syntax becomes vexed at precisely those points which concern the domain of such a procedure. In particular, we do not know how rich the syntactic structures are from which semantic representations will be computed, and we do not know what kinds of evidence ought to be considered decisive in answering this question.

It appears, in fact, that a rather unpleasant dilemma may be in the making here. If deep syntactic structures are allowed to be *very* abstract, we can effect a corresponding simplification of the function which maps them onto semantic representations. In the limiting case, we might suppose that it is an identity function, e.g., that sentences have a common deep structure if and only if their behavior is semantically identical. But insofar as the linguistic evidence supports such abstract analyses, a problem is posed for the psychologist concerned with syntax recovery: the more abstract deep structures become, the more computation will be required for their recognition. The prima facie interests of the psychologist and the semanticist thus appear likely to be at odds in this repect, and this bodes ill for anyone who has the best interest of both disciplines at heart.

c.   Throughout this discussion we have assumed that the appropriate vehicle for entailment is the sentence, and there are notorious philosophical problems with this assumption. We might, for example, wish to suppose that it is statements, rather than sentences used to make statements, that have entailments, thus accounting for such facts as that the entailments of sentences like (4-105) vary depending upon which speaker uses them (if, indeed, this *is* a fact). The point here is that the

4-105   I am ill.

theory of speech acts may finally need to preempt some of the notions we have been assuming belong primarily to the theory of sentences, thus requiring mutual (and possibly drastic) readjustment all along the line.

Our discussion has been devoted almost entirely to speculations about some of the general properties of semantic theories of natural languages. Very little has been said about specifically psycholinguistic problems about semantics. To understand why this is the case, it is only necessary to hark back to the general comments about the character of theories in cognitive psychology that we made in Chapter 1. We argued that such theories consist, on the one hand, of analyses of the concepts at the disposal of an organism and, on the other, of accounts of how these concepts are internalized and applied to their instances. If this approach is generally correct, it is hardly surprising that psychology has thus far failed to produce theories of any importance in the area of semantics. We cannot ask pertinent or insightful (to say nothing of experimentally resolvable) questions about how the semantic system of a speaker-hearer is used, or about how it is learned, until something substantial is known about the properties of that system. The part of theory construction which consists in conceptual analysis is, in this sense, methodologically prior to the part which considers questions about the application or assimilation of concepts. It is highly probable, though doubtless depressing, that specifically psychological work on semantics will continue to be largely impertinent until a great deal more theoretical insight has been gained about the structure of formal semantic theory than is currently available.

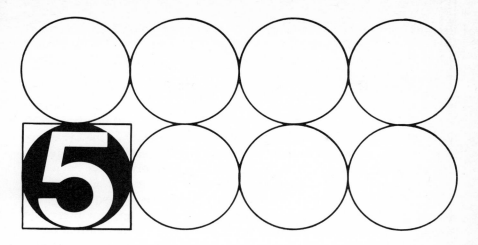

THE PSYCHOLOGICAL
REALITY OF
GRAMMATICAL STRUCTURES

PSYCHOLOGY AND THE "NEW GRAMMAR"

Among the more striking changes in the style of psycholinguistic research after the advent of transformational grammars was the proliferation of experiments on details of syntactic structure. Earlier work tended to treat "language" as a homogeneous field of behavior, paying relatively little attention to the psychological consequences of the structural differences sentences exhibit. As we pointed out in Chapter 2, for example, Hullean psycholinguistics emphasized the links between behavioral and linguistic theories. But except for their concern with the effects of varying the redundancy of messages, psychologists in this tradition showed little interest in how structural features of sentences affect psychological processes in the comprehension, production, or acquisition of language.[1]

There are several reasons why the development of transformational theory should have stimulated an interest in the psycholinguistic consequences of details of syntactic structure. First, earlier accounts of grammar did not begin to suggest the full complexity of the organization of sentences: transformational grammars revealed "language behavior" to be far more richly organized than had previously been suspected. Second, most psychological theories that were at all concerned with language tended to place primary emphasis on explaining the learning process. But there was nothing in learning theory which could account for the remarkable differentiation of verbal behavior that transformational treatments revealed. In this respect, generative syntax represented a new and very much more detailed case of an old embarrassment for American psychology. As Osgood (1953) had pointed out,

> When perceptual phenomena are treated in behavioristic texts it is usually from a strictly descriptive point of view, with little or no attempt at integration or interpretation. The fact that triangular forms are perceived as such, that the colors of recognized objects show constancy, that objects are seen as three dimensional, is vaguely attributed to "learning", but there the matter usually ends. It is assumed that since perceptions are learned behaviors, they must follow the same principles as other responses—they must display habit formation, generalization, inhibition, and so on—but no attempt has been made to apply these principles to perceptual phenomena in any detail. The reason for this is certainly not elusive: almost by definition perceptual events are neither exclusively dependent upon manipulable stimulus variables nor reflected in readily recorded overt movements—they are mediation processes [pp. 208-209].

Thus, classic problems about the organization of perception and action were revived by the development of a new linguistic formalism which offered both an indefinite body of examples of such organization and a disciplined theory of the generalizations which underlie the examples.

---

[1] The report of the Summer Seminar on Psycholinguistics (Osgood and Sebeok, 1954) issued a call for empirical work on linguistic relativity, transitional probabilities among items of different lexical classes, the relation of associative structure to linguistic structure, the cross-cultural generality of meaning systems, etc. But there seems to have been little or no feeling that experiments in which syntactic structure was the manipulated variable might yield interesting results. Diebold's (1969) review of the ensuing decade of work makes it clear that widespread interest in studying how details of syntactic structure affect the recognition, production, and learning of linguistic materials was attributable largely to the impact of generative grammar on psychological research.

This combination was unique in the history of psychology,[2] and it had the effect of making the problem of recognition and production of structured forms the central one in the psychological study of language.

So, in the late 1950s and early 1960s, we find experimenters beginning to ask whether the structures which grammars postulate are psychologically "real" and, if so, what procedures the speaker-hearer uses to manipulate them. The present chapter is primarily devoted to a review of experiments on the first of these questions. The common theme of these experiments is the attempt to determine whether syntactic structural descriptions correspond to the representations which speaker-hearers use in understanding, producing, or remembering sentences. In later chapters we will review what has been learned about the computational operations involved in the construction of such representations in speaking and listening.

THE DISCOVERY OF SYNTAX

In 1950 Miller and Selfridge demonstrated an effect of language structure on the recall of strings of words. They showed that recall improves as one increases the order of approximation of such strings to the statistical regularities of English. At the time, Miller and Selfridge interpreted this result in terms of the view that sentence structure is determined by a series of left-right associative dependencies between successive lexical items (or pairs, or triples, etc., of such items). A decade later, however, Miller and Isard (1963) [and subsequently Marks and Miller (1964)] were using quite similar stimulus materials to demonstrate the effect of specifically syntactic (nonstatistical) factors in the perception and recall of sentences. A fundamental change in the way psychologists think about language was implicit in this difference in the way the manipulated variable was interpreted in these studies.

Miller and Isard constructed a set of fifty sentences, each of which contained five principal content words, and each of which was fully grammatical and meaningful; for example, (5-1). By systematically in-

5-1 Accidents kill motorists on the highways.
Bears steal honey from the hive.

terchanging content words from these sentences, they constructed an ad-

---

[2]But note that Gestalt psychologists' emphasis on the "good figure" principle and their examples of ambiguous forms have obvious parallels in the grammatical notions of well-formedness and ambiguity in sentences. [See, for example, chapter 10 in Neisser (1967).]

ditional set of fifty stimuli; for example, (5-2). These stimuli were presumed to be syntactically well formed but "semantically anomalous" in at least the sense that the statistical and associative dependencies between adjacent lexical items were weaker than those holding in the first set. A third set of fifty stimuli were derived from the anomalous sen-

5-2   Accidents carry honey between the house.
Bears shoot work on the country.

tences by "haphazardly permuting the positions [within strings] in order to destroy ... syntactic structure" (p. 220); for example, (5-3). Subjects listened to the lists of sentences under various signal-to-noise

5-3   Around accidents country honey the shoot.
On trains hive elephants the simplify.

ratios. The main result was that the three classes of stimulus strings were significantly different in their perceptibility under noise. Normal sentences were the best understood, "semantically anomalous" strings were the next best, and random strings of words were the worst understood. This result was taken to suggest an effect of the syntactic structure of a sentence that is independent of its semantic or associative coherence.

In the experiment by Marks and Miller, similar kinds of stimulus materials were used, but a fourth class of items was added: semantically interpretable scrambled sentences (e.g., "Fatal accidents deter careful drivers" became "Deter drivers accidents fatal careful"). Marks and Miller referred to these as "anagram strings." Their intention was to present strings which had a definite interpretation but which did not exhibit normal syntactic structure. In this very restricted sense, the sentences may be regarded as semantically coherent though ungrammatical. Marks and Miller thus had strings which were syntactically well formed but semantically anomalous, strings which were semantically coherent but syntactically anomalous (i.e., the anagram strings), and word lists. Subjects were presented with tape recordings of mixed lists of these various types of stimulus strings and were required to report immediately as much of each string as they were able. Five successive presentations of each list of stimulus strings were given. The median percent of recall at each trial was tabulated; Figure 5-1 shows the results.

All three of the experiments just discussed varied the "sensibleness" or interpretability of word strings. Although Miller and Selfridge acknowledged the operation of both semantic and syntactic factors in determining the performance of their subjects, the information theoretic model of language on which their work was based did not require or suggest the importance of such a distinction; that model would identify *both* the semantic *and* the syntactic coherence of a string with its redun-

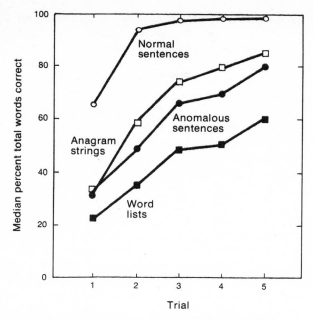

Fig. 5-1. Median percent of total words correct for each of the four types of strings over five trials. A word was counted as correct regardless of its position in the string (from Marks and Miller, 1964).

dancy. The Marks and Miller and the Miller and Isard studies were, however, explicit in their recognition of the possible importance of syntactic structure as a psychological variable distinct from associative relations, redundancy, semantic plausibility, etc. They thus acknowledged a kind of organization in language which is presumably not to be explained by appeal to the sorts of factors that classically function in associative accounts of behavior.

It is certainly possible to doubt that any of these experiments actually succeeded in independently manipulating syntactic and semantic variables. In particular, the assumption that semantic anomalies were produced by the experimental changes yielding (5-2) seems to commit the investigators to an associative account of semantic relations, even though they rejected such an account for syntactic relations. The distinction between (5-2) and (5-3) is probably one of degree of grammaticalness, with sentences like (5-2) exhibiting fewer, and less severe, structural violations than sentences like (5-3). Certainly, the literature provides no principled theoretical grounds for assuming a qualitative distinction between such sentences. [For discussion, see Chomsky (1964) and Katz (1964).] In short, the interesting aspect of these experiments is not that they actually demonstrate a fundamental difference between syntactic and semantic structure, but rather that they are concerned with the importance of the former as a potentially significant psychological variable.

The same historical moral can be drawn from a paper by Mandler and Mandler (1964). They showed that the bowed serial position curve characteristic of the learning of lists of nonsense syllables does not appear when the stimulus lists can be interpreted as sentences. Here again, the linguistic organization of the stimulus string has a strong influence on the character of the subjects' performance, an observation that previous researchers might have granted[3] but would probably have considered irrelevant to their main theoretical concerns. Psychologists studied learning of nonsense strings precisely because in real sentences the presence of previously learned linguistic structure obscures the formation of new associations, and it was the latter process in which psychologists were primarily interested. It is indicative of the change in the psychological climate that the previous decade's irrelevancies became the object of overt inquiry in the 1960s. [For a review detailing a similar trend in experimentation on word-list learning, see Bower (1970).]

THE PSYCHOLOGICAL REALITY OF INTERSENTENTIAL RELATIONS

We saw in Chapter 3 that transformational grammars provide means for representing the fact that sentences which differ in their constituent structure may nevertheless be syntactically related. Transformations impose a taxonomy upon the sentence types of a language: sentences are interrelated insofar as they share portions of their transformational histories. A number of early experiments, initially inspired by the work of George Miller, fixed upon this aspect of the function of transformations. The reasoning was that if the taxonomy implied by the transformational system predicts the similarities that speaker-hearers actually perceive among sentence types, the claim that the transformational mechanisms are themselves psychologically real is correspondingly supported.

These early studies differed in the experimental paradigms they employed, but they were quite similar in the linguistic structures they investigated and in the grammatical assumptions that motivated them. Most of these assumptions should seem quite natural, given the discussion in Chapter 3. One of them, however, requires special comment.

It was assumed in much of the early psycholinguistic research that

---

[3] Indeed, Thorndike (1930) discussed this fact.

one sentence form, the simple, active, affirmative, declarative (hereafter called a "kernel"), was of preeminent theoretical significance. This was because of the role which kernel sentences played in the grammars with which the experimenters were working.

In Chapter 3 we argued that transformations like passive, negative, etc., are mandatory and are triggered by markers in the base structure of the sentences to which they apply. This account is largely attributable to Katz and Postal (1964) and is widely accepted in "standard" analyses. An alternative, earlier view [see Chomsky (1957)] is that such transformations are optional and apply to a base structure which is literally indistinguishable from that which underlies simple declaratives. In this view, a base-structure tree could be optionally "passivized," "questioned," "negated," etc., by the application of the relevant transformational rules. Given that none of these "optional singulary" transformations were applied to a base tree, it was automatically transformed into a kernel sentence by mandatory rules.

Given such a formulation of the grammar, the assumption of special psychological significance for kernel sentences is easy to understand. Such sentences are the most direct expressions of the underlying form from which the related members of a sentence family are derived.[4] Moreover, kernel sentences are always the syntactically simplest members of their sentence family, since they are the only ones in which options for transformational elaboration have not been exploited. The assumption that kernel sentences are special in these ways holds not only for the research on perceived similarities between sentences that we are about to review but also for a class of memory studies which we will discuss later in the section on the coding hypothesis.

Miller, McKean, and Slobin (reported in Miller, 1962b) performed the first experiment aimed at testing the psychological reality of the taxonomy of sentences implied by transformational grammars. They attempted to do this by determining the times taken to produce one member of a sentence family as a response, given some other member as stimulus. In particular, they asked whether these response times could be predicted as a function of the transformational distance between the sentence forms.

Figure 5-2 displays the presumed relations among the members of the sentence family formed by the optional singulary transformations and their combinations. The transformational distance between any

---

[4] By "sentence family," we refer to a group of sentences which are all transforms of the same base-structure tree (including its lexical formatives). For example, the sentences in (3-30) constitute such a family.

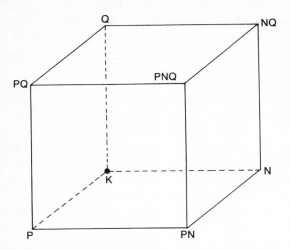

Fig. 5-2. Relations between members of a sentence family
formed by the optional singularies passive, negative, and question (after Miller, 1962b).

two sentences is represented by a path along the edges of this cube;
each vertex of the cube corresponds to a sentence type. For example,
this diagram represents *K* (kernel) sentences and *PNQ* (passive, negative, question) sentences as maximally dissimilar: three steps are
required to move from the *K* vertex to the *PNQ* vertex (the diagonals of
the space being undefined). Similarly, *P*, *N*, and *Q* are represented as
equidistant from *K*.

We will see that the detailed justification of experimental predictions
based on this representation of the transformational distance between
sentence types turns out to be rather difficult. As a first approximation,
however, one can use the cube in Figure 5-2 to generate predictions
about the time required to interrelate a pair of sentences as follows:
such times should be proportional to the shortest distance between the
sentences along the edges of the cube.

In the initial experiment, subjects were presented with a page containing two columms of sentences; the sentences in the two columns
differed depending upon the experimental condition to which the subject was assigned. For example, a sentence in one column might have
been, "Jane liked the old woman" (*K*), while its counterpart, which appeared somewhere in the other column, would be "The old woman was
liked by Jane" (*P*). Subjects were instructed to locate, in the target column, the sentence corresponding to a designated transform of each sentence in the source column. *K* and *P*, *K* and *N*, *K* and *PN*, *N* and *P*, *N* and
PN, and *P* and *PN* were all tested. Base search times were determined by
having subjects match *un*transformed versions of sentences in two

scrambled lists—as, for example, two lists of the same K sentences in different orders.

Two of the types of sentences studied by Miller et al., were presumed to be related by two transformational operations, and four were presumed to be related by a single operation. For instance, where a P sentence was called for and an N sentence was given, it was assumed that the subject "undid" the work of the negative transformation and then applied the passive, thus requiring two transformational steps. However, for the same initial condition (given an N sentence), but with a PN target sentence, it was assumed that only one step was required. (Since the initial sentence is N, the subject need only apply the passive transformation to produce PN.) Subjects' performance showed just the order predicted by these assumptions. It thus appeared that the model of sentence relations given in Figure 5-2 could be used to predict the psychological difficulty of relating sentence types to one another.

A modified replication of this experiment was conducted by Miller and McKean (1964). In this version, the sentences were individually presented tachistoscopically; when a subject decided he had performed the required transformation, he pressed a button which presented the search list. The results of this version of the experiment were generally comparable to those of the paper-and-pencil method, and we will rely on it for the details of the subsequent discussion.

As Table 5-1 shows, the sentence pairs whose members differ by two transformations are interrelated less rapidly than are the pairs whose members differ by only a single transformation. Within the two sets (i.e., single-transformation relations and double-transformation relations) the orderings are quite uniform: the negative transformation is in every case easier than the passive transformation; and, in every case, pairs which include a K as the source or target are easier than corresponding pairs which test the same transformation but do not include a K sentence. Further, the data suggest that the transformations may produce a linearly additive complication of the stimulus sentences: for example, sentences which involve both the negative and passive transformations appear to require a time approximately equal to the sum of the average time required for negative or passive applied separately.

Miller and McKean's results also show no significant difference attributable to the direction of transformation. For example, subjects were required to transform K sentences to N sentences as frequently as they were required to transform N sentences into K sentences. There is very little evidence of any difference in search time as a function of this difference in direction.

It would be well to pause at this point and reflect on the impressiveness of this pattern of results. The grammatical formalism which provided the basis for the predictions was in no way intended to afford

TABLE 5-1. CONVERSION TIMES FOR SOME OPTIONAL SINGULARY SENTENCES

Average presentation times, sec

Rows are labeled according to syntax of sentences presented; columns are labeled according to syntax into which it had to be transformed (experimental condition) or which also occurred on the same subtest (control condition).

	K	N	P	PN
Experimental:				
K	....	1.81	2.20	2.49
N	2.08	....	3.60	2.73
P	2.51	3.51	....	2.20
PN	2.92	2.72	2.37	....
Control:				
K	....	1.42	1.46	1.35
N	1.68	....	1.80	1.70
P	1.63	1.68	....	1.80
PN	1.58	1.73	1.93	....
Differences:				
K	....	0.39	0.74	1.14
N	0.40	....	1.80	1.03
P	0.88	1.83	....	0.40
PN	1.34	0.99	0.44	....

Source: After Miller and McKean, 1964.

an index of the facility with which speaker-hearers manipulate linguistic objects. Rather it was intended to represent those aspects of the syntactic organization of a sentence upon which its semantic interpretation is dependent; the ones which mediate the relation between form and meaning. The experimental finding that the psychological distance between sentences can be predicted from transformational distance thus represents a surprising and nonobvious convergence of psychological and linguistic results. The thesis that grammatical transformations are in some sense psychologically real—that they correspond in some very close way to mental operations—seems strongly supported by the results of these two experiments. So too is the thesis that K sentences are "special," since their presumed simplicity and centrality in the grammar is reflected in the relative facility which subjects showed in manipulating sentence pairs that included a K.

There are, however, two cautionary notes. The first is that the evidence so far relates to only a very limited class of grammatical operations. Indeed, the items tested do not even exhaust the potentialities of the cube in Figure 5-2. The second point is that we have yet to examine closely the argument which derives the experimental predictions from the grammatical assumptions: the thesis that the operations that subjects performed in these experiments were in fact those specified by grammatical transformations.

Construct validity of the Miller and McKean model.   The question we wish to take most seriously at this point is: How closely does the pattern of results in these experiments bear on the question of the psychological reality of the grammatical rules used in the derivations of the stimulus sentences? Given that the experimentally determined distances between the sentences correspond to the taxonomy of sentences implied by a transformational grammar, can we explain the correspondence by assuming that subjects actually employ syntactic transformations in carrying out the experimental task? To answer this question, we will need to discuss some properties of the transformational rules themselves. The discussion will apply with equal force to the "standard" version of these rules and to the Chomsky (1957) version.

Let us consider the sequence of operations a subject would presumably have to carry out if his computations in the Miller and McKean experiment were to correspond to the operations specified by a transformational grammar. In so doing, we must bear in mind that transformations are ordered with respect to one another in grammatical derivations. Thus, if Miller and McKean's subjects were to apply the grammatical transformation T to a given stimulus sentence in the experimental task, they would first have to recover a representation of the sentence structure as it appears in the derivation *prior* to the application of any rule ordered later than T. When we take this requirement into account, however, we predict relations among the sentence types that are quite different from those obtained experimentally. The clear inference appears to be that Miller and McKean's subjects could not have been using the grammatical transformations to perform the experimental task.

Consider some cases which illustrate the problem. In Miller and McKean's formulation, the translation of N to P is more complex than the translation of N to NP; this is because, in the first case, it is assumed that the subject must undo the effect of the negative transformation as well as apply the passive. But in the second case, this is not necessary; passive is assumed to apply directly to the negated form. In fact, however, in order to perform the passive transformation, one must perform the inverse negative transformation in *both* cases. This is because in the grammar, the operation of the negative transformation is ordered *after* the operation of the passive transformation. The justification of this ordering is that applying negative *before* passive would result in ungrammatical strings. For example, if we assume that the negative transformation applies to an underlying string, (5-4a), we will get the string shown

5-4   a.   {John *Aux* kiss Mary}

in (5-4b). If we now apply passive to this string, we get (5-4c), which

5-4 b. {John *Aux Neg* kiss Mary}

5-4 c. {Mary *Aux Neg* be + en + kiss by John}

corresponds to the ungrammatical surface form (5-4d). Thus, a string to

5-4 d. *Mary didn't be kissed by John.

which the passive transformation is applied must not be one to which the negative transformation has previously applied. The implication for the N to PN case is that if the subjects are using the transformational rules as specified by a grammar, the order of application must be to detransform negative, then passive, and then negativize. Hence *three* operations, rather than one, are required to convert N into PN (although our way of counting agrees with Miller and McKean in requiring only two transformations to interconvert negatives and passives: detransform negative, then passivize, or conversely). Similarly, P to PN requires only one transformation, as compared with the three required for N to PN, since negation *can* be applied to a passivized string in the grammar.

Table 5-2 lists the transformations or their inverses (both optional and obligatory in terms of the 1957 grammar) for the sentences investigated by Miller and McKean which involve P, N, and K. We have included in this tally the effect of *do*-support, a mandatory transformation which inserts *do* into sentences where "tense" is the only auxiliary element. This transformation operates after *Aux* inversion in the formation of such questions as "Does John eat," or "Did John eat," and it operates after *Neg* placement but before *affix* movement to produce such sentences as "John didn't eat." It is an anomaly in Miller and McKean's results (as in other results that we shall presently review) that the operation of *do*-support characteristically does *not* contribute to the obtained intersentence distances. This is another consideration which militates against interpreting these results as providing direct experimental support for the psychological reality of transformations.

The remarks we have been making about P and N apply also to the sentence pairs involving Q. Roughly, passive must apply prior to the question transformation because it affects the character of the auxiliary which is moved by Q (e.g., *Did John be eaten by the shark?). In fact, the passive transformation is literally undefined for structures to which Q has applied, since the formulation of the passive rule assumes that the elements of the auxiliary are in the positions that they occupy before Q applies to rearrange them. (See the discussion in Chapter 3.) Thus, if P, Q, and PQ were included in our table (as they are in Figure

TABLE 5-2. TRANSFORMATIONS AND THEIR INVERSES REQUIRED TO INTERCONVERT *K, N, P,* AND *PN*

	Number of transformations	Total
K to P:		
1. Inverse affix movement (i.e., recover base needed to satisfy structured index of *P*)	1*	
2. Apply passive transform	(2)†	3
3. Affix movement		
P to K:		
1. Inverse affix movement		
2. Inverse passive transform	1	
3. Affix movement	(2)	3
K to N:		
1. Inverse affix movement		
2. Negative transform	1	
3. *Do*-support transform	(3)	4
4. Affix movement		
N to K:		
1. Inverse affix movement		
2. Inverse *do*-support transform	1	
3. Inverse negation	(3)	4
4. Affix movement		
P to PN:		
1. Inverse affix movement		
2. Negative transform	1	
3. Affix movement	(2)	3
PN to P:		
1. Inverse affix movement		
2. Inverse negative	1	
3. Affix movement	(2)	3
N to PN:		
1. Inverse affix movement		
2. Inverse *do*-support		
3. Inverse negative	3	
4. Passive transform	(3)	
5. Negative transform		6
6. Affix movement		
PN to N:		
1. Inverse affix movement		
2. Inverse negative		
3. Inverse passive	3	
4. Negative transform	(3)	
5. *Do*-support		6
6. Affix movement		

(Continued)

TABLE 5-2. *Continued*

	Number of transformations	Total
K to PN:		
1. Inverse affix movement		
2. Passive transform	2	
3. Negative transform	(2)	4
4. Affix movement		
PN to K:		
1. Inverse affix movement		
2. Inverse negative	2	
3. Inverse passive	(2)	4
4. Affix movement		
N to P:		
1. Inverse affix movement		
2. Inverse *do*-support	2	
3. Inverse negative	(3)	5
4. Passive transform		
5. Affix movement		
P to N:		
1. Inverse affix movement		
2. Inverse passive		
3. Negative transform	2	
4. *Do*-support	(3)	5
5. Affix movement		

*Optional.
†Obligatory.

5-2), $P \leftrightarrow PQ$ would require one step (apply the question transformation) while $Q \leftrightarrow PQ$ would require three steps (apply the inverse of the question transformation, passivize, then apply the question transformation).

We have argued that it is dubious whether Miller and McKean's subjects were in fact employing grammatical transformations in the experimental task; hence, it is dubious whether the experiment provides evidence for the psychological reality of transformations. We shall presently see that this view is compatible with holding that Miller and McKean's results do provide evidence for the psychological reality of the taxonomy of sentences that standard transformational grammars imply. First, however, we shall review some studies which suggest that Miller and McKean's results are reliable in the sense that they hold across a variety of experimental paradigms and sentential materials.

Generality of the results obtained by Miller et al. The experiments by Miller et al. concern only three sentence types and one variation on a single experimental paradigm. We can begin to inquire into the generality of these findings by considering other studies of the optional singulary transformations. There are two that are especially relevant: Clifton, Kurcz, and Jenkins (1965) and Clifton and Odom (1966).

Clifton, Kurcz, and Jenkins investigated the same kinds of sentences as Miller and McKean (K, P, N, PN) but employed a different experimental task. The response measure they used was an adaptation of a technique developed by Mink (1963) for testing the effects of "semantic generalization." In this paradigm, subjects are first exposed to a training list of sentences for some specified number of presentations; during the presentation of the training list, the subject presses a button (which sounds a buzzer) immediately following the presentation of each stimulus sentence. In the test phase, subjects are presented with a new list of sentences which includes the training-list sentences either in their original form or in some transformed versions. Also on the test list are control sentences—sentences which did not occur on the training list and are not transforms of training-list sentences. Subjects are instructed to press the telegraph key during the test list whenever they recognize a sentence from the training list. The number of instances in which subjects erroneously press the key in response to the presentation of either a control sentence or a transformed version of a training-list sentence provides an index of generalization.

Clifton et al.'s subjects exhibited a substantial amount of generalization to transformed versions of the training-list sentences as compared with the control sentences. False positive responses to control sentences averaged .03, while the response frequency to transforms of the training-list sentences ranged from .17 to .85.

More importantly, there were also significant differences among the levels of generalization as a function of the particular transformational relations that connected training- and test-list sentences. Clifton et al. interpreted these generalization data in terms of a distance metric. As Figure 5-3 indicates, the results are similar to those obtained by Miller and McKean with one exception: the unexpectedly large distance between K and N sentences. Barring that, the comment made about the Miller and McKean results might also be made here: sentences which differ by two transformations show less generalization (i.e., have a greater separation in the distance metric) than sentences differing by a single transformation, and a transformation and its inverse appear to contribute in the same measure to the distance function. A third property of Miller and McKean's results—additivity—is, of course, complicated in Clifton et al. by the disproportionate distance between K and N (though it seems to hold for other comparisons).

The intent of the Clifton and Odom (1966) experimentation was more ambitious than that of Clifton et al. Like all the studies thus far reviewed, Clifton and Odom sought to determine the relation between

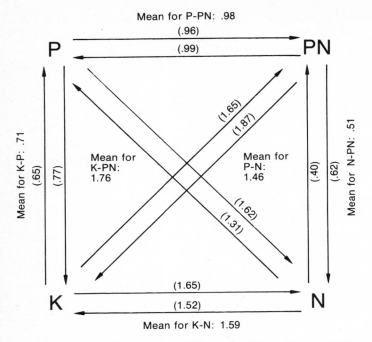

Fig. 5-3. "Distances" between some optional singulary members in a generalization task (after Clifton, Kurcz, and Jenkins, 1965).

syntactic descriptions of sentences and the psychological similarity of sentence types. But they were also interested in contrasting the predictions of two syntactic models and in assessing the effects of changes in experimental paradigms. In particular, the Chomsky (1957) model, which treated negative, question, passive, etc., as optional singulary transformations was contrasted with the Katz and Postal (1964) model according to which such transformations are obligatory.

It will be recalled that "standard" theory distinguishes the members of a sentence family not only in their transformational history but also in the base configurations which underlie them. The representation of the sentence family, as Clifton and Odom interpreted the Katz and Postal suggestion, is given in Figure 5-4. This figure should be understood somewhat differently from the cube in Figure 5-2; here the dimensions correspond to the presence of "universal grammatical markers" (that is, *P, Q, N*) in the base; thus the "prism" representation is tantamount to a claim that questions and negative questions are more similar *in their base structures* than, say, passives and negative passives.

Clifton and Odom performed several experiments, most of them employing the technique adapted from Mink by Clifton, Kurcz, and Jenkins. Multidimensional scaling techniques were used to achieve a

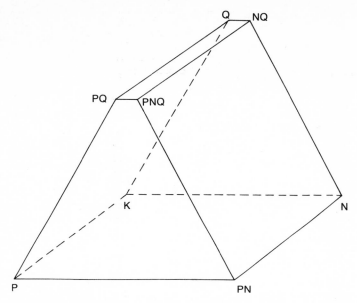

Fig. 5-4. Relations between optional singulary members on the Katz-Postal theory (after Clifton and Odom, 1966).

spatial representation of the data from each of the experiments. The full set of sentences, involving all the interactions of *P*, *N*, and *Q*, were tested in one way or another. A brief description of their experiments follows.

In their first study, Clifton and Odom obtained explicit judgments of sentence similarity. Subjects were presented successively with several sets of eight sentences (each set constituted a sentence family). From each of these sets a single sentence was selected as a standard against which subjects assigned each of the remaining seven a similarity rank. In a second experiment, the same stimuli were tested in the generalization paradigm described for Clifton, Kurcz, and Jenkins. In a third experiment, subsets of the sentence families were tested by the generalization method in order to determine both the reliability of the scaling results from the previous experiments, and the effect of the choice of the comparison set upon a subject's judgments. Five subsets were tested corresponding to faces of the cube in Figure 5-2. (The omitted face is the one tested in Clifton, Kurcz, and Jenkins—*K*, *P*, *N*, and *PN*.) In a fourth experiment, the *K*, *P*, *N*, *PN* set was tested with repetition of training and test trials; but more importantly, a variation in the auxiliary was introduced: the sentences were run in the past perfect tense as opposed to the simple past. This variation was intended to provide a control for possible effects of the surface similarity of sentences, since it was as-

TABLE 5-3

Proportion of possible presses to test list sentences (experiment 2)*

Test-list construction	Training-list construction							
	K	**P**	**N**	**Q**	**PN**	**PQ**	**NQ**	**PNQ**
K	0.77	0.50	0.33	0.58	0.19	0.35	0.46	0.23
P	0.60	0.85	0.40	0.54	0.52	0.71	0.44	0.52
N	0.33	0.21	0.65	0.27	0.50	0.33	0.40	0.38
Q	0.27	0.29	0.35	0.60	0.21	0.38	0.44	0.29
PN	0.17	0.27	0.50	0.27	0.73	0.46	0.31	0.46
PQ	0.25	0.38	0.27	0.35	0.44	0.58	0.48	0.69
NQ	0.33	0.29	0.54	0.60	0.48	0.52	0.71	0.56
PNQ	0.29	0.46	0.38	0.40	0.54	0.56	0.50	0.79

Rotated configuration (experiment 2)

Construction	Dimension		
	Passive	**Negative**	**Question**
K	0.00	0.00	0.00
P	1.10	0.00	0.00
N	0.42	1.75	0.00
Q	0.31	0.74	1.11
PN	1.54	1.59	−0.02
PQ	1.46	0.74	0.77
NQ	0.39	0.94	1.16
PNQ	1.44	1.14	1.29

*Source: From Clifton and Odom (1966).

sumed that present perfect versions of sentences belonging to a given family were more physically similar to one another than are those in the simple past tense (they have more words in common and there are no irregular forms in the main verb). Table 5-3 and Figure 5-5 summarize some of Clifton and Odom's main findings.

The first remark to make about the results is their striking consistency across the several experimental paradigms. There is an impressive correspondence between the structures achieved through similarity rankings and those based on the generalization tests of Clifton and Odom and of Clifton, Kurcz, and Jenkins. Moreover, the generalization results do not appear to be especially sensitive to experimental "context" (i.e., to which member of its optional singulary family a sentence is compared with); the relations among sentence types obtained with relatively limited comparison sets are very much the same as those obtained by measures taken across the entire family.

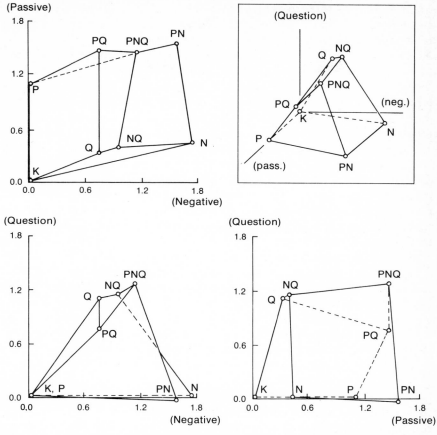

Fig. 5-5. Two-dimensional projections of experiment 2 configuration, with oblique projection inset (from Clifton and Odom, 1966).

Second, the effects of physical similarity between sentences as tested by comparing the behavior of simple past and past perfect do not appear to be great. The degree of generalization from training list to test lists was somewhat higher for the past perfect sentences, but the pattern of relations among the various sentence types was almost exactly the same as for the simple past. There are, as Clifton and Odom and others have pointed out, other arguments against explaining the obtained patterns of generalization by appeal to superficial similarities between surface sentence structures; in particular, the K and N sentences differ by only a single lexical item, whereas the P and K sentences differ by at least two words and a reordering. Yet the latter pair is judged to be more closely related in these experiments than is the former.

The most interesting result, however, is that the prism model of Figure 5-4 appears to correspond more closely to the generalization and similarity data than does the cube of Figure 5-2. Thus, apparently, the representation of the relations among the sentences given by the standard analysis more closely predicts the subjects' behavior in these experiments than does the 1957 grammar. This suggests that features of the base structures of these sentences may be more important to the determination of their similarities than are transformational operations.

If just the forms K, P, N, PN and K, P, Q, and PQ are considered, the relations among the sentence types are predictable from the similarities and differences between their transformational histories. When Q and N interact, however, the effects are different from those that would be predicted on this basis. The Katz and Postal theory allows us to rationalize this difference, since in their analysis the transformation that produces negative questions is *not* triggered by a deep-structure negative marker. In particular, the N that appears in NQ and PNQ is not a realization of the deep-structure negative element that occurs in N, PN, etc. This assumption is alleged to account for the fact that negative questions are not "true" negatives (e.g., they are in some sense synonymous with the corresponding affirmative questions). If the Katz and Postal analysis is accepted, and if we assume that the degree of similarity between sentences in a family is determined by the number of deep-structure markers they share (rather than by the number of transformations common to their histories) we can account for the Clifton and Odom results: Q and NQ have the same deep-structure markers (namely, Q) though they differ in their transformational histories. Thus, a theory which takes deep-structure markers to be the basis of sentence similarity will predict that Q and NQ are more alike than will a theory which uses a transformational index of similarity. This pattern of explanation also has the advantage of accounting for the fact that transformations like *affix* movement and *do*-support characteristically have little or no effect on obtained intersentence differences (see the analysis in Table 5-2). These transformations, like NQ, are not associated with characteristic base-structure markers.

SUMMARY

The experimental evidence we have thus far reviewed argues strongly for the psychological reality of the taxonomy of sentences implied by transformational syntax. The derived intersentential distances which emerge from the studies seem to be reliable both within and across experimental paradigms, and they correspond closely to the distances predicted from the grammar when the number of deep-structure markers a pair of sentences share is used as the index of their similarity.

However, only in the case of the matching experiments of Miller and

McKean did this confirmation of the grammatical taxonomy of sentences appear to provide direct experimental support for the psychological reality of *transformations*, for only in those experiments did it seem necessary to assume that the subjects' performance of the task required them to transform and detransform sentences. We have seen, however, that when the logic of the matching experiments is investigated closely, the hypothesis that the operations that the subjects performed *were* grammatical transformations is actually disconfirmed by the data, since the rules the subjects were using did not observe the constraints on ordering that transformations obey.

We might characterize the difference between the matching experiments and the Clifton et al. (1965) experiments in the following way: in the matching experiments, the similarity metric was defined over grammatical *operations* (that is, over the number of shared transformations in the history of a pair of sentences); in the later experiments, the simplicity metric was defined over grammatical *structures* (that is, over the number of shared markers in the deep structure of a pair of sentences). It is the latter, rather than the former, metric which the experimental results tend to confirm.

This is a pattern of results which will recur throughout our survey of the experimental findings on generative grammars: experiments which undertake to demonstrate the psychological reality of the structural descriptions characteristically have better luck than those which undertake to demonstrate the psychological reality of the operations involved in grammatical derivations. Why this should be so is a question of considerable theoretical interest.

SEMANTIC INTERPRETATIONS OF THE SENTENCE SIMILARITY STUDIES

The discussion thus far suggests that the number of base-structure markers that a pair of sentences have in common contributes to determining their similarity. There is, however, a serious objection that may be raised against this conclusion: in the experiments reviewed so far, the metric of sentence similarity derived from the number of shared base-structure markers is coextensive with the similarity metric derived from the *semantic* relations among the sentences. In particular, with the exception of cases which involve the passive, two sentences in a family differ in their base markers if and only if they differ semantically. This is because transformations which are not triggered by base-structure markers (such as *affix* movement, *do*-support, and NQ in the Katz-Postal account) also do not affect the semantic properties of sentences to which they apply. Conversely, barring passives, sentences which differ by transformations that are marked in deep structure (N, Q, etc.) are semantically different, and the magnitude of their semantic difference is arguably proportional to the magnitude of the transformational difference.

One might thus attribute all the variance in the sentence-similarity experiments to the semantic relations among the stimulus items, holding that syntactic structure does not contribute to similarity relations at all. This sort of skepticism could take either a weak or a strong form. In the strong form, it might deny that there is any psychological reality even to the notion of a sentence family. In this view, sentences belonging to such a family are similar to one another just to the extent that their semantic properties are similar. For example, one might argue that a sentence like "John sold the picture to Mary" is no more closely related to one like "The picture was sold to Mary by John" than it is to "Mary purchased the picture from John." On this account, the syntactic relation that transformational grammars acknowledge between an active and its passive is just a special case of the relation between pairs of synonymous sentences. Similarly, one might deny that there is any relation between "John died" and "John didn't die" which does not also hold between "John died" and "John survived."

The less radical version of the view that it is semantic (not syntactic) properties of sentences that account for their perceived similarity might hold only that *within sentence families* sentences are similar just to the extent that they are semantically similar. In this view, one would admit that pairs like affirmatives and their negations have a special relation to one another in addition to being contradictories, that actives and passives have a special relation to one in addition to their synonymy, etc. One could thus acknowledge the psychological reality of sentence families but still claim that within families it is semantic relations like synonymy and contradiction that determine degree of similarity.

Clearly the strong form of semantic hypothesis is less plausible than the weak form, and there is some experimental evidence which suggests that it is incorrect. For example, Smith (1965) used an experimental task similar to that of the initial study of optional singularies (Miller and McKean). He compared the process of making syntactic alterations, such as changing actives to passives or affirmatives to negatives, with process of making lexical substitutions which had semantic effects comparable to those of the syntactic changes. For example, given the sentence "the boy paints the inside of the house," some subjects were asked to passivize and some were asked to substitute "brother" for "boy" in the response sentence. These operations were presumed to have comparable semantic effects, at least in comparison with such alterations as negating the sentence or substituting "girl" for "boy." Differences in the ease of the two types of operations might thus suggest that constructing a response sentence belonging to the same family as the stimulus sentence is different from constructing a syntactically comparable response sentence belonging to another family. Such differences would thus indicate the psychological reality of the sentence-family construct.

In general, Smith (1965) found that the effects of lexical change were both smaller and less consistent than the effects of syntactic change. In addition, he found that the response time for making two-word lexical alterations was not greater than the response time for one-word lexical alterations. This contrasts with the finding that the time required to change a sentence into another member of its family was proportional to the number of deep-structure markers that must be altered, as in Miller and McKean. In short, Smith's results suggest that within-family sentence relations have properties that distinguish them from across-family sentence relations and this cannot be explained by reference to the semantic features of the sentences alone.

Koplin and Davis (1966) produced another experimental comparison of effects of semantic similarity and syntactic relatedness. They used a pencil-and-paper version of the Clifton et al. (1965) generalization procedure; however, instead of measuring response latencies, Koplin and Davis used confidence ratings of S's judgments that the stimulus item on the recognition list had or had not appeared on the training list.

Sentence types from the optional singulary family were used together with sentences related periphrastically but not transformationally (for example "the play pleased me" and "I liked the play," or "I regard John as pompous" and "John strikes me as pompous"). The results were similar to those of Clifton and Odom for the members of sentence families. The synonymous, but syntactically unrelated, pairs also showed significant amounts of generalization when compared with control sentences, but such pairs were significantly *less* effective in producing generalization than were the syntactically related members of a sentence family. This was true even for *non*synonymous within-family cases; for example, negative was more closely related to other members of its sentence family than those sentences were to their paraphrases.

The results of these two experiments suggest that sentences belonging to the same family have a coherence over and above what can be explained by their semantic properties. Whether or not sentences mean the same thing seems less important to the determination of subjects' perception of sentence similarity than is the fact that the sentences are syntactically related. (We shall see, however, that there are reasons for supposing that the generality of this result is limited.)

These data are, however, compatible with the *weak* version of the semantic explanation of the sentence similarity results. That is, the pattern of similarity that subjects see among sentences *of the same family* may be determined entirely by the semantic relations among such sentences. In that case, the apparent correlation between the perceived similarity of two sentences and the number of deep-structure markers they share might be an artifact of the correlation between semantic relatedness and overlap of deep-structure markers. Clearly, the critical case for evaluating this proposal is the passive. If within-family judgments of sentence similarity are entirely semantic, then passives should be psychologically indistinguishable from their corresponding actives. However, we have seen that passive *does* contribute to judged distances between sentences in a way that is roughly comparable to Q and N; thus the results with passives suggest a specifically syntactic, nonsemantic, source of variance in determining the perceived similarity of sentences.

This argument, of course, presupposes that actives and passives do not differ in any important semantic properties; if they do, then their perceived dissimilarity might be attributed to that semantic difference. We saw in Chapter 4 that there is some question whether actives and passives are synonymous in the case of sentences containing mixed quantifiers. What is critical for evaluating the findings on sentence similarity, however, is whether passivization yields synonyms in the kinds of stimulus sentences used in the similarity experiments.

There is some evidence which suggests a semantic difference between actives and passives which might account for the asymmetries between them that sentence-similarity studies typically reveal. For example, Clark (1965) found significant differences in the variability of lexical items selected by subjects for active and passive sentence "frames," e.g., there was less variety in subjects' selection of nouns for the agent NP in active frames than for the agent NP in passive frames. In discussing his results, Clark focused on a particular semantic property of the nouns selected by his subjects, namely, their animacy. This feature was asymmetrically distributed in the test frames. [(5-5) and (5-6) give the frequencies of occurrence of animate nouns used in such frames by Clark's subjects.]

5-5   The (81.5 percent) $V + ed$ the (26.7 percent).

5-6   The (45.8 percent) was $V + ed$ by the (68.3 percent).

M. Johnson (1967) found a compatible pattern of results in the semantic differential ratings which subjects assigned to nonsense syllables presented in active and passive sentence frames, e.g., "The NIJ hurt the GAQ," etc. In active frames, nonsense syllables used as object-NP's were rated less active and potent than were syllables used as subject-NP's. But this contrast between the two positions was less marked in the passive frames. This is just the sort of result that might be expected from the distribution of animacy in Clark's experiment given that "animacy" is associated with "activity" and "potency."

Both Clark and Johnson interpret their results as indicating an important semantic difference between actives and their corresponding passives. If they are right, then the asymmetry between actives and passives found in the sentence-similarity experiments may not be attributable to purely structural differences between the base structures of the sentences involved. However, the results of the Clark and Johnson studies are not unequivocal. In fact, their data are compatible with there being no semantic differences between actives and passives at all.

Suppose, for example, that there is a stylistic principle, "all things being equal, animate NP's are in the topic position (i.e., the surface subject) in English." Now consider the types of deep-structure relations exhibited by sentences in the Clark and Johnson studies. The possibilities are

1. Animate noun, verb, animate noun
2. Inanimate noun, verb, inanimate noun
3. Animate noun, verb, inanimate noun
4. Inanimate noun, verb, animate noun

Of these cases, only 3 and 4 are asymmetric for animacy. If the stylistic principle we have assumed is correct, 3 is normally realized as a surface active. That is, passives can inherit subject/object relations that are asymmetric for animacy only from case 4. However, case 4 is satisfied by only a relatively small number of verbs; there are few verbs which permit a deep-structure animate object and inanimate subject compared with the number of verbs which permit deep-structure animate subjects and inanimate objects. This fact, taken together with the presumed stylistic principle which favors animate topics, predicts less asymmetry for subject/object animacy in active sentences than in passives, even on the assumption that there is *no* semantic difference between actives and passives. We do not, of course, claim that this is the right analysis of Clark's and of Johnson's findings but only that the reduction of animacy-asymmetry in the passive frame does not point unequivocally to a semantic difference between actives and passives.[5]

There is a further feature of passives which may be of particular relevance in these experiments: the agent position in the frames that were

---

[5] Since verbs govern the selection of noun features, it is crucial to examine results like those of Clark (1965) and M. Johnson (1967) for each type of verb separately. For example, verbs like "surprise, worry, amaze" prohibit inanimate nouns in the surface-object position in sentences like (5-5) and in surface-subject position in sentences like (5-6): clearly, if the experimental materials Clark and Johnson had used had been verbs of this type only, then the results would have been quite different.

intended to be construed as passives *can* be occupied by locative expressions (for example, "the intersection" is a possible completion of "the man was hit by _____"). Insofar as subjects assigned this sort of structure to frames like (5-6), they would be free to place inanimate nouns in the second noun position.

SUMMARY

The results of the work on sentence similarity can be summarized as follows:

1. The notion of a sentence family is apparently psychologically real. Sentences belonging to the same family are recognized as having a special interrelationship which is not predictable from their semantic properties alone.

2. Within a sentence family, the perceived similarity of sentences is predictable from the number of base-structure markers they have in common. That this is, in fact, the effective variable is suggested by the case of passives. In nonquantified sentences, passives are at least roughly synonymous with their corresponding actives. Yet the perceived dissimilarity between passives and actives is comparable to the perceived dissimilarity of questions and actives, negatives and actives, etc.

3. Just as semantic relations yield a less adequate account of perceived sentence relations than number of shared base markers do, so, in critical cases, overlap of transformational histories fails to yield a good index of perceived relatedness. In particular, differences between transformational histories in a sentence family apparently affect perceived similarity only for transformations which, like *Q, P, N*, etc., are triggered by deep-structure markers. Transformations like *NQ, do*-support, *affix* movement, etc., which do not have a representation in deep structure, appear to contribute negligibly, or not at all, to perceived dissimilarity between sentences.

THE PSYCHOLOGICAL REALITY OF SURFACE AND UNDERLYING PHRASE STRUCTURE

Contemporary with the research on sentence similarity were a number of experiments which sought to demonstrate the psychological reality of surface-constituent structure. This section begins with a review of some typical examples of such studies. It will become clear, however, that the findings often implicate deep-structure relations, so that experimental investigations of the reality of deep and surface structures tend to merge into one another.

Some effects of surface-constituent structure.   Epstein (1961) reports a study which appears to show that subjects impose constituent analyses on linguistic stimuli. Epstein contrasted the learning of nonsense syllables which were grammatically inflected with the learning of the same string of nonsense syllables without the grammatical tags. For example, (5-7) as compared with (5-8). The finding was that, in spite of the greater

5-7   The yigs wur vumly rixing hum in jegest miv

5-8   The yig wur vum rix hum in jeg miv

length of the inflected strings, they were learned much more easily than the uninflected ones.

The explanation of this phenomenon seems to be related to a subsequent demonstration by Glanzer (1962). Glanzer first showed that pairs consisting of a nonsense syllable and an English word are learned more readily when the word is a "content" word than when it is a "function" word. Thus, "yig-food" is learned more readily than "kex-and" or "tah-of." This finding is compatible with an absolute difference in learnability between function words and content words. But it is also compatible with the view that the learning of the pairs is facilitated to the extent that they resemble constituents. That the latter interpretation is probably the right one is shown by the fact that when Glanzer embedded the function words in a nonsense context with which they formed constituent-like structures, the relative speed of learning for function words and content words was reversed. So, for example, "mef-think-jat" or "yig-food-seb" were learned more slowly than "woj-and-kex" or "tah-of-zum." This suggests that the important variable is not the contrast between function words and content words *per se* but rather whether the stimuli are readily interpretable as similar to grammatical constituents. This analysis is, of course, fully compatible with Epstein's (1961) findings.

A good deal of subsequent research has been carried out with the Epstein paradigm. The upshot appears to be that the presence of grammatical morphemes is facilitating only so long as the subject perceives the inflected strings as having linguistic structure. For example, Forster (personal communication) showed that the facilitation fails to occur if the presentation of the items is slow enough so that subjects do not notice that a linguistic structure can be imposed upon the string. Facilitation is, however, immediately restored if the experimenter points out to the subject that the strings will accept such an analysis.

Not all the experimentation which suggests a facilitative effect of constituent structure on recall tasks involves nonsense stimuli. For example, Anglin and Miller (1968) showed that printed prose passages in which the end of each line corresponds to a constituent boundary are easier to learn than passages in which that correspondence does not obtain.

Similarly, Suci (1967) segmented a set of sentences in three different ways. The first segmentation respected the largest constituent boundaries. The second segmentation corresponded to the positions at which pauses occurred when the sentences were read aloud. [This corresponds roughly, but not perfectly, with a segmentation into major constituents (see Chapter 7).] The third segmentation was random. Subjects were required to learn lists of the sentence segments so produced. The order of ease of acquisition was: random segmentation, hardest; constituent segmentation, next hardest; and pausal segmentation, easiest. Evidently, preserving constituent structure provides a significant enhancement of Ss' performance; and constituent structure is not the only factor. Similar findings are reported in a study by R. Johnson (1970).

Recoding. Studies of the sort just discussed suggest that imposing a constituent analysis (or "parsing") facilitates the learning of nonsense material, and that respecting constituent analysis facilitates the learning of linguistic material. Results like these seem analogous to such familiar facts as that giving a telephone number in two groups of digits makes it easier to remember. Why should such an effect occur?

Practically the only hypothesis in the field is one suggested by Miller [see, for example, chapter 10 in Miller, Galanter, and Pribram (1960)]. The basic idea is that facilitation by parsing is a species of facilitation by "recoding." Two examples will clarify this latter notion.

Suppose one has to learn a list consisting of the pairs "dog-two, house-two, of-two, calendar-two, phonograph-two." Clearly, one can save himself effort by taking account of the obvious generalization that the second word of each pair is "two." That is, what would presumably be learned is a recoding of the list into a sublist and a rule: the list is "dog, house, of, calendar, phonograph," and the rule is "every word in the list is followed by 'two'." Learning the generalization thus reduces the number of items of rote material that must be assimilated. Analogously, most adults will learn the following test list in one trial: "January, February, March, April, June, May, July, August, September, October, November, December." The point here is that most of what needs to be "learned" is already available in permanent store. All the subject needs do is recode the list as "the months of the year in order with May and June reversed."

Miller, Galanter, and Pribram (1960) suggested that the facilitating effect of constituent structure depends on recoding. "As the learner groups and renames the elements in the list to be memorized, *he effec-*

tively shortens the length of the list" (p. 132). [See also Miller (1956a).] However, it is difficult to see how this could be the correct explanation.

The examples just given illustrate the two kinds of savings that recoding can effect: it can permit us to memorize short generalizations instead of long lists, and it can permit us to use information already available in long-term storage in order to recall current inputs. The present point is that *neither* of these things can be going on in cases of the type investigated by Epstein (1961) or by Anglin and Miller (1968). On the one hand, there is no generalization that permits us to recover the lexical content of the stimulus material given only its parsing tree. That is, these cases are not like the first example. But neither is the stimulus item already available in the subject's long-term memory in these experiments. Both Epstein's nonsense strings and the Anglin-Miller sentences are presumably novel items for the subjects. Thus learning them cannot be a matter of selection from a previously stored repertoire.

The question thus arises: How can recoding effect savings in this sort of case? Miller, Galanter, and Pribram put their finger on the precise issue when they remark that "A list of N words requires $N-1$ associations if we learn them as a chain. If we organize them into groups and form associations between those groups, we simply add to the number of associations we need. Isn't this just a make-work proposition? The efficient solution should be to use as few new associations as possible" (p. 131). The problem is: why is adding constituent structure to word sequences *not* a make-work proposition as well? We know that adding constituent structure to lists does facilitate learning, even where a list is novel and cannot be generated by a rule. But why such facilitation occurs is not explained by length of the lists.

What these observations show is that the virtues of recoding cannot be explained in terms of how much material has to be stored. A reasonable alternative approach is that recoding allows a more efficient *transfer* of information into long-term storage and that, unlike short-term storage, there are no practical limits on the amount of material that can be stored permanently. This, of course, places the burden of explanation on an account of why the imposition of structure enhances the transfer of information into long-term storage, and this is presently an unsolved problem.

Some further studies of constituent structure. Whatever the explanation of the effect of constituent structure in facilitating learning may be, there is now a variety of independent experimental evidence which leaves the question of its psychological reality beyond doubt. Some of these experiments provide us with a relatively detailed picture of important aspects of constituent structure. We turn to a review of a portion of this work.

N. Johnson (1965) reported the first of a series of studies exploring

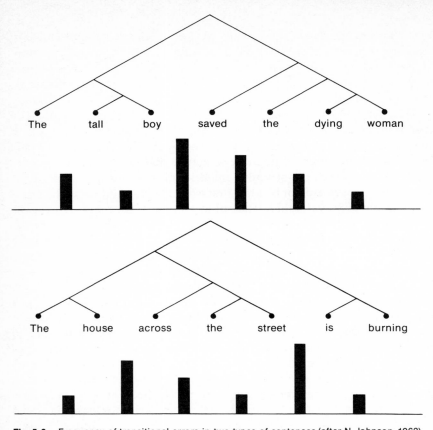

Fig. 5-6. Frequency of transitional errors in two types of sentences (after N. Johnson, 1963).

the relation of constituent structure to patterns of errors made in learning lists of sentences. Johnson devised a measure called the TEP (transitional error probability) such that the value of TEP for a particular word in a sentence is a function of the probability that the word is *in*correctly recalled given that the preceding word is recalled correctly. Johnson's major finding is that TEP typically exhibits a significant increase for the first word in each of the major phrases in a sentence. This suggests that subjects learn sentences in phrase groups; when a part of a phrase is learned, the rest of it tends to be learned as well. One of Johnson's histograms of the distribution of errors in his data is reproduced as Figure 5-6.

Johnson notes that even though the level of error is highest between major phrase groups, there is also significant variation in error level internal to constituents. He suggests that this may be explained by the decomposition of major constituents into the minor constituents of which they are composed. However, there seems to be little regularity in the error levels internal to constituents, other than a tendency to separate articles from the nouns they introduce (especially where the noun is complex or preceded by an adjective). We shall see that this difference between the major and minor constituent boundaries in a sentence can be found in experimentation with several different paradigms. It is, in fact, a type of finding whose theoretical significance will be of some concern in Chapter 6.

Johnson's central findings—that major constituents tend to be learned as units—also emerges from a study by Suci, Ammon, and Gamlin (1967) with the "next-word" probe technique. In their experiment, subjects were presented with a sentence immediately followed by a word which occurred in the sentence. Their task was to respond as quickly as possible with the succeeding word from the sentence. For example, a subject presented with the sentence "The big boy eats red apples" and the probe word "boy" would be expected to respond with the word "eats." The major finding was compatible with Johnson's. The longest response times were found when the probe was the final word in a major constituent. Again, as in Johnson's study, there appears to be no regular relation between the response delay and minor constituent structure. Several other investigators (Kennedy and Wilkes, 1968; Ammon, 1968) have employed the next-word probe technique with generally similar results.

A different paradigm, which illustrates surface-constituent effects, is that of Mehler and Carey (1967). They demonstrated that it is possible to develop in subjects a set or expectation for a specified surface-structure configuration. Subjects were presented with a series of eleven sentences heard in noise. In the control condition, all eleven sentences had the same constituent structure. In the experimental condition, the first ten sentences were syntactically homogeneous (e.g., all were like "they are forecasting cyclones") but the eleventh had a contrasting phrase structure (e.g., "they are conflicting desires"). Subjects in the experimental condition did not understand the eleventh sentence as well as subjects in the control condition. Mehler and Carey attribute this effect to a perceptual set induced by the phrase structure of the first ten sentences in the list.

In still another experiment on the effects of surface constituency, Stewart and Gough (1967) used a "two-word" probe technique in a task where reaction time was the dependent variable. In this paradigm subjects hear a stimulus sentence and are then presented with *two* words. They are required to respond with a decision whether or not both the words had occurred in the stimulus string. Stewart and Gough compared response latencies for cases in which the pair of probe words "straddled" a constituent boundary with those for cases in which it did not. Thus, for a pair of sentences like (5-9) and (5-10), the probe was

5-9   **The presidents of large corporations pay millions of dollars in taxes each year.**

5-10   **When profits are large, corporations pay millions of dollars in taxes each year.**

"large corporations." In (5-9), "large" and "corporations" are members of the same immediate constituent, whereas in (5-10), they are not. Response latencies reflected this difference: they were significantly greater for sentences like (5-10) than for sentences like (5-9). Note that, in this experiment, there is no confounding of the effect of constituent structure with the effect of the serial position of the probed items or with the lexical content of the probes, since the same probe is used at the same serial position in both stimulus sentences.

Another experimental paradigm, derived from work by Ladefoged and Broadbent (1960), has provided evidence for the psychological reality of constituent structure. In their study, Ladefoged and Broadbent found that subjects were surprisingly inaccurate in locating the position of a short burst of noise (approximately 30 milliseconds) embedded in speech. Moreover, the subject's accuracy was affect by the character of the speech material. Accuracy levels were lower when the materials used were sentences than when they were digit strings. Ladefoged and Broadbent interpreted this as evidence that the units of perceptual analysis used by the subjects in processing the digit strings were smaller than the units of analysis they used in processing the sentences.

In a subsequent experiment, Fodor and Bever (1965) demonstrated that the patterns of errors in "click location" made by subjects when listening to sentences were related to the constituent structure of the sentences. For example, Fodor and Bever's stimulus material contained recordings of the sentence (5-11) in versions of which a click was located before, after, or in the major constituent break [indicated by the carets

5-11   **That he was happy was evident from the way he smiled.**

in (5-11)]. There was a significantly greater error for location of clicks not objectively placed at the major boundary than for those which objectively occurred at the boundary. There was, moreover, a significant tendency to place mislocated clicks at the major constituent break. [Similar findings are reported in Garrett (1965).]

In this and subsequent experiments with the click paradigm, it was argued that the pattern of results was evidence for the effect of constituent structure upon the perceptual segmentation of sentences. That question will occupy us in Chapter 6. For present purposes it is a matter of indifference whether the error is strictly perceptual in the sense that it occurs during the process of computing the structure of the sentence, whether it is a memory effect in the sense that it occurs during the interval between the subject's identification of the sentence and his response, or, indeed, whether the errors are the reflection of some re-

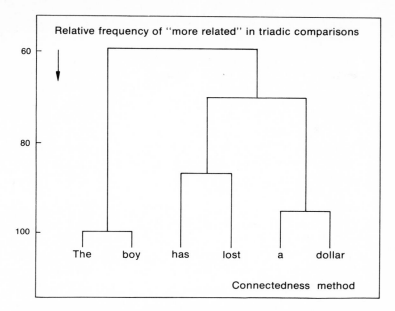

Fig. 5-7. HCS solution (connectedness method) for "The boy has lost a dollar" (triadic comparisons data) (from Levelt, 1970).

sponse bias. In any case, the errors are clearly sensitive to the constituent structure of the stimulus material [Garrett (1965), Scholes (1969), Holmes and Forster (1970), Berry (1970), Seitz (1972)] and the paradigm thus provides further evidence for the operation of specifically syntactic factors in sentence processing tasks.

The final demonstration of the psychological reality of constituent structure that we will consider here is perhaps the most direct. This is a study by Levelt (1970) of the parameters of subjects' judgments of relatedness among the lexical items in a sentence. The approach is very much in the spirit of the first experiment in Clifton and Odom (1966). Subjects were simply asked to rate the degree of relatedness between pairs of words taken from a sentence, such judgments being obtained for all the word pairs that can be formed from the lexical material in the sentence. A spatial representation of the similarity judgments was provided by the use of hierarchical clustering analysis (HCS). Thus a subject of Levelt's scaling experiment might be presented with the sentence (5-12). The subject is then given the list of word pairs and a seven-

5-12 The boy has lost a dollar.

point scale on which to judge the degree of relatedness for each pair. These are the data subjected to scaling. An example of the results of Levelt's work is presented in Figure 5-7. The similarity between the

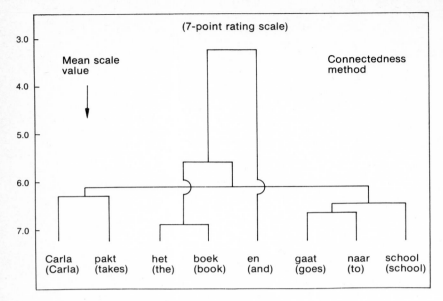

Fig. 5-8. HCS solution (connectedness method) for

Carla pakt het boek en gaat naar school
(Carla) (takes) (the) (book) (and) (goes) (to) (school)

(7-point rating scale data) (from Levelt, 1970).

scaling structure and the surface-structure analysis of the sentence is apparent.

Deep-structure effects. For some of the sentences which Levelt examined, however, the correspondence between the scaling results and the surface-constituent analyses was less satisfactory. For example, the scaling structure for (5-13) is given in Figure 5-8. The untidiness of this

5-13 Carla takes the book and goes to school.

structure can be seen by noting that the verb in the second conjunct is as closely related to the first noun as is the verb in the first conjunct. As Levelt points out, we might expect problems with such representations for sentences in which there have been deletions of repeated elements. In (5-13) the single surface occurrence of the word "Carla" was judged by Levelt's Dutch subjects as almost equally related to the two surface verbs "takes" and "goes." In the hierarchical representation only one of the two relations can be expressed; thus we have the result shown in Figure 5-8. However, when Levelt took the deletion into account in his scaling procedures, the structure was as is shown in Figure 5-9.

Clearly, the subjects in Levelt's scaling experiment were not responding *only* to the surface phrase structure of the sentences. Rather,

THE PSYCHOLOGICAL REALITY OF GRAMMATICAL STRUCTURES

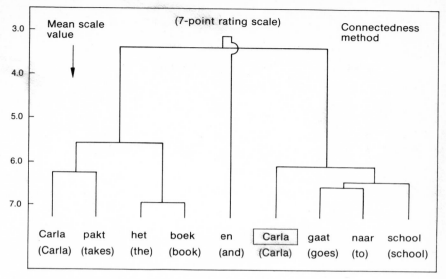

Fig. 5-9. HCS solution (connectedness method) for expanded matrix of

Carla   pakt   het   boek   en   Carla   gaat   naar   school
(Carla) (takes) (the) (book) (and) (Carla) (goes) (to)   (school)

(Carla added) (from Levelt, 1970).

their judgment of the relatedness among the lexical items was affected by their perception of the underlying grammatical relations in the sentence. Where those relations are reflected in the surface constituency, no conflict arises; but where suppressed or deleted underlying elements are involved, the scaling technique must be adjusted to take account of that fact.

Precisely the same point can be made about the experiments with double probes conducted by Stewart and Gough (see page 251). In the example we discussed, the data were straightforwardly interpretible by appeal to the principle that word pairs which straddled major constituent boundaries yielded longer latencies than did pairs drawn from within a constituent. However, Stewart and Gough also tested sentences like (5-9) and (5-10) with probes like "corporations pay." In this case, the response latencies were faster for (5-10) than for (5-9), and this asymmetry cannot be explained simply in terms of the immediate constituent structures of the two sentences. [In particular, if one attends to the surface bracketings (see Figure 5-10), one notices that in *both* sentences "corporations" is separated from "pay" by an *NP/VP* boundary attached to the highest node in the sentence.] It seems plausible that the explanation of the asymmetry in response latencies should appeal to the difference in grammatical relations between "corporations" and

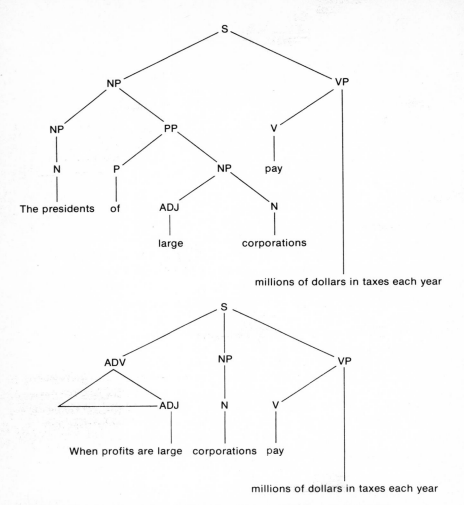

Fig. 5-10. Diagrams of sentences in Stewart and Gough, 1967 (from Walker, 1969).

"pay" in the two sentences, since the response latencies are lower where the probed items are related as grammatical subject and main verb.

In a subsequent effort to evaluate the effect of underlying grammatical relations on latency to double probes, Walker, Gough, and Wall (1968) contrasted the effects of surface-structure adjacency with those of underlying grammatical relations. Walker, et al. used sentences of the type shown in (5-14). They compared latencies for the following kinds of

5-14 The scouts the Indians saw killed a buffalo.

probes: e.g., "scouts killed," "scouts saw," "Indians saw," and "Indians

TABLE 5.4. RESULTS OF WALKER ET AL. (1968)

Response latency, sec

	Verb in probe	
	Embedded (saw)	Matrix (killed)
Noun in probe:		
Matrix (scouts)	1.06	1.02
Embedded (Indians)	1.06	1.12
E.g., The scouts the Indians saw killed a buffalo.		

killed." Table 5-4 provides a sample of the probe materials and of the results. Note first that grammatically related pairs like "scouts killed" yield shorter latencies than grammatically unrelated pairs like "Indians killed," though the former are further apart in surface serial position than are the latter. In general, it seems clear that there is an effect of grammatical relatedness on response latency: probe pairs which contain grammatically related words are significantly faster than those which do not. What is *un*clear is whether this experiment shows an effect of *surface* constituency. The fastest probe type does not involve words drawn from the same surface constituent; moreover, given that both items in the probe come from the same deep sentoid, response latency is not affected by whether or not they also occur in the same surface constituent. For example, both "Indians saw" and "scouts saw" come from the embedded sentoid "the Indians saw the scouts," but only the former belong to the same surface constituent. Yet response latency for "Indians saw" is not significantly faster than the response latency for "scouts saw."

This discussion of the Levelt and the Walker et al. results suggests the difficulty of providing a clear experimental dissociation of the effects of surface and deep linguistic structure. On the contrary, when the details of experiments on surface-constituent analysis are examined, one finds evidence for interactions with grammatical relations of the kind that standard syntactic theory represents as holding among *deep* constituents. Most experimental paradigms thus far devised appear to be sensitive both to surface and to deep-structure relations if they are sensitive to either. We shall see in Chapter 6 that this probably holds for the "click" paradigms as well as for the ones just discussed.

A number of studies other than Walker et al. intentionally manipulated grammatical relatedness of the stimulus items. For example, Davidson (1969) compared TEP's for items in two kinds of sentences: full passives (like "Important messages were dispatched by governments") and truncated passives with adverbial phrases (like "Important messages were dispatched by wire"). The results did not distinguish the TEP of the two sentence types for words (major lexical classes only) drawn from adjacent surface-structure constituents. For example, TEP for pairs like "dispatched governments" was not distinguished from TEP for pairs like "dispatched wire." However, TEP for pairs that are related in the underlying structure like "governments dispatched" was lower than TEP's for pairs that are unrelated like "wire dispatched." This comports with the grammatical analysis according to which the main verb of a passive is more closely related to the *NP* from its agent *by phrase* (which forms its deep subject) than to the *NP* from its adverbial *by phrase.*

Experiments by Blumenthal (1967) and by Blumenthal and Boakes (1967) also assessed the psychological reality of underlying grammatical relations. The first experiment studied prompted recall for stimulus materials similar to those used by Davidson (1969). Stimulus sentences included cases like (5-15) and (5-16). The dependent variable was the subjects' accuracy of recall of the sentence when prompted with the

5-15   **Gloves were made by tailors.**

5-16   **Gloves were made by hand.**

word "tailors" as compared with his accuracy of recall when prompted with the word "hand." Since accuracy of prompted recall is generally superior to accuracy of free recall, one can estimate the relative effect of the prompts by comparing the increment in performance each produces over the subject's performance in a free-recall task. Blumenthal found that "tailors" produced a significantly greater increment of response accuracy over free-recall levels in sentences like (5-15) than did "hand" in sentences like (5-16).

This result is compatible with a variety of interpretations. Blumenthal suggests that the higher the deep-structure node which immediately dominates the prompt word, the better prompt that word will be ("higher" here refers to the number of nodes intervening between the top *S* node and the prompt word). The idea is that if deep subjects like "tailors" are more intimately implicated with their sentences than nouns in adverbial phrases, like "hand" (a conclusion that the Davidson study also suggests), this is because the former derives from a higher position in the deep tree than does the latter. An alternative interpretation is simply that when a prompt is drawn from the same deep sentoid as the material it cues, it is more effective than when it is not: (5-15) has a one-sentoid deep structure, but it is doubtful whether (5-16) does.

It is conceivable that Davidson's and Blumenthal's results ought not, after all, be attributed to the deep-structure relations among the items in their stimulus materials but merely to the kinds of adverbial phrases that they used. Perhaps there is a difference between passive adverbial

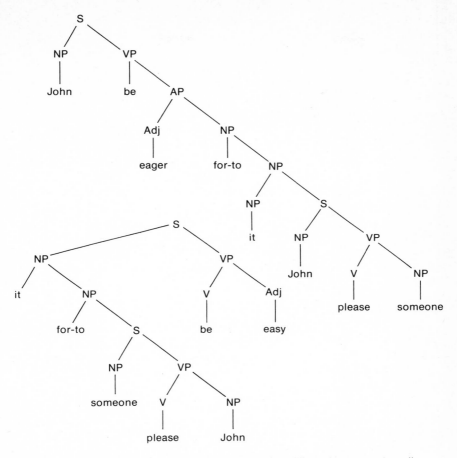

Fig. 5-11. The deep structures for "John is easy to please" and "John is eager to please."

phrases and all others that somehow explains the obtained asymmetries. To test the generality of the deep-structure interpretation, Blumenthal and Boakes (1967) did a study in which the experimental technique was identical to Blumenthal (1967) but which did not involve the passive. Stimuli were pairs of sentences like (5-17) and (5-18). The

5-17 John is easy to please.

5-18 John is eager to please.

effects of prompting with "easy" versus "eager" were compared, as were the effects of prompting with "John" for the two types of sentences.

The result in the latter comparison is readily interpretable. "John" is a better prompt in "eager" sentences than in "easy" sentences. If one considers the respective deep structures, one can see why this should be so. (See Figure 5-11.) It is both the case that "John" appears in a

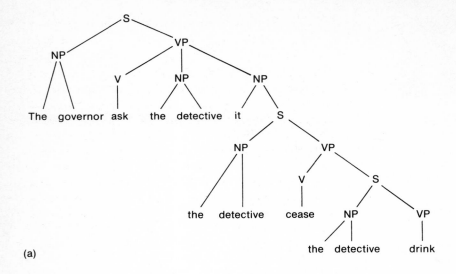

(a)

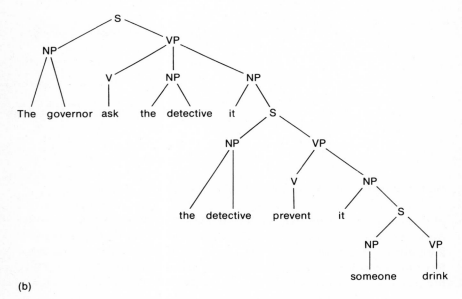

(b)

Fig. 5-12. (a) The deep structure for a "cease" sentence (from Wanner, 1968).
(b) The deep structure for a "prevent" sentence (from Wanner, 1968).

higher sentoid in "eager" sentences than in "easy" sentences, and that
"John" appears more frequently in "eager" sentences than in "easy"
sentences. We have thus at least two potential explanations of why
"John" should be a better prompt for the former sentences than for the
latter.

A second result of Blumenthal and Boakes is, however, harder to understand. They found that "easy" is a better prompt than "eager," and this result cannot be explained by the relative height of the prompts in their deep trees (both are predicates in the highest sentoids) or by the frequency with which the items appear in the deep trees (each appears twice). Blumenthal and Boakes suggest that the critical fact is that "easy" (unlike "eager") modifies the entire proposition in sentences in which it occurs; i.e., in the deep-structure tree for (5-17), all the content material is subordinated to "easy," but this is not the case for "eager" in the deep structure of (5-18). This explanation, however, needs to be considered with some caution, since it predicts, for example, that "surprisingly" should be the best prompt for a sentence like "Surprisingly, John left town," and it seems unlikely that this is true.

We remarked above that there are at least two explanations which might account for the observation that "John" is a better prompt in "eager" sentences than in "easy" sentences: one refers to the height at which the item occurs in the deep tree, and the other to the frequency with which it occurs in the deep tree. Wanner (1968) performed an experiment designed to test the latter of these explanations. He used a prompted recall paradigm in which sentences like (5-19) and (5-20) were compared. In the critical case, the prompt was "detective." To see why

5-19 **The governor asked the detective to prevent drinking.**

5-20 **The governor asked the detective to cease drinking.**

this is relevant to the frequency hypothesis, consider the deep trees for the two sentences given in Figure 5-12. The important fact is that "detective" occurs three times in the deep structure of the "cease" sentence but only *twice* in the deep structure of the "prevent" sentences. The "frequency in deep structure" hypothesis thus predicts that "detective" should be a better prompt in the former than in the latter, and this is what Wanner found. (See Figure 5-13.) It should be added that the obtained asymmetry cannot be explained by reference to the inherent memorability of (5-19) and (5-20). There was *no* difference in the level of recall for the two sentences in a control condition in which "governor" was used as the prompt. (Note that "governor" occurs equally often in both structures.)

It is worth noting the impressive intimacy with which results like Wanner's relate to the grammatical formalism. What is being demonstrated is not just that there is some psychological reality to the grammatical relations that deep structure represents, for that could be admitted without admitting that grammatical relations should be represented by tree structures of the kind transformational analyses employ. If we are to account for Wanner's findings, however, we need to appeal to detailed properties of the notation that the standard theory uses to repre-

Mean RPS

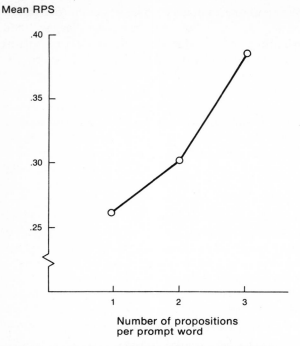

Fig. 5-13. Relative prompt success (RPS) as a function of the number of propositions per prompt word (from Wanner, 1968).

sent grammatical relations—properties as detailed as the frequency with which a constituent appears in a deep-structure tree. Blumenthal and Boakes's (1967) and Wanner's findings thus appear to provide persuasive evidence for the notion that the speaker-hearer's internal representation of grammatical relations is mediated by structures that are isomorphic to those the grammatical formalism employs.

Two more recent experiments which employ Blumenthal's paradigm throw light on the generality of Wanner's finding of a relation between the repetition of linguistic elements in deep structure and the efficacy of those elements as prompts in a recall task.

Franks, Nesbitt, and Clayton (1971) have shown that the prompt efficacy of a noun is a function of the number of adjectives which modify it in surface structure. This would be predicted on the view that phrases of the form adjective + noun are transformationally derived from deep sentences, so that "the tired old soldier" comes from "the soldier is old and the soldier is tired" (i.e., from a representation in which the noun occurs once for each adjective that modifies it). However, though this study seems compatible with the sorts of results we have just been reviewing, its interpretation is obscured by the possibility that the specificity or imagibility of an item in a sentence is a factor in facilitating recall; presumably the specificity and imagibility of what a noun denotes increases, at least roughly, with the number of modifiers of that noun. [For a discussion of some effects of imagibility upon recall, see Pavio (1969, 1971).]

The second experiment, by Lesgold (1972), is interesting because it does *not* show a relation between prompt efficacy and syntactic structure in a kind of sentence where such a relation might have been expected. Lesgold compared sentences like (5-21) and (5-22), prompting with each of the italicized items. He found that sentences like (5-21)

5-21 The *aunt* was *senile* and she *ate* the *pie*.

5-22 The *aunt* was *senile* and Alice *ate* the *pie*.

were better recalled overall than sentences like (5-22). But he found no difference between the relative effectiveness of the first nouns as prompts in the two types of sentences as compared with the relative effectiveness of any of the other paired prompts: though "aunt" was a better prompt in (5-21) than in (5-22), it was so only to the extent that "senile," "ate," and "pie" were. This is surprising on the assumption that the first noun occurs twice in the deep structure of (5-21) while all the other probes occur only once in their deep structures. If frequency in deep structure is an index of prompt effectiveness, this difference ought to differentially facilitate recall of (5-22) given "aunt" as prompt.

It should be emphasized, however, that this argument presupposes that pronouns are *not* deep-structure elements (that they enter sentences as replacements for iterated deep-structure noun phrases). The current linguistic evidence does not tend to support this assumption; in fact, "Bach's paradox" is usually taken to be a decisive argument on this point. Bach (1968) pointed out that unless deep structures contain pronouns, there is no way of assigning a transformational source to sentences like "the man who deserved it won the prize he wanted."

We conclude this section by citing one further study which yields a differential effect from surface and deep properties of sentences. MacKay and Bever (1967) tested subjects' ability to detect ambiguities in sentences when specifically instructed to search for them. Three types of ambiguous sentences were used: "lexical" ambiguities (like "the soldiers took the port at night"); surface-constituent ambiguities (like "They talked about the problem with the mathematician"); and ambiguities of grammatical relations (like "The mayor asked the police to stop drinking"). Response time for the detection of an ambiguity was found to be characteristic of the level of analysis at which the ambiguity occurred: lexical ambiguities were detected significantly faster than surface-structure ambiguities, and surface-structure ambiguities were detected significantly faster than ambiguities of grammatical relation. It seems clear from such results that subjects are sensitive to grammatical relations as well as relations at the levels of lexical and constituent analysis. It seems equally clear that the representation of grammatical relations must be distinct from the representation of lexical and constituent relations in the mind of the subject, just as it is in the grammar; otherwise, how explain the observed differences in response time?

THE CODING HYPOTHESIS

To show that linguistic representations are psychologically real, it is necessary only to demonstrate that the way subjects respond to sentences depends on the properties of linguistic representations. Most of the studies we have been reviewing are, in this sense, demonstration experiments. They show that linguistic structures engage psychological processes in some way, but they do not seek to explore the character of the interactions. Clearly, the latter question is the more difficult and the more interesting of the two. The studies we will examine now were directed toward specific claims about the role which linguistic structures play in one psychological process, namely long-term recall. We will argue that although these studies seemed to show an intimate relation between permanent memory and deep syntactic trees, they probably succeeded only in providing further demonstrations of the psychological reality of structural descriptions.

It has long been known that recall for grammatically well-formed, meaningful material is characteristically unlike rote recall. The form in which linguistic material is retrieved is related only abstractly to the input form, and it is not predicted by the kind of decay curve typical of rote lists of unrelated materials. [See the discussion of Mandler and Mandler and on page 226 in Chapter 2. See also Bartlett (1932) and the review of the traditional literature in Blumenthal (1970).] Presumably, these facts are to be explained by reference to the character of the representation of a sentence which we store when we remember it. The coding hypothesis suggested that the stored representation of a sentence can be identified with its base structure.

To understand the development of work on the coding hypothesis, it is essential to bear in mind that it assumed the 1957 account of singulary transformations. Rules like negative, question, passive, and so forth were held to be optional and to apply to deep structures literally indistinguishable from those which underlie simple, active, affirmative declaratives.

Given this view of the grammar, we can identify the coding hypothesis with the following claims:

1. The base-structure tree of a sentence is stored independently of the representation of the transformations which applied to it.
2. The representations decay independently.
3. The representation of the transformational history of a sentence decays more rapidly than does the representation of its base-structure tree.

Since it was assumed that an otherwise untransformed base tree has a simple, active, declarative sentence as its surface expression, it follows that all sentences should tend, over time, to be recalled as kernel sentences.

While the assumptions of the coding studies are intimately related to those of the studies of intersentential relations reviewed above, the theoretical issues involved are distinct. It is quite possible that syntactic parameters should be one of the determinants of perceived relatedness among sentences without its being true that the long-term memory representation of a sentence is its syntactic base structure. On the other hand, where generalization or recall paradigms are used to measure intersentence relations, the experimental implications of the two hypotheses may become indistinguishable: it is presumably the common features of the memory representation of a pair of sentences which determines the extent to which subjects confuse them in recall.

The earliest study of the coding hypothesis is by Mehler (1963), first reported in Miller (1962b). Mehler tested the coding hypothesis in both free- and prompted-recall paradigms using as stimulus material randomized lists of eight sentences of the same general type as were employed by Clifton and Odom (1966). He scored for recall of construction type, lexical content, and grammatical relations. (Presumably, correct recall of construction type indicates retention of the transformational history of a sentence, while correct recall of lexical content and grammatical relations indicates the retention of its base structure.)

The following results emerge from Mehler's data:

1. The number of transformations in a sentence is inversely related to the probability that it will be correctly recalled. (Correct recall means retention of construction type, lexical content, and grammatical relations.)
2. Among errors that affect construction type simplifications preponderate: given that such an error is made, it is more likely that a transformation will be dropped than that one will be added.
3. More errors involve loss of transformational information than loss of information about grammatical relations or lexical content.

4. The recall of a given transformation is independent of the recall of any other.
5. If we discount the effects of lexical content, the confusion matrix for recall of the sentences is, in general, representable by a space in which the distance between two sentences (i.e., the probability that they will be confused) is monotonically related to the number of transformations by which they differ.

These results may profitably be compared with some others which we have already reviewed.

First, Mehler's finding that recall tends towards simplification is compatible with Miller and McKean's (1964) finding that operations on kernel sentences are faster than operations on their transformed counterparts; both results suggest some sort of psychological centrality for the kernel form.

On the other hand, Clifton and Odom (1966) find no general tendency toward simplification. In their data, the tendency to generalize from a relatively complex construction to a simpler one is no greater than the tendency to generalize from a relatively simple construction to a more complex one. (For example, passives are recalled as passive negatives no less frequently than passive negatives are recalled as passives or negatives.) Thus, Clifton and Odom found no tendency for representations to decay in the *direction* of the kernel, though they did find a tendency to produce kernels rather than other constructions. That is, the only appearance of simplification in their data might be viewed as produced by a response bias for kernels.

Finally, as we remarked earlier, Clifton and Odom's (1966) data differ from what Mehler (1963) reported in that Clifton and Odom found the distance between negatives and kernels to be larger than the mean distance for structures separated by one transformation, while the difference between negatives and negative questions, and between questions and negative questions, is smaller. Clifton and Odom claim further that Mehler's data also yield these effects upon reanalysis.

What is the status of the coding hypothesis in the light of Mehler's (1963) findings? The evaluation of Mehler's results and of their bearing upon the coding hypothesis is extremely difficult.

In the first place, the use of a rote-memory paradigm with only a small number of types of sentences encourages the subject to use a strategy which may lead to an artifact. As Miller (1962b) has pointed out, given sentence families as stimulus material, "the subject quickly gets the impression that about half the sentences are negative, half are passive, half are questions; in recall, therefore, they try a little probability matching. If a transformation is forgotten, it is not simply omitted; instead, a guess is made, based upon the overall impression of how often each transformation should be applied" (pp. 760–761). If, however, this is what accounts for the observed response distribution, the experiment is telling us more about the betting strategies of subjects than about the form in which sentences are stored.

Second, it should be noted that, of findings 1 to 5, only the first three are directly relevant to the evaluation of the coding hypothesis. In particular, the finding that transformations decay independently and that the distance between sentences varies with the difference between the number of transformations they contain are both neutral on the question of whether it is base structure which tends to be recalled over the long run.

Third, we have remarked that the coding hypothesis was originally elaborated against the background of a grammatical model on which the kinds of transformations examined in Mehler's study were viewed as optional and as unmarked in the base. But if one accepts the arguments given in Chapter 3, according to which singulary transformations are obligatory and triggered by the presence of deep-structure markers, it is difficult to see how the coding hypothesis is to be formulated. We can no longer say, for example, that the tendency over time is to retain the base structure of a sentence while losing information about its transformational history, because, in the current view, the transformational history of a sentence is determined by its base structure in the kinds of cases that Mehler studied.

Some of these objections are met by an experiment of Bever and Mehler (1967) in which memory for sentences containing *sentence* adverbs (i.e., adverbs which are attached to S in deep structure, like "probably" and "surprisingly") was compared with memory for sentences containing *verb-phrase* adverbs (i.e., adverbs which are attached to VP in deep structure, like "slowly" or "carefully"). Both kinds of sentences were presented in a memory task like the one Mehler used; both kinds of adverbs occurred in initial- and within-sentence positions in the stimuli. The finding was that sentence adverbs tended to be remembered in sentence-initial positions and VP adverbs tended to be recalled in the position adjacent to the verb; that is, there was a tendency toward errors which locate adverbs in their deep-structure positions.

This finding is not prejudiced by the syntactic revisions associated with standard theory, since even in the standard theory, "stylistic" transformations like adverb movement are not marked in the base structure. Moreover, sentence length and sentence meaning are entirely unaffected by adverb movement, and this is not true of many of the transformations Mehler tested.

There are, nevertheless, some caveats that need to be put forth. First, the effect was found *only* in the late trials, which may suggest some artifact of the experimental design. Second, the experiment was uncontrolled for response bias so that the findings may have nothing whatever to do with memory. It is quite possible that subjects prefer sentences in which adverbs take their base-structure position to sentences in which the adverbs have been moved.

ALTERNATIVES TO THE CODING HYPOTHESIS

The coding hypothesis identifies the representation of a sentence that is stored for long-term recall with one of the representations provided by a transformational syntax, namely, with a deep structure. We have seen that some of the data on sentence recall support this proposal, but we have also seen that these data are not unequivocal.

There are at least two alternatives which share with the coding hypothesis the view that the stored representation of a sentence is one of its linguistic representations but which differ as to which representation this is. We turn to a discussion of these alternative proposals.

Surface variables: the depth hypothesis.   We first consider a proposal made by Martin and Roberts (1966) to account for the recall of linguistic materials. Their theory is based on a suggestion made by Yngve (1960) that short-term memory load for any portion of a sentence can be indexed by a metric defined over its surface phrase tree. In particular, Yngve argued that the demands that a given word in a sentence places upon immediate memory is a function of the number of left branches which must be traversed to connect that word to the highest S node in the parsing tree of the sentence. This number (referred to as "depth" by Yngve) presumably represents the degree of "structural embeddedness" of the word in the sentence. For example, sentence (5-23) has depth numbers assigned to each of its lexical items. Martin and Roberts simply averaged the depths of the words in each of their stimulus sentences and identified "mean depth" with a complexity metric for the long-term memory of the sentences [e.g. mean depth for (5-23) equals 1.29]. They predicted that sentences which are relatively complex by this measure should be correspondingly difficult to recall.

5-23   They were not prepared for rainy weather.
    1   3   2   1   1   1   0

In their initial experiment (free-recall lists mixed with respect to both depth and syntactic type), Martin and Roberts (1966) indeed found that high-mean-depth sentences were recalled more poorly than low-mean-depth sentences. Thus, for the stimulus sentences they used, there appeared to be a significant relation between a metric defined over the *surface* phrase tree and levels of recall. This argues that the stored form of sentences preserves important aspects of their surface geometry and is thus not the sort of result one would expect if the coding hypothesis is true.

Martin and Roberts also varied sentence type in the way Mehler (1963) did. Surprisingly, they found a significant effect of sentence type that was primarily attributable to *inferior* recall of K sentences as compared with the other types tested (N, P, short passive, PN). This failure of the Martin and Roberts results to replicate even the direction of Mehler's finding makes comparison of the studies difficult. Moreover, it should be noticed that the mean-depth analysis does not make a prediction about the *kind* of recall error subjects will make, while the coding hypothesis does. Thus one of the primary empirical tests of the coding hypothesis is irrelevant to testing the mean-depth analysis; comparison of the hypotheses must rely on the ability to predict gross accuracy of recall.

To add to the confusion, various other studies of the mean-depth hypothesis have yielded mixed results. Martin, Roberts, and Collins (1968), for example, found a significant effect of mean depth, but in the *reverse* of the predicted direction. Perfetti (1969) and Perfetti and Goodman (1971) found significant effects in experiments which manipulated mean depth across a greater range of values; they found inconsistent patterns as well, however—low-mean-depth sentences were in some circumstances recalled more poorly than high-mean-depth sentences.

Gallagher (1969) reported an experiment in which both mean depth and sentence type were manipulated. She tested active and passive sentences in both high- and low-mean-depth versions. Consistent effects of the transformational and mean-depth variables were not found on the usual scoring (e.g., Mehler, 1963). For example, she found a significant effect of the active/passive difference only on the number of sentences wholly omitted (passives were omitted more often); she found no consistent pattern related to mean depth.

Gallagher also found significant interactions between the manipulated variables and the order of presentation of the lists, and the use of mixed or unmixed lists. It appears, in short, that Miller's (1962b) earlier quoted observation about the importance of the hypothesis formation of subjects in the Mehler experiments may be of equal relevance here. Whether or not the syntactic variables which the experimenter focuses on are reflected in the patterns of subjects' performances may be largely determined by such apparently insignificant facts as the succession of sentence types in the training lists.

Finally, we should note a methodological difficulty with the mean-depth experiments. As Rohrman (1968) has pointed out, the surface-structure changes Martin and Roberts employed in order to manipulate depth also have consequences for the deep-structure representation of the sentences. Typically, depth is increased by the addition of adjectives or adverbs, and these additions complicate the base as well as the surface structure of the stimulus sentences. Thus, even if the results of the experiments on mean depth were consistent, it would be unclear what property of the structural description to attribute them to.

It seems fair to say that the hypothesis that the memory representation of sentences can be captured by surface phrase structure does not receive strong support from the studies we have reviewed. This is not to deny that subjects *can* recall surface phrase structure; under appropriate circumstances they will undoubtedly do so. Under "normal" circumstances, however, they probably do not. Of course, it does not follow that if the surface-structure hypothesis is false, the coding hypothesis must be true. The currently available data provide no convincing evidence that *any* syntactic description of a sentence is isomorphic to its representation in long-term memory.

Semantic variables. In discussing the psychological reality of intersentential relations, we remarked that so long as the deep structure is assumed to be that syntactic representation of a sentence which is semantically interpreted, hypotheses about the psychological effects of deep-structure features tend to be confounded with hypotheses about the psychological effects of semantic relations.

A similar remark is pertinent to the coding hypothesis: the claim that base structure is what we remember of a sentence is hard to disentangle from the claim that what we remember about a sentence is what it means (i.e., its semantic representation). Indeed, claims for the effect of semantic variables seem even more plausible in the context of memory experiments than in the context of experiments which require subjects to make judgments about how similar sentences are. It is hard to believe that differences of form shoud not contribute *something* to the variance in the latter case, but it is easy to imagine that semantic content could be the only relevant factor in memory for messages over relatively long periods.

In the case of memory, there is some evidence favoring the semantic hypothesis over the syntactic one. Sachs (1967) used a recognition paradigm for sentences presented in continuous texts. She reports only a negligible effect of syntactic form as opposed to semantic content; in general, her subjects did not preserve such semantically irrelevant syntactic information on whether the sentence to be recalled occurred in the active or in the passive. Similarly, Fillenbaum (1966) reported that subjects in a recognition task show little ability to distinguish between approximately synonymous sentences which differ in lexical content and syntactic form (e.g., "The postman is not alive"; "The postman is dead"). Bregman and Strasburg (1968) also provided evidence for a nonsyntactic, semantic form of sentence storage in a memory task. They used sentence families in a free-recall paradigm in which subjects were allowed second guesses when their first guess was incorrect. They found a significant correlation between the character of the first guess and the character of the second, which appears to be dependent on the *semantic* features of the sentences involved. Subjects whose first guess was a passive tended to provide an active version of the same lexical content as a second guess, and vice versa. This fact is explicable if one assumes that the stored information specified semantic (but not syntactic) features of the input sentences. Roughly, the subject's strategy is as follows: if the first guess is wrong, try, as a second guess, some sentence which satisfies the same *semantic* description but differs in syntactic form. In this view, it is a stored semantic representation that is controlling the subjects' behavior.

An experiment by Bransford and Franks (1971) graphically illustrates this tendency of subjects to recall an interpretation of a sentence rather than its syntactic structure. They constructed sets of complex sentences like (5-24). Each of the complex sentences was analyzed as containing

5-24   **The rock which rolled down the mountain crushed the tiny hut at the edge of the woods.**

four simpler sentences, e.g., (5-25), (5-26), (5-27), and (5-28). The train-

5-25   **The rock rolled down the mountain.**

5-26   **The rock crushed the hut.**

5-27   **The hut was tiny.**

5-28   **The hut was at the edge of the woods.**

ing list actually presented to subjects consisted of simple sentences, various simple-sentence combinations, or both [e.g., (5-29) is a "combination" of (5-26) and (5-28) and is the sort of sentence that appeared on the training list]. But though the sentences presented in the training list

5-29   **The rock crushed the hut at the edge of the woods.**

exhausted the semantic content of the complex source sentence, that sentence never itself occurred in training. That is, subjects received training sentences like (5-25) to (5-29) but never received training sentences like (5-24).

Subjects were tested for recall by presentation of a recognition list which contained combinations not used in the training lists, including full source sentences like (5-24). They were required to give confidence ratings for each of their judgments about whether or not a sentence on the recognition list had appeared on the training list. Bransford and Franks found that their subjects' confidence that a given test sentence had been on the training list was positively correlated with the extent to which it exhausted the full semantic content of the source sentence. In particular, the full complex sentences were assigned the highest confidence ratings in spite of the fact that no such sentence occurred during training. Subjects were evidently not remembering the form in which information was presented to them but rather a representation which integrated semantic content across sentences in the training list.

While the experiments just reviewed certainly suggest an important contribution of semantic content to sentence recall, it should be emphasized that the available data by no means present a uniform and coherent picture. For example, we have already mentioned an experiment by Koplin and Davis (1966) which suggests that there is more generalization between nonsynonymous sentences that are syntactically related than between synonymous sentences of unrelated syntactic forms. This hardly comports with the view that what one recalls about a sentence is just its semantic representation. This diversity of findings is, perhaps, less surprising than it might appear. It seems obvious that, depending upon how subjects interpret the demand characteristics of the experimental situation, they can produce anything from a rough paraphrase of the stimulus sentence to a verbatim report. There is some experimental evidence for this point.

Johnson-Laird (personal communication) investigated recall of materials like (5-30) to (5-33). In the case of such sentences, one has pairs which belong to the same family contrasted with pairs that do not,

5-30   The duchess sold the painting to John.

5-31   John purchased the painting from the duchess.

5-32   The painting was sold to John by the duchess.

5-33   The painting was purchased from the duchess by John.

semantic content being held roughly identical throughout. Briefly, Johnson-Laird found a specifically syntactic effect [(5-30) conflated with (5-32) more frequently than either is with (5-31) or (5-33)] only when subjects were specifically informed that they were participating in a memory experiment; i.e., when the experimental instructions placed a premium upon the retention of input form.

Similarly, Wanner (1968) found that a subject's knowledge that he would be required to recall the stimulus material affected the accuracy with which he could report stylistic properties of sentences, but had no important effects upon the recall of their content. It is thus entirely possible that the various experiments on linguistic effects in sentence recall may not really be comparable. Experimental manipulations which emphasize attention to linguistic detail yield the kinds of results that are classically taken to support the coding hypothesis. Experimental manipulations which do not emphasize such accuracy yield results in which semantic content is the effective variable. Thus, one typically gets the former sort of result in studies where subjects are asked to rank the similarity of sentences, or to give rote recall of sentence lists; one typically gets the latter sort of result when the stimulus is continuous text and the subject is not instructed that he will be required to recall the material. In either case, the decisive factor seems to be not just the linguistic structure of the stimulus material but rather the subject's construal of the demand characteristics of the experimental task.

In light of these remarks, it should be emphasized that there is no a priori reason why *any* linguistic representation of a sentence (surface, deep, syntactic, or semantic) ought to be isomorphic to the one stored for recall. There is a literature dating at least to Bartlett (1932) which suggests that what subjects remember about a text is a complicated function of the literal text and their beliefs and values. Insofar as this is true, there is no reason to suppose that any purely linguistic theory could specify a representation of sentences which would predict the form in which they are recalled. A recent experiment by Bransford, Barclay, and Franks (1972) serves to make this point with considerable clarity. They showed that subjects who had heard a sentence like "Three turtles rested on a floating log and a fish swam beneath it" did not distinguish it in a memory task from a sentence like "Three turtles rested on a floating log and a fish swam beneath them." What seems to be going on is that the representation subjects stored is neutral between the sentence they actually heard and certain of its logical consequences. (In the present case, a consequence mediated by the transitivity of "beneath.") There is no likelihood that such a representation would be linguistically motivated at *any* level of grammatical description.

CONCLUSION

There are three morals one might reasonably draw from the welter of early experiments on generative grammars. They are the following.

1. The parameters of sentences which linguistic descriptions mark enter, in one way or another, into a variety of psychological processes concerning language. There seems no serious doubt that *structural descriptions* are, in this sense, psychologically real; they specify at least some of the descriptions under which linguistic messages are interpreted and integrated.

2. The direct evidence that the integration and recognition of sentences is governed by the *computational processes* specified by transformational grammars appears considerably weaker. So far, the arguments for the existence of such processes depend largely

upon methodological and simplicity considerations like those reviewed in Chapter 3. In particular, the experimental evidence for the psychological reality of deep and surface trees is considerably stronger than the experimental evidence for the psychological reality of transformations.

3. Though the experiments we have been discussing provide ample evidence for the interaction of psychological mechanisms with features of structural descriptions, they tell us very little about which mechanisms interact with which features. In particular, these experiments do not provide an account of the role of structural features in sentence processing. It is primarily to this kind of question that the next two chapters are addressed.

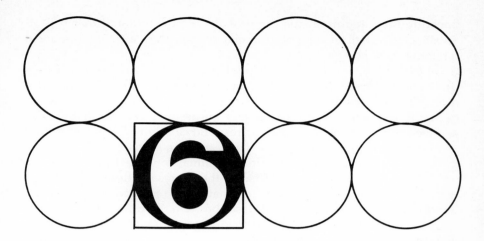

SENTENCE PERCEPTION

INTRODUCTION: GRAMMATICAL MODELS AND RECOGNITION MODELS

The output of a generative grammar of a natural language consists of an infinite set of representations of sentences. If the grammar is to be an adequate theory of the language, each distinct sentence must receive precisely one such representation, and that representation must provide whatever grammatical information is relevant to understanding the sentence. In Chapter 3, we surveyed a number of considerations which suggest that some form of transformational grammar capable of meeting these requirements can probably be devised and that it is almost certain that no type of grammar weaker than a transformational grammar will be able to meet them.

In Chapter 5, we discussed a number of experimental results which indicate that transformational grammars generate structural descriptions of sentences that are "psychologically real." Many of the findings we reviewed seem inexplicable unless one assumes that the distinctions subjects make among sentences correspond closely to the parameters of syntactic structural descriptions. Thus, one can envision the construction of an *optimal* transformational grammar for which the following might be claimed. On the one hand, the representations it generates provide whatever grammatical information is required to understand the sentences of the language it describes. On the other, the representations are articulated in terms of theoretical constructs whose psychological reality can be demonstrated. Given such a grammar, it would seem rational to view the speaker-hearer's recovery of the structural description it assigns a sentence as essential to his understanding of that sentence.

The same point might be put slightly differently. An optimal grammar of a language specifies the set of sentence types which constitutes the language. (The reader will recall that a sentence type is an abstract object such that two events count as tokens of the same sentence type if and only if they are utterances, inscriptions, etc., of the same sentence.) A grammar specifies the sentence types characteristic of a language by generating precisely one structural description for each such type.

Now, as we remarked in Chapter 1, understanding an utterance (or inscription) of a sentence requires at least the identification of the sentence being uttered: to understand a sentence token, we must assign it to a sentence type. If, then, we have a system of structural descriptions that specifies the sentence types, a natural hypothesis is that understanding an utterance of a sentence involves pairing it with one of the structural descriptions belonging to that system. Any empirical evidence for the psychological reality or the linguistic adequacy of such a system of representations tends to increase the plausibility of that hypothesis.

We can put these remarks more formally by characterizing the relation between three concepts: "grammar of L," "ideal sentence recognizer of L," and "real sentence recognizer of L." We begin with the first two.

A grammar of L is a mechanism which takes as input a dummy symbol S and provides as output an infinite set of structural descriptions of sentences of L. An ideal sentence recognizer is a mechanism which takes as input any waveform that is in fact a token of a sentence type in L and produces as output the structural description of the sentence.

There are thus intimate logical relations between an optimal grammar and a model of an ideal sentence recognizer for the language the grammar describes. Since the latter device assigns each utterance one of the structural descriptions that the former device generates, the output of the optimal grammar constrains the output of the ideal sentence recognizer. It should be emphasized, however, that the grammar does *not*, in that sense, constrain the operations that the recognizer employs in *computing* its output. It is an open question, and one with which we shall be concerned throughout this chapter, what operations an ideal sentence recognizer must run through in assigning structural descriptions to utterances.

It may help to grasp the conceptual relation between grammars and models of ideal sentence recognizers if one compares it to the relation between formal systems and feasible proof procedures. If one learns the axioms and inference rules of a formal system, for example Euclidean geometry, one has learned a finite representation of a certain infinite class of theorems. That is, the result of applying all the rules of inference to all the axioms in every possible way will be the enumeration of the theorems. But when one actually attempts to prove a theorem of geometry, one doesn't do it by randomly applying the inference rules to the axioms. On the contrary, much of what one learns when one learns how to "do" Euclidean geometry consists of systematic procedures for starting with a formula and devising a proof. Such proof procedures are logically related to the corresponding formal systems in that they must *not* "recognize" (assign proofs to) any string of symbols which is not a theorem, and they must recognize every string of symbols which is a theorem. But learning the formalism is quite different from learning to do proofs, and devising a mechanical proof procedure relative to a given axiomatic system need by no means be a trivial (or even a solvable) problem. This, then, is the sort of situation that faces a psychologist interested in devising a recognition model relative to a grammar. The grammar specifies the entire set of structural descriptions characteristic of a language, so that it is known antecedently that any utterance of a sentence of the language must be assignable to one or another of the representations that the grammar generates. What is required are feasible procedures for effecting that assignment.

Thus far we have been discussing the relation between an optimal grammar and a model of an ideal sentence recognizer. It must now be noticed that both these devices are to be distinguished from a model of the *real* sentence recognizer. This distinction is, in fact, one of several that are referred to as "the" *performance-competence* distinction in the standard linguistic literature.

An ideal sentence recognizer can transduce any of indefinitely many utterances into their appropriate structural descriptions. But the capabilities of a real sentence recognizer are clearly finite. An ideal sentence recognizer is, presumably, a failure-proof device in both the following two senses: first, there is no sentence in the range of the corresponding grammar that it is incapable of recognizing; second, it makes no mistakes, i.e., it never assigns the wrong structural description to an input. It is patent that the real speaker-hearer is not failure-proof in either of these respects. Again, an ideal sentence recognizer computes every structural description of an ambiguous input and every aspect of every structural description of any input. But a real speaker-hearer presumably often fails to compute structural information when it is not task-relevant, or when he is fatigued, or when he is insufficiently motivated. Finally, a real speaker-hearer, unlike his ideal counterpart, works, by definition, in real time.

These remarks point to the ways in which models of an ideal sentence recognizer really are idealizations. The behavior of speaker-hearers is not only a product of their language-handling capacities but also a result of the operation of psychological variables, including memory, motivation, beliefs, and so on, which are not specifically linguistic in nature. The model of an ideal speaker-hearer abstracts from the effects of these variables, as it must do if problems in psycholinguistics are to be isolated from the ultimate problem of simulating the total behavior of the organism.

We thus assume that a model of the real speaker-hearer is an extension of a model of the ideal speaker-hearer; the real speaker-hearer is conceptualized as an ideal speaker-hearer suffering under such "performance" constraints as mortality, motivation, and memory. In some barely conceivable future psychology, one can imagine predicting aspects of concrete verbal behavior on the basis of knowledge of the interactions between language-handling capacities, current inputs, and nonlinguistic psychological faculties. For present purposes, however, this is a pipe dream, and the characterization of ideal speaker-hearers must be the primary object of rational concern.

Thus far, we have thought of the ideal sentence recognizer simply as a function from utterances (strictly, from acoustic or orthographic representations of utterance tokens) onto structural descriptions. Trivially, if there is any such function, there must be infinitely many, and the problem in psycholinguistics is to choose between them. We close these prefatory remarks with some observations on how this choice is to be made.

An *empirically adequate* model of an ideal sentence recognizer is constrained in at least three important ways. We have seen that one such constraint is formal compatibility with an optimal grammar; the model must recognize whatever structural descriptions the grammar enumerates. It may be added that there are other constraints that the relation between the sentence recognizer and the grammar could plausibly be expected to satisfy. For example, given an optimal grammar of a natural language, it should be possible to construct the corresponding model of a sentence recognizer by a universal algorithm. This must be true in any account which holds that it is fundamentally the speaker-hearer's mastery of the grammar which enables him to use the language. (For further discussion, see Chapter 8.)

A second constraint on an empirically adequate model of an ideal sentence recognizer is the requirement that it prove compatible with models of other psychological faculties. Eventually, we shall have to have a theory of how linguistic capacities are embedded in the matrix of psychological (and, presumably, neurological) properties of the organism. Any model of the ideal speaker-hearer which is incompatible with whatever is known about the rest of human psychology is ipso facto disconfirmed.

Finally, and most important for the practical purposes of psycholinguistics, an empirically adequate model of an ideal speaker-hearer is constrained by relevant experimental data about how people in fact handle sentences. Whatever we can discover about the relative perceptual complexity of sentences, the order in which features of structural descriptions are recovered, the salience of features of sentences for the transmission of grammatical information, and so on, is grist for this mill. To take just one example, it is a striking fact that the length of a sentence is not per se a good predictor of the difficulty of understanding the sentence. Among the infinity of possible sentence-recognition devices, there is surely a large subset that is ruled out by this fact alone.

We turn now to a discussion of recognition models for several different levels of linguistic structure and of some of the experimental evidence currently available for their evaluation.

PART ONE. PERCEPTUAL MODELS FOR PHONETICS

What we have said thus far implies that optimal sentence recognizers must compute a representation of each input at each psychologically real level of description acknowledged by the grammar. As we noted in Chapter 2, a grammar provides a phonetic level of representation, and the phone is a perceptual entity at least in the sense that a phonetic transcription of a sentence must represent the way the sentence sounds to speaker-hearers. Hence, the sentence recognizer must include procedures for assigning phonetic representations to each utterance token in the language.

It is useful to consider these procedures in abstraction from the ones that are involved in the assignment of such higher-level descriptions as lexical analysis, surface constituent analysis, deep-structure analysis, semantic analysis, etc. But it should be noted that this abstraction is artificial. The assignment of a phonetic representation to a waveform is demonstrably responsive to decisions about higher levels of structure. That this must be the case is shown by the fact that the intelligibility of a speech signal is highly sensitive to its redundancy in context. As we shall see, a wide variety of experimental studies attest to this fact. This means, of course, that the speaker-hearer's decisions about the phonetic analysis of the input are sensitive to his hypotheses about its lexical, syntactic, and semantic analysis.

In fact, it is plausible to suppose that decisions at *every* level of analysis are subject to feedback from decisions at higher levels as well as feed-forward from decisions at lower levels. What one finally chooses as a structural description for a waveform would thus be the "best hypothesis" given all the available information about the input. In effect, the representation at each level is adjusted to comport with considerations of overall optimality. A finished theory would thus have to say something about the order in which representations are computed, the ways in which feedback is employed in adjusting them to one another, and the character of the weighting function in terms of which "overall optimality" is defined. It seems to us that this identification of perceptual analysis with the choice of a best hypothesis about the structure of a sensory array probably holds quite generally, and is in no way restricted to the perception of language.

At present we must consider the perceptual analysis of each level of representation in relative isolation from the others, simply because little is known about how decisions at the various levels may interact. Moreover, this idealization is not entirely arbitrary. It is *possible* for the hearer to identify speech sounds in isolation, though he normally does so less accurately than when higher-level constraints are simultaneously imposed. What we are thus aiming at, at a minimum, is a theory of the performance of the sentence recognizer in the limiting condition in which the only input information pertinent to phonetic analysis is a description of the acoustic character of a waveform.

The "naïve" speech-perception model.   We are interested, then, in characterizing the information flow in a "voice typewriter": a device which accepts as input waveforms that are in fact utterances of sentences and provides as outputs appropriate phonetic transcriptions of the waveforms.

The most natural hypothesis about the operation of such a device derives from the assumption that phones are acoustically defined. More specifically, what we shall call the naïve theory of speech perception assumes that each phone is associated with a list of criterial values of acoustic parameters. This list specifies the properties that a speech signal must exhibit if it is to be perceived as an utterance of the phone in question. The operation of the recognizer is essentially that of matching the acoustic properties of an input signal against those which define the phones and of categorizing the signal appropriately.

Patently, this view of the nature of phone recognition is capable of liberalization. For example, one could think of a given set of acoustic properties as characterizing an ideal, or modal, phone from which real-speech events are allowed to diverge in certain ways, or within certain limits, or both; the probability of an event being recognized as an utterance of a given phone would then be a function of the character or the extent of such divergence. Or one could imagine a system which relativizes the definition of a phone to the gross acoustic properties of the productions of individual speakers, thus allowing for acoustic differences across voices. Such liberalizations of the model are of some intrinsic interest, and we shall return to them.

For present purposes, the crucial question is whether to accept a theory according to which there are purely acoustic criteria for classifying a speech event as a certain phone. Notice that this is the sort of view of the relation between speech events and phones that was widely accepted by taxonomic linguists. We saw in Chapter 2 that the conditions upon "free variation" of subphonetic elements (i.e., the conditions under which an n-tuple of elements are interchangeable in a linguistic environment without alteration of the phonetic value of the message) are supposed to be defined in terms of overlap between the acoustic properties of the variants of a phone.

To summarize: the most primitive model of the relation between acoustic events and the phones that represent them holds that for each phone there is a list of criterial acoustic properties which are speaker- and context-independent. The first of these assumptions says that every speaker who intelligibly utters a given phone must produce a signal exhibiting the criterial attributes for that phone. The second assumption says that each intelligible utterance of a given phone must exhibit those attributes in whatever linguistic environment it occurs.

If these two assumptions are true, they dictate the general character of a model for a phone recognizer. Consider a recognition device consisting of (1) a bank of detector elements (filters) tuned to the presumed criterial values of acoustic parameters in terms of which the phones are defined, (2) a hierarchy of Boolean logic elements which receives inputs from the filter bank, and (3) an output system which commands a phonetic vocabulary. Some such device will recognize phones insofar as the latter are identifiable with Boolean functions of criterial acoustic features. It will do so by scanning its acoustic input for the relevant criterial invariants and producing a phonetic output determined by the acoustic properties it finds.[1]

A great deal of early work on speech recognition was aimed at the construction of just such a device. The acoustic dimensions in terms of which the recognizer analyzed the signal were assumed to be frequency, intensity, and time. The computational operations performed by the device consisted primarily of matching its input against specifications of ideal phones given in terms of those dimensions.

As we remarked above, the sophistication of such a model may be increased in a variety of ways. For example, in real-life situations the acoustic quality of an input may be degraded by such factors as ambient noise and careless articulation. However, the recognizability of a linguistic signal is clearly not linearly related to the extent of such degradation. An utterance of a phone may be entirely recognizable even when it does not exhibit the full criterial acoustic array presumed to be associated with that phone; witness speakers' ability to understand speech under the sort of distortions encountered on the telephone or at cocktail parties.

The explanation of this fact is fairly obvious: connected speech exhibits an enormous amount of informational redundancy. In particular, an utterance of a phone in connected speech may diverge widely from the paradigm so long as the phonetic value of a given segment of the utterance is predictable from its context. The plausibility of a speech-recognition model of the kind we have been discussing can thus be increased if we allow it to take advantage of redundancy.

The theoretical framework we have been discussing thus leads to two sorts of psychological experimentation: (1) experiments to determine the criterial acoustic features for the perception of phones in isolation from ongoing speech and (2) experiments which investigate the interaction between the redundancy of a phone and various distortions of its acoustic representation, with a view toward determining which kinds of distortions can be tolerated at various levels of redundancy of the signal. We now turn to a review of some typical findings in these areas.

---

[1] The interest of this kind of model is by no means limited to the psychology of phone recognition. Indeed, the assumption that something like it is true has been almost ubiquitous in the psychological literature on perception. The "criterial-invariant" view is, in fact, the most natural alternative to the sort of "best-hypothesis" acount of perception tentatively endorsed above. It seems to be the common theme of theorists who have as little else in common as Selfridge (1959), Bruner (1957), Hebb (1949), and Vygotsky (1965), and it has been read as the moral of such neurological findings as those of Hubel and Weisel (1963). Indeed, it is a large part of what connects psychological theorizing about perception to the empiricist tradition in philosophy.

EARLY STUDIES OF THE ACOUSTIC REPRESENTATION OF PHONES

What we have been calling the naïve theory of speech perception was widely prevalent in both psychology and linguistics long before the first serious attempts at experimental determination of the presumed acoustic invariants for phones. Such experimentation was made feasible by advances in acoustic science during and after the Second World War, which permitted the reliable analysis of the acoustic character of a speech signal. In particular, the invention of the "sound spectrograph" permitted experimenters to investigate previously inaccessible properties of such signals.

The sound spectrograph provides a continuous display of the changing distribution of acoustic energy in the speech spectrum. Its output, for a given utterance as input, is a "speech spectrogram," i.e., a graph of the intensity of the signal at various frequencies across time.

Since much of the work which suggests a lack of acoustic invariants corresponding to phones is based on spectrographic analyses, and since it is always conceivable that such invariants might turn up under some different acoustic transformation of the speech signal, it is worth noticing two reasons for taking results obtained with spectrography seriously. The first is that it is fairly certain that the peripheral auditory system of humans does provide a frequency by time by intensity analysis of its inputs (cf. von Békésy, 1960). Thus, there is reason to believe that the kind of information preserved by spectrographic analysis is available to speaker-hearers for employment in phone recognition. Second, speech spectrograms preserve sufficient information to determine perceptually recognizable phones. That is, a device which synthesizes utterances from specifications of their spectrographic properties produces recognizable speech.

Among the earliest purposes to which speech spectrography was put was the attempt to discover acoustic invariants for the vowels. For example, Potter, Kopp, and Green (1947) noticed that utterances of vowels appear to have characteristic modal regions of energy concentration. Figure 6-1 gives spectrograms for representative vowels. The regions of energy concentration are called "formants." For example, utterances of the vowel [æ] characteristically display energy concentrations at 700 hertz (f_1), at 1,600 hertz (f_2), and at 2,460 hertz (f_3).

Formant analysis has played a considerable role in discussions of the acoustic properties of speech, and a variety of considerations suggest that the formant structure of a segment is the most important acoustic determinant of its phonetic analysis. For one thing, the location of formants is determined by the resonance frequencies of the vocal tract, so that shifts in the arrangements of formants are at least roughly interpretable in terms of changes in the configuration of the organs of speech.

Each Front Vowel Has a Distinct Pattern

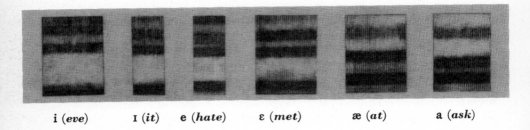

i (*eve*)   ɪ (*it*)   e (*hate*)   ɛ (*met*)   æ (*at*)   a (*ask*)

Each Back Vowel Has a Distinct Pattern

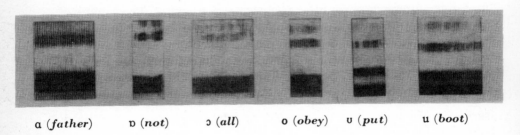

ɑ (*father*)   ɒ (*not*)   ɔ (*all*)   o (*obey*)   ʊ (*put*)   u (*boot*)

Each Mid-Vowel Has a Distinct Pattern

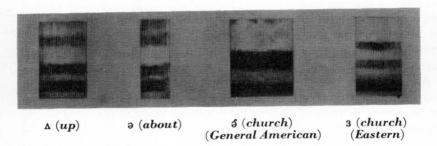

ʌ (*up*)   ə (*about*)   ɝ (*church*) (*General American*)   ɜ (*church*) (*Eastern*)

Fig. 6-1. From Potter, Kopp, and Green (1943, pp. 66, 72, and 69).

Again, it is an important consequence of studies in speech spectrography that although the formant analysis of a speech sound represents only a part of the information present in the speech sound, a specification of the behavior of f_1 to f_3 normally provides sufficient information for the synthesis of an intelligible artificial speech signal.

A number of investigations have attempted to describe speech sounds as spectrographic patterns [see, for example, Heintz and Stevens

(1961); for a review, see Jakobson, Fant, and Halle (1963)]. Common to all such studies was a degree of success in discovering acoustic features in terms of which the phonetic representations of speech events might be identified by a device incorporating a suitably tuned system of filters.

There were, however, difficulties. In the first place, the level of accuracy of the phone identifications that can be attained by monitoring for such "invariants" as these studies discovered was not especially high compared with the accuracies routinely achieved by human hearers. For example, the recognition system employed by Hughes and Halle (1956) was required to distinguish only among the three unvoiced fricatives [f], [s], and [ʃ]. Using three acoustic criteria, at least two of which were applied to each signal, permitted correct identifications ranging around 80 percent.

Second, the filter systems appropriate for the automatic recognition of vowels do not turn out to be appropriate for consonants. Consonants, unlike vowels, are not, in general, identifiable with steady states of the spectrographic display, nor do they invariably exhibit formant structure. More significant still is a point to which we shall return for lengthy discussion: the filter values appropriate for the recognition of a given consonant in one syllabic environment may be radically different from the values appropriate for the recognition of that same consonant in a different syllabic environment. In short, it appears that recognition devices which filter for such spectrographic invariants as have thus far been identified are neither fully capable of providing accurate identifications in the domain for which they are specifically designed nor generally useful outside that domain.

There are further reasons for adopting a pessimistic view of such success as early studies had in isolating acoustic invariants for the phones. Investigations which suggested the existence of such invariants characteristically abstracted from the problem of interspeaker variation. When such variations *are* taken into account, it turns out that filter values appropriate to the acoustic realization of a given speech sound by a given speaker may differ quite dramatically from the values appropriate to the identification of the same sound in the productions of a different speaker. Figure 6-2 compares relations between f_1 and f_2 in the vowel systems of two speakers of English. It is apparent that the formant structures which define vowels for speaker A are not the ones which define the same vowels for speaker B. Of special interest in this regard is the observation that spectrographic patterns for children and adults producing the same linguistic forms are characteristically grossly different. [See the spectrograms in Lenneberg (1967).] This makes it difficult to believe that what the child is learning when he masters the acoustic-phonetic correspondence characteristic of his language is a set of criterial acoustic values for each of the phones.

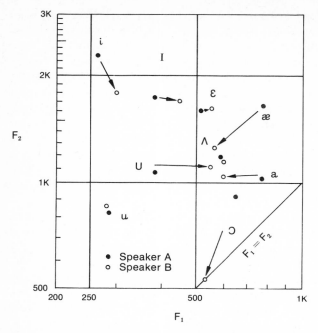

Fig. 6-2. Vowel systems of two individual speakers (from Fairbanks and Grubb, 1961).

It thus appears that the hearer is somehow able to relativize his criteria for phone identification to the general acoustic properties of a speaker's voice. Ladefoged and Broadbent (1957) have provided a striking experimental demonstration of this fact. A tape recording which is heard as "bit" when it follows the sentence "Please say what this word is," spoken in one voice, is heard as "bet" when it follows the same sentence spoken in a different voice. Evidently the analysis of the vowel is being relativized to the acoustic properties of the two voices. According to the authors, "the linguistic information conveyed by a vowel sound does not depend on the absolute values of its formant frequencies, but on the relationship between the formant frequencies for that vowel and the formant frequencies of other vowels pronounced by that speaker" (p. 98).

The view that a speech sound is characterized by a unique combination of acoustic properties across speakers is difficult to maintain in the face of such observations as those just cited. A variety of proposals for relativizing the acoustic analysis of speech sounds to the idiosyncratic properties of speakers is to be found in the literature, though it is probably fair to say that none of them provides an adequate account of the hearer's tolerance of interspeaker variation. One such proposal, for example, maintained that the important acoustic property that is preserved across speakers, at least for the case of the vowels, is the *ratio* of formant frequencies. In this view, though there is a difference in the absolute location of the formants for speakers A and B in Figure 6-2, the ratio between f_1 and f_2 should be constant. Moreover, if this proposal were correct, phonetically distinct vowels produced by a given speaker would never exhibit the same formant ratios. In fact, however, neither of these consequences of the "constant-ratio" theory of vowel identification is confirmed by the data. A 45° line in Figure 6-2 expresses a constant ratio; the reader can confirm by inspection that utterances of a given vowel by the two speakers do not invariably fall on the same constant-ratio line. Moreover, speaker A has distinct vowels [ʊ] and [u] that do fall on the same constant-ratio line, so that constant-ratio relations do not predict either vowel identity across speakers or vowel distinctness for a given speaker. Addition of f_3 information does not substantially alter the situation.

The kinds of difficulties we have thus far surveyed were, of course, known to investigators seeking to find acoustic invariants for the phones; and the investigators were not insensitive to the dilemma such difficulties pose for filter models of phone recognition. How could filter models be maintained, given the failure to find acoustic invariants across speakers or across syllabic environments in the linguistic forms produced by a given speaker? One way of coping with these difficulties is to think of the effects of interspeaker variation and of syllabic environment as analogous to noise in the signal [cf. Denes and Pinson (1963)]. The ability of the hearer to recover the appropriate phonetic analysis despite the lack of acoustic invariants could then be attributed, at least in some part, to his exploitation of the redundancy of the input.

We will argue presently that this account of the hearer's ability to provide phonetic analyses for signals which do not exhibit acoustic invariants is defective. The problem is not that the invariants are *distorted* in the speech signal; it is rather that there often turn out to be no such invariants. Nevertheless, the view that real speech consists of noisy approximations to acoustically defined phones did lead to a variety of interesting experimental results on the relation between signal distortion, signal identifiability, and signal redundancy in speech perception. The common feature of these experiments is the suppression of one or another aspect of the normal acoustic pattern. The effects of this distortion on the recognition of connected discourse is then determined for stimulus materials exhibiting various degrees and kinds of redundancy. Of the large number of experiments of this kind to be found in the literature, we shall discuss only a few that are paradigmatic.

Experiments on the effects of redundancy and distortion on speech perception. Experiments with filtered speech provide one of the simplest and most striking demonstrations of the fact that much of the acoustic information in continuous speech is redundant. Figure 6-3 shows the functions for recognition of phonetically balanced word lists under high- and low-pass filtering. With a low-pass filter (i.e., one which passes only the portion of the spectrum below a specified frequency), the recognition score increases with increase of the cutoff frequency; the converse is the case with a high-pass filter. The interesting point about this figure is that the functions are symmetric and that they cross (at approximtely 1,900 hertz); thus the spectrum above 1,900 cycles is redundant given the lower portion and the spectrum below 1,900 cycles is redundant given the upper portion. The recognition scores at the crossover point are 60 percent for isolated words. If the same test is performed with connected discourse, however, the recognition scores are virtually perfect.

Analogous results have been found in the investigation of "time-compressed" speech. Time compression is effected by sampling the speech signal in time; by one or another process, very short stretches of the speech signal (say, about 20 milliseconds) are periodically excised and the residual sequences are abutted. The effect is to increase the rate at which information is carried by the signal. The usual finding is that a reduction of about 55 percent in the time used to present the signal is compatible with correct identifications of about 90 percent of single words in isolation—hence, that something like half the material in the speech signal is redundant. What is striking is the suggestion that the subjects' inability to tolerate higher rates of presentation may be due to the saturation of his short-term memory (i.e., to his inability to *recall* the stimulus materials) rather than to failure of perceptual resolution. [See Foulke (1969)].

It seems that information relevant to the phonetic decoding of the speech signal is widely distributed across the frequency spectrum and across time, so that large portions of the signal turn out to be dispensible without significant loss of intelligibility. As Licklider and Miller remarked in their (1951) review of the literature on speech recognition:

> Apparently no single dimension of speech is critical. Speech power can be varied over a range of a billion to one. Conversations are intelligible with only the upper half of the spectrum, but there is nothing unique about this half because we can throw it all away and get along equally well with only the lower half. The waveform can be distorted to a series of square waves or turned off half the time without severe effects.... Changes in the intensity, the fundamental frequency, the waveform, the envelope of the wave, or the spectrum do not affect intelligibility until the change is so great the spectrographic pattern is markedly altered [pp. 1068–69].

Thus far we have mentioned experiments which show that much of the acoustic character of the speech signal is predictable; the signal is *acoustically redundant* in the sense that the information relevant to phone perception is simultaneously represented by values of many dis-

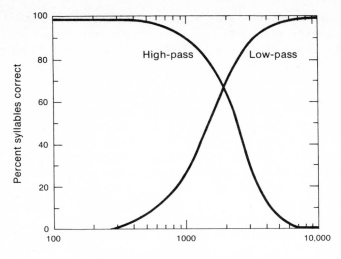

Cutoff frequency, cycles per second

Fig. 6-3. Functions relating nonsense-syllable articulation scores to the cutoff frequency of high-pass and low-pass filters. For example, with a 100-hertz high-pass filter 90 percent are correctly heard; with a 1000-hertz low-pass filter only 27 percent are correct (from Miller, 1951).

tinct acoustic parameters. There is another large group of experiments in the literature which show that the recognizability of distorted speech varies as a function of what might be called message redundancy—i.e., with the extent to which the linguistic representation of a portion of the speech stream is predictable given knowledge of the linguistic representation of the prior segments. We have, in fact, already noted instances of this effect. For example, we remarked that the recognition scores at the intersection of the curves in Figure 6-3 increased from approximately 60 percent to approximately 100 percent when connected discourse is substituted for word lists in the stimulus material. Presumably this change is caused by the fact that message redundancy is relatively higher in connected discourse than in word lists.

A similar experiment by Miller, Heise, and Lichten (1951) investigated the intelligibility of speech heard under noise as a function of the presence or absence of linguistic context. The fundamental finding was that words in sentences can be correctly understood at considerably higher levels of noise than the same words presented in isolation. It is also likely that effects of *non*linguistic, situational context on the perceptibility of speech are comparable to the effects of acoustic and message redundancy. Knowledge of the speech situation, of the topic of conversation, and so on, can clearly be used by the hearer to facilitate his comprehension of the speech signal.

The upshot is that the perceiver's tolerance for distortion of the input appears to be vast so long as the signal is sufficiently redundant at one or another level of analysis. However, it is important to understand the relation of these investigations to our primary question—the adequacy of filter models of speech perception. The studies we have mentioned do not challenge the assumption that the optimal utterance of a phone is characterizable in terms of some set of criterial acoustic features; they only argue that, given the redundancy of speech events, phonetic values can often be determined even for utterances that are not acoustically optimal. That is, these studies only demonstrate that *if* there are criterial acoustic features for phones, speakers can use redundancies to predict which such features a given utterance *would have exhibited had it been acoustically optimal*. They leave open the question of whether acoustic criterial features can in fact be stated for the optimal phone.

The situation can be summarized as follows. The naïve speech-perception model may be made more sophisticated by supposing that it has available not only a list of acoustic definitions of optimal utterances of phones but also a catalog of relevant information about acoustic and message redundancies. The model is presumed to be capable of searching its input for occurrences of relevant criterial features and of tolerating distortions of such features insofar as the signal is redundant. It is tautological that this sort of model is appropriate only if the optimal utterance of a phone can in fact be acoustically characterized, for only in that case will there be some characteristic acoustic display for whose presence the device can search the input signal. We thus return, once again, to the question of whether, in the optimal case, the phone is definable by some Boolean function of values of acoustic parameters.

To assume that each phone is characterizable by reference to some set of acoustic invariants is to make the following predictions: (1) Utterances of distinct phones should differ in the criterial acoustic properties in all linguistic environments. (2) Utterances of a given phone should exhibit the criterial acoustic properties across all linguistic environments. (3) Phones should exhibit a segment-by-segment correspondence to portions of the acoustic signal: i.e., if phone a precedes phone b in the phonetic transcription of an utterance, then the portion of the acoustic input which corresponds to phone a should precede the portion of the acoustic input which corresponds to b. (4) The probability that two signals which differ only along a given criterial acoustic parameter will be identified as distinct phones should be roughly proportional to the magnitude of that difference. It is worth remarking again that these are precisely the sorts of conditions which we saw were presupposed by taxonomic approaches to phonetics. This suggests, correctly we think, that the notion that there could be a mechanical, acoustically determined discovery procedure for phonetic theories is intimately related to the notion that a filter bank could be an adequate speech recognizer. Both inherit the consequences of the doctrine that the optimal phone is acoustically definable.

It has been shown, in large part by experiments carried out at the Haskins Laboratory, that in all probability none of the above consequences of the assumption that there exist criterial acoustic invariants for phones is true. The implications of this discovery for the entire theory of speech recognition are, of course profound: in particular, it suggests that no "passive" model of speech perception is going to work. The characteristic feature of filter models, for example, is that they reject information; i.e., they assume that the criterial invariants are present in optimal acoustic inputs, and that the perceptual problem is to abstract them out of the accompanying noncriterial information. The experimental demonstration that such invariants do not exist suggests that the perceptual problem is not that of *rejecting* irrelevant information present in the signal but rather that of *adding* information in terms of which the signal can be properly decoded—that is, speech perception involves a perceptual constancy in the sense of Chapter 1: the phonetic analysis of the speech signal represents an integration of acoustic information with background knowledge available to the hearer. We return to these remarks after a brief survey of some of the relevant experimental results.

The diversity of acoustic representations of phones.   Among the most striking results on the acoustics of speech is the discovery that very different signals—signals which are highly discriminable when they occur in isolation—may nevertheless be heard as perceptually identical utterances of one and the same phone when they occur in the speech stream. The most interesting examples of this phenomenon concern the perception of stop consonants.

Utterance of *stop consonant + vowel* syllables have a characteristic type of formant structure. The signal normally consists of an initial component, in which frequency values of the formants are rapidly modulated, followed by a signal of relatively steady state. Very roughly, this pattern is explicable by reference to the sequence of articulatory gestures involved in the production of such syllables: the vocal apparatus moves rapidly from a position of relative or complete closure involved in the production of the stop to an open and relatively stable condition involved in the production of the vowel.

We may therefore expect that, at least for syllables spoken in isolation, the major acoustic difference between utterances of such sequences as /da/, /ga/, /ka/, and /ba/ will be located in the character of the initial formant inflection. Thus, Liberman, Harris, Hoffman, and Griffith (1957) showed that varying the initial inflection of an otherwise steady-state signal will yield what is perceived as a sequence of different stop consonants followed by the same vowel.

To investigate the relation between a stop consonant and its acoustic representation in various vowel environments, experimenters have used synthetic speech signals. For example Figure 6-4 shows an array of spectrographic patterns sufficient for the synthesis of /d/ before a variety of vowels. A number of interesting points emerge. First, the position of the second formant (the structure which contains the primary information for distinguishing between consonants) varies through a range of some 1,000 hertz. It would appear, in fact, that the absolute-frequency value of the formant structure associated with the consonant is determined almost entirely by the absolute frequency of the formant structure of the following vowel. Second, it is noteworthy that even the *direction* of slope of the modulated portion of the signal varies as a function of the choice of the vowel. Roughly, /d/ before high vowel is associated with a rising second-formant structure and /d/ before low vowels is associated with a falling second-formant structure. Finally, it must be emphasized that the differences between the acoustic patterns associated with these perceptually identical /d/ signals are much larger than the discrimination threshold for frequency. Indeed, the same acoustic objects which are heard as utterances of /d/ when they occur as the initial portion of signals like those in Figure 6-4 will be heard as highly discriminable glides if they are isolated from their vowel environment. As Liberman, Cooper, Shankweiler, and Studdert-Kennedy (1967) remark,

> How different these acoustic features are in nonspeech perception can be determined by removing them from the patterns [Figure 6-4] and sounding then in isolation. When we do that, the transition isolated from the /di/ pattern sounds like a rapidly rising whistle or glissando on high pitches, the one from /du/ like a rapidly falling whistle on low pitches. These signals could hardly sound more different from each other. Furthermore, neither of them sounds like /d/ nor like speech of any sort [pp. 435–436].

It may be added that these sorts of results are not specific to /d/ but are the general case for the stop consonants.

Such anomalies in the behavior of the stop consonants have generated classic puzzles in phonetic theory. We remarked in Chapters 2 and 3 that there is a dialect of English in which the segments /t/ and /d/ are represented by the identical velar flap [D] in such words as "writer," "rider"; "latter," "ladder"; etc. What is heard as a /t/ and /d/ contrast in these environments is in fact acoustically represented by a linguistically conditioned lengthening of the preceding vowel. If we consider this finding in the light of those described above, we have evidence for multiple failures of isomorphism between the acoustic and phonetic representations of the utterance: among the acoustic proper-

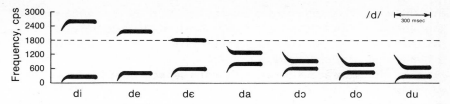

Fig. 6-4. Spectrographic patterns sufficient for the synthesis of /d/ before vowels. (Dashed line at 1800 hertz shows the "locus" for /d/.) (From Libermann, Cooper, Shankweiler, and Studdert-Kennedy, 1967).

ties that may suffice to determine the perception of a consonant, we must include not only a wide variety of formant transitions but also temporal features of the preceding vowel. Moreover, in the present case, there is patently nothing like a segment-to-segment correspondence between the acoustic signal and its phonetic transcription, since the perceptual difference associated with the consonant is signaled by an acoustic difference associated with the *prior* phone.

It is noteworthy that, insofar as the difficulty we have been discussing involves the effects of a phone's syllabic environment upon its acoustic realization (e.g., the effect of the character of the succeeding vowel upon the consonant in a *CV* syllable), it could be resolved by assuming that the syllable is the perceptual unit and that there are acoustic invariants for the identification of syllables. This suggestion has been seriously proposed in the literature (e.g., Savin and Bever, 1970) and cannot by any means be dismissed out of hand. However, there are at least four difficulties that it has to cope with.

1. The notion of a syllable is not itself entirely well defined, so that there is a corresponding vagueness in the claim that syllables are perceptual units. What, for example, is the correct syllabification of "writing"? Is it [rayt-ing] or [ray-ting]? In general, there is a problem about whether intervocalic consonants should be assigned to the preceding or to the following vowel.

2. Syllables are *heard* as having internal structure, e.g., "bad" and "bet" are heard as beginning with the same phone. A model of speech perception will thus have to render a phonetic transcription at some point, whether or not it takes the syllable to be the first unit recovered in the order of speech processing.

3. It is not known how much acoustic distortion a syllable receives as a result of the character of *its* syllabic environment, but it is clear that some intersyllabic effects exist. There is thus no guarantee that moving the perceptual unit "up" from the phone to the syllable will locate an invariant acoustic counterpart to a linguistic unit. Notice, for example, that the writer-rider case discussed above appears to involve *inter*-syllabic effects which determine the phonetic representation of an acoustic event. Indeed, there is every possibility that characterizing the ways in which the acoustic realization of a syllable depends on its environment will require the *same* theoretical apparatus needed to characterize the ways in which acoustic representations of phones are environment-dependent. This is because some of the acoustic interactions between syllables surely depend on the character of their phonetic content.

4. The standard explanation for the existence of a phonetic level in language is that it permits the recognition of speech with a relatively small bit-per-unit information load. This explanation is lost to a theory which takes the syllable as the unit of perceptual analysis. Thus, every recognition of an allophone of English involves identifying one entity from a pool of about a hundred in fully nonredundant signals. If we assume that syllables are the first-recognized objects, the information load associated with each unit goes up dramatically. There are about 5,000 English syllables, so that recognizing a syllabic unit in completely nonredundant speech would cost about twelve bits.

In short, many of the problems associated with the definition and recognition of phones recur for syllables, and the assumption that the syllable is the perceptual unit involves problems of its own.

Finally, a special caution is required in interpreting the data which show that information about the syllabic environment of a speech signal is essential to its perceptual identification. These data per se do not show that the syllable is the perceptual unit in speech. What they do suggest is that characteristically no stretch of speech signal shorter than a syllable can receive a reliable phonetic interpretation. It is important to notice that these two claims are different. To see this, compare the case of handwriting recognition. We often need a rather long stretch of handwriting before we are able to provide a secure identification of any of the words or letters. It does not follow, however, that orthographic invariants in handwriting are associated with very long texts, or that the unit of analysis in handwriting is anything larger than the individual letter. What seems to be the case is rather that we accept hypotheses about the identity of individual letters and words only if they yield a sensible interpretation of longer sequences like phrases and sentences. The fact that we need to examine longer sequences in order to analyze shorter ones may thus reflect not on the size of the units of analysis but rather on the character of the data we require our analyses to conform to.

The diversity of phonetic interpretation of acoustic cues. Thus far we have mentioned results which suggest that a given phone may be identified with a variety of distinct acoustic representations depending upon its syllabic environment; e.g., that acoustic signals which are discriminably different in isolation may nevertheless be heard as representations of the same phonetic element when they occur in the speech stream. The converse is also true. That is, a given acoustic event may be subject to a variety of distinct phonetic analyses depending on the character of the speech stream in which it is embedded, so that an acoustic signal which is interpreted as one phone in a given syllabic environment will be interpreted as a different phone when the environment is changed. We have, in fact, already mentioned one such case: Ladefoged and Broadbent's demonstration that the phonetic interpretation of a vowel sound can be made to vary with variation of the speaker who utters it. But the same kind of effect can be obtained *without* speaker variation.

Suppose that one has recorded the sequence /pi/. It is possible to locate roughly the portion of the tape corresponding to the consonant and to splice it to a recording of some different vowel like /a/ or /u/. If /p/ is identified with an acoustic invariant, the prediction is that the new tapes will be heard as /pa/ and /pu/ respectively. In fact, however, the tape composed of the /p/ clipped from /pi/ and the /a/ recorded in isolation is consistently heard as /ka/, whereas the tape composed of the /p/ clipped from /pi/ and the /u/ recorded in isolation is heard as /pu/ (Schatz, 1954). The same result is obtained with artificial speech where energy bursts prior to the steady-state portion of the signal simulate the consonant in a *CV* syllable. "Bursts of noise that produce the best /k/ or /g/ vary over a considerable frequency range depending on the following vowel. The range is so great that it extends over the domain of the /p,b/ burst, creating the curiosity of a single burst of noise at 1,440 cps that is heard as /p/ before /i/ but as /k/ before /a/" (Liberman et al, 1967, p. 439).

This is by no means a special case. Consider the variety of percepts that can be engendered by introducing acoustic "pause" into the speech stream. It is possible to convert a recording of the word /slit/ into a stimulus that will be heard as an occurrence of /split/ simply by the introduction of about 75 milliseconds of blank tape between the /s/ and the /l/. Thus, in certain environments, pause can have the phonetic value /p/ (Liberman, Harris, Eimas, Lisker, and Bastian, 1961). Analogous operations will, however, convert /sore/ to /store/, so that /t/ is also among the phonetic values of a pause in appropriately chosen environments (Bastian, Eimas, and Liberman, 1961). Nor do these cases exhaust the perceptual consequences of brief silent intervals in the speech signal. Bolinger and Gerstman (1957) showed, for example, that the introduction of a pause at the morpheme boundary between /t/ and /h/ will have the effect of converting a phonetic string with the perceived stress /light#house#keeper/ (i.e., lighthouse keeper) into a string with perceived stress /light#house#keeper/ (i.e., light house keeper). A number of similar findings have been reported. Thus we have comparable silent intervals effecting contrasts in both perceived stress and perceived phonetic value.

Failures of segment-by-segment correspondence between acoustic and phonetic representations. Several of the observations already reviewed point to an important difference between the formal character of the phonetic and acoustic representations of a speech signal: it is not generally the case that when one phone precedes another, the acoustic information relevant to the identification of the first will invariably precede the acoustic information relevant to the identification of the second. Rather, such information may be "spread out" over a relatively long stretch of the signal. Thus, paradigmatically, we have seen that the information relevant for the identification of a consonant in a *CV* syllable may be in part represented by the absolute-frequency characteristics of the vowel.

A striking consequence of this fact is that attempts to assemble an intelligible speech signal from a stockpile of prerecorded phones have characteristically proved unsuccessful. Several investigations have attempted to synthesize words by combining taped fragments of approximately phonetic length clipped from continuous speech; e.g., to produce an intelligible recording of /kat/ by concatenating appropriate fragments from recordings of other words containing /k/, /a/, and /t/. We have already seen, however, that the perceived phonetic value of an acoustic signal is characteristically heavily dependent on the environment in which that signal occurs. If, therefore, we attempt to cut the acoustic signal at points corresponding to boundaries between the perceived positions of phones, the results of recombination of the fragments are in general unsatisfactory. Either the speech so synthesized is unintelligible or the segments fail to have the same acoustic value as they did in the speech from which they were derived (cf. Harris, 1953).

It is interesting that the most successful attempt at this kind of speech synthesis (Peterson, Wang, and Sivertsen, 1958) used fragments containing two phones whose "mutual influence" occurs in the middle of the fragment, thus preserving at least some of the acoustic information which determines environmental effects on perceptual identification. That is, such success as Peterson et al. enjoyed derived precisely from *violating* the assumption that the perceptual and acoustic phone correspond segment by segment. It is also of interest that some eight thousand fragments were required to synthesize a single idiolect of

American speech; this figure should be compared with the usual estimate that the phonetic population of American English consists of about forty elements.

The categorical character of speech perception.   If one assumes that the identification of a phone is a matter of detecting its invariant acoustic counterparts, it is also natural to make the following assumption. Suppose we have two phones, $/\alpha/$ and $/\beta/$, which differ just in that their optimal utterances are associated with different values of a certain acoustic dimension D; thus the optimal utterance of $/\alpha/$ is associated with the value D_α, and the optimal utterance of $/\beta/$ is associated with the value D_β. Now consider an utterance U, whose acoustic representation falls on some value D_U between D_α and D_β. In a forced choice situation, the probability of identifying U as an utterance of the phone α ought to increase roughly monotonically with decrease in the distance between D_U and D_α. Correspondingly, the probability of identifying U as an utterance of $/\beta/$ should increase monotonically with decrease in the distance between D_U and D_β. In particular, these are the predictions we get if we think of each phone as a normal probability distribution around some optimal acoustic value: e.g., as an acoustic template associated with a "jitter function."

This hypothesis is experimentally testable. Like the other consequences of the identification of the phone with an acoustic invariant discussed above, it turns out to be false, at least for the case of the noncontinuant speech sounds. Apparently the perception of such sounds involves imposing relatively sharp cutoffs on the continuously variable values associated with their acoustic realizations. In this respect, the behavior of the speech-perception system is strikingly similar to that of an analog to digital converter which employs threshold mechanisms to encode a continuous signal into one whose elements are discrete.

Consider, for example, the following experiment.

In CV syllables uttered in isolation, the perceptual distinction between voiced and voiceless stops ($/d/$ versus $/t/$; $/b/$ versus $/p/$; $/k/$ versus $/g/$, etc.) seems to be largely determined by the temporal relations between the onset of the first and second formants. For example, Liberman, Harris, Kinney, and Lane (1961) demonstrated that a progression from identification of signals as $/do/$ to identification as $/to/$ can be obtained simply as a consequence of changing the point of onset of f_1 relative to the onset of f_2. In the case of synthetic speech, an optimal voiced stop is achieved when the onset of f_1 is simultaneous with the onset of f_2; the optimal unvoiced stop is obtained when the onset of f_2 precedes the onset of f_1 by about 60 milliseconds.

Synthetic signals have been prepared in which the disparity between f_1 and f_2 onset is systematically manipulated; in particular, an array of signals is generated in which this disparity is increased by intervals of 10 milliseconds starting with an optimal /do/ and ending with an optimal /to/. Given such tapes, the subject's decoding of the signal can be experimentally studied as a function of variation in the disparity between formant onsets. The results of this experiment are of considerable interest. In the view that the phone is an acoustic template associated with a jitter factor, it would be reasonable to expect that the consequence of adding 10 milliseconds of disparity to any signal between optimal /do/ and optimal /to/ would be a constant increment in the probability that the signal will be recognized as /to/. The observed result is, however, quite different. The probability of identification of the signal as either /do/ or /to/ is quite insensitive to manipulation of the disparity between formant onsets except through a highly critical range of values. In this range, 10 milliseconds increase produces a shift from 75 percent responses as /do/ to 75 percent responses as /to/. (See Figure 6-5.)

What is still more striking is the result of imposing a curve which represents the *discriminability* of these signals upon the curve which represents their *identifiability*. Normally, subjects are able to discriminate between a vastly wider set of signals than they can identify. The standard result in psychophysical studies of nonspeech stimuli is that, if minimal error is demanded, identification of signals differing on only one dimension is limited to about seven (cf. Miller, 1956b), while the normal subject can discriminate between several thousand acoustic inputs which differ in frequency, amplitude, duration, etc.

In the present case, however, we have the unusual finding that the subject's ability to discriminate between speech signals differing in formant onsets is of approximately the same order as their ability to identify them: that is, subjects can tell that two such signals differ only when they assign them distinct phonetic analyses. Figure 6-6 shows the result of predicting discrimination curves for these signals from their identification; the discriminability peak falls in the same range of values that are critical for determining identification: discriminability is high only at phone boundaries. In short, the perception of these signals seems to approach being fully categorical: to a first approximation, all signals falling within a phone are heard as identical to one another and as distinct from all signals falling outside that phone.

It may be added that the same sort of finding has been made for the perception of a variety of other kinds of speech signals: the categorical perception of the /slit/ and /split/ distinction can be demonstrated by incremental variation of the amount of pause between /s/ and /l/, and the categorical perception of the /b/, /d/, and /g/ contrast in *CV* syllables can be demonstrated by incrementally varying the slope of the second-formant onset while holding the steady-state portion of the signal fixed. Finally, recent work by Stevens et al. (1969) has suggested that

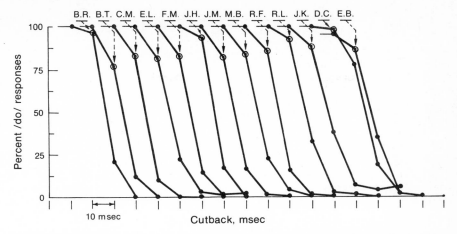

Fig. 6-5. Response functions for each of the 13 S's, showing how phoneme labels were assigned to the stimuli. The circled points represent, for each S, the percentage of /do/ responses to the stimulus that had 20 msec of cutback. So that the functions might be better separated for the eye, each one has been started just beyond the point that would represent the results at 0 msec of cutback. The /do/ responses at that point (100 percent for 10 S's, 99 percent for 2 S's, and 96 percent for 1 S) can, however, be inferred from the graphs (from Liberman, Harris, Kinney, and Lane, 1961).

while vowel perception is noncategorical for signals heard in isolation, it may be categorical for vowels heard in continuous speech. [For a discussion and criticism of work on the categorical perception of speech, see Ades (in press).]

SPEECH PERCEPTION AS A PERCEPTUAL CONSTANCY

The results we have been surveying do not, of course, show that the speech signal carries insufficient acoustic information for the determination of a unique phonetic analysis. On the contrary, we have seen that the phonetic representation of a speech event is usually massively overdetermined: the relevant acoustic information is present with enormous redundancy, so that the signal will remain comprehensible even after gross acoustic distortion.

What these findings suggest is rather that the formal properties of phones considered as perceptual entities are very different from the formal properties of phones considered as acoustic events. An occurrence of a given phone will be more or less perceptually identical with any other occurrence of that phone across syllabic environments. Phones are perceptually discrete and, barring "supersegmental" phones, they are well ordered in time. None of these properties are true of the acoustic representation of the phone. The moral would appear to be that the re-

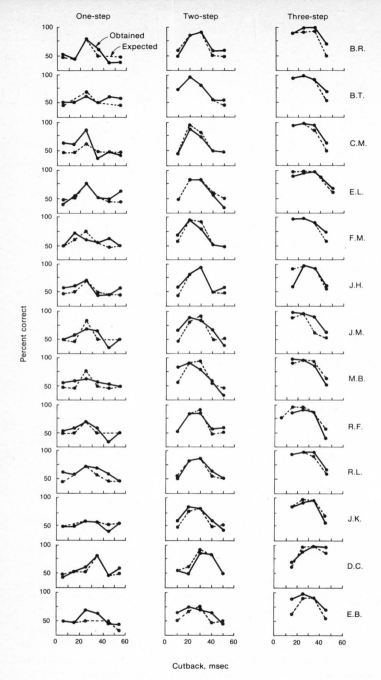

Fig. 6-6. Obtained discrimination functions compared with expected functions based on identification results for the one-, two-, and three-step differences among the synthetic speech stimuli (from Liberman, Harris, Kinney, and Lane, 1961).

covery of the phonetic analysis of a speech input must involve quite complicated data processing upon the acoustic representation of that input. The perceptual phone is an object engendered by applying some decoding procedure to the acoustic event; since the disparity between the phones and their acoustic representations appears to be considerable, we must hypothesize that the decoding procedures are correspondingly intricate. To suggest a homely analogy: the detective may be able uniquely to determine the identity of the criminal from the clues, but it does not follow that there is a characteristic clue for every criminal. That is, the possibility of solving the crime from the clues does not presuppose that each criminal leaves one and only one kind of clue. But, insofar as this correspondence fails, and the mapping from clues to criminals is complicated, the detective's inferences will have to be complicated too. The more indirectly the criminal is implicated by the clues, the more subtle must be the cerebrations of the detective.

Clues like fingerprints, which are mapped one to one onto criminals, make the deduction easy. The interesting case is where a given type of clue might have been left by any of a number of criminals or where a given criminal might have left any of a number of different types of clue. In such cases, the detective's background information must come into play. The acoustic representative of a phone turns out to be quite unlike a fingerprint. It is more like the array of disparate data from which Sherlock Holmes deduces the identity of the criminal. Reconstructing the phonetic analysis is rather like reconstructing the crime. Given the acoustic information available, the phonetic representation may be uniquely determined, but it is so only relative to the computational procedures and background information the hearer brings to the analysis.

In retrospect, it is perhaps not surprising that this should be true. To see why, let us consider what must happen in the speech-*production* process whereby the phonetic message is encoded into an acoustic event.

THE "BACKGROUND INFORMATION" FOR SPEECH PERCEPTION

We have assumed that the process of encoding a message involves computing its phonetic representation and that this representation can be identified with a distinctive feature matrix of the kind discussed in Chapter 3. We further assume, for purposes of simplifying the exposition, that each phonetic distinctive feature corresponds to a control parameter of the vocal apparatus. This last assumption is in fact likely to be true for at least some of the classic distinctive features. For example, the plus value of the feature "voiced and unvoiced" apparently corresponds to a tensing of the vocal chords across an airflow. Similarly, according to Jakobson, Fant, and Halle (1963) "the stops have complete closure followed by opening. The constrictives have incomplete closure ... the continuant liquids ... combine a median closure with a side opening...." etc. What we are assuming is that each of the characteristic gestures of the vocal apparatus involved in speech production is controlled by a characteristic pattern of input to the vocal apparatus, and that each such input is representable as a value of a distinctive feature.

Figure 6-7 suggests the information flow for an ideal speech producer on these assumptions. The output of the phonetic component is represented as sequences of decisions about values of distinctive features. These decisions are imposed, in parallel, upon appropriate subsystems of the vocal apparatus. The result of the activity of the vocal apparatus is a waveform.

The consequences of this pattern of information flow are worth considering. We know from the phonetic theory that the distinctive feature matrix which excites the vocal apparatus has several linguistically significant characteristics. First, a given feature may change its value "instantaneously" as we move from left to right across its row in the matrix. For example, we can go instantaneously from "plus" to "minus" on the feature "voicing" in the first two phones of a word like "ask." Second, with certain kinds of exceptions that are irrelevant to the present discussion, the value of simultaneous cells (those in the same column) in the matrix is independent; any cell belonging to a phone can be *plus* where any other cell belonging to that phone is *minus*. Finally, the values of the phonetic matrix are assumed to be binary. Every cell is either plus or minus and no cell is both.

None of these properties, however, is true of the vocal apparatus. Values of phonetic features may change instantaneously, but states of the vocal apparatus cannot. Damping of resonators, movement of the lips and tongue, opening and closing of the velum, etc., all take time, so that it is plausible to expect that the configuration of the vocal apparatus that is actually produced by any given set of instructions will be determined, at least in part, by the character of the immediately preceding configuration. In fact, we know that it is also partly determined by the character of intended succeeding configurations, a point to which we shall presently return.

The upshot, for present purposes, is that the physical character of the vocal apparatus imposes what might be called "lateral noise" upon the phonetic decisions it transduces. While the value of a cell in a phonetic distinctive feature matrix is independent of the value of cells to its left and right, the configuration of the vocal apparatus that corresponds

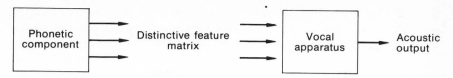

Fig. 6-7. Schematic characterization of the information flow from the phonetic component to an acoustic output.

to that value is massively subject to environmental contamination.

Again, we said the value of a cell representing a phone is characteristically independent of the values of other cells representing that phone. We have assumed that each distinctive feature corresponds to a characteristic set of instructions to the vocal apparatus. What we must now notice is that these instructions will often overlap in the sense that the same organ of the vocal apparatus may be "called" by the instructions associated with more than one of its distinctive features. For example, a vowel may be either *high* or *low*, *front* or *back*, so that the tongue position involved in realizing a vowel is simultaneously determined by the values of at least *two* cells in the distinctive feature column representing it. By hypothesis, these instructions are orthogonal at the phonetic level. But there is every reason to expect them to interact at the articulatory level, e.g., the height of the tongue when it is realizing the instructions "high back" may differ systematically from the height of the tongue when it is realizing the instruction "high front."

In short, we have seen that the intrinsic physical characteristics of the vocal apparatus may determine interactions between gestures associated with values of horizontally adjacent cells in a phonetic distinctive feature matrix. Our present point is that they may also determine interactions between the gestures associated with values of cells belonging to the same column of such a matrix, thereby imposing what might be called "vertical noise" on the correspondence between the input instructions and the acoustic output. To put it succinctly, the organs of the vocal apparatus are neither inertia-free nor infinitely plastic, but a physical system would have to have the former property if it were to preserve the orthogonality of decisions about the feature values of successive phones; and it would have to have the latter property if it were to preserve the orthogonality of decisions about the value of features belonging to the same phone.

Finally, we have remarked that the values of a phonetic matrix are binary. But clearly the values of parameters of the vocal apparatus are not. A vowel is either front or back, but tongue position can vary along a continuum. A consonant is either closed or liquid, but the vocal apparatus can assume indefinitely many degrees of constriction. If, in short, the *perceptual* system is a device for quantizing a continuously varying signal, the production system is a device for generating a continuously varying signal corresponding to a set of binary instructions. This symmetry is, of course, no accident. If the perceptual system is to recover the matrix of phonetic instructions which controls the output of the production system, the former must be so organized as to compensate for distortions produced by the functioning of the latter.

Thus far we have been assuming that the set of instructions corresponding to values of a phonetic distinctive feature matrix is read onto the vocal apparatus in a strictly left-to-right manner. That is, if α and β are values of features in a phonetic matrix, then if α appears in a column to the left of the column in which β appears, the instructions corresponding to α are imposed upon the vocal apparatus prior to the instructions corresponding to β. This assumption is, however, certainly false. Instructions to the vocal apparatus are not programmed in the order in which they occur in the phonetic distinctive matrix. Rather, they are often temporally reordered and the result is a further complication of the correspondence between the phonetic and acoustic representation of an utterance.

At least two sorts of evidence for this kind of scrambling are worth mentioning. In the first place, we noticed above that the acoustic realization of a consonant in a *CV* syllable is characteristically highly sensitive to the acoustic realization of the *succeeding* vowel. This means that we have contamination of the acoustic realization of a cell in a distinctive feature matrix not only as a consequence of the values of the cells to its left but also as a consequence of the values of cells to its right. Instructions for *CV* syllables are apparently programmed onto the vocal apparatus more or less as a unit, so that the articulatory configuration which realizes the column for a given consonant will depend, at least in part, on the vowel to follow.

A second kind of evidence that articulatory instructions are not imposed upon the vocal apparatus in an order that strictly reproduces the left-to-right relations in a distinctive feature matrix can be seen from the following demonstration experiment. Pronounce the word "sloop" and then the word "slip," attending in each case to *where* the lips begin to round or flatten. Clearly, from a phonetic point of view, the rounding and flattening is associated with the vowels: i.e., rounding distinguishes /u/ from /i/. For most speakers, however, the onset of rounding in utterances of /sloop/ occurs at the *beginning* of the word, and similarly for the flattening in utterances of /slip/. In this case, the character of an utterance is being determined by features of a phonetic matrix two columns to the right of the segment being uttered. It is a consequence of this preplanning of the articulatory positions that utterances of /sloop/ differ from utterances of /slip/ not only in that the latter contains a flat vowel whereas the former contains a rounded vowel but also in that the /sl/ in /sloop/ is rounded whereas the /sl/ in /slip/ is flat. This distortion is perceptually tolerable (in fact characteristically goes unnoticed) presumably because rounding and flattening are not contrastive for fricatives and liquids. It is, however, quite easy to hear the difference between, e.g., a flat and a rounded /s/ if they are pronounced out of the speech stream. [We wish to thank A. Liberman for bringing this example to our attention (personal communication).]

We may summarize this discussion by an appropriate alteration of Figure 6-7. Figure 6-8 shows the revised information flow: from the phonetic distinctive matrix, through a scrambler which functions to produce an "instruction matrix" (in which the left-right order of cells may differ from the order displayed in the phonetic representation), to the vocal apparatus, and finally into a waveform. We do not by any means suppose that this is all the recoding that goes on between the phonetic and acoustic representations of an utterance; it is rather an attempt to establish a reasonable lower bound on the complexity of that relation.

Lenneberg (1967) has suggested that a scrambler may play an important role in preserving what homologies there are between the vertical relations of cells in a phonetic distinctive feature matrix and simultaneity relations among the gestures of the vocal apparatus involved in producing the speech sound corresponding to a phone; in effect, that the system purchases fidelity to the vertical relations in a phonetic distinctive feature matrix at the price of infidelity to the horizontal relations. Since the various articulatory organs are at different distances from the (presumptive) control centers in the motor cortex, and since neural im-

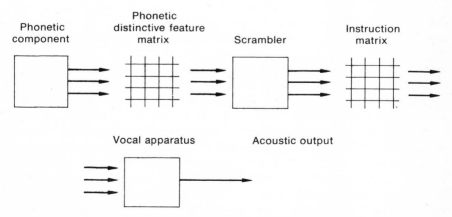

Fig. 6-8. Schematic representation of information flow from the phonetic component to an acoustic output.

pulses (presumably) travel at a fixed rate, the simultaneous activation of speech organs that are neurally distant from one another (like the voicing apparatus and the tongue) can be accomplished only if instructions to relatively remote organs are dispatched *earlier* than instructions to relatively proximal ones. In this view, the production of a syllable like /ba/, where simultaneous voicing and lip closure are called for, would require that the voicing instruction be imposed earlier than the closure instruction. This suggests that the scrambler must have access to a display of the phonetic matrix which is, at any event, several columns wide. It may then shuttle back and forth across this display, reading out instructions in whatever order is required to promote appropriate sequencing of articulatory gestures. It would be of considerable interest to know how wide this display is, and whether it is determined by a temporal constant, an informational load, an upper bound on the number of phones (or higher linguistic units) that can be simultaneously represented, etc. The data on articulatory errors to be reviewed in Chapter 7 have some bearing on this issue.

We have suggested repeatedly that speech perception is a perceptual constancy; that is, that it involves interpreting an acoustic object in terms of background information that the hearer brings to the perceptual process. Given the preceding, rudimentary sketch of some of the recodings involved in going from a phonetic matrix to a waveform, we are in a position to make some preliminary suggestions about what this background information is like.

The perceptual device will somehow have to take account of the transformations which are imposed upon the message in the process of encoding the phonetic matrix into an acoustic object. This is tantamount to saying that a speech recognizer will have to include models of the devices that perform these transformations: in particular, of the vocal apparatus and of the scrambler. In cases of perceptual constancy, the subject recognizes a signal by relating the physical display to his background knowledge of the general character of the stimulus domain from which the display is drawn. Ideally, he chooses the hypothesis about the analysis of the display which best comports with both its physical properties and the background information. The present suggestion is that, in the case of speech perception, this background knowledge is information about the character of the transducers which transform phonetic matrices into acoustic objects. If this is true, then the psychological problem in modeling human speech recognition is to give a general account of the information about the production system that the device must have at its disposal, to give a corresponding account of how this information is used to interpret the acoustic signal, and to suggest how the information may have been assimilated by a child learning to speak a language.

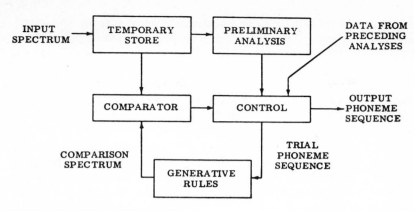

Fig. 6-9. From Halle and Stevens (1964).

MOTOR THEORIES AND ANALYSIS BY SYNTHESIS

The most serious attempt thus far to characterize a device which interprets acoustic representations of speech signals in light of the character of the articulatory mechanisms which produce them (thereby accounting for the perceptual constancy of phones) is the *analysis-by-synthesis* model of speech perception.

We have seen that the problem is to recover the sequence of articulatory instructions which corresponds to the phonetic matrix underlying a waveform. The device which does this must somehow take account of the distortions that a human articulatory system imposes upon such sequences. The heart of the present proposal is the supposition that the sentence recognizer contains an internal representation of the articulatory mechanisms and that this representation is employed for the generation of candidate analyses of an input signal.

Consider a device (see Figure 6-9) which consists of the following essential components (cf. Halle and Stevens, 1964): (1) a "preanalyzer" which accepts physical signals as inputs and provides acoustic analyses as outputs; (2) a "grammar" considered as a generative source which enumerates well-formed phonetic matrices (for the sake of simplicity, we can think of such matrices as abbreviated by strings of phones); (3) an articulatory model which converts such strings into representations of waveforms; (4) a "comparator" which tests internally generated representations of waveforms against representations of the acoustic properties of the input; (5) a "strategy" which determines that successive candidate analyses converge on the "correct" analysis of inputs.

We can think of the device as operating in the following manner. A given input receives a preanalysis into some description given in acoustic parameters (e.g., a time-frequency-energy graph). The grammar is then used to provide a source of phonetic sequences generated in what may initially be thought of as a random order. These phonetic sequences are transduced by the articulatory model into representations in whatever vocabulary is employed by the preanalyzer. Such internally generated representations are then compared, seriatum, with the acoustic analysis of the input signal until a match is achieved. Given a match between an internally generated signal and an input, the phonological description of the input is simply the set of feature values that were used in producing the internal candidate analysis. Given a mismatch between an internally generated signal and an input, the strategy component must operate so as to reduce the distance between the input and succeeding candidate signals.

There are a number of interesting features of this sort of model. In the first place, it is an analysis-by-synthesis routine in the sense that it uses a grammar to synthesize signals as part of the computational process involved in speech recognition. It thus assumes an extremely concrete relation between a grammar and a speech recognizer: the derivation by the grammar of a phonetic sequence is assumed to be literally part of the process of speech recognition. This is an extremely important notion and one to which we shall repeatedly return.

Second, this sort of model, unlike the filter models discussed above, is appropriately thought of as an *active* perceptual device. Whereas filter models function primarily to reject noncriterial input information, the present model interprets the input in light of background information about the general character of the stimulus domain from which it is drawn; in particular, information about such properties of speech signals as are determined by the character of the transducers employed in producing them.

Finally, the model we have sketched is a *motor theory* of speech perception in the weak sense that it incorporates a representation of the articulators as part of the sentence-recognition loop. That is, the computational routine derives phonetic representations of utterances from their acoustic representations by reference to the manner of operation of the articulatory system. But the present view is not thereby committed to any of the stronger versions of the motor theory which have been proposed from time to time.

The notion of accounting for perceptual constancies by reference to motor integrations implies that we arrange our perceptual schemata in terms of motor feedback loops. In the case of speech perception, this would mean that speech analysis requires subvocal activation of the speech organs (cf. Liberman, Delattre, and Cooper, 1952). This suggestion is, of course, far stronger than the claim that speech perception involves accessing a model of the transformations of phonetic matrices that the speech organs produce. For the former theory, there exists literally no evidence whatever. That is, there is no evidence that subvocalization plays a significant role in speech perception. On the contrary, paralysis of the speech organs produces no measurable decrement in language perception, and children who are totally mute have, nevertheless, learned to understand their language (Lenneberg, 1962).

There is another sense in which the sort of model we have been discussing makes weaker assumptions than classic motor theories of speech perception do. We have assumed that there is a point in the speech-recognition process at which something like the imposition of a set of articulatory instructions upon a model of the vocal apparatus takes place. It is *not* suggested, however, that the phones are identifiable with invariant configurations that the articulatory apparatus assumes as a result of their excitation by such instructions. On the contrary, the present model envisages the perceptual and articulatory representation of the phones as converging only at the highest levels: possibly at the level of instructions to the vocal apparatus; certainly at the level of phonetic matrices. No stronger assumptions seem to us to be warranted, since the same sorts of considerations which render acoustic definitions of the phone impossible make it correspondingly unlikely that the phone can be identified with gestures or configurations of the articulatory organs. As Liberman et al. (1967) have remarked,

> If we take into account the structure and function of the articulatory system, in particular the intricate linkages and the spatial overlap of the component parts, we must suppose that the relation between [muscle] contraction and resulting shape is complex, though predictable. True encoding occurs as a consequence of two further aspects of this conversion; the fact that the subphonemic features can be, and are, put through in parallel means that each new set of contractions (a) starts from whatever configuration then exists...and (b) typically occurs before the last set has ended, with the result that the shape of the tract at any instant represents the merged effect of past and present instructions. Such merging is, in effect, an encoding operation [p. 447].

It is just this sort of "merging" which has frustrated a long series of attempts to find invariant configurations of the vocal apparatus corresponding to each of the phones (see Fant, 1960).

It is worth stressing the ambiguities in the notion of "*the* motor theory of speech perception." What all versions of the motor theory have in common is the assumption that, at some level, the motoric and perceptual representations of a speech signal are identical. More or less "attenuation" of the theory takes place in proportion as the common level of representation is assumed to be more or less remote from the actual perturbation of articulatory organs. We have already observed that the most perpheralistic versions of the theory are certainly false. On the other hand, the version that says that motor and perceptual representations converge at the phonetic matrix seems to amount to very little more than an endorsement of the psychological reality of phones; if it were false, speech recognition could not be the perceptual recovery of a phonetically encoded message.

For purposes of exposition, we ourselves have assumed a mildly tendentious version of the motor theory according to which each phone corresponds to a distinct battery of instructions to the motor apparatus. As we mentioned above, this might turn out to be true; but it is also possible that there are one or more levels of encoding between the output of the phonetic system and the input to the vocal apparatus. Among the types of empirical evidence relevant to this question are electromyographic (EMG) recordings of muscle potentials in the speech organs. If each change of muscle potential corresponds to a characteristic change in the articulatory instruction imposed upon the muscle, then the claim that such instructions are in one-to-one correspondence with distinctive features implies that there should also be electromyographic invariants corresponding to distinctive features.

In fact, the experimental evidence on EMG increasingly suggests that the required invariances are not to be found. In a recent review of these data, MacNeilage (1970) remarks that "the main result of the attempt to demonstrate invariance at the EMG level has not been to find such invariance but to demonstrate the ubiquity of variability. For example, MacNeilage and DeClerk (1969) found that in an inventory of 36 consonant-vowel-consonant monosyllables, some aspect of the motor control of every phoneme differed with the identity of the previous phoneme, and almost every phoneme differed in some respect depending on the following one" (p. 184).

Moreover, there are serious difficulties with assuming that such invariances *should* exist. Consider utterances of the syllables /awk/ and /eek/. Presumably, in both cases, the /k/ is realized by a velar constriction effected by the tongue. Notice, however, that to make this constriction, the tongue has to retract and lower in the case of /eek/, whereas it must raise in the case of /awk/. It is difficult to see how these quite diverse gestures could be associated with the same set of motor commands. If this sort of argument is correct, then it strongly suggests a level of encoding between the phonetic matrix and the matrix of instructions to the vocal apparatus. Hence it suggests corresponding attenuations of the motor theory. An analogous point has been made by Lieberman (personal communication), who stresses that a variety of different patterns of muscle activity may effect such convergent consequences as lip closure in the production of bilabial stops. Insofar as this is true, there must be a level of recoding between the phonetic level, in which bilabial closure is uniformly represented, and the articulating level at which it is heterogeneously achieved.

It is, in short, by no means evident that the articulatory and perceptual phone converge at *any* level lower than the phonetic feature matrix: that matrix may be the lowest level at which the output of the speech recognizer and the input to the speech production system are identical. In this view, the phonetic matrix is the least abstract informational structure common to speech perception and speech production; the least abstract informational structure that is conceptually neutral in the sense discussed in Chapter 1. In particular, it is possible to endorse an analysis-by-synthesis account of speech recognition without being required to assume what stronger versions of the motor theory typically do assume: that the correspondence between phones and states of the production system is, in general, better than the correspondence between phones and acoustic features.

The recognition of prosodics. The basic conclusions of the preceding discussion are the following: (1) The correspondence between phonetic elements and their acoustic representatives in the speech stream is, in general, extremely complicated. (2) The recovery of the phonetic representation of an acoustic event is, in all probability, not a matter of filtering for invariants. Rather, it involves integrating an acoustic representation of the signal with some rather rich system of background information at the disposal of the hearer. (3) Part of this information would appear to be a representation of the transducer characteristics of the vocal apparatus.

These same points would, in general, seem to hold for the recovery of information about the prosodics of an utterance. In fact, we have already had reason to mention the work of Bolinger and Gerstman (1957) which suggests that there is a relation between acoustic pause and the perception of linguistic stress. The complexity of the interrelation between the acoustic and perceptual representations of prosodic features is, apparently, like the complexity of the relation between acoustic and perceptual representation of phones. In both cases it is a consequence of the hearer's integration of the acoustics with some sort of background information.

This is suggested by an experiment of Lieberman (1965). Lieberman asked several linguists to judge the stress pattern of a number of sentences in a language known to them. In this situation, reliability across judges was good at four degrees of stress. "However, when the linguist heard [just] fixed vowels that were accurately modulated with the fundamental frequency and amplitude contours of the original speech signal, he was unable to transcribe accurately more than two degrees of stress, stressed or unstressed" (p. 53). It appears, then, that some of the information that the linguist is using to mark stress levels other than primary stress is not carried by the fundamental frequency, amplitude, or duration of the segments in the speech signal. It is plausible to assume that the information is in fact being "supplied" by the linguist on the basis of what he knows about the stress rules of the language.

The implication that a model of the motor transducers is part of the perceptual system which recovers prosodic information is suggested by a variety of data. For example, consider the apparent intensity of speech. The vowels of a language differ in acoustic energy in the sense that two vowels produced with the same amount of effort will not, in general, exhibit the same amplitude envelope: a high vowel like /i/ will contain less energy than a low vowel like /a/ simply because the production of the former involves filtering out part of the low-frequency spectrum, where the largest proportion of the acoustic energy is concentrated.

However, adjacent vowels in a speech stream do not, in general, sound as though they are varying in amplitude. What accounts for this perceived constancy is apparently that hearers judge the amplitude of a vowel by estimating the amount of work that is required to produce it as well as the acoustic energy it exhibits. Indeed, what correlates best with perceived equality of amplitude is estimated equality of effort. Lehiste and Peterson (1959) demonstrated this effect in a well-known experiment. They recorded a randomized list of vowels under conditions where

> The speaker watched a VU meter in the recording room and produced all vowels at the same VU level. Some vowels required considerably greater effort than others. A tape was then prepared, in which various vowels produced with equal effort were mixed at random with vowels produced with unequal effort but which were equal in pressure level as measured by the VU meter. The vowels were arranged in random pairs and were presented to listeners, who were asked to judge the relative loudness of the two paired vowels. ...Almost invariably, the listeners identified the vowels that were produced with a greater amount of effort ... as louder than vowels having greater intrinsic amplitude, but produced with normal effort [p. 431].

Further evidence that the hearer's estimate of the states of the speaker's vocal apparatus determines the perception of prosodics derives from a study of intonation contour by Lieberman (1967). The upshot of this work is that the hearer's judgment of whether an utterance of a sentence ends in a rising intonation (as in a yes-no question) or a falling intonation (as in declaratives) is determined, in part, by his estimate of the relative subglottal air pressure available to the speaker at the end of the sentence. Roughly, the terminal pitch required to produce an apparent question is lower in sentences which have used more breath (i.e., for which the subglottal pressure available to the speaker is relatively low by the end of the sentence). It can thus be shown that precisely the same acoustic object that is interpreted as exhibiting a question contour in sentences which terminate in relatively low subglottal pressures will be perceived as carrying a declarative intonation in sentences which do not.

These results, like much other work on prosodics, seem to confirm the morals we have drawn from the data about the perception of phones. The recognition of prosody, too, seems fundamentally to be a perceptual constancy, and one of the kinds of information the hearer uses in making his judgments would appear to be his knowledge of the character and functioning of the vocal apparatus.

PART TWO.   SYNTAX RECOGNITION

We remarked at the beginning of this chapter that it is a primary goal of theory construction in psycholinguistics to provide recognition models for the recovery of each psychologically real level of linguistic structure. Thus far we have discussed only the part of the recognition process which performs the analysis of acoustic waveforms into phonetic segments together with their prosodic features. In the present section, we will discuss the recognition process which maps strings of formatives onto syntactic analyses. We will not consider such intermediate levels of structure assignment as the mapping from phonetic strings to deep phonological analyses, or the mapping from sequences of phonological matrices onto strings of formatives. None of these processes has been systematically investigated and nothing at all is known about their nature, about the order in which they occur, or even about whether they exist as psychological processes distinct from those involved in other aspects of sentence recognition.

What does seem to be clear, however, is that the perceptual analysis of a sentence involves the recovery of a level of structure at which the semantically relevant syntactic relations among the parts of the sentence are exhibited. In generative grammar this representation has usually been identified with the deep structure of the sentence, although, as we have seen in Chapter 4, there is evidence that some aspects of surface structure may also be involved in determining semantic representations. At any event, we shall assume in what follows that the recognition of a sentence involves the operation of a device which computes deep structures from strings of words.

TWO APPROACHES TO RECOGNITION ROUTINES

Analysis by analysis.   Since an ideal syntax recognizer is required to recover precisely the structures that an optimal grammar enumerates, it is natural to suppose that their computational characteristics may be very similar. In fact, it is a natural first guess that the sentence recognizer is simply the grammar "run backward." That is, the grammar maps from the symbol S through a series of intermediate representations onto a string of words. One might initially suppose that the sentence recognizer performs the same kind of mapping, but backward, starting with the sequence of words, computing the intermediate representations in reverse order, and terminating with the symbol S. This sort of proposal may be called "analysis by analysis" to distinguish it from the more widely discussed "analysis-by-synthesis" account of syntax recognition which we shall consider below. There are a number of difficulties with analysis by analysis, to which we now turn.

The fundamental conception underlying the notion of analysis by analysis is that the rules of a generative grammar are literally to be applied backward in the recognition of sentences. Every grammatical rule can be thought of as an ordered pair: a structural description of the tree to which the rule applies (i.e., of its domain), and a structural description of the tree it produces (i.e., of its range). In the analysis-by-analysis approach, at each stage of the recognition process, we search through the rules of the syntax until we find one with a range satisfied by the tree under examination. This tree is then rewritten so as to satisfy the domain of the rule in question. The class of representations generated by iterating this process is the structural description of the strings.

The basic idea can be seen easily in an example from context-free phrase-structure grammars. Suppose we have the following grammar:

Grammar	Analysis-by-analysis syntax recognizer
1. $S \rightarrow NP + VP$	7. soup $\rightarrow N$
2. $NP \rightarrow T + N$	6. likes $\rightarrow V$
3. $VP \rightarrow V + NP$	5. boy $\rightarrow N$
4. $T \rightarrow$ The	4. the $\rightarrow T$
5. $N \rightarrow$ boy	3. $V + NP \rightarrow VP$
6. $V \rightarrow$ likes	2. $T + N \rightarrow NP$
7. $N \rightarrow$ soup	1. $NP + VP \rightarrow S$

We saw in Chapter 3 how this sort of grammar can be utilized for the generation of sets of trees from the initial symbol S. It may now be noted that by simply reversing the direction of each of the arrows, the grammar may be used for sentence recognition. In particular, given a sentence in the output of the grammar, like "the boy likes the soup," the appropriate tree can be reconstructed by applying the rules backward in the order 7, 6, 5, 4, 2, 2, 3, 1.

This approach to using the grammar for sentence recognition seems a perfectly natural one for context-free phrase-structure grammars. If, however, we attempt to extend it to the construction of recognition models for transformational grammars, it becomes much less plausible.

In the first place, the range of transformations is defined over trees, not over strings of symbols. This means that there is no way of determining whether the range of a transformation is satisfied by an object which consists solely of a string of words. Therefore, if we want to carry out sentence recognition by applying transformations backward, we will first have to provide a surface-tree analysis of each of the input strings. There is, however, a principled objection to this sort of approach. The number of well-formed surface trees (that is, the number of surface trees which satisfy the range of some transformation in an adequate grammar) is a minute subset of the possible, arbitrary bracketings of the sequences of words that are generated by the grammar. For example, given a sequence like "John likes the soup," we have not only the well-formed bracketing (John) (likes(the soup)) but also a large variety of ill-formed bracketings like (John likes) (the) (soup), (John) (likes the soup), (John) (likes the) (soup), etc. Indeed, the number of ways of arbitrarily bracketing a sentence goes up exponentially with the length of the sentence in words. This means that if we attempt first to bracket the strings arbitrarily and then apply reversed transformations to those bracketed strings that happen to be well formed, each step in the analysis will require a search through an enormous space of trees, most of which are in fact *ill* formed in the sense that they do not have deep-structure counterparts.

We might attempt to meet this objection by using some preanalysis system which supplies only those types of initial bracketings which have some reasonable chance of satisfying the range of some transformation in the grammar. The possibilities for the construction of some such preanalyzer have been discussed by Herzberger (in press) and Petrick (1965), among others. Suffice it to say here that the closer the preanalyzer comes to producing *only* trees which satisfy the range of transformations, the more powerful the rules it employs must be. That is, the more the preanalyzer does, the less the model resembles a grammar run backward.

It should be added that the notion of "reversing" a transformation is a good deal less clear than it may at first appear. Suppose a transformation T functions in a certain grammar to map the class of structures C_1 onto the class of structures C_2. It need not be self-evident how to construct from T a "reverse transformation" which will have the precise effect of mapping any member of C_2 onto the corresponding member of C_1. Suppose, for example, that T allows us to delete an element e wherever it occurs. (The transformation which deletes relative pronouns in English approximates applying this freely.) Then the structural index of this transformation will be XeY, where X and Y are any sequence of strings, the structural change will be $e \Rightarrow \phi$, and the output will be XY. But how shall we specify the reverse transformation for this case? If we choose $XY \Rightarrow XeY$, we are saying, in effect, that e may be introduced between any pair of elements. But most of the trees produced by such an insertion will not be well formed; from the fact that an element may be deleted wherever it occurs, it does not follow that it can occur everywhere. In particular, the class of structures we get by employing this reverse transformation is not the domain of T. Probably the best we can do by way of specifying a reverse transformation is to construct rules with a range that is a superset of the trees in the domain of the original transformations. If this is true, then at every stage of the recognition process, the output of reverse transformations will somehow have to be searched for those trees that happen to be well formed. It goes without saying that a model of sentence recognition should avoid this sort of iterated search if possible.

Analysis by synthesis for syntax recognition.   We have seen that an analysis-by-analysis procedure assumes that the recognition device employs at least one component which is not found in a generative grammar, i.e., a "preanalyzer" which functions to assign surface trees to lexical strings. In this sense, the analysis-by-analysis approach assumes a relatively complicated relation between a generative grammar and the corresponding recognition device. Not only is it the case that the rules employed by a grammar must be run "backward" to effect recognition, but it is an open question of how the preanalyzer is to be constructed.

Another way of realizing a grammar as part of a perceptual device is to employ, at the syntactic level, the kind of analysis-by-synthesis procedures discussed in the section on phone recognition. In such a procedure, the grammar is used to generate a "search space" of candidate structural descriptions which are tested one by one against the input string. This comparison procedure halts when a match is effected between the internally generated signal and the input, and the structural analysis of the input is determined by reference to the grammatical rules employed in generating the successful matching signal. Thus, on the analysis-by-synthesis account, a grammar is literally a part of a sentence recognizer, and the grammatical generation of a sentence is literally part of recognizing it. This "conservative" approach to the relation between grammars and sentence recognizers has attracted many theorists to analysis by synthesis. For example, Neisser (1967) has remarked "If [the analysis-by-synthesis view] is accepted, there can no longer be any doubt that the study of syntax is an integral part of cognitive psychology. We deal with the sentences we hear by reformulating them for ourselves; we grasp their structure with the same apparatus that structures our own utterances" (p. 252). Analysis by synthesis thus purports to provide a clear, concrete answer to the fundamental question we are investigating in this book: what is the relation between a theory of what the speaker-hearer knows about his language and a theory of the procedures by which he exploits his knowledge?

It should be noted, moreover, that analysis-by-synthesis procedures are, in principle, capable of being made failure-proof. Appropriate formal maneuvers, which involve a limitation on the number of items that transformations can delete and a disciplined order of generation for the candidate analyses, will guarantee that analysis-by-synthesis procedures will find the correct grammatical description of any input within a finite amount of time. Thus, such procedures are provably capable of providing a representation of the capacity of an ideal hearer. The important question is whether they are capable of providing an empirically adequate representation.

Despite their many attractive features, there are a number of difficulties with analysis-by-synthesis recognition procedures. The first, and most serious, is simply that the size of the space of candidate structures that will need to be searched is very large if we are to be guaranteed an analysis of an arbitrarily selected input. In fact, the search space increases exponentially with the length of the input. Miller (1965) has calculated that the number of twenty-word sentences in English is of the order of the number of seconds in the lifetime of the universe; it is obviously impossible that the recognition of any given twenty-word sentence involves searching a space of that many derivations.

Again, pure analysis-by-synthesis routines make extremely inefficient use of the input data, since all they are allowed to ask about the input is whether or not it matches some internally generated representation of a sentence. If one took this literally as a psychological model, one would be forced to predict that speaker-hearers can make no determinations of the linguistic properties of an input until they have decided which sentence it encodes. But this is clearly absurd; one normally recognizes the first word of a sentence, for example, long before the sentence is over.

In short, though the analysis-by-synthesis approach has the advantage of allowing us literally to embed a grammar in the perceptual routine, what we pay for that advantage is that the information the grammar encodes is extremely inefficiently exploited. In general, there is reason to be wary of any approach to perception which states: "Generate the space of possible percepts and search it."

These sorts of objections are perhaps not decisive, but they do suggest that no *pure* analysis-by-synthesis procedure will afford a reasonable model of sentence recognition. Some heuristics will need to be employed to drastically reduce the size of the space to be searched. Two types of heuristics suggest themselves immediately: the first is a preanalysis of the input strings which might provide a representation more abstract than a sequence of words, thereby constraining the initial "guesses" of the recognizer. Second, pure analysis-by-synthesis proce-dures provide only a yes-no decision on whether a given candidate anal-ysis matches the input. It would be much more efficient to suppose that error signals are somehow refined in a way which constrains the subsequent search; i.e., that the device somehow not only "knows" that there is a mismatch between the input and a candidate analysis, but knows something about the nature of the mismatch.

It is not currently clear whether such heuristic procedures can in fact be constructed, or whether an analysis-by-synthesis device con-taining such procedures would provide a plausible model of sentence recognition. What does seem obvious is that the more powerful the computational procedures employed in reducing the search space are assumed to be, the less clear and concrete is the relation between the grammar and the sentence recognizer envisioned by the analysis-by-synthesis approach. This is precisely the same observation we made about recognition models based on analysis-by-analysis routines. In both cases, when one tries actually to construct such systems, the role of the grammar tends to be displaced by that of the preanalysis heuristics.

In short, the psychological plausibility of the analysis-by-synthesis model seems to rest rather heavily on the availability of heuristic procedures for narrowing the space of candidate analyses that needs to be searched, and discussions in the literature have suggested that much of this heuristic structure is to be located in the preanalyzer. Roughly, preanalysis categorizes the input string as having some theoretically relevant structural property, and computational savings are effected by searching only that set of derivations which produce sentences with the property in question.

There is, however, a difficulty. We can use the kind of heuristic procedure just outlined only if we have a technique for constraining a grammar to produce only derivations which satisfy some predetermined characterization. But such techniques are not, in general, available.

To see what the problem is, imagine that we have a preanalyzer capa-ble of sorting sentences into those which contain subordinated clauses and those which do not. We can use this preanalyzer to reduce the search space in analysis by synthesis insofar as we are able to constrain a grammar to produce only derivations of sentences which have that prop-erty. In fact, however, nothing at all is known about how to restrict the sentences produced by grammars to only those which have some ante-cedently designated feature; and the problems involved in formalizing such restrictions may clearly be formidable depending upon which fea-tures we select. How, for example, could one constrain a grammar to produce only derivations of sentences containing, say, a nominalization as their third most embedded sentoid in surface structure? If there were a *general* answer to this sort of question, the sentence-recognition problem for syntax would thereby be solved, since to assign a structural description to a given morpheme sequence, all we should have to do is constrain the grammar to generate only derivations which terminate in that morpheme sequence. This shows that the proposal that we cope with the inefficiency of analysis by synthesis by somehow adding heuristics which reduce the number of candidate derivations is less a solution of the recognition problem than a restatement of it. The point is that the flowcharts which show preanalyzers feeding useful information to analysis-by-synthesis loops conceal an array of problems which have in fact gone almost totally unexplored.

EMPIRICAL CONSTRAINTS ON SENTENCE-RECOGNITION MODELS

Thus far we have been considering only very gross conditions upon the adequacy of a model of the sentence recognizer: primarily, that it should not be committed to the unguided investigation of exponential search spaces as a routine part of sentence recognition. But, much more detailed empirical constraints can and should be placed upon such models. For example, any theory of sentence recognition must be committed to an array of testable predictions about the relative complexity of sentences of different grammatical types. This follows from the consideration that each such model will have to run through a fixed number of operations for the recognition of each sentence; if the computations of the model are taken as representing the mental operations of the hearer, then the more such operations the model must run through in recognizing a certain sentence, the more complicated the sentence is predicted to be.

These considerations have a direct application to the empirical evaluation of analysis-by-analysis and analysis-by-synthesis approaches to sentence recognition. We have seen that analysis by synthesis assumes that the grammatical generation of a sentence is part of its recognition; correspondingly, analysis-by-analysis procedures postulate the application of a "backward" rule in the recognition of a sentence for each application of a standard rule in its grammatical derivation. It follows that, on the most natural interpretation of these sorts of models, they predict that the more grammatical operations involved in generating a sentence, the more difficult it ought to be to understand the sentence. (It is true, however, that this correspondence might turn out to be quite loose on any model which exploits a rich preanalyzer. Indeed, any predictive consequence whatever can be derived from analysis by analysis *or* analysis by synthesis by making the appropriate assumptions about the computational effects of unknown heuristic procedures.)

A number of early psycholinguistic studies of generative grammar appear to have been motivated precisely by the hypothesis that the complexity of a sentence is measured by the number of grammatical rules employed in its derivation. We shall call this hypothesis the *derivational theory of complexity* (DTC).

DTC can be made explicit in the following way. Consider a generative grammar G_i of the language L and a sentence in the range of G_i. It is possible to define a metric that specifies for every such sentence the number of rules, n, that G_i requires to generate it. (For present purposes it does not matter whether the metric is based on the number of grammatical rules which are required by the derivation or on the number of elementary operations these same rules employ. Though this is an important distinction, these measures generally give convergent predictions for the studies we shall discuss.) DTC in its strongest form is the claim that n is an index of relative sentential complexity. In particular, other things being equal, two sentences assigned the same value of n should be equally complex, and of two sentences with different values, the one assigned the larger number must be the more complex.

Since the truth of DTC appears to be predicted by both analysis-by-synthesis and analysis-by-analysis approaches to sentence recognition, we may begin our discussion of the character of the sentence-recognition device by examining the status of the experimental evidence for DTC. If we can show that DTC is true, then it is reasonable to argue that a recognition model using the grammar in an analysis-by-analysis or analysis-by-synthesis routine is empirically plausible. If, on the other hand, we can show that DTC is false, we have some reason for rejecting both models and, indeed, any model in which grammatical derivations form part of the recognition process.

A variety of psycholinguistic studies may be interpreted as relevant to DTC. However, to understand these studies, it is necessary to bear in mind that many of them were designed on the grammatical assumptions that underlay the research on sentence similarity and on the "coding hypothesis" (Chapter 5). That is, they assumed the 1957 view that all sentences belonging to a common sentence family have the same base tree and that the least transformationally elaborated form of that tree is the simple active declarative forms.

Experiments relevant to DTC. We have seen that a considerable number of experimental investigations have concerned themselves with the effects of properties of the transformational history of sentences on such tasks as recall of the sentences, transfer of training between sentences, sorting of sentences, and so forth. In the present section, we review those studies which seem to bear primarily on the truth of DTC, namely, on the relation between the number of grammatical operations involved in the derivation of a sentence and its perceptual complexity.

Of experiments whose results tend to confirm DTC, McMahon's (1963) is paradigmatic. This experiment was a continuation of the line of research on the psychological reality of grammatical transformations inaugurated by Miller and McKean (1964) and discussed in Chapter 5. McMahon used active, negative, and passive sentences and required subjects to judge whether a presented sentence was true or false. His sentences were of the type: "5 precedes 13," "3 is preceded by 7," or "13 is not preceded by 6." McMahon found that both negatives and passives required a longer time to evaluate than active affirmatives. Table 6-1 gives the order of McMahon's sentences from easiest to most difficult. These findings are compatible with the DTC hypothesis on the

---

TABLE 6-1

Active affirmative	
	Small difference
Passive affirmative	
	Large difference
Active negative	
	Small difference
Passive negative	

---

following assumptions: first, that there are fewer grammatical operations involved in the derivation of active sentences than any of the others and, second, that the variance is due to differences in the difficulty of *understanding* the sentences. This last assumption is somewhat questionable given the fact that evaluating the truth of negative propositions generally appears to be harder than evaluating the truth of affirmative propositions (see Wason, 1965, for example).

A similar pattern of results, with a variation in the experimental paradigm, was found by McMahon (1963) and by Gough (1965). In both cases, the experimental task involved presenting a sentence and a picture; S was required to say whether the picture made the sentence true or false. In Gough's experiment, sentences were of the type "the boy kicked the girl," "the girl was not kicked by the boy," etc. Among the results relevant to the evaluation of DTC were the following: passive took longer to verify than active in both affirmative and negative versions; negative took longer to verify than affirmative in both active and passive versions. It is of interest that while the syntactic prediction is confirmed, there is a residual interaction of response time with the truth or falsity of the sentence, which suggests that some purely semantic variable is operative. Gough notes that DTC must be "elaborated with respect to the verification process [to account for the interaction with truth value]. But otherwise the data are entirely consistent with the assumption that the hearer of a complex sentence transforms that sentence into its underlying kernel, and that understanding of the sentence waits upon such transformation" (p. 110). Thus Gough takes his results to suggest that the processes in sentence recognition are in some relatively simple relation to those involved in the grammatical derivation of the sentence.

In a subsequent experiment Gough (1966) controlled for a possible confounding of the syntactic prediction with sentence length, i.e., for the possibility that the verification of passive is slower than the verification of active simply because passive sentences are longer than actives. In this experiment Gough showed that the verification time for *short* passives (i.e., passives with deleted agents, like "the boy was hit") is longer than the verification time for corresponding actives like "the boy hit the girl." There are, however, two facts that must be borne in mind in interpreting the significance of these findings for DTC. First, it is notable that the syntactically predicted differences persist even when a 3-second delay is introduced between the presentation of the sentence and the presentation of the picture. Gough himself argues that this militates against the assumption that the differences are solely an effect of the relative difficulty of comprehending the stimulus sentences. Second, it is unclear that *NVN* sentences are the relevant control for short passives. It can be argued that a better one is *N be ADJ* (e.g., "the vase was red"). We do not, however, know of any experiment in which the relative complexity of short passive and predicate adjective sentences has been systematically compared.

Another study that can be interpreted as relevant to the evaluation of DTC was conducted by Savin and Perchonock (1965). It represents an attempt to relate the short-term-storage requirements of various sentences to the length of their transformational histories. Their assumption was that the greater the complexity of a sentence's description, as measured by the number of rules required for its derivation, the greater would be the demands its retention places on short-term storage. Savin and Perchonock sought to determine this difference by requiring subjects to recall both a sentence and a set of words. Each subject was presented with a sentence followed by a string of eight unrelated words. He was to repeat the sentence and then as many of the eight words as he could recall. The number of words correctly recalled when the sentence was also correctly recalled was the measure of storage requirements for that sentence type. They used the same sentence types as Mehler (1963) (reviewed in Chapter 5) with the addition of emphatic forms (involving heightened stress on *Aux* or on *wh* forms): e.g., *"What* has Morris solved?"; "Morris *did* solve the problem"; etc.

The ordering of sentence types in this experiment was compatible with results of the other experiments just reviewed. In every instance, sentences involving relatively fewer transformational operations required relatively less storage (i.e., interfered less with recall of word lists) than did sentences involving relatively more operations; simple active affirmative declaratives interfered least of all. Savin and Perchonock also reported constant effects for given transformations: that is, a given transformational operation apparently took the same storage space regardless of the other transformations with which it was associated (for example, a question added the same degree of difficulty whether it occurred with a passive, active, or emphatic).

Finally, there is an experiment by Compton (1967) that revealed roughly the same ordering of these sentence types as was found by Savin and Perchonock. In this case, subjects transcribed sentences heard through a low-pass filter. The accuracy of their transcription was generally a function of the number of transformations in the derivation of the sentences.

The results of these studies provide evidence of a relation between aspects of the derivational history that grammars assign sentences and the relative complexity of the sentences. In particular, they support a view of the relations between syntactic variables and sentence complexity similar to that formulated by DTC, and thus are compatible with both analysis-by-synthesis and analysis-by-analysis accounts of the sentence-recognition process. Yet despite these experimental findings, and despite the intrinsic appeal of the models, there are serious considerations that militate against accepting DTC. First, there are a number of experimental and intuitive facts about the relative complexity of sentences which DTC simply fails to account for. Second, there is increasing theoretical and experimental evidence that if we are to understand the psychological processes underlying sentence perception, we must postulate a far more abstract relation between the grammar and the sentence recognizer than is envisioned in either analysis by synthesis or analysis by analysis. This, in turn, predicts a more abstract relation between sentence complexity and length of grammatical derivation than is implied by DTC. We shall discuss these points in order.

In unpublished experiments, Bever, Fodor, Garrett, and Mehler (1967) found a variety of cases in which increases in complexity are *not* uniformly associated with increases in the length of the derivational history of a sentence when meaning and length in morphemes of the compared sentences are fully controlled. In a task for which the assumptions were roughly similar to those of Savin and Perchonock (1965), subjects were required to determine which of a series of four tones heard before the presentation of a sentence was identical to a single tone presented immediately following the sentence. Under this condition, no complexity differences were reliably associated with transformational differences like the one between "John phoned up the girl" and "John phoned the girl up" or "The bus driver was nervous after the wreck" and "The bus driver was fired after the wreck." Notice that the second member of each of these pairs is transformationally more complicated than the first; in the former case, particle movement has been applied, and, in the latter case, both passivization and agent deletion have been applied.

In a separate experiment on immediate recall, Bever and Mehler (1967) [reported in Bever (1968)] found that sentences with the adverb at the beginning and the particle at the end ("slowly the operator looked the number up)" are simpler in a short-term-recall task than sentences with the adverb and particle adjacent to the verb ("The operator slowly looked up the number"). Insofar as these results illuminate the relative complexity of the sentences, they are in direct contradiction to DTC since, in both cases, we find that the more transformationally elaborated of a pair of sentences turns out to be easier for subjects to deal with.

In an unpublished experiment by Jenkins, Fodor, and Saporta (1965), similar kinds of structural differences were evaluated for their effects on complexity: for example, such variants of the comparative construction as "John swims faster than Bob swims," "John swims faster than Bob," "John swims faster than Bob does." If DTC is true, relative complexity should increase from the first to the third sentence, since the first sentence is fewer transformational steps from its base structure than either of the others, and the third sentence requires one step more than the second for its derivation (namely, the *do*-support transformation which applies after deletion of the second occurrence of "swims"). When tachistoscopic thresholds were measured for such sentences, however, the first type turned out to be most difficult, whereas the other two types were indistinguishable. Similar tests for difference between sentences with displaced particles and those particles in the untransformed positions showed no significant differences.

A (1967) experiment by Fodor and Garrett was devised specifically to test a prediction based on DTC. In this experiment, the length of the transformational history of a set of doubly self-embedded sentences was increased by adding an adjective to each of the first two noun phrases. These sentences were then compared in a paraphrase task with identical sentences not containing adjectives.

To understand the point of this experiment, we must remind the reader of the standard syntactic analysis of adjective-noun sequences which we discussed in Chapter 3. Consider, in particular, the sequence "tired soldier" occurring in the sentence "The first shot the tired soldier the mosquito bit fired missed." The underlying structure can be represented by the configuration in Figure 6-10. The order of operations in the derivation is roughly the following: "Relativization" produces "The soldier who is tired"; "who is" is deleted to yield the intermediate form "the soldier tired"; a mandatory permutation of the adjective with the noun then yields "the tired soldier."

Each of the two added adjectives thus introduced three transformations in the derivation of the test sentences, so that each such sentence has six more transformations in its derivational history than does its adjective-free control version. If increase in the length of the derivational history by one transformation is presumed to account for the observed difference in complexity between, e.g., actives and passives, negatives and affirmatives, etc., then increases in the length of a derivational history by *six* transformations ought to make subjects' performance on the sentences with adjectives far worse than their performance on controls. In fact, however, there was found to be no significant effect of the experimental manipulation; the sentences with adjectives exhibited no tendency to inhibit subjects' accuracy on the paraphrase task. This result is of some importance since, as we shall see below, other syntactic manipulations of the same self-embedded sentences did prove to exert control over the subjects' performance. [McMahon (personal communication) has also failed to find an experimental effect of adjectives on the perceptual complexity of sentences.]

Finally, it is worth mentioning an instructive study reported by Slobin (1966). In this picture-verification study, conducted with 6- and

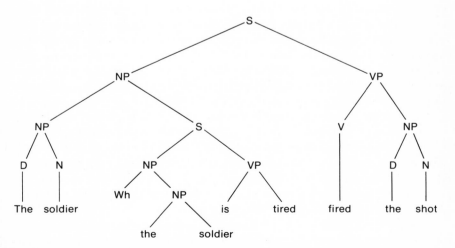

Fig. 6-10. Schematic deep-structure tree for the sentence "The tired soldier fired the shot."

7-year-old children, Slobin found a complexity difference between actives and comparable passives, *only* when passives were "reversible." A reversible passive is one which "makes sense" when its subject and object noun phrases are interchanged. Thus, "the girl was hit by the boy" would be considered reversible, but "the kite was flown by the child" would not. The same sort of finding was made in a "probe latency" study with adults by Walker et al. (1968): subjects decided faster whether a probe word occurred in an active sentence than in a passive. But the asymmetry held only when the passive was reversible.

These results are of special significance in that they point to a general problem about the interpretation of much of the experimentation concerning DTC. The difficulty arises in the following way. DTC has usually been tested by comparing the complexity of sentences which have relatively few grammatical transformations in their derivational histories with the complexity of sentences that have a relatively large number. The experimental prediction is characteristically that the latter sentences will prove more difficult than the former in experimental tasks. Unfortunately, however, the effect of the application of a transformation in the derivation of a sentence is normally to deform the structures to which it applies. The typical effect of transformation is to destroy tree structure.

Now, it is precisely the deep syntactic structure upon which the semantic interpretation of a sentence is presumed to depend. Thus, as we *increase* the transformational distance between the base and surface structure of a sentence, we normally *decrease* the extent to which its surface structure exhibits the grammatical relations among the parts of a sentence in the appropriate form for semantic interpretation. If, for example, we passivize a sentence, we add a grammatical operation to its derivational history. But we also produce a linguistic object which departs from the "canonical" (base-structure) English sentence order in which the first noun phrase is the subject and the second noun phrase is the object. There is thus a problem with the many experimental results which tend to demonstrate the increased complexity of passive sentences as opposed to their active counterparts: they fail to tell us whether the increase in complexity is due to the addition of a transformation to the derivational history of the sentence, or to the fact that the surface structure of the passivized sentence is not in the canonical form for semantic interpretation. In short: does the hearer find passives relatively difficult because grammatical operations are psychologically real and the derivational history of the passive is one grammatical operation longer than the derivational history of the active? Or does he find them relatively difficult because his heuristics for the decoding of English sentences treat the cases in which the first noun phrase of a sentence is the subject noun phrase as the canonical case? Slobin's and Walker's findings suggest that the latter story may be the correct one. When the logical subject and object of the sentence are redundantly marked (i.e., when they are indicated not only by the syntactic form of the sentence but also by its semantic character), the added difficulty associated with the passive apparently washes out.

We have been reviewing a variety of experimental results which suggest grounds for doubting DTC. We conclude this review by mentioning some informal considerations which lead to the same conclusion.

There are types of sentential structures which seem to be intrinsically difficult for subjects to deal with, but in which the difficulty is quite certainly *not* traceable to features of the length of the derivational histories. Paradigmatic of such cases are doubly self-embedded sentences like the ones used in the experiment by Fodor and Garrett (1967) discussed above. In the case of such sentences one has the impression that the addition of any transformation which helps to break up the structures makes the sentences *easier* to understand. (Compare "the first shot the tired soldier the mosquito bit fired missed" with "the first shot fired by the tired soldier bitten by the mosquito missed." The second sentence, in which passivization has applied twice, seems the easier to understand.) Thus one finds types of sentences whose complexity relations appear to run counter to what DTC would lead one to predict. [For an extensive discussion of why the center-embedded sentence is difficult, see below; see also Miller and Chomsky (1963, pp. 470–471), Fodor and Garrett (1967), and Bever (1970, pp. 333–341).]

Second, there are pairs of sentence types which, unlike many of the ones discussed above, have not been extensively examined in experiments employing specifically perceptual tasks, but which look like good candidates for reversing the complexity ordering that DTC predicts. We have remarked that the standard theory derives adjectives from relatives, hence DTC would appear to be committed to the view that "the small cat is on the dirty mat" is *more* complicated than "the cat which is small is on the mat which is dirty." Analogously, according to the standard theory, the sentences "that John left the party quickly amazed Bill" and "it amazed Bill that John left the party quickly," derive from the same base, but the former is transformationally simpler; thus one would predict that the latter sentence must be the more complex. Sentences in which full subordinated clauses appear to the left of main clauses in surface structure have attracted considerable psycholinguistic attention for a variety of different reasons, and we shall return to them in several different contexts. Suffice it to say here that intuition does not support the direction of complexity assymmetry predicted by DTC, and that the data available also point in the opposite direction. Finally, there are sentence pairs like "John seemed to be in a hurry" and "it seemed that John was in a hurry." It is hard to see how one could avoid a treatment of such pairs in which the second is closest to the deep structure; the obvious analysis is that "John" has been transformationally raised from deep subject of the subordinated sentoid to superficial subject of "seem." Once again, however, the intuitive complexity differences do not go in the right direction from the point of view of DTC. The point is not that the DTC prediction is known to be false. It is rather that it is hard to believe that there could be an asymmetry in the predicted direction that is of the magnitude of those discovered in the experiments which compared actives with passives, passives with passive negatives, etc. But unless there is such an asymmetry, DTC is in trouble.

THEORETICAL ALTERNATIVES TO ANALYSIS BY SYNTHESIS AND ANALYSIS BY ANALYSIS

Perhaps the fairest summary of the evidence for and against DTC is that it fails to yield a decisive resolution. This is not solely because of shortcomings in the experiments. Any test of DTC must be predicated on *some* assumptions about the grammar, and it is always possible that such assumptions might turn out to be false. If, for example, the sequence *Adj N* is a base-structure form, then Fodor and Garrett (1967) is not an argument against DTC.

In the present section, we will discuss what seems to us to be the strongest reason for being suspicious of DTC; namely, that more plausible accounts of sentence recognition would not predict that it is true.

We remarked above that DTC is intimately connected with theoretical commitments to sentence recognizers that employ grammatical information in a fairly concrete way; e.g., they assume that each grammatical operation has a counterpart in the mental operations involved in sentence recognition. We will now consider aspects of a sentence-recognition system which is considerably less conservative in its approach to the grammar. In particular, we shall outline a number of processes for whose centrality in sentence recognition there appears to be theoretical and experimental evidence. It is characteristic of these processes that, although they use the syntactic information expressed in a grammar, they employ it in a form quite different from the form in which standard grammars do. Thus, postulating that those processes play an important role in sentence recognition is tantamount to accepting a recognition model which does *not* entail a commitment to DTC.

We have assumed throughout that the essential problem about sentence recognition at the syntactic level is to account for the recovery of deep structure. The deep structure of any sentence is, by hypothesis, a tree composed of one or more "sentoids." (It will be remembered that a sentoid is a subtree of the base structure whose highest node is S and which contains no embedded sentences.) We can, therefore, think of the process of recovering the deep structure of a given sentence as involving the recovery of information which answers the following questions:

What sentoids are there in the deep structure of the sentence; in particular, which parts of the surface string belong to the same sentoid?

What grammatical relations hold among the elements of each sentoid?

How are the sentoids in the deep structure of the sentence arranged relative to one another?

For example, given an input sentence "John believes Mary is a friend," the recovery of its deep structure involves at least determining that "John believes" and "Mary is a friend" belong to different sentoids; and that the sentoid containing "John believes" dominates the sentoid containing "Mary is a friend." In what follows, we will argue for a view of sentence recognition in which listeners use heuristic strategies to make direct inductions about those aspects of base structure in terms of which answers to these questions can be stated. We shall review evidence for psychological processes in sentence recognition which may be interpreted as reflecting the operation of such heuristics, and we will try to say something about their character.

CLAUSAL ANALYSIS

We have suggested that one process involved in the assignment of a deep structure to an input sequence of words involves grouping together those words which are members of a common sentoid. There exist a variety of experimental results which suggest that this process does in fact go on, and which illuminate its general character.

Much of the evidence tending to support the hypothesis that surface items belonging to a single sentoid are grouped together in the process of sentence recognition derives from experiments on the perceptual effects of surface *clause boundaries,* since these positions in surface structure typically mark the boundaries between material drawn from different deep-structure sentoids. (The position between "John believes" and "Mary is a friend" is such a boundary in the sentence "John believes Mary is a friend." But the positions between, e.g., "John" and "believes" or between "Mary" and "is" are not.) These experiments suggest that the boundaries between clauses have a unique and characteristic role in the perceptual organization of sentences, a role compatible with the view that they mark the boundaries of the perceptual units in terms of which the sentence is analyzed. This is, of course, precisely what would be predicted on the hypothesis that an early process in sentence recognition involves grouping together items from the same sentoid.

Among the experimental results upon which this conclusion rests, several derive from exploitation of the "click" paradigm introduced by

Ladefoged and Broadbent (1960) and described briefly in Chapter 5. In this paradigm, subjects hear stimuli consisting of words or sentences, during which there occur short bursts of noise (clicks). After each such stimulus, subjects are required to report the word or sentence and the position of the click. Ladefoged and Broadbent showed that errors in reporting the click position were larger and more frequent when the click occurred in a sentence than when it occurred in nonsentential word sequences. They interpreted this finding as related to the subject's perceptual segmentation of the stimulus strings. The suggestion is that clicks are displaced from their objective positions to the boundaries of perceptual units, and that the character of such displacements can be employed to estimate the size of these units. This interpretation takes click displacement to be a species of the well-known phenomenon of perceptual "closure"—the tendency of perceptual units to resist inter-ruption. If it is correct, then the Ladefoged and Broadbent results show that the size of perceptual units is larger in the processing of sentences than in the processing of nonsentential sequences of words.

A more precise hypothesis about the character of the perceptual units in sentence recognition can be formulated, however: namely, that such units can be defined in terms of the constituent structure of a sentence. As we remarked in Chapter 5, a relation between constituent structure and click location has been found by many investigators. In general, there is a significant tendency to displace clicks into or toward major bounda-ries, and the position of clicks which are objectively located at such boundaries is perceived more accurately than is the position of clicks which interrupt constituents.

This sort of finding prompted a variety of experimental investigations directed toward two major questions: First, is the relation between con-stituent structure and click location a perceptual effect or an effect of non-perceptual factors (e.g., of a response bias)? Second, precisely *which* as-pects of the structure of a sentence are related to click location? It is this latter question which bears on the hypothesis that clausal analysis is an important process in sentence recognition; we return to it after a brief review of experiments which study the question of whether the click ef-fect is the result of a bona fide perceptual process.

Several hypotheses have been put forth as alternatives to the suggestion that click displacement reflects the subject's perceptual segmentation of a sentence. The first concern is that the effect may somehow reflect a re-sponse bias of the subject. For example, it has been suggested by Reber and Anderson (1970) that the location errors reflect a serial position bias, in particular, a bias to choose the middle of a sentence (or of any other sound sequence) as the probable locus of interference. Though there clearly are serial position effects on listeners' judgments of click location (see Ladefoged and Broadbent, 1960), they do not provide a plausible account of the observed correlations between constituent structure and click location. For example, Bever, Lackner, and Kirk (1969) treated the ordinal position of the major constituent boundary as a manipulated variable and found no tendency for the click effect to be enhanced when that boundary was coincident with the middle of the sentence. Moreover, in most experiments that have focussed on syntactic variables serial position has been controlled for (i.e., a given serial position is tested under different constituent analysis).

A more persuasive alternative to the suggestion that click location is a perceptual effect is that it is determined by a response bias operating in conjunction with a memory error. In particular, it is suggested that the effect occurs only when the subject forgets the position in which he heard the click. In such circumstances, response bias operates and the subject reports a click in a major constituent boundary. The evidence for this interpretation rests on the claim that subjects told that they are listening to a sentence containing a "subliminal" click, whose position they are asked to guess, exhibit some tendency to locate the click in a major constituent boundary; Ladefoged (1967) reports this result for sentences which in fact contain no click whatever.

It is clear that the important part of this interpretation is the suggestion that memory error plays a critical role in determining click locations. After all, there is no question that subjects have a "bias" to locate their responses at major constituent boundaries: that is precisely what the original experimental results on clicks showed. The interesting question is: What causes the bias? In particular, is a significant proportion of the bias produced by interaction of the perceptual analysis of a sentence with the perception of a click? If the contribution of memory error can be shown to be inessential, the existence of a response bias favoring major constituent boundaries is fully compatible with—indeed, is demanded by—the theory that click location is a perceptual phenomenon.

There are, in fact, a number of experimental findings which suggest that memory error does not play an essential role in producing click-location effects.

First, there is no significant reduction in the tendency to locate clicks at constituent boundaries when memory demand is decreased by substituting a recognition task for a recall task: Garrett (1965) and Holmes (1970) found that subjects who are provided with a written version of the stimulus sentence following its auditory presentation produce the same pattern of responses as subjects who are required to write out the sentence before indicating the click position. In another experimental variation aimed at reducing memory load, a significant constituent-structure effect was found even where the only response the subject produced was a judgment of identity or difference in the location of clicks in successively presented recordings of a sentence (Garrett, 1965). It is also notable, in this connection, that within wide limits (six to twenty-two words) there appears to be little relation between sentence length and magnitude of click errors, although such a correlation *does* exist for nonsentential stimuli (Garrett, 1965). These results hardly comport with the suggestion that the occurrence of syntactically determined error patterns depends on memory failures.

Still more directly to the point is the finding by Holmes and Forster (1970) that reaction times to clicks are affected by the proximity of a major constituent boundary. Clicks internal to major constituents are responded to more slowly than clicks that are immediately adjacent to a major constituent boundary. Presumably, reaction time is a measure which abstracts from memory effects if any measure does.

Again, if a response bias coupled with a memory error is the explanation of the syntactic effects on click location, one would expect a negative correlation between syntactically conditioned errors and a subject's confidence in the accuracy of his response. But confidence ratings typically show no such correlation (Fodor and Bever, 1965).

Finally, a series of experiments (Bever, 1973 and forthcoming) addressed the question originally raised by Ladefoged: What happens when subjects must report a click location for a sentence which in fact contains *no* click. In these studies, subjects heard sentences in one ear, and in the other clicks were presented in masking noise. Signal-to-noise ratio was varied for the click channel, and there were some cases in which that channel contained only noise. In all other cases, a click occurred one syllable before a major syntactic boundary, in the boundary, or one syllable after it. The effects of response bias were assessed by comparing the no-click cases with the one in which a click was present.

Three response conditions were compared. In the first (the one usually used in click studies) subjects listened to the sentence and then wrote it out, indicating the click position. In a second response condition, a subject was provided with a transcript which he could follow *while* he listened to the stimulus material. His task was to indicate the click position on the transcript. The results for these first two response conditions were the following: in the first condition there was a significant difference between the distribution of responses to sentences which contained clicks and the distribution of responses to those which did not; the former exhibited a greater proportion of clicks reported at the major break. But no such asymmetry was found in the second response condition where subjects were supplied with transcripts. This is taken to indicate that there *is* a click-displacement effect over and above any response bias, but *only for subjects who are required to attend to the content of the sentence.*

There is a possible objection to this interpretation, however. When a subject actually heard a click, he might remember its rough location, and if he did, then his responses would tend to cluster at the objective click positions. Subjects who heard sentences with no click would show no such clustering. In principle, their responses should be dispersed over the entire sentence. Suppose there *is* a response bias to place clicks in breaks, but that it operates only for clicks antecedently believed to be near a break. This bias would operate for those sentences with clicks but no others. Hence one could predict that the click-present condition would result in more in-break responses than the no-click condition; and there would still be no necessity to assume any click-displacement effect other than a response bias.

The third response condition was designed to permit evaluation of this possibility. On any given trial, in this condition, a subject did not know whether he would have to write out the sentence; this ensured that he would always attend to the sentence. On critical trials, the subject was given a transcript of the sentences *after* he had heard it. The transcript indicated the approximate click location within four syllables and the subject had to say where, within the indicated portion of the sentence, he thought the click had actually occurred. The effect of this response condition was to provide subjects with the information that the appropriate response was near or in the break in both the trials where clicks were present and the trials where they were not. If the explanation of the click effect is that a response bias operates only for clicks believed to be near the break, the click and no-click conditions should have produced equal numbers of in-break responses when this response window was provided. In fact, they did not. In this condition, as in the first, significantly more in-break responses were given when a click was present than when it was not. This seems clearly to rule out the claim that the displacement effect is due to a response bias.

Though the studies we have just reviewed make it reasonable to relate click-location errors to the perceptual analysis of sentences, we have yet to discuss which aspects of that analysis are revealed. We turn now to a discussion of experiments which are relevant to this question: what aspects of sentence structure control click-location errors, and therefore (by hypothesis), determine the perceptual segmentation of sentences?

We may begin with an observation which both indicates that click location does reflect the "grouping" in a string of words, and suggests a hypothesis about click location in sentences that requires examination. There is reason to believe that structure can be imposed on an otherwise unrelated string of words (e.g., a string of digits or nonsense words) by introducing pauses or intonation contours to the string. In

Chapter 5, for example, we discussed the phenomenon of facilitation of recall as a consequence of such grouping. This is germane to our present concerns because there is some evidence that clicks tend to be displaced into pauses in spoken digit strings (Garrett, 1965). This indicates the sensitivity of the paradigm to whatever structure may be present in a string, but it also raises the possibility that the tendency to displace clicks into major constituent boundaries is to be explained in terms of acoustic pauses occurring at such boundaries. Fodor and Bever (1965) attempted to evaluate this possibility by showing that there was no correlation between the objective decrease in acoustic energy at the major constituent boundary of a sentence and the magnitude of the click effect for that sentence. But though this seems to rule out the attribution of the effect to the occurrence of silent intervals in the speech stream, there remains the more general worry that acoustic correlates of prosodic features (e.g., intonation contour and stress pattern) are the major determinant of the syntactically patterned location responses. Two experiments are directly relevant to evaluating this possibility: in one the acoustic indicants of prosody are destroyed and in the other they are equated for sentences of different constituent structure.

Abrams and Bever (1969) constructed stimulus sentences by splicing together individual words that had originally been recorded as members of a list. This procedure produced stimuli in which there were no stress, intonational, or pausal cues to the constituent structure of the sentences. The location of clicks in such stimuli showed the familiar pattern: a significant tendency to mislocate clicks as occurring in the immediate vicinity of the major constituent boundary.

Garrett, Bever, and Fodor (1966) controlled for acoustic artifact by constructing stimulus sentences in which constituent structure of a lexical sequence was altered by varying the initial portions of the sentence. For example, a stimulus pair like sentences (6-1) and (6-2) was constructed by splicing the italicized fragments onto the common fragment. Thus, click-location responses could be related to the differing

6-1 *As a direct result of their new invention's* influence the company was given an award.

6-2 *The retiring chairman whose methods still greatly* influence the company was given an award.

constituent structure of acoustically identical sequences. Figure 6-11 shows the observed distribution of responses for this sentence pair for clicks objectively located at the center of the phrase "the company" and the center of the word "was"; the modal error position in each case is the major constituent boundary. A similar result was found for eleven of twelve such contrasting pairs tested in the experiment.

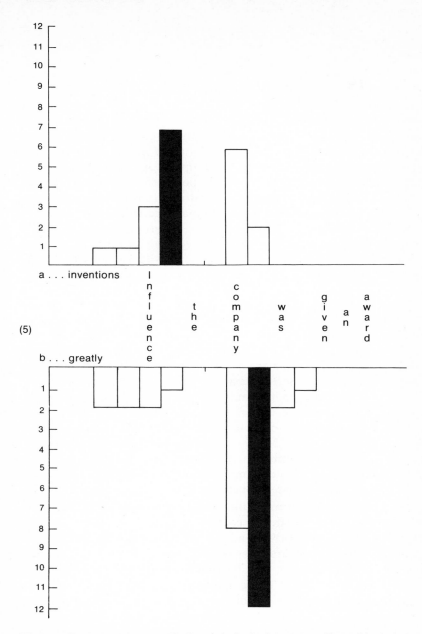

Fig. 6-11. Responses to an acoustically matched pair of sentences. The positions of response concentration predicted by variations in the constituent boundaries are darkened areas in the graph (Garrett, Bever, and Fodor, 1966).

The results just reviewed suggest that the click effect is not attributable to acoustic artifacts. Therefore, we may assume that the perceptual segmentation that subjects impose upon sentences is dependent on properties more abstract than the acoustic reflections of its syntactic and prosodic structure. What, precisely, do click effects indicate the perceptual segments of sentences to be?

In their (1965) paper, Fodor and Bever argued that all constituents in the surface structure can function as perceptual units, so that the probability that any point in a sentence will function as the boundary of a perceptual unit is proportional to the number of constituents which have their termini at that point. It should be noted, however, that their experimental data for this claim came entirely from the assessment of the perception of clicks located near or in major constituent boundaries in complicated sentences. When, in later experiments, the effect of minor constituent boundaries was assessed, the original suggestion turned out to require revision. In particular, Bever, Lackner, and Stolz (1969) found no difference between the *NP-V* boundary and the *V-NP* boundary inside a sentoid bracketed ((*NP*) ((*V*(*NP*))). Yet a difference is predicted by the hypothesis that all derived constituents correspond to perceptual units, since clicks between *NP* and *V* interrupt fewer constituents of such sentences than clicks between *V* and *NP*. Analogously Bever, Lackner, and Kirk's (1969) data reveals no correlation between the frequency of click displacements toward a boundary and the number of constituents coterminus at that boundary. What was discovered, both in these experiments and in a reexamination of earlier click data, was that much of the variance is contributed by a tendency to displace clicks into surface boundaries which mark the ends of embedded sentences. This finding seems compatible with the notion that the perceptual processing of sentences involves a procedure in which surface material belonging to a common sentoid is grouped together and segmented from surface material belonging to other sentoids.

An experiment by Chapin, Smith, and Abrahamson (1972) bears on this hypothesis. They sought to contrast the effect of major surface boundaries which do *not* correspond to sentoid boundaries with that of minor surface structure boundaries which do; e.g., boundaries 1 and 2 respectively in the sentence, "All those who own cars[2] with cash[1] can step to the head of the line." These investigators found that, in general, the main subject-predicate break of a sentence (when it was putatively not a sentoid boundary) exerted a greater effect on click location than did a minor structure break (when it was putatively a sentoid boundary). Thus, rather than the interpretation we suggested above, Chapin et al. propose that it is surface structure, and in particular the subject-predicate boundary, that determines perceptual segmentation of sentences.

We think this is doubtful, however. To begin with, some of Chapin et al.'s stimuli may have been misanalyzed. In the example sentence given above, it is our strong intuition that the phrase "with cash" must be given a parenthetical intonation to be acceptable, and it is at least a moot question whether that phrase is a part of the main sentoid, or whether it should be derived transformationally from a subordinated sentoid "who are with cash." This problem is typical of the stimulus material used by Chapin et al.; by our analysis, more than half of the main subject-predicate boundaries tested are also sentoid boundaries. Moreover, by our analysis a number of the boundaries that were intended by Chapin et al. to mark a juncture between sentoids do not (e.g., boundary 2 in "All three of the cooks[1] noticed[2] the cake plate"). These two problems with the stimuli vitiate the intended contrast between what is prima facie the most important nonsentoidal surface boundary and sentoidal boundaries of lesser surface significance.

Beyond this, there is other experimental evidence on the question of the effects of clausal structure which seems to run counter to the conclusions of Chapin et al. Notice, for example, that the contrast between sentences (6-1) and (6-2) affords at the second break tested (i.e., the one between "company" and "was") something like the test Chapin et al. were after. In *both* versions of the test sentence the test boundary is the subject-predicate break, but in the (6-2) version, that break coincides with a sentoid boundary while in the (6-1) version it does not. This was the case for each of the six pairs of sentences tested; and in every case the subject-predicate break that was *also* a sentoid boundary was the more effective one. If the primary perceptual segmentation of a sentence depends solely on its surface tree, it is hard to see why there should have been this difference.

A good summary of the click results discussed so far would appear to be that the boundaries of surface clauses determine the perceptual segmentation of sentences. However, note that every boundary between surface clauses corresponds to a boundary between deep sentoids; and, in most cases, the converse is also true: the surface structure reflex of a boundary between deep sentoids will be a clause boundary. For such cases, the hypothesis that the perceptual unit is the surface clause will be extensionally identical with the hypothesis that perceptual units are determined by surface reflexes of deep sentoids. There are, however, cases which may allow a choice between these hypotheses and there is some relevant experimental data. An experiment by Bever, Lackner, and Kirk (1969) was directed precisely at comparing surface boundaries which coincide with junctures between sentoids with surface boundaries which do not.

Consider the sentences "John persuaded Bill to leave" versus "John expected Bill to leave." It seems plausible to maintain that both sentences have essentially the same surface structure, namely something like Figure 6-12. However, as we saw in Chapter 3, there is evidence

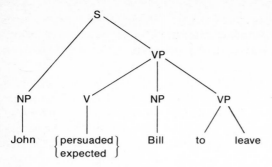

Fig. 6-12. Surface structure for the sentences "John persuaded Bill to leave" and "John expected Bill to leave."

that they differ in deep structure. In particular "John persuaded Bill to leave" and "John expected Bill to leave," contrast in their deep structures in the way Figure 3-14 contrasts with Figure 3-10. Thus the position between "expected" and "Bill" marks a sentoidal juncture in deep structure, but the position between "persuaded" and "Bill" does not. If the click effect is primarily sensitive to constituent boundaries which mark the junctures between sentoids, then we would expect the magnitude of the effect to be significantly larger following the main verb in the "expect" type of sentence than at the corresponding position in the "persuade" type. If, on the contrary, the click effect is mainly sensitive to surface clauses, then we should expect no difference between sentences of these two types. It was, in fact, the former result that Bever et al. obtained. Insofar as this analysis is accepted, it indicates that surface clauses act as perceptual units only insofar as they indicate the decomposition of the input into deep sentoids.

There is an important point to bear in mind about the experiment of Bever et al. just discussed: the conclusion that it is the *underlying* clausal structure which determines the perceptual salience of a surface constituent boundary rests on the assumption that the surface structure of *NP*-complements (with "expect"-type verbs) and *VP*-complements (with "persuade"-type verbs) is the same. It is possible to find a difference in the effects of these complement types of the sort found by Bever et al. and still maintain that the perceptually salient boundaries in a sentence depend on its surface structure. In particular, one might claim: (1) that in *NP*-complements, but not in *VP*-complements, there is a surface clause boundary immediately after the main verb, and (2) that it is surface clause boundaries which are the primary determinants of click effects. At present, there are no conclusive linguistic arguments which will resolve this issue. There are, however, some additional findings with click location which indicate that surface-structure features do influence the magnitude of click effects in cases where deep clausal structure is held constant.

In a modified replication of the study by Bever et al., Fodor, Fodor, Garrett, and Lackner (1974) tested both the contrast between *NP-* and *VP-*complements and the effects of relative clause reduction. This study found the same relation between *NP-* and *VP-*complements as did Bever et al., but in the tests with relatives, it was found that the deletion of the surface indicants of a sentoid boundary reduced the influence of such boundaries on click location. For the position immediately following the italicized *NP* in sentence pairs like, "This time of year, *anyone* who is rich enough takes a vacation in the Carribean," versus "This time of year, *anyone* rich enough takes a vacation in the Carribean," the boundary effects were stronger in the *unreduced* version. Note that the underlying relation between the italicized *NP* and the material which follows it is the same for both sentences. This finding does not rule out the hypothesis that underlying clausal structure determines perceptual segmentation, but it does rule out the claim that only that class of variables is relevant. Moreover, it suggests an effect of surface clause boundaries per se, since presumably the primary consequence of relative clause reduction is the "pruning" of a surface S-node (see Ross, 1967). Perhaps the best way to summarize the findings we have been reviewing is that they indicate that surface constituent boundaries which correspond to junctures between sentoids define the *potential* points of perceptual segmentation of sentences; whether any such point is in fact taken as the boundary of a perceptual unit may depend on a variety of other structural features.

Thus far, we have been examining the experimental evidence for two closely related hypotheses. We have argued that a process of grouping together surface elements belonging to a common sentoid occurs in sentence recognition, and that a consequence of this effect is to make the surface boundaries that mark sentoid junctures perceptually prepotent. A number of results with experimental paradigms other than clicks is relevant to assessing these hypotheses. We consider first a pair of studies which suggest a correspondence between the underlying clausal structure of a sentence and its perceptual analysis. We then turn to investigations which bear on the explanation of this correspondence.

Whatever perceptual units are, they should have the property that the more of them some object contains, the more complicated the object is. If clausal structure determines perceptual units, increasing the number of clauses should complicate sentences. A series of experiments by Forster (1970) and by Forster and Ryder (1971) suggest that this is the case.

These experiments employ a technique which Forster calls RSVP (rapid serial visual presentation). Subjects are presented with stimulus sentences one word at a time on successive frames of a film strip. By varying the rate of presentation, it is possible to affect the error rate. When Forster compared error rates for sentences controlled for length in words, he found that those with two underlying sentoids are, in general, more complicated than those with only one. For example, "Betty will send Mary the letter" and "The rabbit jumped into the truck" are less complicated than "Knowing Jim made Betty very happy" and "The kitten nobody liked was young." Forster and Ryder replicated this finding and showed that it is not dependent upon the semantic plausibility of the stimulus sentences.

In an experiment by Wingfield and Klein (1971) we find some additional support for the claim that clauses have a special perceptual salience in the analysis of sentences. In this experiment, subjects were required to localize the point at which a monaurally presented speech signal was switched from one ear to the other. Accuracy in the localization of the switch point and accuracy of recall of the sentence were the dependent variables. Manipulated variables included syntactic and prosodic features.

The stimulus sentences used by Wingfield and Klein were constructed in a manner similar to Garrett et al. (1966); i.e., a string of words constituting a sentence fragment was spliced to two contexts which yielded different constituent structures for the fragment [see examples (6-1) and (6-2)]. Since, however, intonational neutrality was explicitly *not* maintained, it was possible to compare cases where the intonation was compatible with the structure determined by the spliced context with cases where it was not. In short, for each sentence fragment there were two pairs of stimulus items, one pair for each constituent structure; members of each pair consisted of a sentence with the intonation appropriate to its structure, and a sentence with the intonation appropriate to the structure of the opposite pair. The stimulus sentences thus prepared were presented to subjects with switch points preceding, at, and following a clause boundary.

The experiment thus provides an opportunity to study the interaction between intonation and syntactic structure in determining the perceptual organization of a sentence. It turned out, as in the click experiments, that overall the subject was most accurate in locating interruptions that occur at clause boundaries. However, there was no significant effect favoring accuracy at the major clause boundary in the case of the abnormally intonated sentences. On the contrary, for such sentences accuracy increased not at the *objective* clause boundary, but at the *apparent* boundary indicated by the intonational cues. This might suggest a disagreement between the results for the switching paradigm and those for the click paradigm, since the former seem to show that the entire burden of determining the perceptual segmentation of the input is being carried by prosodic (as opposed to syntactic) features of the signals. But this appearance turns out to be misleading upon investigation of the behavior of the other dependent variables. For example, if we look not at the *accuracy* of the response (i.e., the frequency with which the subject correctly locates the switch point) but at the *distribution* of erroneous responses, we find a modal response at the clause boundary for the normally intonated sentences and a *bi*modal distribution for the abnormally intonated ones. The two modes in the latter case are of equal size and occur at the objective (syntactic) clause boundary and at the intonationally indicated boundary. This suggests that the error responses are controlled both by prosodic and by structural features of the sentences. Supportive of this interpretation is the nature of the errors that subjects make in recall of the stimuli. In the case of the normally intonated sentences, syntactic structure is generally preserved and errors are either substitutions or omissions of lexical items. In the inappropriately intonated sentences, the error pattern is quite different; 38 percent of the errors involve a restructuring of the syntax of the sentence to make it correspond to the intonational pattern of the disambiguating fragment. The other responses preserved the objective syntactic structure of the stimulus string. In short, these results appear to support two findings with clicks: first, clause boundaries impose a perceptual segmentation on the signal, and second, they tend to do so even in the absence of appropriate intonational cues.

All the studies we have just been reviewing seem to indicate that clausal structure determines the units of perceptual analysis in sentence processing. A number of other studies throw some light on the ways in which such clausal units are implicated in the perceptual processing of sentences. First, it appears that the processing load on the perceptual system is particularly high just at the ends of clauses. Accordingly, reaction times to clicks are relatively slow in such positions, when compared with reaction times to clicks objectively located just after the clause boundary (Abrams and Bever, 1969). Similarly, the detectibility of clicks is found to be lowest at the position just before the break in experiments in which click position and click amplitude are the manipulated variables (Bever, 1968).

Such results allow us to reject at least one important kind of explanation of the way in which clauses function as perceptual units. It might be supposed that the peculiar effects of clause boundaries in perception depend on the fact that the redundancy of sentential material increases as we approach a clause boundary and decreases sharply as we pass the clause boundary. In this sort of theory, a clause functions as a perceptual unit because it is a structure within which the hearer can use his knowledge of linguistic redundancies to make successful predictions about the content of the sentence he is hearing.

If this explanation were true, however, one could expect that the processing load on the perceptual system would *de*crease at the ends of clauses and *in*crease at the beginnings. This prediction is, however, precisely contrary to the results just reviewed (assuming that the positions in a sentence where the subject is able to predict the linguistic material are the ones where he is free to divide his processing capacity between monitoring the sentence and attending to extraneous signals like clicks). It is also inconsistent with a finding of Bever, Lackner, and Stolz (1969) in which the redundancy of the stimulus sentence was explicitly manipulated. Decreasing the transitional probability between items in a sentence showed no tendency to increase the magnitude of click displacements into boundaries between those items.

An alternative account of the way clauses engage the sentence-processing mechanisms can be developed by considering a persistent question in recent psycholinguistics: Why are center-embedded sentences like "The man the boy the girl knew liked got sick" harder to understand and to recall than are their right-branching counterparts like "The girl knew the boy who liked the man who got sick." Clearly, if one is to understand either sentence one must gather together surface elements which derive from common sentoids. In particular, one must determine which *NP*'s go with which *VP*'s. Thus, Schlesinger (1968) was able to show that the difficulty of understanding self-embedded sentences was markedly decreased when there were strong semantic associations between *NP* and *VP* belonging to the same sentoid. (Compare "the boy the girl the man liked hated died" with "the water the fish the man caught swam in was polluted.") The point appears to be that by facilitating the task of grouping together materials from the same sentoid, we correspondingly facilitate the understanding of the sentence.

Schlesinger's result helps explain why some center-embedded sentences are easier than others. But it does not explain why center-embedded sentences are harder than their right-branching counterparts. Such an explanation is forthcoming, however, if we assume, first, that there is only a limited amount of short-term memory available for the perceptual processing of sentences, and second, that no constituent of a sentence can be dismissed from short-term memory until it has been assigned to a sentoid. It follows from this assumption that center-embedded sentences ought to be harder to understand than right-branching ones since, in the former case, we must store all the *NP*'s belonging to the sentence before we can assign any constituent to any sentoid (in particular, before we can assign any *NP* to its *VP*). But, in the latter case, we do not have to store more than a single *NP* before we encounter the *VP* of the sentoid to which it belongs.

The following picture of sentence processing emerges from these considerations. As the sentence is received, it is assigned to a short-term store where the fragments that constitute each of its sentoids are collected together. Material is dismissed from this storage as soon as it can be assigned to a completed sentoid. It is because each sentoid is dismissed from this store en bloc that the clause functions as a unit of speech perception.

There exist a variety of types of evidence for this account other than the behavior of multiply center-embedded sentences. First, we noted above some evidence that processing demands are higher at the ends of clauses than at their beginnings. This is what one would expect if the perceptual system contains a buffer storage which cannot be cleared until it reaches the end of a sentoid and must be cleared thereafter: the closer one is to the end of a clause, the closer this buffer will be to saturation.

Second, notice that if immediate memory is cleared at the end of each clause, it ought to follow that the accessibility of lexical materials for recall is inversely related to the number of clauses between the occurrence of the lexical material and the point at which recall is attempted. Two recent experiments suggest that something like this may be the case.

In a series of studies, Jarvella (1971) presented listeners with short stories which were interrupted at various points. The listener's task was to recall verbatim as much of the preceding material as he could. The results showed that rote recall was best for the clause immediately preceding the interruption and that the performance dropped off markedly for rote recall of words occurring before that clause. There was, however, no significant effect of serial position within clauses. That is, of two clauses, the second is better recalled than the first; but for two words within the same clause, serial position does not predict recall. In short, items appear to decay clause by clause, so that the accessibility of a word is determined primarily by the clause to which it belongs. This is precisely what one would expect on the assumption that the unit of transfer from one memory system to another is the clause.

Jarvella also tested recall of the meaning of his materials. Here the dependent variable was the subject's ability to answer questions about the content of the stimulus items rather than his ability at rote recall. In this task, virtually no difference in performance was found as a function of the number of clauses intervening between the material to be recalled and the point at which the interruption occurred. Jarvella concludes that when a clause is dismissed from immediate memory it is "recoded" into some semantic representation. It is this representation that is stored for long-term recall.

A result which provides similar support for the view that the completion of a clause is the condition for dismissing linguistic material from immediate memory is reported by Caplan (1972). In this experiment the dependent variable is decision time to determine whether a probe word presented at the end of a two-clause sentence did or did not occur somewhere within the sentence. Stimulus sentences were constructed by tape splicing as in Garrett et al. (1966), so that the clause in which the probe word occurred was manipulated without varying intonational cues or serial distance from the end of the sentence. For example the word "oil" was probed in both (6-3) and (6-4). The response time for sen-

6-3 **"Now that artists are working in oil, prints are rarer."**
6-4 **"Now that artists are working fewer hours, oil prints are rare."**

tences like (6-3), in which the probed word appears in the first clause, was regularly higher than the response time for sentences like (6-4), in which it appears in the second clause. This is the result one would expect if the completion of a clause is the condition under which lexical material is transferred from the most accessible memory system to one that is less accessible.

IMPLEMENTATION OF CLAUSE ANALYSIS

Thus far we have been reviewing experimental results which suggest that an important process in syntax recognition is the grouping together of surface elements that belong to a common sentoid. We have, however, said very little about how this grouping is accomplished; that is, about what kinds of information in the input hearers might use to determine which material to assign to which sentoid. Wingfield and Klein's results, for example, suggest that the prosody of a sentence can provide clues for its clausal decomposition. When constituents belonging to the same sentoid are adjacent in surface structure, they often exhibit a characteristic intonation, and it is worth noting that this sort of prosodic pattern (unlike many others) is sometimes acoustically marked (for example, by acoustic pauses at the end of the clause). Since, however, we can understand prosodically neutral material, or material whose prosody is not acoustically marked, the question remains open what structural features of the input might be exploited to effect its analysis into clauses. It is this question that we now consider.

The "canonical-sentoid" strategy. An early stage in the perceptual analysis of linguistic material is the identification of the sentoids of which the input sentence is composed. By hypothesis, each such sentoid will consist of a *subject-NP* and a verb which may or may not have an object. If we now look at surface sequences, at least for English, we notice a striking fact. There are few surface structures which exhibit this canonical-sentoid form (i.e., which have the form *NP, immediately* *followed by V, immediately followed by NP*) where the surface constituents are not, respectively, the subject phrase, the verb phrase, and the object phrase of a common deep-structure sentoid. If, as we have supposed, the hearer is interested in gathering together surface material which belongs to a common deep sentoid, it would be reasonable for him to employ what we shall call the canonical-sentoid strategy: whenever one encounters a surface sequence *NP V (NP)*, assume that these items are, respectively, subject, verb, and object of a deep sentoid.

One way of determining whether hearers do employ this strategy is to ask whether sentences for which it gives the *wrong* analysis are difficult to understand. We shall presently consider some experimental evidence that suggests that they are. Notice, first, however, the following anecdotal fact. There are sentences like "the horse raced past the barn fell" which exhibit the required surface configuration but which are misanalyzed by the canonical-sentence strategy. It is of some interest that such sentences are hard to understand and that the characteristic misperception is one which seeks to make "the horse" the subject of "raced past" and "the barn" its object. (In fact, of course, the sentence is a reduced form of "the horse which was raced past the barn by someone fell.")

Experimental support for the canonical-sentoid strategy. The first indication that unelaborated surface sequences of the form *NP V (NP)* are characteristically interpreted as sentoids in sentence-recognition tasks comes from a widely noted fact about subjects' performance with doubly self-embedded sentences. If one asks which grammatical relation between constituents the hearer is most likely to interpret correctly in dealing with such a sentence, it turns out that it is invariably the subject-verb relation between the rightmost *NP* in the sequence and the leftmost *VP*. It is therefore notable that this is the only pair of constituents in the sentence to which the hearer can apply the strategy of interpreting *NP V (NP)* sequences as sentoids.

Bever (1968) conducted an experiment designed specifically to demonstrate the effects of the canonical-sentoid strategy. Bever compared "normal" self-embedded sentences with a specially constructed stimulus list having the property that the second *NP* in the sentence was a homophone of some transitive verb. Thus sentences like "The editor the authors the newspapers hired liked died" were compared with sentences like "The editor authors the newspapers hired liked died." In every case, the sentence containing the noun-phrase homophonic to a verb received far fewer correct paraphrases than its control. Moreover, analysis of the incorrect responses showed a significant tendency to misinterpret sequences like "the editor authors the newspaper" as sentoids (i.e., to assign them the interpretation *subject, verb, object*), and this tendency was resistant to learning effects. Apparently the tendency to employ a canonical-sentoid strategy is both strong and unlabile in this sort of situation.

The same sort of observation can be made about sentences which have only a single center embedding; in this case the effect of the canonical-sentoid strategy should be to make *object relatives* (i.e., sentences where the relativized *NP* is the embedded object) harder than *subject relatives* (i.e., sentences where the relativized *NP* is the embedded subject). Compare, for example, sentences like "the girl who kissed John blushed" with sentences like "the girl whom John kissed blushed." The former sentence is a subject relative, while the latter is an object relative. Wanner and Maratsos (1971), who used a modification of Savin and Perchonock's (1965) technique, and Walker (1969), who used a probe latency task, both found some evidence that the subject relative form is easier than the object relative. Presumably the explanation lies in the fact that, in the case of subject relatives, the surface order of constituents parallels the deep order so that the canonical-sentoid strategy can be applied successfully to such sentences. In the case of object relatives, however, the order of surface constituents is: object of embedded sentence (subject of matrix sentence), followed by subject of embedded sentence, followed by embedded *VP*, followed by matrix *VP*. Clearly, the canonical-sentoid strategy does not apply here. It may be worth mentioning that the data which show that passives are harder than the corresponding actives may have an analogous explanation in terms of the hearer's preference for structures to which the canonical-sentoid strategy applies. It is an interesting speculation that "Who has John kissed?" ought to be harder than "Who has kissed John?" if the canonical-sentoid theory is generalizable to sentences which do not contain embeddings.

Thus far we have suggested that the canonical-sentoid strategy will operate given a surface string of the form *NP V (NP)*. It may be added that hearers apparently tend to employ this strategy even for the case of sequences which do *not* have this analysis. That is, there seems to be a tendency to "preanalyze" strings into the *NP V (NP)* form wherever possible, and then to employ the canonical-sentoid strategy on the preanalyzed string. Thus, Blumenthal (1966), in an error analysis of responses to doubly self-embedded sentences, found a dominating tendency to try to treat the initial *NP NP NP* sequence of his stimulus sentences as though it were a compound noun phrase, and the subsequent *VP VP VP* sequence as though it were a compound verb phrase, thus imposing an analysis like that in Figure 6-13 on the whole string. A typical paraphrase for a sentence like "The man the girl the boy liked hated laughed" might thus be "The man, the girl and the boy liked, hated and laughed."

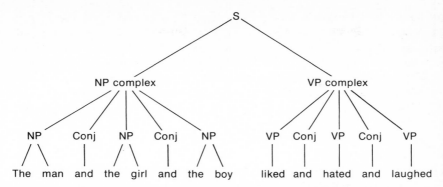

Fig. 6-13. Analysis of paraphrase responses in Blumenthal's experiment (1967).

This tendency to force inputs into forms to which the canonical-sentoid strategy can be applied also explains a finding of Bever and Mehler (1967). They investigated sentences containing verb-particle constructions and adverbs in both immediate and delayed recall. They found *no* tendency for subjects to report sentences with the adverbs and the particles in their presumptive base-structure positions in the immediate recall task. On the contrary, the significant tendency was for all particles and all adverbs (sentence adverbs *and* VP adverbs) to be displaced to the beginning or end of the sentence. For example, a sentence like "The waiter quickly brought back the order" tended to be remembered as having the form "Quickly the waiter brought the order back." (This tendency was reversed with the same materials in the delayed recall task. See Chapter 5.) It thus appears that preanalysis tends to favor any form of the input to which the canonical-sentoid strategy can be applied. In short, the stages in processing appear to be to first reduce the input to the form *NP V (NP)* and then apply the canonical-sentoid strategy.

This line of analysis would seem to be supported by studies like that of Moore (1972). Moore found that subjects who are required to make grammaticality judgments under time pressure look for relations between subject, verb, and object before they look for relations that implicate modifiers on the subject or the object. This would be predicted on the view that main sentoid relations are established early in the recognition process.

Two further remarks should be made about the canonical-sentoid strategy. First, it cannot be the *only* heuristic hearers have available for clausal analysis, since, as we have noted, there are a number of types of sentences for which it fails to yield the right base structures. It is a question of some interest what supplementary strategies might be employed in such cases. Second, the hypothesis that the canonical-sentoid strategy is widely used in sentence analysis predicts certain asymmetries of sentence complexity which are not intuitively obvious and have not yet been experimentally tested. For example, compare "they wanted John killed," where the canonical-sentoid strategy would misanalyze the sequence "John killed" as *subject, verb,* with "they wanted John dead," where no such misanalysis would be forthcoming. The prediction is thus that the first kind of sentence is harder to understand than the second, but there is at present no experimental evidence either way.

LEXICAL ANALYSIS

Suppose that by employing techniques like the canonical-sentoid strategy, the hearer has effected a preliminary determination of the sentoids to which the material in the surface structure of an input belong. Clearly, this determination cannot solve more than part of the sentence-recognition problem. To reconstruct the base structure underlying a sentence, it is necessary to know not only which sentoids occur in that structure but also how they are arranged relative to one another. In this section, we discuss one of the computational procedures that appears to be involved in making decisions about such questions of arrangement.

Let us assume that the speaker-hearer has internalized a *lexicon* which classifies the lexical items in his language according to the deep-structure configurations that they are able to enter. We saw in Chapter 3 that some such assumption is independently plausible on syntactic grounds since lexical insertion transformations must be sensitive to such constraints in determining whether a given lexical item can be inserted into a given sentence frame. The lexicon may be thought of as effecting these classifications by assigning syntactic features to each lexical item. Each such feature, in turn, is thought of as designating a partially specified deep-structure tree. [In effect, the features referred to here are the ones which determine strict subcategorizations in the sense of Chomsky (1965).]

Thus, verbs might receive features like *plus transitive, plus that-complement, plus infinitival complement,* etc. To say of a given verb that it has such a feature is to say of certain deep-structure trees that they are well formed when they appear with that verb as their main verb. Thus, for example, to say of the verb "hit" that it is *plus transitive* is to say that trees like the one in Figure 6-14 are well formed. To say of the verb "expects" that it is *plus that-complement* is to say that trees like the one in Figure 6-15 are well formed, etc. It may be remarked that the claim that lexical items are cross-classified for the sort of base structures in which they appear is one that has considerable empirical import. We could, for example, imagine that the system worked the other way around: that speakers cross-classify types of clauses by the lexical items which can select them. That this is not the case is strongly

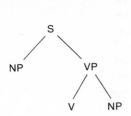

Fig. 6-14. Transitive verb's deep structure.

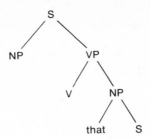

Fig. 6-15. *That*-complement verb's deep structure.

suggested by such considerations as the following. It was noticed by Forster (in press) that subjects find considerable difficulty in completing left-deleted sentences like "_____ the man come running through the trees." ("Completion" here means supplying any phrase in the blank which renders the whole a grammatical sentence.) On the other hand, the completion of the following left-deleted sentence is relatively easy: "_____ saw the man come running through the trees," as is the completion of the right-deleted sentence "John saw _____." (See Chapter 7 for a discussion of this paradigm.)

The explanation is apparently that certain verbs (in particular, perceptual verbs like "see," "hear," "feel," etc.) govern subordinated clauses in which tense is neutralized. In principle, this is a fact which the speaker-hearer might represent in either of two ways: as a constraint upon the class of verb which can be chosen given that one has chosen a subordinate clause with neutralized tense, or as a constraint on the class of subordinated clauses that can be chosen, given that one has chosen a perceptual verb. In fact, the performance asymmetry just cited strongly suggests that the technique of representation actually employed is the latter one. Given only a subordinated structure with neutralized tense, subjects find it difficult to select a verb compatible with that structure. However, given the dominating verb, subjects find relatively little difficulty in supplying subordinated phrasal material which satisfies the strict subcategorization restrictions associated with that verb. The moral appears to be that subjects cross-classify lexical items by the material they dominate and not vice versa.

Experimental evidence for this point comes from a study by Moore (1972). We referred briefly to an aspect of that study in our discussion of the canonical-sentoid strategy. In Moore's procedure, subjects were presented with a sentence from which one of the content words had been deleted. A "candidate" word for the blank was then presented and decision times for determining the grammaticality of the resultant sentence were measured. The time taken to determine the compatibility of a verb with a given *subject-* or *object-NP* was significantly greater than the time for the corresponding decision about an *NP* given a frame with the verb specified. This result would follow given that verbs are cross-classified by the types of phrases they select.

For these and related reasons, we assume that the lexical items of a language are associated, in the speaker-hearer's lexicon, with sets of constraints on the deep structures in which these items can appear. If this is correct, then a plausible assumption is that the hearer employs the lexicon in sentence recognition by postulating for a given sentence just those types of deep structure compatible with the lexical items that the sentence contains. Since, moreover, it appears to be the verb of a sentence which often dictates the more general features of the geometry of the deep structure, we may assume, as a first approximation, that an early step in sentence recognition involves postulating any deep structure for a sentence that is compatible with the lexical analysis of its verbs.

Experimental investigations of the lexical analysis strategy.   Fodor, Garrett, and Bever (1968) performed two related experiments designed precisely to test the hypothesis that the postulation of deep structures compatible with strict subcategorization restrictions on lexical items is among the processes involved in syntax recognition. They argued as follows.

There is a difference between the lexical analysis of "slap," and similar verbs, and the lexical analysis of "like," and similar verbs. While "slap" can occur only in transitive constructions, "like" can occur not only with a direct object but also with a variety of complements. Thus verbs of the latter kind are compatible with a wider range of hypotheses about the deep structures of sentences in which they appear than verbs of the former kind. This suggests, in turn, that sentences containing verbs like "like" ought to be more difficult for subjects to understand than sentences containing verbs like "slap." In short, if the sentence-recognition routine exploits information about the lexical structures of a sentence's verbs as a source of hypotheses about the base structure of the sentence, then we might expect that the greater the variety of deep-structure configurations that the lexicon associates with a verb, the more difficult will be understanding sentences containing the verb.

This hypothesis was tested with self-embedded sentences in a paraphrase task and with sentences of a variety of structural types in an anagram task. In the first experiment, stimulus materials included pairs of sentences like "The box the man the child *liked* carried was empty" and "The box the man the child *slapped* carried was empty." It should be noticed that, in both these sentences, the manipulated verbs are appearing as transitives; that is, both sentences have precisely the same type of deep structure. The relevant difference is just that whereas "slap" occurs only in transitive constructions, "like" *can* appear both in transitive constructions and with a variety of types of complements. If we assume that the lexical analyses of "slap" and "like" are contributing hypotheses about the possible base structures of the stimulus sentences, then we must predict that the sentence containing "like" will be harder than the sentence containing "slap." This was, in fact, the observed result; subjects were significantly less accurate in immediate paraphrase of self-embedded sentences of the "like" type than those of the "slap" type.

Not all the comparisons in Fodor, Garrett, and Bever were between sentences with pure transitive verbs and sentences containing verbs which take both direct objects and a large variety of complements. There were also sentences containing an intermediate type of verb (like "see," "know," "decide") which enter more types of deep structure than verbs like "slap" but fewer types than verbs like "like." Bever (1970) reanalyzed Fodor, Garrett, and Bever's data and showed that the complexity ordering predicted by these considerations was in fact borne out. Subjects were most accurate with sentences containing verbs like "slap," next most accurate with sentences containing verbs like "see," and least accurate for sentences containing verbs like "like."

Experiments with doubly self-embedded sentences are always suspect simply because of the oddity of the stimulus materials. Fodor, Garrett, and Bever attempted to deal with this difficulty by performing an experiment in which the contrast between sentences containing verbs like "like" and verbs like "slap" was examined in constructions other than self-embeddings. Stimulus sentences included pairs like "the letter which the secretary expected was late" and "the letter which the secretary mailed was late." The words constituting such sentences were typed on small pieces of file card and were placed haphazardly before the subject, who was required to arrange them serially to form a grammatical and meaningful sentence.

The data were analyzed according to the number of correct completions, the number of erroneously reported completions, and response times for acceptable completions. Differences between the lexical analyses of the manipulated verbs did not predict differences in response time, but they did predict differences in error scores. For verbs compatible with a relatively large number of types of deep structures, subjects produced significantly more errors and failures to complete the task than they did for verbs compatible with a relatively small number of types of deep structures. Moreover, informal analysis of the errors revealed the interesting fact that mistakes involving verbs of the latter type tended to be minor misorderings or substitutions, while errors with verbs of the former type tended to be major violations of syntactic form.

The finding that center-embedded sentences containing verbs which accept a relatively large variety of deep structures are harder to paraphrase than sentences with simple transitive verbs was replicated by Hakes (1971). However, Hakes did *not* find an influence of verb complexity on the "monitor task" (in which the dependent variable is the subjects' reaction time for the detection of an antecedently specified phoneme in the test sentence). Clearly this negative result is a source of difficulty for the present hypothesis, since reaction times in the monitor task do generally seem to vary with the syntactic complexity of stimulus sentences (see Foss, 1969).

Though the monitor-task results of Hakes must temper our confidence in the effects of lexical complexity, the results of work by Holmes and Forster (1972) with the RSVP technique provide some additional evidence for a lexical-analysis strategy in sentence perception. Holmes and Forster found that one-clause sentences with complex verbs are more difficult than one-clause sentences with simple verbs precisely as the lexical analysis would predict. Their results for two-clause sentences are more difficult to assess, however. First of all, Holmes and Forster did *not* find an overall complexity difference between two-clause and one-clause sentences. Yet such a difference would be predicted both from their own finding that the verbs used in the two-clause sentences were in general more complex than the verbs of the one-clause sentences, and from the results of Forster (1970) discussed earlier (see page 339). In fact, the failure to find the expected difference between one- and two-clause sentences is attributable to a striking difference in the effects of the complement types that were tested: *VP for-to* complements (like "John persuaded Bill to leave") turned out to be substantially easier than *NP for-to* and *NP that* complements; indeed, not significantly more difficult than one-sentoid sentences. As Holmes and Forster point out, the *NP*-complement verbs are compatible with a wider range of structures than are the *VP* complements and, hence, the contrast among the types of complements is in accord with the lexical-analysis strategy; the ease of the two-clause *VP* complements relative to the one-clause sentences is not.

Thus far we have been speaking in a way that may suggest that the strategies of segmentation and lexical analysis are distinct and ordered in real time, so that the application of the former precedes the application of the latter. This is, however, implausible on a priori grounds, since it is clear that strict subcategorization information about lexical items can be used in determining segmentation. That some such process does go on is suggested by the results of Bever et al. (1969) and

Fodor et al. (1974). We mentioned above that these studies demonstrated a difference between click displacements for *NP* and *VP for-to* complements at the position immediately following the complement verb. The boundary effects were significantly stronger for the *NP* complements. We now note that for Bever et al. this difference arose almost entirely to shifts in the position of clicks objectively located *in* the verb. This pattern of results is plausibly explained by reference to the lexical analyses of the two verbs. For example, sentences containing "expect" as a main verb will almost invariably exhibit a sentoid boundary immediately after that verb. Contrariwise, sentences containing "persuade" as a main verb will always have an *NP* direct object in deep structure. It is plausible to assume that subjects use this information in sentence processing to achieve a sentoidal decomposition of the input. Roughly, given an *NP V* sequence where the verb is "expect," postulate an *S*-boundary after the *V*; given an *NP V NP* sequence where the verb is "persuade," postulate an *S*-boundary after the *object-NP*. The assumption that subjects do in fact employ some such strategy will explain Bever, Lackner, and Kirk's data. Moreover, such obvious counterxamples as "John expects Mary" are no embarrassment to the plausible hypothesis that they derive from deep structures like {John expects Mary (to come)}.

SURFACE-STRUCTURE ANALYSIS

We have thus far discussed two kinds of strategies that hearers may employ in recovering the deep structure of an input sequence: clause analysis, which is concerned with determining the sentoidal decomposition of the sentence; and lexical analysis, which is concerned with determining the dominance relations that hold among its sentoids.

Even considered as a first approximation, however, this clearly cannot be the whole story. For, a given lexical item may, if we consider its entire distribution across the language, be compatible with a wide variety of types of deep-structure trees. But, barring cases of ambiguity, only one deep-structure tree will represent the appropriate analysis of any given sentence in which the item occurs. Thus, suppose we grant that the hearer appeals to a lexicon to assign putative deep structures to a sentence, and that the putative analyses he assigns must be compatible with, and are determined by, the lexical entries for the words in the sentence. We have left open the question of how the hearer decides between analyses when a lexical item appearing in a sentence is compatible with more than one deep-structure assignment. It is obvious that the surface structure of a sentence must contain sufficient material to permit such decisions and that the hearer must be in possession of computational procedures adequate for the exploitation of that material.

Thus, for example, in analyzing a sentence like "John expected Mary to leave," we assume that the subject must ask which of the deep-structure configurations possible for "expect" the sentence exemplifies. In particular, we assume that the subject knows that "expect" can take *infinitival* or *that* complementation, or, possibly, a direct object. Since he is capable of determining which of these patterns is exemplified by any unambiguous sentence containing "expect," we must assume that the subject has and applies tests for each of the various base-structure configurations the verb may enter. It is at this stage that the appeal to surface-structure features presumably plays its role. Thus, it is self-evident that the analysis of "John expected Mary to leave" as an example of *for-to* complementation must be facilitated by the presence of "to" in the surface structure of that sentence. Similarly, the *poss-ing* interpretation of "John expected Mary's leaving" must be facilitated by recognition of the surface *s, ing,* etc. In such cases we might say that the surface material is a "spelling" of certain deep-structure features and configurations much as /z/, /iz/, and /s/ are possible spellings of the English plural morpheme. On this analogy, the heuristics available to the hearer must specify *which* surface configurations spell which deep configurations in the language he speaks.

The action of surface-structure markers in facilitating the recognition of deep-structure features like complement type can sometimes be quite dramatic. For example, *that* complements are the only ones in English which satisfy both of the two following conditions. First, they govern subordinated clauses which contain tense ("He thinks that John will be late" but not "*He hopes for John to will be late"); and second, they contain deletable complementizers ("He thinks *that* John is an idiot" versus "He thinks John is an idiot"). In particular, complements like *whether*, which also govern subordinated sentences containing tense, are *not* deletable. Thus, we have "I wonder whether John will come" but not "*I wonder John will come."

Since *that* is the only deletable complementizer which can govern subordinated structures containing tense, it is plausible to hypothesize that the presence of marked tense in a subordinated structure should be an extremely efficient clue to *that* complementation in sentences where the complementizer has been deleted. There are some examples that are persuasive on this point. Notice that "He felt the child trembled" is heard as a reduced form of "He felt that the child trembled" and as unrelated to the (tenseless) "He felt the child tremble." Correspondingly, "He felt the children tremble" is ambiguous between the two types of complement, depending on whether "tremble" is heard as tensed. In these cases, it seems perfectly evident that an effective clue to the analysis of the complement is being given by the presence or absence of tense in the surface structure of the subordinated clause. In fact, since "He felt the child trembled" and "He felt the child tremble" form, in the relevant respect, a minimal pair, it seems evident that *only* the presence of marked tense in the subordinated clause can be relevant to the operation of whatever perceptual heuristics are involved in distinguishing between them.

In short, the present suggestion is that one procedure that ought to lead to increasing the performance complexity of sentences is the elimination, or confounding, of surface-structure features which can serve to "spell" features of the deep structure underlying the sentence. A body of experimental and anecdotal literature is rapidly developing on this point.

Consider first some gross facts about relative complexity. We remarked above that in a sentence like "John felt the girl trembled," the recovery of the underlying form of complementation depends upon recognizing the tensed or tenseless character of the subordinated verb. In these sentences, that would appear to be the only clue hearers have to the relevant deep structure, and it is interesting that subjects very often find such sentences difficult to understand. In particular, many subjects have some difficulty in "hearing" the *that*-complement version correctly. It is equally interesting that this difficulty can be remedied simply by increasing the redundancy with which deep-structure information is specified in the surface structure. The most obvious way of doing this is by restoring the lost "that" to the reduced sentence. Indeed Hakes (1972), using the monitor task, found that with the target phone on the first content word of the *subject-NP* in a *that* complement reaction times are significantly less when the complementizer is present than when it has been deleted. For the present kind of example, however, there is also a more interesting way of increasing the redundancy with which the character of the underlying complement structure is marked in the surface material.

For-to-complement constructions take pronouns in the object case as the subject of the subordinated sentence, but *that* complements take pronouns in the subjective case in that position. Thus, we have "John believes *her* to be an idiot" but not "*John believes *she* to be an idiot," and conversely we have "John believes that *she* is an idiot" but not "*John believes that *her* is an idiot." *That* complements continue to differ from infinitival complements in this way even after reduction of the complementizer. Notice the difference between "John hoped *she* left" and "John asked *her* to leave."

In short, the case of pronouns in a sentence is sometimes determined by the complement structure of the sentence. It is therefore interesting to notice the striking intuitive difference in complexity between "John felt the girl tremble" and "John felt the girl trembled," on the one hand, and "John felt her tremble" and "John felt she trembled," on the other. It seems immediately obvious that by introducing pronouns whose case is determined by the complement structure of the sentence, we increase the richness with which deep-structure relations are marked in surface structure, and get a corresponding decrease in perceptual complexity.

Another result which points to the same conclusion depends on the optional deletion of relative pronouns. Fodor and Garrett (1967) found that the elimination of relative pronouns in center-embedded sentences (e.g., differences like the one between "The man that the girl knew got sick" and "The man the girl knew got sick") increased the difficulty subjects have in paraphrasing such sentences. This finding for paraphrases was replicated by Hakes and Cairns (1970). Both Hakes and Cairns and Hakes and Foss (1970) also found a significant increase in monitor-task times as a function of relative pronoun deletion.

These results make it fairly clear that the unreduced versions of sentences with relative clauses are easier for subjects to process than the corresponding reduced sentences. Presumably, the facilitation ought to be attributed to the fact that the relative pronoun provides a surface-structure coding of the subordination relations among the sentoids in the deep structures of the sentences.

It is clear, in any event, that a proper comprehension of sentences requires not only segmenting them into clauses and labeling the grammatical relations among the phrases they contain but also specifying the relations of subordination and superordination which hold among the clauses themselves. Apparently, attending to the presence of a relative pronoun provides one kind of strategy for establishing such relations, and the analysis of the lexical structure of verbs, discussed above, may provide another. We turn now to a third strategy for analyzing surface structure which may be used in recovering the subordination relations among clauses in a sentence. The direct experimental evidence that subjects use (6-5) in the perceptual analysis of sentences is modest at best.

6-5 **Take the verb which immediately follows the initial noun of a sentence as the main verb unless there is a surface-structure mark of an embedding.**

But there are some purely distributional facts about English which might be accounted for on the assumption that some such strategy is implicated in sentence perception.

Consider first the experimental data. If subjects normally assume that the first verb of a sentence is its main verb, sentences for which this assumption is false should, in general, be more difficult than those for which it is not. There is some indication that this is true. For example, Clark and Clark (1968) reported that sentences in which a subordinate clause preceded a main clause were more poorly recalled than those with the reverse clause order. There is also a relation between the surface order of main and subordinate clauses and subjects' ratings of the comprehensibility of sentences. For judged ease of comprehension,

Weksel and Bever (1966) found that nominals in subject position ("That Mary was happy surprised Max") are rated as harder to understand than nominals in object position ("It surprised Max that Mary was happy"); that preposed adverbials ("When Mary left, Max was happy") are rated as harder than normally positioned adverbials ("Max was happy when Mary left"); and that sentence initial subordinated conjuncts ("Although Mary had left, Max was happy") are ranked harder than sentence final ones ("Max was happy although Mary had left"). Subjects' judgments of the relative comprehensibility of sentences have been shown to correlate with various indices of their structural complexity (Schwartz, Sparkman, and Deese, 1970). Thus the rating differences reported by Weksel and Bever (and the recall findings of Clark and Clark) may be tentatively taken as an indication that the surface order of main and subordinate structures is significantly related to their ease of comprehension, and that the order *main + subordinate* is easier than the order *subordinate + main*.

There is only one available direct test of the perceptual effects of the order of main and subordinate clauses; using the RSVP technique, Holmes (1973) found that sentences with preposed adverbial clauses were more difficult than those with normally positioned adverbials, and similarly for *NP* complements in subject and in object positions. ("The girl's leaving home so suddenly amazed all her friends" was more difficult than, e.g., "The lawyer resented my aunt giving orders to the staff.") However, Holmes did *not* find this pattern for center-branching versus right-branching relative clauses (e.g., relatives which are subordinated to the *subject-NP* of a sentence versus those subordinated to the *object-NP*).[2]

These results suggest a perceptual consequence of the order of main and subordinate clauses that is compatible with the existence of a strategy like (6-5); if subjects normally take a sentence initial *NV* sequence as containing the main verb, then rejection of that perceptual assumption would presumably increase comprehension difficulty. But it should be emphasized that the experimental results do not demand such a conclusion. Subjects' preference for surface structures of the form *main clause, subordinate clause* may be only a special case of a more general preference for placing elaborately branched subtrees (so-called "heavy

---

[2] Center-branching relatives (in which the subordinate clause precedes the *VP* of the main clause) were significantly *easier* than right-branching relatives. This reversal of the pattern found for adverbials and *NP* complements might be attributed to special characteristics of the RSVP technique (see Holmes, 1973) or to some special property of such sentences—e.g., that a portion of the main clause precedes the subordinated structure even though the subordinated clause precedes the main verb.

structures") at the end of the surface sentence. If this is true, then the pattern of results we have tentatively attributed to a perceptual strategy may in fact have a quite different explanation. (We shall return to this question in Chapter 7.) Suffice it to say here that the findings we have just surveyed do not allow us to choose between a theory which explains the preference for the order *main clause, subordinate clause* in terms of a perceptual strategy and a theory which explains the bias in terms of short-term-memory limitations. These two explanations are not mutually exclusive of course; subjects may find difficulties both with structures which violate a perceptual strategy and those which place a heavy demand on short-term memory.

What makes the perceptual strategy view appealing is primarily its apparent relation to constraints that English syntax imposes upon the structure of sentences whose first surface clause is an embedding: namely, that such clauses must be marked *as* embeddings in surface structure. Indeed, Bever and Langendoen (1971) have argued that this constraint on English may itself be an instance of a linguistic universal, stated in (6-6). Bever and Langendoen provide some cross-language evidence for the

6-6 A subordinate clause is marked as subordinate by the end of its verb phrase if it is the first clause in a sentence, but may go unmarked if it follows the main verb.

universal status of (6-6). We will restrict ourselves to the situation in English.

In English, a heterogeneous set of syntactic restrictions apparently fulfill the function of ensuring that subordinated clauses are so marked when they are the first clause in surface structure. For example, consider the behavior of the complementizers "that" and "the fact" in sentences in which the complement clause is *not* initial, as in sentences like (6-7). One might conclude from such examples that the complementizers can be freely deleted; that such a conclusion is incorrect is shown by the examples in (6-8). The generalization here is clear: when the subordinated clause occurs first in surface structure, one of the complementizers can be deleted *so long as the other remains.* However, no such restriction applies when the complement clause follows the main verb. We can explain this asymmetry by reference to the presumed strategy of taking the first *NV* sequence as containing the main verb. So long as the initial *V* in sentences like (6-8) is explicitly *marked* as subordinate by some property of the sequence, this strategy will not apply; conversely, if sentence initial subordinate *NV* sequences were not so marked, such sentences would be misanalyzed.

6-7 John noticed the fact that Sam is a fool.
   ?John noticed the fact Sam is a fool.
   John noticed that Sam is a fool.
   John noticed Sam is a fool.

6-8   The fact that Sam was a fool was noticed by John.
      That Sam was a fool was noticed by John.
      ?The fact Sam was a fool was noticed by John.
      *Sam was a fool was noticed by John.

A similar account of syntactic constraints on deletion of relative pronouns also seems reasonable. Note that the relative pronoun in (6-9)
may be deleted while that in (6-10) may not. This is just the constraint
one might expect, given a perceptual heuristic that takes an unmarked
sentence initial *NV* sequence as containing the verb of the main clause.
Note that cases like (6-11) in which *relative pronoun + is* is optionally
deletable are not exceptions to this interpretation since the embedding
is marked (by the progressive ending on the verb in the absence of an
auxiliary). However, structures like that of (6-12) with a passive embedding do provide counterexamples to the deletion constraint we have
been considering. Truncated passives with *wh + is* deletion can yield
surface structures in which a sentence initial embedding is not marked
as such.

6-9   The boy (who) Mary kissed blushed.
6-10   The boy who kissed Mary blushed.
6-11   The man (who is) leaving Chicago plays basketball.
6-12   The boat (which was) floated down the river (by *NP*) sank.

It might seem that there are only two possible reactions to the existence of examples like (6-12). Either the kinds of positional constraints
on deletion that we have been discussing are not universal, or they are
not attributable to the operation of a perceptual strategy like (6-5). It certainly must be admitted that since there are exceptions to (6-6) even in
English, (6-6) can at best be a statistical universal. Indeed, even if there
were no examples like (6-12), the existence of sentences like (6-13)
would be enough to show that (6-6) does not hold with perfect generality. In such cases, complementizer deletion is *mandatory* after fronting a
that complement [i.e., sentences like (6-14) are ungrammatical].

6-13   Bob is leaving, said Bill.
       Mary is neurotic, it seems.

6-14   *that Bob is leaving, said Bill
       *that Mary is neurotic, it seems

On the other hand, in many cases deletions do appear to be constrained in the way that (6-6) predicts, and the exceptions for English
are either restricted to passive embeddings with weak verbs like (6-12)
or intonationally marked like (6-13). Since it is conceivable that structural features of languages should reflect the sentence-processing strategies of speaker-hearers but that the correspondence between the syntax and the heuristics should be less than perfect, the question of the
universal status of such generalizations as (6-6) is extremely difficult to
evaluate.

For the present discussion the question of whether (6-6) is a universal is less interesting than the question of whether the deletion constraints on relatives and complements in English do provide evidence for the existence of some such perceptual heuristic as (6-5). Notice that the existence of (6-5) is, in fact, supported by cases like (6-12). That sentence is hard to understand in just the way that (6-5) predicts; listeners tend to assign main-clause status to the sequence "the boat floated down the river" and are thus unable to assign a function to the last verb ("sank") without recomputing the structure of the sentence. The attribution of this effect to a heuristic like (6-5) is reinforced by the straightforward intelligibility of (6-15), where the embedding uses a strong verb whose past and past participle forms differ; the overt marking of the embedding blocks (6-5) and listeners do not misanalyze the initial sequence.

6-15   The fish eaten in Boston stank.

In several of the examples we have been considering, inflections prevent misanalyses which would otherwise arise from the application of perceptual heuristics like (6-5). As we remarked above, exactly this same observation can be made about the constraint on the deletion of relative pronouns from sentences like (6-9). Bever and Langendoen (1971) have argued that these phenomena are connected in that the historical development of restrictions on the deletion of relative pronouns was correlated with the disappearance of inflectional markings for embeddings. At one stage in the history of English, sentences like (6-16a) could appear as versions of sentences like (6-16b). Such sentences would not be misanalyzed because NP's like "the girl" were generally marked by inflections when they occurred in the nonsubjective case. As such inflections dropped from the language, such sequences presumably became perceptually confusing; Bever and Langendoen argue that it is the possibility of this confusion which underlies the emergence of restrictions that require the relative pronoun to be present whenever there is a danger of the $N+V$ sequence being misinterpreted as a surface clause. Once again, however, even if this explanation is correct, the correspondence between structural facts and perceptual heuristics which such historical changes effect is clearly less than perfect. Modern English permits sentences like (6-17), which contain a surface $N+V$ sequence whose elements are drawn from different sentoids. If the language is constructed to avoid such sequences' being interpreted as *subject + verb*, one might expect a constraint on the reduction transformation which derives (6-17) from (6-18), corresponding to the constraint which does block the derivation of (6-16a) from (6-16b).

6-16   a.   I like the girl is here
b.   I like the girl who is here.

6-17 **They wanted Bill shot.**
6-18 **They wanted Bill to be shot.**

To summarize: though the experimental facts are thus far in-conclusive, such studies as there are support a heuristic like (6-5), and examples like (6-12) versus (6-15) strongly suggest that English speakers do employ such a strategy in perceptually analyzing sentences. It is in-triguing to speculate further that the compatibility of certain constraints on English-deletion transformations may actually be explicable by ref-erence to the assumption that (6-5) functions in sentence processing and, more generally, that some linguistic universals may be explicable by reference to the computational procedures that speaker-hearers use to process sentences. Clearly, as things now stand, this *is* speculative; first, because our knowledge of sentence-processing heuristics is at present rudimentary, and second, because the predicted effect of processing heuristics on syntax would be at best imperfect, and we have no a priori measure of *how much* convergence is required to prove the hypothesis that the properties of the language reflect the heuristics that speaker-hearers use. In spite of these limitations, however, it seems to us that this kind of teleological analysis provides an interesting way of integrating linguistic and psycholinguistic findings and, for that reason, deserves to be pursued. At the very least, arguments from the existence of linguistic universals to the innateness of language compe-tence presuppose that not all syntactic universals have teleological ex-planations (see Chapter 8). Until cases like the ones we have been dis-cussing are thoroughly examined, the status of that presumption will remain unclear.

THE PERCEPTUAL EFFECTS OF AMBIGUITY

The discussion of perceptual strategies in syntax recognition that we have provided clearly does not amount to a general theory of how speakers recover information about the syntactic structure of utterances in their language. Nevertheless, some of the principles we outlined may have fairly broad application to problems in psycholinguistics. We turn now to one such case.

Most sentences contain some ambiguous parts, and many sentences are fully ambiguous. Yet the effect of context in selecting among read-ings of ambiguities is normally so efficient that ambiguities are rarely noticed and do not obviously increase the difficulty of sentences in which they occur. Psycholinguists have long been interested in describ-ing the way the sentence-processing system handles ambiguous mate-rial, though they have encountered numerous frustrations in attempt-ing to do so.

There are, patently, two broad theoretical options. One the one hand, one might imagine that the perceptual system is a parallel processor in the sense that given a portion of a sentence which has n possible linguistic structures, each of the n structures is computed and "carried" in short-term storage. If a disambiguating item is encountered, all but one of the n analyses are rejected, with the residual analysis being the one which is stored. If no disambiguating material is encountered, all n analyses are retained, and the sentence is represented as ambiguous in n ways.

Alternatively, one might suppose that the system is a serial processor in the sense that given a portion of a sentence which has n possible linguistic structures, only one of the n structures is computed. This structure is accepted as the correct analysis unless disambiguating material incompatible with it is encountered. If such material *is* encountered, then the processor must go back to the ambiguous material and compute a different analysis.

There are obviously a variety of modifications and blends of these two proposals that one might consider. Nevertheless, practically any model which is parallel in spirit will differ in an important way from any model which is fundamentally serial: parallel theories predict that the computational difficulty of a sentence ought, in general, to increase as a function of the number of unresolved ambiguities it contains; serial theories do not. This is because parallel theories claim that each time we encounter an n-ways ambiguous portion of a sentence, we must compute and store n paths of analysis, with n reducing to one only if disambiguating material is encountered. On the serial model, however, ambiguity should cause increased computational loads only when the first analysis assigned turns out to be the wrong one; i.e., only when the character of the subsequent input is incompatible with whatever reading was assigned to the ambiguous material.

A number of experiments have been addressed to the question of whether the occurrence of ambiguous material in a sentence does, in general, increase the difficulty of the sentence. The results are superficially equivocal. We shall briefly report some studies that make it look as though the answer is "yes"; then we shall report some others that make it look as though the answer is "no." We will then suggest a possible resolution of the dilemma which depends on the kinds of perceptual mechanisms we outlined above.

Consider first three experiments which support the view that the presence of ambiguous material does increase performance difficulty on tasks which involve understanding sentences. MacKay (1966) found that the time required to complete an ambiguous sentence fragment (e.g., "After taking the right turn at the intersection, I...") is longer than the time to complete a corresponding fragment which is not ambiguous (e.g., "After taking the left turn at the intersection, I ..."). This result held for subjects who did *not* report noticing the ambiguity of the stimulus fragment during the experiment. It can thus be viewed as evidence for the parallel account if one assumes that the increased latency is attributable to response interference (i.e., interference from the unnoticed, but presumably computed, reading of the ambiguity).

Foss (1970) used the phoneme-monitor task to investigate the effects of ambiguity on sentence comprehension. He contrasted reaction times for phoneme detection in corresponding environments immediately following ambiguous and unambiguous sequences in sentences. He found that reaction time was slower following the ambiguous material. We noted earlier (page 352) that phoneme-monitor times appear to be related to the computational load imposed by a sentence during its processing; the increased reaction time in this experiment presumably reflects an increase in computational load in the period immediately following an ambiguity. Thus Foss's result and MacKay's result would seem to have the same explanation: multiple readings for the ambiguous material are computed at the point of occurrence of the ambiguity (or shortly thereafter).

A different kind of demonstration of the simultaneous availability of both readings of an ambiguity comes from an experiment by Lackner and Garrett (1973). Subjects were dichotically presented with an ambiguous sentence and a disambiguating context sentence (i.e., ambiguous sentence in one ear and, simultaneously, biasing context in the other). Subjects were told to attend to the ear to which the ambiguous sentence was presented, and attention to the ambiguous sentence was further assured by presenting it at a level 5 to 10 decibels more intense than the context sentence. Immediately following the presentation, subjects were required to provide a paraphrase of the attended sentence. Under these conditions, subjects were unable to report any information about the content of the unattended channel other than that it was speech;[3] in particular, they did not notice either that there were ambiguities in the attended channel or that there was a relation between the content of the two channels.

Thus, so far as the conscious reports of the subjects are concerned, there appears to have been total isolation of the two sentences. Yet Lackner and Garrett found a strong effect of the biasing contexts on the readings assigned to the ambiguous sentence (determined from the paraphrases Ss gave). For example, when the ambiguous sentence "Visiting relatives can be a bore" was presented with a neutral context

---

[3] At the levels used in the experiment, either message presented monaurally was easily understandable.

("the car is being repaired"), slightly more than half the subjects (0.54) assigned the subject nominal reading (R1: the relatives visit), and slightly less than half (0.46) assigned the object nominal reading (R2: someone visits the relatives). When presented in the R1 bias context ("I hate relatives who visit often"), 0.80 of the subjects assigned the R1 reading; when presented in the R2 bias context ("I don't like to visit relatives"), only 0.17 of the subjects assigned the R1 reading (i.e., 0.83 assigned the R2 reading). A substantial majority of the sentences tested showed this pattern; i.e., the proportion of subjects who assigned a reading compatible with the bias context was greater in the bias condition than in the neutral condition. This overall pattern of confirmation was preserved when the ambiguities were considered by type: lexical, surface bracketing, and deep structure.

It is hard to see how this result could have arisen unless subjects were in fact computing both interpretations of the ambiguities. Without such a parallel computation, subjects would not be in a position to determine the relevance of the biasing materials (i.e., there would be nothing for the bias context to affect). This assumes, of course, that subjects did not consciously alter their interpretations to correspond to the context after presentation of the stimuli. Such an assumption seems reasonable, given that subjects produced their paraphrases immediately following the stimuli and given their inability to provide any report of the content of the biasing channel.

These experiments argue for a behavioral effect of unnoticed ambiguities; there are, however, experiments which seem to support the opposite conclusion. For example, Foss, Bever, and Silver (1968) report a result which indicates that only one reading of an ambiguous sentence is normally available to a given subject at a given time. This conclusion is hard to reconcile with the parallel account, on which all readings of an ambiguity are assumed to be simultaneously available. Foss et al. presented both unambiguous and ambiguous sentences immediately followed by pictures. Subjects were asked to decide whether the picture made the sentence true or false. Pictures were sometimes pertinent to the more frequently favored reading and sometimes pertinent to the less frequently favored reading. The relevant finding is that response latencies for the ambiguous sentence were longer than latencies to the unambiguous controls only in the latter condition. Foss et al. concluded that their results "support a model of normal sentence comprehension which states that Ss typically assign only one immediate interpretation to an ambiguous sentence. Only if that interpretation is found to be incorrect does S reinterpret the sentence" (p. 306). Foss et al. has recently been replicated by Cairns (1970) using a paradigm in which the picture is replaced by a disambiguating sentence. (It should be remarked, however, that these results could be interpreted as compatible with a model in which the readings of an ambiguous sentence are computed in parallel but tested for truth value serially, with the most-favored reading tested first.)

Carey, Mehler, and Bever (1970) used the same experimental paradigm as Foss et al., except subjects were preset to expect a sentence with one of the two phrase structures illustrated in Figure 6-16. Subjects then heard an ambiguous sentence like "They are lecturing doctors" followed by pictures which made the sentence true or false on one of its readings. Two results are pertinent to the present discussion. First, subjects who heard the ambiguous material as having the structure for which they had been set exhibited latencies essentially indistinguishable from those of subjects with analogous unambiguous material; that is, their behavior appears to have been completely uninfluenced by the existence of the unattended reading. Second, subjects who heard the ambiguous sentence as having the structure for which they had *not* been set, exhibited characteristically *longer* latencies than did subjects who were set for the reading they heard. This increase in latency is not easy to explain on a parallel model, which holds that both readings ought to be simultaneously available.

How are these apparently conflicting results to be reconciled? It will be remembered that a main conclusion of our discussion of sentence recognition is that the clause is the primary unit of analysis, and that the segmentation of a sentence into clauses is an important early step in computing its structural description. Specifically, we suggested that material is recoded and dismissed from short-term storage in sentence recognition on a clause-by-clause basis.

The application of these remarks to the perception of ambiguous material is straightforward. If the kind of model we have been arguing for

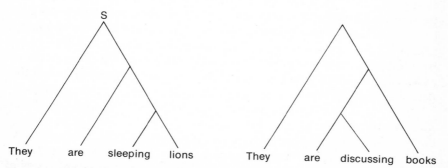

Fig. 6-16. Examples of structures Ss were presented with for the two experimental conditions testing the sentence "They are lecturing doctors" (from Carey, Mehler, and Bever, 1970).

is correct, higher-level decisions about input material, including semantic decisions, are in general made after the assignment of that material to a clause. We might therefore expect that decisions about the disambiguation of ambiguous items will be left open within clauses but closed after the clause boundary. To put it slightly differently, this model predicts that if ambiguous material increases computational load, this will be revealed only if tested prior to the immediately following clause boundary. Several considerations recommend this view.

First, there is no conflict between the ambiguity studies reviewed above, given the assumption that clause boundaries establish limits beyond which interpretive decisions about ambiguous materials are not delayed. A common feature of the studies which found no increase of difficulty associated with the presence of ambiguity was that the testing occurred *after* the completion of the clause containing the ambiguous material (in fact, after the end of the sentence). Conversely, in the experiments which *do* show an effect of ambiguity, a common feature is the demand that subjects determine their response *before* the end of the stimulus sentence. MacKay's experiment, for example, illustrates this interaction between the locus of the response demand and the effect of ambiguity. In a (1968) reanalysis, Bever showed that most of the effect of ambiguity in the data MacKay reports derives from cases in which the sentence fragment presents an ambiguity *in an incomplete clause.*

The interpretation of clause boundaries as limiting points for measurable effects of ambiguity was tested by Bever, Garrett, and Hurtig (1973). They used a sentence-completion task similar to that of MacKay but explicitly varied the clausal character of the stimulus fragments in which the ambiguities were presented: one-third of the fragments ended internal to a clause (e.g., "Although the solution was clear in...."), at a clause (e.g., "Although the solution was clear in class...."), and internal to a new clause (e.g., "Although the solution was clear in class, it...."). Completion times for ambiguities were contrasted with those for unambiguous controls (e.g., "Although the answer was clear in....") in each of the fragment types. Significantly slower completion times for the fragments containing an ambiguity were found only in the incomplete-clause condition. This is the result found in the reanalysis of MacKay's data and suggests that the increase in computational difficulty associated with ambiguity is limited by clausal boundaries.

There are a number of questions about the effects of ambiguity on sentence processing that we have not considered. For example, most of the experiments tested three types of ambiguity: lexical, surface bracketing, and deep structure. Results have varied across these types, and, indeed, there is good reason to believe that the different types of ambiguity should have different effects on the perceptual analysis of sentences.[4] Similarly, we have not explored one other interesting consequence of a parallel processing view: namely, if one accepts such a view, there should be performance tasks for which the presence of an ambiguity is *facilitating*. There is some evidence that this is so. See Bever, Garrett, and Hurtig (1973) for discussion of both these points.

Finally, we should note that a variety of paradigms have been used to test the effects of ambiguity, and it is not perfectly clear which effects ought to be associated with on-line sentence analysis and which with subsequent interpretive or evaluative processes. However, the significant results of Foss with the phoneme-monitor task and those of Lackner and Garrett with the dichotic-listening task make a fairly strong case for the claim that there is an increase in computational load associated with ambiguity, and that some sort of parallel processing is what accounts for that increase. The question of whether such effects are limited by clause boundaries internal to sentences is at present an intriguing, but less clearly established, claim.

CONCLUDING REMARKS

A grammar associates every sentence with a syntactic and phonological representation. The problem of sentence recognition is that of characterizing a device which takes an acoustic representation of an utterance as input and provides the appropriate syntactic and phonological analyses as output.

We saw in our discussion of phonological analysis that the recognizer apparently must have at least three kinds of information at its disposal: information about the acoustic properties of the signal it is processing; information about the phonetic population of the language being spoken; and information about the properties of the articulatory system that produced the signal. The latter kinds of information may be thought of as determining a perceptual "set"—a system of assumptions that the recognition device makes about the properties of the signals it is required to recognize. These assumptions are, roughly, that the linguistically distinctive properties of the signal can be represented by a phonetic distinctive feature matrix, and that the articulator of the signal has the physical characteristics of human articulatory systems. The

---

[4]For example, MacKay found effects for all three types, while Bever et al. found significant effects only for deep-structure ambiguities. However, MacKay found the largest effects for deep-structure ambiguities; and though Bever et al. found nonsignificant differences, they did find trends for the lexical- and surface-structure ambiguities. Thus, the overall order of effects in the two experiments may be comparable.

problem of characterizing the recognition device thus bifurcates. First, there is the problem of precisely stating the content of these assumptions. Second, there is the problem of characterizing whatever computational procedures are employed in bringing this information to bear on the analysis of particular signals, i.e., the computations which allow the speaker to decide upon a best hypothesis about the analysis of the input signal relative to his background information.

The same sorts of points apply, with even greater force, to the recognition of syntactic structure. In order to recover the syntactic analysis of a given sequence of words, the recognition device almost certainly must employ information about the grammatical structure of the language from which the sequence is drawn. The structural analyses to be recovered are, after all, precisely the trees that a grammar generates. It would thus be incredible if the recognition procedures did not somehow employ the kind of information that is represented by grammatical rules. The question of primary theoretical concern throughout the discussion has been: In what form is this information used in sentence recognition?

We have proposed a model which does not posit a very intimate relation between the form in which grammars represent linguistic structure and the form in which sentence recognizers do. In particular, we have seen that both the theoretical and experimental arguments for a perceptual model in which the grammar is concretely realized appear dubious. To review the relevant considerations briefly:

1. There exist no suggestions about how a generative grammar might be concretely employed as a sentence recognizer in a psychologically plausible model.

2. Experimental investigations of the psychological reality of linguistic structural descriptions have, in general, proved quite successful. But experimental investigations of the psychological reality of grammatical rules, derivations, and operations—in particular, investigations of DTC—have generally proved equivocal. This argues against the occurrence of grammatical derivations in the computations involved in sentence recognition and hence against a concrete employment of the grammar by the sentence recognizer.

3. On the other hand, there appear to be phenomena in sentence recognition which are not, in any direct way, predictable from the grammar and which presumably must be attributed to the character of the recognition device. The effects of clause analysis, for example, are not predicted by the grammar, since the grammar makes no claim whatever about what the perceptual unit in

speech must be. But we have seen that the existence of strategies like clause analysis substantially influences the behavior of subjects in sentence-recognition tasks. Whatever else one says about the relation between grammars and recognition models, it now seems clear that the latter will have a considerable amount of structure which is not specified by the former.

This conclusion represents a rather marked deviation from the earliest speculations generative grammarians made about the relation between grammatical models and models of psycholinguistic processes. In the earlier view, psychological models were largely concerned with explaining the interactions of linguistic competence (as represented by a grammar) with relatively unsystematic nonlinguistic variables like memory, motivation, and attention. Observed behavior was supposed to be the consequence of such interactions.

The present view is that the sentence-recognition system has a complex structure of its own, and that behavior in sentence-recognition tasks is not, in general, explicable as the consequences of interactions between grammatical knowledge and *unsystematic* variables. This is a way of saying that in theories of language behavior the question "what computational systems mediate the organism's application of concepts to their instances?" is likely to prove fully as substantive as the question, "what concepts does the organism have at its disposal?" The discovery that psycholinguistics has a subject matter—a body of phenomena which are systematic but not explicable within the constructs manipulated by formal linguistics—is, perhaps, the most important result of the last decade of psycholinguistic research.

This result, however, suggests an extremely serious theoretical problem about the relation between linguistic and psychological models, to which much future research will need to be directed. We have been arguing that an optimal grammar generates the set of internal representations of sentences that speakers encode and hearers recover in linguistic exchanges. We have also argued that the grammar is probably not concretely realized in the perceptual model; that, even though the decoding processes compute the same structural descriptions that a grammar does, the information they use for these computations is not represented in the same form in which a grammar represents it. We noticed in Chapter 3, however, that there are linguistic universals which serve precisely to constrain the form in which information is represented in grammars (i.e., the form of grammatical rules). The question is: If these universals do not also constrain the form in which linguistic information is represented in a sentence-processing system, how is their existence to be explained? Surely, if universals are true of anything, it must be of some psychologically real representation of a language. But what could such a representation be if it is not a part of the sentence encoding-decoding system?

One can imagine a variety of possible answers to this question. We are by no means certain about how one ought to choose between them, or even that one *can* choose between them in the present state of the art.

1. The line of argument we have been pursuing is wrong. The grammar *is* concretely represented in the recognition system and linguistic universals therefore constrain the form in which speaker-hearers finitely represent the infinite set of structural descriptions characteristic of their language. Certainly, none of the evidence that we have been surveying to the contrary is so strong as to rule this suggestion out of consideration.

2. The linguists are wrong. Such linguistic universals as appear to constrain the form of rules in a grammar are either artifacts or can be explained away in one of the following fashions: by showing that they are misdescriptions of what are actually universal properties of the sentence-recognition–production system; or by showing that they are misdescriptions of what are actually universal properties of structural descriptions. Notice that it is the psychological reality of grammatical derivations, and not that of structural descriptions, that the discussion in this chapter has questioned. Hence while universals which constrain the form of rules employed in derivations are in jeopardy, those which constrain structural descriptions are not.

3. The line of argument we have been pursuing is partly wrong. The language-processing system does contain heuristic procedures whose form is not constrained by grammatical universals. But these procedures are not failure-proof. That is, there exist some well-formed sentences to which they will not assign correct structural descriptions. Such sentences must be recognized by resort to "brute-force" (e.g., analysis-by-synthesis) problem-solving routines in which the grammar *is* concretely employed. Linguistic universals thus *do* describe systems that are psychologically real. In particular, they describe the form in which information about the language is stored in this backup recognizer.

A question that is crucial in evaluating this possibility is whether evidence can be found that the construction of "intermediate" trees ever plays a role in sentence processing. Intermediate trees are those representations of a sentence which are produced by transformations in the course of syntactic derivations but which are not either deep or surface trees. (For example, the tree structure in Figure 3-12 is an intermediate tree, since it is in the domain of an obligatory transformation.) Intermediate trees are "uninterpreted" syntactic structures in the sense that, so far as anyone knows, neither semantic nor phonological rules are ever sensitive to their properties. They are thus not part of the syntactic structural description of a sentence in the usual use of that term. If intermediate trees can be shown to be psychologically real, then there can be no argument but that the transformational mechanisms of the grammar are intimately implicated in the production-perception of sentences. On the current proposal, for example, intermediate trees would have to be computed on at least those occasions when heuristic procedures fail to yield the right analysis. This is clearly an area that begs for experimental treatment, but so far as we know, there are at present literally no data available one way or the other.

4. Everyone is right. In this view, both the grammar and the processing heuristics are psychologically real. The function of the grammar is to provide a "library" of information about the structures in a language, and the functioning of (some of the) heuristics is to *access* the grammar, i.e., to ask what the grammar says about the structure of the particular string of morphemes to which the hearer is attending. Such a relation between the grammar and the perception system is compatible with the negative data on DTC so long as the heuristics access the grammar by some means other than using it to actually run through grammatical derivations. If, in fact, there is an objection to this approach, it is only that there is, at present, no positive reason for believing it is true, and such sentence-processing heuristics as are supported by the available data are not of this kind.

5. Everyone is right but in a slightly different way. Recognition procedures can be constructed by a simple and general algorithm from grammars that satisfy the universals and *only* from such grammars. The process of learning a (first) language involves internalizing the grammar and applying this algorithm to construct the corresponding recognition procedure.

This last hypothesis has obvious virtues. It allows us to hold that the linguistic universals describe psychologically real systems, and it allows us to account for the divergences between grammars and recognizers that we have been stressing through much of this chapter. Moreover, some of the heuristic procedures we have been discussing suggest exactly this sort of relation between grammars and recognizers.

For example, we saw that, in determining the appropriate base structure for a sentence like "John felt the child trembled," the subject apparently uses information about the kinds of derivations that are possible in English; in particular, the information that a derivation in which complement reduction has applied to a tense-marked complement is possible only when the complementizer is "that." That is, the subject is using information that might be appropriately represented as a metatheorem about the possible derivations in an English grammar. It is precisely this metatheoretic character of the subject's information that is interesting. There is no single grammatical rule which corresponds directly to the heuristic that the subject appears to be employing. Rather, the heuristic is viable because of certain features of the ways that several grammatical rules interact in the course of permissible derivations. Derivations do not, in short, occur in the course of the recognition procedure, though the recognition procedure works only because certain facts are true about the derivations which the grammar permits.

The critical question for this approach is, of course, whether it is possible to construct a computational procedure which, given a grammar in normal transformational form, will compute the appropriate metatheorems about the possible derivations in that grammar; i.e., a computational procedure which will construct a recognition device from a transformational grammar which satisfies the universals. As things stand, no one knows the answer to this question, since no one knows in detail what universals there are or how recognition devices work, and the possibility of constructing recognizers from grammars surely turns on both. Perhaps the best that can be said is that a reasonable goal for theory construction in linguistics and psycholinguistics would be to determine whether it is possible to constrain grammars and recognition models to satisfy this condition without loss of naturalness and generality.

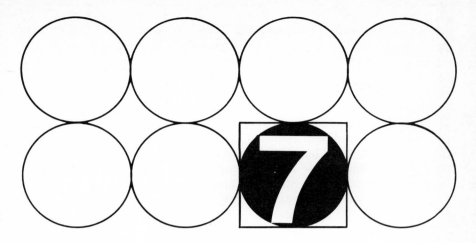

SENTENCE PRODUCTION

It should be clear from the discussion in the preceding chapter that almost every aspect of sentence recognition remains unsettled despite the experimental attention that the problem has recently received. There are, nevertheless, grounds for satisfaction in the fact that we can *state* the problem in what seems to be a revealing way: the hearer must compute a linguistic structural description of an utterance from some acoustic description of that utterance. The psychologist must provide an account of these computations which is responsive to such "performance parameters" as the relative difficulty of the task and the speed, accuracy, etc., with which it is carried out. Thus, the terms of the recognition problem are set by acoustics and linguistics insofar as the former science provides the theoretical vocabulary for characterizing the input to the recognizer and the latter science constrains the characterization of its output.

In the sense in which the recognition problem is relatively well defined, the production problem, unfortunately, is not. Merely stating the production problem requires raising questions about the relation between thought and language which are traditional cruxes in cognitive psychology. Though we have no hope of answering these questions here, we shall attempt to outline a conceptual framework within which issues about sentence production may profitably be discussed.

THOUGHT AND LANGUAGE

The recognition problem is well defined because we can plausibly identify the hearer with a transducer whose inputs and outputs are descriptions of utterances of sentences in theoretical vocabularies that are independently motivated by acoustics and linguistics. Suppose we attempt to characterize the production problem in an analogous way.

It seems clear enough what the output of a sentence-production device must be. The pertinent consideration is that whatever object is *output* by a sentence producer must be the *input* to a sentence recognizer. If, then, a sentence recognizer is a device which recovers the structural description of an object with a specified acoustic description, the output of a production device must be acoustic objects that satisfy such structural descriptions. Briefly, the production system must be a device for constructing acoustic encodings of sentences. But what is the *in*put to such a device?

Common sense invites the view that what happens in sentence production is this: a speaker starts with a message he wants to communicate. By exploiting some sort of encoding procedure, he constructs a linguistic form which is an appropriate vehicle for the transmission of that message. In effect, this is viewing speech production as a matter of *translation*: the speaker's knowledge of his language somehow constitutes a routine for translating the messages he wants to communicate into sentences. But what sort of thing is a "message"? And are we not begging the question of how a speaker chooses to utter a linguistic form if we say that the choice is contingent upon an (unexplained) previous choice of a message to communicate? There is a school of philosophic criticism which claims a vicious regress in explaining the production of a sentence as the encoding of a prior, nonlinguistic thought. [For an extended discussion of these and related issues, see the exchange between Harman and Chomsky in Hook (1969).] Nevertheless, it seems to us that there is much to be said for the old-fashioned view that speech expresses thought, and very little to be said against it. What follows is simply a version of that view.

Talking is a kind of acting and, presumably, the factors which determine what we say are fundamentally the same as the determinants of nonverbal rational action. Such factors typically include the beliefs and utilities of the actor. In particular, deciding upon an action typically involves using background information and current environmental inputs to determine which actions are likely to be possible, and then evaluating the various possibilities in light of some system of preferences. The action chosen is the one which achieves some sort of balance between estimated feasibility and estimated utility. This is, of course, very much idealized; but there is no particular reason to deny that it is a first approximation to an account of reasoned choice. Indeed, no alternative account of rational choice which is even remotely plausible has ever been proposed.

If anything like this view is correct, then deciding on an action is, among other things, a *computational* process. In particular, it presupposes that the agent has access to a system of representation in which the various behavioral options can be formulated and assessed. To this extent, deciding upon an action itself involves the use of a language-like system, and this is true whether or not the action up for consideration happens to be a speech act.

These sorts of arguments suggest attributing to the organism an "internal" computing language ("mentalese," as it were) and thinking of the choice of an utterance as determined by computations which take place in this language. For example, we might imagine the following sequence of events underlying the performance of speech acts. (1) A variety of candidate messages are formulated in mentalese. As a zero-order approximation, candidate messages may be supposed to be chosen at random. But a better approximation is that the selection of candidate messages is determined by what the speaker is attending to, by what his motivational state is, by what the contents of his memory are, etc. (2) The speaker attempts to predict the consequences of communicating one or another of the candidate messages. ("If I say so and so, she will take it that I believe that such and such. . . .") (3) The utility of bringing about these various situations is evaluated and compared. ("If she takes it that I believe that such and such she will admire me, which is all to the good. . . .") (4) A best candidate is chosen. (5) A translation procedure is employed to find the English-language sentence which best expresses the best candidate message. (6) The sentence is uttered.

It is obvious, once again, that this model is highly idealized. For example, one does *not* always choose the best way of saying what one intends to say, so (5) should be liberalized. Again, one does not always consider the consequences of what one says; still less does one always choose to say whatever would optimize the probable payoff. Granting these sorts of points, however, comes only to admitting that speakers are not ideally rational. Such objections are not, therefore, principled grounds for rejecting the sort of model expressed by statements 1 to 5. A principled objection would need to show that 1 to 5 are not the *kinds* of computational procedures which underlie speech production in the paradigmatic cases. But what are the theoretical alternatives?

We said that the claim that language expresses thought is thoroughly old fashioned. It is worth remarking upon the persistence, in the psychological literature, of the related notion that there is a language "of thought" (or "of the neurons") which is different from the languages we speak, and that speaking involves the encoding of messages which are originally formulated in that language. [For an up-to-date version of this sort of theory, see Pribram (1971).] It must also be noticed, however, that there is a traditional alternative to that sort of view, namely, that the language of thought *is* natural language: that thinking is simply inhibited overt speech.

The notion that natural language is the vehicle of thought, rather than a means for its expression, can be found in writings as various as Vygotsky (1965), Ryle (1949), and Harman (1968). It is open to a theorist who accepts this notion to agree with everything we have said about the computational processes underlying rational action with the exception of 5. For such a theorist, there can be no question of "translating" from the language of thought to natural language, since the two are identical: thinking and speaking are continuous except that the latter is de facto a matter of overt utterance whereas the former is not.

It seems reasonably clear that there are cases in which a natural language *does* serve as the vehicle of thought; in such cases, thinking consists in merely saying to oneself bits of natural language which one might equally well have said aloud. The rehearsal which often goes on in short-term-memory tasks (repeating in one's head the telephone number one has just gotten from information) is a persuasive example of this kind, and it is not implausible that some of the thinking that goes on in problem solving might consist in saying to oneself sentences or sentence fragments in one's language. Perhaps one might even want to say that *all* conscious discursive thinking is of this sort.

But whatever we may want to say of conscious discursive thought, it seems quite clear that underlying many mental capacities, there must be computational processes which are carried out in codes other than natural languages. The computations underlying problem solving and the integration of percepts and motor gestures in nonverbal organisms must be of this kind, and so too, on pain of infinite regress, must the computational processes involved in human first language learning. If, in short, there is such a thing as mentalese, the fact that natural languages are learned and that rational activities are often pursued by nonverbal organisms strongly suggests that mentalese cannot be, e.g., English.

We are, in effect, commending a view of the cognitive organization of organisms which borrows heavily from the actual organization of multipurpose computers. Such devices typically perform their computations in an "internal" language which may be quite different from the languages in which they accept their inputs and encode their outputs. Access to the internal language is achieved via translation systems (compilers) which mediate between the peripheral and the central codes. One consequence of this kind of organization is that the same machine can be responsive to a variety of different kinds of input, since messages in all the different input languages have translations in the same central computing language. Conversely, given appropriate compilers, a given message in the central language may be "read out" as any of a variety of kinds of displays (typeouts, images on a cathode tube, etc.).

There would seem to be obvious analogies to organisms. For example, most higher organisms have a routine ability to interpret information in any one input mode in terms of information in any other. What we see often determines how we take what we hear; the way things smell affects the way they taste, and vice versa; and so on. It is thus tempting to think of the various sensory channels as transducing stimulus data into a central computing language rich enough to represent visual, tactual, auditory, gustatory, and olfactory information as well as whatever abstract conceptual apparatus is involved in thought. In such a language are performed the calculations involved in evaluating the auditory implications of visual inputs, the gustatory implications of olfaction, etc. It is, at any event, self-evident that the language in which we integrate visual and auditory information cannot itself be either the language of vision or the language of audition, though it must contain both.

One is tempted to extend the analogy. Just as the kinds of data which can impinge upon thought are at least as various as the kinds of sensory channels available to the organism, so too the kinds of *en*coding available for a given thought are rarely, if ever, restricted to a single mode. One can not only describe a triangle, but imagine (i.e., *image*) one as well; and surely the information about triangles used to do the one is the same information used to do the other. Once again the picture of a neutral central language with mechanisms for translating into a variety of different peripheral codes seems practically irresistible. That there should be biological systems which can provide either discursive or idetic readout of the same centrally stored information is a hypothesis which must be taken seriously, inasmuch as it is already possible to build computers with these capacities.

Insofar as one accepts the kind of picture we have been discussing, one is lead to think of a natural language as in certain respects analogous to a sensory mode; i.e., as providing a channel through which input data can gain access to the central information handling systems, and through which the results of computation can be expressed. For example, linguistic inputs, like sensory inputs, are integrated and interpreted in light of memories and current nonverbal experience (for the integration and interpretation of which they are in turn available). Presumably the computations underlying these integrative processes are typically effected in the central code. If this is so, then the production and comprehension of speech involves translating between this central code and a natural language.

Whatever virtues such views may lack, they have at least the advantage of providing a framework within which we can raise a number of profound questions about cognition. For example, if mentalese is a language, what kind of language is it? In particular, what, if anything, can be said about its syntax and its vocabulary? And if talking involves translating from mentalese to a natural language, what can be said about the character of the translation procedures? Such questions may seem hopelessly beyond the range of empirical inquiry, and it is true that they are probably not, in the first instance, *experimental* questions. Nevertheless, quite a lot can be said about the general characteristics that mentalese must have if it is to be the vehicle of thought, and much of what can be said has been known for centuries. (For a more elaborate treatment of these topics than will be provided here, see Fodor, forthcoming.)

For example, though it is plausible to say that human beings have the ability to *display* centrally stored information in the form of images, it has been clear since Berkeley (1710) that no system of representation which can serve as the vehicle of thought could *consist* of images. This is because whatever code we think in must have some means for expressing abstract ideas, and the content of abstract ideas cannot be expressed by images (see the discussion in Part I, Chapter 4). Such considerations show us how to establish a sort of lower bound on the richness of the means of representation which must be available in mentalese; they can be extended in ways that are implicit in a number of other observations we have already encountered in this book.

Consider, for example, the question about the syntactic structure of mentalese. If we assume that the intended content of a communication in a natural language is typically a message in mentalese, it follows that mentalese must be sufficiently rich that whatever can be communicated by a sentence in natural language can be expressed in mentalese. But this is simply a roundabout way of saying that mentalese must at least be rich enough to permit the representation of semantic interpretations. One way to explore the character of mentalese is thus to ask "what is the minimal syntactic structure we need to assume for a formal system in which semantic interpretations can be represented?" We can be certain that any syntactic mechanism that is essential to such a system must be available to mentalese.

Thus, some of the considerations we raised about semantic representations in Chapter 4 converge upon questions about the character of mentalese. For example, any argument which tends to show that semantic interpretations can, or cannot, be represented in a certain formalism tells us something about the possible adequacy of that formalism *as a theory of mentalese*. Mentalese cannot be first-order logic if the semantic interpretations of English sentences cannot be represented in first-order logic. Mentalese cannot be a list of features if the meaning of English words cannot be expressed by a feature system. To put it briefly, it is rational, in the present view, for psychologists to be interested in semantics, since it is rational to believe that studying the structure of the system of semantic representations is studying the structure of the language of thought.

To know something about the syntax of a language in which semantic interpretations can be expressed is to be in a position to make at least informed guesses about the syntax of mentalese. Similar considerations apply to the relation between the *vocabulary* of mentalese and the vocabulary of a system of representations for semantic interpretations. To establish the latter is to set a lower bound on the richness of the former.

Once again the discussion returns us to issues we first encountered in Chapter 4. We there reviewed arguments that some forms which occur as single lexical items in the surface sentences of English may correspond to phrases at the level of syntactic deep structure and, a fortiori, at the level of semantic interpretation. This is to say that the entries in the lexicon of English may be a superset of those in the lexicon of mentalese.

Consider, for example, a verb like "to doubt." There are a number of respects in which this verb acts as though it "contains" a negative element. Thus, there is a striking parallelism between (7-1) and (7-2). This

7-1   **There isn't anyone coming.**
      There is someone coming.
      ***There is anyone coming.**
      ?There isn't someone coming.

7-2   John doubts that anyone is coming.
      John thinks that someone is coming.
      *John thinks that anyone is coming.
      ?John doubts that someone is coming.

symmetry can be captured on the assumption that the alternation be-tween "some" and "any" is conditioned by *negative* and that "doubts" is a negative context; e.g., that there is a level at which "John doubts that *P*" is represented as "John thinks that *neg-P*." Quite aside from the semantic plausibility of this suggestion, it appears that "doubt" in-teracts with *surface* negative elements in very much the way that this proposal would predict. Thus, "John doesn't doubt that Bill is in-telligent" sounds complicated in the same way as "John doesn't think that Bill isn't intelligent," and this would be expected in the view that "doubt" contains a negative element at some level in its derivation. These intuitive complexity judgments for sentences with the verb "doubt" have, in fact, been experimentally verified by Sherman (1969). His subjects were required to determine (as rapidly as possible) whether or not a presented sentence was "reasonable" (pragmatic fac-tors were the basis for assigning an answer; e.g., "Few people believe the world is round," is an "unreasonable" sentence); as previous research would suggest (see Wason, 1962, for a discussion), sentences containing overt negatives were more difficult than those with affirma-tives. But in the same experiment Sherman found that the verb "doubt" increased processing difficulty fully as much as did the presence of an overt negative. In general, he found that cases of implicit negation (i.e., cases which have syntactic reflexes of *negative* of the sort discussed above for "doubt"; see Klima, 1964) increased decision latency for his task.

Our point is not that such arguments are conclusive; they clearly are not. We are making the more modest claim that there are distributional considerations which might lead one to suppose that some surface lex-ical items are "analyzed" (i.e., represented by a phrase) at some level of syntactic representation. Since, presumably, being analyzed at some *syntactic* level is a sufficient condition for being analyzed at the *semantic* level, and since mentalese is supposed to be the language in which semantic representations are couched, such considerations bear on hypotheses about the primitive vocabulary of mentalese; analyzed forms need not be assumed to occur in that vocabulary.

It is possible to press this line of thought further. We might ask whether being syntactically analyzed is a *necessary*, as well as *sufficient*, condition for being analyzed in mentalese. There are the following pos-sibilities: every lexical form which is syntactically unanalyzed corre-sponds to a primitive expression in mentalese; or alternatively, some syntactically unanalyzed forms are represented by *definitions* at the level of mentalese. (For example, there is no syntactic evidence that "bachelor" is an analyzed form; one might nevertheless want to deny that "bachelor" corresponds to a primitive term in mentalese. Why not let it be represented by the mentalese equivalent of "unmarried man"?) To all intents and purposes, the first of these proposals amounts to saying that a word corresponds to a primitive lexical item at the level of mentalese if and only if it corresponds to a primitive lexical item at the level of syntactic deep structure. The second proposal amounts to saying that some words which are primitive at the level of syntactic deep structure are defined at the level of mentalese.

Surprisingly enough, there are empirical considerations which bear even on this recondite issue, although as usual, these considerations are suggestive rather than conclusive. To begin with, many production errors—slips of the tongue—consist in the conflation of lexical items which have semantic properties in common. Similarly, when one attempts to recall a word which is on the "tip of one's tongue," one often recovers items which are semantically—rather than morphologically—related to the word that one is looking for (see Brown and McNeil, 1966). Data like these are extremely valuable since they provide, together with complexity data, one of the few sources of nondistributional evidence for theories about the character of the most abstract levels of representation. When we get conflation between items in speech production, it is reasonable to assume that there is some level at which the representations of the items are either identical or overlapping. Unless one makes some such assumption, it is hard to imagine how one could explain production errors in which one "calls" one of the items and gets the other. Presumably, in these cases, the level of representation is the level at which messages are specified. The theoretical consequence of the existence of semantically based slips is thus to lend some support to the assumption that distinct but semantically similar lexical items receive overlapping representations in messages.

There is another kind of experimental data which tends to support the view that items that are unanalyzed at the syntactic level may nevertheless correspond to complexes (phrases) at the level of mentalese. These are data that come from so-called sentence verification tasks. As one example we may take an experiment by Clark and Chase (1972) in which subjects were asked to decide on the truth or falsity of sentences like (7-3a and b), in situations where they were presented with vertical

7-3 a. **The star is above the cross.**
      b. **The cross is below the star.**

arrays of stars and crosses. The critical finding, for our purposes, is that the decision time for sentences like (7-3b) was regularly higher than the decision time for sentences like (7-3a). This is interpretable on the assumption that "below" is represented as "not above" at the point where subjects compare the linguistically given information with the visual array. There is, however, no distributional evidence that "below" is a syntactically analyzed form. In particular, "below" and "above" are *not* related as marked and unmarked terms,[1] nor does "below" exhibit any of the characteristic syntactic reflexes of a negative context (unlike such surface words as "doubt," which we discussed above). In fact, the two terms are not even contradictory, though it may be argued that the subject is willing to treat them as such for purposes of the experimental situation. (Indeed, some such assumption will have to be made if the experimental data are to be taken as confirming the claim that "below" is represented as "not above" at *any* level.[2])

Note that adjective pairs which *do* show some reflexes of syntactic analysis also show the kind of complexity relation Clark and Chase report for "above" and "below." For example, Sherman (1969) compared the effects of marked adjectives with those of both overt and implicit negation. His results are compatible with those of Clark and Chase in that he did find a significant increase in sentence difficulty for marked as opposed to unmarked adjectives. (See also Clark and Card, 1969.) Thus, we have some evidence that syntactically *un*analyzed forms contribute to complexity in a way comparable to that of superficially similar forms which may be syntactically analyzed.

If one wishes to accept this sort of experimental finding as bearing on the character of the subject's internal representation of sentences, then the data support the claim that there are syntactically unanalyzed forms which receive analyses at the level of mentalese. In this respect they run parallel to the data on slips of the tongue and tip-

---

[1] Compare "near" and "far," which *are* related as unmarked and marked. "How far is it?" doesn't presuppose that it's far, and this is the classic test for an unmarked form. But "how (much) above *x* is *y*?" *does* presuppose that *x* is above *y*, and "how much below *y* is *x*?" presupposes that *y* is below *x*. Hence both "above" and "below" fail the test for unmarkedness. The adjectives used by Sherman, however, do seem to satisfy the tests for markedness. (It should be noted that the sense of "marked" at issue in the contrast "marked-unmarked" is *not* the marked one in which a form is said to be marked if it constitutes an exception to some rule or generalization. Both usages are found in the linguistic literature.)

[2] This last consideration suggests one of the ways in which one must be cautious in interpreting results on sentence verification as even relevant to the question of how sentences are understood. Clearly, the latter process is not identical to the former, since it is perfectly possible to understand a sentence and have no beliefs about whether or not it is true. The fact that subjects appear to be willing to accept such rough-and-ready equivalences as "above = not below" for purposes of the verification task suggests that the task may elicit context-specific behaviors which have very little to do with the exercise of linguistic knowledge in the perceptual analysis of sentences.

of-the-tongue phenomena discussed above; all three suggest a level of representation at which words are replaced by (something like) their definitions.

The kinds of facts we have just been discussing thus argue that the vocabularies of mentalese and natural languages are, in general, quite different: natural-language lexical items often correspond to complex objects in mentalese. There are, however, broadly empirical reasons for questioning this conclusion.

Suppose we assume that processing a sentence involves computing its representation in mentalese and that, in the course of this computation, natural-language lexical items are replaced by their mentalese definitions. Then it seems to follow that the more complicated the definition of the items in a sentence is, the greater will be the computational load associated with understanding, producing, or storing the sentence. The indicated experiments have not been run, but it seems unlikely that this prediction will be borne out. Cases like "doubt" which comport with it would seem to be the exception rather than the rule. For example, "square" is presumably defined in terms of "line," but "that's a square" is not noticeably more difficult to understand, produce, or remember than "that's a line." This suggests that "line" and "square" are both available items at whatever levels of encoding are employed in understanding, storing, and producing sentences; e.g., that understanding "that's a square" does *not* involve computing a mentalese formula which corresponds to "that's a four-sided closed figure whose sides are straight lines of equal length which meet at right angles."

To put it the other way around, these considerations suggest that both "square" and "line" appear in the vocabulary of mentalese and that the semantic relations between them are mediated by principles of inference that apply to mentalese formulas. This account would predict, what seems plausible, that complexity differences between squares and lines should turn up in processes that involve reasoning about them rather than in processes that involve understanding sentences that mention them.

We have been arguing that questions about the character of mentalese, however hopelessly metaphysical they may at first appear, are not entirely beyond the reach of the combined methodologies of psychology and linguistics: we can imagine data which would bear directly upon such questions. The state of the art is such that even though almost nothing of interest can be said about the factors which lead us to choose to transmit one message or another, we are beginning to get some leverage on the question of what messages are like—at least insofar as this can be identified with the question of what semantic representations are like.

Similarly for the question which will primarily concern us in the rest of this chapter: What psychological processes are involved in translating from messages in mentalese to surface forms of a natural language? While very little is known about how this question should be answered, it is at least becoming possible to characterize some of the properties a reasonable answer will have to have.

We shall presently turn to a more detailed discussion of the problems involved in translating mentalese into surface forms and of such data as are currently available for illuminating the problems. It is, however, impossible to conclude a discourse on "the relation between thought and language" without saying something about the issue most often discussed under that heading: the so-called "Whorf hypothesis." Our remarks will be relatively brief.

LINGUISTIC RELATIVITY

Stated crudely, Whorf's hypothesis is that one's cognitive structure is largely determined by the structure (including the vocabulary) of the language one speaks. It is, for example, the language one has learned (rather than any innate characteristics of the mind) which accounts for the way one individuates events, for the patterns of similarity and difference that one perceives among objects and their properties, and, in general, for one's ontological commitments, however such a notion may be defined.

It is notorious that this thesis is hard to state clearly and that the arguments that Whorf provides for it tend to be circular. This latter point was put persuasively by Black (1959) in his review of Whorf (1956):

> [Whorf] makes much of the fact that the statement "It is a dripping spring" (an odd example, by the way) is expressed in Apache by a very different construction, inadequately rendered by "As water, or springs, whiteness moves downwards." Whorf adds: "How utterly unlike our way of thinking!" But what is the evidence that the Apache *thinks* differently? The difficulty is that the hypostatized structural concepts are so bound to the defining grammatical constructions that it becomes hard to conceive of any extra-linguistic verification. Having the concept of a predicate (for all except the linguist or the philosopher) is about the same as using a language that insists upon the use of predicates, and Whorf's contention reduces to saying that one cannot speak grammatically without using a particular grammar. It is a far cry to the assumption that to speak grammatically is to mold "reality" into a structure isomorphic with the grammar [p. 232].

If, in short, one is going to explain differences in the cognitive organization of speakers by reference to differences in the grammatical organization of their languages, one had better have some way of demonstrating the existence of the former that does not depend solely upon the existence of the latter. There is some literature devoted to the experimental investigation of Whorf's hypothesis, though the main concern in these experiments has been with the possible cognitive effects of the vocabulary of a language rather than with those of its syntax. If we are seeking noncircular arguments for or against linguistic relativity, these experiments are the place to look.

According to Whorf's hypothesis, the way one organizes one's experience is a function of the language one speaks, and the concepts one has are those one's language insists upon. It seems to follow that whatever stimuli the language calls by the same name should be homogeneous for cognitive purposes, and vice versa. Clearly this is not entirely true, since we can take note of vastly many distinctions for which we do not have contrasting names. The question is thus whether there is anything to be said for the claim at all. Experiments which have sought to answer this question have often involved the perception and recall of color-chips as the dependent variables. To understand these experiments, it is necessary to understand the assumptions the experimenters made about the stimulus materials.

Consider the way the vocabulary of a language divides up the color spectrum. Since there are no physical discontinuities in the spectrum (one color grades continuously into the next), it would seem to be entirely a matter of linguistic convention where the boundaries between the colors are placed. Contrast this case with that of, for example, rabbits: one feels very strongly that it is "natural" for a language to distinguish between rabbits and nonrabbits, since (1) there is a sharp boundary where each rabbit ends and everything else starts, and (2) when a rabbit moves, he takes his boundary with him. There are thus plausible grounds for the cognitive salience of rabbits which would hold even in the absence of languages. "The world" would pull against a language which failed to place object boundaries on both sides of a rabbit. In this sense, however, there is nothing "natural" about having color boundaries on both sides of brown, and nothing "unnatural" about failing to have a color boundary between blue and green.

And, in fact, there are languages which locate color boundaries in places other than the ones that English chooses. Iakuti has a single word for what we distinguish as the blues and the greens (see Brown, 1958) and Dani uses a basic two-term color vocabulary corresponding to what we call the distinction between light and dark (see Heider, 1970). In short, it looks as though, in the case of colors, *only* language is at bottom of our notions about where one stops and the next begins. Hence, if there are any cognitive consequences of linguistic conventions about individuation, we should expect to find them here.

The classic study in this field is the work of Brown and Lenneberg (1954), which demonstrated an effect of the "codability" of a color upon memory for that color in a short-term-recognition task. Roughly, the codability of a color in a language is indexed by (1) whether that color has a one-word name in the language (less codable colors are named by phrases, e.g., "brown" versus "somewhere between brown and orange"), (2) the degree of consensus speakers of the language show on what the color should be called (with greater consensus indicating greater codability), and (3) the speaker's latency for judgments about what the color is called (with shorter latencies indicating higher codability). Brown and Lenneberg's work showed that insofar as a color is highly codable in English, it is relatively easy for English speakers to remember.

The fact that codable colors are memorable seems to provide at least some support for the Whorfian views, for it suggests that good examples of linguistic categories are good examples of cognitive categories. Indeed, one can imagine an obvious mechanism for producing correlations between memorability and codability. If what subjects remember about a color is its *name*, one might expect that longer names would go with worse recall, that what can't be named unequivocally can't be recognized unhesitatingly, and so on.

The crucial test would, of course, be the cross-cultural demonstration that memorability of a given stimulus color varies from one language community to the next as a function of the codability of the color in each language. Brown and Lenneberg thought that this might be the case. "The Zuni color lexicon codes the colors we call orange and yellow with a single term. Monolingual Zuni Ss in their recognition task frequently confused the orange and yellow colors in our stimulus set. Our English speaking Ss never made this error.... Interestingly, bilingual Zunis who knew English fell between the monolingual Zuni and the native speaker of English in the frequency with which they made these errors" (p. 461). [See Lenneberg and Roberts (1956) for details of the study on which these remarks are based.]

It thus seems that the organization of the vocabulary of a language may affect at least one cognitive task: recognition tests for short-term recall of colors. However, recent work by Heider (1972) and by Heider and Olivier (1972), in which cross-cultural effects were very carefully examined, suggests that even the marginal support for Whorf's hypothesis which Brown and Lenneberg's study provided may need serious reevaluation.

To begin with, it is apparently *not* true that there is as much difference in the way that languages articulate the color space as most investigators have assumed. Cross-cultural linguistic investigation (Berlin and Kay, 1969) suggests that the basic color vocabulary of languages always draws on the same spectral areas, with the "focal" colors centering in the areas black and white, red, green, yellow, blue, pink, orange, brown, and purple. Languages *differ* in where they put boundaries and in the number of focal colors that are named. But one does not find languages whose basic color words denote nonfocal colors. This rather suggests that Whorf's hypothesis may have the relation between codability and cognitive salience backward. It may well be that their universal cognitive salience leads to the universal codability of the focal colors rather than the other way around.

Two results of Heider's suggest that this counter-Whorfian account is probably the right one. First, Heider has shown that even for Dani subjects, focal colors are more memorable in a short-term-recognition task than nonfocal colors are. In this case, the memorability of focal colors cannot be a consequence of their codability since, as we remarked above, Dani has a basic color contrast only for the brightness-darkness dimension: chromatic distinctions are not coded in the Dani vocabulary at all.

Second, Heider showed that despite the differences in their color vocabularies, the pattern of memory errors for colors is comparable for English and Dani speakers. Clearly, the Whorfian view makes the opposed prediction: the Dani should tend to indiscriminate confusion of color on the chromatic dimension since their language does not code distinctions in this dimension. What in fact happens is that both Dani and English *recognition* errors show the same general profile that one gets from scaling the subjects' judgments of *similarity* among colors; this is, the colors which get confused in recall are, roughly, the ones that subjects say look alike rather than the ones which their language groups under the same name. To put it succinctly, it appears that the Dani are quite sensitive to the difference between, say, light red and light green, though their language does not happen to provide them with labels for this distinction.

Such experimental results as these do not argue for the Whorfian view. It may be worth adding that if the view we have been presenting about mentalese is true, then one would not expect that cognitive structure should prove to be indefinitely plastic to linguistic experience in the way that Whorf's hypothesis appears to require. Whorf, after all, begins with the assumption that the organism imposes no endogenously determined structure upon its experience. Even what we have referred to as "natural" distinctions between objects and their ground are not inevitable for the committed Whorfian since radical linguistic relativity would entail that cognitive salience is *learned*. Given this assumption, it becomes essential to ask where the relatively orderly epistemology of the adult comes from. The structure of his language offers a plausible candidate, with the corollary that different linguistic structures ought to impose different cognitive organizations.

We have supposed, on the other hand, that the nervous system comes equipped with a language in which it does its computations, and that learning a natural language involves learning to translate into and out of this computational code. This assumption exactly reverses Whorf's predictions, since the source of cognitive organization may now be supposed to lie in the inherent structure of our internal language; and this language is presumed to be part of the common human endowment. Thus, where Whorf predicts conceptual pluralism, the present account predicts that such conceptual differences as can be attributed to acculturation should prove to be relatively slight. It is, for example, compatible with the present view that natural languages should be intertranslatable, a state of affairs that would be simply inexplicable if the cognitive structures of their speakers could differ without limit. It's worth mentioning that radical linguistic relativists like Quine (1960) have in fact denied the possibility of translation between historically unrelated languages.

Similarly, where Whorf's account suggests that natural languages should differ from one another arbitrarily, it is compatible with the present suggestion that they should turn out to be quite alike. For, according to our view, every natural language must be such that the semantic interpretations of its sentences can be represented in mentalese. Depending on what the character of mentalese turns out to be, it is entirely possible that this should prove to be a substantive constraint on the possible natural languages.

If, in short, Whorf's hypothesis were true, it would pose a serious objection to the entire conceptual framework we have assumed in stating the sentence-production problem. The best current evidence suggests, however, that Whorf's hypothesis is probably not true. Hence, the view that sentence production is translation from an internal code which is not itself a natural language is compatible with such evidence as is currently available. We therefore return to the sentence-production problem so construed.

PRODUCERS, PERCEIVERS, AND GRAMMARS COMPARED

We shall take it for granted in what follows that the problem of speech production *is* the problem of characterizing a device which translates mentalese into English. It should be clear that what one says about the structure of such a device will depend, in part, upon what view one holds of the relation between semantic representations and syntactic deep structure. If, for example, one takes the "generative semantics" position, according to which deep structures and semantic representations are identical, then the problem of translating from mentalese to English is the problem of selecting a surface form corresponding to a deep structure. Throughout this book, we have preferred the view that deep structure is an interlevel between surface forms and semantic representations; the so-called standard theory of generative grammar. If this latter theory is correct, then the speech-production problem is correspondingly altered: it becomes an empirical hypothesis that the production of a sentence involves the construction of a representation of that sentence which corresponds to its (standard) deep-structure tree. In this hypothesis, the translation function from mentalese to English maps (1) from formulas in mentalese to deep structures and (2) from deep structures to surface forms. And there may be a third factor, namely, a mapping from mentalese directly to surface forms, in case there are properties of sentences that are represented at the semantic and the surface level but not in deep structure. We shall return to these points. Suffice it to remark here that the assumption that producing a sentence involves computing its standard deep structure is a substantive one, for which there is at present very little by way of direct psychological evidence. We will make that assumption partly for purposes of exposition and partly because it seems sensible to assume symmetry between the mechanisms of production and those of perception wherever there is no evidence to the contrary.

We are now in a position to summarize the view of the relation between production devices, recognition devices, and grammars that has been implicit in our discussion thus far.

In the first place, the objects whose relations must be computed by the production model are precisely those with which the recognition model is concerned. In both cases the problem is to interrelate surface forms, deep structures, and messages. In this respect, the production problem as we have outlined it here is symmetrical with the perception problem as we discussed it in Chapter 6. But even though the production and perception devices relate the same levels of linguistic description, the direction of information flow is different for the two. Thus, with respect to the present assumptions, the production device must compute a deep structure given a message as input, and must compute a surface sentence given a deep structure as input. A perceptual device, on the other hand, computes deep structures from surface sentences and messages from deep structures.

It is often remarked that direction of information flow makes no difference in a grammar. According to Chomsky (1971), "the standard theory generates quadruples [of phonetic representations, surface structures, deep structures and semantic representations]. It is meaningless to ask whether it does so by 'first' generating [a deep structure then mapping it onto a semantic representation (on one side) and a phonetic representation on the other]. At this level of discussion... there is no general notion 'direction of mapping' or 'order of steps of generation' to which one can appeal..." (In Steinberg and Jakobovits, 1971, pp. 187–188). Such points are plausible when made about grammars, since all that a grammar undertakes to do is specify a certain correspondence between sets of objects: namely, to specify the representation each sentence has at each level of linguistic description. In the case of performance models, however, the situation is quite different, as Chomsky himself remarks. A performance model attempts to specify the actual sequence of computations which underlies the speaker-hearer's production and recognition of sentences. For such models, the direction of information flow is critical.

Because of the differences in the direction of information flow, it is risky to commit oneself to any a priori assumptions about structural similarities between grammars, producers, and recognizers. For example, one might assume that the way the speaker copes with the problem of producing an acoustic form which has a structural description appropriate to the message he wants to encode is simply to "run through" his internalized grammar. On this assumption, the production device consists of the rules of the grammar plus some algorithm for applying them.

Note that the production system must be a device which constructs sentences corresponding to messages. But the grammar begins every derivation with the same symbol: the input to the grammar is always S. Evidently, a production system cannot simply *be* a grammar. We need some procedure for producing derivations which correspond to particular messages, and this the grammar per se does not do.

In short, if we begin to take a standard grammar seriously *as part of a production device*, we must begin to do what grammarians typically do not: namely, to interpret the direction of information flow in the grammar. A completed standard grammar would provide a procedure for constructing a semantic interpretation given a specified deep-structure tree; the semantic component of a standard grammar is usually thought of as a mapping from deep-structure trees onto semantic representations. It would not, however, provide any mechanism for constructing a deep-structure tree corresponding to a specified semantic interpretation. That is, it provides no mechanisms for doing what a production model is required to do.

Analysis by synthesis again.   The most obvious proposal for incorporating a grammar in a performance theory is the use of analysis by synthesis (ABS). In ABS for perception, comparisons are made between a phonetically coded input string and the internally generated output of the phonological component of a grammar (see Chapter 6). But the grammar is as suited for use in an ABS production system as it is for use in an ABS perceiver; we need simply alter the objects between which the comparisons are made. In particular, an ABS producer would function by comparing messages with the output of the semantic component of the grammar.

Figure 7-1 suggests the organization of such a system. It should be noticed that Figure 7-1 *assumes* that mentalese is the language in which semantic representations are couched: i.e., that the output of the semantic component is in the same language as the messages which are input from the message source to the recognition loop. The effect of this assumption is to allow comparisons between these messages and the semantic representations generated by the grammar. It is, of course,

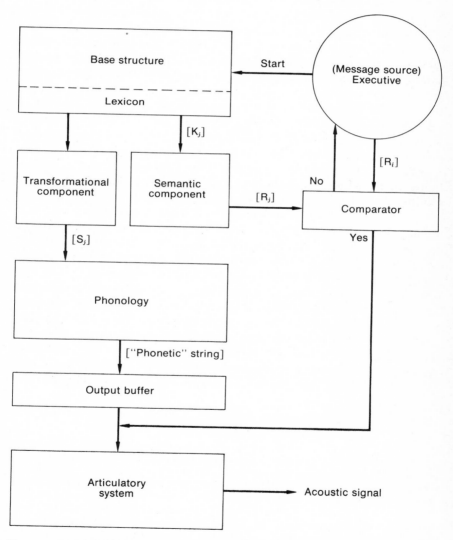

Fig. 7-1. Analysis by synthesis for production. [S], [K], and [R] refer to surface phrase structures, base phrase structures, and semantic readings respectively. When $[R_j] = [R_i]$, the structure corresponding to $[R_j]$ is output.

possible that this assumption is too optimistic; that there is an interlevel between messages and the kind of semantic representations that grammars generate. This would be unfortunate, since it would mean that linguistic semantics is telling us less than one might hope about the structure of mentalese. It is, however, a contingency which models like Figure 7-1 can accommodate, since nothing prohibits a recoding operation between the message source and the comparator.

How seriously should we consider an ABS production system that incorporates the grammar given that there are grounds for rejecting such ABS recognizers? It might be argued that the fact that language perception and production are rarely if ever dissociated suggests that the same fundamental computational mechanisms must underlie both.[3] Unfortunately, this argument cuts both ways: if we had substantive empirical grounds *for* adopting something like an ABS production system, we should have to reconsider the arguments *against* ABS recognizers. If there were grounds for incorporating the grammatical rules into the computational machinery of production, it would be extraordinarily difficult to justify their exclusion from the mechanisms of recognition.

Moreover, it should be kept clearly in mind how strong a claim is being made when one opts for fundamentally analogous models of production and recognition. To claim that these devices overlap in important ways is to claim that, for the most part, the computational machinery is identical in both cases, and that the same sequence of mental events that underlies the production of a sentence also underlies its recognition. On grounds of simplicity we might expect this sort of coincidence, but we ought not to be too surprised if we fail to find it. Nor would one wish the issue to be decided for reasons of simplicity alone. These are empirical questions, and it is a challenge to the methodology of psycholinguistics to find data upon which they can be made to turn.

The upshot of these remarks is that, all things being equal, one would favor an account which makes the production and perception systems similar, and this holds for ABS models that incorporate the grammar as well as any others. But, the arguments which suggest there

---

[3] It has been claimed that lesions of Broca's area produce aphasic dissociation between speech perception, which remains intact, and speech production, which does not. However, the available evidence suggests that insult to Broca's area primarily affects the motor implementation of speech. Since there is no reason to suppose that the computational procedures underlying the encoding of messages is implicated in such cases, they provide no evidence against the claim that those procedures are fundamentally the ones employed in recognition.

are fundamental homogeneities among the performance systems are not overwhelming. It would, for example, be unwise to reject ABS for production *merely* on the grounds that it is implausible for recognition.

What *can* be argued, however, is that neither recognition nor production can depend upon exhaustive searches through the output of a grammar. In particular, the same considerations which suggest that ABS recognition systems would have to employ heuristic procedures to cut down the number of candidate analyses to be tested also apply to ABS production models. And again, in both cases, as these heuristics become more sophisticated, the importance of the synthesis loop becomes less clear. With production as with recognition, the limit of such elaborations on ABS models is a straight-through heuristic system.

HEURISTIC PROCEDURES FOR SENTENCE PRODUCTION

Even if there is a synthesis loop in the production process, it is likely that the heart of that system will be heuristic procedures for associating messages with linguistic encodings. About the character of such heuristics, however, nothing is presently known. In this section, we shall explore some of the theoretical issues which make the characterization of production heuristics such a difficult problem.

As we remarked above, we shall be assuming that the construction of a sentence which encodes a message involves the construction of a standard deep structure for that sentence. If this assumption is correct, then the production system should embody procedures which (1) pair messages with deep structures, (2) pair deep structures with surface forms, and (3) pair messages with surface forms in case there are properties of sentences which are represented at the semantic level and in surface structure but not at deep structure. We will discuss each of these procedures in turn.

From messages to deep structures. How does one construct the deep structure which corresponds to a semantic representation? It seems clear that a standard deep structure displays two kinds of information that have semantic import: its lexical content and those features of its geometry which represent grammatical relations. If, then, we are to *construct* a deep structure corresponding to a message, we must find principles which constrain the geometry and lexical content of that structure by reference to the properties of the message to be encoded. In short, we want heuristic principles of the general form "if the message has the property P, then the corresponding deep structure has the property D," where values of D specify geometric and lexical features of deep structures.

What might such principles be like? Clearly, that depends on what kind of representation corresponds at the *semantic* level to what appear as grammatical relations and lexical contents at the deep-structure level. This, however, is where the discussion bogs down, since serious answers to these questions are not yet forthcoming.

For example, there is a traditional proposal which says that the semantic counterparts of the grammatical relation *subject-verb-object* are *actor-action-acted upon*. In this view, a semantic representation would have to contain a specification of such information as who counts as the actor, what the actor does, and who, or what, he does it to. The production heuristics would then have to insure that the part of the message which refers to the actor is encoded by the highest deep-structure *NP*, the part which refers to the action by the highest *VP*, and the part which refers to the object of action by the highest *NP* dominated by *VP*.

It seems unlikely, however, that strong support can be mustered in favor of the traditional account of the semantic import of grammatical relations. Consider sentences like "John forgot the appointment." "Forgetting" is obviously not an action, and there seems to be no sense in which an appointment is acted upon when it is forgotten. Indeed, recent syntactic discussion has tended to the conclusion that *subject* has no stable semantic import at all, and hence that it does not need to be represented in deep structure. (See Fillmore, 1968; but see also Chomsky, 1970a.) Analogously, it is entirely unclear what semantic features correspond to such syntactic relations as, e.g., those between a subordinating and a subordinated sentence, or those between a verb of propositional attitude and a sentence within its scope.

Our present point is that if production heuristics are to construct deep trees corresponding to semantic messages, the geometry of the trees they construct will have to be at least partially determined by whatever semantic features correspond to grammatical relations. But as things now stand, no one knows what such features are.

Nor do we know how such features are *represented* at the level of messages. If, for example, *actor* is a semantic category, then one can imagine any of a variety of notations that mentalese might use for specifying which things are in that category: for example, *actor* might be represented by a feature, or by some geometric property of formulas in mentalese, or by some interaction between the two. The point is that this difference matters for the formulation of the heuristics which map from mentalese to deep structures.

Precisely analogous problems arise in attempting to specify the procedures which determine the lexical content of a deep-structure tree. We know that some semantic properties of messages are encoded by geometric features of deep trees and that some are encoded by lexical items. This means that among the procedures for constructing deep trees from messages, there must be some which select lexical items in the natural language, given the corresponding formulas in mentalese. But, again, what are such formulas like and how is the selection made?

In short, there seem to be two major problems in characterizing rules which construct deep trees corresponding to messages. There must be some procedure for encoding the semantic counterparts of grammatical relations as geometrical properties of deep trees; and there must be some procedure for coding properties of messages as lexical items. But until we have an account of the form that messages can take, we cannot characterize the domains in which these rules operate.

From deep structure to surface structure. A standard grammar provides a formal procedure for constructing a surface structure corresponding to a given deep structure; that is, apply the transformations. Thus, if we have a deep structure which encodes a given message, it is always possible to find a corresponding surface form by simply using the transformational mechanisms that the grammar makes available. It should be noticed that proceeding in this way does *not* involve analysis by synthesis, since no comparison step is required. Every transformational route which starts with a well-formed deep structure will yield an appropriate well-formed surface structure.

If there is any objection to this way of coping with the problem of constructing surface forms, it is simply that it constitutes a relatively uneconomical performance model. For at each step in the derivation, the structure being computed must be checked against all the structural indices of all the transformations. Clearly this is computationally expensive, and heuristic procedures which narrow the set of transformations that need to be searched would be desirable.

Such procedures would most naturally take the form of a cross-classification of the transformations. For example, we know that there are transformations which apply only to structures containing more than one sentoid (for example, all embedding transformations). Similarly, there are a variety of transformations (*Neg, Q, Imp,* etc.) which apply to only one S at a time. It seems obvious that these sorts of facts could be used to reduce the computational load in a production system; if we are computing a surface structure corresponding to a deep tree which contains only one sentoid, there is no point in testing the applicability of embedding transformations to that tree. In general, the more sophisticated the cross-classification of transformations available to us, and the more abstract the description of structural indices under which transformation can be "called," the more we can hope to eliminate consideration of groups of transformations all of whose structural indices fail to be satisfied at a given point in the derivation.

Thus, one way of dealing with the deep-structure-to-surface-structure computation is to use the transformational apparatus, preferably in conjunction with some system for cross-classifying the transformations. Another kind of solution is more closely parallel to what we suggested in the case of the recognition problem: namely, it may be possible to specify direct, but heuristic, correspondences between aspects of deep structures and aspects of their corresponding surface structures. Such heuristics would be similar in form to recognition heuristics, although it is left open that they might be quite different in content.

As things stand, we have no way of telling which, if either, of these kinds of systems provides a reasonable model of sentence production. In part this is because we do not have data on production complexity comparable to those available on recognition complexity. Such data are critical since they would allow us to test the length of the grammatical derivation of a sentence against the difficulty of producing it. It will be remembered from Chapter 6 that it was primarily the failure to find a close correlation between the length of derivations and the complexity of a sentence in *perceptual* tasks that led us to doubt that grammatical transformations are closely implicated in recognition.

It should also be remarked that neither of the types of production systems we have been discussing will account for the intuition that the integration of sentence structure proceeds, at least roughly, from left to right; i.e., that the parts of a sentence which are produced first are normally integrated first. It is, of course, an open question how far this intuition should be trusted. Verbal slips in which parts of the sentence that should come late are inverted with parts that should come early suggest that there may be a less strongly left-to-right bias in the production system that one might at first suppose. (Compare errors like "they don't make shirts that skort" with the intended "they don't make skirts that short.") Moreover, the effect of a left-to-right production system could always be mimicked by one which contains a low-level store in which the whole sentence is simultaneously displayed, together with a left-to-right readout. Such data as are available on this question will be reviewed later in the chapter. Our present point is that production systems based closely on the grammar will presumably not exhibit *any* inherent tendency toward planning a sentence in an order that corresponds to the output order, and this might well be taken as a prima facie objection to such models.

From messages to surface structures. Even if there is an interlevel of deep structure between messages and surface forms, there is reason to believe that not all semantically relevant features of the syntactic organization of a sentence are displayed by its representation at that level. In particular, deep structure represents those features which depend on grammatical relations and lexical content, but there is nothing at the level of standard deep structure which corresponds to topic, presupposition, focus, etc. (See the discussion in Chapter 4, Part 2.) It is possible that such features are represented only at the level of messages and surface structures. On this assumption, a production system will need techniques for constraining features of surface syntactic form in light of features of messages.

Only the notation changes if we accept a generative semantics position, where features like topic and presupposition *are* marked at a level to which syntactic transformations apply. Such systems require "derivational constraints" which reject otherwise well-formed surface structures in case they do not have the topics, presuppositions, etc., which their deep structures require. For example, one would reject the route from {John hit Mary} to the surface sentence "It was Mary John hit" if "John" is marked as topic in {John hit Mary}. In effect, whether one takes the generative or the standard view, the production model will need to select between well-formed surface structures according to which topics, presuppositions, etc., they express, and this selection will have to be constrained by semantic properties of the messages being encoded.

To summarize: Both the conceptual and the empirical issues in the most interesting areas of the production problem are largely unsolved. This is primarily because these problems tend to hinge on the character of semantic representations, and this is itself not fully known. Moreover, even where the issues are clear enough so that data might choose between competing theories of production, the facts are usually unavailable. Getting the data we need (e.g., on the relative production complexity of sentences of different syntactic types) would involve somehow getting the subject spontaneously to produce sentences of an antecedently specified message or form, and there is no very satisfactory procedure for doing this.

In the rest of this chapter, we shall review the experimental findings currently available on the production issue. Considering the difficulties involved in obtaining the relevant facts, we think that some of this material is quite interesting. There are two kinds of experiments to be reviewed. The first attempts to isolate stimulus variables which govern the form and content of utterances, and the second attempts to elucidate the effects of structural variables on the mental processes involved in producing sentences.

EXPERIMENTAL STUDIES
OF SENTENCE PRODUCTION

ENVIRONMENTAL VARIABLES

A natural way for an experimental psychologist to begin his inquiry into sentence production is by trying to establish correspondences between the linguistic form or content of an utterance and features of the environment in which it is produced. This is an especially natural strategy if one assumes, as much of modern psychology has done, that the really important determinants of behavior are the stimuli impinging upon an organism. Nevertheless, the experimental literature on the environmental control of linguistic responses is surprisingly sparse, and the examples of such control cited in the literature are largely anecdotal. Excepting analyses of exchanges between patient and therapist in analytic interviews—which we ignore here because they are primarily concerned with identifying stimuli that elicit paralinguistic (e.g., emotive) properties of verbalizations—it is difficult to think of a body of literature on the environmental control of verbal behavior which does not consist primarily of *gedanken* experiments.[4]

For example, Skinner (1957) remarks:

> We set up an occasion for a tact with the form *pencil* by putting a very large or unusual pencil in an unusual place clearly in sight—say, half submerged in a large aquarium or floating freely in the air near the ceiling of the room. . . . Under such circumstances it is highly probable that our subject will say *pencil* [p. 254].

Probably no one has ever done an experiment to test this. Nor is it easy to believe that learning whether Skinner's prediction is true would cast even a glimmer of light on the relation between a speaker's utterances and environmental stimuli. It is worth asking why this is so. We will see that the same considerations which make it uninteresting to test the prediction that an English speaker will say "pencil" when confronted

---

[4] Experiments on "verbal conditioning" are not counterexamples. What such experiments seek to show is that verbal responses can be converted into conditioned operants by the manipulation of reinforcers. They do *not* show (or even suggest) that the language behaviors which the subject brings to the experimental situation are themselves conditioned operants under the control of specifiable environmental variables. To achieve operant control over a verbal response is to demonstrate not that verbalization is a conditioned response but merely that it is a response that can be conditioned. There are, of course, many kinds of behaviors other than conditioned operants which can be brought under operant control. Eye blink and EEG are apparently cases in point.

with a gigantic pencil hold also with respect to some subtler experiments on stimulus effects in production.

The prediction that English speakers will, in fact, utter the word "pencil" in the circumstances Skinner describes turns on three assumptions.

1. "Pencil" is a locution standardly used to refer to pencils in English.
2. When English speakers talk about pencils, they are likely to use a standard English locution to do so.
3. A situation in which "a very large or unusual pencil (is) . . . clearly in sight" is one in which speakers will often want to talk about pencils.

Now, the first two of these assumptions are not in doubt. Item 1 represents an extremely trivial part of the linguistic analysis of English, and 2 follows from the remark that speakers of English frequently obey the rules of their language when they talk. So, if Skinner's experiment is relevant to testing any hypothesis, it must be item 3. Notice, however, that 3 is a hypothesis not about the linguistic forms a speaker will utter but rather about the topics of conversation he will choose. In particular, 3 has nothing to do with the relation between environmental stimuli and the exercise of any particular verbal capacity. This can be seen from the fact that our reasons for believing that 3 may be true of a speaker are entirely independent of any assumptions that we make about what language he speaks. (That is, while 1 is true only of English, and 2 is true only of English speakers, 3 is presumably true of everybody if it is true at all.) To put the point briefly, the linguistically relevant experimental hypothesis is 1; and 1, as we have seen, is not in doubt in the kind of case that Skinner describes—hence the intuition that Skinner's experiment would not be worth trying.

The general objection to experiments like Skinner's is simply that the environmental property which is shown to be "in control" of a linguistic form is one that is related to that form *by a linguistic rule*. Hence, if the experiment succeeds, we are shown no more than that the speaker knows the rule and is adequately motivated to apply it. If it fails, we learn nothing at all. The moral is the following: A generalization of the form, "if the stimulus situation is of type *S*, adequately motivated subjects will use the linguistic form *w*," will be an interesting comment on the environmental variables which control *w* only if, "*w* is a linguistic form appropriate to situation *S*," is not itself a rule of the subject's language. It is pointless to run an experiment which shows that if something is a pencil, appropriately motivated English speakers will call it "pencil." Anyone who knows English knows that already.[5]

So far as we know, there is only one experiment (Osgood, 1971) in which a systematic attempt was actually made to manipulate the spontaneous productions of speakers by varying the eliciting environmental stimuli. Several of the results in this study are subject to the same difficulty we identified in Skinner's example; but others are not, and it is important to examine the difference.

Osgood performed a series of brief and very simple vignettes before an audience that was instructed to write descriptions of the scenes they had just observed. Subjects were told to put their description in a single sentence simple enough for a child to understand. The scenes that were to be described involved the experimenter's manipulation of objects on a table placed at the front of the room. The objects included small plastic balls, rings of various colors, a saucer, poker chips, etc.; and the experimenter's performance involved such actions as rolling one of the colored balls along the table to strike one of the others, placing a poker chip in the saucer, or selecting a single colored poker chip from a stack of white chips. Osgood sought to demonstrate a correspondence between the character of such performances and a number of syntactic and lexical properties of the sentences subjects produced in their descriptions.

For example, some of the objects were used by the experimenter repeatedly and in immediate succession across a series of scenes, while other objects appeared only once or only at widely separated points in the experimental series. Osgood found that the subject's use of definite and indefinite articles was heavily determined by this feature of the experimental presentation. Roughly, when an item appeared for the first time, it was referred to with the indefinite article. Successive appearances separated by short intervals elicited the definite article. A similar effect was observed in cases which involved selecting an item from a contrasting set. If the experimenter selected a white poker chip from a ring of chips all but one of which were white, subjects described the performance as "the man takes a white chip." But, when the experimenter selected a chip with a feature which distinguished it from its reference

---

[5] To put this point more precisely: the difficulty with Skinner's experiment is that the manipulated variables are specified *under the same description* in the experimental hypothesis (pencils elicit utterances of "pencil") and in a rule of the subject's language ("pencil" refers to pencils). It *would* be interesting to test hypotheses about environmental control in which the manipulated variables are specified in some proprietary vocabulary (e.g., a vocabulary whose terms refer only to physical properties of inputs). Unfortunately, no one knows of any such hypotheses that are plausible enough even to be worth testing.

set, the performance was described as, e.g., "the man takes *the* blue chip." Other findings included the following.

1. The use of pronouns to refer to an object was dependent on such factors as the number of immediately successive actions in which the referent occurred, so that "whereas about half of the observers who perceived two actions of the same entity used *it* for the second reference to THE BALL, none of the single-action perceivers produced a pronoun" (p. 510).

2. The form of the auxiliary employed in descriptions was affected by whether the events described were perceived as completed or as continuing actions.

3. If an expectation was established by a series of vignettes, negative constructions appeared in subjects' descriptions when the expectation was *dis*confirmed. For example, after having seen a table serve as the setting for a variety of events, subjects described the situation in which only the table was present as "there is nothing on the table" rather than "there is a table at the front of the room."

4. Some of the experimental manipulations produced alternations between active and passive constructions. For example, in scene 1, the experimenter rolled a ball on the table. In scene 2, he placed the same ball on a plate. All subjects described scene 1 by constructions in which "the ball" occurred as surface subject ("the ball is rolling on the table," for example). In scene 2, however, 19 percent of the responses were in the passive voice (e.g., "the ball was placed on the plate"). Presumably, subjects who provided passive responses perceived the ball in scene 2 as *both* the focus of attention *and* the object of action.

5. Alternations between predicate-adjective constructions and constructions containing postnominal adjectives were produced by experimental manipulations which apparently affected the presuppositions of the subjects' descriptions. For example, subjects described a scene consisting solely of a black ball resting on the demonstration table with such forms as "there is a black ball on the table," but never with such forms as "the ball on the table is black." If, however, the experimenter went through a process of sorting through his sack of props, exposing a red cup, and then selecting a green one for display on the table, subjects used locutions like "the cup on the table is green," but never forms like "there is a green cup on the table." Osgood suggests, in effect, that in the second case, subjects assume that the "point" of the experimenter's actions is to choose between cups on the basis of their color. Thus subjects use descriptions in which the cups are

presupposed and their colors are asserted. Roughly, presupposition is controlled by perceived contrast, and the choice between pre- and postnominal adjectives is controlled by presupposition.[6]

It will be noticed that many of these results suffer from the difficulty we pointed out in discussing Skinner's speculations about pencils. The circumstances of the scene which subjects were exposed to *did* have a direct effect on their selection of lexical and syntactic forms. But insofar as the manipulated variable is one which is linked to the covarying linguistic form *by linguistic rule*, the experiments tell us little or nothing about stimulus control of verbalization. For example, in Osgood's study the past-tense morpheme was only elicited in descriptions of past events. One is inclined to find this unremarkable, since its use in referring to past events is precisely what makes a form like *ed* a past-tense morpheme.

But even when such experiments tell us little about stimulus control, they may still be informative. When we know that a linguistic form is connected to a certain situation by rule, not much is gained by showing that such situations elicit the form from appropriately motivated subjects. There are, however, cases in which it is precisely the linguistic rule that is in doubt; not every rule is as obvious as is" 'pencil' is used to refer to pencils." To take one example, it is plausible, but by no means self-evident, to argue that the semantic function of passivization is to shift focus from the logical subject of a sentence to its logical object. One can test this sort of hypothesis by showing, as Osgood did, that situations in which subjects are induced to shift (perceptual) focus bring about corresponding shifts from active to passive. Indeed, it would be interesting to extend this kind of experimentation by showing that manipulations which elicit passives in preference to actives tend also to elicit other transformations (like topicalization) which

---

[6] In fact, it seems likely that these results should be analyzed somewhat differently. Though there *is* a difference in presupposition between "the cup on the table is green" and "the green cup is on the table," that difference is associated with the scope of the definite article "the," *not* with the contrast between pre- and postnominal adjectives. Roughly, noun-phrase material (including adjectives) is presupposed when it occurs in the scope of the definite article. Shifting from predicate adjectives to prenominal adjectives thus alters presuppositions *when it involves moving the modifier into the scope of a definite article;* when it does not, presupposition is unaffected. Notice that a *post*nominal adjective will be presupposed when it occurs in the scope of a definite (e.g., "The boy who is sick won a prize."). Notice too that while "the green cup is on the table" presupposes a green cup, "a green cup is on the table" does not. In short, one would expect that the kinds of manipulations Osgood performed would control the selection between pre- and postnominal adjectives only in the very special case of movement into the scope of a definite article.

linguists identify as affecting focus. Such a demonstration would tend to show that the linguists are right in supposing that there *is* a uniform phenomenon of focusing which is common to a variety of otherwise distinct sentential forms.

There is a final remark that should be made about how stimulus control functions in experiments of this sort. What the experimenter must manipulate to gain control over the form or content of subjects' productions are their psychological states. For example, the difference between the conditions in which subjects use "the" and those in which they use "a" involves the speakers beliefs (or assumptions) about what is contextually definite for the hearer (very roughly, one does not say "*the* cat is on the mat" unless one believes one's hearer knows of some cat that it is the one being referred to). Thus, the "environmental" conditions upon which the choice between "the" and "a" turns are not *stimulus* conditions in the Skinnerian sense but rather conditions which involve *the speaker's construal of the stimulus situation.* To put it the other way around, we cannot achieve stimulus control over the speaker until we can determine how he will construe the speech scene; i.e., until we have stimulus control over his beliefs about his inputs. This is a point on which Osgood, unlike Skinner, is entirely clear. It is Osgood's reiterated insistence that what his experimental operations affect in the first instance is the subject's perceptual analysis of the stimulus array. Control over verbalization, when it is achieved at all, is achieved only via this analysis.

STRUCTURAL VARIABLES IN SENTENCE PRODUCTION

There is no theory about the way environmental variables determine what sentence is uttered for the same reason that there is no theory about how context variables determine the way a sentence is understood: in both cases, the entire psychology of the organism—motivation, set, belief, etc.—mediates between the input and its consequences. Clearly, if there is to be progress in psycholinguistics, we must avoid formulating the goals of the discipline in ways that presuppose the general psychology of the organism. In the case of sentence recognition, progress was made when we limited the problem to that of characterizing the interactions between perceptual routines and structural properties of sentences. The analogous move may prove profitable in the case of sentence production. Instead of asking for a theory which uses environmental information to predict the form of what the speaker will say, we set the more modest goal of characterizing the integrative processes involved in the organization of utterances. In particular, we may ask what representations of a sentence are computed in the course of its production, and what procedures are involved in such computations. In this way the kinds of questions to be investigated in the experimental analysis of production parallel those raised in Chapters 5 and 6.

In Chapter 5, we considered evidence from experimental tasks in which hearers are shown to be responsive to features of syntactic structural descriptions. Such evidence, taken together with the kind of distributional arguments reviewed in Chapter 3, establishes a prima facie case that structural variables play a corresponding role in speech production, since what the hearer must recover to understand a sentence presumably corresponds closely to whatever representations of that sentence the speaker encodes. It would, nevertheless, be extremely useful to find direct experimental evidence for the representation of surface and deep structural features in sentence production. It is this sort of evidence which we shall now review.

Clearly, the first thing to be established in an investigation of the relation between sentence production and structural variables is that syntactic structure per se does have an effect upon sentence production. Some of the evidence previously reviewed is suggestive in this respect. In particular, Miller and McKean (1964) used a sentence-production task in what they took to be an evaluation of sentence complexity, and it is likely that the outcome of their experiment was affected by integrative as well as perceptual processes. However, as we remarked in Chapter 5, it is unclear what correspondence we should claim between the subject's task in Miller and McKean's paradigm and normal sentence processing.

What is needed is a paradigm in which structural variables are manipulated independent of content variables in a production task. Of course, the speaker's choice between sentence forms is presumably not random, even in cases where the choice involves synonymous sentences. The best we can expect to show, then, is that pairs of sentences whose only semantic differences either are stylistic or involve features of focus, topic, etc., differ in production tasks in ways that can be predicted from their syntactic analyses. For example, the data from Osgood's study suggest an intimate relation between passivization and shift of focus. In all other relevant respects, unquantified actives and passives are apparently semantically equivalent linguistic forms. A production task which balances for change of focus and still finds an active-passive difference would thus suggest the psychological reality, for the speaker, of the syntactic properties of passives. In particular, such a finding would provide grounds for rejecting the hypothesis that all the variance in production tasks is contributed by content variables.

Experiments on the contribution of structural variables to production tasks are relatively scarce compared with the corresponding literature on sentence perception. Indeed, few paradigms for such experiments are available, simply because of the difficulty of eliciting responses of a specified syntactic form in anything approaching a natural task. But although it was not specifically designed to meet this problem, Tannenbaum and Williams' (1968) study can be construed as providing one such paradigm.

In their experiment, synonymous but structurally different sentences were produced on cue by speakers in a task where response latency was the dependent variable. Tannenbaum and Williams focused the subject's attention on one or another NP by having them read a paragraph in which that NP was the topic. After reading the paragraph, subjects were required to provide immediately either an active or a passive description of a line drawing, using the NP from the paragraph. It was thus possible to manipulate independently the surface form of the subject's response (by instruction) and the focus of his attention on the line drawing. In particular, the NP which was the topic of the paragraph could refer either to the actor or to the object of the line drawing for a trial on which the subject was instructed to produce either an active or a passive response. (The experimenter also provided a neutral focus condition as a control. In this condition, the topic of the paragraph referred neither to the actor nor to the object of action in the line drawing.)

Response times for the complete response were recorded. The results are summarized in Figure 7-2. In the neutral focus condition, active sentences show shorter latencies than passives. This is what would be predicted from the analogous studies on perception and is worth remarking upon, since it suggests not only that the structural differences between active and passive affect production but also that the effect is in the same direction as in perception. It would be of considerable interest to know whether this symmetry is general across syntactic structures.

It might be argued that the observed difference between active and

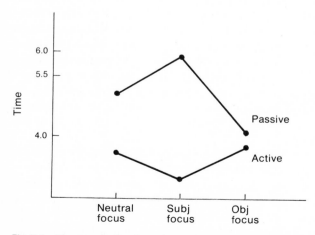

Fig. 7-2. Mean production times for actives and passives in three conditions of focus (after Tannenbaum and Williams, 1968).

passive in the neutral condition is explained by the fact that the latter is used to place a special emphasis on focus and is thus inappropriate in circumstances where the focus of the message has not been specified. In linguistic terminology, this would be accounting for the difference by arguing that passive is "marked" for focus but active is not. The data do bear out the claim that passive is marked for focus. In circumstances where the focus is on the logical subject, the discrepancy between active and passive is even greater than in the neutral condition; but in circumstances where focus is on the logical object, the difference between active and passive is not significant. This is just what would be predicted from the view that the passive is appropriate only where focus is on the logical object. The fact of primary interest from our point of view, however, is that active in the neutral focus condition is faster than passive in the object focus condition. This suggests a structural effect present even when considerations of focus are controlled.

There is, however, an obvious difficulty in interpreting Tannenbaum and Williams' results as relevant to the effect of syntactic variables in production: namely, that it requires making direct comparisons between latencies for actives and passives. Since latencies were measured to the *end* of subjects' responses, and since passives are longer than their corresponding actives, it is conceivable that the observed latency differences are mere artifacts of the length differences. So far as we can tell, however, if one assumes that the subjects produced syllables of normal duration, the critical difference between neutral focus actives and object focus passives remains even when one subtracts out the times required for uttering the extra syllables in the passives.

Had Tannenbaum and Williams been interested in syntactic effects rather than focusing effects, the appropriate dependent variable would have been latency to the initiation of response rather than latency to response completion. The former measure, unlike the latter, is insensitive to the length of the response. As things stand, it cannot be claimed that Tannenbaum and Williams' work provides a decisive demonstration of a purely structural effect in production. It does, however, provide a paradigm in which structure can be manipulated in relative independence of content, and this alone suffices to make the work methodologically interesting.

SURFACE-STRUCTURE VARIABLES IN PRODUCTION

Yngve (1960) proposed a model for the production of sentences which has provided the basis for considerable experimental inquiry. We have already seen (Chapter 5) that the notion of sentence "depth," which derives from Yngve's model, has played a role in experiments on sentence memory and perception. We argued, in discussing those experiments, that their theoretical bases were insecure. The available evidence suggests that a complexity metric defined over surface structure ought to have relatively little predictive power in memory paradigms, since it seems unlikely that surface representations of sentences are stored for long-term recall. Analogously, there is reason to posit a relatively direct induction of deep structures from very superficial surface analyses in sentence perception. If this is correct, then it would be unlikely that complexity metrics which are sensitive to details of surface trees will be confirmed in recognition tasks. And, in fact, the empirical support for the importance of sentence depth in memory and recognition is, by and large, not convincing.

However, Yngve's proposal must be taken quite seriously in a discussion of sentence production; indeed, it was in that context that the proposal was originally made.

Yngve's model entails an interaction between the surface structure of sentences and the short-term-storage demands on a speaker who utters them. The character of this interaction is determined by three assumptions about the integrative processes involved in the construction of a surface tree: namely, that the nodes in the tree are chosen from top to bottom, that they are chosen from left to right,[7] and that the load on memory at any point in the tree is proportional to the number of stored, yet-to-be-expanded nodes dominating that point. The basic idea is that each such node represents a structural commitment undertaken by the speaker, and that memory is exhausted to the extent that the speaker is required to keep track of such commitments. Thus, in the production of the tree fragment in Figure 7-3, there will be two unelaborated nodes (N and VP) at the point where the speaker says "the." The substance of Yngve's theory is that such unelaborated nodes must be stored—hence that they contribute to the memory load that the tree imposes upon the speaker.

In Figure 7-4, we have two roughly synonymous sentences analyzed for memory load as predicted by Yngve's theory. The important thing to notice is that the complexity value associated with each lexical item in the sentence is equal to the number of unelaborated nodes dominating the item, which is in turn equal to the number of left branches dominating the item. The main empirical consequence of Yngve's model is

---

[7] To put this assumption more precisely: let $(Y,Z)_X$ be any subtree such that X immediately dominates Y and Z and such that Y is to the left of Z. Then the assumption that processing is top to bottom requires that the choice of X be prior to the choice of either Y or Z; and the assumption that processing is left to right requires that every node dominated by Y be chosen before the choice of any node dominated by Z.

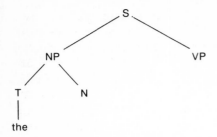

Fig. 7-3. According to Yngve's model, there are two stored nodes at the point in the production of this tree where the speaker says "the."

precisely that left branching plays a special role in determining the memory demands upon speakers.

Yngve's proposal has been criticized on linguistic grounds because it utilizes a surface grammar, and on psychological grounds because it makes opposed complexity estimates for speakers and hearers. The former criticism seems to us to be beside the point, since it is quite compatible with Yngve's account that what controls the production of a surface-structure tree may be a deep-structure tree (or some other abstract representation of a sentence) that the speaker has in mind. That is, Yngve's proposal is not *incompatible* with the psychological reality of deep structure; it is neutral. The only linguistic considerations relevant to evaluating Yngve's model would seem to be whether the surface trees he assumes are well motivated.[8]

The psychological objection is, however, more serious. On Yngve's account a natural assumption about *perception* is that it proceeds left to right and bottom to top and that an item is dismissed from storage as soon as it is assigned to a phrase. The consequence of these assumptions is, however, that left-branching structures ought to be easier than right-branching structures from the point of view of the perceiver. For

---

[8] Yngve's model does imply that the operations employed in constructing the surface tree which corresponds to some deep tree must determine their output in a certain order: namely, top to bottom and left to right. It should be emphasized that syntactic transformations do not have this property. The notion of the temporal order in which output elements are produced is not defined for transformations (or, for that matter, for any other syntactic rule; there is, for example, no definite sense to the question "does the rule $S \rightarrow NP + VP$ produce the NP or the VP first?"). On the other hand, it should be possible, in principle, to embed the transformations in a production model which would accept deep trees as input and construct surface trees in the order required by Yngve's theory. In this sense, Yngve's model is neutral on the psychological reality of transformations, just as it is neutral on the psychological reality of deep structure.

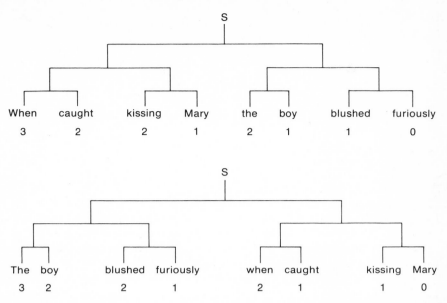

Fig. 7-4. The number of stored nodes at each point in the production of two semantically similar sentences. Notice how the storage demands associated with a given lexical item vary depending on the shape of the subtree dominating that item.

example, in Figure 7-5, the shortest phrase that contains A is 3. Thus, if the tree is being processed left to right and bottom to top, A can be dismissed from store as soon as B is recognized. In Figure 7-6, however, the shortest phrase that contains A is 1. Thus, A cannot be dismissed from store until B, C, D, and all the intermediate nodes have been recognized. Clearly, the model predicts that complexity is proportional to right branching for the perceiver, just as it predicts that complexity is proportional to left branching for the producer.

It seems, then, that a depth model does not provide a plausible account of recognition. But then, there is no particular reason why one should demand that it provide such an account. As we have noticed, there is no reason to suppose that sentence recognition does involve the recovery of a fully elaborated surface tree, and in this respect, it may be that the speaker and the hearer are asymmetric. For example, it is imaginable that the only way that producers can satisfy the output-order constraints characteristic of their language is by actually integrating the surface tree which dominates the output string. If this is so, and if the heuristics at the disposal of the hearer allow him to ignore surface detail in favor of relatively direct inductions of deep structure, it might well turn out that a complexity metric based on depth works for production but not for perception.

There is, in fact, experimental evidence which suggests that left

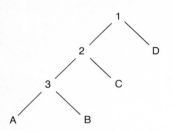

Fig. 7-5. Left-branching constituent structure tree. See text.

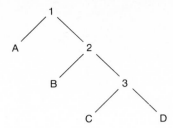

Fig. 7-6. Right-branching constituent structure tree. See text.

branching does play a prominant role in production tasks. This evidence supports Yngve's model or, indeed, any model on which surface constituents are chosen from top to bottom and elaborated from left to right.

The first piece of evidence suggesting the existence of an effect of sentence depth in a production task comes from a study by N. Johnson (1966). Johnson had subjects learn paired associate lists, where the first member of each pair was a digit and the second a sentence. The sentences were matched for lexical content but so constructed as to vary the number of surface nodes dominating their initial lexical items. (See, for example, Figure 7-4.) After trials in which the lists were learned to criterion, Johnson administered test trials. In both the learning and the test trials, the digit member of each pair served as a prompt for the corresponding sentence. The dependent variable was latency to the *initiation* of the sentence response, and the experimental prediction was that this latency would vary with the depth of the initial lexical item in the sentence.

Johnson's prediction was in fact confirmed. Comparisons between sentences matched for lexical content showed greater latencies for the versions whose initial segments had the higher depth. This provides some support for the notion that the elaboration of left branches in a surface tree does affect the amount of computational activity required for the production of the sentence.

There are, however, caveats that obscure the interpretation of this experiment. First, the sentences Johnson contrasted are arguably very different in acceptability. Those with the higher depth are also more awkward (consider "the boy who stood near me. . . ." versus "the boy near me who stood. . . ."). It is entirely possible that this difference in acceptability directly influenced production latencies or that it produced a difference in the degree of original learning of the stimulus list.[9] Thus, while Johnson's results are suggestive, they cannot be considered decisive.

The most persuasive body of evidence for the significance of the branching characteristics of surface trees in a production task comes from a series of experiments by Forster (1966, 1967). All these studies are variations on a paradigm in which the subject is required to complete a fragment of a sentence either by adjoining material to its left or by adjoining material to its right. Fragments of the former sort are called left-deleted (LD) and fragments of the latter sort are called right-deleted (RD). Thus "_____ the woman in a state of great agitation" is LD and "On his return to the house he found _____" is RD.[10]

It seems obvious that any model of sentence production which claims that the integrative processes involved are predominately left to right will predict that the speaker has more experience with supplying the last part of a sentence given a specification of its first part than with supplying the first part of a sentence given a specification of the last part. That is, any such model will predict that completing an RD ought to be easier than completing an LD. Moreover, almost any conceivable sentence-production model will be biased toward left-to-right processes at some levels of integration simply because speech is deployed in time. Even a theory which supposes that every part of a surface tree is planned prior to the utterance of any lexical items will still have to acknowledge a left-to-right readout of the lexical items themselves.

In light of these remarks, it is perhaps not surprising that Forster did find an asymmetry between LD and RD, with shorter latencies reliably associated with the latter. Forster constructed his stimuli by selecting a set of forty sentences, ten to sixteen words in length, from novels, magazines, etc. Each sentence was divided in the middle to yield fragments of equal length in words. Thus, each of the source sentences provided

---

[9] Johnson takes note of the possibility that the stimulus items were not equally well learned and argues against it on the grounds that latencies in the first ten of the twenty test trials are not significantly different from those in the second ten. This suggests that no further learning was taking place during the test trials, hence that all the items were equally well learned during training. However, inspection of Johnson's published data suggests that the lack of statistical significance should not lead us to embrace the null hypothesis; there does appear to be a possible serial decrease in latency over test trials.

[10] In most of the experiments, subjects were constrained to supply one word for each of the blanks. Forster (1968b) shows that removing this constraint does not alter the results in any interesting ways.

both an LD and an RD. The dependent variable was the number of fragments completed during a standard test interval of 75 seconds. The results were clear: mean score for RD was 5.49; mean score for LD was 3.27.

Given this finding, there are several questions to raise. First, we need to establish that the difference between LD and RD is reasonably language-specific and not merely an instance of some general fact about the way subjects cope with serially ordered material. Second, if the phenomenon is to be related to the Yngve model, we need to show that the difference between LD and RD is not just a consequence of the fact that the lexical contents of a sentence are ordered in time. That is, we need to show that the difference between LD and RD indicates left-to-right production processes at some level higher than lexical readout. These hypotheses are not independent, since any demonstration that the magnitude of the phenomenon is specifically related to the syntactic structure of the stimulus fragments would tend to confirm both.

What is the evidence for a relation between syntactic structure and LD-RD effects? Suppose one assumes that the subject's task in the experimental situation is essentially one of finding a completion which satisfies whatever constraints are imposed by the stimulus fragment. Then it ought to follow that both completion latencies and the magnitude of the LD-RD asymmetry is proportional to the number of such constraints. Now, if we can show that this is true for constraints defined at levels more abstract than the lexical level, we have an argument that these abstract levels are themselves computed in a roughly left-to-right fashion. For it will be remembered, it was precisely the fact that the speaker has more experience with left-to-right processes than with right-to-left processes which is assumed to account for the LD-RD asymmetry in the first place.

Forster (1967) attempted to show that LD-RD effects were determined by constraints defined at the level of surface phrase structure. Roughly speaking, he assumed that such constraints are imposed whenever the stimulus fragment contains an interrupted surface constituent. In order to estimate the number of such constituents interrupted by a given stimulus fragment, Forster assigned surface-structure trees to each of his source sentences. Since LD and RD items are constructed by making a cut at the midpoint of a source sentence, such trees can be used to estimate the number of constituents the subject will have to reconstruct to complete either of the fragments. This number is the *t-node count* for the fragments. Notice that, by definition, the *t*-node count will be identical for a pair of fragments which derive from the same sentence. Hence it cannot be used to predict differences between the LD and RD fragments of a given source. What one can do, however, is ask whether latencies vary as a function of *t*-node value in either LD or RD fragments. Ideally, one would predict (1) that there is a covariation between *t*-node count and latency for both LD and RD; (2) that the magnitude of the LD-RD difference increases with increase of the *t*-node count, since the higher the count is, the more the subject's differential experience with left-to-right processes should affect his performance. To find both these results would be to show, with some certainty, that production involves left-to-right processing of constituent structure.

In fact, the observed results were the following: *t*-node counts showed the expected relation with latencies for LD items but were not significantly correlated with latencies for RD items. In these circumstances, it is impossible independently to assess prediction (2). Since there is a correlation between *t*-node count and LD but not between *t*-node count and RD, it follows trivially that the size of the asymmetry between LD and RD must increase with increase in *t*-node count.[11]

Two points seem to emerge from these data. First, it is reasonably clear that there is *some* sort of interaction between the constituent structure of the fragment and the dependent variable. This argues against the view that the LD-RD asymmetry is attributable solely to the subject's experience in producing *lexical items* in left-to-right order. On the other hand, the theory that surface trees are produced left-to-right predicts a correlation between *t*-node count and RD, and this correlation is not observed. It is conceivable, however, that the failure of this correlation may be an artifact of the magnitude of the asymmetry between LD and RD; subjects may find RD so easy that no variance is detectable with the kind of measure Forster used. Some such conclusion is, in fact, suggested by the results in Bever, Garrett, and Hurtig (1973) discussed in Chapter 6. In that experiment, latency to the initiation of a sentence-completion response (rather than number of responses per unit time) was the dependent variable. A significant tendency *was* observed for subjects to exhibit longer latencies for RD completions of fragments with interrupted constituents as compared with their latencies for RD fragments with intact constituents.

The experiments just reviewed suggest surface-structure effects in sentence production, and they may suggest generally left-to-right construction of surface trees. They do not, however, tell us much about *which* properties of surface structure affect the speaker's performance.

---

[11] For LD items, the mean value of the correlation is .52; for RD items, the mean value of the correlation is .23. It is worth remarking that computing the *t*-node count from the sentences subjects actually gave as completions (rather than from the source sentences the experimenter used to construct the fragments) had no significant effect in increasing the RD correlations. On the contrary, this analysis yielded LD correlations of .50 and RD correlations of .06.

In particular, they do not tell us whether left branching plays the role in sentence production that would be predicted by Yngve's model. In general, experiments on *t*-node count cannot reveal asymmetries between left- and right-branching structures, since there will not, in general, be any relation between the *t*-node count for a fragment and the direction in which the fragment branches.

There is, however, another series of studies with the sentence-completion paradigm, also done by Forster (1968a), which throws some light on the specifics of Yngve's model. Forster argued as follows. In producing a left-branching structure from top to bottom and from left to right, one is in effect choosing certain items which appear relatively late in the structure before one chooses items that appear relatively early (i.e., the right-hand expansion of each node is chosen and stored before the subtree dominated by the left-hand expansion of that node is elaborated). This means that the production of a left-branching structure may often involve suiting items on the left side of that structure to constraints imposed by items on the right. Forster concluded from these considerations that speakers of languages which contain many types of left-branching sentences should be relatively experienced at selecting the early part of a sentence given a determination of the later parts. This should give speakers of such languages an advantage in coping with LD items. Forster therefore ran an experiment to show that a subject's performance with LD fragments is proportional to the amount of left branching in his language.

Forster used speakers of Turkish, Japanese, German, and English. While it is difficult to provide an entirely objective procedure for estimating the amount of left branching a language contains, most linguists apparently would rank these languages in the order just given. Every effort was made to equate the stimulus material and test conditions for the different language groups. The results are given in Figure 7-7. The obvious moral is that while there is an LD-RD difference for all the groups, the magnitude of this difference is relatively small for speakers of left-branching languages. (All interlanguage differences are significant except German versus Japanese.) That this is really an effect of language variables rather than subject variables is strongly indicated by the results of Forster and Clyne (1968); essentially the same experiment was run with English-German bilinguals fluent in both languages. The experiment showed the subjects' performance to be characteristic of the language in which the stimulus fragments occurred. That is, RD-LD differences were smaller for German fragments than for English fragments even where the fragments were completed by the same subjects.

There is one further study that bears mentioning at this point in a discussion of the order of integrative processes in speech production, since it may throw light on Yngve's theory.

Jarvella (1972) asked subjects to construct sentences containing

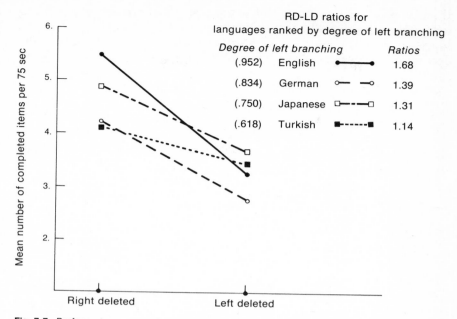

Fig. 7-7. Performance on completion of left-deleted versus right-deleted sentence fragments by speakers of four different languages (after Forster, 1968a).

specified pairs of verbs. Each such pair consisted of one complement verb and one noncomplement verb. In some conditions subjects were instructed that their sentences should contain the verbs in the order of presentation; in other conditions, subjects were free to reorder the verbs if they desired to do so. In general, subjects preferred to produce sentences of the surface form *main clause followed by complement clause,* where the complement verb functioned as the main verb of the first clause. This was largely independent of the order in which the verbs were presented, so that a verb pair like "die, believe" might elicit some such response as "they don't believe that John will die."

The interesting point about this finding is that *it holds even when verbs which take subject complements are included in the stimulus pairs.* Thus, a verb like "surprise," which takes a deep sentential *subject,* elicited the same sort of surface sentence as a verb like "believe," which takes a deep sentential *object.* In effect, subjects preferred to produce extraposed forms (like "it surprised Bill that John hit Mary") to nonextraposed forms (like "that John hit Mary surprised Bill") despite the fact that the latter are closer to the base tree than are the former.

What accounts for subjects' reluctance to produce complement constructions in the surface subject position? Jarvella makes the reasonable suggestion that what is happening is that subjects *are constructing deep-structure trees from top to bottom, sentoid by sentoid.* For this production strategy, the matrix sentence will be produced first because it is encountered first, and this will be true whether the matrix verb takes a subject complement or an object complement. Thus, a device constructing the deep tree in Figure 7-8 from top to bottom will encounter the sentoid containing "amaze" before it encounters the sentoid containing "go." Compare a device which constructs that tree from left to right for which the reverse prediction will be true.

If Jarvella's explanation is correct, it is important, for almost nothing is known about the order of planning at the level of deep structure. Unfortunately, however, there are a number of fairly strong considerations which militate against this account.

Subject Complementation

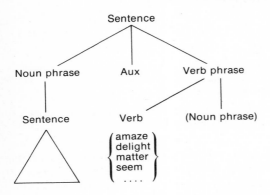

(1) That he went amazed me.
(2) I'm delighted you came.
(3) It doesn't matter we lost.
(4) It seems he likes pizza.
(5) He amazed me by going.
(6) It'd delight me if you came.

Object Complementation

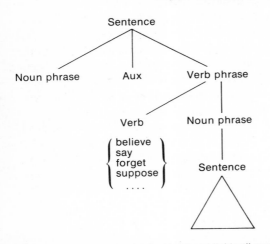

(1) I believe he's right.
(2) Say we can leave now.
(3) I forgot to bring it.
(4) It's O.K., I suppose.
(5) It's believed he left.
(6) If you say so, I'll go.

Fig. 7-8. Deep structures for "subject" and "object" complements (from Jarvella, 1972).

First, as we noted in Chapter 6, a preference for surface structures with the clause order *main + subordinate* extends to tasks which do not involve sentence production; in particular, to memory tasks, to ratings of sentence complexity, and, in most cases, to performance in the RSVP paradigm. It is hard to see how these findings could be explained by a theory which appeals to the order of operations in *producing* a sentence, and it seems arbitrary to assume that the speaker's clause-order biases are attributable to a different source from those of the hearer.

Second, the top-to-bottom-through-deep-structure theory makes the same prediction for relatives on *subject-NP's* that it does for *subject complements*. But extraposed relatives are avoided by most speakers. Thus, most speakers prefer "the rug which you spilled wine on has been dry-cleaned" to "the rug has been dry-cleaned which you spilled wine on." Yet a top-to-bottom-production device encounters the sentoid "the rug has been dry-cleaned" before it encounters the sentoid "you spilled wine on the rug," so if the top-to-bottom theory predicts a preference for extraposed subject complements it ought also to predict a preference for extraposed subject relatives.

Third, the preference for extraposition that Jarvella's subjects exhibit is indistinguishable from a preference for avoiding left-elaborated surface structures, since surface subject complements branch to the left. Indeed, Yngve has suggested that the reason extraposition exists as a transformation is to reduce the amount of left branching that speakers have to contend with. Like Jarvella's account, Yngve's fails to explain the bias against extraposed relatives. But insofar as there is independent evidence that left-branching surface structures are hard to produce, we do not also require assumptions about the ordering of deep-structure processes to explain data like Jarvella's. To provide a convincing argument that his data indicate top-to-bottom processes at the deep-structure level Jarvella would have to show that subjects prefer the surface order *matrix clause + subordinate clause* to the surface order *subordinate clause + matrix clause* even where the total left elaboration of the two structures is controlled. As things now stand, there is no evidence that this is true, and there is some indication to the contrary.[12]

---

[12] Indeed, there are some considerations other than simplicity that militate against Jarvella's explanation and in favor of Yngve's. We remarked in Chapter 6 that the preference for extraposed subject complements may be simply a special case of the preference speakers have for moving "heavy" NP's to the end of sentences (see Ross, 1967). This tendency would seem to be quite independent of subordination relations; for example, it operates to select the form $(V \; Part \; NP)_{NP}$ over the form $(V \; NP \; Part)_{VP}$ when the NP is elaborate. The overall effect of this preference would appear to be that of reducing the number of surface structures in which elaborate subtrees depend from left branches.

A recent study by Rochester and Gill (1973) provides some results which may be relevant to this question. In a corpus of spontaneous speech, they counted the numbers of "disruptions" (i.e., nonfluencies of various sorts) associated with *the-fact-that* complements (e.g., "The fact that the woman was aggressive threatened the professors") and those associated with relatives (e.g., "the book which was written by Millet was lauded by all"). These cases have roughly the same left elaboration, but here too, Rochester and Gill's results show evidence for the same dissociation of complements and relatives that we remarked above. The former structures had significantly more disruptions associated with them and, Rochester and Gill infer, were more difficult to produce than the relatives. It is difficult to tell from their report just how closely the cases Rochester and Gill analyzed corresponded to the properties of their example sentences, but to the degree that they did, it counts against the generalization we were seeking in Jarvella's results. We should also note that independent of their bearing on Jarvella's hypothesis, the results of Rochester and Gill suggest an interesting (but otherwise unverified) possibility that complements and relatives differ in the ease of their production.

The studies we have been reviewing— particularly the cross-language experiments by Forster — provide the clearest evidence so far available for the theory that surface trees are elaborated roughly in the order that Yngve's model requires: from left to right and from top to bottom. It is therefore notable that this evidence is all indirect. The experimental literature still lacks an entirely convincing demonstration that left-branching sentences are harder to produce than their right-branching counterparts; i.e., that depth as such contributes to complexity in a production task. What the experiments do seem to demonstrate unequivocally is that there is an involvement of surface-structure configurations in sentence production; hence that that level of linguistic structure is "psychologically real" for the speaker.

Before concluding this discussion, something should be said by way of reconciling the remarks we have been making here with our previous observations about the order of events in sentence processing. We said in Chapter 1 that both intuition and the existence of phenomena like verbal slips argue that the order of output of lexical items in a sentence is not the order in which the parts of the sentence are chosen. How is this compatible with the inclination we have evinced here to accept a left-to-right model of the construction of surface trees? The answer should be obvious: a surface tree is not the only representation of a sentence which must be computed in the course of producing the sentence. If it were, the

Yngve model would have such bizarre consequences as the following: since the tree is elaborated from top to bottom, its general structure must be chosen before its lexical contents; hence we must know the form of what we are going to say before we know what we are going to talk about. The way out of this paradox is to assume that the process of constructing a surface tree is guided by some more abstract representation of the sentence, and that this representation is available in more or less simultaneous display at the point when the surface tree is integrated. On the basis of current data there is no reason to reject the hypothesis that this representation is a deep structure.

PLANNING UNITS IN SENTENCE PRODUCTION

If sentences are not planned entirely from left to right, the question arises about what the size of the planning unit is. Another way of putting this question is: How much of the material to be uttered is present to the mind of the speaker at a given point in the production of a sentence, and at what level of analysis is the preplanned material available? This question is entirely analogous to one we raised about sentence recognition; just as we wanted to determine the size of the units into which sentences are segmented for purposes of perceptual analysis, so here we are asking about the size of the units in terms of which sentences are planned for purposes of behavioral integration. We will see that the available evidence favors the surface clause as a unit of sentence planning, just as it favors the surface clause as a unit of perceptual analysis.

Perhaps the best sources of information from which to infer sentence-production processes are cases in which the functioning of the production system is less than optimal. Spontaneous speech is characteristically nonfluent and replete with traces of the speaker's changing decisions about what to say and how to say it. Consider the following passage of transcribed speech (Valian, unpublished research):

Uh, my earliest, earliest memory
    Uh, my birthday is November 15 and my earliest memory of my only birthday. It's the only really mem—good memory I have, like the birthday that I remember the best (laugh). Can I start again? O.K. Uh, uh, O.K. My birthday is November 15, and uh, I remember my fourth, my fourth birthday the most. I didn't know it was my fourth birthday until about three weeks ago because I happened to ask my mother what happened to this, uh, red chicken that I used to play with when I was a kid and she told me uh, you know, the one that you got on your fourth birthday and, uh, I didn't realize it was my fourth birthday until then, but I always have memories of it because that chicken was, uh, like I used to sleep with it all the time and I remember the time that I first learned how to dance with that chicken, at my fourth birthday party, because I then the Lindy was the big dance and, uh, I wanted to learn how to do it and all my relatives were doing it.

It is hard to escape the conclusion that the production process is often a continuous series of approximations to the speaker's communicative intent. At least some of the false starts and hesitations and lapses of grammar and pronunciation that are so striking when one listens for them in spontaneous speech presumably represent on-line decision making by the speaker. They may thus provide a relatively direct indication of the character of sentence planning.

Though there are many types of speech error that might be examined, two such phenomena have received most of the experimental attention: hesitation pauses and slips of the tongue (or "spoonerisms"). We will see what implications these and related behaviors have for theories of sentence production.

Hesitations and other pausal phenomena.   Not all pauses in the stream of speech are hesitations, nor are all hesitations marked by pauses. For example, people frequently use stock phrases like "you know," "I mean," "it seems to me," etc., to buy time while formulating their message, and it is usually the case that the vowel preceding a hesitation pause is lengthened, possibly for the same reason. Quite often this lengthening is the principal acoustic analog of what is perceived as a hesitation pause (Martin, 1970). Conversely, many pauses that are acoustically indistinguishable from hesitations may be phonetically or syntactically conditioned and have nothing to do with sentence planning. An example of the former is the 80- to 120-millisecond silence between the closure and the release of a stop consonant. An example of the latter is the pause of several hundred milliseconds in duration which normally surrounds a parenthetical expression. There is no general "operational" procedure for sorting out true hesitations from these other phenomena. But barring evidence to the contrary, it seems reasonable to trust the intuition all speakers have that some of their pauses mark loci of subjective indecision and that others do not. There is also a reasonable objective basis for this distinction: syntactically and phonetically conditioned pauses do not drop out when we read aloud, nor do pauses for breath or pauses for emphasis. But hesitation pauses do.

In short, it is clear why hesitations have been of interest to psychologists—they have face validity as indicants of sentence-planning activity. It is also clear that the most obvious and frequently employed experimental technique for indexing hesitations (namely identifying them with acoustic pauses of some predetermined minimal duration) has at best only a rough construct validity.

Perhaps the earliest serious suggestion about the way pauses are distributed is speech derives from Lounsbury (1954). The suggestion is that hesitations occur at points of high statistical uncertainty in the speech stream, where uncertainty is assessed by determining transitional probabilities from word to word. There are two hypotheses implicit in this proposal: first, that words are the primary planning units in the integration of sentences and second, that the speaker's subjective uncertainty about what he is going to say mirrors the statistical uncertainties characteristic of his language. It is, to put it mildly, not self-evident that either of these suppositions is true.

The most frequently cited evidence that lexical uncertainty is the chief determinant of the distribution of hesitations derives from a study by Goldman-Eisler (1958a). She selected a set of twelve sentences from a large sample of spontaneous speech. By employing the Shannon guessing-game technique, she determined the predictability of each of the content words in these sentences, given the rest of the sentence as context. She then compared this assessment of uncertainty with the distribution of pauses in the original sample. (Her sole criterion for the occurrence of a hesitation pause was the existence of a silent interval of greater than 250 millisecond duration. Sixty such pauses occurred during the utterance of the sentences.) Goldman-Eisler's major finding was that hesitations in her corpus occurred significantly more frequently before high-uncertainty lexical items than before low-uncertainty items. (Compatible findings were obtained in Goldman-Eisler, 1958b.)

This study appears to support the view that hesitation is primarily a function of lexical uncertainty and suggests, though it does not demand, that the integration of the sentence is word by word. There are, however, problems with Goldman-Eisler's experiment. In the first place, the sample of sentences used was very small and hardly representative of normal spontaneous speech. (The sentences examined were required to be perfectly grammatical and directly related to the topic which was under discussion during the interviews from which the sample was drawn.) Second, the criterion adopted for the occurrence of a hesitation confounded juncture pauses and respiration pauses with true hesitations. Indeed, given that the sample of sentences was selected with a premium on well formedness and topicality, one might question the likelihood that any large number of true hesitations could have been included in the sample. Certainly a mean of five per sentence would seem to be unreasonably high. Finally, as Boomer has pointed out, the statistical significance of Goldman-Eisler's findings is sensitive to her decision to exclude from treatment all lexical items whose predictability from their left context was not approximately equal to their predictability from their right context. It is hard to see what justifies such a decision. (For a review of this and similar work by Goldman-Eisler, see Boomer, 1970). On balance then, it is unclear whether or not the Goldman-Eisler studies provide very strong evidence that lexical uncertainty determines the distribution of hesitations.

The principal remaining source of experimental support for this view comes from a finding of Maclay and Osgood (1959). In contrast to the small samples typically used by Goldman-Eisler, Maclay and Osgood analyzed 50,000 words of spontaneous speech. Moreover, in their study, only cases which independent judges took to be clearly hesitations (rather than junctural pauses or pauses for effect) were included in the analysis. Of relevance to the issues about lexical redundancy was the result of categorizing this material into "function words" (e.g., prepositions, conjunctions, relative pronouns, and determiners) and "content words" (nouns, verbs, adjectives, and adverbs). Maclay and Osgood argued that since content words are much less predictable than function words (as estimated either by a Cloze test or by taking account of the relative number of words of the two kinds), hesitations should precede content words more often than they precede function words if it is indeed lexical uncertainty that determined their distribution. This is the result they found: 59 percent of the total hesitations in their sample preceded content words; only 41 percent preceded function words.

Though Maclay and Osgood's study seems to be methodologically superior to Goldman-Eisler's, it is not immune to criticism. In the first place, the observed asymmetry, though significant, is not large. Moreover, it is unclear how much of the effect may be attributable to sampling error. There were more content words than function words in Maclay and Osgood's sample; one might therefore argue that there was not an equal a priori probability of occurrence of hesitations preceding the two classes of items (Valian, 1971). There is another factor which may inflate the asymmetry between content and function words which we will discuss when we review the results of Boomer (1965) below.

It should also be remarked that while the high relative frequency of pauses before content words supports the lexical redundancy theory of hesitations, there are other findings that Maclay and Osgood report which do not. Maclay and Osgood counted not only hesitations but also false starts and repeated items. They found, for example, that when a speaker changes his mind about the item he has uttered, he does not simply alter that item. Rather, he typically returns to the beginning of the *phrase* that contains the item and repeats it, changing only the offending word. This strongly suggests a unit of sentence encoding longer than single words, a suggestion that is strengthened by Boomer (1965).

Boomer segmented a corpus of spontaneous speech into "phonemic clauses." The phonemic clause is defined as "a phonologically marked macrosegment which, according to Trager and Smith, contains one and only one primary stress and ends in one of the terminal junctures /I, II, III [rising, loud, falling]/" (p. 150). Such units correspond well, but not perfectly, with surface-structure clauses (the most notable exceptions being certain kinds of nominalizations). Boomer's corpus contained

1,593 phonemic cluases, and 713 of them contained one or more pauses. In the analysis of the data, every position between words in a phonemic clause (including the position preceding the first word) was considered to be a possible pause location; see sentence (7-4). Boomer tabulated both "filled pauses" (e.g., "um," "er," "ah," etc.) and unfilled pauses exceeding 200 milliseconds in duration. Juncture pauses, which occur at the ends of phonemic clauses, were noted but excluded from the primary analysis.

7-4 $_1$And$_2$the$_3$weather$_4$was$_5$hot

Boomer compared the actual distribution of hesitations at each position in a clause with the chance distribution. The estimate of chance distributions assumed equiprobable occurrences at each position for clauses of a given length. As Figure 7-9 shows, the finding was that the location of hesitations did bear a regular relation to the structure of the phonemic clause; hesitations occur with a frequency greater than chance only toward the beginning of such clauses. This finding militates against the hypothesis that the distribution of hesitations is determined by lexical uncertainty since, as Boomer observes, the items receiving primary stress are characteristically the least predictable words in phonemic clauses, and such items tend to occur late in the clause rather than early.

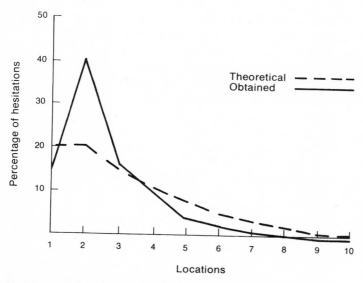

Fig. 7-9. Comparison of theoretical and obtained total percentages of hesitations occurring at successive boundary locations (Boomer, 1965).

What is surprising, however, is the fact that it is apparently the position *after* the first word in the phonemic clause rather than the position before that word which provides the modal pause location for every clause length from two words to ten. If the regular relation between the structure of the phonemic clause and the location of hesitations is due to the fact that the sentence is being integrated in clauses, why don't hesitations occur primarily at the initiation of the clause? There are at least two plausible explanations. Boomer's exclusion of juncture pauses from the analysis, though entirely defensible on the grounds that such pauses are syntactically conditioned, may also be overly conservative. It is possible, for example, that some of the pause time at syntactic junctures is in fact contributed by hesitation. If so, it would not be revealed by Boomer's treatment of the data. Yet, to the extent that juncture pauses include hesitation time, the difference between positions 1 and 2 in Boomer's analysis may be inflated. At any event, if juncture pauses are added to the analysis, the modal pause position is 1.

Second, the salience of position 2 may be partly attributable to the fact that that position will often separate a conjunction or a complementizer from a succeeding clause. For example, "that Mary had left" is a phonemic clause in "John was certain that Mary had left" and "and the weather was hot" is a phonemic clause in "the sun was out and the weather was hot." But if a new syntactic clause is often being introduced at position 2 of a phonemic clause, then Boomer's data can be taken to suggest that syntactic (rather than phonemic) clauses are the unit of sentence planning. In short, from a syntactic point of view, the selection of the phonemic clauses as the object of experimental analysis is not particularly well motivated, despite the clear relation between phonemic clauses and prosodic patterns. Of course, a unit defined in terms of juncture and stress may turn out to be more relevant to the analysis of production than a unit defined in terms of surface or underlying syntactic structure. On the basis of the present data, one simply can't tell.

The final observation to make about Boomer's results is that they bear on the interpretation of Maclay and Osgood's findings. The significantly greater likelihood of hesitation following the first word of a clause would tend to inflate the difference between content and function words that Maclay and Osgood report, since the first word of a phonemic clause will less often be a content word than will the second.

The available data suggest that some clause-like structure determines the distribution of hesitations during speech, though the results are hardly conclusive. Moreover, the induction from this (presumptive) fact to a theory about the size of units of production must be extremely cautious. It is quite likely that planning goes on simultaneously at several levels of abstractness, some of which may affect hesitation and some of which may not. Boomer remarks that "the hesitations in phonemic clauses are most likely to occur *after* at least a preliminary decision has been made concerning its structure and *before* the lexical choices have finally been made" (p. 156). But, of course, the coincidence of hesitation with phonemic clauses is neutral in this sort of speculation. For example, such a coincidence is compatible with the possibility that lexical choices are made *before* the point of hesitation; perhaps hesitations reflect decisions in the integration of a surface tree, and perhaps such integrations are guided by previously chosen deep-structure representations, which include some or all lexical contents. The fact is that we cannot tell what planning is reflected in the hesitation at the beginning of a phonemic clause, though the evidence suggests that it is not merely the planning of the next lexical item.

Studies of breathing. We have just seen that hesitations may be related to the clausal structure of speech. A related conclusion emerges from a consideration of breathing pauses.

There are two striking facts about respiration during speech: first, in fluent speech, people tend strongly to breathe at major constituent boundaries; second, in nonfluent speech, they tend *not* to breathe at hesitation points. Roughly, the relation between breathing and hesitation can be summarized as follows: breathing occurs where punctuation would be appropriate; hesitation occurs one word later. Thus, in a sentence like "In his yard, the boy found an apple," the natural locus for a breath would be between "yard" and "apple," and the natural locus of hesitation would be between "the" and "boy."

One might dismiss the correspondence between breath points and clause boundaries were it not for the failure of correspondence between breathing and hesitation. For, one might argue, speakers have an interest in fluency and therefore choose to interrupt the flow of speech by breathing only at points where pauses are prosodically natural. The boundaries of clauses are just such points; not only are prosodic pauses common there, but pauses at the boundaries of syntactic units are perceptually less salient than pauses elsewhere in the speech stream (see Boomer and Dittman, 1962, for discussion).

But, of course, hesitation pauses provide an opportunity to breathe that would be no more disruptive for the hearer than is the hesitation itself. Thus, the failure of speakers to breathe at hesitation pauses (which often are of a second or more in duration) cannot plausibly be attributed only to the speaker's desire to maintain a fluent output. This suggests, in turn, that the coincidence of breathing with syntactically defined units reflects true integration of respiration patterns with sentence-planning activities. If one does not know what one intends to say, one cannot plan one's breathing to synchronize with it; and similarly if one does not know when one will need to breathe, one cannot plan for respiration.

The data which motivate these speculations derive from experiments on the relation between breathing and speech. We turn first to experiments which indicate some sort of interaction of respiration with syntactic structure and some sort of complementarity between the location of hesitation and the location of respiration.

For example, Henderson, Goldman-Eisler, and Skarbek (1965) report a study which relates breathing patterns to the structure of read and spontaneously spoken messages. They examined the distribution of the silent intervals in their sample which were in excess of 100 milliseconds. The sum of such intervals determined what they referred to as the "pause time" for a sample. In the spirit of much of Goldman-Eisler's work, Henderson et al. thought of the production process as yielding alternating phases of planning (in which speech is nonfluent in the sense that there is a high ratio of pause time to vocalization) and readout of the preplanned material (in which speech is fluent in the sense that there is a low ratio of pause time to verbalization).

The interesting point, for our present purposes, is that Henderson et al. found a different relation between syntax and the location of respiration points in the fluent and nonfluent portions of the corpus. Breathing in fluent passages was similar to breathing during reading; in both cases, it is concentrated at syntactic boundaries (78 percent of respirations took place at major syntactic boundaries during fluent speech and 100 percent during reading). However, breathing in nonfluent free speech occurred at grammatical boundaries only 54 percent of the time.

The points Henderson et al. designated as grammatical boundaries were primarily clause boundaries. One cannot tell from the way the data are reported where subjects breathed when they did not breathe at one of the categorized positions. In particular, one cannot tell from the reported figures what the relation between hesitation pauses and breathing is, since the surprisingly low (100 millisecond) criterion for pauses surely includes not only hesitations but some pauses which are phonologically conditioned and all juncture pauses.

Earlier work by Goldman-Eisler (1956) does, however, indicate that there is a reduced amount of respiration during hesitation pauses; and two more recent studies suggest that speakers tend *not* to breathe at artificially induced pauses except when such pauses occur at major constituent boundaries. Webb, Williams, and Minifie (1967) conducted an experiment in which subjects had to read a passage aloud. Hesitations were induced by requiring subjects to fill in a one-word blank which occurred in the middle of the passage. The blank occurred either just after a sentence boundary or in the middle of a sentence. Subjects were in conditions of "high respiratory need" (impounded air equal to 50 percent of vital capacity) and "low respiratory need" (impounded air equal to 75 percent of vital capacity). No effect of respiratory need was found, but subjects breathed significantly less at within-sentence blanks than at between-sentence blanks. That is, hesitation affected respiration primarily when it was syntactically conditioned.

Fodor, Forster, Garrett, and Hakes (1974) also investigated the respiratory activity of speakers reading aloud. The passages were typed in groups of five words on file cards, regardless of punctuation. Thus, when subjects read aloud, they encountered "card boundaries" every five words; some of these boundaries corresponded to clause boundaries and some did not. The results were that subjects rarely breathed at a card boundary that was not also a major syntactic boundary, and all breathing not at card boundaries was syntactically conditioned. See, for example, Figure 7-10.

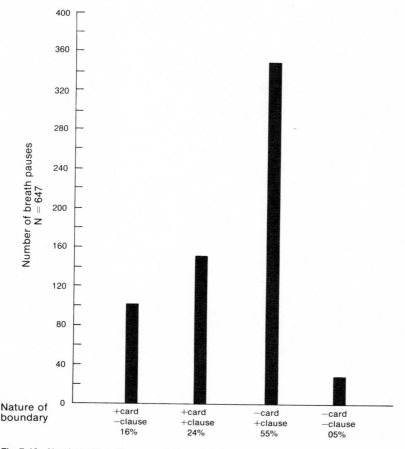

Fig. 7-10. Number of breath pauses at clausal and nonclausal boundaries for text in five-word groups on file cards. Breaths taken between cards are indicated +*card*; those taken internal to a card are indicated −*card*.

To summarize: If one assumes that hesitations mark the locus of planning, it seems that respiration is inhibited during planning. Similarly, it seems entirely clear that there is a strong relation between both hesitation and breathing and the clausal structure of speech, though the two relations are arguably different; that is, it may be that the distribution of breathing is determined primarily by the surface syntactic clause while distribution of hesitations is determined primarily by the phonemic clause. There have been a substantial number of studies of hesitation phenomena which we have not discussed here, but none of these studies materially affect the conclusions we have drawn from the experiments surveyed in the present context.

The data we have been discussing do not allow us to estimate the extent to which breathing is preplanned to match the syntactic structure of the intended message. In fact, they leave open the possibility that speakers do not preplan respiration but merely stop to breathe when they come to boundaries. This interpretation is all the more plausible in light of data like Webb et al., which suggest that the physiological constraints on respiration leave considerable latitude in the choice of breath points. But if the coincidence of breathing with clausal structure is not due to the clause-by-clause integration of the sentence, why does breathing respect the integrity of clauses? And, how are we to account for the complementarity of breathing and hesitation?

Spoonerisms and other slips of the tongue. Some of the morals we have drawn from the work on hesitation and respiration are supported by investigations of speech errors. The most popular source of such errors is the eponymous Reverend William Spooner (1844–1930), erstwhile dean of New College at Oxford, England; and not without reason, for the reported slips of Spooner's tongue always made a bumbling sort of sense. Witness such passages as these (addressed to a student):

> You've hissed (missed) all my mystery (history) lectures.
> I saw you fight (light) a liar (fire) in the back quad.
> In fact, you've tasted (wasted) the whole worm (term).

And memorably, on a windy day:

> Oh please, will nobody pat (pick) my hiccup (hat up)?

In fact, however, errors of the sort attributed to Spooner are not at all typical; apparent phone and syllable metatheses occur, and with some frequency, but full metatheses, in which the exchange results in two actual words, are relatively rare. Most exchanges result in nonwords [in about the ratio of 3 nonwords to 2 actual words on the basis of the published cases from Fromkin's corpus (1971) and a collection of sound metatheses by Garrett and Shattuck (1974)]. On these grounds alone, it seems reasonable to attribute most spoonerisms not to an unconscious Freudian desire to say something scandalous but rather to the temporary malfunction of the speech-control system which effects the serial deployment of words and phrases.

On the other hand, though many slips take place at levels less "deep" than a Freudian might suppose, it is also clear that many do not take place at the most superficial levels of integration. This can be seen from such facts as that many spoonerisms are morphophonemically conditioned: that is, one or both of the exchanged elements take on the morphophonological characteristics typical of their new environments. This means that the rules which determine the morphophonemic shape of an element must apply at a point in the integration of the sentence that is *later* than the point where the slip occurs. Consider such spoonerisms as "What the specifity of speech add [∧ps] to" for "What the specificity of speech [ædz] up to." What has happened here is that the tense element has been displaced from the end of "add" to the end of "up" and has been morphophonologically conditioned to agree with its new environment by a rule which makes tense unvoiced following an unvoiced element. Precisely the same accommodation with the opposite effect is shown by an example from Fromkin (1971). She reports "tap [stabz]" for "tab stops," in accordance with a rule which makes the plural morpheme voiced when it follows a voiced element.

In fact, order errors apparently occur at practically all levels of analysis including distinctive features, phones, syllables, morphemes, words, phrases, and semantic features. They thereby somewhat confusingly provide support for the psychological reality of nearly every level of linguistic analysis known to man. Before considering some of the implications of this embarrassment of riches, we will review data on the size and nature of the units such errors can subtend. Of all the data on spoonerisms, these are probably the least clear. However, they throw the most direct light on the problem of decision units in production.

Boomer and Laver (1968) analyzed the recorded proceedings of conferences in order to amass a corpus of about 100 speech errors. Two of their findings are of special interest. First, sound exchanges most often took place between elements of the same phonemic clause; second, the most likely source of intrusive sound was the "tonic" (i.e., the most highly stressed) word of the clause.

It is a condition upon the first of these findings' being of the theoretical interest that it does not simply represent a decrease in the incidence of exchanges as a function of an increase in the separation of the exchanged items. In particular, one wants to be sure that the probability of exchanging items separated by a given number of elements is significantly smaller when a clause boundary appears between the elements

TABLE 7-1. FREQUENCY OF SOUND EXCHANGES BY SEPARATION IN SYLLABLES AND BY WORDS

Number of separating syllables	Number of observed errors	Number of separating words	Number of observed errors
0	72	0	103
1	66 (1)	1	57 (1)
2	19	2	4
3	6	3	2
4	5	4	2
‹4	2 (1)	‹4	2 (1)

Entries in parentheses are errors which spanned clause boundaries.

than when it does not. This is apparently the case. Table 7-1 (Garrett and Shattuck, 1974) gives the distribution of sound-exchange errors as a function of syllable and word separation between the elements involved. Note, for example, that none of the exchanges between adjacent elements crosses a clause boundary. In fact, in the entire corpus, only two sound exchanges do so.

The natural interpretation of an exchange of elements in an utterance requires that they be simultaneously available when the first of the exchanged items is uttered. On this assumption, the interpretation of the first of Boomer and Laver's findings seems transparent: the unit within which exchanged items are simultaneously displayed is the phonemic clause; items not within a clause are not simultaneously displayed and hence not exchanged.

The second finding—that the stressed item in a phonemic clause is the most probable source of the intruding material in a slip—is open to several possible interpretations. It may be that there is an intrinsic connection between prosody and slips. This interpretation is favored both by Boomer and Laver and by MacKay (1970); the suggestion is that the tonic item has a stronger neural representation than any other word in a clause simply by virtue of its heavy stress. However, there is another possible reading of these data. The item with the heaviest stress in a construction will normally be the head of that construction, and it is conceivable that heads of constructions are chosen earliest, the rest of the material in the construction being organized around them. Since material that is chosen first is available longest, it is reasonable to argue that such material should provide the source of most intrusions.

There are two arguments which favor the latter interpretation over the former. First, phrasal stress is not distorted by exchanges; exchanged material exhibits the stress level characteristic of its *new* location. If it is tonic stress on an item which determines whether it is moved, then one would expect that the tonic material would retain its stress level when it is exchanged. Consider examples like (7-5).

7-5　How bad things were → How things bad were (Boomer and Laver)

　　What's the point of beating your brick against a head wall? (Garrett and Shattuck)

The second argument, which suggests that it is not their high stress per se which causes tonic items (or material within them) to be anticipated, comes from considerations of the characteristics of slips in which whole words (or phrases) are exchanged. Such slips, like sound exchanges, tend to select the stressed item in a construction. However, unlike sound exchanges, word and phrase exchanges *do* cross clause boundaries, and when they do so, they tend to preserve the syntactic subcategorization of the exchanged items.

Interestingly enough, this fact seems to hold not only for exchanges which cross surface clause boundaries but also for exchanges which cross deep-structure sentoid boundaries. In neither case does one find verbs exchanged with nouns, nouns with adjectives, etc. See, for example, slips like (7-6).

7-6　I wouldn't buy macadamia nuts for the kids → I wouldn't buy kids for the macadamia nuts. (Fromkin)

　　A fall in pitch occurs at the end of the sentence → An end of the sentence occurs at the fall in pitch. (Fromkin)

　　I saw a lot of trucks down there towing cars away → I saw a lot of cars down there towing trucks away. (Garrett and Shattuck)

　　Everytime I put one of these buttons ón, another one comes óff → Everytime I put one of these buttons óff, another one comes on. (Garrett and Shattuck)

Although the rarity of full word or phrase exchanges makes interpretation difficult, what seems to be happening is that elements that come from different sentoids are exchanged only when they have corresponding node labels. When the elements are in the *same* sentoid, the exchange may take place between different form classes—i.e., exchanges between members of different form classes behave in the same way as sound exchanges, as in (7-7) (from Garrett and Shattuck).

7-7　It couldn't have anything to do with the.... → It couldn't have to do anything with the....

　　You're not allowed to mix meat with milk.... → You're not allowed to meat mix with milk....

　　Does your store close at six.... → Does your close store at six....

This pattern of results clearly favors temporal priority rather than heavy stress as the feature of tonic items which accounts for their being anticipated in exchanges. What seems to be happening is that heads of constructions (in effect, major-category content items) are chosen at some level of representation before the integration of the surface form of the utterance. This material is present to the mind during the course of surface integration, which latter process is essentially left to right and surface clause by surface clause. These assumptions provide for all the major observations. On the one hand, phenomena likely to be the consequences of late integrations (like sound-structure changes) observe surface clause boundaries, while phenomena which are represented in early integrations (like lexical choices) do not. On the other hand, the syntactic category of words exchanged between clauses is preserved, and this is what one would expect if surface integrations are guided by abstract representations which are themselves syntactically subcategorized. Once again, we have a picture of the sentence-production processes which is compatible with the view that surface integrations are guided by something like previously chosen deep structures. It goes without saying that while the data seem compatible with this view, they do not *demand* it; theorizing at this stage of investigation is extremely hazardous because it is largely unconstrained.

Slips and the psychological reality of linguistic elements. In most of our discussion, we have been interested in slips as a source of insight into the psychological processes which underlie the integration of relatively long stretches of speech. But slips can also be viewed as providing a source of evidence for the psychological reality of linguistic constructs. When items are regularly exchanged, one suspects an underlying identity of representation. Insofar as the exchanges respect a grammatically motivated taxonomy, this factor argues for the psychological reality of the classes that the taxonomy postulates.

There are, for example, regularities in slips which provide an abundance of support for units of linguistic analysis smaller than phrases. We have already seen cases of the independent movement of stem and affix. Another, particularly striking illustration is (7-8), where quite clearly, the stems have been moved and the affixes left behind.

7-8   He made a lot of money *installing* telephones → He made a lot of money *intelephoning* stalls. (Garrett and Shattuck)

Just as slips provide evidence for segmentation of complex words into stem and affix, so too they provide evidence for the psychological reality of syllables. In particular, sound exchanges obey a "law of syllable place," such that sounds which come from initial syllables permute with one another, as do sounds from medial syllables and sounds from syllable final position (see Fromkin, 1971, where data about spoonerisms are brought to bear on a variety of questions of the psychological reality of various aspects of phonological descriptions).

One of the more interesting aspects of the slip data is that they appear to provide evidence for distinctive features (as opposed to phones) as the relevant apparatus for the description of speech sounds. This may appear paradoxical, since one's first impression is that most spoonerisms involve precisely the permutation of phonemes. ("Phonemes" rather than "phones," since, as we have already observed, transposed speech sounds are accommodated to their new phonetic environment.) There are, however, two arguments which favor the distinctive feature analysis: first, there are a variety of cases in which the best analysis seems to be that what is exchanged is not a pair of whole phonemes but just one or more of their features; second, the probability of an exchange between two speech sounds appears to be fairly directly related to the number of features they have in common (MacKay, 1970; Nooteboom, 1967). With respect to the first claim, consider such cases as (7-9). If one wanted to try

7-9   **Errors span greater distances than. . . . → Errors / skræn bej ɚ / distances than. . . .**

to represent this slip in the terminology of phones and phonemes, one would have to say that p and g are permuted and that the /g/ must then be altered because of a phonological constraint which prohibits the sequence / # s g——/ in English. This account, however, doesn't explain why /g/ has gone to /k/ (as opposed to, say, /l/ or /h/). Moreover, and more important, it does not explain why /p/ goes to /b/ in the environment / # ____æt ɚ / (note that /pæt ɚ / is phonologically well formed). In the feature analysis, however, all these facts are easily accommodated, e.g., by assuming that what permutes is not /p/ with /g/ but rather all the elements of their feature matrices except *voicing*, which is, as it were, left behind. There are alternative possible analyses in terms of features, but it is hard to see how any explanation which does not appeal to the internal structure of phones could account for slips where the exchanged items exhibit the sort of complementarity illustrated by this example. (For similar cases, see Fromkin, 1971, pp. 35–36.)

A second argument for the feature analysis of slips is that the probability of an exchange between elements is roughly proportionate to the number of features they have in common. According to MacKay, 56 percent of reversed consonants in the corpus he studied differed by only one feature; only 2 percent differed in as many as four features. This is not to say, however, that we can predict the distribution of slips just by counting shared features; there are apparently qualitative as well as quantitative considerations involved. For example, one almost never gets permutations of consonants with vowels, however many shared features a given consonant and a vowel may exhibit. As Fromkin remarks, "the only conclusion that one can draw from the examples of feature switching . . . is that at least some of the proposed distinctive features are independent behavioral units . . . but an examination of the errors . . . definitely shows a hierarchy or independence of certain features" (p. 37).

SUMMARY

Practically anything that one can say about speech production must be considered speculative even by the standards current in psycholinguistics. We have assumed that speech production is a matter of computing a sequence of encodings of a message; that this sequence starts with a representation which formally characterizes the speaker's communicative intent; and that it ends with a surface form. The first is presumed to be at least as abstract a representation as linguistic semantics provides for sentences and to be in the language in which central data processing occurs. The last is assumed to be interpretable as a sequence of instructions to the vocal apparatus. It is a research problem what interlevels of encoding occur between these two and in what order these interlevels are computed.

We have seen that there is considerable data favoring the view that surface constituent structure is one such interlevel, and that the process of constructing surface trees is roughly left to right, top to bottom, and clause by clause. For a number of reasons, this process must be guided by a more abstract representation than surface syntax affords. We noted that some of the data from slips suggest that this abstract representation is itself syntactically organized at least to the extent of marking major categories of lexical items and phrases. The data are thus compatible with the assumption that deep structure is psychologically real for the speaker and that the integration of the surface tree of a sentence is guided by a previously computed representation of its deep tree.

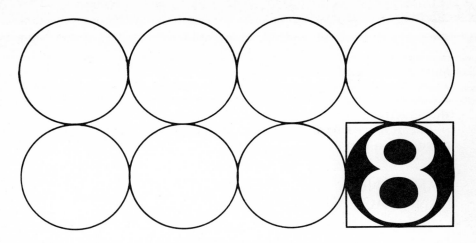

FIRST LANGUAGE LEARNING

This chapter is divided into three parts. In Part 1, we explore one of the fundamental differences between approaches to psycholinguistics within the tradition of generative grammar and earlier accounts of language in American psychology. It was a cardinal principle of those schools of psychology which descended from philosophical empiricism that language learning is essentially homogeneous with the learning of nonverbal behaviors in infrahuman organisms, so that the concepts available within general behavior theory are powerful enough to provide the basis for an account of language development. An alternative view, that has been typical of much of current psycholinguistics, is that the mechanisms of language learning are largely species-specific and task-specific—in particular, that they are not instances of universal principles of learning.

In Part 2, we assume a generally nativistic account of language acquisition and discuss some recent proposals about the character of the underlying innate endowment.

In Part 3, we survey some of the data which bear upon the theories discussed in Part 2.

PART ONE. THE SPECIFICITY OF LANGUAGE SKILLS

It is sometimes said, in a rough-and-ready way, that while the American tradition in psychology is largely empiricist, the view of language learning characteristic of psycholinguists working in the tradition of generative grammar is nativistic. This way of talking is harmless unless it leads one to suppose that empiricist theories of learning are somehow able to do without assumptions about the character of the innate information that organisms bring to learning tasks. It is important to understand that no theorist whose views of learning are coherent can avoid such assumptions [for a discussion of this issue, see Harman (1969) and Chomsky (1969)]. We shall presently see that there *is* a real disagreement between the American tradition in learning theory and the views most psycholinguists now hold about the nature of language acquisition; our present point is that the disagreement is not properly captured by saying that one position is nativistic and the other is not.

For the empiricist, the learning of languages is primarily a matter of discrimination learning: the ability to distinguish between utterances of sentences and nonsentential sounds is treated as a learned perceptual discrimination, and the ability to produce linguistically regular utterances is treated as a learned response discrimination. To understand why any such theory must be committed to fairly strong assumptions about the innate contribution of the organism to its performance in learning tasks, we must consider the discrimination-learning paradigm in some detail.

Whenever an organism learns a discrimination as the result of training, certain very general conditions must be satisfied. In the first place, there must be a *training period* during which the organism experiences correlations between reinforcement and certain other events. In typical discrimination-learning experiments, these "other events" are stimulus-response pairs. Second, it is a logically necessary condition for the occurrence of discrimination learning that the responses of the organism toward some potential future stimuli must be modified as a result of training. Finally, it is a logically necessary condition for the occurrence of discrimination learning that there be potential stimuli toward which training does *not* modify the organism's behavior. (A response that transfers to everything is not a discriminated response.)

Let us call the set of events with which reinforcement is coincident during the training period the *positive training set*. We will say that other events experienced by the organism during the training period constitute the *negative training set*. Finally, we will call the events toward which the organism's future behavior is modified by training the *positive transfer set* and the events toward which the organism's future behavior is *not* modified the *negative transfer set*.

We may now think of what happens in discrimination-learning experiments as a "game" the psychologist plays with the experimental organism. This game is played in the following way: the experimenter specifies the training sets by manipulating the reward contingencies. The experimental animal is then required to choose a corresponding transfer set. The animal wins (i.e., continues to be reinforced) if the positive transfer set it chooses is related to the positive training set in the right way (i.e., if it shares with the members of the positive training set those properties upon which reward is, in fact, contingent). On the other hand, the animal loses (i.e., ceases to be reinforced) if it chooses a positive transfer set whose members do *not* exhibit those properties upon which reward is contingent.

In short, what happens in the discrimination experiment is that the animal "bets" on which positive transfer set a given positive training set belongs to. There is, however, a more illuminating way of looking at it: having experienced a set of reinforced events, the animal is required to decide which properties the members of that set share with one another, but not with unreinforced events.

Notice that these two ways of characterizing the animal's problem are actually equivalent. This is because each hypothesis that the animal can devise about what property distinguishes unreinforced from reinforced training trials automatically determines a pair of positive and negative transfer sets. Thus, if the animal bets that ϕ is that property, it thereby chooses events exhibiting ϕ as belonging to the positive transfer set.

Now, given any finite set of reinforced events, there are obviously indefinitely many properties its members have in common with one another but not with the unreinforced events the animal has experienced. That is, there are indefinitely many hypotheses that will be true of all reinforced events and no unreinforced events, whatever the objective schedule of reinforcement happens to have been. Here then is the puzzle that a substantive theory of learning must solve. There are indefinitely many distinct bets that the animal can, in principle, make about what property defines the positive training set. Each such bet determines a different pattern of transfer: i.e., each bet determines a projection of the positive training set onto a different positive transfer set. Hence for any given training set there are infinitely many corresponding transfer sets among which the animal much choose. Question: What determines the choice?

In the case of animals in Skinner boxes, the empiricist may plausibly argue that the organism doesn't do anything like choosing among an infinity of possible transfer sets when it learns. It may be, says the empiricist, that there are an infinity of *predicates* that the events in the positive training set satisfy and that are not satisfied by the events in the negative training set. But it is a fallacy to think of the animal as somehow sorting through these predicates in order to find the one which names the property upon which reinforcement is contingent. For of that infinity of possible descriptions of the positive training set, there is only one (or only a few) that the animal could be conceived of as entertaining. Thus descriptions of the reinforcement set that refer, for example, to the abstract numerical properties of its members, to their geographical properties, or to their astrological properties simply do not occur to the animal. What does occur to it (or, to put it less tendentiously, what the animal does respond to) is things like color, sound, odor, rudimentary configurational properties, motion, and whatever other sensory properties it has sensory mechanisms for detecting. Only if the reinforced property of the members of the positive training set is one of these, or perhaps a simple Boolean function of them, does the animal learn. In short, there is no problem of "choosing a transfer set" because the choice is determined by the organism's *peripheral physiology*.

It is important to notice, however, that this way out of the problem (which, so far as we know, has been accepted by every psychologist who has discussed the problem at all) is itself nativistic. The suggestion, after all, is simply that the organism comes prewired to choose its transfer sets in a certain way (by reference to the sensory properties of its members) and not in other ways (not by reference to their number-theoretic or astrological properties). It is obvious, moreover, that the nativist move is the right move to make here. Unless one makes it, one creates an insuperable difficulty about how the organism ever makes the right induction from the observed contingencies of reinforcement.

Indeed, the most profound students of learning, be they empiricists or nativists, have generally acknowledged that there can be no explanation of generalization of training which does not eventually refer to the innate organization of the organism. Pavlov assumes as a matter of course that the pattern of generalization typical of a species must reflect the "spread of neural excitation," the character of which is in turn determined by the local organization of the organism's nervous system. Similarly, the philosopher Quine argues that the possibility of learning presupposes, on the part of the organism, an innate quality space and an innate distance measure. The argument in both cases is essentially the same: there cannot be coherent transfer of training unless there are some general principles that determine which transfer set is selected by a given training set; and, on pain of infinite regress, we cannot assure that these principles themselves are all learned.

We can summarize the preceding discussion as follows: *Any* theory of discrimination learning must consist of two components. The first answers the question, What hypotheses does the organism have available for defining possible relations between training sets and transfer sets? The second answers the question, What considerations determine which of two such hypotheses the organism chooses in a specific learning situation? Answers to the latter question are generally given by theories constructed in terms of reinforcement variables. Such theories can profitably be construed as partial specifications of confirmation metrics, according to which the probability that the organism will accept a hypothesis is taken to be some complicated function of the frequency with which acting upon that hypothesis has yielded "confirming" data (i.e., rewards). Practically all traditional learning theory has this character, except that "probability of acceptance of a hypothesis" is usually called "response strength," "habit strength," etc.

The first kind of question is widely ignored in the learning theoretic tradition. However, as we have seen, any theory of learning must make some assumptions about the range of hypotheses available to the organism in the learning situation, and, in the long run, the assumptions one makes must be determined by what one supposes the innate cognitive structure of the organism to be. It is in this sense that no one can avoid being nativistic about learning, and it is in this sense that the controversy between classic and contemporary views of language acquisition is *not* a controversy over nativism.

But while it is a conceptual point that any organism which learns must have inherent principles for projecting its past experience to new cases, it is a question of brute fact whether such principles are species-specific, task-specific, or both. For example, it is a factual question whether the learning principles that underlie human-language acquisition are similar to those which underlie the acquisition of birdsong or, for that matter, the acquisition of nonlinguistic skills in humans. *It is, in short, the questions of species-specificity and task-specificity, rather than the question of innateness, that underlie the current disputes between empiricists and psycholinguists.* It is to these questions that we now turn.

THE SPECIES-SPECIFICITY OF LANGUAGE

A good one-sentence summary of the traditional American view of the psychology of language might be: "Verbal behavior differs in complexity but not in kind from learned behavior in animals." The consequences of this view were pursued with relentless consistency by American learning theorists. For example, Mowrer (1960) argued that given the essential homogeneity of verbal and nonverbal learning, the fact that humans and no other animals have achieved speech can be attributed only to the relatively advanced development of motor control of the vocal system in man. "It can hardly be doubted that the greatest single 'mutation' which separates man from other anthropoids consists precisely of this: new and more abundant neural connections between the speech center in the brain and the speech organs!" (p. 111).

Indeed, the literature of this period abounds in attempts to train animals to talk, thereby demonstrating the essential homogeneity of human-language learning with infrahuman learning of motor skills. It seems to have been assumed that success in teaching language to an infrahuman organism is a critical experiment in demonstrating the interspecific character of the learning mechanisms involved in language acquisition.

These early attempts to teach animals to talk were, however, uniformly unsuccessful (cf. Kellogg and Kellogg, 1933; and the review by Brown, 1970). Nevertheless, theorists were surprisingly willing to draw morals for human-language learning from the putative facts about animals.

> It is apparent that birds learn to talk when and only when the human teacher becomes a *love object* for them, ... In terms of psychoanalytic theory, the bird, as a result of developing "positive cathexis" (love) for its human trainer or "foster parent," identifies with or tries to *be like* that person.... So far as can be determined at present, essentially the same account holds, at least up to a point, for acquisition of speech by human infants. ... Human infants, like birds, are vocally versatile creatures and in the course of random activities in this area will eventually make sounds somewhat similar to those which have already acquired pleasant connotations [Mowrer, 1960, pp. 79–80].

Whatever one may think about the advisability of applying psychoanalytic theory to mynah birds, it *is* clear that the early failures to teach speech to animals are equivocal. For organisms that can produce speech-like sounds (parrots, mynah birds, etc.) are not remarkably plausible candidates for learning complex symbolic systems. Conversely, organisms whose general intelligence seems even remotely comparable to that of man (chimpanzees and possibly dolphins) have articulatory systems that are not well adapted to the production of speech sounds.

Two recent studies (both still in progress) have attempted to circumvent these difficulties by teaching a nonverbal language to chimpanzees. We shall briefly review these studies, concentrating on what they show about the chimpanzee's ability to master syntactic structures comparable to those found in human languages.

Washoe.   The first of the two attempts to teach chimpanzees some nonverbal coding of natural language is reported in Gardner and Gardner (1969). The Gardners raised the year-old female chimpanzee Washoe in a linguistic community of speakers of American Sign Language: a system of signing that relies predominantly on word signs rather than a sign alphabet.

Perhaps the most interesting feature of the Gardners' methodology was the decision not to employ stringent and regimented training procedures. Brown (1970) comments that Washoe was "raised as a child" (p. 210). Though operant reinforcement and imitation were occasionally employed by Washoe's teachers, the primary training program consisted in surrounding Washoe with humans who used the signs to communicate with one another and with the chimpanzee. In this respect, Washoe's linguistic apprenticeship was reasonably comparable to that of a human child. The Gardners summarize their methods with the remark that "Washoe has been exposed to a wide variety of activities and objects, together with their appropriate signs, in the hope that she would come to associate the signs with their referents and later make the signs herself" (Gardner and Gardner, 1969, p. 667).

The results of this procedure appear to have been mixed. By the time Washoe was about 3 years old, she was in control of some thirty-five different signs. These signs not only were "intelligible" to Washoe in the sense that she appears to have understood them when they were produced by others but were also produced spontaneously by Washoe in appropriate circumstances. Moreover, the pattern of generalization of these signs were strikingly "human." "In general, when introducing new signs we have used a very specific referent for the initial training—a particular door for 'open,' a particular hat for 'hat.' ... Washoe has always been able to transfer her signs spontaneously to new members of each class of referents. ... The sign for 'flower' is a particularly good example of transfer, because flowers occur in so many varieties, indoors and outdoors, and in pictures, yet Washoe uses the same sign for all" (pp. 670–671).

As the Gardners themselves remark, these results seem to be continuous with familiar achievements of domestic animals. Anyone who has lived with dogs knows about their ability to learn (and sometimes to invent) characteristic begging gestures and "out" gestures and to use these in circumstances that seem "appropriate" from the human point of view. The "out" gesture "generalizes" from one door to another but not, say, from doors to tomatoes. This suggests that nonhuman animals perceive similarities and differences between situations in ways that are sufficiently like those of humans to be comprehensible to us (a fact which ought not, perhaps, to strike us as surprising, though it raises difficulties for a Whorfian who sees our perceptual categories as themselves a consequence of the structure of our language).[1] Moreover, though the Gardners had explicitly hoped that Washoe would learn "not only to ask for objects but to answer questions about them and also to ask us questions. . . . " (p. 665), Washoe's signing, like that of domestic animals, appears to have remained resolutely nonconversational. Washoe didn't chatter with her trainers in the way that children chatter with their parents, nor did she use her language to make spontaneous reports of the state of her nonlinguistic environment.

What *is* striking in the Gardners' results, however, is the fact that at about 2 $^1/_2$ years of age, Washoe began to communicate with *sequences* of signs. Thus we begin to find not only occurrences of the sign for "up," "tickle," "flower," and so forth, but also sign sequences like "Give please food," "hurry open," "more tickle," etc. Does this mean that Washoe's language is beginning to develop a "syntax"?

Brown has made two points which he thinks argue that Washoe's sign sequences really should be construed as primitive sentences. First, the mean length of Washoe's sequences appears to be gradually increasing with time. Brown argues that this fact would be inexplicable if the individual signs which constitute these sequences were not somehow in construction with one another; if they were merely independent gestures that happen to be temporally concatenated, there is no particular reason why short sequences should appear in Washoe's repertoire before long ones do. However, the same argument would show that members of a list are in construction with one another, since digit span increases with age in human children. Clearly, this observation about Washoe's development does not decisively show that the sign sequences she produces are sentences.

The second observation is that Washoe's sign sequences yield intelligible interpretations on the assumption that they express some sort of semantic relations. Brown believes that Washoe's sequences express

---

[1]See, further, Herrnstein and Loveland's demonstration (1964) that pigeons can be trained to respond selectively to human figures in photographs. There are, however, apparently limits to interspecific similarities in the perceptual organization of the environment. Tinbergen (1969) remarks upon the release of the male stickleback's territorial response by a distant view of a red post office truck. In the normal ethology of the stickleback, this response is released by the red spot on other male sticklebacks. The moral seems to be that for certain species-specific purposes, the stickleback divides the world into small red patches and everything else—a kind of parsing that humans do not find particularly natural.

at least the relations agent-action, action-object, action-locative; it is notable that these are a subset of the relations Bloom (1970) finds in the sentences of children at the two-word stage (see below). In short, Washoe's production of sequences like "listen dog" (when a dog barked) or "Roger Washoe tickle" (when Washoe craved tickling) suggests that she is in control of a representation of messages in terms of relations like actor-action-agent. This does seem to imply that Washoe's sign sequences are not mere lists.

The difficulty, however, is that there is so far no evidence that Washoe represents the *semantic* relations between the signs in her sequences as *syntactic* relations between parts of a sentence; indeed, there is no evidence that such relations are in *any* way coded by stable properties of the syntactic organization of "sentences" in Washoe's language or even that sentences in Washoe's language *have* a syntactical organization.

Human languages characteristically signal grammatical relations by some combination of constituent order and inflection; in Washoe's training language, constituent order bears the entire burden. Since the training language distinguished sentences like "Roger tickle Washoe" from sentences like "Washoe tickle Roger," it would seem that a respect for constituent order would be the least evidence that Washoe could give to show that she treats relations like actor-action, action-object, action-location, etc., as *grammatical* relations (i.e., that they are coded by configurational properties of her productions). It is, for example, a striking fact about the early productions of children that they rarely include constituent orderings that are ungrammatical in the adult language, and even when they do, the orderings they produce are usually restricted (Brown, 1970). Washoe's productions, however, apparently approximate complete freedom of sign order. According to Brown, "The Gardners have kept careful records of all the occurrences of each combination of signs ... they report that the signs in a combination tend to occur in all possible orders. And that order often changes when there is no change in the non-linguistic circumstances" (p. 226). Since Washoe has no inflectional system available for the signaling of grammatical relations, it seems fair to say that there is as yet no evidence that such relations are encoded by *any* formal properties of her sign sequences. If this is correct, then Washoe's "language" differs from human languages in what is surely an essential respect: the lack of a syntactic representation of grammatical relations.

In short, Washoe has learned a relatively large number of signs which may or may not relate to their significates in the way that (some) human words relate to their referents. Her patterns of generalization of signs, and her employment of semantic relations like actor-action-object of action, suggest that she sees the world in categories rather like human categories: there are events, objects, properties, actions, etc., in Washoe's ontology as in ours. But there is no evidence that this epistemological similarity between Washoe and us shows up in a corresponding similarity between her language and ours. It is characteristic of human languages that certain of the relations we perceive are coded by configurational properties of the sentences we use, and Washoe's productions, thus far, give no indications of such a system of encoding.

Sarah. The second recent attempt to teach a chimpanzee a system that might reasonably be called a language is the work of David Premack. In some respects, Premack's approach is the opposite of the Gardners'. Where Washoe was raised in an environment which approximated the speech environment of a child, Premack's chimpanzee Sarah was subjected to rigorous operant training procedures; so rigorous that Premack speaks of such procedures as potentially providing a "recipe" for teaching an organism to talk.

The kinds of techniques Premack used will thus be generally familiar to students of the operant learning literature. "Words" in Sarah's "language" consist of magnet-backed plastic counters of a variety of shapes and colors which either Sarah or the trainer can affix to a board. Training begins by establishing "reference" relations between each word and a nonlinguistic object. "One day ... the trainer places an element from the language system, a piece of colored plastic, alongside [a] piece of fruit.... The animal is induced to make a prescribed response with the language element, in this case, place it on the language board, after which she is given the fruit" (Premack, 1969, p. 10). Having established that the chimpanzee must place the counter on the board as a condition for getting the food, the range of cases in which the response will be produced can now be manipulated by appropriate operant training which

> consists of making simultaneous changes in some aspect of the [nonverbal] transaction and in some aspect of the language system, so as to establish a correspondence between the two systems. For example, we may start with the fruits that are offered. The set of possible objects is defined by offering different fruits on different trials and each time with a corresponding change in the language element. When the fruit is banana the plastic chip is of one kind, when apple of a different kind, and when orange, still a third kind. On each trial the chimp's task is the same, place the piece of plastic that is alongside the fruit on the board before receiving the fruit [p. 11].

With a repertoire of "words," thus established, discrimination training can now be applied to word sequences, and at this level Premack performs prodigies of operant conditioning. Thus Sarah can be taught the difference between "Randy give apple Sarah" and, say, "Sarah give apple Randy" by explicit training in which she receives the apple as reinforcement for the production of the first sequence but not for the production of the second. Moreover, it can be shown that the training is not specific to the particular items constituting the trained sequence since, in appropriate circumstances, Sarah will spontaneously substitute other items in her vocabulary into this sequence. For example, if bananas are on view and if "banana" is a previously learned word for Sarah, she will spontaneously produce "Randy give banana Sarah." Similarly with substitutions for the other words in the sequence.

Premack thus constructs a system of "sentences" in which Sarah is responsive to both order constraints and lexical contents and which are productive in the sense that Sarah can substitute words in her vocabulary for words in the trained sentences. It is now possible to make this system look more like a language in the following ways: a negative element can be added by, in effect, reversing the reward conditions for a sentence which contains that element.[2] An interrogative element can be introduced in essentially comparable ways. Teach the chimpanzee a task in which she responds positive to "$X R X$" and "$X S Y$" but negative to "$X S X$" and "$X R Y$" for any desired substitutions of X and Y in her vocabulary. R can now be taken as the identity element, and S as the nonidentity element. One now introduces a new element, say, ? which will function as the interrogative marker. If ? appears in the sequence "$X ? X$" or "$Y ? Y$," the chimpanzee is reinforced for replacing ? with R. If ? appears in "$X ? Y$" or "$Y ? X$," the chimpanzee is reinforced for replacing ? with S. In effect, the chimpanzee is being asked "what is the relation between X and X" and "what is the relation between X and Y," and reinforced if it chooses identity in the first case and nonidentity in the second.

There is, of course, no reason why the operation of the question element, thus introduced, needs to be restricted to the relation term in a sequence, or, for that matter, why the relation need be restricted to identity. Suppose that the chimpanzee has been trained on color words and fruit words, and trained to respond positive to Cx only when C names the color of the fruit designated by x. Then we can use the interrogative element to ask the chimp $?x$, where reward is contingent on replacing ? by choosing a chip that names the color of x. Premack

---

[2] Since Premack's usual paradigm is a two-choice-response task, the logical force of negation is largely exhausted by its behavior in arguments of the form $(PvQ, -P : Q)$. That is, if the chimpanzee is to choose token A from the set AvB in response to sign sequence S, then B will be the reinforced response to the sign sequence $negative$-S. The result of this limitation on the logical behavior of negation is that we have no evidence that the chimpanzee ever thinks of Neg-S as meaning that S is *false*.

reports the introduction of various other complications in Sarah's language, but the preceding should give some idea of the techniques involved.

Sarah has certainly learned something. Has she learned something like a natural language? This question can be raised about two aspects of Sarah's system: we can ask whether its syntax is like that of a language and we can ask whether the counters in the system function semantically like words. We will consider these questions in turn.

It seems fairly clear that the system Sarah has mastered is not syntactically comparable to a natural language. To begin with, there is only very fragile evidence that the sequences in the language have phrase structure. Premack has taught Sarah to respond differentially to such sequences as "Sarah insert banana pail apple dish," where the correct response is one in which the banana goes into the pail and the apple into the dish, and not vice versa. From this Premack infers that Sarah perceives "banana pail" and "apple dish" as more intimately related than, say, "banana dish" and "apple pail," *and* that this suggests that Sarah must be imposing some sort of constituent analysis on the sentence. But both steps in this analysis are dubious. Premack himself remarks that the appearance of constituent structure could be an artifact of Sarah's using a simple order strategy (putting the fruit in the first container mentioned to its right). Moreover, and far more important, it is unclear what the experiment would show about the constituent structure of the sequence even if there were adequate controls for serial effects.

The point is that constituent structure is not a matter of the relative intimacy of the relations between items designated by elements of a sentence. It would be quite unreasonable to argue, for example, that if John kisses Mary, Mary is somehow closer to the action that John is. Nevertheless, the constituent structure of "John kisses Mary" is ((John) (kisses (Mary))). This is because of the pattern of substitutions for parts of the sentence that can occur in the language, preserving well-formedness and similarity of syntactic type. Thus, we can substitute either a word or a phrase for any constituent of the sentence (e.g., for "John" we can substitute either "Tom" or "the boy next door"; for "kisses Mary" we can substitute either "died" or "does it again and again"; etc.). But there is no one-word substitution for "John kisses" which produces a well-formed sentence structurally similar to "John kisses Mary."

These points are not, of course, intended as a definition of constituency. Rather, they emphasize the way that the notion of a constituent is connected with the distributional patterns that are permitted in a language. Thus, what would be relevant to showing that Sarah has mastered a system of constituent analysis would be evidence that her productions exhibit the appropriate distributional properties. It is worth emphasizing that such evidence *can* be cited in support of the claim that human children learn the constituent structure of sentences in their language. Brown (1970), for example, has remarked that "it is quite wonderful" how one finds that in Finnish as in English children, there is a regular pattern in the progression from two- to three-word utterances: "one term, the nominal, in two-term relations, which is in the early period always a single noun, begins frequently to be elaborated into a two-word noun phrase. These noun phrases fill all of the positions originally occupied by single nouns.... In fact, then, the elaboration of the noun term is accomplished by filling noun positions with just those two-term operations and relations which are noun phrases and which have been long practiced as independent utterances" (p. 223). It is precisely this productive alternation between words and phrases of the same syntactic type which is the characteristic mark of a constituent-structure system.

But Sarah's language permits few such alternations, and there is no evidence that Sarah uses productively those which it does permit. This issue is of central importance; since Sarah's training-language contains no productive transformational mechanisms, the question of whether she has mastered a productive system of constituent structure is equivalent to the question whether her language is productive at all.

So far as we can tell from the data Premack has published, the following list exhausts the cases in which a phrase can alternate with a word in Sarah's language.

1. *R* alternates with *Neg-R* in sentences of the form *X R Y* (so we have both "apple identical apple" and "apple not identical apple").

2. Lists alternate with words (so we have both "Sarah take apple" and "Sarah take apple and pear and peach").

3. Modifier + noun alternates with noun (so we have both "Insert apple in dish" and "Insert apple in red dish"). Since this is the most striking of the alternations permitted in Sarah's language, it is significant that the evidence that Sarah understands *any* *modifier* + *noun* constructions is thus far inconclusive (Premack, 1971).

4. *Be* alternates with *be* + *plural* to agree with compound subjects of predicative sentences. (This alternation can be ignored in assessing the extent to which Sarah has grasped a productive phrase-structure system, since it cannot, even in principle, apply iteratively to generate a productive class of structures.)

5. *Quantifier* + *noun* alternates with *noun* ("some apples" as well as "apples").

The striking fact about Sarah's language is thus how limited its productive mechanisms are. Of the three major sources of recursion in human language, two (complementation and relativization) have no analogs whatever in Sarah's system, and the third (conjunction) leads at best a marginal existence.[3]

Whether the productive mechanisms available in this system are too limited to make it comparable to a human language is a question one might argue about. But it is unnecessary to become involved in this issue, since the important question is not what productive mechanisms Sarah's language offers her but rather which, if any, of these mechanisms she has learned to employ productively. With the exception of one case to be discussed below, there is no evidence that Sarah has ever gained control of *any* of the productive mechanisms potentially available in her language. It seems fair to say that the syntax of the language that Sarah can actually use is exhausted by two fixed sentence forms [roughly *x be Pred* and $X R Y (Z)$, where R is a one-word verb, *Pred* is a one-word adjective, and everything else is a one-word noun, except that two-word sequences can alternate with one-word sequences as substitutions for certain of the variables].

In this respect, it is of prime importance to notice the difference between what Sarah does and what Brown says children do when they develop alternations of single words with two-word phrases. For the children, the production of *modifier + noun, possessive + noun*, etc., in linguistic environments that were previously restricted to one-word nouns is an untrained, spontaneous performance. For Sarah, however, such alternations never occurred spontaneously; rather, each case where a two-word sequence replaced a single word had to be specifically trained. Having been taught that $X R Y$ was well formed, Sarah had then to be taught that $X (Neg\text{-}R) Y$ was well formed; having been taught that $X R Y$ and Y *is Pred* were well formed, Sarah had then

---

[3] Sarah's language contains two other kinds of conjunctions that are, in principle, capable of producing productive classes of phrases which are not lists—i.e., which have internal constituent structure. These are the conjunctions of prepositional phrases mentioned above, and the kind of sentence conjunction involved in formulas like *S implies S* ("Mary takes grape implies Sarah takes candy"). As we remarked, however, it is dubious whether Sarah does, in fact, understand any prepositional conjunctions. And the general point that, with the exception of lists, the potentially productive mechanisms of her language are never productively employed by Sarah holds for these cases too. In particular, both *V (preposition noun) (preposition noun)*, and *S implies S* are specifically trained forms, and there is no evidence of any inclination on Sarah's part to capitalize on the possibilities for recursion that they introduce. For example, there is no evidence of generalization from training on *S implies S* to the use of such forms as *S implies (S implies S)*.

to be taught that $X R (Pred (Y))$ was well formed, etc. In short, there is no reason to attribute any of the cases in which phrases do alternate with words in Sarah's productions to a grasp, on her part, of the fundamentally productive character of constituent structures. The sole exception to these remarks is the alternation of lists with single items specified in rule 2. It really does seem that forms like "Sarah take apple, and candy, and banana" belong to a productive class of sentences; having learned to deal with the two-conjunct cases, Sarah did not need to be specifically trained in three, four, or more, conjunct cases. Since this is apparently the *only* case of the productive use of a syntactic form in Sarah's repertoire, it is of some interest that the alternation of words with lists generates only phrases with no *internal* constituent structure.

To summarize: so far as we can tell, except for the alternations of lists with single lexical items, *all* of what Premack calls productivity in Sarah's use of language consists in her "generalizing" from the trained sentence form to other sentences of the *same* form but different lexical content. In the data available to us, there is no indication that Sarah has ever done the most characteristic thing that a productive syntax permits human speakers to do: namely, use a sentence of a syntactically novel form without being specifically trained on sentences of that form. Productivity in human languages exploits iterative syntactic mechanisms which generate *novel constituent sequences*. Productivity in Sarah's language consists fundamentally of the substitution of novel lexical items into fixed constituent sequences. If so, it has the striking consequence that the "language" that Sarah has mastered is fundamentally nongenerative; it specifies only a finite number of sentences, which could be exhausted by performing all the permissible substitutions of lexical items for variables in the basic sentences $X be Pred$ and $X R Y (Z)$.

In fairness to Premack, it should be noted that he is apparently more interested in the question of whether the tokens in Sarah's language are really symbols than in the question of whether what Sarah talks is, from the syntactic point of view, really a language. It is, however, extremely difficult to answer the first question. Sarah uses her counters to do some of the things we do with some words, and she apparently knows that the counters are "arbitrary" in the sense that the properties of the counters are independent of those of the things the counters refer to. Whether that makes the counters words is a question which can be seriously raised only against the background of a comparably serious theory about which functions of words are the essential ones. But of course there exists no such theory, and none appears to be forthcoming.

SUMMARY

What has the work with Washoe and Sarah shown us? This question divides four ways: What has it shown us about chimpanzees? What has it shown us about whether chimpanzees can learn languages? What has it shown us about the species-specificity of the mechanisms involved in human-language learning? What has it shown us about human languages?

—What have the chimpanzee studies shown us about chimpanzees? Primarily, that chimpanzees are intelligent animals, and that they parse the world more or less the way that we do. In a variety of circumstances, Sarah and Washoe make discriminations and identifications in ways that make sense to us. Perhaps it is some comfort to have our ontology seconded by one of the higher primates. At any event, it is clear that the methodological decision to allow the chimpanzee to use nonverbal responses in signaling its classifications has been more than justified by the results.

—What have the chimpanzee studies shown us about the chimpanzees' ability to learn human language? Neither Washoe nor Sarah appears to have mastered a productive syntactic system; in neither case do the animals' responses give clear evidence of constituent structure, to say nothing of transformational structure. In Washoe's case, it is at best extremely doubtful that any of the human grammatical relations are syntactically coded in her language. In Sarah's case, constituent order clearly performs such a coding, but perhaps only because discrimination training was explicitly employed to distinguish the reward conditions associated with distinct constituent orders. Since Sarah mastered none of the mechanisms that her language provides for generating novel constituent sequences, this factor demonstrates only that chimpanzees can be conditioned to discriminate ordinal relations and apparently has no other significance.

We do not, of course, claim that no one will ever succeed in training an animal to use a language with a productive syntax. But it is remarkably clear from the studies of Washoe and Sarah that learning such systems is not a natural and spontaneous accomplishment for chimpanzees; apparently, that is, years of exposure to a language environment is not sufficient. The best one can say is that the present experiments provide no evidence that chimpanzees can learn a formal system in any important way similar to a natural language.

—What have the chimpanzee studies shown about the species-specificity of language-learning capacities in humans? It seems to us that the answer must be that these studies would not have been relevant to that question even if they had been fully successful.

Linguistic information is innate in humans if and only if it is represented in the gene code. Whether other animals can be taught to talk is irrelevant to answering this question. If they cannot be taught to talk, it need not be because they lack the relevant genetic endowment but only that they lack, for example, the relevant motivation. Conversely, if they can be taught to talk, they may still lack whatever innate species-specific language-handling capacities humans are endowed with; e.g., they may learn to talk in a different way from the way that humans do.

This last point is rather more than a quibble, since there are very many clear cases in which an organism with one kind of innate endowment can be trained to mimic the behavior of an organism with a quite different kind of innate endowment. The fact that a dog can be trained to walk on its hind legs does not prejudice the claim that bipedal gait is genetically coded in humans. The fact that we can learn to whistle like a lark does not prejudice the species-specificity of birdsong. It is hard to see, then, why a successful attempt to teach a chimpanzee to talk should have any bearing on the innateness of language in people.

—What have the chimpanzee studies shown us about language? Literally, nothing.

Given that the chimpanzee studies provide no decisive evidence against the claim that the human ability to talk a language is based on a species-specific genetic endowment, what positive arguments can be adduced in favor of the view that language skills are species-specific? The claim at issue is that when humans learn their language, they exploit a genetic endowment that other types of organisms do not have. It is to the character of this endowment, rather than to their "general intelligence," that the human capacity for language is attributed.

As Lorenz (1965) has remarked, the standard ethological method for establishing that behavior is species-specific, in the sense of being the consequence of specific phylogenetically adapted mechanisms, is the employment of the deprivation experiment. In such experiments one withholds "from the young organism information concerning certain well-defined givens of its natural environment" (p. 83). Behavior patterns which the organism exhibits in spite of this sort of deprivation are considered to be genetically coded.

This method cannot be applied in the study of language learning: the crucial experiment, in which the character of the child's exposure to linguistic inputs is systematically manipulated, cannot be run. Moreover, the nativist need not claim that the human infant deprived of linguistic inputs would nevertheless exhibit verbal behavior. There are a variety of ethological precedents for the claim that the appearance of innately specified behavior is sometimes triggered only when the environment provides appropriate "releasing" stimuli. Very often the character of the stimuli that can serve to release innate behavior may itself be innately specified, either diffusely or in considerable detail (cf. Tinbergen, 1969, for examples). Thus the nativist and the empiricist can agree that experience is essential for the development of language behavior even though they disagree over the kind of role experience is alleged to play. For the empiricist, whatever information the organism uses to structure its behavior is abstracted from regularities in its environment. For the nativist, environmental information serves largely to elicit behavior whose principles of organization are genetically coded.

It is clear, at any event, that claims for species-specificity of language-learning mechanisms in humans cannot rest upon the relatively direct evidence that deprivation experiments provide. There are, however, five kinds of indirect evidence that can be brought to bear. We turn now to a review of this evidence.

1. There are a number of types of evidence which suggest a degree of dissociation between cognitive and linguistic development. For example, we have already seen that chimpanzees exhibit no clear ability to learn language. The mental age of a mature chimpanzee is usually said to be comparable to that of a 3-year-old child, and 3-year-old children are verbal organisms. Similarly, there is evidence that the child's acquisition of language skills proceeds in roughly the same fashion in normal and pathological populations. This suggests that the character of language development is not particularly sensitive to general cognitive impairment and hence that language development is not simply an expression of general intellectual development.

Investigators have remarked upon the relatively unlabile character of certain features of language development in brain-damaged children and in children with congenital neurological disorders: the types of linguistic structures available to a child of a given *mental* age appear to be similar for pathological and normal groups. There are at least two relevant studies. The first is by Lenneberg, Nichols, and Rosenberger (1964), who examined 84 Mongoloid and feeble-minded children. A number of interesting findings emerged. For example, Lenneberg et al. found that the same sort of correlation between motor and linguistic development typical of normals also holds for Mongoloids. Thus even though handedness emerges much later for Mongoloids than for normals, it is correlated with the earliest predominance of words and phrases over random babbling in both groups. Moreover, analysis of errors produced by Mongoloids and young normals on sentence-repetition tests again suggests that the ontogenetic sequencing for the Mongoloids is similar to that of normals of comparable mental age.

> When very young children (24 to about 30 months) are compared with the mongoloids in terms of their respective performance on the sentence repetition test, we are impressed with the similarity. Unfortunately, there is no reliable method available at present to quantify this impression, but the inaccuracies, mistakes, and occasional forays into parroting-strategies appear to be strikingly alike. Thus the intellectual limita-

tion does not produce bizarre language behavior; it merely results in arrest at primitive, but "normal," stages of development [Lenneberg, 1967, pp. 319–320].

In an analogous study, Lackner (1968) investigated the linguistic capacities of five grossly retarded children of mental ages 2-3 (2 years, 3 months); 2-11; 3-0; 4-9; and 8-10. These retarded children were compared with a group of normal children of corresponding mental age. Lackner found that the grammatical structures that had been mastered by brain-damaged children of a given mental age were, in general, also available in normal children of corresponding mental age. However, the grammatical structures that had been mastered by brain-damaged children of more advanced mental age were not, in general, comprehensible to the younger normals. From this Lackner infers that the *order* of development of syntactic forms is essentially the same for the two groups, i.e., that the primary difference between the groups is in the *rate* of development and the point at which development stops. As Lackner remarks,

> These results are noteworthy in that an ordering is maintained between the complexity of the grammars and the mental ages of the retarded children and the chronological ages of the normal children. This result should not be interpreted as meaning that the language behavior of a retarded child of a given mental age is equivalent to that of a normal child of a particular chronological age. Rather, these findings suggest that the language behaviors of normal and retarded children are not qualitatively different, that both groups follow similar developmental trends, but that the most severely retarded children become arrested in their development and remain at a lower level of normal language acquisition [p. 309].

There is another sort of indirect evidence which bears on the question of the genetic determination of the process of human-language acquisition by suggesting that there is a restriction on the period of a child's life during which "normal" language learning can take place. There may be a "sensitive period" during which first language learning *must* occur if it is to occur at all. If so, then the capacity for language acquisition exhibits a cutoff for which general cognitive development offers no obvious analog.

Lenneberg (1967) provides strong evidence for such a claim through an analysis of the symptoms and recovery rates for victims of traumatic aphasias. Lenneberg notes that the likelihood of a full recovery from aphasia is strikingly different for pre- and postpubescent populations. Children who suffer an aphasia as the result of cerebral damage incurred roughly before age 11 show almost 100 percent recovery, and the younger the child, the more certain this becomes. For older aphasics, however, the rate of full recovery is much lower—60 percent at best.

The symptomatology in these cases is also revealing. For the very young children the course of recovery is often a recapitulation of the normal ontogenetic sequence, i.e., the child appears to be able to "start from scratch" and follow the normal course of language acquisition for a second time. This is never true of adult recovery, however. Lenneberg remarks:

> When aphasic symptoms subside in the adult patient, he does not traverse the infant's stages of language learning. There is no babbling, single-word stage followed by a two-word-phrase stage. There is no semantic overgeneralization nor a gradual emergence of the more complex grammatical constructions. . . . Recovery from aphasia . . . means arrest of interference with established habits. This is very different from the emergence and assembly of speech and language phenomena throughout the synthesizing process of language acquisition [pp. 143–144].

We have had occasion to refer to the observation that the order of stages in the language development of retarded children parallels the order of developmental stages in normal children. It may now be added that the termination of language development in retardates also honors the "critical period" for language acquisition in normals. Both Lackner (1968) and Lenneberg (1967) note that retardate language development proceeds until about the onset of puberty, at which point progress is arrested and no further elaboration of basic grammatical skills takes place; the retarded child can learn a great deal after this period, but *not* about the syntax of his language. His general problem-solving abilities continue to enable him to learn, but the mechanism which mediates the establishment of basic linguistic skills apparently ceases to function. [There is much more to the discussion of both the developmental sequence and symptomatology of language skills in aphasics and retardates than we are able to present here. Further information can be found in Lenneberg (1967), Thorpe (1961), and Penfield and Roberts (1959).]

Finally, under the general head of the relative independence of language learning from the development of intelligence, we may briefly consider the anecdotal evidence that the learning of a *second* language is easier for monolingual children than for monolingual adults. If this is true, it cannot be simply a matter of greater or lesser "retroactive inhibition," since both groups—children and adults—have fully functional linguistic skills. If language acquisition is to be accounted for simply in terms of general intelligence, it is difficult to understand why a mature organism should be *less* adept at learning languages than an immature one.

In fact, the linguistic facility of the 5-year-old as compared with that of the 15-year-old would appear to be a severe embarrassment for any traditional learning theoretic account of language acquisition. Clearly, inasmuch as the capacity for language acquisition appears to operate independently of general problem-solving skills, or survives their gross impairment, it ought not to be considered a special case of the application of those skills. The alternative hypothesis would appear to be that at least some important features of language acquisition are determined by fixed, autonomous, species-specific biases that the human infant brings to the language-learning situation but which are unavailable to the adult humans just as they are unavailable to intelligent infrahuman organisms.

2.   The second line of empirical evidence consonant with this hypothesis stems from the existence of linguistic universals: i.e., of profound formal and substantive similarities between all natural languages, including those that are, presumably, historically unrelated.

As we saw in Chapter 3, natural languages resemble one another in rather surprising ways. For example, they share properties with one another that they do not share with artificial "languages" like the ones we use for talking to computers and the ones we use for formalizing logical inferences. There is, of course, no way of *proving* that such resemblances between natural languages are not the product of convergence brought about by similar environmental, cultural, or cognitive pressures operating on historically unrelated and initially heterogeneous codes. In fact, we saw in Chapter 6 that there are some universal linguistic properties for which precisely this sort of explanation appears plausible. But in most cases it is difficult to see why time should preserve, or the environment select, the quite arbitrary kinds of features that seem to be characteristic of natural languages. At the very least, we have no a priori grounds for rejecting the suggestion that there are linguistic universals because there are genetic universals: e.g., that human languages are similar to one another for very much the same sorts of reasons that bee "languages" are similar to one another, the common behavioral properties being in either case dictated by a common genetic endowment.

3.   There is surprisingly little evidence that reinforcement, or indeed any sustained form of explicit teaching, plays an important facilitating role in language learning. Indeed there exists some experimental evidence which suggests that explicit instruction in the child's first language fails to be facilitating. If reinforcement theory is the alternative to the view that language learning is the expression of species-specific genetic mechanisms, this evidence supports the latter rather than the former theory.

Luria and Yudovich (1959), for example, found short-term acceleration due to a program of first-language training but apparently failed to produce lasting differences between trained twins and their siblings. Thus *ten* months after the initiation of training, the differences between the trained and untrained twins were less striking than the differences after *three* months of training; that is, the control twin was catching up with the experimental one, despite the special attention afforded the latter. Luria and Yudovich remark: "Special speech training, which made speech the object of conscious perception, accelerated the conscious application of speech and helped the child to acquire an extended grammatical structure of speech; nevertheless, it is clear that the special training played only a subsidiary role, leaving the leading place to the formative influence of direct speech communication" (pp. 75–76).

It may be remarked that this pattern of short-term acceleration without significant long-term effect is often also observed in cases where attempts are made to employ training to speed the child's mastery of performances which, like walking and climbing, are patently genotypically determined.

> Gesell and Thomson (1929) introduced the now famous co-twin method of study [for the investigation of maturational vs. environmental variables]..., observing the progress of identical twins T and C. When the twins were on the verge of climbing activities, twin T was given ten minutes of training every day for 6 weeks, while the control twin C received no training and was prevented from climbing stairs. At the end of the six weeks, twin C was given a brief 2 week training period. Performances of the twins were then compared. On the initial tests, twin T was more skillful, but twin C also managed to climb the stairs unaided. Two weeks later twin C was just as proficient as her sister [Zubek and Solberg, 1954].

A study by Cazden (1965) is directly relevant. Her results suggest that explicit correction of the child's speech in the form of "expansions" of his "telegraphic" utterances tends actually to inhibit grammatical development. Children in Cazden's experimental group received daily sessions in which the experimenter provided the fully grammatical adult sentence corresponding to each abbreviated sentence the child uttered. (Thus, for example, if the child were to utter a sequence like "train run," the experimenter would provide an utterance like "the train runs" or "the train is running.") Children in a second group received analogous daily periods of topic-oriented free conversation with the experimenter, but received no expansions. Cazden found that at the end of the experiment, the children who had received expansions had made significantly *less* progress in grammatical development, as measured by a variety of test procedures, than the children who had received no expansions.

This study suggests that the richness of the child's verbal environment and the extent of his opportunities to engage in conversation with adults have more impact upon his grammatical development than does the occurrence of explicit training. A more recent study of Cazden's strengthens this suggestion. Cazden examined a corpus consisting of dialogues between three mothers and their children. She compared the correlation between the child's mastery of three syntactic variables (the use of prepositions and prepositional phrases, the ability to respond appropriately to *wh*-questions, and the use of noun and verb inflection) with the extent to which the mother provided expansions of each of these forms and with the frequency of each of these forms in the mother's speech. The result of this comparison appears to be that frequency variables correlate better with developmental variables than does the mother's tendency to provide expansions. For example, the child whose mother produced the smallest proportion of expansions of the child's uninflected utterances was the one who was most advanced in the use of inflections. Cazden (1967) remarks that "it is hard to reconcile this finding with our original hypothesis that expansion should provide the most usable information for the acquisition of all types of functors" (p. 64). It is also hard to reconcile this with any account of language which makes *training* an important factor in the child's linguistic development. As is often the case with the maturation of endogenously determined behaviors, language development apparently makes only quite diffuse demands upon the character of the environment in which the learning occurs: the structure of the mature behavior reflects the mental structure of the organism rather than the detailed organization of its environment.

It is, in short, difficult to find evidence that the normal development of syntax requires any sort of training or reward on the part of the adult community. Perhaps that is why the adult community does not normally selectively reinforce syntactic well-formedness, learning theorists to the contrary notwithstanding. As Ervin-Tripp (1971) remarks in commenting on Staats (1971):

> Reinforcement appears to play a strong role in Staats' theory of acquisition. I can't imagine what kind of interaction he has been watching, but it is rarely the case that we spend much effort correcting the formal structure of children's speech. . . . Adults listening to children speak are usually listening to the message, just as they are when they listen to adults. Our evidence is that they comment on the form only in the case of socially marked deviations such as obscenities, lower class nonstandard forms, and in the case of black families, forms believed to be "country speech." Such formal correction occurred much more when the children were five or older than at the age of interest here [p. 196].

Learning theories which have not supposed that reinforcement is the primary mechanism of language acquisition have tended to coopt that role for imitation (sometimes construed as a "self-reinforcing" activity). However, the available evidence does not support the claim that imitation plays an essential role in acquiring a first language any more than it supports the claim that reinforcement does.

To begin with, it seems clear that imitation cannot be an essential mechanism in first-language learning since it appears that many normal children do not spontaneously imitate linguistic forms. (Cf. Leopold, 1939, and Bloom, in press.) Again, if the child's tendency to imitate adult forms is to play any important role in his learning of the adult language, this tendency must at least be "progressive" in the sense that the child must frequently imitate forms which he has not previously mastered. But it is unclear whether or not children's imitations satisfy even this prerequisite to relevance in language learning. Though it is known that children can be trained to imitate forms that are grammatically more mature than their freely produced speech (see Frazer, Bellugi, and Brown, 1963), it is quite doubtful that they regularly do so spontaneously. For example, Ervin (1964) compared the grammatical maturity of spontaneously produced imitations by five children with the grammatical maturity of their free speech. In four of the five cases, the level of maturity was identical (i.e., the child's imitations were not progressive). In the fifth case, the imitations were *more primitive* than the free speech. In light of this kind of finding, McNeill concludes a recent discussion of the data on language imitation with the remark that "the contribution of parental speech to language acquisition is not to supply specimens for children to imitate" (1970, p. 107).

It may be added that however the empirical findings about the progressiveness of imitation turn out, appeals to imitation are incapable on purely conceptual grounds of accounting for the important features of the child's performance in learning his language.

There are two points to notice in this regard. The first is that theories of language learning which are based on imitation are, by that very fact, incapable of accounting for the child's mastery of productive systems. What the speech community offers the child as models for him to imitate are, at best, *examples* of sentences. (Probably what it offers are often examples of nonsentences, i.e., of sentence fragments.) At any event, the speech community does *not* offer the child examples of the structural facts that underlie sentences. If, then, the child's behavior is ever to go beyond rote repetition to the production of novel sentences, he must somehow learn from the examples he hears not just the conditions under which an imitation of this or that sentence is acceptable but also the general conditions an utterance must satisfy if it is to be in his language. In short, for the child to learn to talk, he must determine the relation between the sentences he hears and the possible sentences of his language. Even if it were true that the child imitates correctly *every* sentence he hears, reference to that fact would shed no light whatever on the question of how this relation is learned.

Imitation, then, obviously cannot account for the learning of productive systems. A less obvious, but equally important, conceptual point is that the imitation model fails even to provide a convincing answer to the question of how the child learns to repeat utterances. The relevant consideration is that the relation between an utterance and its repetition is often extremely abstract: in this respect there is a difference between repetition and mimicry. One way to put it is that the conditions for accurate repetition cannot be given in terms of *acoustic* correspondences between the child's utterances and those of the adult model since what is necessary and sufficient for one utterance to be a repetition of another is that they have the same *phonetic* representation. The question that the imitation theory begs is thus: How does the child learn the formidable system of abstractions required to master the correspondences between acoustic and phonetic descriptions?

It is clear, in point of fact, that the child *does* master this system. Spectograms of children imitating the utterances of their parents exhibit radical acoustic disparities between the signal produced by the adult and the signal produced by the child. If the child is to learn to imitate, he must learn to tolerate this disparity; *how* he learns this is, however, a question about which the imitation model has nothing whatever to say.

None of this discussion, of course, denies that the tendency to imitate may play an important, or even essential, role in facilitating language acquisition in some children: e.g., in fixing attention and in providing occasion for rehearsals. The present point is that even if imitation *were* to prove an essential condition for language learning, an explanation of how the child learns a language could not consist primarily of an appeal to the tendency to imitate. [For speculations about the roles that imitation and rehearsal may have in facilitating language learning, see Weir (1962).]

One final remark should be made about the inadequacies of selective reinforcement and imitation theories of language learning. The most striking feature of a child's productions is clearly their spontaneity. By this we mean not only that the child, like the adult, is master of a productive system of rules rather than a fixed inventory of responses but also that the utterances of the child (even when he "imitates") diverge regularly and reliably from anything he hears in his speech community. Thus, for example, Ervin (1964) notes:

> Omissions bulked large in our cases of imitation. These tended to be concentrated on the unstressed segments of sentences, on articles, prepositions, auxiliaries, pronouns, and suffixes. For instance: "I'll make a cup for her to drink" produced "cup drink"; "Mr. Miller will try," "Miller try"; "Put the strap under her chin," "Strap chin." Thus the imitations had three characteristics: they selected the most recent and most emphasized words, and they preserved word order [p. 169].

When one considers the child's free, as opposed to imitated, utterances, the disparity between his linguistic preferences and those of the adult are still more striking. Bellugi (1967), for example, has noted a preference for uncontracted forms in the dialect of the children she studies (thus her children said "do not" and "have not" whereas their parents regularly said "don't" and "won't"); and Slobin (in press) states that the phrase-order preferences of Russian children differs systematically from those of adult Russian speakers: children employ the "base-structure" order *subject phrase verb phrase object phrase,* whereas for the adult order is essentially free. Analogously, Bellugi has demonstrated a systematic and orderly development of the negative in children's speech, where almost all the early forms that children typically use are ungrammatical, and presumably never occur in the adult dialect. Forms like "no daddy hat," are regular in the child's earliest negative productions and surely have no models in the adult language. Examples of this sort are legion; everyone knows that children speak a special dialect—the dialect we attempt to mimic when we talk "baby talk."

It is extremely difficult to see how a shaping model, or an imitation model, could account for this spontaneity in the child's productions. In the latter case, the best we can hope to do is to explain rote repetition. In the former case, *random* variability in verbal behavior is assumed; but this is not to the point, since the child's dialect is apparently quite regular even though it diverges from that of the adult speech community. In short, there appears to be structure in the child's productions which is in no obvious sense a copy of the structure on display in his verbal environment. A natural way to answer the question, "Where does this structure come from?" is by appealing to endogenous organismic variables.

4. There exists very little *direct* experimental evidence on the hypothesis that some features of the child's linguistic competence are determined by his innate species-specific genetic endowment. However, some recent work has been done on the perceptual constancies involved in phone recognition, and these results do point in the direction of a nativistic account.

It will be recalled from the discussion in Chapter 6 that it is characteristic of adult speech perception to impose discrete categories on continuously varying physical magnitudes. A classic case is the voiced-voiceless distinction among stop consonants. Apparently, one of the important acoustic cues for this distinction is the relation of temporal onset between f_1 and f_2. In the optimal voiced consonant, onset of f_1 and f_2 is roughly simultaneous; and in the optimal unvoiced consonant, f_2 precedes f_1 by about 60 milliseconds. The important point for the present discussion is that the degree to which two stimuli are likely to be perceived as differing in voicing is not proportional to the magnitude of the physical difference between their formant onset relations. Rather, any signal with an onset relation roughly between 0 and 25 milliseconds will tend to be perceived as voiced, and any signal with an onset relation of longer than 25 milliseconds will tend to be perceived as unvoiced.

In a recent experiment, Eimas, Siqueland, Jusczyk, and Vigorito (1971) undertook to show that infants' perception of such signals is categorical in very much the same way as is adults'. The experimental procedure consisted of playing recordings of signals with varying formant onset relations to infants of between 1 and 4 months. The signals were what adults hear as either [b] followed by vowel or [p] followed by vowel. Subjects were habituated to each such signal and tested for generalization of habituation to each of the others. The extent of generalization was determined by monitoring changes in the infant's sucking response.

Eimas et al. found less generalization of habituation when two stimuli were drawn from categories that were phonetically distinct for adults than otherwise. This was true even where differences in the absolute magnitudes of the onset relations were equated across stimuli. This discontinuity of discriminability at the same region that marks the adult phoneme boundary should be taken as evidence that speech sounds are categorized by the preverbal infant and that his categories are similar to those of the adult.

A demonstration with the same point was provided by Fodor and Garrett (in press) using differential reinforcement of head-turning responses in 3- to 4-month-old infants. It will be recalled that there are striking cases of variation in the acoustic properties of a given consonant when it appears in different vowel environments (see Chapter 6, page 291). Fodor and Garrett found that their infant subjects responded selectively to a given phone across several different vowel environments (e.g., that they identified /p/ in the environment /a/ with /p/ in the environment /i/). This indicates that infants' perceptual capacities allow them to respond to syllables in terms of the internal phonetic structure that permits a segmental analysis of adult speech. This study and that of Eimas et al. thus provide evidence that quite complex kinds of information about the linguistic analysis of speech are available at an age when infants could *not* have had experience with the distributional evidence required to infer those analyses. It seems inescapable that most of this information is endogenously determined.

5. What probably has had most effect in convincing psychologists of the specificity of language-learning mechanisms is simply complexity of the information that is internalized as a result of the operation of these mechanisms. There is, of course, no way to quantify this concept. But it does seem clear that the child must internalize an extremely elaborate generative system in an extremely short time if his language acquisition is to proceed normally. To the extent that parts of this system are assumed to be innately given, the remarkable facility with which children learn to talk is rendered corresponding intelligible.

We have reviewed some of the evidence for and against the claim that the mechanisms of language acquisition are species-specific. It seems to us that the most persuasive of these arguments is the one which seeks to explain language universals as the expression of the genetic endowment of speaker-hearers. If grammars do have the universal form that transformational theory says they do, that fact will have to be explained; and it is hard to believe that an exhaustive explanation could be couched largely in terms of environmental variables.

What can be said with certainty is that language acquisition is not explicable by reference to the intraspecific learning mechanisms to which empiricists have usually appealed: selective reinforcement and imitation. It is conceivable that some account of first-language learning in terms of other intraspecific mechanisms will eventually be forthcoming. If so, it will have to be quite different from anything that has yet been proposed.

THE TASK-SPECIFICITY OF LANGUAGE SKILLS
The question of whether there is a *species*-specific contribution to the processes involved in first-language learning should be distinguished from the question of whether such processes are *language*-specific. As we have seen, the literature contains every conceivable view on the former question. On the latter, however, there seems to be a fairly substantial consensus. Many psychologists and philosophers hold that the procedures whose operation eventuates in the child's mastery of his language are really simply special cases of cognitive mechanisms which operate throughout the child's mental development. In this view, the child's acquisition of language is simply an expression of his general cognitive growth. For example, Brownowski and Bellugi remark: "We see that small children whose cognitive powers are limited in many respects show a remarkable ability to reconstruct the language they hear, just as they reconstruct (give structure to) their experience of their physical environment; the process and the capacity are not specifically linguistic, but are expressions of a general human ability to construct general rules by induction" (1970, p. 672). Similar sentiments have re-

peatedly been expressed in the philosophical literature by Goodman (1967), Putnam (1961), and Harman (1967, 1969).

Despite the popularity of these kinds of views, it seems to us that the theoretical and conceptual issues involved in sorting out the relations between cognitive and linguistic development are extremely unclear, and that the data available for choosing between alternative accounts are both fragmentary and indecisive. We regard the following remarks as preliminary.

There is at least one respect in which it is not an empirical hypothesis but a mere truism that language development depends upon cognitive development. It is (roughly) a sufficient condition for having mastered a concept that one be able correctly to apply a linguistic form which expresses that concept. Conversely, it is (roughly) a necessary condition for being able to apply a linguistic form correctly that one should have mastered the concept that the form expresses. In short, if a child is able to use the word "dog" to refer to dogs, it follows that he must have the concept of "dog." In this sense, it is certain that there is at least one linguistic skill (applying a term correctly) which cannot be attained without the attainment of a corresponding level of cognitive sophistication (mastery of the concept the term expresses).

But while these remarks are doubtless true, they are quite uninteresting. For example, it does not follow from the fact that language development is contingent upon cognitive development in this way that we can infer the order of the child's acquisition of concepts from the order of his employment of the forms which express these concepts. English-speaking children acquire negative sentence forms later than they acquire affirmatives, and they acquire action nominals (like "John's leaving the party") long after they acquire negatives. Presumably, affirmatives characteristically express assertions, negatives characteristically express denials, and action nominals characteristically denote events. Our present point is that these observations do *not* necessarily allow the inference that children have the concept of an affirmation before they have the concept of a denial, or that they have the concept of a denial before they have the concept of an event. Though these data are *compatible* with that assumption, they are equally compatible with such radically nativistic assumptions as that all three concepts are available to the child at birth, and that the ontogenetic order of the corresponding linguistic forms is determined entirely by their relative *grammatical* complexity.

It is interesting in this respect that Slobin (1973) has investigated a case in which the emergence of locative locutions in a bilingual child occurs at different chronological points for the two languages he speaks; since the child must have had the concept of a location by the time he was able to use locatives in the first language, the ontogenetic sequence must reflect the fact that the syntactic constraints on the expression of locatives are more demanding in one language than in the other.

There are, in short, at least two broadly opposed options available for interpreting an observed ontogenetic sequence in the child's ability to use a linguistic form correctly. One may take the relatively late emergence of such a capacity either as data for the correspondingly late acquisition of a concept or as data for the relative complexity of the linguistic form which expresses the concept. It is quite possible that there is no single right answer to the question of which of these options one ought to choose: ontogenetic sequencing may indicate conceptual development in one case (cf. the relatively late acquisition of the term "electron") and linguistic sophistication in another (cf. the relatively late acquisition of action nominals). The only way to tell for sure is by finding an experimental task which tests cognitive skills without requiring either linguistic responses or responses that are linguistically mediated. Such tasks are notoriously hard to come by.

To take a case in point: there is a controversy in the observational literature on child language development over the character of the child's acquisition of such concepts as "agent of an action." The relevant data seem to be these: if the child's earliest one-word utterances are analogous to any adult sentences, they are predicate adjectives and predicate nominals. If the child who says "mommy" is making a statement at all, then so far as one can tell from the context of the utterance, he is making the same statement that an adult would make by saying, e.g., "Here is Mommy." Later one-word utterances may, or may not, be interpretable as expressing agentive relations, depending on whom one reads and what principles of interpretation one's methodology allows [for the former view, see Greenfield (in press); for the latter, see Bloom (in press)]. By the time the child's mean length of utterance approaches two, however, one gets overt *NV* sequences of the *subject-verb* form: the *N* and *V* are in grammatical construction with one another and the context of the utterance makes it hard to doubt that a relation of actor to action is intended (Bloom, 1970).

What do these data tell us about the mastery of the relational concept *actor-action* and of the grammatical relation *subject-verb* which English uses to express this concept? It is hard to believe that they tell us anything very decisive. McNeill (1970) has suggested that the syntactic definition of the grammatical relations are specified as part of the child's innate linguistic endowment, and that the child's developing grasp of the actor-action analysis of events is somehow grounded in this specifically syntactic information. Bloom (in press) accepts a Piagetian account that the development of the concept of an agent is a relatively late phenomenon which depends upon the child's sensory-motor engagements with his environment. In this view, the child's initial failure to use sequences of the syntactic form *subject-verb* is explained by assuming that he does not have the concept that the form is used to express. Development consists of the child's (somehow) mastering the concept *actor-action* and then (somehow) learning that the concept is expressed in English by the relation between subject and verb.

Our present point is that the data about ontogenetic sequence do not really choose between Bloom's view and McNeill's, nor do they preclude the possibility that it is the actor-action notion that is innate and the corresponding grammatical relation that is learned. Indeed, the available data do not preclude the view that both grammatical relations and the concepts they express are specified in the child's innate endowment, and that the observed ontogenetic sequence is a purely maturational phenomenon.[4] If it turns out that cross-cultural data show the order of the child's mastery of the concepts expressed by grammatical relations to be a universal, it might well be this last view that one should adopt.

To summarize the discussion thus far: it is tautological that linguistic development presupposes cognitive development in the uninteresting sense that one cannot express a concept that one doesn't have. But this uninspiring notion of the dependence of language on thought is compatible with any observed ontogenetic sequencing whatever in the child's developing capacity to use linguistic forms.

Part of the consensus that language development is an expression of

---

[4] For example, the child's ability to use what it innately knows might depend upon the maturation of short-term memory adequate to integrate the linguistic forms with which to express its concepts. Bloom (in press) argues that the child's failure unambiguously to express grammatical relations at the one-word-utterance stage cannot be attributed to computational limitations, but her evidence for this claim seems weak. It turns on the fact that the child whose one-word productions she studied did use some two-word sequences. In such sequences, the second item was the nonce word /wid ə/. Bloom argues that the regular production of —— /wid ə/ forms shows that the child has the computational capacity for grammatically structured two-word utterances; hence the failure to produce such utterances must be attributable either to the lack of the concepts which grammatical relations express, to the lack of the grammatical relations themselves, or to both.

We think this argument is unconvincing since, first, there is no evidence that /wid ə/ was in construction with the other word in —— /wid ə/ utterances. If it was not, then one cannot infer from the child's ability to produce —— /wid ə/ that he had the computational capacity to produce two-word sequences whose elements are grammatically related. Second, there is no evidence that /wid ə/ carried any semantic load in the child's utterances; Bloom is herself explicit in saying that she was able to find no consistent interpretation for its occurrences. But, again, it does not follow from the fact that the child has the necessary computational capacity for producing sequences of two items *one of which is a dummy* that it has the computational capacity to produce sequences of two items both of which are content words.

cognitive development may, in short, rest on the confusion of a truism with an empirical hypothesis. There are, however, a number of theorists who have quite clearly *not* been guilty of this confusion; most notably, those who have approached language development with Piagetian presuppositions. Such theorists typically hold that the linguistic development of a child is an expression of the *cognitive stage* he has attained. A cognitive stage is specified by enumerating the logical properties of the computational operations available to the child at that stage; i.e., by characterizing the types of rules the child can employ. It is clearly a substantive, and extremely interesting, hypothesis that the formal character of the computational procedures available to a child for nonlinguistic problem solving at a given developmental stage determines the formal character of the rules that order the child's language at that stage.

But while this hypothesis is interesting, it is also extremely dubious. To begin with, the existence of cognitive stages in the sense of sequentially ordered developmental periods *characterizable by reference to the formal properties of the child's concepts* is itself by no means a foregone conclusion. Granted that the cognitive capacities of children change over time, it is an open question whether this is because the formal character of their concepts changes or, e.g., because of the growth of the child's capacity to *use* his concepts in the kinds of computations that underlie problem solving.

Second, just as it is not a settled issue whether there exist stages in the formal character of children's nonlinguistic concepts, it is also unclear whether there are, in this sense, stages in the development of the child's language. For example, we will see below that it is an open question whether children *ever* use grammars that are formally distinct from those specified by adult universals. If the answer to this question turns out to be negative, then there is at least one aspect of the child's linguistic development—syntax—which does not exhibit developmental stages in the Piagetian sense of the term. In this account, the number of rules available to the child changes with time, as does the complexity of the computations in which he can employ the rules. But the formal character of the rules is fixed and the child's syntactic development cannot be viewed as a progress through a succession of stages.

These remarks are almost entirely speculative for the simple reason that practically nothing is known about the formal character of the computational principles underlying any area of linguistic or cognitive functioning. Questions about the formal character of conceptual systems can barely be raised before one has considerable detailed information about the concepts belonging to the system; and there is no area of cognitive psychology in which reliable information of this sort is available. Not surprisingly, there are no more than a handful of experiments which even purport to be relevant to the question of whether stages of linguistic development express stages of cognitive development; and these experiments are not, in general, persuasive. For example, there is a study by Sinclair. We quote from the summary given by Piaget (1970).

> First she established two groups of children. One group consisted of conservers; that is, they realized that, when a certain amount of liquid was poured from a glass of one shape into a glass of another shape, the quantity did not change in spite of the appearances. The other group consisted of nonconservers. . . . Mme. Sinclair proceeded to study the language of each of these groups of children by giving them very simple objects to describe. . . . She found noticeable differences in the language used to describe these objects according to whether the child was a conserver or a nonconserver. ... [From the syntactic point of view, the most important difference seems to have been a preference for comparative constructions on the part of the former group.] She [then] undertook to give linguistic training to the nonconserving group. ... She taught these children to describe the objects in the same terms that the conservers used. Then she examined again the children who had previously been nonconservers but who had then learned the more advanced linguistic forms to see whether this training had affected their operational level. . . . Well, in every case she found that there was only minimal progress after the linguistic training. . . . *Mme. Sinclair's conclusion on the basis of these experiments is that the intellectual operations appear to give rise to linguistic progress, and not vice versa* (Italics added.) [pp. 48–50].

But, glaringly, the conclusion is not warranted by these observations. Notice that there are *three* possibilities: either linguistic development determines general cognitive development, or general cognitive development determines linguistic development, *or their development is independent*. Sinclair's observations bear on the first of these hypotheses, but they have no bearing whatever on the decision between the last two. If language development is paced primarily by the maturation of language-specific mechanisms, then the natural prediction is that it should be relatively unaffected by training in nonlinguistic, cognitive skills and vise versa. There is nothing in Sinclair's observations as Piaget describes them which suggests that this prediction is false.

It appears, in short, that there is no decisive evidence for an interesting dependency of language development upon cognitive development or that stages of linguistic development express stages of cognitive development. Conversely, the data thus far available are compatible with a view of language development as paced by the maturation of task-specific computational procedures. This is not to say that the data *demand* this treatment, only that at this point, a serious preference for either view would be largely dogmatic. Brownowski and Bellugi (1970) are right to remind us that language learning, like learning of any other kind, involves the induction of general rules from particular instances. But the view that only one kind of inductive principle underlies learning has no more a priori plausibility than the (historically related) view that there is only one kind of warranted inductive procedure in science. Philosophers are beginning to think that the attempt to find a general form of nondemonstrative argument of which all empirical inferences are special cases was ill advised. It may well turn out that the search for a single principle of induction to account for all species of learning is equally so. Just as the principles of empirical inference a scientist accepts seem inextricably bound up with the detailed content of the theories he believes to be true, so too the principles involved in the child's extrapolations of linguistic rules may be intimately determined by the detailed character of his innate beliefs about the structure of his verbal environment. Like the empirical data, the analogies between learning and induction are interesting but they fail to yield an unequivocal moral on the question of the task-specificity of language-learning processes.

PART TWO. SOME THEORIES ABOUT THE INNATE ENDOWMENT IN LANGUAGE ACQUISITION

What traditional language-learning models have in common is their failure to exploit the possibility that the child brings to the learning situation a rich system of hypotheses about the kinds of structural regularities that can underlie the sentences that adult speakers produce. It seems increasingly clear that no account of first-language learning which does not make some such assumption has much chance of success. The interesting question is less *whether* the child brings such information to the language-learning task than what the character of the information he brings might be. In this section we consider a number of recent proposals which have sought to characterize that information.

Four conditions must be satisfied in any account which seeks to answer the question: What information does the child bring to the language-learning situation by virtue of which he is able to arrive at an internal representation of the adult language? First, the hypothesized information must be *adequate* in the sense that an organism which had it would be able to develop a correct representation of the structure of a natural language if subjected to relevant environmental stimulation (like presence of a linguistic corpus, the occurrence of appropriate reward, etc.). Second, an organism employing the hypothesized information must be proficient at learning *any* natural language since, so far as anyone knows, children learn with approximately equal ease any language to which they are exposed. Their linguistic capacities are not biased toward, e.g., Russian rather than Bantu. Third, the postulated information should at least *contribute* to an explanation of the stages through which children proceed in the process of learning their language. Ontogenetic regularities in language learning which are not specific to particular cultures or particular languages may be consequences of the character of the learning strategies children employ; hence it is reasonable to require that theories about these strategies lead to an explanation of such regularities. Finally, a characterization of the structure children bring to language learning should throw light on language universals. Insofar as there exist common structural properties of historically unrelated languages, and insofar as such universals are not explicable as convergences determined by social, pragmatic, or other environmental pressures, it seems plausible to attribute them to the inherent biases of language learners. Hence there ought to be a very close relation between what we hypothesize about the procedures children use to learn languages and what can be demonstrated about universal features of languages.

It is sometimes claimed that insofar as accounts of language learning attribute the child's capacity more to endogenously determined structures than to the operation of environmental variables such accounts must be empirically unconstrained. The absurdity of such a claim should be clear. We have enumerated four minimal conditions that an account of the endogeneous language-learning mechanisms must meet. It provides some insight into *how* difficult it is to satisfy these conditions that there does not exist in the literature on language learning a single theory that meets any one of them. The problem is not that there are too many ways to satisfy the minimal demands upon a nativistic theory of language acquisition; the problem is that, as things now stand, there aren't any.

CHOMSKY'S ACCOUNT OF INNATE MECHANISMS

The most explicit attempt thus far to characterize the general nature of the innate contribution to language learning is found in Chomsky (1965). Chomsky's suggestion is worth investigating at length: first, because it makes clear one way in which theories about the child's linguistic endowment can be related to theories about linguistic universals (i.e., to what Chomsky calls "general linguistic theory"); and second, because there are interesting parallels between Chomsky's treatment of language learning and the sort of analysis-by-synthesis models of speech perception reviewed in Chapter 6. We shall see that the question of how language is learned is more like the question of how language is perceived than it might at first glance appear to be.

In *Aspects of the theory of syntax*, Chomsky writes as follows:

> Let us consider with somewhat greater care just what is involved in the construction of an "acquisition model" for language. A child who is capable of language learning must have
>
> ...(i)   a technique for representing input signals
>
> (ii)   a way of representing structural information about these signals
>
> (iii)   some initial delimitation of a class of possible hypotheses about language structure
>
> (iv)   a method for determining what each such hypothesis implies with respect to each sentence
>
> (v)   a method for selecting one of the (presumably, infinitely many) hypotheses that are allowed by (iii) and are compatible with the given primary linguistic data
>
> Correspondingly, a theory of linguistic structure that aims for explanatory adequacy must contain
>
> ...(i)   a universal phonetic theory that defines the notion "possible sentence"
>
> (ii)   a definition of "structural description"
>
> (iii)   a definition of "generative grammar"
>
> (iv)   a method for determining the structural description of a sentence, given a grammar
>
> (v)   a way of evaluating alternative proposed grammars
>
> Putting the same requirements in somewhat different terms, we must require of such a linguistic theory that it provide for
>
> (i)   an enumeration of the class $s_1, s_2, \ldots$ of possible sentences
>
> (ii)   an enumeration of the class $SD_1, SD_2, \ldots$ of possible structural descriptions
>
> (iii)   an enumeration of the class $G_1, G_2, \ldots$ of possible generative grammars
>
> (iv)   specification of a function f such that $SD_{f(i,j)}$ is the structural description assigned to sentence s_i by grammar G_j for arbitrary i,j,
>
> (v)   specification of a function m such that $m(i)$ is an integer associated with the grammar G_i as its value (with, let us say, lower value indicated by higher number) [pp. 30–31]

[For a statement of essentially similar views, cf. Katz (1966).]

In effect, Chomsky assumes that the child must have five distinct types of information available to him if he is to be able to learn the grammar underlying the corpus of utterances to which he is exposed. The picture Chomsky has in mind appears to be the following. Consider the set of all sequences of phones. Clearly this is an infinite set, and clearly it can be partitioned into subsets, one of which contains all and only the sequences of phones that satisfy universal phonetic constraints and the other of which is its complement. (Thus, for example, "boy" and "garcon" and phonetically regular nonwords like "trok" or "irkflugles" belong to one set but phonetically impossible sequences like "pbtdkg" and "sftrzdk" belong to the other.) Such a partitioning is tantamount to a definition of the notion "possible phonetic sequence in a natural language," and condition *i* states that the child brings to the language-learning situation a knowledge of this partitioning.

Analogously, consider the set of all possible sequences of constituent-structure trees; clearly there is some partitioning of this set into subsets, one of which contains all the sequences of trees which can be derivations of a sentence in some real or possible natural language and one of which is its complement. Thus, for example, one set contains the union of the derivations of all sentences in French, German, Bantu, Latin, Urdu, etc. But, on the assumption that there is no sentence in any language of which the deep and surface structure are identical, the complement set contains all (but not only) derivations which consist of a single tree. (Similarly, on the assumption that transformations never introduce structure, the complement set contains all but not only sequences of trees such that some tree in each sequence has more nodes than a preceding tree in that sequence.) Such a partitioning is tantamount to a definition of the notion "possible syntactic derivation in a natural language," and condition *ii* states that the child has innate knowledge of this partitioning.

Now consider the infinite number of possible axiomatic representations of relations between structural descriptions and phonetic sequences for any real or possible natural language. Clearly there is a partitioning of this set into those representations which satisfy universal linguistic constraints and those which do not. For example, no representation which employs only unordered rules will appear in the former set, and all representations which employ only unordered rules will appear in the latter set. Such a partitioning is tantamount to a "super-grammar": an enumeration of the possible grammars of natural languages; and condition *iii* states that the child has innate knowledge of this partitioning.

Condition *iv* states that the child has a universal recognition routine for transformational grammars. That is, the child has a device which takes as input any sequence of phones that satisfies condition *i* and gives as output the structural analysis assigned that sequence of phones by any grammar which satisfies condition *iii*. In short, the recognition device is equivalent to an infinite set of triples, the first member of which is a phonetic sequence, the second member of which is a grammar, and the third member of which is the structural analysis that phonetic sequence receives from that grammar. [The third member of such a triple will be null in each of infinitely many cases where the phonetic input is not in the range of the grammar (i.e., is not a well-formed sequence in the language that the grammar describes).]

To summarize thus far: the field of hypotheses that the child brings to language learning consists of a representation of all the possible structural descriptions and all the possible grammars. His problem is construed as that of sorting through the possible grammars to find the one which provides the best analysis of the regularities underlying his corpus. Since the procedures for phonetic analysis are assumed to be innate, the corpus is itself construed as a finite set of phonetic representations of utterances.

In Chomsky's view, then, the child is faced with a task analogous to that of a field linguist confronted with an alien language. Both are required to construct a characterization of the regularities underlying a certain set of phonetic strings (equivalently, a theory of the linguistic competence of the speakers who produced these strings) where the relevant form of characterization is a generative grammar. Like the field linguist, the child does not come to his task empty-handed: ideally, both are in possession of a "linguistic theory" which constrains the candidate analyses of the corpus to those which *could* be true of some natural language. In the case of the linguist this information is likely to be held as an explicit theory of grammar; in the case of the child it is the implicit information described by conditions *i* to *iii*. In either case the problem is that of discovering which of the infinitely many grammars that satisfy universal constraints on form and content of linguistic rules is the best one for the language from which the corpus is drawn.

Given the assumption that the child's a priori information about language structure is what conditions *i* to *iii* suggest, what mechanisms might be hypothesized for the recruitment of this information? What is being asked for here is an account of the computational procedures whereby the child goes about analyzing a corpus in terms of his innate information about grammatical structure. The problem is formally analogous to the one concerning how the hearer applies his information about the structure of his language in order to recover the structural descriptions of utterances; in either case, a range of possible analyses of the input is assumed to be available to the organism, and the problem is to describe the computational procedures involved in determining which of these hypotheses provides the best description of the organism's experiences.

Chomsky probably intends that condition *iv* should yield a solution to this problem, since it provides a partial definition of the notion of "confirmation of a candidate grammar." That is, the hypothesis that a given grammar is the optimal analysis of the regularities underlying the child's corpus is partially confirmed for the child whenever he discovers in his corpus some phonetic sequence which is, in fact, generated by that grammar. Condition *iv* simply states that the child has at his disposal techniques for determining, about any phonetic sequence he hears, whether it *is* generated by the particular candidate grammar he happens to be testing.

Notice, however, that as we have developed Chomsky's proposals thus far, certain important problems about confirmation of candidate grammars have been left unresolved. This is because, even though condition *iv* allows the child to determine whether a given grammar predicts a phonetic sequence that he discovers in his corpus, and even though it permits the child to determine which structural description the grammar assigns that phonetic sequence, Chomsky has provided the child with no way of determining when a given candidate grammar assigns the *correct* structural description to a phonetic sequence.

The nature of the difficulty can be seen from the following example. Imagine a child exposed to a corpus of English. Let us suppose that on a given occasion, this child hears an utterance having the phonetic shape [How's the wife and kids]. Suppose too that the child is considering as a candidate grammar for his corpus the grammar G_i, which has the property of being weakly equivalent to the hypothetical correct grammar of English. That is, G_i enumerates the same set of phonetic sequences that the correct grammar does but does not assign to them the same structural analyses. Suppose, for example, that G_i assigns to the phonetic sequence [How's the wife and kids] a structural description which includes the feature *imperative*. The problem the present theory must face is how the child is to determine that G_i is *not* the correct grammar of English; in particular, how is he to determine that the structural analysis G_i assigns to [How's the wife and kids] is incorrect?

It is clear upon inspection that there is nothing in principles *i* to *iv* which permits him to do this. In particular, principle *i* allows the child a phonetic transcription of his input. Principle *iv* allows him to ask whether an observed phonetic sequence is in the output of a given candidate grammar. Hence by applying *i* and *iv*, the child can determine that G_i predicts [How's the wife and kids]. Principle *iv* also allows the child to determine that G_i analyzes [How's the wife and kids] as an imperative. The difficulty is that Chomsky has provided no way for the child to determine that this analysis is wrong. It appears that the best that principles *i* to *iv* can do is select a set of weakly equivalent candidate grammars, one of which is the correct grammar of the child's language. Given only the information specified by *i* to *iv*, the child has no way of determining which of these grammars is the correct one.

Adding principle *v* does not materially alter the situation. Principle *v* is apparently intended to provide the child with a confirmation metric, i.e., a function which determines which of *n* grammars is to be preferred, given a certain corpus. But since the only observations that *i* to *iv* permit the child to make are observations about the phonetic content of the corpus, principle *v* must work essentially by choosing between weakly equivalent grammars *on formal grounds alone*. Now it is doubtless conceptually possible that some metric over formal properties of a grammar should yield a choice among the indefinitely many weakly equivalent grammars that could be formulated for a natural language. But while this is logically possible, it is extremely unlikely to be true. We know, for example, that a vast amount of information about, e.g., speakers' intuitions of ambiguity, relatedness of grammatical structure, similarity of meaning, etc., is required by linguists if they are to choose between weakly equivalent analyses. It is, indeed, characteristic of the methodology of the generative movement that data of this sort, as well as data about which phonetic strings are intuitively well formed, are routinely taken into account in deciding between descriptions of a language. But Chomsky's proposals provide no way for the child to bring these kinds of considerations to bear on the construction of his theories of language.

Chomsky remarks:

> A language acquisition device that meets conditions (i)-(v) is capable of utilizing ... primary linguistic data as the empirical basis for language learning. This device must search through the set of possible hypotheses $G_1, G_2 ...$, which are available to it by virtue of condition (iii), and must select grammars that are compatible with the primary linguistic data, represented in terms of (i) and (ii). It is possible to test compatibility by virtue of the fact that the device meets condition (iv). The device would then select one of these potential grammars by the evaluation measure guaranteed by (v). The selected grammar now provides the device with a method for interpreting an arbitrary sentence by virtue of (ii) and (iv). That is to say, the device has now constructed a theory of the language of which the primary linguistic data are a sample. The theory that the device has now selected and internally represented specifies its tacit competence, its knowledge of the language. The child who acquires a language in this way of course knows a great deal more than he has "learned." His knowledge of the language, as this is determined by his internalized grammar, goes far beyond the presented primary linguistic data and is in no sense an "inductive generalization" from these data [1965, pp. 32–33].

But, in fact, as we have seen, it is highly doubtful whether a device of the kind Chomsky describes could, even in principle, do better than select an indefinite set of weakly equivalent grammars, one of which is the correct grammar of the language. And it is far from obvious how the device might be supplemented so as to choose the unique best grammar from among this set.

There seems, indeed, to be a paradox inherent in Chomsky's position. If the child is appropriately to constrain the grammar he chooses, he must know more about the grammatical structure of the utterances in his corpus than merely their correct phonetic description. He needs such information to determine whether his candidate grammar is assigning the correct structural description to items in the corpus. But he could *have* the relevant grammatical information about the utterances he hears only insofar as he knows the grammar of the language. (By hypothesis, a necessary condition for being able to assign the correct structural analysis to a phonetic sequence is knowing which grammar correctly describes the language that sequence is drawn from.) In short, it is possible to argue that a child having the innate endowment Chomsky's theory specifies could learn only the grammar of a language he already knows.

It looks as though something has gone seriously wrong. It helps in understanding the difficulty to make explicit certain striking analogies between Chomsky's proposal for the structure of a language-acquisition device and the analysis-by-synthesis account of sentence recognition which we discussed in Chapter 6.

Analysis-by-synthesis models assume that the perceiver exploits a generative grammar as a source of candidate analyses of input signals and that he accepts a given such analysis in case it satisfies some predetermined criterion for a match between the internally generated signal and the input. Analogously, in Chomsky's proposal, the child is assumed to have innate knowledge of a sort of supergrammar (i.e., of a recursive enumeration of the grammars of possible natural languages). The child is imagined to run through these grammars in some determinate order comparing the output of each with his corpus. We have seen that principle *iv* (together with the assumption, implicit in principle *i*, that the child has available automatic procedures for phonetic analysis) permits the child to determine whether any given candidate grammar correctly predicts the phonetic sequences he hears. Clearly, the process of searching through possible *grammars* and comparing the output of each with the phonetic content of a *corpus* is formally analogous to the analysis-by-synthesis procedure of searching through possible *derivations of sentences* and comparing them with some *phonetic representation of an utterance* whose syntactic structure is to be computed.

Like the analysis-by-synthesis model of speech perception, this account deserves to be taken seriously. In the first place, it gives an explicit representation of the information a child is hypothesized to bring to the language-learning task, just as the analysis-by-synthesis model given an explicit representation of the information the speaker is assumed to bring to the task of speech perception. Thus the former model avoids vague references to language-learning sets, just as the latter one avoids vague references to speech-perception sets. In each case, the character of the information employed in computation is precisely specified.

However, Chomsky's proposals about language learning share not only the virtues of the analysis-by-synthesis model of speech perception but also its defects. Roughly speaking, like the analysis-by-synthesis model of speech perception, Chomsky's model uses the input data in only the most inefficient manner. In effect, the only question that the child is allowed to ask about his corpus is whether it matches the predictions of some candidate grammar *at the phonetic level*. Though there is no reason for denying that distributional facts, semantic facts, facts of discourse structure, etc., may play a role in determining the child's developing picture of the grammar of his language, it is difficult to see how Chomsky's model could accommodate this possibility.

It should be emphasized that this difficulty is inherent not in the notion that the child has innate information about the language he has to learn but rather in the suggestion that the information is organized in the form of a recursive enumeration of the possible grammars. For example, these sorts of problems vanish if it is assumed that the child's innate information is organized as a set of "discovery procedures" for operating on a corpus to *construct* candidate grammars. Again, we return to a point quite similar to one we made in our discussion of speech recognition. We suggested in that discussion that at least some of an adult speaker's syntactic knowledge is organized as a set of computational procedures which operate directly upon morphologically characterized inputs to yield analyses of their deep structures. By allowing these strategies to take detailed cognizance of features of lexical content and arrangement in the surface structures of sentences, we hoped to avoid the more wasteful characteristics of analysis by synthesis. Indeed the more powerful we assumed the procedures for analyzing lexical and serial features of the surface string to be, the smaller the number of candidate analyses of the deep structure underlying that string the perceiver was required to entertain.

Precisely the same sort of point is relevant in the case of language learning. The more data-processing procedures the child is assumed to have available for analyzing his corpus, the more constraints he can place upon candidate grammars of that corpus. The ideal procedure is the limit of this series; that is, the case where the child's data-handling procedures automatically produce the unique best grammar, given an adequate corpus as input.

Indeed, Chomsky is himself forced to suppose that the child has *some* procedures for the direct analysis of his corpus at his disposal: unless the child were allowed to "automatically" convert a corpus into its phonetic representation, he would have *no* data against which to test his candidate grammars. However, the assumption that the choice of a grammar is effected by constructive procedures up to the phonetic level but proceeds by analysis by synthesis at higher levels would seem to be quite unmotivated.

We can conclude our discussion of Chomsky's suggestion by remarking that it is not obvious that the model, as it is outlined in *Aspects of the theory of syntax*, would satisfy *any* of the conditions which we suggested a theory of language learning should meet. The first such condition was simply that the device exhibit the appropriate input-output relations, i.e., that given an adequate corpus of data about a natural language, it be demonstrable that the device would, in fact, produce a unique best grammar of that language. We have just seen, however, that there is no reason to suppose that this model will ever select the correct grammar of a language from among the indefinite number of weakly equivalent grammars compatible with conditions *i* to *iv*.

Second, the model does not demonstrably satisfy the condition that it be equally proficient at learning any natural language; while it is an important advance over previous approaches to language learning in that it provides a way of reducing the child's hypotheses about his input to those that could be true of *some* natural language, the order in which candidate grammars are generated is left entirely undetermined. The difficulty here is in the nature of a dilemma. On the one hand, candidate grammars cannot be generated at random if the device is to converge on the correct grammar in real time. But on the other hand, it is completely unknown how to provide principles for determining the order in which candidate grammars are tested that will not bias the device toward learning one natural language more easily than another. At any event, the model, as it stands, is compatible with any hypothesis whatever about the relative difficulty of natural languages.

Third, the postulated model fails, for the same sorts of reasons, to make predictions about the stages through which the child passes in learning his language. As Chomsky remarks, the model treats the language-learning process as "all or none": each candidate grammar either does or does not properly describe the phonetic content of the corpus, and if it does not, it is rejected in favor of the next candidate. It should be emphasized that this sort of treatment is inherent in the analysis-by-synthesis approach and that for this reason, that model looks to be especially unilluminating as an account of language learning.

Such implications as the model does have for the prediction of developmental stages are not supported by the available data. For example, if we take literally the suggestion that the information the child brings to language learning has the form of recursive enumeration of the possible grammars of natural languages, we ought to be able to predict that a child never assigns to his corpus a structure that is incompatible with linguistic universals that hold for adults. For, on Chomsky's view, the child's source of candidate analyses for the input corpus is restricted to the formalisms which constitute possible adult grammars. But while it is a plausible *hypothesis* that the dialect that children speak satisfies, at every stage, the universal constraints on natural languages, it is by no means clear that this hypothesis is in fact true. There exist data which suggest that at least some children go through stages during which the hypotheses they formulate do *not* assume that the corpus is drawn from a language for which adult universals hold. For example, many investigators appear to agree with Braine's (1963b) characterization of the early productions of the child. At about 2 years of age, when the child begins to produce utterances longer than one word,

> ... there are two-word classes: pivots and X-words [often referred to as "open" class words]. The pivots are few in number; they tend to occur in several word combinations, and each is associated with a particular utterance position. Thus two subclasses [of pivot words] are definable, P_1 associated with initial position, and P_2 with final position. The X-class is a large open class containing the child's entire vocabulary except for some of the pivots. X-words tend to recur in relatively few word combinations and do not appear to be tied to a particular utterance position; they occur alone or in the position complementary to that of the pivot word [p. 9].

It seems clear that the formalism Braine describes differs in radical ways from that which underlies the grammar of adult natural languages. Indeed, it is characteristically the case that both the pivot and the open class contain lexical material which, from the point of view of the adult taxonomy, is completely heterogeneous. In short, if Braine's description is accurate, then there is at least one stage during which at least some children impose upon their primary linguistic data a structural analysis which violates universals that hold for the adult language. It is unclear how this can be explained if we assume that the child's innate information about languages is exhausted by a specification of the adult universals or by a recursive enumeration of the possible adult grammars. We will return to the issues raised by Braine's analysis of early grammars later in this chapter.[5]

Finally, the analysis-by-synthesis model, as it stands, fails with respect to the requirement that the theory of language learning should contribute to an explanation of the linguistic universals. Indeed, the model makes no prediction about linguistic universals other than that they must exist. This is partly a consequence of the fact that no completed linguistic theory is presently available, so that we do not know what properties a satisfactory recursive enumeration of the possi-

---

[5] There are, however, several caveats which must be observed in interpreting Braine's data. First, there is now some question about its generality. Bowerman (1968), for example, finds no such stage in the development of the Finnish-speaking children she investigated. Second, as we shall see in our discussion of Bloom (1970), the superficial homogeneity of the two-word *pivot* + *open* sentence may conceal a deeper heterogeneity; *pivot* + *open* sentences can apparently express a wide variety of relations between their constituents. Finally, it is important to emphasize that Braine's grammar, like most of those that have been written for childrens' speech, is based entirely on distributional features of the child's productions. For example, it makes no use of the child's intuitions about sentences.

ble grammars would exhibit. But it is also entirely possible that languages may exhibit some universals whose explanation lies in the character of the strategies that children employ to learn them. If this should prove true, the analysis-by-synthesis model of language learning would be in the position of having part of its explanatory power rest on inexplicit assumptions about which such strategies these happen to be.

McNEILL'S ACCOUNT OF THE CHILD'S INNATE HYPOTHESES ABOUT LANGUAGE

There are a variety of other formulations about the information children bring to language learning which deserve to be discussed. Many of these views are not so much alternatives to Chomsky's formulation as they are derivatives from it. The basic property they share is the assumption that the language-learning device maps from a corpus to a transformational grammar and that it does so by exploiting information that amounts to a general definition of the form of such grammars. What distinguishes these views from Chomsky's is their account of how this information is applied: less emphasis is given to analysis-by-synthesis proposals, and a more detailed characterization of the strategies for the construction of grammars is attempted.

For example, McNeill (1966) has proposed the following sort of model. The child's hypotheses about the structures underlying his corpus include (1) a universal hierarchy of syntactic categories, (2) a definition of the grammatical relations, and (3) a definition of "transformational rule" and "phrase-structure rule." Let us consider these in turn.

1. McNeill (1966) suggests that we

Imagine that we have before us a complete transformational grammar of English. We would find that the rules are expressed in terms of very narrow categories of words ... that embody such distinctions as animate and inanimate nouns. ... Suppose that above this level is another that categorizes the same words more broadly. And above this level suppose yet another that classifies the same words more broadly, and so on until at the top there is just one class containing all the words of English. ... The system of levels can be abstractly pictured by the tree graph in [Figure 8-1] [p. 33].

McNeill suggests that this hierarchy may be part of the conceptual equipment that is required for language learning and that learning the language involves assigning vocabulary items to the increasingly subtle syntactic subclasses that the hierarchy defines. "In a child's subsequent development, the differentiation of P [pivot] and O [open] [i.e., of initial classifications of the formatives] may consist of moving down the hierarchy to more narrowly defined categories" (p. 35).

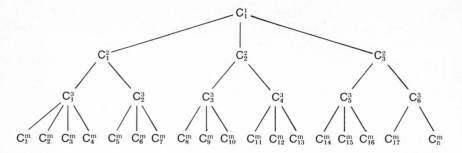

Fig. 8-1. An abstract hierarchy of syntactic categories. (McNeill, 1966, fig. 2).

How the child determines which items in his language belong to which of these categories is not discussed by McNeill. There are, however, two empirical consequences of McNeill's hypothesis that are susceptible to direct test. First, if McNeill's proposal is right, then typical "errors" on the part of language learners ought to consist of the production of well-formed sequences of classes with the wrong substitution instances (e.g., "the stone bit the idea," but not "all gone book"). There is, however, no evidence for this prediction.

Second, if the process of ontogenesis consists in assigning formatives to successively refined subclasses, it ought to be the case that the class to which the adult assigns a word is a "descendent" of the class to which the child assigns it. That is, there ought always to be a route through the tree diagram in Figure 8-1 such that the child's assignment is to a node which lies on the route to the node that directly dominates the adult assignment; the process of differentiation cannot in principle yield cases where a word is assigned first to a class on one side of the tree and then to a class on the other side. Here again, however, the data do not support the prediction. Thus as remarked above, in the initial pivot-and-open-class assignments, it is notable that words from arbitrarily various adult lexical classes can appear in either class. This suggests that crossing must take place in the process of ontogenesis and hence that a view of that process as consisting primarily in the differentiation of lexical class assignments cannot be correct.

2.   McNeill assumes that the child has available the universal definitions of fundamental grammatical relations such as "subject of," "object of," etc. As we remarked in Chapter 3, however, it should be noticed that these definitions are given in terms of relations between *phrases* in *base-structure* trees. There are, for this reason, a number of problems con-

cerning how such definitions could be *applied* to primary linguistic data.

In the first place, grammatical relations are relations between phrases, but McNeill has assumed a hierarchy of *lexical* classes in terms of which the child's input is to be interpreted. On this assumption, the best a child could do with an input string is to assign it to a tree which gives "higher and higher classifications of the words." McNeill does not discuss how the child is able to make the step from a *lexical* tree (i.e., a definition of the lexical classes) to an assignment of *phrase structure* to his inputs.

Second, the definitions of grammatical relations are given in terms of *base* trees; thus McNeill's proposal requires some way for the child to represent the distinction between deep and derived structure. McNeill seems to have two views about this problem. The first is that, in fact, the very young child understands only those sentences whose derived structure happens to exhibit the base-phrase orderings that define subject, object, and other grammatical relations. But second, McNeill believes that at some later point the "ontogenetic clutter" that is generated by the child's failure to make the base-structure—surface-structure distinction forces him, somehow, to the development of a transformational grammar.

3.   The child is assumed to have available definitions of such notions as transformational rule, phrase-structure rule, etc. It is by virtue of this information that he is enabled to "simplify" his initial surface-structure grammar by developing a transformational analysis of his primary linguistic data. However, McNeill provides no indication of how the child goes about constructing the *right* transformations; that is, the putative innate definition of "transformation rule" must be equally well satisfied by the transformations of any conceivable natural language. The question is: How do the child's primary linguistic data interact with his innate endowment to insure that he constructs the transformations characteristic of the language of his speech community?

It should be noticed that references to children's presumed need to "simplify" the phrase-structure grammars with which McNeill suggests they first describe their data provide no insight into this question. We have nothing approaching a simplicity metric that will automatically choose English transformations as the simplest description of an English corpus, Turkish transformations as the simplest description of a Turkish corpus, etc. It might be supposed that the child *does* have such a metric available to him, but that assumption lacks any force as an explanation of how the child learns the language, since the entire problem of characterizing the language-learning procedures can be restated as a problem about characterizing the metric. Indeed, if the assumptions about the simplicity metric are sufficiently rich, no other a priori knowledge of the form of possible grammatical rules need be attributed to the child at all, since his (presumptive) innate preference for a transformational grammar can be represented as a feature of the ordering which his simplicity metric imposes upon hypotheses.

Thus there does not seem to be anything in the proposals made by McNeill which will *explain* how a child who starts by using sentences that correspond (roughly) to base structures might eventually learn to use sentences which do not. But, of course, this does not show that no such process takes place. What would help McNeill's position would be evidence that there is a stage at which children grasp the fundamental grammatical relations marked in base structure but have no transformational system. Relevant data are hard to come by, but the best case that has thus far been made for the view that children's very early utterances express the adult grammatical relations is by Bloom (1970) (see the discussion below). Bloom takes her data to show that transformational structure is present even in the child's earliest sentences though, as we shall see, the situation is far from clear.

As we have reconstructed it thus far, McNeill's position assumes, but does not explain, a correspondence between the earliest productions of the child and base-structure constituent order. McNeill sometimes writes as though he thinks there *is* an explanation for the hypothesized correspondence: namely, that the child has innate knowledge of the base-structure rules.

This is, of course, a much stronger claim than the one which says that "the child has innate knowledge of the *concept* of a base-structure rule." The latter suggestion implies that the *form* of the base-structure rules must be universal, but the former implies that the rules themselves must be, i.e., that all languages have the same base structures. This is an hypothesis McNeill apparently thinks may be true.

It is, however, next to impossible to evaluate this claim, given the fluidity of the treatment of base structure in contemporary syntactic theory. We saw in Chapter 4 that there is an intricate problem of adjudicating between the claims of the base component, the lexicon, and the transformational component in general linguistic theory. Roughly, grammars that employ very powerful transformational components use relatively simple lexicons and permit very abstract base structures generated by a relatively small number of base-structure rules; conversely, systems that use highly elaborated lexicons characteristically assume that the base tree of a sentence is rather closely related to its surface tree, and hence that the base component must be rich enough to specify a relatively large number of types of structures. Given that questions of this degree of generality remain open in linguistics, it seems to us premature to indulge in psycholinguistic speculation about the innateness of any particular set of base-structure rules.

PART THREE.   SOME EMPIRICAL STUDIES OF LANGUAGE ACQUISITION

The account of the child's innate endowment that Chomsky gives assumes that the output of a language-acquisition device is a transformational grammar. That is, it assumes that grammatical rules and operations are psychologically real for the adult speaker and that the problem of language acquisition is characterizing a system of hypotheses which would permit the child to select or construct an appropriate grammar of his language given a corpus of primary linguistic data.

Quite explicit statements of this view can, in fact, be found elsewhere in the literature. Menyuk (in press), for example, has maintained that

> despite the fact that the child is producing non-grammatical structures he seems to have the capacity for recognizing sentences versus non-sentences and possible versus not possible phonological sequences. He may produce utterances which do not follow the rules of a structure to completion ... but he does not easily produce or understand [sequences whose production would require violating or amending the rules of the adult grammar]. That is, the not completely well-formed structures he produces can be generated by using the rules of the grammar of his language. He does not produce structures which are derived from sets of rules outside this grammar.

Menyuk supports this hypothesis by reference to such examples of children's productions as "It's for to eat," "You say it what's happening," and "I dream about I got new toys." Each of these structures corresponds to a form produced as an "intermediate tree" in the adult English grammar. That is, each of them would be grammatical except that a mandatory transformation or sequence of transformations has failed to be applied (the rule which reduces "for" in the first case; the rule which replaces "it" by "what's happening" in the second case; and the rule which nominalizes "I get" in the third case). The fact that children are observed to produce sequences of this kind would thus appear to support the hypothesis that their linguistic development is primarily a matter of obtaining mastery over more and more of the adult transformations, and that having mastered a particular set of such rules, the child uses them in some quite direct way to produce sentences. Misproductions are cases where either the child has not learned the late rules required to complete a derivation or he knows the rules but somehow fails to employ them. In either case, the assumption is that the process of grammatical derivation is psychologically real.

We saw in Chapter 6, however, that the adult speaker-hearer's exploitation of the information represented by a standard generative grammar is probably mediated by a complex of heuristic procedures for encoding and decoding sentences, and that the grammar per se provides very little insight into the character of those procedures. That is, while the optimal grammar represents the linguistic knowledge of the adult speaker-hearer in the sense that it specifies a set of structural descriptions that he can encode-decode, it appears to provide very little information about the computations which actually underlie encoding and decoding.

If grammar is only very abstractly related to a model of the adult sentence producer-perceiver, considerable caution must be exercised in employing the grammar as a source of predictions about ontogenesis. Clearly, such predictions have theoretical warrant only if one assumes both that the grammar represents the information a language learner has to internalize and that it represents the information in the *form* in which it is internalized. It is thus incumbent upon investigators to consider whether the ontogenetic data supports the hypothesis that linguistic competence at a given stage can, in general, be specified by reference to some portion of the adult grammar that the child has mastered by that stage.

There are three kinds of predictions which follow naturally from the claim that linguistic development is a matter of increasing mastery of the rules that appear in the transformational grammar of the adult language. The first prediction is that structures that are introduced in the adult grammar by a single rule, or by a number of interrelated rules, are mastered more or less simultaneously by the child. The second prediction is that the productions of the child ought themselves to permit a natural representation by a transformational grammar. The third prediction is simply the ontogenetic analog of what we called in Chapter 6 the derivational theory of complexity. If what the child is learning is a grammar, then the grammatical complexity of a structure, as measured by the number of rules required for its derivation, should be a predictor of the ontogenetic stage at which the structure is mastered, with grammatically simpler structures becoming available to the child earlier than grammatically complicated ones.

About the first of these predictions (although it is clearly of critical importance) there is very little known. There exists in the current literature only one detailed longitudinal study of the emergence of a group of interrelated grammatical structures. This is the study by Bellugi (1967) and Klima and Bellugi (1966) of the development of the auxiliary and negative system in English. And though, as Bellugi remarks, "it is the fact that much of the apparatus comes in in a relatively short period of time and appears in a variety of structures" (1967, p. 90), the data by no means unequivocally point to a close correspondence between ontogenetically simultaneous structures, on the one hand, and structures that fall within the domain of a single grammatical rule, on the other.

There are more data available on the second two predictions, to which we now turn.

THE TRANSFORMATIONAL REPRESENTATION OF CHILDRENS' LANGUAGE

In a previous section, we remarked upon the view that for some children, the earliest structured word strings produced (starting at about 18 months of age) have the form *pivot* + *open* or *open* + *pivot*. *Pivot* and *open* denote word classes, and the grammar usually exhibits two important properties: the pivot class is smaller than the open class; and the order of the classes is relatively stable for a given child—that is, children who produce *pivot* + *open* do not produce *open* + *pivot*, and vice versa.

It is important to notice that if this analysis of the child's productions is correct, it counts against both Chomsky's and McNeill's approach to language development. For, if children start out with a *pivot* + *open* grammar, then at least one of the systems of representation produced by the innate language-acquisition device is *not* a transformational grammar and does not satisfy the linguistic universals that hold for the adult grammar. It is also important to notice, however, that the analyses on which the claims for pivot-open grammars are based are purely distributional. That is, the procedure involved is the collection of corpora of utterances which are then taxonomized solely in terms of the privileges of occurrence of the lexical material.

It is, of course, possible to take a different approach. In a recent longitudinal study, Bloom (1970) analyzed the verbalizations of three young children, using not only distributional data but also information about the (apparent) intention of the child when he produced the utterances. Commenting on the methodology of her study, Bloom remarks: "...evaluation of the children's language began with the basic assumption that it was possible to reach the semantics of children's sentences by considering nonlinguistic information from context and behavior in relation to linguistic performance. ... evaluation of an utterance in relation to the context in which it occurred provided more information for analyzing intrinsic structure than would a simple distributional analysis of the recorded corpus" (p. 10).

When analyzed in light of such information about the context of utterance, the child's language, even at the *pivot* + *open* stage, suggests far more structure and systematicity than merely distributional studies disclose. For example, Bloom finds no less than five distinct relations which can be expressed by the surface sequence $N + N$ in the corpus of a child at the *pivot + open* stage.

> There were five possible structural descriptions that could explain the semantic relationship between constituents in utterances with the surface description Noun + Noun at Kathryn I: (1) *Conjunction,* where the two constituents named simultaneous aspects of the same referent or two referents within the bounds of a single utterance, with no connection between them, as in "umbrella boot." (2) *Attributive* construction, where the initial-position noun was an attribute of a matrix noun that occurred in second position, as in "party hat." (3) *Genitive* string, where the initial-position noun was a possessor-noun and the second-position noun was a possessed-object-noun, as in "Kathryn sock." (4) *Subject-locative* string, where the initial noun was the subject of a locative predication and the second-position noun was the relational locative constituent, as in "sweater chair." (5) *Subject-object* string, where the initial-position noun related to the whole string as sentence-subject, and the subsequent noun represented the predicate of the subject—a direct object [p. 62].

It should be noticed that each of the relations between nouns which Kathryn expresses by a surface $N + N$ sequence corresponds to a "grammatical relation" in the sense of Chomsky (1965). Since grammatical relations are defined over configurational properties of base trees, Bloom assumes that at least five different base structures must underlie the $N + N$ surface strings in Kathryn's corpus. Thus, underlying the *subject-object* utterances of $N + N$ constructions, Bloom postulates deep trees like that in Figure 8-2, where the two N's are the ones which occur in the observed utterance, and the Δ is a hypothesized, but unexpressed, verb. Similarly, a proposed deep structure for $N + N$ sequences like "sweater chair" where the second N is a locative is as shown in Figure 8-3.

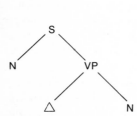

Fig. 8-2. Hypothesized deep structure for two-word ($N + N$) sequences which express a subject-object relation (after Bloom, 1970).

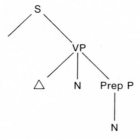

Fig. 8-3. Hypothesized deep structure for two-word ($N + N$) sequences which express an object-locative relation (after Bloom, 1970).

The decision to postulate distinct deep-structure geometries corresponding to the different relations between nouns expressed by $N + N$ surface structures has, as an immediate consequence, the requirement that one assume a transformational system underlying sentences even at the *pivot + open* stage. In particular, since the overt "sentences" contain only two constituents and the hypothesized deep structures may contain many more, a transformation must be postulated which reduces complex deep trees to $N + N$ surface strings. "...a reduction transformation was postulated that operated to delete category constituents that dominated forms that were not expressed in surface structure, for example, the VP or Δ symbol postulated as an intervening constituent in *subject-object* strings" (Bloom, 1970, p. 71). Bloom has, in fact, an ingenious distributional argument for the operation of some form of deletion in the production of overt two-item sequences. If one looks at a stage slightly later than the one characterized by $N + N$ constructions, but where the mean length of utterance is still only 1.9 words, one finds two-word sequences in which nouns, verbs, adverbs, etc., may occur. "Looking at the entire group of sentences, it could be seen that when the subject of the sentence was expressed, either the verb, the object, the adverbial phrase, or more than one of these was not expressed. ... Characteristically, elaboration of what preceded or followed the verbal position was accompanied by a deletion of some or all other constituents" (p. 146). In short, at this stage, one gets a reasonable characterization of the distribution of overt utterances by assuming that there is a complex underlying structure from which the child must choose not more than about two elements in producing a surface form. The existence of $N + V$, $V + N$, and $N + N$ as well-formed surface structures points clearly to an underlying $N + V + N$ form from which constituents are deleted.[6]

Part of the interest of Bloom's work is that it provides us with an analysis of the two-word stage in children's utterances which suggests that the child's internal representation of his language is far richer than one would have supposed from the *pivot + open* grammars. This is im-

---

[6] Bloom considers this reduction to be a true transformation operation, but it seems more plausible to regard it as merely the mechanical effect of a limitation on immediate memory. Notice, in particular, that its operation is apparently *not* sensitive to either configurational or lexical features of the structures it applies to. That is, it applies indifferently to all the various deep structures Bloom postulates. If the reduction operation has any counterpart in the adult grammar, it would be that of a "surface constraint" rather than a true transformation. (See Perlmutter, 1968.)

It is also worth emphasizing in this respect an observation of Brown (quoted by Greenfield, 1968). Since the constraint on surface sentence length is relaxed as the child gets older, treating it as a true transformation commits us to the mildly paradoxical conclusion that the child's syntactic development involves the *loss* of transformations over time.

portant because, if Bloom's analysis is correct, we shall have to make correspondingly rich assumptions about the character of the learning mechanisms that the child is employing at this stage. In particular, on the basis of Bloom's analysis there is no reason to believe that these mechanisms ever lead the child to postulate a grammar which does not contain a base component and a transformational component.

How, then, are we to choose between the picture of the two-word stage that holds that it is organized by some sort of phrase-structure grammar and the one we get from Bloom? It is immediately evident that Bloom's grammar is sensitive to a far wider body of data than are the early grammars that were based on purely distributional facts. Sentences that the latter grammars represent as structurally homogenous, the former represents as differentiated at both the syntactic and semantic level. Bloom's grammar can thus represent a variety of features of the child's use of two-word sequences that constituent-structure grammars cannot. It may thus seem prima facie obvious that Bloom's grammar should be preferred, and that we should accept the very rich picture of the child's language-learning mechanisms that it implies.

There is, however, a serious difficulty about Bloom's methodology which makes it hard to choose between her grammar and a relatively superficial distributional analysis of the child's early productions like the *pivot* + *open* one. Bloom takes it as a matter of methodological principle that relations between constituents which would count as grammatical relations in the *adult* grammar should be represented by geometrically distinct deep-structure configurations in the child's grammar. This principle is, however, hard to justify.

The existence of a level of the adult grammar at which the different grammatical relations are represented by geometrically distinct objects is, after all, an empirical hypothesis rather than a mere methodological assumption. In particular, it is claimed that a level which acknowledges trees exhibiting distinct configurations corresponding to distinct grammatical relations will also provide the best domains for independently motivated syntactic transformations. This coincidence is among the strongest arguments for the existence of a distinct level of deep linguistic structure; the transformations are motivated by the need to capture the surface forms of the language, and the deep trees needed to provide domains for the transformations turn out to be simply those which permit the representation of grammatical relations. In short, in the adult grammar, it is the demands of the transformations which justify postulating the types of deep-tree structures in terms of which the grammatical relations are defined: one can justify distinguishing between the geometry of deep trees only by showing that some transformation applies or fails to apply to them by virtue of their difference in form. Demonstrating a semantic difference between the sentences the trees underlie is insufficient since there are clearly a wide variety of kinds of semantic differences between sentences which are *not* encoded by features of their deep geometry.

If, however, we compare the case with children's language as analyzed by Bloom, we see that the decision to represent distinct grammatical relations with distinct base structures is, in fact, simply that: a methodological decision. In particular, Bloom cannot show that the distinctions she wishes to draw between the base structure of sentences which express distinct semantic relations among their constituents can be independently motivated by reference to the requirements of the transformations which apply to those structures. At the stage Bloom studies, there is only one type of surface sentence available to the child, which is to say that there is no way of motivating transformations which apply differentially to the different kinds of base structures Bloom distinguishes.

To summarize: In the case of the adult grammar, we postulate transformations to account for the available surface forms, and we make distinctions between configurational properties of base structures in order to provide domains for those transformations. We then *discover* that the structures which provide such domains are compatible with those required for the definition of grammatical relations. But in the case of children's grammars, there is no evidence for transformations which apply differentially to the base structures Bloom distinguishes. Hence, there is no independent evidence supporting the postulation of distinct base structures corresponding to distinct interpretations of two-word outputs. This is hardly surprising; one cannot reasonably hope to have distributionally justified transformations for a language all of whose sentences have the same surface form.

What, then, do Bloom's data actually *show*? First, they provide plausible arguments for the view that the child's overt output is characteristically some reduced version of an underlying structure. This is a special, and interesting, case of the widely made suggestion that children's internal representation of their language is richer than what a purely distributional analysis will reveal. Second, they show that even at the two-word stage, children represent such distinctions as subject versus object versus genitive, versus attributive, versus locative, etc., *somewhere*; i.e., that they have available, at a very early age, a considerable subset of what turn out, in the adult language, to be grammatical relations. What the data do *not* show is that these relations are represented in the child's grammar by configurationally distinct deep structures. For example, the data are fully compatible with the view that the child represents these relations by distinct semantic or conceptual structures, all of which are expressed by the *same* tree structure at every level in the child's language. Bloom objects to generating $N + N$ sentences of the kind she finds in her data with the rule $S \rightarrow N + N$ primarily on the grounds that "the rule cannot explain the differences in underlying semantic relationship between the constituents—that different combinations of noun forms 'mean' different things" (1970, p. 64). If, however, we press this objection wherever it applies, we are committed to misanalyses even in the case of the adult grammar, since here the same *grammatical* relations often serve to express a wide variety of different *semantic* relations. "John touched Mary" and "John forgot the appointment" are both of the subject-verb-object form, and they presumably derive from deep trees having precisely the same geometry. Yet the semantic relations these sentences express differ as much as do any of those expressed by the two-word sentences in Bloom's data.

It is thus compatible with Bloom's observations that the syntax of the children she studied is almost as uncomplicated as the surface character of their sentences makes it appear to be, e.g., that the child represents all sentences by simple $((N)\ (V)\ (N))_S$ structures which are reduced to two-word surface forms by a mechanical computational constraint. What Bloom has demonstrated is only that if such is the case, then the children are using a language in which very limited syntactic means express a wide variety of semantic relations. At any event, it does not seem that Bloom's work provides decisive grounds for believing that the early productions of the child have their most natural representation in a transformational grammar, though it is perhaps more strongly suggestive of such a view than any other study of the speech of very young children.

DTC PREDICTIONS OF CHILDRENS' LANGUAGE

We said that the third prediction relevant to assessing Chomsky's claim that the output of the child's language-acquisition device is a transformational grammar is the ontogenetic equivalent of DTC. Just as much of the early psycholinguistic work on syntax recognition attempted to demonstrate some relatively simple relation between the grammatical complexity of a sentence and its psychological complexity, so has much of the early work on the ontogenesis of syntax attempted to demonstrate some relatively simple relation between the number of rules in a derivation and the order in which grammatical structures are mastered. The motivations were essentially the same in both cases. To show that grammatical complexity predicts difficulty of recognition or production in the adult is to provide evidence that the operations postulated by a grammar closely parallel the mental operations involved in recognizing or producing a sentence. Analogously, to show that the number of rules required to specify a grammatical structure predicts the stage at which the structure is mastered is to provide evidence that the representation of his language the child is acquiring is closely parallel to the representation afforded by the grammar.

The most direct statement of this view appears in a paper by Brown and Hanlon (1970). They sought to predict the order of appearance of certain types of sentences from a complexity measure based on the number of transformations required to specify them. Brown and Hanlon, however, are careful to restrict their comparisons to instances of what they refer to as "cumulative complexity." That is, they predict an ordering between two types of sentences only in the case where every transformation required in the derivation of one appears in the derivation of the other, but not conversely. Given two such sentence types, the cumulative complexity of the former is said to exceed that of the latter. Brown and Hanlon explicitly reject any account of sentence complexity which simply counts the number of transformations required to generate two sentences and predicts that the one which has the greater number of transformations in its history will be the more complex.

How strongly do the data support the prediction about ontogenetic ordering based on relative cumulative complexity? Brown and Hanlon investigated the appearance of eight different constructions in the child's speech. The constructions are related in various "chains" of cumulative complexity by the following transformations: question, negative, and sentence truncation. They present the eight kinds of sentences in the following paradigm. (We indicate the transformations which apply to each construction.)

1. Simple, active, affirmative, declarative (*SAAD*). For example, "We had a ball."
2. Simple, active, affirmative, interrogative (*Q*). For example, "Did we have a ball?" (*Q*)
3. Simple, active, negative, declarative (*N*). For example, "We didn't have a ball." (*N*)
4. Simple, active, affirmative, declarative, truncated (*Tr*). For example, "We did." (*Tr*)
5. Simple, active, negative, interrogative (*NQ*). For example, "Didn't we have a ball?" (*N, Q*)
6. Simple, active, affirmative, interrogative, truncated (*TrQ*). For example, "Did we?" (Also used as affirmative tag.) (*Q, Tr*)
7. Simple, active, negative, declarative, truncated (*TrN*). For example, "We didn't." (*N, Tr*)
8. Simple, active, negative, interrogative, truncated (*TrNQ*). For example, "Didn't we?" (Also used as negative tag.) (*N, Q, Tr*) (Brown and Hanlon, 1970, pp. 18–19)

TABLE 8-1

SAAD < Q < NQ, TrQ, TrNQ	Four predictions
SAAD < N < NQ, TrN, TrNQ	Four predictions
SAAD < Tr < TrQ, TrQ, TrN, TrNQ	Four predictions
SAAD < NQ < TrNQ	Two predictions
SAAD < TrQ < TrNQ	Two predictions
SAAD < TrN < TrNQ	Two predictions
SAAD < TrNQ	One prediction

The relative cumulative complexity of these sentence is given in Table 8-1 (where < means "is less complex than").

Brown and Hanlon point out that the sentence types are not fully ordered for cumulative complexity; in particular, we do not have an order for the following pairs: Q and N; Q and Tr; N and Tr; Q and TrN; N and

TABLE 8-2. PREDICTIONS (IN BROWN AND HANLON) CONFIRMED (+), DISCONFIRMED (−), AND UNSETTLED (?) FOR DERIVATIONAL COMPLEXITY AND ORDER OF ACQUISITION

	Adam			Sarah			Eve		
	+	?	−	+	?	−	+	?	−
SAAD < Q	✔			✔			✔		
#Q < TrQ	✔			✔			✔		
* Q < NQ	✔			✔			✔		
#Q < TrNQ	✔			✔			✔		
SAAD < N	✔			✔			✔		
#N < TrN					✔				
* N < NQ	✔			✔			✔		
#N < TrNQ	✔			✔			✔		
#SAAD < Tr	✔			✔			✔		
Tr < TrQ†	✔			✔			✔		
Tr < TrN		✔			✔		✔		
* Tr < TrNQ†	✔			✔			✔		
#SAAD < TrQ	✔			✔			✔		
* TrQ < TrNQ		✔		✔					✔
#SAAD < TrN	✔			✔			✔		
* TrN < TrNQ†	✔			✔			✔		✔
SAAD < NQ	✔			✔			✔		
#NQ < TrNQ		✔				✔	✔		✔
#SAAD < TrNQ	✔			✔			✔		
Totals‡	16	1	2	15	2	2	16	3	
Totals§	13	1	2	11	2	2	14	2	

†Prediction not made for tags (TgQ or TgNQ).
‡Appropriate totals if doubtful cases are TrQ and TrNQ.
§Appropriate totals if doubtful cases are TgQ and TgNQ.

TrQ; Tr and NQ; NQ and TrQ; NQ and TrN; TrQ and TrN. If the facts of partial ordering are kept in mind, then the following representation of the overall order is helpful:

$$SAAD < \left\{ \begin{matrix} Q & NQ \\ N & < TrQ \\ Tr & TrN \end{matrix} \right\} TrNQ$$

For each of three children under intensive study, Brown and Hanlon found that the predictions derived from the summary above were quite strongly confirmed: that is, the greater the cumulative complexity of a sentence, the later it appeared in the child's utterances (see Table 8-2).

At first glance, these results would appear to confirm the hypothesis that cumulative complexity is related to the order in which constructions emerge in children's speech. However, they are, in fact, equivocal between this interpretation and an interpretation based on the explicitness with which underlying structure is represented by surface structure in the various sentence types. This is another instance of the conformity of predictions based on the derivational complexity of sentences to predictions based on the extent to which their surface form distorts their deep form; a kind of confounding which, as we pointed out in Chapter 6, makes equivocal much of the perceptual experimentation on sentence complexity.

Notice that nine of the nineteen comparisons in Table 8-2 predict the late appearance of a construction in which relevant deep-structure information has been deleted as compared with a construction which does not involve deletion (these predictions are marked with a #). An additional five hypotheses (marked *) involve the relatively late appearance of constructions with the negative question form. As we remarked in Chapter 5, the linguistic analysis of NQ is very much in doubt: in particular, it is dubious where NQ *is* a compound of N and Q. If it is not, then we have no way of ordering N, Q, and NQ for cumulative complexity, and no way of predicting their ontogenetic sequencing.

All the remaining predictions of Brown and Hanlon involve comparing an affirmative form either to a question or to a negative. It seems clear to us that any theory of complexity must take into account the naturalness and prominence of affirmatives over other sentence types. While the derivational theory of complexity attempts to account for this by reference to the added transformations in nonaffirmative constructions, one could offer the following account with equal plausibility: (1) negatives and questions involve an interruption or reordering of the basic deep-structure constituent relations, and (2) if the standard analysis is accepted, processing negatives and questions requires the recovery of deleted information, i.e., N and Q markers. On both grounds, one might predict greater complexity for N and Q than for $SAAD$. But neither prediction commits one to the psychological reality of the negative and question transformation; only to the reality of the structures they relate.

These considerations suggest that Brown and Hanlon's findings, though compatible with some ontogenetic version of DTC, is also compatible with the kind of view of psychological complexity discussed in Chapter 6: namely, that a significant determinant of the complexity of a sentence is the extent to which features of its base structure, or clues to features of its base structure, are present in its surface structure.

There is one further remark to make on the generality with which the notion of cumulative complexity predicts ontogenetic ordering. Brown and Hanlon's study investigated only a relatively small number of sentence types. However, Brown (1973) provides a rich source of data on developmental stages in language acquisition, which summarizes many of the findings from experimental and observational studies that have been reported in the literature. An investigation of those data reveals at least the following cases in which a sentential form regularly appears earlier than its transformational source in the child's productions.

Verbs with displaced particles precede *Verb + Part* constructions.
Adjective + noun constructions precede relatives.
Passives precede structures with main verb "have."
"Wanna," "gonna," and "hafta" appear as main verbs with reduced infinitival complements in sentences like "I wanna go" before the appearance of such unreduced complements as "I want John to go."
Short passives precede long passives.

In a recent discussion of the Brown and Hanlon results, Brown (1970) remarks: "[Brown and Hanlon] explores the role of grammatical complexity in child speech. Are constructions mastered in an order of increasing complexity? The answer turns out to be 'yes'—for the set of sentence-types [they] studied. . . . One year later, with more knowledge of the facts of acquisition, I find that I can make quite a long list of exceptions to the rule" (p. 156).

SENTENCE-PROCESSING ACCOUNTS OF CHILDRENS' LANGUAGE

We have been considering studies which explore the hypothesis that the output of the child's language-acquisition mechanisms is a transformational grammar. According to this hypothesis, transformational rules (as well as syntactic structural descriptions) are psychologically real for the adult, and the child's ontogenetic career is viewed as the gradual assimilation of the rules of the adult grammar. Since the language-acquisition device is construed, in large part, as a specification of the universals of adult grammar, the expectation is that the child's productions should always be organized by a system which satisfies those universals, and that the transformational complexity of a linguistic form ought, in general, to predict the stage at which that form will be mastered.

We have suggested that the experimental support for this view is not compelling. But whether or not the view is true, it is obvious that a transformational grammar cannot be the *only* output of the child's language-acquisition mechanisms; computational procedures for effecting the production and comprehension of sentences must also be developed. In particular, the growth of child language appears to be, at least in part, explicable as a developing mastery of sentence processing heuristics of the general kind discussed in Chapter 6. There is a growing body of data which suggests that just as simple correspondences between the surface and deep analysis of a linguistic form facilitates the perceptual recognition of that form in the case of the adult, so it also predicts relatively early acquisition of the form on the part of the child. Conversely, sentences whose surface organization exhibits deep-structure relations only in a relatively distorted way appear to be ontogenetically late for the child, just as they are perceptually difficult for the adult. The suggested conclusion is that at least part of the child's ontogenetic career involves the development of heuristic procedures for "reading" deep-structure relations from features of the surface string, which is precisely the conclusion one would expect on the assumption that such procedures play an important role in the adult's exercise of his linguistic competences.

One of the first studies which suggests that the child's linguistic maturity may be indexed in part by the extent of his mastery of heuristic procedures for relating specific surface features of sentences to properties of their deep organization is that of C. Chomsky's (1969). Chomsky studied the ability of children between 5 and 10 years of age to understand a variety of sentences of rather complicated syntactic structure. Among the questions she investigated was the correlation between the degree of reduction a structure has undergone and the difficulty children have in understanding it.

The sentence types studied included a number in which the verbs "ask" and "tell" play a central role; for example, such sentence pairs as (8-1) on the one hand and (8-2) on the other. The second member of

8-1 **Ask her what you should do.**
     Ask her what to do.

8-2 **Ask her what the color of the ball is.**
     Ask her the color of the ball.

each of these pairs of sentences is, in an important way, reduced with respect to the first. In the case of (8-1), the second sentence does not make explicit the subject of the subordinated verb "do"; i.e., the hearer must restore the deleted pronoun "you." In (8-2), the important reduced element is the interrogative morpheme. In "Ask her what the color of the ball is" the surface structure makes it clear that the sentence is a question embedded in an imperative. In the case of "Ask her the color of the ball," however, the underlying interrogative character of the embedded sentence is relatively less perspicuously marked in surface structure.

The relevant finding is that in both kinds of cases, the child is able to handle the more fully elaborated version before the more reduced one. While Chomsky herself emphasizes that her samples are very small and that her investigations are preliminary, transcripts like the following are striking.

E: Laurie, ask Peter the color of the doll's dress.
S: Red.
E: Ask Peter what color this tray is.
S: What color's it? (1969, p. 80)

E: Ask Christine her last name.
S: I don't know.
E: Ask Christine what the doll's name is.
S: What is her name? (1969, p. 90)

In these kinds of exchanges it appears that if the subordinated interrogative is reduced, the child tends to confuse "ask" and "tell." When, however, the subordinated interrogative appears in the surface sequence, the child keeps the distinction between "ask" and "tell" clear. The same sort of thing also occurs in the case of the reduction of the subordinated pronoun. We find protocols like the following:

E: Ask Joanne what to feed the doll.
S: The hot dog.
E: Now I want you to *ask* Joanne something. *Ask* her what to feed the doll.
S: The piece of bread.
E: Ask Joanne what *you* should feed the doll.
S: What should I feed the doll? (1969, p. 90)

A similar study of the effect of reduction of deep-structure information has been reported by Olds (1968). In a game-playing situation, Olds investigated the relative abilities of children to follow such instructions as "Ask your opponent which piece to move one space" versus "Ask your opponent which piece you should move one space." Once again, the sentence in which the embedded pronoun was reduced proved to be the more difficult for the children. "Of the 30 children who failed to interpret the first instruction with 'ask' minus pronoun correctly, 16 interpreted a succeeding instruction with 'ask' plus pronoun correctly, and 12 of those subjects then interpreted the final instruction (again 'ask' minus pronoun) correctly. In other words, in a relatively large number of cases, the presence of the pronoun ... helped the children to interpret the instruction correctly" (p. 90). Olds also reports that the presence of the relative pronoun in embedded constructions facilitates the speed (though not the accuracy) with which children follow such commands as "the piece which your opponent just moved may be moved two spaces backwards." (For the role of relative pronouns in adult perceptual heuristics, see Chapter 6.)

Each of these studies emphasizes the degree to which explicitness of base relations in a sentence facilitates the child's ability to comprehend it. Parity of argument would suggest that the lexical character of major formatives in the sentence ought also to affect its position in the ontogenetic sequence, since we saw in Chapter 6 that lexical structure may be a determinant of complexity for the adult.

The studies on lexical structure reviewed in Chapter 6 largely concerned cases in which a given word could govern more than one type of deep tree. We suggested that, in such cases, the complexity of a sentence in which the word occurs varies with the number of kinds of deep structures in which it can appear. There is, however, another way in which lexical structure may affect complexity. To understand what is at issue, we need the notion of a *marked* lexical item.

There is a rule in English which governs the relation between noun phrases in matrix and constituent sentoids of a complex sentence. Roughly, this rule states that the noun phrase of a subordinated sentence deletes under identity with the noun phrase closest to the subordinating verb in deep structure. [For detailed discussion, see Rosenbaum (1967).] Thus, for example, in "John ordered Mary to leave the room," the subject of "leave" (like the object of "ordered") is "Mary." Again, in "Mary was ordered by John to leave the room," the subject of "leave" and "order" is Mary, because in the deep structure (*before* passivization) Mary is the *NP* nearest "leave." Notice, however, that this rule works *only* for sentoids related by complementization. "John saw Mary walking to the store" can mean "John saw Mary while *he* was walking to the store."

It turns out, however, that certain complement verbs are exceptions to this principle and will be required to be so marked in the lexicon. Thus "John promised Mary to leave the room" means that John promised Mary that *John* would leave the room not that John promised Mary that *Mary* would leave the room: this is an exception to the general complement deletion rule, because in the deep structure the NP closest to the subordinated occurrence of "John" (which deletes) is "Mary." That is, the deep structure is: ((John promised Mary) (*John* leave)) and the deletion transformation acts on the italicized occurrence of "John."

We may now consider the following hypothesis, to which Chomsky's data are relevant: Sentences containing marked lexical items are, characteristically, more complicated than sentences containing unmarked lexical items, and will appear later in the child's competence.

Chomsky investigated this hypothesis as it bears on the verbs "ask," "promise," and "tell." She predicted that the marked verb "promise" ought to be more difficult than the unmarked verb "tell," and that the unmarked verb "ask$_q$" (i.e., the query sense of "ask" which appears in constructions like "John asked whether it would rain") should be less difficult than the marked verb "ask$_r$" (i.e., the request-for-permission sense of "ask" which appears in constructions like "John asked the teacher to leave the room").

Chomsky's data are, in fact, compatible with both these predictions. She finds one stage in which all her subjects respond correctly to imperatives with main verb "tell" and none respond correctly to imperatives with main verb "promise." Significantly, the kinds of errors that subjects make in this stage involve confusions about which NP has been deleted: given a sentence of the form NP_1 *promises* NP_2 *to Verb*, subjects tend to interpret the sentences as meaning that NP_2 is to perform the action specified by *verb*.

Thus we find protocols like the following:

E: Donald tells Bozo to hop across the table. Can you make him hop?
S: (Making Bozo hop.) Bozo, hop across the table.
E: Bozo promises Donald to do a somersault. Can you make him do it?
S: (Making Donald do the somersault.) I promised you you can do a tumblesault.
E: Would you say that again?
S: I promised you you could do a tumblesault. (C. Chomsky, 1969, p. 40)

The same preference for the unmarked as opposed to the marked lexical form is evident in Chomsky's comparisons between "ask$_q$" and "tell" and "ask$_q$" and "ask$_r$."

There are two additional studies which bear on the generality of Chomsky's findings. Cromer (1970) has reported results with the "eager"-"easy" contrast which parallel the results just discussed. Cromer finds that the *NP is eager* type of construction is mastered earlier than the *NP is easy* type. It is not obvious that a theory based on relative complexity of derivational histories would predict this result, but it *is* clear that one based on the explicitness with which surface structure marks deep structure does so: the surface relations between "John," "easy," and "please" misleadingly suggest that "John" is the logical subject of the verbs rather than their logical object.

In another study, Kessel (1970) replicated the finding that sentences with "tell" are easier for children to understand than parallel sentences with "ask," though the only subject populations with which Kessel found this difference were children under 7 years; that is, children younger than those Chomsky studied. Kessel also found an "easy-eager" asymmetry which parallels the findings of Cromer just mentioned. He did not, however, find an asymmetry as a result of pronoun deletion in the "ask-tell" sentences; for the children Kessel studied, sentences like "the boy asked the girl which bird to feed" were no harder than sentences like "the boy asked the girl which bird he should feed." It may be that this nonreplication is attributable to the relative simplicity of Kessel's task as opposed to Chomsky's. The response Kessel required was to choose between pictures, whereas Chomsky required the child not only to understand the sentence but to act it out.

The studies just reviewed suggest that the child does develop strategies for the induction of deep-structure relations from surface form in the course of his developing mastery of language. In particular, they suggest that linguistic forms that constitute exceptions to relatively general procedures for sentence processing are hard for the child to learn just as they are hard for the adult to understand. There are also several studies which illuminate the ontogeny of these procedures. Some of these studies indicate the existence of stages in the development of the procedures available to the child for inducing the grammatical relations of sentences from their surface organization.

The perceptual heuristics whose ontogeny has been most intensively studied are those used to determine which *NP* in a sentence is its logical subject. The major finding appears to be the following. At about age 2, children interpret any noun immediately preceding the main verb of a sentence as the logical subject of the sentence. At about age $3^1/_2$ children interpret the first noun of a sentence as the actor, independent of its surface relation to the verb.

The experimental paradigm on which these findings are based is one in which children are asked to "act out" simple sentences with dolls. Three structural contrasts have been investigated: actives versus pas-

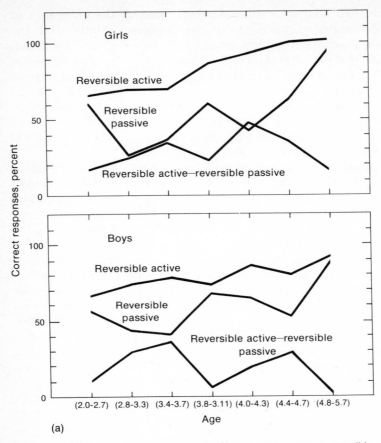

Fig. 8-4. (a) The proportion of correct performance by age and sex to reversible active and passive sentences (each child acted out three sentences of each kind). The bottom line in each graph represents the difference between the performance on actives and passives, and thus is a measure of the children's dependence on the "actor-action-object" order. (b) The same kind of data display as in (a) for a different subject group; responses are to reversible cleft sentences with subject NP first (analogous to actives in a), versus those with object NP first (analogous to passives), (from Bever, 1970, pp. 309 and 310, figs. 6 and 7).

sives (like "The cow kisses the horse" versus "The horse is kissed by the cow"), subject versus object clefts (like "It's the cow kisses the horse" versus "It's the cow the horse kisses") and NNV versus VNN nonsense sequences (like "The cow the horse kisses" versus "Kisses the cow the horse"). The performance on these constructions is displayed by age in Figure 8-4. The pertinent observation in the case of a 2-year-old is that he interprets the noun directly preceding the main verb as

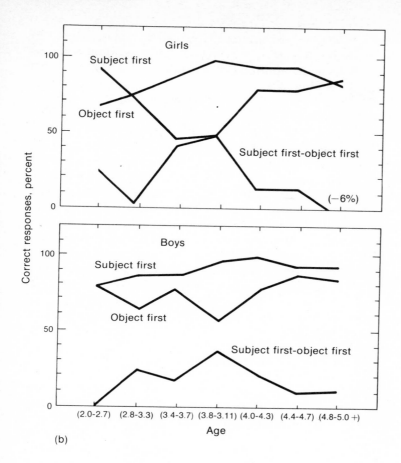

(b)

the logical subject with a frequency greater than chance in all the types of stimulus materials where there *is* a noun immediately preceding. the main verb. In the case of passives, and of *VNN* sequences, where this strategy will not apply, the level of performance is at chance.

As the child grows older, his performance gets better on sentences in which the first noun is the actor, and he gets worse on sentences in which it is not, in both cases irrespective of the noun's immediate adjacency to the main verb. Parallel to this course of development is an increasing tendency to take the first noun as the actor in both the *VNN* and the *NNV* sequences. This tendency peaks at about age 3½, after which children tend increasingly to perform correctly on all constructions while persisting in the first-noun-equals-logical-subject interpretation of *NNV* and *VNN*.

These results were originally obtained by Bever, Mehler, Valian,

Epstein, and Morrissey (in preparation) [replicated in Maratsos (1972); for discussion, see Bever (1970)]. Analogous findings for the active-versus-passive contrast are reported by DeVilliers and DeVilliers (1972), where mean length of utterance rather than chronological age is the independent variable. There is also a study by Sinclair de Zwart and Bronkhard (1972) that uses *NNV* and *VNN* materials in French. Thei found a dominant tendency to treat *NN* sequences as complex *NP*'s, e.g., as analogs to constructions like "the boy and the girl"; however, if one considers only responses in which one *N* was taken as subject and the other as object, the same developmental trend emerges as in Bever et al.: as the child gets older, he exhibits an increasing tendency to interpret the first noun as the logical subject. Finally, Ervin-Tripp (1970) reports a study in which simple actions were performed for children who were then asked questions like "Who did he kiss?" or "Who kissed him?" The finding was that younger children did better on questionns like the first than did older children, though all children performed well on questions like the second. This is consistent with the view that older children prefer an analysis in which the first noun is the logical subject; that analysis yields the wrong result in sentences in which a questioned object appears in surface subject position.

SUMMARY

The main issue in recent studies of syntax acquisition parallels the one that arose in the discussion of sentence perception in Chapter 6: How plausible is it to view the grammar as psychologically real? In the case of perception, this issue was central for analysis-by-synthesis recognition models. In the case of language learning, it arises in the context of theories which hold that a standard transformational grammar is the output of the child's innate language-acquisition mechanisms.

We have argued that neither the empirical nor the theoretical basis for this view of language acquisition is secure. There exist no satisfactory models of a language-acquisition device capable of inducing a grammar from a corpus, and there is very little unequivocal evidence that such an induction does, in fact, take place. On the other hand, it seems clear that some of the child's developing linguistic capacity is organized into perceptual heuristics for projecting structural analyses, and that these heuristics have specifiable ontogenetic careers.

CONCLUSION

The impression that the reader should form from this chapter is that there exists no account of grammar acquisition for which theoretical coherence and empirical support can plausibly be claimed. We have seen that there are grounds for supposing that the mechanisms of language acquisition are species-specific and that there are no grounds for rejecting the claim that they are task-specific. However, attempts to characterize such mechanisms have thus far met with no noticeable success.

Part of the problem may be that the more serious work on theories of language acquisition has taken the psychological reality of grammatical rules for granted. The notion that the output of a language-acquisition device is a transformational grammar has been common ground for almost all recent research on the problem of syntax learning. However, we have seen that the direct evidence for this view is unpersuasive and that even if the view is true, the child's developing linguistic capacities include mastery of sentence-processing procedures which such grammars do not specify.

The situation is one that we have seen before in this book. We can make some sense of the child's behavior if we assume that he is interested in inducing the underlying structure of sentences from the surface forms he hears. We can make some sense of the child's development if we assume that he is learning procedures for making such inductions. But there exists no acceptable account of these procedures and it is unclear how they relate to the kinds of derivational processes that are explored in transformational theory.

CONCLUSION

We said in the Preface that psycholinguistics has provided a test case for the possibility of an experimental mentalism. It is now appropriate to ask how far psycholinguistic research has succeeded in advancing the mentalist program.

Gestalt doctrine distinguished between the distal and the proximal stimulus and insisted upon the psychological efficacy of the latter. In the kinds of cases that concern cognitive psychologists, the behavioral effect of the environment is mediated by its representation in the mind of the organism and depends upon the character of that representation.

When perception is veridical, the organism is viewed as choosing an internal representation from among the indefinitely many descriptions that are true of the distal stimulus and as responding in light of the properties which that representation assigns. Misperceptions occur when the organism's internal representation assigns properties to the distal stimulus which it does not, in fact, possess. In either case, the distal stimulus has its effect only indirectly, by means of its proximal representation, so a theory of proximal representations is an essential first step in explaining the ways in which the behavior of an organism is affected by the character of its environment. Since it turns out that a given distal object may receive any of a wide variety of proximal analyses depending upon such factors as the genetic endowment of the organism, its previous experiences, and its current motivational state, it seems safe to assume that any such theory must be either extremely nontrivial or false.

One might say that mentalists are committed to the view that the behavior of an organism is contingent upon its internal states—in particular, upon the character of its subjective representation of the environment. This formulation has the virtue of connecting the kinds of remarks we have been making with new-look views in the psychology of perception. What is wrong with it is only that it may suggest an invidious ontological distinction between the "objective" properties of the physical stimulus "out there" and the "(merely) subjective" properties assigned by the mental representation "in here." This implicit reductionism ought to be resisted; it stems from a vicious ambiguity in the notion of a subjective variable which has caused great confusion in cognitive psychology.

It is a typical doctrine of mentalism that what counts in the etiology of behavior is the way that the organism construes its input. The mentalist is thus committed to the importance of "subjective" variables in the sense in which such variables contrast with those which range over properties of the physical environment. But though the perceptual analysis that the organism imposes upon a stimulus is subjective in *that* sense, the properties it assigns to the stimulus may perfectly well be objective in the sense in which "objective" means "real." The mentalist view is precisely that objective properties of the stimulus have their behavioral effects mediated by the organism's subjective system of representation. This does not, however, make mentalism a species of solipsism. To stress the significance of the organism's beliefs in determining its behavior is not to deny the distinction between true beliefs and false ones.

For the mentalist, then, it is the perceptually analyzed stimulus which is immediately implicated in the causation of behavior. Perceptual analysis typically involves computing representations of the stimulus at many different levels of description, and the representation assigned to the stimulus at each such level marks a variety of its properties. In principle, any property so marked may play a role in the organism's selection of a behavioral response depending, for example, on how the utilities of the organism are arranged. There is thus no reason why the properties of the stimulus which affect behavior should be "stimulus properties" in the technical sense of that notion. That is, there is no reason why the description of the stimulus to which the organism attends in selecting its response should be its *physical* description. A motorist buys gasoline because he knows it's needed to make his car run, not because gasoline is a complex of hydrocarbon. The first property of gasoline is as objective as the second, and is in fact the one which directly explains the motorists behavior in purchasing it.

Often, then, the character of the behavioral response will be determined by the relations that the stimulus is perceived to have to the organism's personal history, background knowledge, values, motives, preferences, and so on. When this is true, the psychologist who is interested in understanding the mental processes which mediate the relation between stimulus and response has no alternative but to try to learn enough about what the organism knows and values to determine what perceptual analyses it will impose. This is a hard doctrine, for it says that the attempt to short-circuit the organism in specifications of stimulus-response relations will not work. One cannot, in the long run, dispense with the organism's contribution to its own behavior.

Psycholinguistics has been most successful when it has hewn most closely to the implications of this sort of view. Presumably that is because the analysis imposed upon a speech signal is determined not only by the stimulus properties of the signal but also by its relation to the background information which constitutes the speaker-hearer's knowledge of the structure of his language. To review some of the main points of our discussion: recent theorizing has pictured the speaker-hearer as using what he knows about his language to compute a series of representations of the overt speech event and as integrating his behavior in the light of the results of such computations. For the hearer, the initial member of this series is an analysis of the phonetically relevant acoustic properties of the utterance. Such an analysis may conveniently be thought of as the output of the peripheral auditory transducer. Some relatively late member of the series specifies the semantic properties of the sentence type of which the utterance is a token. "Semantic representation" is here used in a technical sense to mean a representation which formally determines the entailments of the sentence to which it is assigned. It is a useful working hypothesis that such representations are articulated in the data language in which memory information and nonlinguistic perceptual information are also coded and in which cognitive operations are carried out; i.e., that a representation of a sentence which is semantic in the technical sense will also serve to specify what we informally think of as the information that utterances of the sentence standardly convey. But whether or not this is true, it seems clear that the speech event must at some point be assigned an analysis in such a central language, and that the object of the elaborate series of recodings which underlies speech perception is precisely to effect the assignment. Utterances can communicate thoughts only because hearers know how to translate them into the language in which thinking is done.

The converse considerations hold from the point of view of the speaker. The central fact about the production of speech is surely that speakers are somehow able to make the sounds they utter conform to their communicative intentions. Speakers intend the utterances they produce to convey certain messages, and they select the syntactic and lexical properties of their utterances in light of the messages they intend to convey. Typically, the message that the speaker has in mind cannot be specified in a language whose vocabulary items denote only parameters of articulatory events. Yet the vehicles *by which* speakers communicate are precisely utterances of strings in such a language (i.e., utterances of phonetic strings). The computational problem in speech production is thus to encode from a language rich enough to specify the intended message into a language whose symbols have an articulatory-acoustic interpretation. What one learns when one learns to talk must be, in large part, the computational procedures for effecting such encodings.

In short, psycholinguistics is built on a certain account of how it is that utterances can serve as vehicles of communication between speaker and hearer: According to this account, hearers have access to procedures for recovering precisely those proximal representations of sentences that guide speakers in the production of utterances. It is a fundamental empirical hypothesis in the discipline that these procedures effect a number of encodings between the message and the speech event and that each such encoding belongs to one of a fixed set of levels of description. To a first approximation, every signal receives a representation at each level, and every level may itself be represented by a formal language with a characteristic vocabulary and syntax.

If all of this is true, then the theory of the internal structure of the speaker-hearer can be viewed as having two components. The first, which corresponds to what we called in Chapter 1 a "conceptual analysis," consists of a precise characterization of each of the descriptive levels. The goal of theory construction is to write a grammar for each such level which specifies the vocabulary, syntax, and intended interpretation of the formal objects which represent sentences at that level. The second, which corresponds to what we called in Chapter 1 a "theory of mental operations," consists of a specification of the mapping rules which take a given signal from its representation on one level of description to its representation on the next. These two components, taken together, ought ultimately to have the character of a simulation—a computational routine for encoding from messages to articulatory events, and vice versa, which (1) provides a representation of the speech signal at each psychologically real level of description, and (2) predicts the value of "performance" parameters of the speaker-hearer's behavior.

Thus far we have been emphasizing the aspect of psycholinguistic theory which relates it most clearly to the mentalist tradition in psychology: that is, its emphasis upon the significance of the proximal representation and the complexity of the operations by which such representations are assigned to distal objects. If psycholinguists are committed to the assumption that it is both possible and essential to provide a systematic account of proximal stimuli and the transformations they undergo, so too are most other theorists who accept a mentalist approach to psychology.

What has given a special twist to psycholinguistic theorizing is the notion—common to both Hullean and generative approaches—that some of the levels at which distal stimuli receive *internal* representations may be identifiable with levels of *abstract* representation in the linguist's sense of that term, i.e., to levels of grammatical description. The deplorable tendency of some theorists to use "abstract" and "internal" as equivalent modifiers ought not blind us to the thoroughly empirical character of the assertion that grammars provide (at least partial) theories of the proximal stimulus. Grammatical analyses proceed from the assumption that distributionally similar items should receive identical analyses at some level of description. To identify the analyses so engendered with proximal representations of speech signals is to *explain* the grammatical properties of sentences by reference to the character of the encodings that speaker-hearers assign to them: the grammar predicts the observed distributions *because* the structural relations it postulates are the ones that speaker-hearers manipulate in encoding-decoding sentences. Clearly, no methodological fiat can guarantee that a grammar will support explanations of this kind. If, as we have argued, there are reasons to believe that transformational grammars do so, these are matters of fact, not method.

We have emphasized that the convergence of the levels of description which transformational grammars postulate with those which are psychologically real for the speaker-hearer is an empirical hypothesis. The syntax might have turned out to be no more than a set of classificatory conventions, as many taxonomic grammarians assumed that it would. Indeed, if grammarians had seriously observed the constraint that *only* distributional data can motivate grammatical analyses, syntax probably *would* have turned out that way. If the goal is psychological reality, distributional data probably underdetermine grammatical theories. What tipped the balance was the decision to take into account perceptual judgments of ambiguity, structural relatedness, well-formedness, similarity of meaning, etc. Such data reveal the character of the analyses that speaker-hearers impose upon utterances in their language. What the experiments on the psychological reality of syntactic structural descriptions primarily show is that a theory which accommodates the speaker-hearer's intuitions about the organization of sentences will often be led to postulate the kinds of psychological structures which account for the intuitions.

There are, in short, two hypotheses with respect to which the mentalist program in psycholinguistics has had a history of almost unmixed success: first, that the behavior of speaker-hearers is complexly dependent upon the properties of proximal representations of speech signals; and second, that the character of such representations is revealed by structural descriptions of the kind that transformational grammars provide. We have seen throughout this book that claims for the psychological reality of the major structural relations postulated by transformational grammars have, in general, received extensive experimental support. In consequence, we now know a great deal about some of the levels of description at which speaker-hearers encode sentences. (For example, that at least one such level is populated by distinctive feature matrices and at least two others are populated by trees; that the vocabulary at the former level contains such predicates as "voiced-unvoiced" and "vocalic-consonantal," and that the vocabulary at the latter two contains *article, noun, sentence, constituent, verb phrase,* etc.) Nowhere else has psychology approached so closely a rigorous theory of the proximal stimulus. The joint achievements of grammar and psycholinguistics in formulating and testing this theory thus represents an impressive vindication of the mentalist program: an account of the concepts which figure in the organization and perception of verbal behavior appears to be methodologically possible and called for by the experimental data. Given such an account, we can explain details of the speaker-hearer's performance in ways that were simply impossible without a characterization of the mental structures by which the performance is mediated.

What we do *not* have is a plausible theory of the operations which take signals from one level of encoding to another—i.e., a theory of the mental operations in speech perception-production. We have seen, in the course of our discussion, that a great deal of experimental work in psycholinguistics has been directed toward testing (and, finally, disconfirming) the suggestion that the grammar is itself such a theory. That this should have been the first hypothesis about transformational grammars which psycholinguists took seriously was, perhaps, inevitable. Such grammars apparently do enumerate some of the representations of utterances that are transduced in speech exchanges, and they effect the enumeration (in part) by defining mappings from one descriptive level to another. (Thus surface trees are enumerated by reference to transformations defined over deep trees; phonetic matrices are specified by transformations defined over phonemic matrices; and so on.) As it turns out, however, these mappings do not appear to have any very direct relation to the data processes which associate speech signals with their proximal representations. Syntactic transformations were not constructed to carry any given acoustic form onto a corresponding message, or any given message onto a corresponding acoustic form. When one attempts to adapt them to that purpose (to "realize a grammar as a performance device"), one gets unnatural psychological models. What's worse, one gets models that the experimental data do not support.

These having been the major successes and failures of the last decade of work, where do we go from here? In the first place, if the grammar does not provide a model of the mental operations in speech production-perception, we need a theory that does. Much future research in psycholinguistics will surely be directed to that end. We now have reason to believe that understanding and producing a sentence is not a matter of running through grammatical derivations; that grammatical operations are not, in this sense, psychologically real. But to say that heuristic procedures must be implicated in language performance is not to say much. What is required is an account of how the heuristic systems that speaker-hearer's use are related to grammatical formalisms which account for the distributional data; in particular, we need a theory that explains how there can be universal constraints on the form of grammatical rules if grammatical rules are not what the speaker-hearer uses to compute structural descriptions.

As we remarked in our discussion of the perception problem, very few of the available options have received serious examination in the psycholinguistic literature to date. For example, it is compatible with the negative data on the psychological reality of grammatical *operations* that grammatical *rules* are internalized by speaker-hearers. One might imagine that a transformational grammar is the normal form for the internal representation of a language, and that the role of heuristic procedures is primarily to *access* that information: to provide computational mechanisms for determining what structure the internally stored grammar assigns to particular sentences in its domain. In this view, the relation of the heuristic procedures to the grammar is rather like the relation of a librarian to his books: even if the books contain the information he requires, it is a rational undertaking to devise and execute efficient methods for getting the information out. Random search is a zero-order approximation to a theory of the way that librarians solve their access problem, just as it is probably a poor approximation to an account of intelligent behavior in sentence processing. At any event, a virtue of looking at things this way is that it accommodates both the psychological reality of structural descriptions and the observed non-correspondence between transformational complexity and perceptual complexity, these being the major experimental findings in psycholinguistics thus far.

To put it slightly differently, the experimentation to date has provided evidence for the psychological reality of structural descriptions and against the psychological reality of grammatical operations. But it is largely neutral on answering intimately related questions like the reality of uninterpreted syntactic structures (such as the trees intermediate between deep and surface structure in syntactic or phonological derivations) or that of ordering conventions, or even of the rules themselves, insofar as they may be supposed to play some role in the production-perception process different from the one they play in grammatical derivations. Conservative views of the relation between grammars and performance models predict positive results for all such inquiries. Experimental techniques are required for carrying out these investigations, since their consequences will bear directly on how one construes the relation between psychology and grammar.

Second, although the hypothesis that levels of grammatical description correspond closely to psychologically real levels of encoding has thus far often been vindicated, it cannot be relied upon indefinitely. Even as a source of information about the entities which populate descriptive levels, the standard techniques of syntactic analysis may finally be running dry. We have seen that the kinds of constraints that have thus far been brought to bear within syntax seem to be compatible with a variety of assumptions about the degree of abstractness of deep structure. This clearly suggests that the constraints need to be tightened. Since the adequacy of a grammar depends on the psychological reality of the structural descriptions it postulates, it may well be that only direct experimentation on psychological reality will ultimately choose between competing syntactic theories.

In short, work on the psychological reality of syntactic structures has just begun, though one can anticipate that this work will ultimately be concerned less and less with the vindication of independently motivated linguistic analyses and more and more with choosing between candidate analyses where the linguistic arguments are equivocal. A relation between psychology and linguistics in which each uses its bootstraps to lift the other may make bad physics, but it is excellent methodology. However, the condition upon psychology's playing this role is the existence of refined experimental procedures whose validation in clear cases is undisputed. It is more than likely that the development of such paradigms will continue to be a major occupation of psycholinguists for the future.

Finally, we need a theory of how the perception-production system is internalized—a kind of theory which thus far psycholinguistics has been quite unable to provide. We have seen that the character of such a theory must be intimately determined by the character of linguistic universals, and that one's views about the status of the universals will itself turn on one's views about the psychological reality of grammatical rules. In this way, many of the deepest problems about the psychology of language converge, ultimately, on the problem of how languages are learned. Thus far we have no theory of ontogenesis which does convincingly any of the things that such a theory ought to do, i.e., account for the universals, explain the child's eventual mastery of adult capacities, and provide a reasonable taxonomy of the developmental data. This area is wide open for future research, and its potential significance is enormous, since basic issues concerning the character of cognitive development and the innate endowment of human beings appear to be inextricably involved.

Given that there is so much left to do, it is worth emphasizing what the past decade of research has achieved. What emerges from the empirical details is a new way of looking at human mental processes; or, rather, an old way of looking at them which psychologists appear to have rejected in undue haste. We can now begin to make something substantial of the traditional notion that human beings are largely self-determining systems whose actions are typically calculated responses rather than conditioned reflexes. Just as common sense has always supposed, people act out of their construal of the situations in which they find themselves, and such construals are normally the consequence of very complicated perceptual and cognitive integrations. There is nothing novel in this view; what is new is only the technical apparatus for developing a psychology that takes it seriously. The moral of this book is that the mentalists were right: People think. There is no substitute for human intelligence.

REFERENCES

ABRAMS, K., and BEVER, T. G. Syntactic structure modifies attention during speech perception and recognition. *Quarterly Journal of Experimental Psychology*, 1969, **21**, 280–290.

ADES, A. Categorical perception and the speech mode. *Cognition*, in press.

AMMON, P. The perception of grammatical relations in sentences: A methodological exploration. *Journal of Verbal Learning and Verbal Behavior*, 1968, **7**, 869–875.

ANGLIN, J. M. *The growth of word meaning. Research Monograph 63.* Cambridge, Mass.: M.I.T. Press, 1970.

ANGLIN, J. M., and MILLER, G. A. The role of phrase structure in the recall of meaningful verbal material. *Psychonomic Science*, 1968, **10**, 343–344.

ASCH, SOLOMON E. The doctrinal tyranny of associationism: Or what is wrong with rote learning. In T. R. Dixon and D. L. Horton (Eds.), *Verbal behavior and general behavior theory*. Englewood Cliffs, N.J.: Prentice-Hall, 1968. Pp. 214–228.

BACH, E. Nouns and noun phrases. In E. Bach and R. Harms (Eds.), *Universals in linguistic theory*. New York: Holt, 1968.

BAR-HILLEL, Y. Review of *The Structure of Language* by J. A. Fodor and J. J. Katz. *Language*, 1967a, **43**(2), 526–550.

BAR-HILLEL, Y. Dictionaries and meaning rules. *Foundations of Language*, 1967b, **3**, 409–414.

BARTLETT, F. C. *Remembering*. First published, 1932. London: Cambridge University Press, 1961.

BASTIAN, J., EIMAS, P. D., and LIBERMAN, A. M. Identification and discrimination of a phonemic contrast induced by silent interval. *Journal of the Acoustical Society of America*, 1961, **33**, 842(A).

BELLUGI, U. The acquisition of negation. Unpublished doctoral dissertation, Harvard University,1967.

BERKELEY, G. *The principles of human knowledge*. First published 1710. G. J. Warnock (Ed.) London: Fontana Library, 1962.

BERLIN, B., and KAY, P. *Basic color terms: Their universality and evolution*. Berkeley: University of California Press, 1969.

BERLYNE, D. E. *Structure and direction in thinking*. New York: Wiley, 1965.

BERRY, R. A critical review of noise location during simultaneously presented sentences. Unpublished doctoral dissertation, University of Illinois, 1970.

BEVER, T. G. A survey of some recent work in psycholinguistics. In W. J. Plath (Ed.), *Specification and utilization of a transformational grammar: Scientific report number three*. Yorktown Heights, N.Y.: Thomas J. Watson Research Center, International Business Machines Corporation, 1968.

BEVER, T. G. The cognitive basis for linguistic structures. In J. R. Hayes (Ed.), *Cognition and the development of language*. New York: Wiley, 1970.

BEVER, T. G. Serial position and response biases do not account for the effect of syntactic structure on the location of brief noises during sentences. *Journal of Psycholinguistic Research*, 1973, **2**(3), 287–288.

BEVER, T. G., FODOR, J. A., GARRETT, M. F., and MEHLER, J. Transformational operations and stimulus complexity. Unpublished, M.I.T., 1966.

BEVER, T. G., FODOR, J. A., and WEKSEL, W. On the acquisition of syntax. *Psychological Review*, 1965a, **72**(6), 467–482.

BEVER, T. G., FODOR, J. A., and WEKSEL, W. Is linguistics empirical? *Psychological Review*, 1965b, **72**(6), 493–500.

BEVER, T. G., GARRETT, M. F., and HURTIG, R. Ambiguity increases complexity of perceptually incomplete clauses. *Memory and Cognition*, 1973, **1**, 279–286.

BEVER, T. G., LACKNER, J. R., and KIRK, R. The underlying structures of sentences are the primary units of immediate speech processing. *Perception and Psychophysics*, 1969, **5**, 225–231.

BEVER, T. G., LACKNER, J. R., and STOLZ, W. Transitional probability is not a general mechanism for the segmentation of speech. *Journal of Experimental Psychology*, 1969, **79**, 387–394.

BEVER, T. G., and LANGENDOEN, D. T. A dynamic model of the evolution of language. *Linguistic Inquiry*, 1971, **2**, 433–463.

BEVER, T. G., and MEHLER, J. The coding hypothesis and short-term memory. *AF Technical Report*, Cambridge, Mass.: Harvard Center for Cognitive Studies, 1967.

BEVER, T. G., MEHLER, J., VALIAN, V., EPSTEIN, J., and MORRISSEY, H. Linguistic capacity of young children, in preparation.

BEVER, T., and WEKSEL, W. (Eds.) *The structure and psychology of language*. The Hague: Mouton, in press.

BLACK, M. Linguistic relativity: The views of Benjamin Lee Whorf. *Philosophical Review*, 1959, **68**, 228–238.

BLOOM, L. *Language development: Form and function in emerging grammars.* Cambridge, Mass.: M.I.T. Press, 1970.

BLOOM, L. *One word at a time: The use of single word utterances before syntax.* The Hague: Mouton, in press.

BLOOMFIELD, L. *Language.* New York: Holt, 1933.

BLUMENTHAL, A. L. Observations with self-embedded sentences. *Psychonomic Science*, 1966, **6**, 453–454.

BLUMENTHAL, A. L. Prompted recall of sentences. *Journal of Verbal Learning and Verbal Behavior*, 1967, **6**, 203–206.

BLUMENTHAL, A. L. *Language and psychology.* New York: Wiley, 1970.

BLUMENTHAL, A. L., and BOAKES, R. Prompted recall of sentences, a further study. *Journal of Verbal Learning and Verbal Behavior*, 1967, **6**, 674–676.

BOLINGER, D. L. The atomization of meaning. *Language*, 1965, **41**, 555–573

BOLINGER, D. L., and GERSTMAN, L. J. Disjuncture as a clue to constructs. *Word*, 1957, **13**, 246–255.

BOOMER, D. S. Hesitation and grammatical encoding. *Language and Speech*, 1965, **8**, 148–158.

BOOMER, D. S. Review of F. Goldman-Eisler *Psycholinguistics: Experiments in spontaneous speech. Lingua*, 1970, **25**, 152–164.

BOOMER, D. S., and DITTMANN, A. T. Hesitation pauses and juncture pauses in speech. *Language and Speech*, 1962, **5**, 215–220.

BOOMER, D. S., and LAVER, J. D. M. Slips of the tongue. *The British Journal of Disorders of Communication*, 1968, **3**, 2–12.

BOUTON, L. Identity constraints on the do-so rule. *Papers in Linguistics*, 1969, **1**, 231–247.

BOWER, G. Organizational factors in memory. *Cognitive Psychology*, 1970, **1**, 18–46.

BOWERMAN, M. Acquiring Finnish as a native language: Some selected problems. Unpublished paper, Department of Social Relations, Harvard University, 1968.

BRAINE, M. D. S. On learning the grammatical order of words. *Psychological Review*, 1963a, **70**, 323–348.

BRAINE, M. D. S. The ontogeny of English phrase structure: The first phase. *Language*, 1963b, **39**, 1–13.

BRAINE, M. D. S. On the basis of phrase structure. *Psychological Review*, 1965, **72**(6), 483–492.

BRANSFORD, J. D., BARCLAY, J., and FRANKS, J. J. Sentence memory: Constructive vs. interpretive approach. *Cognitive Psychology*, 1972, **3**, 193–209.

BRANSFORD, J. D., and FRANKS, J. J. The abstraction of linguistic ideas. *Cognitive Psychology*, 1971, **2**, 331–350.

BREGMAN, A., and STRASBERG, R. Memory for the syntactic form of sentences. *Journal of Verbal Learning and Verbal Behavior*, 1968, **7**, 396–403.

BROWN, R. W., *Words and things.* New York: Free Press, 1958.

BROWN, R. W. *Psycholinguistics.* New York: The Free Press, 1970.

BROWN, R. W. *A first language: The early stages.* Cambridge, Mass.: Harvard University Press, 1973.

BROWN, R. W., and HANLON, C. Derivational complexity and order of acquisition in child speech. In Hayes (1970).

BROWN, R. W., and LENNEBERG, E. H. A study in language and cognition. *Journal of Abnormal and Social Psychology* 1954, **49**, 454–462.

BROWN, R. W., and McNEILL, D. The tip of the tongue phenomenon. *Journal of Verbal Learning and Verbal Behavior*, 1966, **5**, 325–327.

BROWNOWSKI, J., and BELLUGI, U. Language, name, and concept. *Science*, 1970, **168**, 669–673.

BRUNER, J. S. On perceptual readiness. *Psychological Review*, 1957, **64**, 123–152.

CAIRNS, H. S. Ambiguous sentence processing. Doctoral dissertation, The University of Texas at Austin, 1970.

CAPLAN, D. Clause boundaries and recognition latencies for words in sentences. *Perception and Psychophysics*, 1972, **12**, 73–76.

CAREY, P. W., MEHLER, J., and BEVER, T. G. Judging the veracity of ambiguous sentences. *Journal of Verbal Learning and Verbal Behavior*, 1970, **9**, 243–254.

CARNAP, R. Meaning and synonymy in natural language. *Philosophical Studies*, 1955, **7**, 33–47.

CARROLL, J. *Language and thought.* Englewood Cliffs, N.J.: Prentice-Hall, 1964.

CAZDEN, C. B. Environmental assistance to the child's acquisition of grammar. Doctoral dissertation, Harvard University, 1965.

CAZDEN, C.B. The role of parent speech in the acquisition of grammar. *Project Literacy Report No. 8*, 1967.

CHAPIN, P., SMITH, T., and ABRAHAMSON, A. Two factors in perceptual segmentation of speech. *Journal of Verbal Learning and Verbal Behavior*, 1972, **11**, 164–173.

CHOMSKY, C. *The acquisition of syntax in children from 5 to 10.* Cambridge, Mass.: M.I.T. Press, 1969.

CHOMSKY, N. Three models for the description of language. *IRE Transactions on Information Theory*, 1956, **2**, 113–124.

CHOMSKY, N. *Syntactic structures.* The Hague: Mouton, 1957.

CHOMSKY, N. Review of Skinner's *Verbal Behavior. Language*, 1959, **35**, 26–58. Reprinted in Jakobovits and Miron (1967).

CHOMSKY, N. Degrees of grammaticalness. In Fodor and Katz (1964).

CHOMSKY, N. *Aspects of the theory of syntax.* Cambridge, Mass.: M.I.T. Press, 1965.

CHOMSKY, N. Linguistics and philosophy. In S. Hook (Ed.), *Language and philosophy.* New York: New York University Press, 1969.

CHOMSKY, N. Deep structure, surface structure, and semantic interpretation. In R. Jakobson and S. Kawamoto (Eds.), *Studies in general and Oriental linguistics presented to Shiro Hattori on the occasion of his sixtieth birthday.* Tokyo: TEC Co., 1970a. Reprinted in Steinberg and Jakobovits (1971).

CHOMSKY, N. Remarks on nominalization. In R. A. Jacobs and P. S. Rosenbaum (Eds.), *Readings in English transformational grammar.* Boston: Ginn, 1970b.

CHOMSKY, N. Some empirical issues in the theory of transformational grammar. In S. Peters (Ed.), *Goals of linguistic theory.* Englewood Cliffs, N.J.: Prenctice-Hall, 1972.

CHOMSKY, N., and HALLE, M. *The sound pattern of English.* New York: Harper & Row, 1968.

CLARK, H. H., Some structural properties of simple active and passive sentences. *Journal of Verbal Learning and Verbal Behavior*, 1965, **4**, 365–370.

CLARK, H. H., and CARD, S. K. Role of semantics in remembering comparative sentences. *Journal of Experimental Psychology*, 1969, **82**, 545–553.

CLARK, H. H., and CHASE, W. G. On the process of comparing sentences against pictures. *Cognitive Psychology*, 1972, **3**, 472–517.

CLARK, H. H., and CLARK, E. V. Semantic distinctions and memory for complex sentences. *Quarterly Journal of Experimental Psychology*, 1968, **20**, 129–138.

CLIFTON, C., KURCZ, I., and JENKINS, J. J. Grammatical relations as determinants of sentence similarity. *Journal of Verbal Learning and Verbal Behavior*, 1965, **4**, 112–117.

CLIFTON, C., and ODOM, P. Similarity relations among certain English sentence constructions. *Psychological Monographs*, 1966, **80** (Whole No. 613).

COLLINS, A. M., and QUILLIAN, M. R. Retrieval time from semantic memory. *Journal of Verbal Learning and Verbal Behavior*, 1969, **8**, 240–247.

COMPTON, A. J. Aural perception of different syntactic structures and lengths. *Language and Speech*, 1967, **10**, 81–87.

CONRAD, C. Cognitive economy in semantic memory. *Journal of Experimental Psychology*, 1972, **92**, 149–154.

CROMER, R. F. 'Children are nice to understand' Surface structure clues for the recovery of a deep structure. *British Journal of Psychology*, 1970, **61**, 397–408.

DAVIDSON, D. The logical form of action sentences. In N. Rescher (Ed.), *The logic of decision and action*. Pittsburgh, Pa.: University of Pittsburgh Press, 1967.

DAVIDSON, R. E. Transitional errors and deep structure differences. *Psychonomic Science*, 1969, **14**, 293.

DEESE, J. *The structure of association in language and thought*. Baltimore: Johns Hopkins, 1965.

DENES, P., and PINSON, E. *The speech chain*. New York: Bell Telephone Laboratories, 1963.

DeVILLIERS, P. A., and DeVILLIERS, J. G. Early judgments of semantic and syntactic acceptability by children. *Journal of Psycholinguistic Research*, 1972, **1**, 299–310.

DIEBOLD, A. R. A survey of psycholinguistic research, 1954–1964. In C. E. Osgood and T. A. Sebeok (Eds.), *Psycholinguistics: A survey of theory and research problems*. Bloomington: Indiana University Press, 1969.

EIMAS, P., SIQUELAND, E., JUSCZYK, P., and VIGORITO, J. Speech perception in infants. *Science*, 1971, **171**, 303–306.

EPSTEIN, W. The influence of syntactical structure on learning. *American Journal of Psychology*, 1961, **74**, 80–85.

ERVIN, S. Imitation and structural change in children's language. In E. Lenneberg (Ed.), *New directions in the study of language*. Cambridge, Mass.: M.I.T. Press, 1964.

ERVIN-TRIPP, S. Discourse agreement: How children answer questions. In J. R. Hayes (Ed.), *Cognition and the development of language*. New York: Wiley, 1970.

ERVIN-TRIPP, S. An overview of theories of grammatical development. In D. I. Slobin (Ed.), *The ontogenesis of grammar*. New York: Academic Press, 1971.

FAIRBANKS, G., and GRUBB, P. A psychophysical investigation of vowel formants. *Journal of Speech and Hearing Research*, 1961, **4**, 203–219. Reprinted in G. Fairbanks, *Experimental phonetics*. Urbana: University of Illinois Press, 1966.

FANT, G. *Acoustic theory of speech production*. The Hague: Mouton, 1960.

FILLENBAUM, S. Memory for gist: Some relevant variables. *Language and Speech*, 1966, **9**, 217–227.

FILLMORE, C. J. The case for case. In E. Bach and R. Harms (Eds.), *Universals in linguistic theory*. New York: Holt, 1968.

FILLMORE, C. J. Entailment rules in a semantic theory. In J. F. Rosenberg and C. Travis (Eds.), *Readings in the philosophy of language*. Englewood Cliffs, N.J.: Prentice-Hall, 1971.

FODOR, J. A. Review of Werner and Kaplan's *Symbol formation*. *Language*, 1964, **40**(4), 566–578.

FODOR, J. A. Review of Carroll's *Language and Thought*. *Modern Language Journal*, 1965, **59**(6), 384–386.

FODOR, J. A. Three reasons for not deriving "kill" from "cause to die." *Linguistic Inquiry*, 1970a, **1**, 429–438.

FODOR, J. A. Troubles about actions. *Synthese*, 1970b, **21**, 298–319.

FODOR, J. A. The ontogenesis of the problem of reference. In Reed (1971).

FODOR, J. A. *The language of thought* (forthcoming).

FODOR, J. A., and BEVER, T. G. The psychological reality of linguistic segments. *Journal of Verbal Learning and Verbal Behavior*, 1965, **4**, 414–420

FODOR, J. A., FODOR, J. D., GARRETT, M. F., and LACKNER, J. R. Effects of surface and underlying clausal structure on click location. *Quarterly Progress Report No. 113*, Research Laboratory of Electronics, M.I.T., 1974.

FODOR, J. A., FORSTER, K. I., GARRETT, M. F., and HAKES, D. T. A relation between syntax and respiration. *Quarterly Progress Report No. 113*, Research Laboratory of Electronics, M.I.T., 1974.

FODOR, J. A., and GARRETT, M. F. Some syntactic determinants of sentential complexity. *Perception and Psychophysics*, 1967, **2**, 289–296.

FODOR, J. A., and GARRETT, M. F. Perceptual constancies for speech sounds in infants. *Quarterly Progress Report No. 113*, Research Laboratory of Electronics, M.I.T., 1974.

FODOR, J. A., GARRETT, M. F., and BEVER, T. G. Some syntactic determinants of sentential complexity, II: Verb structure. *Perception and Psychophysics*, 1968, **3**, 453–461.

FODOR, J. A., and KATZ, J. J. (Eds.) *The structure of language: Readings in the philosophy of language.* Englewood Cliffs, N.J.: Prentice-Hall, 1964.

FORSTER, K. I. Left to right processes in the construction of sentences. Unpublished doctoral dissertation, University of Illinois, 1964.

FORSTER, K. I. Left to right processes in the construction of sentences. *Journal of Verbal Learning and Verbal Behavior*, 1966, **5**, 285–291.

FORSTER, K. I. Sentence completion latencies as a function of constituent structure. *Journal of Verbal Learning and Verbal Behavior*, 1967, **6**, 878–883.

FORSTER, K. I. Sentence completion in left- and right-branching languages. *Journal of Verbal Learning and Verbal Behavior*, 1968a, **7**, 296–299.

FORSTER, K. I. The effect of removal of length constraint on sentence completion times. *Journal of Verbal Learning and Verbal Behavior*, 1968b, **7**, 253–254.

FORSTER, K. I. Visual perception of rapidly presented word sequences of varying complexity. *Perception and Psychophysics*, 1970, **8**, 215–221.

FORSTER, K. I. Linguistic structure and sentence production. In Bever and Weksel, in press.

FORSTER, K. I., and CLYNE, M. G. Sentence construction in German-English bilinguals. *Language and Speech*, 1968, **11**, 113–119.

FORSTER, K. I., and RYDER, L. A. Perceiving the structure and meaning of sentences. *Journal of Verbal Learning and Verbal Behavior*, 1971, **10**, 285–296.

FOSS, D. J. Some effects of ambiguity upon sentence comprehension. *Journal of Verbal Learning and Verbal Behavior*, 1970, **9**, 699–706.

FOSS, D. J., BEVER, T. G., and SILVER, M. The comprehension and verification of ambiguous sentences. *Perception and Psychophysics*, 1968, **4**, 304–306.

FOULKE, E. The perception of time compressed speech. In D. Horton and J. Jenkins (Eds.), *Perception in language*, Pt. I, Proceedings of a Symposium of the Learning and Development Center. Pittsburgh: Pittsburgh University Press, 1969.

FRANKS, J. J., NESBITT, J., and CLAYTON, K N. Deep versus surface structure frequency effects in recall. Paper presented at the Twelfth Convention of the Psychonomic Society, 1971.

FRASER, C., BELLUGI, U., and BROWN, R. W. Control of grammar in imitation, comprehension, and production. *Journal of Verbal Learning and Verbal Behavior*, 1963, **2**, 121–125.

FROMKIN, V. A. The non-anomalous nature of anomalous utterances. *Language*, 1971, **47**, 27–52.

GALLAGHER, T. M. Recall of active and passive sentences as related to mean depth. M. A. thesis, University of Illinois, 1969.

GARDNER, R. A., and GARDNER, B. T. Teaching sign language to a chimpanzee. *Science*, 1969, **165**, 664–672.

GARRETT, M. F. Syntactic structures and judgments of auditory events. Unpublished doctoral dissertation, University of Illinois, 1965.

GARRETT, M. F., BEVER, T. G., and FODOR, J. A. The active use of grammar in speech perception. *Perception and Psychophysics*, 1966, **1**, 30–32.

REFERENCES

GARRETT, M. F., and SHATTUCK, S. R. An analysis of speech errors. *Quarterly Progress Report No. 113*, Research Laboratory of Electronics, M.I.T., 1974.

GESELL, A., and THOMPSON, H. Learning and growth in identical twins: an experimental study by the method of co-twin control. *Genet Psychological Monographs*, 1929, **6**, 1–123.

GLANZER, M. Grammatical category: A rote learning and word association analysis. *Journal of Verbal Learning and Verbal Behavior*, 1962, **1**, 31–41.

GLEASON, H. A. *An Introduction to descriptive linguistics*. New York: Holt, 1955.

GOLDMAN-EISLER, F. The determinants of the rate of speech output and their mutual relations. *Journal of Psychosomatic Research*, 1956, **2**, 137–143.

GOLDMAN-EISLER, F. Speech production and the predictability of words in context. *Quarterly Journal of Experimental Psychology*, 1958a, **9–10**, 96.

GOLDMAN-EISLER, F. The predictability of words in context and the length of pauses in speech. *Language and Speech*, 1958b, **I**(3), 226–231.

GOMBRICH, E. H. *Art and illusion*. New York: Pantheon, 1965.

GOODMAN, N. The epistemological argument. *Synthese*, 1967, **17**, 23–28.

GOUGH, P. B. Grammatical transformations and speed of understanding. *Journal of Verbal Learning and Verbal Behavior*, 1965, **4**, 107–111.

GOUGH, P. B. The verification of sentences. The effects of delay of evidence and sentence length. *Journal of Verbal Learning and Verbal Behavior*, 1966, **5**, 492–496.

GRUBER, J. S. Studies in lexical relations. Unpublished doctoral dissertation, Massachusetts Institute of Technology, 1965.

HAKES, D. T. Does verb structure affect sentence comprehension? *Perception and Psychophysics*, 1971, **10**, 229–232.

HAKES, D. T. Effects of reducing complement constructions on sentence comprehension. *Journal of Verbal Learning and Verbal Behavior*, 1972, **11** 278–286.

HAKES, D. T., and CAIRNS, H. S. Sentence comprehension and relative pronouns. *Perception and Psychophysics*, 1970, **8**, 5–8.

HAKES, D. T., and FOSS, D. J. Decision processes during sentence comprehension: Effects of surface structure reconsidered. *Perception and Psychophysics*, 1970, **8**, 413–416.

HALLE, M. *The sound pattern of Russian*. The Hague: Mouton, 1959.

HALLE, M., and STEVENS, K. N. Speech recognition: A model and a program for research. In Fodor and Katz (1964).

HARMON, G. Three levels of meaning. *The Journal of Philosophy*, 1968, **65**, 590–602.

HARMON, G. Linguistic competence and empiricism. In S. Hock (Ed.), *Language and Philosophy*. New York: New York University Press, 1969.

HARMON, G. Psychological aspects of the theory of syntax. *The Journal of Philosophy*, 1967, **64**, 75–87. Reprinted in Rosenberg and Travis (1971).

HARRIS, C. M. A study of the building blocks in speech. *The Journal of the Acoustical Society of America*, 1953, **25**, 962–969.

HARRIS, Z. S. From morpheme to utterance. *Language*, 1964, **22**, 161–183.

HARRIS, Z. S. Transformation theory. *Language*, 1965, **41**, 363–401.

HARRIS, Z. S. *Papers in structural linguistics*. Boston: Reidel, 1970.

HAYES, J. R. (Ed.) *Cognition and the development of language*. New York: Wiley, 1970.

HEBB, D. O. *The organization of behavior*. New York: Wiley, 1949.

HEIDER, E. R. Universals in color naming and memory. *Journal of Experimental Psychology*, 1972, **93**, 10–20.

HEIDER, E. R., and OLIVIER, D. The structure of the color space in naming and memory for two languages. *Cognitive Psychology*, 1972, **3**, 337–354.

HEIDER, K. G. *The Dugum Dani: A Papuan culture in the Highlands of West New Guinea*. Chicago: Aldine, 1970.

HEINZ, J. M., and STEVENS, K. N. On the properties of voiceless fricative consonants. *Journal of the Acoustical Society of America*, 1961, **33**, 589–596.

HENDERSON, A., GOLDMAN-EISLER, F., and SKARBEK, A. The common value of pausing time in spontaneous speech. *Quarterly Journal of Experimental Psychology*, 1965, **17**, 343–345.

HERRNSTEIN, R. J., and LOVELAND, D. H. Complex visual concept in the pigeon. *Science*, 1964, **146**, 549–551.

HERZBERGER, H. Perceptual complexity in language. In Bever and Weksel, in press.

HILGARD, E. R., and MARQUIS, D. G. *Conditioning and learning.* New York: Appleton-Century-Crofts, 1940.

HOLMES, V. M. Some effects of syntactic structure on sentence recognition. Unpublished doctoral dissertation, University of Melbourne, 1970.

HOLMES, V. M. Order of main and subordinate clauses in sentence perception. *Journal of Verbal Learning and Verbal Behavior*, 1973, **12**, 285–293.

HOLMES, V. M., and FORSTER, K. I. Detection of extraneous signals during sentence recognition. *Perception and Psychophysics*, 1970, **7**, 297–301.

HOLMES, V. M., and FORSTER, K. I. Perceptual complexity and underlying sentence structure. *Journal of Verbal Learning and Verbal Behavior*, 1972, **11**, 148–156.

HOOK, S. (Ed.) *Language and philosophy.* New York: New York University Press, 1969.

HUBEL, D. H., and WIESEL, T. N. Receptive fields of cells in striate cortex of very young, visually inexperienced kittens. *Journal of Neurophysiology*, 1963, **26**, 994–1002.

HUGHES, G., and HALLE, M. Spectral properties of fricative consonants. *Journal of the Acoustical Society of America*, 1956, **28**, 303–310.

HULL, C. L. *Principles of behavior.* New York: Appleton-Century-Crofts, 1943.

HUME, D. *A treatise of human nature.* Vol. I. Originally published 1739. London: Dent, 1960.

JACKENDOFF, R. An interpretive theory of negation. *Foundations of Language*, 1969, **5**, 218–241.

JACOBS, R. A., and ROSENBAUM, P. S. *English transformational grammar.* Waltham, Mass.: Blaisdell, 1968.

JAKOBOVITS, L. A., and MIRON, M. S. (Eds.) *Readings in the psychology of language.* Englewood Cliffs, N.J.: Prentice-Hall, 1967.

JAKOBSON, R., FANT, G., and HALLE, M. *Preliminaries to speech analysis: The distinctive features and their correlates.* Cambridge, Mass.: M.I.T. Press, 1963.

JARVELLA, R. Syntactic processing of connected speech. *Journal of Verbal Learning and Verbal Behavior*, 1971, **10**, 409–416.

JARVELLA, R. Starting with psychological verbs. Paper presented at the Midwestern Psychological Association, Cleveland, May, 1972.

JENKINS, J. J., FODOR, J. A., and SAPORTA, S. An introduction to psycholinguistic theory. Unpublished, 1965.

JENKINS, J. J., and POLERMO, D. Mediation processes and the acquisition of linguistic structure. In U. Bellugi and R. W. Brown (Eds.), *The acquisition of language.* Chicago: University of Chicago Press, 1964.

JOHNSON, M. G. Syntactic position and rated meaning. *Journal of Verbal Learning and Verbal Behavior*, 1967, **6**, 240–246.

JOHNSON, N. F. The psychological reality of phrase structure rules. *Journal of Verbal Learning and Verbal Behavior*, 1965, **4**, 469–475.

JOHNSON, N. F. On the relationship between sentence structure and the latency in generating the sentence. *Journal of Verbal Learning and Verbal Behavior*, 1966, **5**, 375–380.

JOHNSON, R. E. Recall of prose as a function of the structural importance of the linguistic units. *Journal of Verbal Learning and Verbal Behavior*, 1970, **9**, 12–20.

JOOS, M. (Ed.) *Readings in linguistics.* New York: American Council of Learned Societies, 1958.

KADEN, S. E., WAPNER, S., and WERNER, H. Studies in physiognomic perception: II Effect of directional dynamics of pictured objects and of words on the position of the apparent horizon. *Journal of Psychology*, 1955, **39**, 61–70.

KANT, I. *Critique of pure reason*. Originally published 1781. N. K. Smith (Trans.). London: Macmillan, 1953.

KATZ, J. J. Review of *Semantic Analysis*. *Language*, 1962, **38**, 52–69.

KATZ, J. J. Semi-sentences. In Fodor and Katz (1964).

KATZ, J. J. *The philosophy of language*. New York: Harper & Row, 1966.

KATZ, J. J. Some remarks on Quine on analyticity. *Journal of Philosophy*, 1967, **64**, 36–52.

KATZ, J. J. *Semantic theory*. New York: Harper & Row, 1972.

KATZ, J. J., and BEVER, T. G. The fall and rise of empiricism. Unpublished manuscript, M.I.T., 1973.

KATZ, J. J., and FODOR, J. A. The structure of a semantic theory. *Language*, 1963, **39**, 170–210.

KATZ, J. J., and POSTAL, P. M. *An integrated theory of linguistic descriptions*. Cambridge, Mass.: M.I.T. Press, 1964.

KELLOGG, W. N., and KELLOGG, L. A. *The ape and the child*. New York: McGraw-Hill, 1933.

KENNEDY, A., and WILKES, A. Response times at different positions with a sentence. *Quarterly Journal of Experimental Psychology*, 1968, **20**, 390–394.

KESSEL, F. S. The role of syntax in children's comprehension from ages six to twelve. *Monographs of the Society for Research in Child Development*, 1970, **35**(6), Serial No. 139.

KLIMA, E. S. Negation in English. In Fodor and Katz (1964).

KLIMA, E. S., and BELLUGI, U. Syntactic regularities in the speech of children. In J. L. Lyons and R. J. Wales (Eds.), *Psycholinguistic papers*. Edinburgh: Edinburgh University Press, 1966.

KOHLER, W. *Gestalt psychology*. New York: Liveright, 1947.

KOPLIN, J. H., and DAVIS, J. Grammatical transformations and recognition memory of sentences. *Psychonomic Science*, 1966, **6**, 257–258.

KRASNER, L. Studies of the conditioning of verbal behavior. *Psychological Bulletin*, 1958, **55**, 148–170. Also in S. Saporta (Ed.), *Psycholinguistics*. New York: Holt, 1961.

LACKNER, J. A developmental study of language behavior in retarded children. *Neuropsychologia*, 1968, **6**, 301–320.

LACKNER, J. R., and GARRETT, M. F. Resolving ambiguity: Effects of biasing context in the unattended ear. *Cognition*, 1973, L, 359–372.

LADEFOGED, P. *Three areas of experimental phonetics*. London: Oxford University Press, 1967.

LADEFOGED, P., and BROADBENT, D. E. Information conveyed by vowels, *Journal of the Acoustical Society of America*, 1957, **29**, 98–104.

LADEFOGED, P., and BROADBENT, D. E. Perception of sequence in auditory events. *Quarterly Journal of Experimental Psychology*, 1960, **13**, 162–170.

LAKOFF, G. On the nature of syntactic irregularity. *Mathematical Linguistics and Automatic Translation Report NSF-16*. Cambridge, Mass.: Computation Laboratory of Harvard University, 1965.

LAKOFF, G. Presupposition and relative grammaticality. *The Computational Laboratory of Harvard University Report NSF-24*, 1970, 51–68.

LAKOFF, G. On generative semantics. In Steinberg and Jakobovits (1971).

LANGENDOEN, D. T. *Essentials of English grammar*. New York: Holt, 1970.

LASHLEY, K. S. The problem of serial order in behavior. In L. A. Jeffress (Ed.), *Cerebral mechanisms in behavior: The Hixon Symposium*. New York: Wiley, 1951.

LEHISTE, I., and PETERSON, G. Vowel amplitude and phonemic stress in American English. *Journal of the Acoustical Society of America*, 1959, **31**, 428–435.

LENNEBERG, E. H. Understanding language without ability to speak: A case report. *Journal of Abnormal Psychology*, 1962, **65**, 419–425.

LENNEBERG, E. H. *Biological foundations of language*. New York: Wiley, 1967.

LENNEBERG, E. H., NICHOLS, I. A., and ROSENBERGER, E. F. Primitive stages of language development in mongolism. *Disorders of Communication, Vol.* XLII: *Research Publications.* Baltimore, Md.: A. R. N. M. D. Williams and Wilkins, 1964.

LENNEBERG, E. H. and ROBERTS, J. M. *The language of experience: A case study.* IUPAL Memoirs of the *International Journal of American Linguistics,* No. 13, Bloomington, 1956.

LEOPOLD, W. F. *Speech development of a bilingual child.* 4 vols. Evanston, Ill.: Northwestern University Press, 1939–1949.

LESGOLD, A. M. Pronominalization: A device for unifying sentences in memory. *Journal of Verbal Learning and Verbal Behavior,* 1972, **11**, 316–323.

LEVELT, W. J. M. A scaling approach to the study of syntactic relations. In G. B. Flores d'Arcais and W. J. M. Levelt (Eds.), *Advances in Psycholinguistics.* New York: American Elsevier, 1970.

LEVIN, H., and SILVERMAN, I. Hesitation phenomena in children's speech. *Language and Speech,* 1965, **8**, 67–85.

LIBERMAN, A., COOPER, F. S., SHANKWEILER, D. P., and STUDDERT-KENNEDY, M. Perception of the speech code. *Psychological Review,* 1967, **74**, 431–461.

LIBERMAN, A., HARRIS, K., EIMAS, P., LISKER, L., and BASTIAN, J. An effect of learning on speech perception: The discrimination of durations of silence with and without phonemic significance. *Language and Speech,* 1961, **4**, 175–195.

LIBERMAN, A., HARRIS, K., HOFFMAN, H., and GRIFFITH, B. The discrimination of speech sounds within and across phoneme boundaries. *Journal of Experimental Psychology,* 1957, **53**, 358–368.

LIBERMAN, A., HARRIS, K., KINNEY, J., and LANE, H. The discrimination of relative onset-time of the components of certain speech and nonspeech patterns. *Journal of Experimental Psychology,* 1961, **61**, 379–388.

LICKLIDER, J. C. R., and MILLER, G. A. The perception of speech. In S. S. Stevens (Ed.), *Handbook of experimental psychology.* New York: Wiley, 1951.

LIEBERMAN, P. On the acoustic basis of the perception of intonation by linguists. *Word,* 1965, **21**, 40–54.

LIEBERMAN, P. *Intonation, perception and language.* Research Monograph No. 38. Cambridge, Mass.: M.I.T. Press, 1967.

LOCKE, J. *An essay concerning human understanding.* Vols. 1 and 2. Originally published 1690. London: Dent, 1961.

LORENZ, K. *Evolution and modification of behavior.* Chicago, Ill.: University of Chicago Press, 1965.

LOUNSBURY, F. G. Transitional probability, linguistic structure, and systems of habit-family hierarchies. In Osgood and Sebeok (1969).

LURIA, A. R., and YUDOVICH, F. IA. *Speech and the development of mental processes in the child;* Joan Simon (Ed.). London: Staples, 1959.

MacKAY, D. G. To end ambiguous sentences. *Perception and Psychophysics,* 1966, **1**, 426–436.

MacKAY, D. G. Spoonerisms: The structure of errors in the serial order of speech. *Neuropsychologia,* 1970, **8**, 323–350.

MacKAY, D. G., and BEVER, T. In search of ambiguity. *Perception and Psychophysics,* 1967, **2**, 193–200.

MACLAY, H., and OSGOOD, C. E. Hesitation phenomena in English speech. *Word,* 1959, **15**, 19.

MANDLER, G., and MANDLER, J. Serial position effects in sentences. *Journal of Verbal Learning and Verbal Behavior,* 1964, **3**, 195–202.

MARATSOS, M. P. The use of definite and indefinite reference in young children. Unpublished doctoral dissertation, Harvard University, 1972.

MARKS, L., and MILLER, G. The role of semantic and syntactic constraints in the memorization of English sentences. *Journal of Verbal Learning and Verbal Behavior,* 1964, **3**, 1–5.

MARTIN, E., and ROBERTS, K. H. Grammatical factors in sentence retention. *Journal of Verbal Learning and Verbal Behavior*, 1966, **5**, 211–218.

MARTIN, E., ROBERTS, K. H., and COLLINS, A. M. Short term memory for sentences. *Journal of Verbal Learning and Verbal Behavior*, 1968, **7**, 60–66.

McCAWLEY, J. D. The role of semantics in grammar. In E. Bach and R. T. Harms (Eds.), *Universals in linguistic theory*. New York: Holt, 1968.

McGOECH, J. A. The direction and extent of intra-serial associations at recall. *American Journal of Psychology*, 1936, **48**, 221–245.

McMAHON, L. Grammatical analysis as part of understanding a sentence. Unpublished doctoral dissertation, Harvard University, 1963.

MacNEILAGE, P. Motor control of serial ordering of speech. *Psychological Review*, 1970, **77**, 182–196.

MacNEILAGE, P., and DeCLERK, J. On the motor control of coarticulation in CVC monosyllables. *Journal of the Acoustical Society of America*, 1969, **45**, 1217–1233.

McNEILL, D. *The acquisition of language*. New York: Harper and Row, 1970.

McNEILL, D. Developmental psycholinguistics. In F. Smith and G. Miller (Eds.), *The genesis of language*. Cambridge, Mass.: M.I.T. Press, 1966.

MEHLER, J. Some effects of grammatical transformations on the recall of English sentences. *Journal of Verbal Learning and Verbal Behavior*, 1963, **2**, 346–351.

MEHLER, J., and CAREY, P. Role of surface and base structure in the perception of sentences. *Journal of Verbal Learning and Verbal Behavior*, 1967, **6**, 335–338.

MENYUK, P. Children's grammatical capacity. In Bever and Weksel, in press.

MILLER, G. A. *Language and communication*. New York: McGraw-Hill, 1951.

MILLER, G. A. Human memory and the storage of information. *IRE Transactions on Information Theory*, 1956a, **IT-2**(3), 129–137.

MILLER, G. A. The magical number seven plus or minus two, or, some limits on our capacity for processing information. *Psychological Review*, 1956b, **63**, 81–96.

MILLER, G. A. Decision units in the perception of speech, *IRE Transactions on Information Theory*, 1962a, **IT-8**, 81–83.

MILLER, G. A. Some psychological studies of grammar. *American Psychologist*, 1962b, **17**, 748–762. Also in Jakobovits and Miron (1967).

MILLER, G. A. Some preliminaries to psycholinguistics. *American Psychologist*, 1965, **20**, 15–20. Reprinted in Jakobovits and Miron (1967).

MILLER, G. A. A psychological method to investigate verbal concepts. *Journal of Mathematical Psychology*, 1969, **6**, 169–191.

MILLER, G. A., and CHOMSKY, N. Finitary models of language users. In R. D. Luce, R. R. Bush, and E. Galanter (Eds.), *Handbook of mathematical psychology*. Vol. II. New York: Wiley, 1963.

MILLER, G. A., GALANTER, E., and PRIBRAM, K. H. *Plans and the structure of behavior*. New York: Holt, 1960.

MILLER, G. A., HEISE, G., and LICHTEN, W. The intelligibility of speech as a function of the context of the test materials. *Journal of Experimental Psychology*, 1951, **41**, 329–335.

MILLER, G. A., and ISARD, S. Some perceptual consequences of linguistic rules. *Journal of Verbal Learning and Verbal Behavior*, 1963, **2**, 217–228.

MILLER, G. A., and McKEAN, K. A chronometric study of some relations between sentences. *Quarterly Journal of Experimental Psychology*, 1964, **16**, 297–308.

MILLER, G. A., and SELFRIDGE, J. Verbal context and the recall of meaningful material. *American Journal of Psychology*, 1950, **63**, 176–185.

MINK, W. D. Semantic generalization as related to word association. *Psychological Reports*, 1963, **12**, 59–67.

MOORE, T. M. Speeded recognition of ungrammaticality. *Journal of Verbal Learning and Verbal Behavior*, 1972, **11**, 550–560.

MOWRER, O. H. *Learning theory and the symbolic processes*. New York: Wiley, 1960.

NEISSER, U. *Cognitive psychology*. New York: Appleton-Century-Crofts, 1967.

NOOTEBOOM, S. G. Some regularities in phonemic speech errors, *Institut voor Perceptie Onderzock Annual Progress Report 2*, Eindhoven, 1967.

OLDS, H. F. An experimental study of syntactic factors influencing children's comprehension of certain complex relationship. *Center for Research and Development on Educational Differences*, Report No. 4, 1968, Harvard University.

OSGOOD, C. E. *Method and theory in experimental psychology*. New York: Oxford University Press, 1953.

OSGOOD, C. E. Motivational dynamics of language behavior. *Nebraska Symposium on Motivation*, 1957, **5**, 348–424.

OSGOOD, C. E. On understanding and creating sentences. *American Psychologist*, 1963a, **18**, 735–751. Also in Jakobovits and Miron (1967).

OSGOOD, C. E. On understanding and creating sentences. Mimeo. Institute of Communications Research, University of Illinois, 1963.

OSGOOD, C. E. Where do sentences come from? In Steinberg and Jakobovits (1971).

OSGOOD, C. E., and SEBEOK, T. A. (Eds.) *Psycholinguistics: A survey of theory and research problems*. Supplement to the *International Journal of American Linguistics*, 1954, **20**(4). Reprinted by Indiana University Press, 1969.

PAIVIO, A. Mental imagery in associative learning and memory. *Psychological Review*, 1969, **76**, 241–263.

PAIVIO, A. *Imagery and verbal processes*. New York: Holt, 1971.

PENFIELD, W. and ROBERTS, L. *Speech and brain mechanisms*. Princeton, N.J.: Princeton University Press, 1959.

PERFETTI, C. A. Sentence retention and the depth hypothesis. *Journal of Verbal Learning and Verbal Behavior*, 1969, **8**, 101–104.

PERFETTI, C. A., and GOODMAN, D. Memory for sentences and noun phrases of extreme depth. *Quarterly Journal of Experimental Psychology*, 1971, **23**, 22–23.

PERLMUTTER, D. M. Deep and surface structure constraints on syntax. Unpublished doctoral dissertation, Massachusetts Institute of Technology, 1968.

PETERSON, G. E., WANG, W. S-Y., and SIVERTSEN, S. Segmentation techniques in speech synthesis. *Journal of the Acoustical Society of America*, 1958, **30**, 739–742.

PETRICK, S. R. A recognition procedure for transformational grammars. Unpublished doctoral dissertation, Massachusetts Institute of Technology, 1965.

PIAGET, J. *Genetic epistomology*. New York: Norton, 1970.

POSTAL, P. M. *Constituent structure: A study of contemporary models of syntactic description*. The Hague: Mouton, 1964a.

POSTAL, P. M. Underlying and superficial linguistic structure. *Harvard Educational Review*, 1964b, **34**, 246–266.

POSTAL, P. M. On the surface verb 'Remind'. *Linguistic Inquiry*, 1970, **1**, 37–120.

POTTER, R. K., KOPP, A. G., and GREEN, H. C. *Visible speech*. New York: Van Nostrand, 1947. Reprinted as R. K. Potter, A. G. Kopp, and H. G. Kopp, *Visible speech*. New York: Dover, 1966.

PREMACK, D. A. A functional analysis of language. Unpublished paper based on an Invited Address, American Psychological Association, Washington, D.C., 1969.

PREMACK, D. A. Language in chimpanzee? *Science*, 1971, **172**, 808–822.

PRIBRAM, K. H. *Languages of the brain*. Englewood Cliffs, N.J.: Prentice-Hall, 1971.

PUTNAM, H. Some issues in the theory of grammar. In R. Jakobson (Ed.), *Proceedings of the Twelfth Symposium in Applied Mathematics: Structure of Language and its Mathematical Aspects*, Providence, R.I.: American Mathematical Society, 1961.

QUINE, W. V. O. *Word and object*. Cambridge, Mass.: M.I.T. Press, 1960.

QUINE, W. V. O. Two dogmas of empiricism. In W. V. O. Quine, *From a logical point of view*. Cambridge, Mass.: Harvard University, 1964.

QUINE, W. V. O. On a suggestion of Katz. *Journal of Philosophy*, 1967, **64**, 52–54.

REBER, A. S., and ANDERSON, J. R. The perception of clicks in linguistic and nonlinguistic messages. *Perception and Psychophysics*, 1970, **8**, 81–89.

REED, C. (Ed.) *The learning of language*. New York: Appleton-Century-Crofts, 1971.

ROCHESTER, S. R., and GILL, J. Production of complex sentences in monologues and dialogues. *Journal of Verbal Learning and Verbal Behavior*, 1973, **12**, 203–210.

ROHRMAN, N. L. The role of syntactic structure in the recall of English nominalizations. *Journal of Verbal Learning and Verbal Behavior*, 1968, **7**, 904–912.

ROSENBAUM, P. S. *The grammar of English predicate complement constructions.* Cambridge, Mass.: M.I.T. Press, 1967.

ROSENBERG, J. F., and TRAVIS, C. *Readings in the philosophy of language* Englewood Cliffs, N.J.: Prentice-Hall, 1971.

ROSS, J. R. Constraints on variables in syntax. Unpublished doctoral dissertation, Massachusetts Institute of Technology, 1967.

ROSS, J. R. On declarative sentences. In R. A. Jacobs and P. S. Rosenbaum (Eds.), *Readings in English transformational grammar*. Boston: Ginn, 1970.

RYLE, G. *The concept of mind*. New York: Barnes & Noble, 1949.

SACHS, J. S. Recognition memory for syntactic and semantic aspects of connected discourse. *Perception and Psychophysics*, 1967, **2**, 437–442.

SAVIN, H., and BEVER, T. G. The nonperceptual reality of the phoneme. *Journal of Verbal Learning and Verbal Behavior*, 1970, **9**, 295–302.

SAVIN, H., and PERCHONOCK, E. Grammatical structure and the immediate recall of English sentences. *Journal of Verbal Learning and Verbal Behavior*, 1965, **4**, 348–353.

SCHATZ, C. D. The role of context in the perception of stops. *Language*, 1954, **30**, 47–56.

SCHLESINGER, I. M. *Sentence structure and the reading process*. The Hague: Mouton, 1968.

SCHOLES, R. J. Click location judgments. *Quarterly Report, Department of Speech, University of Florida*, 1969, **7**(1), 33–38.

SCHWARTZ, D., SPARKMAN, J. P., and DEESE, J. The process of understanding and judgments of comprehensibility. *Journal of Verbal Learning and Verbal Behavior*, 1970, **9**, 87–93.

SEARLE, J. R. *Speech acts*. London: Cambridge University Press, 1969.

SEITZ, M. AER and the perception of speech. Unpublished doctoral dissertation, University of Washington, 1972.

SELFRIDGE, O. G. Pandemonium: A paradigm for learning. *Proceedings of the Symposium on the Mechanization of Thought Processes*. National Physical Laboratory, Vol. I. London: Her Majesty's Stationery Office, 1959.

SHEPARD, R. N., and CHIPMAN, S. Second-order isomorphism of internal representations: Shapes of states. *Cognitive Psychology*, 1970, **1**, 1–17.

SHERMAN, M. A. Some effects of negation and adjectival marking on sentence comprehension. Unpublished doctoral dissertation, Harvard University, 1969.

SINCLAIR deZWART, H., and BRONKHARD, J. P. S. V. D. a linguistic universal? *Journal of Experimental Child Development*, 1972, **14**(3), 329–348.

SKINNER, B. F. *The behavior of organisms*. New York: Appleton-Century-Crofts, 1938.

SKINNER, B. F. *Verbal behavior*. New York: Appleton-Century-Crofts, 1957.

SLOBIN, D. I. Grammatical transformations and sentence comprehension in childhood and adulthood. *Journal of Verbal Learning and Verbal Behavior*, 1966, **5**, 219–227.

SLOBIN, D. I. Early grammatical development in several languages with special attention to Soviet research. In Bever and Weksel, in press.

SLOBIN, D. I. Cognitive prerequisites for the development of grammar. In C.A. Ferguson and D.I. Slobin (Eds.), *Studies of child language development*. New York: Holt, 1973.

SMITH, F. Reversal of meaning as a variable in the transformation of grammatical sentences. *Journal of Verbal Learning and Verbal Behavior*, 1965, **4**, 39–43.

STAATS, A. W. Linguistic-mentalistic theory versus an explanatory S-R learning theory of language development. In D. I. Slobin (Ed.), *The ontogenesis of grammar*. New York: Academic Press, 1971.

STAATS, A. W., and STAATS, C. K. *Complex human behavior*. New York: Holt, 1964.

STEINBERG, D., and JAKOBOVITS, L. A. (Ed.) *Semantics*. London: Cambridge University Press, 1971.

STEVENS, K. N , and HOUSE, A. S. Development of a quantitative description of vowel articulation. *Journal of the Acoustical Society of America*, 1955, **27**, 484–493.

STEVENS, K. N., et al. Crosslanguage study of vowel perception. *Language and Speech*, 1969, **12**, 1–23.

STEWART, C., and GOUGH, P. Constituent search in immediate memory for sentences. *Proceedings of the Midwestern Psychology Association*, 1967.

STRAWSON, P. F. *Introduction to logical theory*. London: Methuen, 1952.

SUCI, G. The validity of pause as an index of units in language. *Journal of Verbal Learning and Verbal Behavior*, 1967, **6**, 26–32.

SUCI, G., AMMON, P., and GAMLIN, P. The validity of the probe-latency technique for assessing structure in language. *Language and Speech*, 1967, **10**, 69–80.

TANNENBAUM, P. H., and WILLIAMS, F. Generation of active and passive sentences as a function of subject and object focus. *Journal of Verbal Learning and Verbal Behavior*, 1968, **7**, 246–250.

THORNDIKE, E., *The psychology of learning. Educational psychology. Vol. II*. New York: Teachers College, Columbia University, 1930.

THORPE, W. H. Sensitive periods in the learning of animals and men: A study of imprinting with special reference to the induction of cyclic behavior. In W. H. Thorpe and O. L. Zangwill (Eds.), *Current problems in animal behavior*. London: Cambridge University Press, 1961.

TINBERGEN, N. *The study of instinct*. London: Oxford University Press, 1969.

VALIAN, V. V. Talking, listening and linguistic structure. Unpublished doctoral dissertation, Northeastern University, 1971.

VON BÉKÈSY, G. *Experiments in hearing*. New York: McGraw-Hill, 1960.

VYGOTSKY, L. S. *Thought and language*. Cambridge, Mass.: M.I.T. Press, 1965.

WALKER, E. Grammatical relations in sentence memory. Doctoral dissertation, Indiana University, 1969.

WALKER, E., GOUGH, P., and WALL, R. Grammatical relations and the search of sentences in immediate memory. *Proceedings of the Midwestern Psychological Association*, 1968.

WANNER, E On remembering, forgetting, and understanding sentences: A study of the deep structure hypothesis. Unpublished doctoral dissertation, Harvard University, 1968. See also (same title). The Hague: Mouton, forthcoming.

WANNER, E., and MARATSOS, M. On understanding relative clauses. Unpublished paper, Harvard University, 1971.

WASON, P. C. The contexts of plausible denial. *Journal of Verbal Learning and Verbal Behavior*, 1965, **4**, 7–11.

WASON, P. C. *Psychological aspects of negation*. London: Communications Research Centre, University College, 1962.

WEBB, R., WILLIAMS, F., and MINIFIE, F. Effects of verbal decision behavior upon respiration during speech production. *Journal of Verbal Learning and Verbal Behavior*, 1967, **10**, 49–56.

WEIR, R. *Language in the crib*. The Hague: Mouton, 1962.

WEKSEL, W., and BEVER, T. G. Harvard Cognitive Studies Progress Report, 1966.

WERNER, H., and KAPLAN, B. *Symbol formation*. New York: Wiley, 1967.

WHORF, B. L. *Language, thought, and reality: Selected writings of Benjamin Lee Whorf*. J. B. Carroll (Ed.) New York: Wiley, 1956.

WINGFIELD, A., and KLEIN, J. F. Syntactic structure and acoustic pattern in speech perception. *Perception and Psychophysics*, 1971, **9**, 23–25.

YNGVE, V. H. A. A model and an hypothesis for language structure. *Proceedings of the American Philosophical Society*, 1960, **104**, 444–466.

ZIFF, P. *Semantic analysis*. Ithaca, N. Y., Cornell University Press, 1960.

ZUBECK, J. P., and SOLBERG, P. A. *Human development*. New York: McGraw-Hill, 1954.

INDEX

Abrahamson, A., 336
Abrams, K., 334, 341
Ades, A., 299
Adjectives, 325, 327
  preposing transformation, 120–121
Affix movement, 112–115
Ambiguity, 18–19, 94–95, 99–100, 188
  perceptual effects of, 361–367
Ammon, P., 251
Anagram task, 224, 350
Analysis by analysis, 313–316, 319
Analysis by synthesis (ABS):
  in first language learning, 469,
    475–479
  in perception, 306–313, 316–319
  in production, 390–393
Anderson, J. R., 330
Anglin, J. M., 206, 248–249
Animate nouns, 244–245
Aphasia, 453–454
Articulatory invariants, 304–305,
    309–310
Ash, S. E., 67
Associationism, 25–27, 51–56, 62,
    71–76, 144, 155–159, 161, 166

Bach, E., 263
Barclay, J., 273
Bar-Hillel, Y., 210
Bartlett, F. C., 264, 273
Base structure (see Deep structure)
Bastian, J., 295
Bellugi, U., 458, 460, 462, 467, 484
Berkeley, G., 156–157, 169, 378
Berlin, B., 386
Berlyne, D. E., 61
Berry, R., 253
Bever, T. G., 69, 103, 252, 263, 267, 293,
    323–324, 327, 330, 332, 334–339,
    341–342, 345, 347, 350–353,
    357–358, 360, 364–367, 413,
    500–501
Black, M., 384
Bloom, L., 443, 458, 464–465, 478, 482,
    485–490
Bloomfield, L., 24, 28
Blumenthal, A. L., 23, 258–259,
    261–262, 264, 346–347
Boakes, R., 258–259, 261–262
Bolinger, D. L., 209, 295, 311
Boomer, D. S., 421–424, 429–431

Bouton, L., 200

Bower, G., 226

Bowerman, M., 478

Braine, M. D. S., 61, 69, 71, 478

Bransford, J., 271, 273

Bregman, A., 270

Broadbent, D., 252, 286, 295, 329–330

Bronkhard, J. P., 502

Brown, R., 150, 157–158, 381, 385–386, 440–443, 447–448, 458, 488, 491–494

Brownowski, J., 462, 467

Bruner, J. S., 8, 11, 282

Cairns, H. S., 356, 365

Canonical sentence strategy, 326, 344–348

Caplan, D., 343

Carey, P. W., 251, 365

Carnap, R., 39

Carroll, J., 142, 145

Categorical character of speech, 297–299, 460–461

Cazden, C. B., 456–457

Chapin, P., 336–337

Chase, W. G., 381–382

Chipman, S., 158

Chomsky, N., 23, 61, 81–82, 84, 189–190, 192, 194, 207, 216, 225, 227, 231–232, 236, 327, 348, 374, 389–390, 394, 436, 469–470, 472–477, 479, 483, 485–486, 495–496, 498–499

Clark, E. V., 356–357

Clark, H. H., 244–245, 356–357, 381–382

Class formation:
  in first language learning, 479–481, 485
  mediational account of, 62–63 66–72
  pre-Hullean account of, 63–66
  in taxonomic syntax, 97

Clauses:
  order effects of, 356–357, 417
  perception of, 329–348, 353, 368
  phonemic, 422–425, 428–430
  production of, 419, 424–432

Clayton, K. N., 262

Click paradigm, 252–253, 257, 329–342, 353
  response bias in, 330–333

Clifton, C., 235–241, 243, 253, 265–266

Clyne, M. G., 414

Coding hypothesis, 264–268, 270
  in syntax recognition, 320

Cognitive development and first language learning, 452–455, 462–467

Collins, A. M., 208–209, 269

Comparatives, 92, 182

Complementary distribution, 35, 41–45, 97–98

Complements:
  in first language learning, 497–499
  perception of, 337–338, 352–355
  production of, 415–418
  standard theory of, 121–130

Complex sentences, 118, 271

Compton, A. J., 323

Concepts, 1–13, 21
  in first language learning, 463–466, 479

Conrad, C., 208–209

Constituent boundaries:
  perception of, 329–341, 352–353, 366–367
  psychological reality of, 251–264

Constituent structure (see Phrase structure)

Conventionalism, 148–150

Cooccurrence grammar, 97–105, 109

Coordination, 93–94

Cromer, R. F., 499

Davidson, D., 213

Davidson, R., 257–258

Davis, J., 243, 272

De Clerk, J., 310

Deep structure:
  in first language learning, 488–489, 495, 499
  perception of, 313, 328–329
  production of, 393–396, 404, 408, 415–417
  psychological reality of, 246–264

Deep structure:
  and semantic representation,
    188–195, 219
  standard theory of, 106–110
Deese, J., 206–208, 357
Denes, P., 287
Denotation, 146
Depth hypothesis, 268–270, 406–419
Derivational theory of complexity,
    320–328, 368, 370, 463–464, 484,
    490–494
Descriptive adequacy of grammars,
    81–82, 85–96
De Villiers, J. G., 502
De Villiers, P. A., 502
Dichotic listening task, 363
Dictionary, 183, 204, 211
Diebold, A. R., 222
Discontinuous constituents, 86–88, 90,
    93
Discovery procedure, 31–32, 40, 95–97,
    476
Discrimination-learning paradigm,
    436–439
Distinctive features, 133–137
  perception of, 301–306, 311
  psychological reality of, 433
Do-so transformation, 200, 203
Do support transformation, 232
DTC (*see* Derivational theory of com-
    plexity)

Eimas, P., 295, 461
Empiricism, 152–160, 436–439, 452
Entailment, 175–176, 180–188, 196,
    216–217, 219
Epstein, J., 502
Epstein, W., 247, 249
Ervin, S., 458–459
Ervin-Tripp, S., 457, 502
Explanatory adequacy of grammars,
    81

Fairbanks, G., 286
Fant, G., 284, 302, 309
Fillenbaum, S., 270

Fillmore, C., 195, 212, 394
Filter model of speech perception,
    284–287, 290–291, 308
Filtered speech, 288
Focal colors, 386–387
Fodor, J. A., 69, 162, 177, 190, 195, 199,
    204, 212–213, 252, 323–324,
    327–328, 332, 334–336, 339,
    350–351, 353, 356, 378, 427, 461
Fodor, J. D., 339
Formants, 283–287, 291–292
Forster, K. I., 247, 253, 331–332,
    339–340, 349, 352, 411, 413–415,
    418, 427
Foss, D. J., 356, 363–365, 367
Foulke, E., 288
Franks, J. J., 262, 271, 273
Fraser, C., 458
Free recall paradigm, 265, 271
Free variation, 35, 38–41, 43–45, 96–98,
    281
Fries, C., 28
Fromkin, V. A., 428–429, 431–433

Galanter, E., 6, 248–249
Gallagher, T. M., 269
Gamlin, P., 251
Gardner, B. T., 441–444
Gardner, R. A., 441–444
Garrett, M., 252–253, 323–324, 327–328,
    331–332, 334–335, 339–340, 344,
    350–351, 356, 363, 366–367, 413,
    427, 429–432, 461
Generalization, 64–66
Generative grammar, 79–140
  in first language learning, 481–490,
    502–503
  phonology in, 133–139
  semantics in, 110, 170–219
  in sentence perception, 368
  in sentence production, 388–390
  (*See also* Standard transformational
    grammar)
Generative semantics, 190, 197–203,
    215, 388, 397
Gerstman, L. J., 295, 311
Gesell, A., 456

Gestalt psychology, 159–160, 505
Gill, J., 418
Glanzer, M., 247
Gleason, H. A., 36, 41–42
Goldman-Eisler, F., 421–422, 426
Gombrich, E. H., 150
Goodman, N., 269, 463
Gough, P. B., 251, 255–256, 321–322
Grammar, 21, 58, 80–81, 112
  (*See also* Cooccurrence grammar;
    Generative grammar; Immedi-
    ate constituent grammar; Phrase
    structure; Standard transforma-
    tional grammar; Taxonomic
    grammar)
Grammatical relations, 101, 103
  in first language learning, 443, 465,
    480–489, 499
  psychological reality of, 261–264
  in sentence production, 394
Green, H. G., 283
Greenfield, P., 464–488
Griffith, B., 291
Grubb, P., 286
Gruber, J. S., 190

Hakes, D. T., 352, 355–356, 427
Halle, M., 23, 26, 284, 304, 307
Hanlon, C., 491–494
Harmon, G., 374, 376, 436, 463
Harris, C. M., 296
Harris, K., 291, 295, 297, 299–300
Harris, Z., 28, 43, 96–97, 102–103
Hebb, D. O., 282
Heider, E. R., 386–387
Heider, K. G., 385
Heinz, J. M., 284
Heise, G., 289
Henderson, A., 426
Hernstein, R. J., 442
Herzberger, H., 315
Hilgard, E. R., 163
Hoffman, H., 291
Holmes, V. M., 253, 331–332, 352, 357
Hook, S., 374
Hubel, D. H., 282
Hughes, G., 284

Hull, C. L., 24, 27, 73
Hullean psychology, 24, 27, 51, 53–54,
  63–74, 77
Hume, D., 153–154, 157
Hurtig, R., 366–367, 413

IC grammar (*see* Immediate constitu-
  ent grammar)
Images, 153–159, 167
Imitation in language learning,
  457–460
Immediate constituent grammar,
  83–96, 98–100, 103, 111, 131
Immediate recall task, 347
Imperative transformation, 117–118
Inference rules, 180–185, 188, 195, 213
Internal representation of sentences,
  15–21
Intersentential relations, 226–240
Isard, S., 223, 225

Jackendoff, R., 192, 216
Jakobovits, L. A., 389
Jakobson, R., 133, 284, 302
Jarvella, R., 343, 414–418
Jenkins, J. J., 61, 71, 235–238, 324
Johnson, M., 244–245
Johnson, N., 249–251, 410–411
Johnson, R., 248
Johnson-Laird, P., 272
Joos, M., 80–81
Jusczyk, P., 461

Kant, I., 12–13
Kaplan, B., 160–162
Katz, J. J., 39, 43, 103, 119, 171, 177, 179,
  190, 192, 204, 225, 227, 236–237,
  240, 470
Kay, P., 386
Kellogg, L. A., 440
Kellogg, W. N., 440
Kennedy, A., 251
Kernel sentences, 101–103, 109
  psychological reality of, 227–230,
  265–266, 269

Kernel sentences:
  recognition of, 321
Kessel, F. S., 499
Kinney, J., 297, 299–300
Kirk, R., 330, 336–337, 353
Klein, J. F., 340, 344
Klima, E. S., 380, 484
Köhler, W., 161–162
Koplin, J. H., 243, 272
Kopp, A. G., 283–284
Krasner, L., 166
Kurcz, I., 235–238

Lackner, J., 330, 336–337, 339, 342, 353,
  363, 367, 453–454
Ladefoged, P., 252, 286, 295, 329–332
Lakoff, G., 189–190, 197, 215
Lane, H., 297, 299–300
Langedoen, D. T., 358, 360
Language acquisition models:
  Chomsky's, 469–478, 483
  McNeill's, 479–482
Lashley, K. S., 4, 25
Laver, J. D. M., 429–431
Left- and right-deleted sentences, 349,
  411–414
Left branching, 408–411, 414, 417–418
Lehiste, I., 312
Lenneberg, E. H., 285, 305, 309,
  385–386, 452–454
Leopold, W. F., 458
Lesgold, A. M., 263
Levelt, W. J. M., 253–255, 257
Lexical analysis, 348
  in sentence perception, 350–353
Lexical insertion, 111–112, 131–132,
  139, 214
Lexicalism in semantics (see Seman-
  tics)
Lexicalization transformation,
  198–199, 202
Lexicon, 20, 207–209, 379, 383
Liberman, A., 291–292, 295, 297,
  299–300, 309
Lichten, W., 289
Licklider, J. C. R., 288
Lieberman, P., 310–312

Linguistic relativity, 384–388
Lisker, L., 295
Locke, J., 142, 153, 169
Logical force, 180–188
Logical form, 181
Lorenz, K., 150, 451
Lounsbury, F., 420
Loveland, D. H., 442
Lucretius, 74
Luria, A. R., 455–456

McCawley, J. D., 190
McGoech, J. A., 75
MacKay, D. G., 362–363, 366–367, 430,
  433
McKean, K., 227, 229–231, 234–235,
  241–243, 266, 321, 404
Maclay, H., 422, 424
McMahon, L., 321, 325
MacNeilage, P., 310
McNeill, D., 381, 458, 464–465,
  479–482, 485
Mandler, G., 226, 264
Mandler, J., 226, 264
Maratsos, M. P., 346, 502
Markedness, 382, 497–498
Marks, L., 223–225
Marquis, D. G., 163
Martin, E., 268–269
Meaning, 145–148
  meaning rules, 212–214
  mediational account of, 156
Mediation theory, 27, 53–63, 72–74,
  222
Mehler, J., 251, 265–267, 269, 322–324,
  347, 365, 501
Memory, 155, 268, 270, 288, 342–343,
  407–408, 465, 487
Mentalise, 375–392
Menyuk, P., 483
Messages in sentence production,
  374–375, 383–384, 391–397
Miller, G. A., 6, 206–208, 222, 224–232,
  234–235, 240, 242–243, 248–249,
  265–266, 269, 288–289, 298, 317,
  321, 327, 404
Minifie, F. D., 426

Minimal pair, 29, 31–32, 34–38, 41

Mink, W. D., 235–236

Mongoloids, 452

Moore, T. M., 347

Morphemes, 41–46, 49

Motor theory of speech perception, 306–312

Mowrer, D. H., 143, 440

Naming, 142–148

Nativism, 436, 438–439, 451–455, 460–462, 468–482

Negative sentences:
in first language learning, 493–494
perception of, 321
production of, 380, 382, 401

Negative transformation, 229–232, 240

Neisser, U., 8, 223, 316

Nesbitt, J., 262

Nichols, I. A., 452

Nooteboom, S. G., 433

Observational adequacy of grammars, 81–82, 85–92, 95

Odom, P., 235–240, 243, 253, 265–266

Olds, H. F., 496–497

Olivier, D., 386

One-word utterances, 464–465

Onomatopoeia, 160

Opaque contexts, 147

Operant learning, 444

Operationalist condition on grammars, 31–34, 47–50, 82
(*See also* Taxonomic grammar)

Ordering of transformational rules, 106, 111, 133

Osgood, C. E., 8, 51–53, 56–58, 60–61, 66–67, 163, 222, 400–404, 422, 424

Paivio, A., 263

Palermo, D., 61, 71

Parallel processing, 362–367

Paraphrase task, 324, 350, 352, 356

Passive sentences:
in children, 499–502

Passive sentences:
perception of, 321–322, 326, 346
psychological reality of, 402, 404–406

Passive transformation, 107, 114, 116–118, 129–130
psychological reality of, 229–234, 244–246, 258

Pauses in speech, 420–428

Pearlmutter, D. M., 488

Penfield, W., 454

Perceptual constancy, 7, 291, 299–306, 313

Perchonock, E., 322–323, 346

Perfetti, C. A., 269

Performance-competence distinction, 277–278, 369, 390

Peterson, G. E., 296, 312

Petrick, S. R., 315

Phoneme monitor task, 352, 355, 363

Phonemes, 20
in generative grammar, 133
mediational account of, 69
psychological reality of, 433
in taxonomic grammar, 30, 32–40, 44

Phones:
acoustic representations of, 283–299, 301
articulatory representations of, 309, 311
in generative grammar, 133–139
perception of, 279, 281, 283, 287–291, 295–301, 305
in taxonomic grammar, 29, 32–40, 139

Phonological component, 20, 110, 133–138

Phrase structure:
in first language learning, 448–450
in immediate constituent grammar, 83–85, 93–95
in sentence perception, 314
in standard transformational grammar, 111–115
(*See also* Surface structure)

Piaget, J., 11, 467

Picture-verification task, 325, 364–365

Pinson, E., 287

Postal, P. M., 84, 119, 190, 197, 227, 236–237, 240

Potter, R. K., 283–284

Preanalyzer in syntax recognition, 315–319

Predicate-raising transformation, 198, 202

Premack, D., 445–447, 449

Presuppositions, 215–216, 397, 402

Pribram, K. H., 6, 248–249, 376

Probe latency task, 251–252, 255–257, 326, 344, 346

Projection rules, 204

Prompted recall paradigm, 258–265

Prosody:
    perception of, 311–313, 334, 340–341, 344
    production of, 430

Putnam, H., 463

Quantifiers, scope of, 216

Question transformation, 232, 246

Questions, 87–88, 115, 120, 493–494

Quillian, M. R., 208–209

Quine, W. V. O., 48, 171, 179, 388, 439

Rapid serial visual presentation, 340, 352, 357

Reber, A. S., 330

Recursive rules, 60–61, 218

Redundancy, 282, 287–291, 421–422

Reference, 142–170

Reflexivization transformation, 125

Reinforcement in first language learning, 455–457

Relative clauses:
    in first language learning, 496
    in sentence perception, 346
    in sentence production, 417–418

Relativization, 118–121
    (*See also* Relative clauses)

Reverse transformations, 315–316

Rewrite rules, 83, 97, 111
    (*See also* Phrase structure)

Roberts, J. M., 386

Roberts, K. H., 268–269

Roberts, L., 454

Rochester, S. R., 418

Rohrman, N. L., 269

Rosenbaum, P. S., 497

Rosenberger, E. F., 452

Ross, J. R., 190, 339, 417

RSVP (*see* Rapid serial visual presentation)

Rule-governed behavior, 167–170

Ryder, L. A., 339–340

Ryle, G., 376

Sachs, J. S., 270

Saporta, S., 324

Sarah, 444–450

Savin, H. B., 293, 322–323, 346

Schatz, C. D., 295

Schlesinger, I. M., 342

Scholes, R. J., 253

Schwartz, D., 357

Searle, J. R., 172

Sebeok, T. A., 51, 53, 222

Seitz, M., 253

Selection restrictions, 112, 132, 191

Self-embedded sentences, 324–325, 327, 342, 345–346, 350–352, 356

Selfridge, O. G., 223–224, 282

Semantic anomaly, 224–225

Semantic features, 204–212

Semantic generalization paradigm, 235

Semantics, 217–220
    and deep structure, 188–195
    in first language learning, 442–443, 476, 485, 490
    in generative grammar, 110, 170–219
    and lexicalism, 203–212
    and logical force, 180–188, 507
    psychological reality of, 270–273
    in sentence production, 379–380, 388–394
    and surface structure, 214–217
    (*See also* Generative semantics)

Sentence family, 97–106, 227
    semantic interpretations of, 241–246
    (*See also* Intersentential relations)

Sentoid, 119–120
 (*See also* Clauses, perception of)
Serial order in behavior:
 mediational account, 27, 51–62
 radical behaviorist account, 24–27
Serial processing, 362
Shattuck, S. R., 429–432
Shepard, R. N., 158
Sherman, M. A., 380, 382
Short-term memory, 268, 288, 342–343,
 407–408, 465, 487
Short-term recall task, 324
Silver, M., 364
Sinclair de Zwart, H., 467, 502
Singulary transformation, 118
Siqueland, E., 461
Sivertsen, E., 296
Skarbek, A., 426
Skinner, B. F., 3, 24–25, 54–55, 146,
 398–399, 402–403, 438
Slips of the tongue, 381–382, 396,
 428–432
Slobin, D. I., 227, 325–326, 460, 463
Smith, F., 242–243
Smith, H. L., 422
Smith, T., 336
Solberg, P. A., 456
Sparkman, J. P., 357
Species-specificity of language, 436,
 439–462, 503
Speech recognizers, 276–278, 306–309,
 313
Speech spectrography, 293, 383–385
Speech synthesis, 296
Spooner, W., 428
Staats, A. W., 61, 457
Standard transformational grammar,
 110–132, 139, 236
Steinberg, D., 389
Stevens, K. N., 284, 298, 307
Stewart, C., 251, 255–256
Stolz, W., 336, 342
Strassburg, R., 270
Strategies in sentence perception:
 clause analysis, 329–348
 in first language learning, 475, 479,
 494–502

Strategies in sentence perception:
 lexical analysis, 348–353
 surface-structure analysis, 353–361
Strawson, P. F., 181–182
Strict subcategorization, 348–352
Structural description, 21, 81, 84, 273,
 512
 (*See also* Deep structure; Generative
 grammar; Surface structure; Taxonomic grammar)
Structuralism, 24, 27–29
 (*See also* Taxonomic grammar)
Subject-raising transformation,
 124–125, 129–130
Suci, G., 248, 251
Surface structure, 106–109
 in first language learning, 489,
 493–496, 499, 502
 in generative grammar, 111, 133,
 139–140
 psychological reality of, 246–264,
 268–270
 and semantics, 214–217
 in sentence perception, 329,
 337–339, 353–361
 in sentence production, 395–397,
 404, 406–419, 434
 (*See also* Phrase structure)
Switching paradigm, 340
Syllable, 293–294, 432
Synonymy, 162, 195–196, 204, 212–218,
 242–244, 270, 272

t-node count, 412–414
Tannenbaum, P. H., 404–406
Task-specificity of language skills,
 436, 439, 462–467, 502
Taxonomic condition in grammar, 30
 (*See also* Taxonomic grammar)
Taxonomic grammar, 28, 47–50, 79–80,
 82, 96–97
 morphology, 40–45
 phonemics, 32–40, 64
 psycholinguistic implications,
 51–72
 syntax, 45–47

Tense movement transformation, 113
Thomson, H., 456
Thorndike, E., 226
Thorpe, W. H.,, 454
Time-compressed speech, 288
Tinbergen, N., 3, 442, 451
Tip of the tongue phenomenon, 381
Titchener, E. G., 157–159
Tolman, E. C., 5
Trager, G., 422
Transformational complexity, 227–240, 246
   (*See also* Coding hypothesis; Derivational theory of complexity)
Transformational cycle, 129–131, 139
Transformational grammar (*see* Generative grammar)
Transformations, psychological reality of, 226, 231–234, 240–241, 274
Transitional probability, 51–52, 56–58, 61, 250, 257–258, 420–421
Transitive predicates, 182–183
Truth conditions, 171
Twadell, W., 28
Two-word stage of language development, 443, 448, 464, 478, 487–490

Underlying phrase structure (*see* Deep structure)
Units in sentence perception, 252, 330, 336–343
Universals in language, 139–140, 371, 468–472, 477, 513

Valian, V. V., 419–420, 501
Vigorito, J., 461
Voice typewriter, 280
von Békésy, G., 283
Vygotsky, L. S., 11, 282, 376

Walker, E., 256–257, 326, 346
Wall, R., 256
Wang, W. S-Y., 296
Wanner, E., 261–262, 272, 346
Washoe, 441–444, 449–450
Wason, P. C., 321, 380
Watson, J. B., 24
Webb, R., 426, 428
Weir, R., 459
Weisel, T. N., 282
Weksel, W., 69, 357
Werner, H., 160–162
Whorf, B. L., 71, 384–388
Wh-transformations, 120
Wilkes, A., 251
Williams, F., 404–406, 426
Wingfield, A., 340, 344

Yngve, V. H. A., 268, 406–408, 410, 412, 414, 417–419
Yudovich, F. IA., 455–456

Ziff, P., 43, 171
Zubek, J. P., 456